THE KITCHEN & GARDEN BOOK OF
HERBS
KNOWING · GROWING · COOKING

THE KITCHEN & GARDEN BOOK OF
HERBS
KNOWING · GROWING · COOKING

JESSICA HOUDRET &
JOANNA FARROW

southwater

This edition is published by Southwater, an imprint of Anness Publishing Ltd, 108 Great Russell Street, London WC1B 3NA; info@anness.com

www.southwaterbooks.com; www.annesspublishing.com; twitter: @Anness_Books

If you like the images in this book and would like to investigate using them for publishing, promotions or advertising, please visit our website www.practicalpictures.com for more information.

© Anness Publishing Ltd 2015

Publisher: Joanna Lorenz
Project Editors: Simona Hill and Doreen Gillon
Copy Editor: Jan Cutler
Botanical Consultant: Sarah Wilson
Designers: Ruth Hope, Lilian Lindblom, Patrick McCleavey and Nigel Partridge
Illustrator: Madeleine David
Production Controller: Ben Worley

p.1, clockwise from top left: Bergamot; Herby Fish Pie with Mushrooms; Madonna Lily; herb cordials and decorative herb ice cubes.
p.2: Red and white valerian contrast with the blue of cornflower.
p.3, clockwise from top left: Deadly Nightshade; Tomato, Ciabatta and Basil Oil Soup; Lavender; Coriander Omelette Parcels with Asian Vegetables.
p.4, from left to right: Aubergine Soup with Mozzarella and Herby Gremolata; Saffron crocus; Strawberry and Lavender Sorbet; Buchu; Grilled Swordfish Skewers with Garlic and Oregano.
p.5, from left to right, top to bottom: Orache; Warm Herby Bread; Bay; Fillets of Sea Bream with Sorrel
in Filo Pastry; Holy thistle; Green Fish Curry with Thai Herbs, Chilli and Coconut Milk; Chamomile; Pissaladière with Herbs and Anchovies;
Cistus; Poached Pears in Saffron Scented Honey Syrup.

COOK'S NOTES
Bracketed terms are intended for American readers.
For all recipes, quantities are given in both metric and imperial measures and, where appropriate, in standard cups and spoons.
Follow one set of measures, but not a mixture, because they are not interchangeable.
Standard spoon and cup measures are level. 1 tsp = 5ml, 1 tbsp = 15ml, 1 cup = 250ml/8fl oz.
Australian standard tablespoons are 20ml. Australian readers should use 3 tsp in place of 1 tbsp for measuring small quantities.
American pints are 16fl oz/2 cups. American readers should use 20fl oz/2.5 cups in place of 1 pint when measuring liquids.
Electric oven temperatures in this book are for conventional ovens. When using a fan oven, the temperature will probably need to be reduced
by about 10–20°C/20–40°F. Since ovens vary, you should check with your manufacturer's instruction book for guidance.
The nutritional analysis given for each recipe is calculated per portion (i.e. serving or item), unless otherwise stated. If the recipe gives a range,
such as Serves 4–6, then the nutritional analysis will be for the smaller portion size, i.e. 6 servings.
The analysis does not include optional ingredients, such as salt added to taste.
Medium (US large) eggs are used unless otherwise stated.

PUBLISHER'S NOTE
This book is intended as a source of information on herbs and their uses, not as a practical guide to self-medication.
Neither the author nor the publisher can be held responsible for any specific individual's reactions, harmful effects or claims arising
from the use of the general data and suggestions it contains, whether in recipe form or otherwise. Nor is any responsibility taken
for mistaken identity of any of the plants. Many plants are poisonous, and all herbs can be toxic if taken to excess, especially
in the form of essential oils. Some may cause adverse reactions in certain people. Consult a qualified practitioner
before using herbs medicinally. The use of any information contained in this book is entirely at the reader's own risk.

Contents

Introduction 6

Introduction

Herbs are a diverse and versatile body of plants, which have been appreciated through the centuries for their many uses. In the past they were the main source of raw materials for medicines, nutritional supplements and culinary flavourings as well as fulfilling a wide variety of household needs. They provided fragrance in the home, were added to bath and beauty preparations, used as dyes, cleaning agents, insect repellents and other similar products which we have become used to buying ready made.

Although few people now would presumably want to give up the benefits of modern medical science or the convenience of contemporary technology and goods, there is an increasing revival of interest in herbs and their uses, which has been gathering momentum since the 1980s. Alternative therapies and herbal healing have gained ground and many more people add herbs to their cooking as a matter of course. This may be partly due to a current inclination towards natural products and natural practices, and partly due to increased travel and communications, which have brought the cuisines and ingredients of the world before a wider audience.

In addition, in more recent times, a new element has emerged: herbs have gained respectability. They are no longer seen as solely the preserve of eccentrics, nor are herbal remedies universally dismissed as superstitious nonsense. The reason is that much traditional herbal folklore has been vindicated by modern research. Scientific studies have proved that many herbs have antibacterial, antifungal, antidepressant and other medicinal properties and that some help to lower blood pressure or act on the hormonal systems of the body. Many plants are now recognized by the medical establishment as providing the key to discovering new drugs to combat the major modern illnesses such as cancers and AIDS.

Growing your own herbs is immensely rewarding, with the added advantage of having fresh material to hand, for use in home remedies and recipes, which you know has not been sprayed, adulterated or polluted. This book begins with a background history, ideas for schemes and layouts and a section on growing herbs and making the most of these useful plants in an ornamental setting.

The herb directory gives detailed information on individual plants. Under each entry, the history and traditions of the herb are dealt with first. Some of the stories or myths associated with the herb are mentioned, the origins of the name, or past uses, and, where relevant, how this is linked to present uses, properties and status. The rest of the information covers practical points on growing and usage for today. There is a description to help with identification, a note on where the plant originated (which often helps in the understanding of cultivation needs) and requirements for growth and propagation.

There then follows the recipe section – more than 300 delicious dishes, each illustrated step-by-step to ensure perfect results every time. Recipes range from warming soups, fragrant salads and light meals to robust meat dishes, delicious cakes and impressive desserts, and they all use a range of herbs. Cook's tips and variations are also included, as well as a nutritional analysis of each recipe.

It would take many volumes to detail every plant that could possibly be construed as having herbal properties, even if all of them were known. In remote areas of the world there are many plants not yet classified, some, perhaps, whose medicinal uses are familiar only to a few local healers. So the decision on which herbs to include has necessarily been subjective. The ones chosen are those which are generally the most useful, the most popular, of special historical interest, or of current significance because of properties discovered by modern scientific research.

The aim is to provide accessible information on a wide range of herbs and the inspiration to take pleasure in them, both in the garden and in the kitchen.

Above *Lavender Scones.*

Left *A collection of containers suitable for herbs.*

The Herb Garden

Growing herbs in the garden or in containers adds both colour and fragrance to even the smallest garden. These versatile plants can be used to create or enhance an almost infinite number of planting designs, from informal gardens and raised beds to themed areas such as a cook's or Shakespearean garden. This section provides everything you need to know about growing, harvesting and drying herbs successfully, as well as a detailed directory of over 250 different herbs.

Above, clockwise from top left *Witch hazel; picking mint leaves; olives; Saffron crocus bulbs.*

Left *Box is ideal for formal hedging and topiary, and is also of great interest to current medical research.*

History of Herbs

The first question explored here is what is meant by the term "herb"? This is followed by some guidelines on restrictions in using these powerful plants and a detailed explanation of plant classification, how it began and developed, and the helpfulness of using Latin names to avoid confusion. A background history of herbal knowledge and use through the centuries comes next. The chapter concludes with a summary of some of the landmarks in herbal literature.

Above *A topiary spiral emphasizes the symmetry of the raised stone urns in a small formal herb garden.*

Left *An arched walkway shelters raised beds, thickly planted with herbs, in a reconstruction of a medieval cloister garden.*

What is a Herb?

The definition of the term "herb" has varied over the centuries. At one time it meant primarily grass, green crops and leafy plants. This concept entered into many dictionaries, where the definition was narrowed to a plant that does not have a woody, persistent stem, but dies down to the ground after flowering – a herbaceous plant, in other words. This was clearly inadequate, because it excluded some of the most obvious and common herbal examples such as rosemary, thyme and sage .

A herb is now generally understood to mean a plant, some part of which, roots, stem, leaves, flowers or fruits, is used for food, medicine, flavouring or scent. This wide category covers much more than a few plants with small green leaves; and includes some trees, shrubs, sub-shrubs or woody-stemmed perennials. Annuals, even ferns and fungi, as well as the herbaceous group, could also fit the general description.

Right *Watermint and bogbean in a pond.*

Below *A detailed illustration of St John's wort,* Hypericum perforatum, *from W. Curtis's* Flora Londinensis, *1826.*

Most of the plants included in this book have a long herbal history, their therapeutic uses having been recorded in early manuscripts or published works written by the specialists of the time. Some of these uses seem very far-fetched or downright dangerous in the light of modern knowledge. Expressed in colourfully poetic language, the early records often deal with bizarre conditions and unfamiliar illnesses, from attacks by "flying venom" and "elf-shot" to agues, fluxes and St Anthony's fire – as well as coughs, fevers and more recognizable medical problems.

However, the remarkable fact is that many herbs have been found under modern analysis to vindicate our fore-fathers' faith in them. Recent research studies have established the antibacterial, antiseptic, anti-inflammatory or other medicinal properties of large numbers of common herbs.

Herb chemistry is very complex. Each individual variety of plant is unique in its make-up, even closely related species are quite distinct. They all contain many active constituents which work together to affect the functions of the body, when used for medicinal purposes. This holistic (or synergistic) method of using the whole plant, as opposed to taking a concentrated extract, is the gentlest and safest way to benefit from herbs.

Aconitum napellus, *or monkshood (top), and* Atropa belladonna, *deadly nightshade (above), are highly toxic in any quantity.* Cannabis sativa *(right) is one of the plants subject to legal restrictions in most countries.*

Restrictions on Herbs

Safety in use

Many plants are highly toxic and can be dangerous in use. Self-medication is not advised and it is always best to seek the advice of a qualified medical practitioner before herbs are used as a treatment. Plants can look very similar and common names are often misleading – there is a danger of mistaking one herb for another. Before collecting a herb, ensure that it has been correctly identified and do not interchange similar species for a particular purpose, as they may not have the same properties. It is also essential to use only the part specified, usually the leaf, stem, flower or seed and occasionally root. Some plants classified as herbs are highly poisonous in any form or quantity, monkshood, *Aconitum napellus*, being an example. It should be remembered that many apparently benevolent substances, for example vitamins, can be toxic if taken to excess. This principle applies to herbs too and includes the common culinary ones, such as thyme or rosemary. It is difficult to ingest a harmful amount in the form of the whole leaf, and most are totally safe if used, fresh or dried, in quantities recommended in recipes. However, in the form of essential oils, which are concentrated extracts of the active principle, they can be highly toxic.

Poisonous and toxic plants in this book are shown under a caution box in individual entries.

Legal restrictions

There are legal restrictions both on the use or trade and on the collection or cultivation of various herbs. Restrictions also cover certain herbal extracts and preparations, and their permitted concentrations and doses, as well as those people allowed to administer, prescribe or supply them.

Growing herbs that are capable of producing illegal drugs, or cultivating species considered to be noxious weeds, is against the law in some countries. It is also a criminal offence to collect or uproot wild plants that are protected by law. See the caution box under individual herb entries for plants likely to be restricted by law.

Plant Names

Herbs are listed in this book under their Latin, or botanical, names. This helps to avoid confusion, as most have several common names which vary according to country, or even from one local region to another. Sometimes the common name used in one country refers to a totally different plant in another country. The Latin names have the advantage of being international. *The International Code of Botanical Nomenclature*, set every five years following an international conference, ensures that all countries accept the same botanical names.

In recent years, however, there has been a spate of reclassifications of plants by botanists in the light of new studies or detailed analysis of specimens. For example, the plant always known as *Mentha rotundifolia* var. 'Bowles', (or Bowles' mint), has now become *Mentha x villosa* var. *alopecuroides*. As far as possible the most current name is listed, but changes are ongoing.

Common Names

The most usual common name is also given in this book, along with variations and synonyms where applicable. Both Latin and common names are often a lively indication of a herb's history, properties or use.

Above *Cultivars of* Achillea millefolium.

Plant Classification

The system of plant classification by Latin names in use today was developed by Carl Linnaeus, 1707–1778, a Swedish botanist and professor of medicine at Uppsala University, near Stockholm. He divided plants into groups, according to common characteristics.

Some modifications have since been introduced, but the system remains essentially the same as at its inception. Under the Linnaeus system all plants have a double name. The first is the name of the genus, or wider grouping, to which they belong, and the second denotes their individual species. Generic names, like all Latin names, are either masculine, feminine or neuter.

Thus *Achillea* = genus, *millefolium* = species. The second part of the name also indicates whether a plant is a hybrid or cultivar, or has been subdivided, according to finer differences, as a subspecies, variety or form.

Plant Divisions

FAMILY – A group of plants, made up of a number of genera with characteristics in common, usually decided by the structure of flowers, fruits or seeds e.g., ROSACEAE. Some families have alternative names, such as COMPOSITAE also known as ASTERACEAE. The first is the traditional name, which, although it remains valid at present, is being superseded by a newer name, designed to fit into a standardized system of nomenclature, whereby all family names end with "aceae", preceded by the key genus of the family, as ASTER-ACEAE.

GENUS – A group, made up of a number of related species, such as *Achillea*, but which may also contain only one species, such as *Anethum graveolens* (denoted by the first part of the Latin name).

SPECIES (spp.) – Individual plants that are alike and breed naturally with each other, such as *Achillea millefolium* (the species is denoted by the second part of the Latin name).

HYBRID – A cross between two species, or genera, indicated by a cross, such as *Lavandula x intermedia*.

CULTIVAR – A variant of the species or hybrid that has a special characteristic, such as leaf variegation, developed and maintained under cultivation. For instance, *Melissa officinalis* 'All Gold', a golden-leafed lemon balm. The name of the cultivar is printed in roman type, within inverted commas (single quotation marks).

VARIETY (var.) – A subdivision of species and hybrids, often with a distinctive difference (such as flower or foliage colour), but with only minor variations in botanical structure, such as *Lavandula dentata* var. *candicans*.

SUBSPECIES (subsp.) – A variant of a species, such as *Lavandula stoechas* subsp. *luisieri*.

FORM (f.) – Has only minor, but often noticeable, variations from the species, such as flower colour, e.g. *Lavandula stoechas* f. *leucantha* – a white-flowering form of *L. stoechas*. (Note that, once a genus has been stated, it can then, as here, be represented by its initial.)

System of plant classification

Herbs in History

There is ample evidence of the herbal use of plants by the civilizations of ancient Egypt, over a period from 3000 BC to the reign of Cleopatra, which began in 48 BC. Papyri dating from 2800 BC record the medicinal use of some familiar herbs, including juniper, mint and marjoram. The wall paintings of tombs and temples reveal the use of aromatic plants, spices and gums in religious and funerary rites and on social occasions. Also an inscription in the temple of Karnak relates Ramses III's plea to the god Amun for victory in battle, reminding him of the pharaoh's generous sacrifice of 30,000 oxen, quantities of "sweet-smelling herbs and the finest perfume". Archaeologists have also found the physical remains of plants, flowers and seeds used for food and flavouring, as votive garlands and in cosmetic and embalming ointments.

Offerings made to the sun god Ra, at Heliopolis, included a concoction of 16 herbs and resins. Known as *kyphi* or *khepri*, it was adopted by the Greeks, and then the Romans, and was described by Dioscorides. Later analysis confirmed that it contained among its ingredients *Acorus calamus*, cassia, cinnamon, peppermint, juniper, acacia and henna.

The Greeks, the great period of whose culture overlapped with the end of the Egyptian dynasties, adopted Egyptian skills in making ointments from aromatic plants, as their literature often confirms. The cosmetic use of plants was a frequently described theme:

He really bathes
In a large gilded tub, and steeps his feet
And legs in rich Egyptian unguents;
His jaw and breasts he rubs with thick
palm oil,
And both his arms with extract of
sweet mint;
His eyebrows and his hair with
marjoram,
His knees and neck with essence of
ground thyme.
– Antiphanes

Above *Plants being ground in a mortar, from a 10th-century French herbal.*

The Romans have left many records of their use of herbs for flavouring food, in perfumery, for decoration and strewing at social events. Medicinal uses are discussed in the works of writers such as Pliny. The vast spread of their empire also meant that the Romans took Mediterranean plants to northern areas that had never known them before and where many became naturalized.

After the fall of Rome, in the period sometimes known as the Dark Ages, AD 476–c.1000, herbal knowledge was nurtured and kept alive in Christian monasteries. In Britain during this time, Anglo-Saxon writings show a wide knowledge of herbs and evidence of correspondence with centres in Europe.

The Eastern Connection

During the 10th century a great Muslim empire stretched from the eastern Mediterranean, taking in Arabia, Persia, parts of Spain and North Africa. Arab academics were paramount in the medicinal practice of the time and Avicenna, born in Persia, AD 980, was one of the most famous. He was the first to describe the making of attar of roses by distillation, was instrumental in the discovery of plant essential oils, and his *Canon* became a standard medical text. Crusaders from Britain, who set out to destroy the Muslim influence, brought home the new plants and exotic spices from the Near East.

Above *A relief at the Temple of Karnak in Luxor, Egypt, depicting a botanical garden showing plants brought from Syria by Pharaoh Tutmosis III.*

In India, where so many medicinal and scented plants grow, there is a long tradition of using spices and aromatic herbs in cookery, for perfumes and cosmetics. An 18th-century Italian traveller wrote that "nowhere do the women pay greater attention to their cleanliness than in the East, bathing frequently and massaging all parts of their body with perfumed oils". Ayurvedic medicine, practised in India, is an ancient system based on herbs and shares many similarities of concept with Chinese herbal medicine, whose longest unbroken tradition of practice is often considered to be the most ancient in origin. The Yellow Emperor, Huang Ti, born *c.* 2000 BC, wrote a medical treatise which is often cited as the earliest herbal on record. Chinese herbalism is currently enjoying a revival in the West.

The Renaissance and the Discovery of the New World

With the Renaissance, the great revival of learning marking the birth of modern Europe, came advances in medicine and the study of the healing properties of plants. The 16th and 17th centuries were the age of great herbalists and herbals: Turner, Gerard and Parkinson in Britain; Brunfels, Fuchs and Bock in Germany; Clusius, L'Obel and Dodoens in the Netherlands; Mattioli and Porta in Italy.

Above *A man and woman harvesting sap, from* Le Livre des Simples Médecines, *a 15th-century French herbal.*

Above *Collecting herbs to use in the stillroom.* Spring *by Lucas van Valkenborch, 1595.*

At the same time the use of herbs in cookery, perfumery and for cosmetics was widespread and well documented in many books on household skills, such as Sir Hugh Platt's *Delights for Ladies*, 1594, and T. Dawson's *The Good Housewife's Jewel*, 1585. It should be remembered, however, that the line between perfumery for pleasure and health was a narrow one. It was generally accepted that a fragrant smell was in itself proof against infection and many recipes in the stillroom books for perfumed powders and pot-pourris, which would now be considered fripperies, had a serious underlying purpose.

In the 16th and 17th centuries a huge quantity of new plants, many of which were used by the Native Americans in their traditional medicine, were brought to Europe from the Americas. Seeds were taken the opposite way by the early colonists keen to establish, in their new country, gardens stocked with the familiar herbs of home – including parsley, savory and thyme.

The Modern Era

Up until the 18th century, botany and medicine were closely allied, but with the rise of modern scientific enquiry they drew apart as separate disciplines. During the 19th century the medical establishment turned away from plant-based remedies, and synthetic drugs, produced in the laboratory, began their ascendancy. This is not to say that old herbal remedies and culinary and cosmetic recipes disappeared: traditions were kept alive in many country districts and in some countries never fell from use. In Europe the day-to-day use of herbs remained more widely practised than it did in Britain.

Mrs Grieve, whose famous herbal was published in 1931, did much to promote the renewed interest in herbs in Britain in the 20th century, as did Eleanour Sinclair Rohde, who wrote many books on herbs and became a popular lecturer on the subject in the United States, following World War II.

In the latter part of the 20th century the revival of interest in all things herbal continues. Emigration and accessibility of travel have spread the use of culinary herbs and spices across many countries and cultures. There is wide recognition among scientists today of the value of plants as the basis for drugs to combat major diseases, such as cancer and AIDS, and much research is being carried out. However, the drugs under development depend on isolating and copying active plant compounds. This takes a different direction from the use of the whole plant as practised in traditional herbal medicine.

Old Herbals

Old herbal manuscripts make fascinating reading. They give an insight into how herbs were used in the past and increase our general understanding of the subject. Not all are readily available and are kept in specialist libraries, but some have been reissued in modern editions and facsimiles and many are widely quoted from by modern authors. The following are some of the more important works on herbs written in the West.

Early Manuscript Herbals

c. 320 BC *Historia Plantarum* and *De Causis Plantarum* – by Theophrastus, *c.* 370–286 BC, Greek philosopher and pupil of Aristotle. (Edited and translated as *The History of Plants* and *The Causes of Plants* by Sir A.F. Hort, Loeb Library, 1916.)

c. AD 60 *De Materia Medica* – written by Dioscorides, a Greek physician, living in Rome. Describes 600 herbs and their healing properties. It became the standard work on medicine, influencing most herbals that followed for over 1,500 years. (English translation by John Goodyer, 1655.)

c. AD 77 *Naturalis Historia* – by Pliny the Elder, contemporary of Dioscorides. A massive, 37-volume work, 16 concern trees, plants and medicines.

AD 400 *The Herbal of Apuleius* – Author unknown. Originally written in Latin it drew quite heavily on Dioscorides and Pliny, adding pagan prayers and super-stitions. It was much copied over the years. (Anglo-Saxon translation made in 11th century.)

c. AD 900 *The Leech Book of Bald* – compiled by a Saxon physician. Reveals a wide knowledge of native plants and includes prescriptions sent by the Patriarch of Jerusalem to King Alfred.

c. 1150 *Physica* – by Hildegard of Bingen. Unique as a book on the medicinal properties of plants by a woman and had great influence on the famous German "fathers of botany", Brunfels, Fuchs and Hieronymus Bock.

c. 1248-1260 *De Proprietatibus Rerum* by Bartholomaeus Anglicus, an English-man living in Paris, then Saxony. A huge encyclopedia in 19 sections, number 17 being on plants and trees and their herbal properties.

Printed Herbals

1491 *Hortus Sanitatis* – compiled by publisher Jacob Meydenbach of Mainz. The last of the medieval works on herbs.

1500 *Liber de Arte Distillandi de Simplicibus* – by Hieronymous Braunschweig. The first major work on the techniques of distillation "of the waters of all manner of herbes". (English translation by L. Andrewes 1527.)

1525 *Banckes's Herbal* – anonymous, a quarto volume published by Richard Banckes. Earliest English printed herbal, based on earlier manuscript herbals.

1530 *Herbarum Vivae Eicones* – by Otto Brunfels, a former monk, Lutheran preacher, botanist and also physician. Published in Strasbourg, with realistic illustrations, it began the movement towards a more scientific mindset.

1539 *Kräuter Buch* – by Hieronymus Bock. Rather than repeat Dioscorides, Bock wrote about native plants and was the first to attempt a system of plant classification.

1542 *De Historia Stirpium* – written by Leonhard Fuchs. A scholarly work, which sought to clarify identification of medicinal plants mentioned by Dioscorides, through carefully observed illustrations. Records many new plants introduced to Germany from other parts of the world.

1551-68 *The New Herball* – by William Turner, credited as the "father of English botany". Based on his own observations of native plants but using many of the woodcuts from Fuchs' work.

1554 *Cruydeboeck* – by Rembert Dodoens, physician to the Holy Roman Emperor Maximilian II and professor of botany at Leyden University. A work of botanical importance, which borrowed Fuchs' pictures. (Many English editions, *A Niewe Herbal or History of Plants*, by Henry Lyte in 1578.)

1563 *Coloquios dos Simples* – by Garcia de Orta, a Portuguese doctor who spent time in Goa and produced a book on the plants and medicines of India.

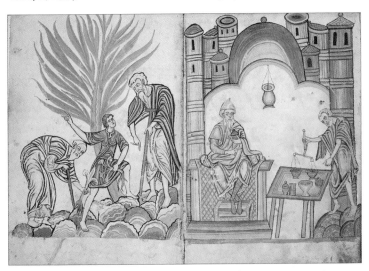

Above *Collecting herbs for the Apothecary's preparations, from a Latin manuscript version of the Herbal of Apuleius.*

Above *Frontispiece to* The Herball, *1597, by John Gerard.*

1569 *Dos libros, el uno que trata de todas las cosas que traen de nuestras Indias Occidentales* – by Nicholas Monardes, a Spaniard, who never himself visited America. His book on the plants of the "New World" became better known by the title of the first English edition: *Joyfull Newes Out of the Newe Founde Worlde*, 1577.
1597 *The Herball or Generall Historie of Plantes* – by John Gerard, gardener and botanist. Based on Dodoens' work, it remains one of the most popular, widely quoted from herbals of all time for the grace of its Elizabethan language.
1629 *Paradisi in Sole Paradisus Terrestris*; **1640** *Theatrum Botanicum* – by John Parkinson. The emphasis in the first is on ornamental planting, the second lists 3,800 plants and their medicinal properties.
1652 *The English Physician* – by Nicholas Culpeper, an astrologer, considered a charlatan by the medical establishment of his day. His book is one of the most popular herbals of all time.
1656 *The Art of Simpling*; **1657** *Adam in Eden* – by William Coles. Less popular,

but more readable than Culpeper, who Coles thought was "ignorant". Includes much herb lore.

Later Herbals

With the break between botany and medicine, few great medicinal herbals appeared after the 17th century. Those of note included:
1710 *Botanologia, The English Herbal or History of Plants* – by William Salmon.
1838 *Flora Medica* – written by John Lindley, botanist and lecturer to the Society of Apothecaries, who wrote several important horticultural works.
1931 *A Modern Herbal* – by Mrs M. Grieve. Seminal work on herbs of the 20th century.

Stillroom Books

As well as the learned tomes, written by the medical men of their day, there is a long tradition of more homely recipe (usually spelled "receipt") books, which include instructions on the culinary and cosmetic uses of herbs as well as medicinal remedies. They are sometimes known as "stillroom books". Throughout the 17th and 18th centuries all the big country houses had their own stillroom and women were supposed to be fully conversant in the art of making herbal and culinary preparations.
1585 *The Good Housewife's Jewel and Rare Conceits in Cookery* – by T. Dawson. A comprehensive, informative compilation of herbal recipes.
1594 *Delights for Ladies* – by Sir Hugh Platt. A book to fit in the palm of the hand, subtitled "to adorne their Persons, Tables, Closets & Distillatories with Beauties, Banquets, Perfumes & Waters".
1654 *The Art of Cookery* – by Joseph Cooper, recipes of Charles I's head chef.
1655 *The Queen's Closet Opened* – by W. M. (cook to Queen Henrietta Maria). Includes perfumed, culinary and medicinal preparations.
1668 *Choice and Experimental Receipts* – by Sir Kenelm Digby, Stuart diplomat, with a side interest in cookery, alchemy and herbalism. **1669** *The Closet of Sir Kenelm Digby Opened*. Many medicinal and fragrance recipes.

1719 *Acetaria* – written by John Evelyn. Cookery book by the prolific author and diarist, with a large section on the virtues of salad herbs, picked from the garden.
1719 *The Accomplished Lady's Delight* – by Mrs Mary Eales (confectioner to Queen Anne). Includes recipes for candying many flowers and fruits as well as for perfumes and scented waters.
1723 *The Receipt Book of John Nott* – competent, often workable recipes of the cook to the Duke of Bolton.
1732 *Country Housewife and Ladies Directory* – by R. Bradley. Intriguing cookery recipes.
1775 *The Toilet of Flora* – Anonymous. The title page states: "The Chief Intention of this performance is to point out, and explain to the Fair-Sex, the Methods by which they may preserve and add to their charms." But it is also for "Domestic Economy" and gives methods of preparing herbal baths, essences, pomatums, powders, perfumes, sweet-scented waters and opiates for preserving and whitening teeth.
1784 *The Art of Cooking* – by Mrs Glasse.
1845 *Miss Leslie's Directions for Cookery* – by Eliza Leslie (published USA). Primarily culinary recipes, but also contains directions for making oil of flowers, sweet jars, perfumes and scented bags.

Above *A medieval garden from* Rustican de Cultivement des Terres, *also known as* Les Livres des Prouffits. *British Library.*

Herb Garden Design

A look at traditional herb gardens and their influence on styles for today, followed by how to choose a design and whether to go for a formal or informal approach. Practical projects include step-by-step instructions on making a knot garden, raised bed and herb wheel. There are examples of themed gardens for inspiration, with detailed plans.

Above *A herb garden bounded by trees and a hedge creates an air of mystery.*

Left *Clipped box hedges, geometric lines and topiary re-create 17th-century formality in this design.*

Traditional Herb Gardens

Herbs have been grown in gardens since ancient times, as evidenced in Egyptian frescoes and descriptions of the Roman *Hortus*. However, it is really the monastery gardens of the early Christian era, following the fall of Rome, which begin the Western tradition of the herb garden.

A plan of the Benedictine monastery of St Gall in Switzerland, dating from AD 812, provided a blueprint of the style of garden attached to religious houses and which became central to their life and ministry. There were three distinct areas in this early plan: A physic garden of medicinal plants, which included sage, rosemary, rue and roses, was close to the infirmary. On the other side of this building was the vegetable garden, divided into 18 plots, each designated a single species of plant, many of which we would call herbs. There were cabbages, lettuce, onions, celery, coriander, dill, poppy, radish, garlic, parsley, chervil and fennel. The orchard adjoined, with a large, cross-shaped path at the centre, and included burial plots. At the centre of the enclosed cloister garden was an

Above *Reconstruction of a Tudor garden, with a central "knot", at Southampton, England.*

area of lilies, roses and scented flowers for decorating the church, often known as a "paradise garden".

Monastery gardens were by their nature enclosed. This was a feature, too, of privy gardens belonging to a palace or castle in the medieval period. However, the emphasis here was on enjoyment, with scents, seats and arbours.

Another characteristic of the monastic gardens, which was carried into the designs of the Renaissance period beginning in the 16th century, is the rectangular layout of symmetrical paths, with the cross as a central motif. It has often been noted, however, that the Islamic and Persian tradition of a garden on a grid pattern (probably set out this way for ease of watering by irrigation channels) was also an influence.

In England the fashion for knot gardens began at the outset of the reign of Henry VIII, in the early 16th century, and was popular for over 200 years. Some of the patterns, depicting interlaced ribbons, were extremely complicated and set out in clipped hedges of wall germander, hyssop, cotton lavender and box, infilled with coloured stones or scented herbs and

flowers. By the 17th century the more expansive and open French parterre, with its elaborate swirls of curls and loops, became fashionable.

It was during the 17th century that a host of new plants arrived in Europe, brought back by explorers and traders. Many of the new arrivals were from North America, including nasturtiums and sunflowers. They were planted in physic gardens and the gardens of the great houses, as well as in large botanical gardens throughout Europe, where the study of botany and medicine still went hand in hand. It was a two-way traffic as plants from the "old world" were also taken to North America.

The landscape movement and "natural" school of garden design in the 18th century swept away the intricate knots and parterres; and physic gardens declined in importance as medicine moved apart from botany. Herbs were still grown, of course, but retreated to the cottage garden. Here, they largely remained until the early 20th century when Vita Sackville-West and Gertrude Jekyll started the fashion for informal planting of old-fashioned species, and restored herbs to centre stage.

Above *An elaborate 17th-century garden, from a painting by Johan Walter, 1660.*

Herb Gardens for Today

When planning a herb garden today there is a vast choice of styles and influences to choose from. As herbs and plants cover such a wide range, they are often grown throughout the garden in ornamental beds and borders or among vegetable plots. But a designated herb garden with a range of medicinal, culinary and aromatic plants and its own boundaries always makes a rewarding feature. In a very small garden, of course, it may well be designed to take up the whole area.

Historical precedents provide much inspiration for a herb garden in the formal style, with rectangular beds, straight paths and edgings of clipped box. It could be based on the medieval garden, with narrow, raised beds filled with a single species, divided by wide alleys. Or you could draw inspiration from the romantic enclave of a castle garden; or a cloister or paradise garden. And the striking pattern of a knot garden or parterre is always effective.

Informal designs based on curves and irregular shapes give scope for imaginative planting schemes with a

Above *A beautiful, scented cloister garden at Château de Vandrimare in France.*

bold use of colour and texture; and the cottage-garden style, with its profusion of plants crammed into a small space, is another option.

In any scheme a place to sit, either a simple bench or intricate covered arbour, is a must. A sundial or urn as a centrepiece provides a good focal point.

Whatever the style, some kind of enclosure adds an extra dimension, setting the herb garden apart. It could be a low fence or herbal hedge or, for a larger area, high trelliswork or a wall may be more appropriate. Herbs may be practical plants, for particular purposes, but they also add a little mystery and magic to the world and deserve a special place of their own.

Left *A sundial makes a traditional focal point in an informal planting of herbs and roses, with a statue in the background.*

Choosing a Design

Working out the design of a new herb garden is an exciting project. But before you begin there are several questions you need to answer to ensure that the end result is a success. Space is the first consideration. How much room are you prepared to devote to herbs? Do you have a large enough area to make a garden within a garden? Perhaps you would like to turn most, or all, of your existing space over to herbs? Or would a bed or border of herbs be more appropriate?

Plan how the design is going to fit in with your surroundings. Think about your house and current garden, as this will dictate the overall style you choose; formal, informal, old-fashioned or state-of-the-art or of the 21st century.

Consider how much time and energy you have for upkeep. Beware of choosing a large and complicated scheme if from a practical point of view your needs are for a low-maintenance garden. A simple knot of box hedging, filled in with gravel needs clipping only twice a year. But be wary of putting in other traditional clipped herbs, such as santolina and germander, unless you are prepared to trim the plants frequently. A formal potager, which needs constant replanting and tending to keep it in shape, can be very time-consuming. But a carefully thought-out border of shrubby herbs and perennials needs little upkeep. Containers of herbs can provide extra space and variety.

Consider which category of herbs is your chief interest – culinary, medicinal or scented and aromatic? Your preference here may dictate size, layout and planting plans. If your main aim is to produce a good supply of culinary herbs, a small, formal patch may be sufficient. But if your ambition is to include as many species as possible, a more extensive scheme is inevitable.

Left *A colourful archway and large containers of pelargoniums mark the entrance to an inviting garden bounded by a high hedge.*

Below *Topiary and architectural plants of contrasting foliage lend height and interest to a mixed scheme of herbs.*

Formal Gardens

Taking their inspiration from the Renaissance gardens of France and Italy, formal designs depend on straight lines and geometric shapes, on symmetry and regularity. Balance is the key, with elements arranged around a central axis. The strict pattern of paths, which form the structure, is all-important. Paths may be of brick, stone, gravel or grass, but make sure they are wide enough to walk on comfortably and to take a wheelbarrow. A metre (about three feet) is a minimum width for straight sections, with some wider areas to create a feeling of spaciousness and for extra manoeuvrability. Planting schemes echo the geometry of the layout, with corresponding blocks of colour filling the beds. Foliage plants, especially those with a dense habit of growth such as thyme, are often more suitable than those with a profusion of flowers and a tendency to sprawl.

Large pots and ornaments or statues provide focal points at the ends of vistas. If placed to line a path edge or in a regular pattern they will provide visual links, drawing the scheme together and reinforcing the regularity. Topiary and plants growing over a shaped framework are used in much the same way. They also introduce a theatrical element which underlines the style. But beware of cramming in too much – for this look to be successful, understatement and simplicity are best.

Above *The low-growing silver thyme in the foreground forms a block of colour to reinforce the geometry of the design.*

This plan is for a garden about 11 x 9.50 m (36 x 31 ft), enclosed by a brick wall to one side and trelliswork at each corner supporting a scented, white-flowered jasmine. If you do not have a site where a wall can be used as one boundary, the trellis can be extended. An archway, clothed in the coppery pink climbing rose, 'Albertine', forms the main entrance, with a bench seat under a jasmine arbour on the opposite side, against the wall. Topiary in pots – box trees clipped in spheres and rosemary globes – mark the points of entry, add height to the scheme and increase the sense of regularity.

A sundial surrounded by a chamomile lawn, of the non-flowering cultivar *Chamaemelum nobile* 'Treneague', makes a focal point at the centre, emphasized by the square beds of creeping thymes, bronze-purple 'Russetings' and the white-flowering *Thymus serpyllum* var. *albus*. Chamomile is quite difficult to establish as a lawn and needs constant weeding, so is best kept on a small scale, as it is here. Paths are of stone slabs with brick or tiling edges to the beds.

The emphasis of the planting is on scented herbs with a purple, silver and white colour scheme predominating. Dark-green hyssop, which has blue flower spikes in summer, along with feathery bronze fennel, provide contrast and texture. Golden hops, trained against the wall, echoed by golden sage, lend brightness. Each of the main beds is edged with a low-growing lavender and has a standard rose at the centre.

Plan for a formal herb garden

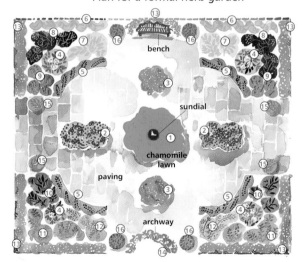

Key to planting plan

1. *Chamaemelum nobile* 'Treneague' – non-flowering chamomile
2. *Thymus serpyllum* 'Russetings' – creeping thyme (mauve-flowering)
3. *Thymus serpyllum* var. *albus* – creeping thyme (white-flowering)
4. *Rosa* 'Félicité Perpétue' – as a weeping standard
5. *Lavandula angustifolia* 'Hidcote' – low-growing lavender
6. *Humulus lupulus* 'Aureus' – golden hops
7. *Salvia officinalis* 'Icterina' – golden sage
8. *Foeniculum vulgare* 'Purpureum' – bronze fennel
9. *Hyssopus officinalis* – hyssop
10. *Salvia officinalis* Purpurascens Group – purple sage
11. *Salvia sclarea* – clary sage
12. *Artemisia absinthum* – wormwood
13. *Jasminum officinale* – jasmine
14. *Rosa* 'Albertine' – rose 'Albertine'
15. *Rosmarinus officinalis* – rosemary trained over a globe frame
16. *Buxus sempervirens* – box trained as a "lollipop"

Formal Beds and Borders

Beds edged with low hedges of clipped, dwarf box are a sure way of providing a formal, structured look. This works well for several beds, each being one element of a larger, overall design, or for a single herb border to stand alone.

A large border may also be subdivided by a pattern of internal hedges for a more interesting effect. The spaces in between construct individual planting areas for different species of herb. Timber or tiling edges are another way to give beds a neat finish in a formal scheme.

Right *Tightly clipped box hedging provides an orderly framework for herbs.*

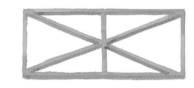

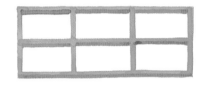

Left *Various designs for long, rectangular borders which are sub-divided by low, internal hedges. Diamonds and squares create satisfying patterns as border divisions and can be filled with a variety of other herbs.*

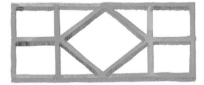

Above *Pyramids of box and tiling edges give beds a neat finish in a formal scheme.*

Clipped Mounds

Plants such as cotton lavender, or golden or variegated dwarf box, may be used as clipped mounds to great effect, either as edgings or to infill a whole bed. This kind of scheme has more impact if punctuated by clipped plants of a contrasting shape and colour: such as a large bed filled with mounds of silvery santolina, set against pyramids of dark-green box bordering a path.

A formal effect can also be achieved by planting blocks of herbs to make up a simple pattern of squares or triangular shapes, which can be repeated. This works most successfully for herbs of contrasting foliage colour and similar heights and habits: silver posie thyme, perhaps, with the dark green of wall germander, or golden and purple sage.

Topiary Herbs

Standard "mop-head" box or bay trees, pyramids or spiral shapes are an instant way to add formality. If you have time and patience you can train your own to shape, but it may be easier to buy them ready-grown. Topiary and citrus fruit trees in tubs were a popular feature in Tudor and Renaissance gardens, and can still work well in a modern scheme. Placed at strategic points in a geometric scheme, they add an old-fashioned touch and increase the sense of order and regularity. They can also be very useful for introducing the all-important dimension of height and visually linking the various elements of a garden.

Effective herbs for potted topiary include: bay, wall germander, mintbush (*Prostanthera rotundifolia*), rosemary, scented-leaf pelargoniums – especially *P. crispum* – myrtle and box.

Right *A bay tree clipped into a spiral emerges from a sea of lavender.*

Below *Box hedging punctuated by finials, tall clipped shapes in the beds and the trim, rounded heads of an avenue of* Quercus ilex *add up to topiary on a grand scale.*

Knot Gardens

Pattern is very satisfying to the eye and a knot garden always makes a stunning feature. The historic ideal consisted of four elements, each of a different pattern, but it would be as well to start with something simpler.

An area 3–4 m (10–13 ft) square will be large enough to contain an interesting, interwoven pattern. If possible it should be sited where it can be viewed from above – an upstairs window, neighbouring mound or raised level in the garden. It could also form an attractive centrepiece of a sunken garden. A sunny position and well-drained soil will suit it best. The old pattern books include a wide variety of hedging plants for knot gardens. To do the job effectively the

plants need to be evergreens with small leaves, dense growth and an ability to withstand close clipping. Although they all have attractive flowers and are not as neat and compact as box, excellent results can be obtained with the following herbs:

Teucrium chamaedrys has glossy, dark-green foliage, shaped like oak leaves. It is fully hardy and tolerates hard trimming, and is easy to grow from cuttings. Plant 23 cm (9 in) apart.

Santolina chamaecyparissus has silvery foliage. This responds well to close clipping and regenerates from old wood. Plant cuttings approximately 23 cm (9 in) apart. *Santolina rosmarinifolia* and *Santolina viridis* have acid-green leaves, treat these as *S. chamaecyparissus*.

Hyssopus officinalis has dark green foliage and is semi-evergreen. This often loses its leaves where winters are hard, but regenerates from old wood. Clip it regularly to avoid straggling and replace plants every four or five years. Plant 23 cm (9 in) apart.

Lavandula angustifolia 'Hidcote' – A low-growing lavender with silvery foliage. Immediately after flowering clip back to shape. However, do not cut into any old wood.

Using box for knot gardens

Box is ideal for knot gardens as its neat habit of growth means that it retains a clipped shape better than most plants. However, it is relatively slow-growing, and an instant finished effect is not easy to achieve.

Buxus sempervirens 'Suffruticosa' has bright-green leaves and is a compact plant, ideal for all edging work.

Buxus sempervirens 'Elegantissima' with small, silver-edged, olive-green leaves is slow-growing and makes a good contrast for darker leaves. *Buxus microphylla* 'Koreana' is low-growing and has dense, dark-green leaves.

It is best to choose compact varieties of box such as these, or the garden will soon grow unwieldy. Using all box makes a more manageable scheme than interspersing other knot garden plants, with different rates of growth and heights when mature.

'Elegantissima'   'Suffruticosa'   'Koreana'

Above *This striking pattern in the form of a foot maze at Hatfield House, England, symbolizes the complexities of following the Christian path through life.*

Right *A stunning and colourful knot garden of clipped box, with spaces between hedges filled with roses, lavender and scented herbs.*

To make a simple knot garden

YOU WILL NEED

Knot garden design
(shown); tape measure;
string; short lengths of
cane with pointed ends;
builder's set square
(in proportions 3:4:5);
plastic bottle and fine
sand; box plants

Tips for success:

• Prepare the site well. Dig in some garden
compost or manure, as it will be difficult to add
organic matter once the plants are established.

• Make sure the area is completely level –
use boards and a carpenter's spirit level.

• Accuracy of measuring out the design and
putting in the plants is essential. A large set
square, made of lengths of wood nailed together
in the proportion of 3:4:5, ensures accurate
90° angles at the corners.

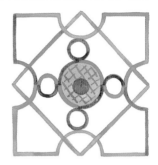

1 *Draw the plan out on
graph paper in measure-
ments to suit your plot (3–4 m
or 10–13 sq ft). Colour in the
design to represent the plants
to be used to achieve the effect
of interwoven ribbons.*

2 *Using the plan as a guide,
mark out the squares on
the ground using the tape
measure, string and short
lengths of cane. A builder's
square will ensure accurate
right angles.*

3 *Find the centre point of
each side of the outer
square and mark the semi-
circles by drawing arcs with
string attached to a cane. The
string should be the length of
the radius of the semi-circles.*

4 *Mark out the semi-circle
with the pointed canes and
attach the string tautly to
define the curve. This
provides an accurate guide to
follow when delineating the
design in sand.*

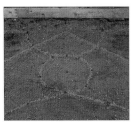

5 *Mark out the rest of the
design with string and
canes, measuring everything
carefully. To define the
pattern, fill a plastic bottle
with fine sand and pour it out
evenly along the lines of the
string and all markings.
Remove the string and canes.*

6 *Put in the plants, spacing
them evenly, 15 cm (6 in)
apart and keeping accurately
to the markings. Follow the
colour code on the plan,
making sure the interwoven
effect is achieved by putting
the right colour plant at the
intersections.*

7 *It will take two to three years for the plants to develop and
close the gaps. In the second year, pinch out the centres and
trim lightly to encourage growth. Once filled out, clip twice a
year (late spring and early autumn). Avoid clipping if there is
any danger of frost, as the new soft growth will be damaged by it.*

Informal Gardens

Designs based on fluid shapes and an irregular layout give plenty of scope for growing a variety of herbs. They often fit better than formal schemes with the style of a contemporary house and surroundings. Paths may be offset and gently curving, with beds and borders placed seemingly at random. Areas of hard material are often broken by greenery and flowers. Plants spill over on to the paths and spring up among the pea shingle; gaps are left among the paving stones of a terrace to be filled with creeping, aromatic herbs. Bare expanses of plant-free gravel are not in keeping with this style of garden.

Planting should be exuberant: forests of poppies, stands of valerian, a vibrant jumble of flowers and foliage. Pruning and trimming are, of course, essential, but the close-clipped look is less acceptable here.

This is not to say that the structure of the informal garden has to be completely irregular. A relaxed look is frequently achieved by the planting schemes as much as by the layout of beds and paths. This has its roots in the cottage garden genre of gardening, where a central path divided two rectangular areas, and lack of space forced an eclectic mix of plants.

In many informal gardens a regular framework works well. But it has to be simple – four rectangular beds, divided by intersecting paths, perhaps. There is little room for complex patterns and rigid symmetry.

Above *Exuberant planting in a cottage garden style.*

Above *Irregular circular shapes and a gently winding path in a display garden at the National Herb Centre, England.*

Plan for an informal herb garden

This has been designed as a peaceful, rustic retreat as well as being an all-purpose herb garden containing a wide variety of plants. A path of circular logs, laid at the side of the central sweep of gravel, leads around the edge of a pond to a wooden decking area for seating and a table. Creeping thymes are planted in pockets among the log paving, and architectural spires of mullein, *Verbascum thapsus*, spring up at random in the gravel.

The borders at either side are planted for colour and to provide a selection of culinary herbs as well. A further collection of culinary herbs in containers is sited near the seating area, and an olive tree in a tub (so that it can be moved to a protected area for winter) is near the entrance. This is surrounded by shrubby herbs: thyme, sage, prostrate rosemary and winter savory in a gravel mulch, which echoes the main area of gravel.

For early summer colour there are swathes of red and white valerian and opium poppies, to be followed later in the season by brilliant red bergamot, *Monarda didyma* 'Cambridge Scarlet'. A broad band of blue catmint, *Nepeta x faassenii*, leads the eye up to the pond, where the fine mossy growth of Corsican mint, *Mentha requienii*, spills over the logs, with clumps of chives and gold and green variegated gingermint nearby. An ornamental form of sweet flag, *Acorus gramineus* 'Variegatus', which does not grow as large as the more authentic sweet flag, *Acorus calamus*, is planted in the pond.

Behind the pond, the spearmint is planted in a bucket with no base to prevent it spreading. Angelica, lovage and fennel provide height and texture as well as being valuable culinary herbs. At the top of the garden, just on its boundaries, is a common elder, with golden and fern-leafed varieties for extra interest.

To complete the countryside feel of the garden and continue the timber theme the boundary could be further defined by traditional wicker screening.

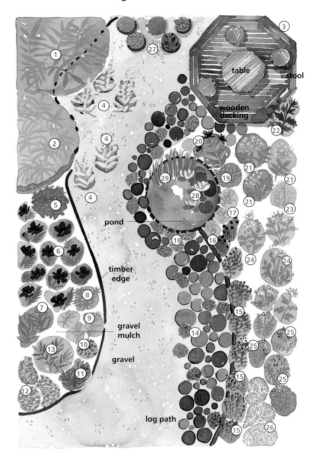

Key to planting plan

1. *Sambucus nigra* – common elder
2. *Sambucus nigra* 'Aurea' – golden elder
3. *Sambucus nigra* f. *laciniata* – fern-leafed elder
4. *Verbascum thapsus* – mullein
5. *Origanum onites* – pot marjoram
6. *Papaver somniferum* – opium poppy has white or lilac flowers, but there are many attractive cultivars in reds and pinks
7. *Salvia officinalis* – common sage
8. *Artemisia dracunculus* – tarragon
9. *Satureja montana* – winter savory
10. *Thymus vulgaris* – common thyme
11. *Rosmarinus officinalis* – Prostratus Group – prostrate rosemary
12. *Thymus vulgaris* 'Silver Posie' – silver posie thyme
13. *Olea europaea* – olive tree
14. *Thymus serpyllum* 'Bressingham Pink' – creeping thymes and *T. serpyllum* 'Coccineus'
15. *Nepeta* x *faassenii* – catmint
16. *Allium schoenoprasum* – chives
17. *Mentha* x *gracilis* 'Variegata' – gingermint
18. *Mentha requienii* – Corsican mint
19. *Mentha spicata* – spearmint
20. *Monarda didyma* 'Cambridge Scarlet' – bergamot, red flowering
21. *Angelica archangelica* – angelica
22. *Levisticum officinale* – lovage
23. *Foeniculum vulgare* – fennel
24. *Valeriana officinalis* – white valerian
25. *Centranthus ruber* – red valerian
26. *Helichrysum italicum* – curry plant
27. A selection of culinary herbs in pots
28. *Nymphaea odorata* – white water lily
29. *Acorus gramineus* 'Variegatus' – variegated sweet flag

Herbal Beds and Borders

Island beds or long borders can make gratifying small herb gardens where space is limited. They are ideal for providing a supply of herbs for cooking, or a colourful medley of medicinal and aromatic herbs for general household use. In larger beds, paths or narrow brick divisions may be appropriate as visual separations and to prevent invasive species from growing into each other. Stepping stones, placed in a random pattern, provide easy access to the plants for picking or weeding.

When planting island beds, tall subjects, such as angelica and lovage, may be placed at the centre, with lower growing plants surrounding them. In a border against a wall or hedge, plant heights look best graduated, with the tallest at the back and dwarf and creeping plants at the front. Introducing height with statuesque plants adds interest. Standards, especially of plants with irregular growth patterns – olive trees, lemon verbena, old-fashioned roses – also add extra height. Scented climbing plants, such as jasmine, hops or honeysuckle, trained over tepees of canes or wooden sticks, make unusual punctuation marks in a large border.

Above *A simple, rectangular border with paved divisions, set in a gravel surround, makes a self-contained herb garden.*

Left *Bronze fennel contrasts well with white-flowering* Galega officinalis *'Alba'.*

Below *A river of creeping thymes, flanked at right by gallica roses (*R.g. *var.* officinalis *and* R.g. *'Versicolor'), makes an imaginative and decorative feature.*

Above *Closely-packed herbs provide a riot of midsummer colour.*

Right *Alternating clumps of purple and green-leafed sage, Salvia officinalis.*

Below *A pocket of mixed thymes, set in golden stone.*

Raised Beds

These have many advantages. They can be used to provide ideal conditions where garden soil is unsuitable. If your garden is on heavy clay, which most herbs dislike, especially the shrubby, Mediterranean varieties, a raised bed can offer the requisite free-draining environment. Where soil is poor and dry, a raised bed can be filled with a good moisture-retentive growing medium for herbs that need damp ground. Beds at a higher level can also make gardening easier and more rewarding for the disabled or elderly. For everyone, they allow plants to be seen from a new perspective so that flowers, foliage and scents can all be appreciated more closely.

Heights of raised beds may be varied according to intended purpose or preference. Old illustrations reveal the popularity from medieval times into the age of the Renaissance garden, of beds raised from the surrounding paths by no more than a few inches. For old-style physic gardens and formal potagers, low raised beds, edged with timber, are both practical and decorative.

Above *A brick-built raised bed provides a free-draining environment, which suits many herbs, especially those of Mediterranean origin.*

There are various materials that can be used for constructing raised beds:
Timber – use planks that are wide enough to sink into the ground. Screw or nail together securely at the corners and treat with wood preservative suitable for plants.

Railway sleepers (railroad ties) can be used for a rustic, informal look. Clean off any tar and preservatives, which are toxic to plants, with solvent. A plastic membrane may be necessary for heavily impregnated sleepers. No foundations are necessary as their weight makes them stable. Lay them flat, rather than on edge, for stability and fix together at the corners with steel rods, driven through them and into the ground.

Bricks are durable and attractive in a variety of settings (especially old bricks). Check they are frostproof as ordinary housebricks may not be suitable.

Above *A raised bed made of timber with feverfew and grasses.*

Above *Marjorams growing in a bed walled with stone.*

Above *Herbs flourish in a brick-built raised bed.*

Making a raised bed

Raised beds can be laid out as functional squares and rectangles, in decorative shapes or made to fit a corner of the garden such as this bed for culinary herbs.

YOU WILL NEED

Short stakes or dowel; string; builder's set square; fine sand or line-marker paint; tape measure; cement; ballast; builder's sand; pointing trowel; approximately 90 bricks; spirit level; waterproof paint; paintbrush; rubble; gravel or pea shingle (pea stone); 3 bags of topsoil; potting medium; a selection of herbs

1 *Mark out the shape of the bed on the ground, using a short, pointed stake or dowel and string. Use a builder's set square to ensure correct right angles. Define the lines with a dribble of fine sand, or use line-marker paint.*

2 *Dig out the soil along the markings to a depth and width of 15 cm (6 in). Fill in with concrete to within 5 cm (2 in) of the top. Firm down, level and leave for 24 hours to set completely. For concrete, use one part cement to four parts ballast.*

3 *Build up four or five courses of bricks, and set into mortar, carefully checking with a spirit level at each stage. (Mortar is one part cement to four parts sharp or builder's sand.)*

4 *Clean up the mortar, while it is still wet, with a pointing trowel. Leave it to harden.*

5 *Before filling with soil, coat the inside of the wall with a waterproof paint.*

6 *Put in a layer of rubble, topped with gravel or pea shingle for drainage. Fill in with bought topsoil and stir in a top layer of a good potting medium.*

7 *Plant up the raised bed with your chosen herbs.*

8 *The completed raised bed planted with a selection of culinary herbs and wild strawberries.*

Herb Wheels

These were a feature of numerous Victorian gardens, when old cart-wheels (wagon wheels) were plentiful. They provided frameworks of little beds containing kitchen herbs, the spokes prevented the different varieties from encroaching on each other. If you are using an old cartwheel, it must be treated with a plant-friendly preservative to prevent the timber from rotting. The spokes may also be a little close together to be practical, so consider removing some of them.

A brick-built wheel is long-lasting and the sections can be more effectively allocated. Choose a location in full sun if possible, and if it is for culinary herbs, put it near the kitchen.

Above *An intriguing design for a herb wheel at the Henry Doubleday Research Association.*

Above *Nasturtiums are good in salads.*

Above *Pot marigolds add bright colour to a herb garden.*

Above *Chives and golden marjoram.*

Herbs for a cook's herb wheel

Medium- to low-growing herbs of similar heights make for a balanced effect.

Perennial selection:

Allium schoenoprasum – Chives. Mild onion flavour herb with attractive, purple flowers.

Origanum onites – Pot marjoram. Warm-flavoured leaves, with pinkish-purple flowers.

Satureja montana – Winter savory. Makes an aromatic, neat pillow of dark-green foliage with white flowers.

Thymus x *citriodorus* – Thyme. Delicious, lemon-scented thyme.

Salvia officinalis Purpurascens Group – Purple sage. Bold purple and green foliage; strong, savoury taste.

Foeniculum vulgare – Fennel. Tall, feathery plant with an aniseed flavour for central pot.

Petroselinum crispum – Parsley. Biennial. It is also suitable for growing as an annual.

Annual selection to sow from seed:

Calendula officinalis – Pot marigold. Well worth including for the brilliance of its flowers. Self-seeds.

Anthriscus cerefolium – Chervil. A delicately flavoured herb, which is fully hardy and can be sown successively for a continuous supply. Self-seeds.

Coriandrum sativum – Coriander (Cilantro). Spicy flavour. Thin out seedlings and keep moist.

Tropaeolum majus – Nasturtium. Grow it for the bright flowers and use them in salads.

Ocimum glabrescens 'Purple Ruffles' – Purple basil. The foliage provides a foil for other green herbs. Good basil flavour.

Satureja hortensis – Summer savory. This is more subtly flavoured than the perennial variety and it goes very well with beans.

Anethum graveolens – Dill. Plant in the central pot for its feathery foliage and delicate taste.

Making a raised brick herb wheel

1 *Using a length of string equal to the radius of the bed, attached to a piece of pointed cane, mark out a circle on the ground. Then shorten the string and mark a small inner circle at the centre. Sink a length of earthenware (clay) sewage pipe (from builder's merchants or building supply stores) in the centre. Then measure off equal points on the circumference to form the spokes, marking them out with canes and string.*

2 *Trace over the whole design with fine sand or line-marker paint.*

3 *Dig a trench for the bricks and fill with sharp or builder's sand.*

4 *Construct as for the raised bed (steps 3–5), putting in one or two layers of bricks, set in mortar, to form the outer circle and spokes.*

5 *Fill in the sections of the wheel and the earthenware pipe with rubble, then gravel or pea shingle, topsoil and compost (soil mix).*

YOU WILL NEED

String; short canes or dowel; earthenware (clay) sewage pipe; fine sand or line-marker paint; tape measure; sharp sand; approximately 90 bricks; cement; builder's sand; ballast; pointing trowel; spirit level; waterproof paint; rubble; gravel or pea shingle; 3 bags of topsoil; compost (soil mix); a selection of culinary herbs

6 *Plant the herb wheel with a selection of culinary herbs such as wild strawberry, thyme, sage, rosemary and lemon verbena.*

Themed Gardens

A themed garden can make a vibrant and colourful display for herbs. In the following section there are plans for various styles of gardens – an old-fashioned medieval garden, a decorative Shakespearean garden with a small knot garden of clipped box, and a pot-pourri garden with many different fragrant herbs and scented flowers. The cook's or kitchen garden is not only productive but will look good too.

The potager is intended mainly for culinary use but with bold use of colour, it makes an excellent ornamental layout. The plan for a traditional apothecary's garden with small, individual plots of medicinal herbs shows how to make a functional, but very eye-catching, herb garden, that needs the bare minimum of maintenance.

Right *A re-creation of a medieval pleasure garden with scented herbs, at Tretower Court, Wales.*

Medieval Garden

Above *Herbs such as valerian and feverfew grow in the raised beds of this medieval-style garden. When gardens like this were laid out, beauty was not a consideration, but with their symmetry, and the colours and shapes of the plants, the effect is delightful.*

In gardens of the Middle Ages herbs were often grown in small beds, each devoted to a single species. This made it easy to tend and harvest the plants, as well as to identify them, and was the chosen style of monastery and physic gardens, whose primary purpose was practical.

By the 12th and 13th centuries pleasure gardens, based on cloister gardens, became a feature of palaces and castles. These usually took the form of a small enclosed "privy" garden, for the benefit of the lady of the house and her attendants. King Henry III installed one for his queen, stipulating that it should have a pleasant herbery and high walls so that no one should enter except the Queen. There are narrow beds at the side, and a seat or an arbour is standard, and often there is a fountain splashing in the corner.

Plan for a medieval garden

This small garden, designed to take up approximately 6 x 8 m (19 x 26 ft), is surrounded by a trellis, with a low fence on one side and a Gothic arch as entranceway. Since a "flowery mead" would be an impractical proposition in this space, the path is made of gravel, with a central bed of pot marigolds, surrounded by a chamomile lawn.

Two chamomile seats, made as raised beds, are separated by a gallica rose, with further gallica roses at opposite corners.

Rosa eglanteria, the eglantine rose of Chaucer's day, climbs over the trellis, but a compromise has been made with the other climbing rose, 'Noisette Carnée'. This rose, unlike the others, is not ancient enough to be a true medieval rose, but has a delicate old-fashioned form and the great benefit of repeat flowering to provide interest over a longer period.

Narrow beds against the perimeter are planted with a froth of lady's mantle, flax (with its profusion of dainty blue flowers),

feverfew, wild strawberries and other plants common at the time – though a modern cultivar, *Achillea millefolium* 'Moonshine', has been substituted for wild yarrow, which would be too invasive for the area and not very attractive. There is a small fountain and shallow pond in one corner, with the moisture-loving *Iris versicolor* planted at its margins. White Madonna lilies, popular in the medieval era as a symbol of purity and associated with the Virgin Mary, are planted in pots.

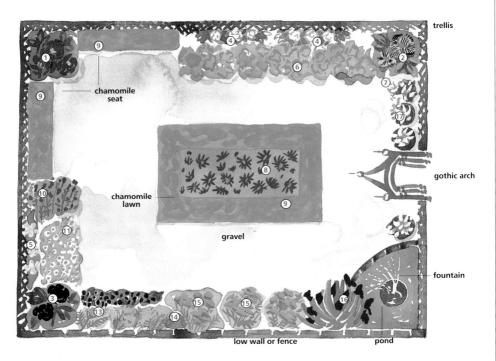

trellis

chamomile seat

chamomile lawn

gravel

gothic arch

fountain

low wall or fence

pond

Key to planting plan

1. *Rosa gallica* var. *officinalis* – the fuschia-pink apothecary's rose
2. *Rosa gallica* var. *officinalis* 'Versicolor' – pink-and-white-striped gallica rose
3. *Rosa gallica* var. *officinalis* 'Tuscany Superb' – dark-crimson, double gallica
4. *Rosa* 'Noisette Carnée' (syn. 'Blush Noisette') – pale-pink repeat-flowering climber

5. *Rosa eglanteria* – sweet briar rose, a vigorous climber with simple, palest pink blooms.
6. *Alchemilla mollis* – lady's mantle
7. *Thymus vulgaris* 'Silver Posie' – thyme with silver-variegated foliage
8. *Calendula officinalis* – pot marigold
9. *Chamaemelum nobile* 'Treneague' – a non-flowering chamomile

10. *Linum usitatissimum* – flax
11. *Tanacetum parthenium* – feverfew
12. *Fragaria vesca* – wild strawberry
13. *Tanacetum vulgare* – tansy
14. *Thymus vulgaris* – thyme
15. *Achillea millefolium* 'Moonshine'
16. *Iris versicolor* – blue flag
17. *Lilium candidum* – Madonna lily

Shakespearean Garden

For those with a literary bent, a garden based on the herbs and flowers included in the works of Shakespeare makes an exciting project. No other poet and playwright can have made so many references to these plants, nor indicated such a delight in them and knowledge of their uses and characteristics. There is also scope for a comprehensive selection, as over 130 plants are mentioned, some under two or three different names.

Culinary herbs include "saffron to colour the warden pies", "a dish of caraways" (caraway seeds) to eat with apples and "parsley to stuff a rabbit". Garlic gets several mentions, usually in connection with its odour on the breath, and onions are linked with tears.

Medicinal uses of plants make frequent entrances – though the portrait of the downtrodden apothecary (in *Romeo and Juliet*) with his "old cakes of roses" and other accoutrements "thinly scattered to make up a show" is hardly a flattering one. The narcotic properties of poppies and mandrake are referred to several times and the myth that mandrakes scream when uprooted is perpetuated. The power of the witch's brew is noted, with its deadly "root of hemlock digged i' the dark". The symbolic associations of herbs are acknowledged such as wormwood for bitterness, and also rosemary for remembrance.

Household uses of herbs include polishing chairs with juice of balm in *The Merry Wives of Windsor*; and the soothing power of scented flowers is memorably evoked in Oberon's description of Titania's bower in *A Midsummer Night's Dream*:

*I know a bank whereon the wild
thyme blows,
Where oxlips and the nodding
violet grows
Quite over-canopied with luscious
woodbine [honeysuckle],
With sweet musk-roses, and with
eglantine.*

Who could resist re-creating this for themselves? For researching the full extent of Shakespeare's references to herbs, *Shakespeare Concordance* by A. Bartlett, 1894, is a great help.

Other works include: *The Plant-lore and Garden Craft of Shakespeare* – by Rev. Henry N. Ellacombe, 1884; *The Flora and Folklore of Shakespeare* – by F.G. Savage (Shakespeare Press, 1923); *The Shakespeare Garden* – by Esther Singleton (William Farquhar Payson, New York, 1931); *Shakespeare's Wild Flowers* – by Eleanour Sinclair Rohde (the Medici Society 1935); *The Flowers of Shakespeare* – by Doris Hunt (Webb and Bower, 1980).

Above *Box and cotton lavender form intertwining ribbons in a garden edging.*

Plan for a Shakespearean garden

The plan is for a garden approximately 9 x 13 m (29 x 43 ft) in the formal style that was popular in Shakespeare's day. At the centre is a small knot garden of clipped box, surrounded by narrow borders of lavender and pinks. Three spacious steps lead to an arbour on a higher level, so that the knot can be viewed from above. Creeping thyme is planted in pockets on the stone slabs in front of the seat, and over the steps. The arbour is clad in honeysuckle and roses and surrounded by the 'wild thyme' and other flowers and herbs of Titania's bower. Raised beds, with brick-retaining walls, form the boundaries and topiary trees in tubs visually link the garden and mark the entrance points. Poisonous plants such as hemlock, henbane, aconitum and others have not been included in this garden for safety reasons. The two rue bushes are at the back of the border, where they are least likely to be accidentally brushed. Rue can cause blistering on contact, but has long been a popular aromatic plant.

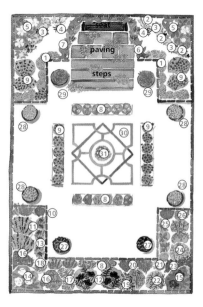

Key to planting plan

1. *Thymus serpyllum* – wild thyme
2. *Viola odorata/Viola tricolor* – violets and heartsease
3. *Primula veris/Primula vulgaris* – cowslips/primrose
4. *Lilium candidum* – Madonna lily
5. *Rosa moschata* – musk rose
6. *Rosa rubiginosa* – sweet briar rose
7. *Lonicera periclymenum* – honeysuckle
8. *Dianthus caesius/Dianthus deltoides* – pinks
9. *Lavandula angustifolia* 'Hidcote' – lavender
10. *Satureja montana* – winter savory
11. *Consolida ajacis* – larkspur
12. *Papaver somniferum* – opium poppies
13. *Calendula officinalis* – pot marigold
14. *Rosa x alba* – white rose of York
15. *Rosa gallica* var. *officinalis* – red rose of Lancaster
16. *Ruta graveolens* – rue
17. *Artemisia absinthium* – wormwood
18. *Hyssopus officinalis* – hyssop
19. *Origanum onites* – marjoram
20. *Mentha* spp. – mint
21. *Carum carvi* – caraway
22. *Foeniculum vulgare* – fennel
23. *Borago officinalis* – borage
24. *Melissa officinalis* 'Aurea' – variegated lemon balm
25. *Petroselinum crispum* – parsley
26. *Sanguisorba minor* – salad burnet
27. *Laurus nobilis* – standard bay
28. *Buxus sempervirens* – standard box
29. *Rosmarinus officinalis* – rosemary (trained as topiary)
30. *Buxus sempervirens* 'Suffruticosa' – dwarf box
31. *Myrtus communis* subsp. *tarentina* – dwarf myrtle

Top *The flower stems of silvery blue* Sempervivums *create an intricate pattern.*

Above *Lavender grows very well in the free-draining soil of a bed with raised timber edge.*

Opposite *An Elizabethan knot garden, closely planted with colourful flowers for a richly embroidered effect, at Stratford-upon-Avon, England.*

Pot-pourri Garden

There is a long tradition of drying scented flowers and aromatic herbs for sweetening the air. Stillroom books of the 17th and 18th centuries include many recipes for scented powders and "perfumes" as pot-pourri was more usually known then. The term as currently used to describe a mixture of dried fragrant petals and leaves did not become common until the 19th century. It comes from the name of a Spanish stew, *olla podrida* (literally meaning "rotten pot"), and the French translation of pot-pourri came to mean any medley or mixture.

An area of scented herbs and flowers, which can be picked for pot-pourri, makes a rewarding garden feature. Stock it with plenty of roses – pink and red ones are best as they retain good colour when dried.

"Rose-leaves ... were gathered even as they fell to make into a pot-pourri for someone who had no garden." (*Cranford* by Mrs Gaskell).

Above *A pergola covered in old-fashioned roses provides plenty of petals for drying.*

Plan for a pot-pourri garden

This plan would fit into an area about 8 m (26 ft) square to make a scented garden with plenty of material to cut for making pot-pourri. The four corner beds, set in a grass path, are edged with dwarf box and filled with colourful flowers and fragrant herbs. The central circular area is brick-paved, with pockets for a low-growing double chamomile and vivid caraway thyme. The gazebo supports a richly perfumed, dark crimson 'Ena Harkness' climbing rose and a cloud of jasmine. There is room beneath it for a seat, or a small table and some stools, and it is surrounded by pots of colourful, scented pelargoniums, pineapple sage and lemon verbena.

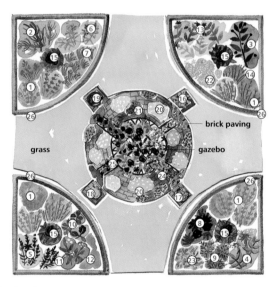

Key to planting plan

1. *Lavandula angustifolia* 'Munstead' – dark blue, low-growing lavender
2. *Rosmarinus officinalis* – rosemary
3. *Myrtus communis* – myrtle
4. *Angelica archangelica* – angelica
5. *Agastache foeniculum* – anise hyssop
6. *Hyssopus officinalis* – hyssop
7. *Dianthus* 'London Delight' – an old-fashioned pink
8. *Paeonia officinalis* 'Rubra Plena' – a rich red paeony
9. *Artemisia abrotanum* – southernwood
10. *Coriandrum sativum* – coriander (cilantro)
11. *Tanacetum balsamita* – alecost
12. *Consolida ajacis* – larkspur
13. *Monarda* 'Croftway Pink' – a pink bergamot
14. *Iris germanica* var. *florentina* – Orris
15. *Rosa* 'François Juranville' – a gold-pink rose, as a weeping standard
16. *Aloysia triphylla* – lemon verbena
17. *Pelargonium tomentosum* – peppermint scented
18. *Pelargonium* 'Lady Plymouth' – scented-leaf geranium, with cream margins
19. *Salvia elegans* – pineapple sage
20. *Chamaemelum nobile* 'Flore Pleno' – dwarf, double-flowered chamomile
21. *Thymus herba-barona* – caraway-scented thyme
22. *Thymus vulgaris* 'Silver Posie' – a silver-leafed thyme
23. *Mentha x gracilis* 'Variegata' – gingermint
24. *Jasminum officinale* –the white-flowering jasmine
25. *Rosa* 'Ena Harkness' – dark-red climbing rose
26. *Buxus sempervirens* 'Suffruticosa' – dwarf box

To make a rose pot-pourri

Making your own pot-pourri is a rewarding and creative experience. The results will have individuality and a more pleasant fragrance than shop-bought.

YOU WILL NEED

3 cups dried rose petals;
2 cups mixed dried flowers;
15 ml (1 tbsp) dried lavender;
1 cup mixed dried herbs: mint,
marjoram, thyme and angelica;
5 ml (1 tsp) cloves; 2.5 ml/½ tsp)
ground allspice; 10 ml (2 tsp)
ground orris root; 5–10 drops
rose essential oil

1 *To dry the plant material, pick everything on a dry day. Spread out on newspaper and leave in a warm, airy place (out of direct sunlight) for 5–7 days, until papery to the touch.*

2 *To make the pot-pourri, combine all the ingredients, mix thoroughly and put them in an airtight container. Leave in a dry, warm place for 2–3 weeks, shaking the container occasionally.*

Above *A traditional rose garden in full bloom and (right) a garden of scented herbs and flowers for making pot-pourri.*

Cook's Garden

A small border or bed can provide a surprisingly good selection of herbs to meet basic culinary needs, especially if supplemented by a few tubs and containers. A sunny location is important as the herbs will thrive and have a better flavour. For convenience the kitchen garden should be sited as close to the kitchen door as possible so that herbs can be harvested without you having to trudge too far.

Plan for a cook's garden of herbs

A semicircular-shaped bed against a wall allows space for 13 useful herbs, with bay, basil and mint in containers: tender basil is much easier to grow in a pot, and mint is inclined to spread into its neighbours. A narrow brick path divides the space and makes it easier to reach the plants when tending or picking them.

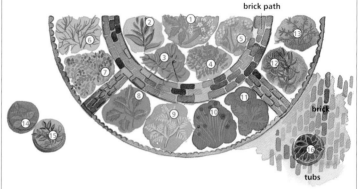

brick path

brick

tubs

Key to planting plan

1. *Angelica archangelica* – angelica
2. *Salvia officinalis* – sage
3. *Artemisia dracunculus* – tarragon
4. *Origanum onites* – pot marjoram
5. *Levisticum officinale* – lovage
6. *Anethum graveolens* – dill
7. *Thymus vulgaris* or *Thymus x citriodorus* – thyme or lemon thyme
8. *Coriandrum sativum* – coriander (cilantro)
9. *Anthriscus cerefolium* – chervil
10. *Allium schoenoprasum* – chives
11. *Petroselinum crispum* – parsley
12. *Rosmarinus officinalis* Prostratus Group – prostrate rosemary
13. *Satureja montana* – winter savory
14. *Ocimum basilicum* – sweet basil
15. *Mentha spicata* – spearmint
16. *Laurus nobilis* – bay

Above left *An informal kitchen herb garden with nasturtiums and coriander (cilantro).*

Far left *A pot of golden and purple sage provides a ready source of leaves for cooking.*

Left *Sweet basil is a traditional complementary flavour for tomatoes.*

Potager

A potager is a garden where vegetables and herbs are grown together in an ornamental layout. Early cooks' gardens contained as many herbs as "vegetables" – as we now call them – with little distinction being made between the two. "Sallet"(salad) herbs in Elizabethan times included a wide variety of unusual leaves and colourful flowers. They were also made into stuffings and uncooked sweet and savoury sauces: flower petals pulverized with ground almonds and sugar, or potent mixtures of green herbs pounded together in vinegar.

Growing herbs and vegetables together is practical and ornamental at the same time. Mixed plantings of this nature suffer less from pests because the bright flowers of many herbs attract beneficial insects, such as lacewings and ladybirds (bugs). At the same time, aromatic plants deter aphids and other insects. If vegetables are intermingled with strong-smelling herbs, rather than planted in huge blocks on their own, they become a less obvious target for the pests normally attracted to them.

As with all vegetable growing, allowance must be made for rotation of crops and there will inevitably be bare patches at intervals to accommodate this. But the garden is afforded a permanent structure by the framework of paths and perennial herbs.

Paths may be of gravel, brick, stone or any hard material. The central one should be at least 1 m (3 ft) wide and the divisions between the beds no less than 0.5 m (20 in). Beds should be no more than 1.5 m (5 ft) wide so that they are easy to reach; timber or tiling edges give them a neat finish and link the elements of the garden together.

Archways for climbing plants at the entrance or at the centre of the garden add height and visual appeal. Espaliered fruit trees at the perimeter make a practical and decorative screen. A tunnelled archway of apples or pears is a traditional feature.

Plan for a potager garden

This potager is both practical and ornamental, with beds about 1.5 m (5 ft) in length and paths 0.5 m(20 in) wide.

The plan below allows for perennial herbs, such as lavender, rosemary and sage, to be planted at the ends of each bed.

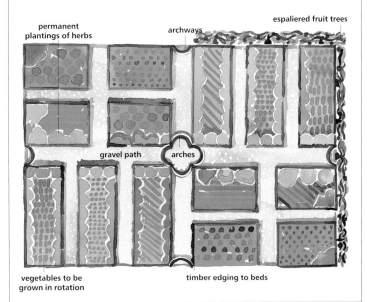

permanent plantings of herbs

archways

espaliered fruit trees

gravel path

arches

vegetables to be grown in rotation

timber edging to beds

Above *A formal potager of box-edged beds, packed with sturdy vegetables, ruby chard (foreground), sweetcorn, marrow and beans, interspersed with aromatic rosemary.*

Apothecary's Garden

Also known as a "physic garden", the apothecary's garden was the source of raw materials for making medicines to heal the sick.

In the tradition of the monasteries, a range of "simples", or medicinal plants, were grown in their own little plots. These were sometimes prescribed to be used on their own, or, more frequently, the apothecary concocted compounds from them, consisting of several ingredients. The advantage of keeping each herb in its separate bed in this way was to make identification easier when it came to picking, as well as being an efficient method of cultivation on a small scale. It also provided easy access for planting, weeding and watering.

When making their remedies, the apothecaries were guided by a variety of herbals: the earliest of which was written in China nearly 5,000 years ago. They also studied the works of the great physicians of ancient Greece – Hippocrates, Galen, Theophrastrus and Dioscorides – and the texts from the Dark Ages which were

copied by generations of monks, and given a new lease of life by the invention of printing in the mid-15th century.

The role and influence of the apothecary began to wane during the 16th century as European herbalists started to base their work on empirical observations of plants. John Gerard's *Herball or Generall Historie of Plantes* was in this tradition of enquiry and was first published in England in 1597. Apothecaries established their own society at the beginning of the 16th century and were the pharmacists of the time, dispensing drugs for the physicians and giving out medical advice to patients.

Above *Herbs growing in little beds, created by gaps in paving slabs, make an attractive and practical medicinal garden.*

Left *A collection of herbs in sunken pots, carefully labelled to ensure correct identification.*

A modern garden of herbs for making home remedies, which draws on the best of these traditions, has understated charm and is a low-maintenance way to grow herbs. Filled with traditional herbs, such as bright gold pot marigolds (*Calendula officinalis*), neatly patterned houseleek (*Sempervivum tectorum*), aromatic lavender, rosemary, thyme and sage, laid out in a simple configuration of beds, it will be both functional and eye-catching.

Top *Houseleek is a useful plant for soothing skin irritations.*

Above *Pot marigolds are picked for drying before they have a chance to go over.*

Plan for an apothecary's garden

This garden of medicinal plants is based on the old idea of individual plots for each herb, but simplified and brought up to date by setting the herbs among paving slabs. The plan is uncomplicated by the need to lay paths, or put in edgings. All that is required is a level, completely weed-free site, some paving slabs and a base of sand and cement to bed them into. The design will fit a space of 4.5 x 6 m (15 x 19 ft).

Key to planting plan

1. *Calendula officinalis* – pot marigold – for soothing creams
2. *Sempervivum tectorum* – houseleek – for chapped skin and insect bites
3. *Myrtus communis* – myrtle – for sinusitis and bronchial infections
4. *Foeniculum officinalis* – fennel – for indigestion
5. *Marrubium vulgare* – horehound – for coughs
6. *Tanacetum parthenium* – feverfew – for migraines
7. *Salvia officinalis* – sage – for mouth and gum infections
8. *Lavandula stoechas* – lavender – for tension headaches
9. *Rosmarinus officinalis* – rosemary - for colds and depression
10. *Thymus vulgaris* – thyme – for sore throats
11. *Origanum onites* – pot marjoram – for arthritis
12. *Allium sativum* – garlic – for warding off colds
13. *Valeriana officinalis* – valerian – for insomnia
14. *Hypericum perforatum* – St John's wort – for anxiety and nervous tension

Boundaries

A herb garden with its own distinct boundaries becomes a secluded retreat, a place to sit and relax away from the pressures of the outside world. The key point is that the enclosing wall, fence or hedge does not have to be very solid, or even high – so as not to cast too much shade, which is usually better for gardens. It is the illusion of a place apart that counts, which can be achieved just as effectively with a low balustrade fence or plant-clothed pergola. And even a low division still provides some shelter, reduces the wind-chill factor and helps to retain and intensify the fragrance of the plants.

Above *A simple construction of posts and cross-rails divides areas of a kitchen garden.*

Above *Trelliswork, in the foreground, makes an effective internal division in a secluded garden bounded by a wall and plant-clothed walkway.*

A garden entirely enclosed by high brick walls enjoys its own warm microclimate. But in order not to be overpowering it has to cover a reasonably large area, as in the walled kitchen gardens of the grand houses of the past. In the smaller gardens of today, it is sometimes possible to make use of a high brick wall as one boundary, but other internal walls are best kept to a height of about 60 cm–1 m (2–3 ft).

Fences are a useful way to provide an instant screen and come in a wide range of materials. Choose one that is sympathetic to the overall style of your herb garden. A simple balustrade fence can work very well, or a traditional picket fence, popular in many American herb gardens: these are often painted white, but also look good with a green or blue finish. Wattle or wicker screens, as used in medieval enclosures, are another congenial fencing material.

Trelliswork, also known as treillage, makes a versatile boundary. It adds elegance and romance and works in formal or informal settings. Trellis comes in different patterns, may be painted in a range of colours and provides a frame for climbing plants. It is important, as for all fences, that the support posts are solid and firmly installed. The easiest and longest-lasting method of securing posts is to bed them into a custom-made pointed metal base set into the ground, or set them into a rubble and concrete base. Timber posts should be treated with preservative – choose one that does not harm plants. (If you use creosote, planting must be delayed for a year, as it can harm plants.)

Pergolas are another way of making a visual boundary, rather than a solid screen, and will suit a small garden as well as a large one. A covered or semi-covered walkway, clothed in plants, was a traditional feature of many 17th-century gardens and it was usually called an "arbour" or "herber". Strictly speaking a pergola should be constructed as a double row to form an arched walkway with a curved or rectangular top. But it can also be made as a single row of posts and cross-rails, to act as a support for climbers and to make an internal fence or division.

Espaliered fruit trees trained flat against a system of posts with wires strained horizontally between them provide an openwork, living screen as a boundary or division. They can be planted in a single row or a double one to form a walk. They also look good trained against a wall. Plant as young trees, removing any side shoots and training the branches along the wires as they grow.

Hedging Plants

Hedges make the ideal boundary for many herb gardens. They divide different areas and delineate paths. They may be formally clipped, or left to a more natural pattern of growth, and reach different heights to provide a high dense screen or a low division. Low, clipped hedges form knot-garden patterns. Choose from a selection of the following:

• *Taxus baccata* – Yew. Slow-growing, but makes a superb screen and its dark green provides a foil for many plants.

• *Buxus sempervirens* – Box. Makes an excellent hedge for a neat, clipped finish. Formal hedges – low to medium height.

• *Buxus sempervirens* 'Suffruticosa' – Dwarf box. Much more compact than the common box, ideal for knot gardens.

• *Santolina chamaecyparissus* – Cotton lavender. A silver plant which responds well to clipping into mounds or low hedges.

• *Teucrium chamaedrys* – Wall germander. The dark-green foliage needs frequent trimming to keep it in shape. Can be grown as an informal hedge and left to flower.

• *Origanum vulgare* 'Aureum' – Golden marjoram. Although it can be clipped to form mounds, its relaxed habit of growth makes it less suitable as a conventional formal hedge.

• *Rosmarinus officinalis* – Rosemary. Can be clipped to a squared-off hedge shape, or trimmed as an informal hedge.

• *Rosa rugosa* – Rose. This forms a dense, impenetrable barrier of medium to full height.

• *Artemisia abrotanum* – Southernwood. Light-green, feathery foliage makes a delightful informal hedge that needs trimming only once or twice a year.

• *Hyssopus officinalis* – Hyssop. It is possible to clip this to a formal shape, but the blue flower spikes make it worth growing in its natural form, lightly trimmed. Cut back in the spring.

• *Lavandula* spp. – Lavender. There are different heights to choose from. Makes a fragrant hedge, needing little attention, apart from cutting back firmly (but not into old wood) after flowering.

Planting a hedge

1 *Dig out a shallow trench along the line of the proposed hedge and fork over the soil at the base of it to ensure good drainage.*

2 *Add plenty of garden compost, digging it lightly into the soil, and just before planting, fork in a sprinkling of blood, fish and bone organic fertilizer, wearing gloves and a respirator mask.*

3 *Mark the centre line of the hedge with string and pegs, put in the plants, spacing them evenly by using a measured length of wood – 23 cm (9 in) apart is suitable for most. Fill in the soil, firming it around each plant, and water.*

4 *The hedge will soon become established, ready for its first trim in the second year. Give it a mulch of compost in subsequent years or add a little organic fertilizer to the soil, watering it in.*

Above *Rosemary forms a good hedge-like boundary in this enclosed herb garden.*

Focal Points

The design of the herb garden will be stronger and have more impact with the inclusion of focal points to draw the eye. They may be in a central position or at the end of a path or vista. A sundial is a traditional feature in many herb gardens. Birdbaths and fountains introduce the soothing element of water. A stone urn overflowing with trailing or flowering herbs is always a simple but effective centrepiece, and standard topiary trees in tubs make versatile and movable points of interest.

An arbour, in the sense of a covered seat or shelter, strikes just the right note in an ornamental herb garden. It provides a focal point as well as being a frame for climbing plants, and introduces the all-important dimension of height. At the same time it adds a hint of mystery and makes a secluded place to sit and enjoy the sights and scents of the surroundings. Sited at the end of a walk, in a far corner or high vantage point, it becomes an inevitable attraction that has to be visited. Arbours may be constructed from many types of materials including posts and rails, trellis, metal frames, or, for a more rustic look, wickerwork.

Archways can be sited to emphasize an important feature, such as a statue, within the garden itself, or to frame a distant view.

Right *The elegant façade of a distant house is framed by an archway of roses.*

Opposite *A fountain makes an attractive centrepiece in a sheltered garden.*

Below *A water-lily pond provides the focal point in the centre of a cloister herb garden.*

Choosing Herbs

When working out planting schemes it pays to think about the colour and texture of the herbs you choose and to group them for best effect. They will flourish and make a better show, too, if given the right conditions – damp or dry, sun or shade. One of the many advantages of a herb garden is that it has quite a long season of interest – often provided by the colour of the leaves (many of which are evergreen). Foliage colours available include silver, or silvery-blue, bronze, purple and gold as well as all the greens.

Ruta graveolens 'Jackman's Blue' – Rue. Steely-blue, strikingly indented foliage.
Salvia officinalis – Sage. Greeny-grey, oval, rough-textured leaves.
Santolina chamaecyparissus – Cotton lavender. A good strong silver, finely indented foliage.
Thymus vulgaris 'Silver Posie' and *T. x citriodorus* 'Silver Queen' – Best of the silver thymes, with delicate variegations.

Bronze and Purple

Ajuga reptans 'Burgundy Glow' – Bronze bugle. Glossy, bronze foliage.

Above *Rue and curry plant in flower.*

Silver

Artemisia abrotanum – Southernwood. Greeny-grey, feathery leaves.
Artemisia absinthium – Wormwood. Silvery-grey, finely indented leaves.
Artemisia ludoviciana 'Silver Queen' – Western mugwort. Fine, silvery lanceolate leaves.
Artemisia pontica – Roman wormwood. Silver, upright, foliage spikes.
Dianthus spp. – Pinks. Foliage colouring varies, most are blue-grey.
Eucalyptus globulus – Eucalyptus. Silvery-blue, smooth oval leaves, round when immature.
Helichrysum italicum – Curry plant. Silver, spiky leaf clusters.
Lavandula dentata var. *candicans* – Lavender. Woolly, finely toothed silvery-grey leaves.
Marrubium vulgare – Horehound. Greeny-grey, rounded, textured leaves.

Above Thymus x citriodorus *'Silver Queen'.*

Above *Feathery, bronze fennel.*

Atriplex hortensis 'Rubra' – Red orache. Purple-red, smooth, pointed leaves.

Foeniculum vulgare 'Purpureum' – Bronze fennel. Golden-bronze foliage.
Ocimum glabrescens 'Dark Opal' – Purple basil. Glossy, purple leaves.
Ocimum glabrescens 'Purple Ruffles' – Purple basil with purple, frilly leaves.
Salvia officinalis Purpurascens Group – Purple sage. Purple-green leaves.
Sambucus nigra 'Guincho Purple' – Purple-bronze elder with indented foliage.

Gold

Many of these are variegated, but the predominant effect is gold.

Above Origanum vulgare *'Aureum'.*

Buxus sempervirens 'Latifolia Maculata' – Golden box. Small golden leaves.
Laurus nobilis 'Aurea' – Golden bay. Smooth, oval golden leaves.
Melissa officinalis 'All Gold' – Golden lemon balm. Bright golden-yellow leaves, splashed with green.
Melissa officinalis 'Aurea' – Variegated lemon balm with gold and green leaves.
Mentha x *gracilis* 'Variegata' – Gingermint. Boldly-patterned gold-and-green-striped leaves.
Origanum vulgare 'Aureum' – Golden marjoram. Yellow-gold, oval leaves.
Salvia officinalis 'Icterina' – Golden sage. Gold and grey-green variegation.
Thymus spp. – Thymes. Several of these have strong gold foliage. Among the best are *Thymus. x citriodorus* 'Archer's Gold', *T. x citriodorus* 'Aureus', *T.* 'Nitidus' and olive-green and gold *T.* 'Doone Valley'.

Above Mentha suaveolens '*Variegata*'.

Variegated

Agave americana 'Variegata' – Agave. Yellow margins to spiky, blue-grey leaves.
Ajuga reptans 'Multicolor' – Bugle. Green, pink and cream variegated foliage.
Armoracia rusticana 'Variegata' – Variegated horseradish. A cultivar with striking, creamy-white stripes on green.
Mentha suaveolens 'Variegata' – Pineapple mint. Creamy-white margins to leaves.
Pelargonium crispum 'Variegatum' – Scented geranium. Crinkly, golden-edged leaves.
Pelargonium 'Lady Plymouth' – Scented geranium. Light-green leaves with creamy margins.
Ruta graveolens 'Variegata' – Variegated rue. Foliage dappled green and cream.
Salvia officinalis 'Tricolor' – Tricolor sage. Striking variegations of pink, greeny-grey and cream.

Above Ruta graveolens '*Variegata*'.

Herbs with Colourful Flowers

Many herbs have colourful flowers which transform the garden when they are in bloom. Even those that do not have large flowers like their cultivated cousins, such as *Hypericum perforatum*, put on a good show in a mass planting.

Above *Red and white valerian with catmint.*

Ajuga reptans – Bugle. Blue flower spikes.
Alchemilla mollis – Lady's mantle. Frothy, greeny-yellow flowers.
Borago officinalis – Borage. Tiny, star-shaped flowers provide a mist of blue when planted en masse.
Calendula officinalis – Pot marigold. Brilliant, orange-yellow blooms.
Dianthus spp. – Pinks. Deep reds and pinks.
Helichrysum italicum – Curry plant. Bright-yellow button flowers.
Hypericum perforatum – St John's wort. Bright-yellow star-shaped flowers.
Hyssopus officinalis – Hyssop. Deep-blue flower spikes.
Inula helenium – Elecampane. Yellow, daisy-like flowers.
Lavandula spp. – Lavender. A range of misty-blues, mauves and purples.
Monarda didyma – Bergamot. There are many cultivars which come in a range of pink, red, purple and white.

Above *Sunflowers and nasturtiums.*

Nepeta x *faassenii* – Catmint. Mauve-blue flowers, spectacular in a mass planting.
Origanum onites, Origanum vulgare – Pot marjoram and oregano. Clusters of purple-red flowers.
Rosa spp. – Rose. Old-fashioned varieties have pink, red and white blooms.
Salvia officinalis – Sage. Massed purple-blue flower spikes.
Santolina chamaecyparissus – Cotton lavender. Bright yellow button flowers.
Thymus spp. – Many of the thymes have mauve to pinkish-red flowers.
Tropaeolum majus – Nasturtium. A range of bright yellows and oranges and a long-flowering season.

Above *Old-fashioned pinks (*Dianthus *spp.).*

Above *A variety of white-flowering herbs.*

Above *Bronze fennel and rosemary standing tall over a bed of low-growing herbs.*

Herbs with White Flowers

A garden of white-flowering herbs has a restful quality, especially if combined with silver-leafed plants and white and green variegated foliage. Many herbs have white flowers, others, such as borage, lavender and sage, have white-flowering forms. This is a selection:

Achillea millefolium – Yarrow. Small creamy-white umbels.
Allium tuberosum – Garlic chives. White star-shaped flowers.
Borago officinalis 'Alba' – A white-flowering borage.
Chamaemelum nobile – Chamomile. White daisy-like flowers.
Digitalis purpurea f. *albiflora* – White foxglove. Creamy-white spires.
Galium odoratum – Sweet woodruff. Small white stars.
Lilium candidum – Inimitable pure-white lilies.
Myrrhis odorata – Sweet cicely. Large white umbels.
Thymus serpyllum var. *albus* – A creeping, white-flowering thyme.
Valeriana officinalis – Valerian. Effective in a mass planting.

Right *Tall herbs – elecampane, fennel and a white-flowering goat's rue at the back of a border.*

Tall Herbs

When it comes to planning beds and borders it helps to know the eventual height and spread of plants. The ultimate size of individual herbs is indicated in this book, but the selection below are a reminder of "what not to put at the front". They are also useful for adding height to a scheme.

Angelica archangelica – Angelica. A classic for adding architectural impact.
Cynara cardunculus Scolymus Group – Globe artichoke. Earns a place in any scheme for the decorative value of its striking, purple heads.
Foeniculum vulgare – Fennel. A graceful feathery plant, which needs plenty of room.
Levisticum officinale – Lovage. Large clumps of glossy, green leaves need space to spread sideways and upwards.
Onopordum acanthium – Scotch thistle. The patterned leaves are relatively low-growing, but the flower stalks rise to a height of 2 m (6 ft 6 in).

Climbers

Another way to add the dimension of height to an otherwise flat design is by training creeping plants over arbours, archways, obelisks and twiggy tepees. Herbal creepers to choose from include:

Humulus lupulus – Hops. There are both green and golden-leaved varieties.
Jasminum officinale – Jasmine. This has star-shaped, perfumed white flowers in midsummer.
Lonicera periclymenum – Wild honeysuckle with creamy flowers, borne throughout summer. There are also many cultivars to choose from.
Rosa rubiginosa – Eglantine rose. Has very short-lived flowers. An old-fashioned climber, such as Mme Alfred Carrière, might be more rewarding. *R. gallica* 'Complicata' reaches 2 m (6ft 6 in) and may be used as a pillar rose.

Above *Creeping thymes make effective and appealing ground cover.*

Top Humulus lupulus *'Aureus'*.

Above *A bay tree with climbing roses.*

Ground-cover Herbs

For the front of a border, to fill an awkward corner, or as paths and lawns, ground-cover plants are invaluable.

Arctostaphylos uva-ursi – Bearberry. A mat-forming evergreen shrublet.
Chamaemelum nobile 'Treneague' – Non-flowering lawn chamomile. A non-flowering cultivar.
Juniperus communis 'Prostrata' – Juniper. Forms a dense, neat carpet, which no weed can penetrate.
Symphytum ibericum – Dwarf comfrey. A fast-spreading plant. Also comes in a gold and green variegated form.
Thymus serpyllum – There are many creeping thymes, ideal for paths, lawns and ground cover.
Vinca minor – Periwinkle. The dark-green leaves form dense, weed-defying cover. Cheerful blue flowers in spring.

Dry or Damp Soil?

It is usually easier to fit the plant to the right environment, rather than the other way about. Changing the soil and microclimate to accommodate a plant's particular preference can often be difficult and costly. The good news is that herbs are relatively easy-going plants and will often adapt to and grow well in conditions they would not choose in the wild. But to make things easier, it usually pays to give them what they want.

Dry, or certainly well-drained, soil suits the majority of plants, especially the shrubby herbs such as rosemary and thyme.

Damp-lovers to watch for include angelica, the *Mentha* genus and *Monarda didyma*. The mints and angelica will also grow happily in shade or semi-shade.

Herb Containers

Growing herbs in containers has many advantages. Where space is limited there is always room for a few pots, even in the smallest of gardens. Sited near the house, they provide the added convenience of being handy for harvesting – important for culinary herbs. As part of a garden scheme, containers can be placed in a bed to fill a temporary bare patch, used as focal points or arranged symmetrically to link different elements of a design.

Their mobility is a definite plus. Of course it must be borne in mind that very large pots, or those made of stone, will be too heavy to move. But, unlike static planting in a bed, small and medium pots, or those made of a lighter material, can be moved around to make a change. This is also useful for plants past their best, which need a less prominent position in which to recuperate. Tender and half-hardy herbs in containers can be moved under cover for winter protection.

Above *Comfrey has deep roots and needs a tall container (left back). Marjoram (centre) and thyme thrive in smaller pots.*

Planting

Growing a single species in a container gives plants room to develop and to provide plenty of leafy growth. For larger specimens, such as bay, sage and lemon verbena, it is essential that they do not

Above *Large pots planted with angelica add impact to a parterre.*

have to share a pot if they are to be left undisturbed for several years. The pot should be large enough to allow roots to spread. Mixed herb pots make very attractive features and are a good way of growing a variety of plants in a small space, but plants are inevitably cramped; roots become congested and annual replanting is usually necessary for a mixed planting.

Good drainage is one of the keys to success. Before you start, check that there is a large hole in the base of the pot, or several holes in the case of plastic pots and troughs. Put in a layer of crocks (broken terracotta pots), then cover with a layer of sand or grit before filling with potting compost (soil mix).

Most herbs flourish in a free-draining environment and, as a general rule, a 3:1 mixture of soilless compost (planting mix) and loam-based compost (soil mix) gives the best results. For shrubby herbs, such as bay, sage and rosemary, and for scented pelargoniums, add a few handfuls of grit to the mix to improve drainage. Do not be tempted to use garden soil; it will not provide enough nutrients and might harbour weeds and pests.

Maintenance

Extra fertilizer must be added after about four weeks, with subsequent weekly feeds throughout the growing season. An organic plant food based on seaweed extract is preferable, but slow-release fertilizer granules save time as they are added when potting up.

Pot-grown plants need frequent watering during the growing season. As a general rule, it is better to let them almost dry out and then give them a good soaking, rather than to keep dribbling in small amounts of water. Water-retaining gel mixed into the growing medium at the time of planting makes watering less of a chore. During the winter months pot-grown perennials should be given the minimum amount of water possible.

Plants that are kept in the same container for several years should have the top layer of compost, about 5 cm (2 in), scraped off and replaced with fresh every year. They will need re-potting in a container one or two sizes larger as roots become congested – try not to leave it until the plant is obviously suffering, with roots bursting out of the pot, yellowing leaves and poor, straggly growth.

Above *Herbs growing in separate pots with* Lavandula stoechas *at rear right.*

Planting a pot of mixed culinary herbs

1 Mix slow-release fertilizer and water-retaining gel, following instructions, into a potting medium made up of 3:1 parts of soilless compost (planting mix) and loam-based compost (soil mix).

2 Put a layer of crocks (broken terra-cotta pots) in the bottom of the pot.

3 Fill to the first hole with the potting medium, settling it evenly.

4 Tap a plant out of its pot and feed it gently through the hole, working from the inside outwards.

5 Cover the roots with more compost and firm it down before adding a further layer of plants.

6 Put in more plants until all the holes are filled and finish with one or two plants on top. Water in thoroughly.

YOU WILL NEED

Slow-release fertilizer; water-retaining gel; soilless compost; loam-based compost; trowel; terracotta pot; crocks (broken terracotta pots); a selection of culinary herbs

Right Marjoram (top), alpine strawberry, thymes and parsley go well together in a pot of herbs for culinary use.

Potting Composts

There are two main types of potting composts (soil mixes): based on sterilized loam, and the soilless composts (planting mixes), based on peat or peat substitutes such as coir. Soilless composts are lighter and easier to handle, but they do not retain nutrients as long as the loam-based ones. They provide a more moist environment, but, if left unwatered, they also dry out more quickly, and are difficult to remoisten. Both types of potting compost are available containing nutrients in a range of proportions: "seed and cuttings" formula contains the least and a "potting" formula the most, with "all-purpose" in between.

Indoor Herb Gardening

Some herbs adapt well to being grown as houseplants. In regions with cold winters which suffer frosts, it is one way of cultivating tender herbs successfully. A conservatory gives scope for keeping a wider range, but is by no means essential. Give indoor plants as much natural light as possible and regular liquid feeds in summer, and do not overwater, especially in winter.

Vigorous and colourful, easy-to-grow scented pelargoniums are a rewarding group to grow this way as they come in such a variety of scents and leaf forms. Don't be afraid to prune them hard if they become straggly and never keep them too damp. Tender pineapple sage (*Salvia elegans*) does well indoors and produces scarlet flowers in late autumn or winter just when colour is welcome. It needs a big pot and more water than most. *Aloe vera* adapts well to an indoor regime, requiring the minimum of attention. A gritty, free-draining compost (soil mix) suits it best and infrequent but thorough watering. Myrtles do not always survive frosts and are another good choice. The dwarf *Myrtus communis* 'Tarentina', having a compact and tidy habit of growth, is eminently suitable, and *Myrtus communis* 'Variegata', being even less hardy, is well worth growing inside.

Herbs on the Windowsill

A supply of indoor culinary herbs is a great convenience. It is possible to grow them on the kitchen windowsill as long as you take into account the stress this puts on the plants. If you put a young plant into a small pot and then keep cutting off its leaves, it will be hard pressed to survive. At the same time, it is being kept short of air, the atmosphere may be too hot and steamy and changes of temperature extreme. From the point of view of flavour, there is little sun to bring out the essential oils.

The best way to counteract these problems is to alternate pots kept on the windowsill with another set left standing outside. Keep the different herbs in individual pots and group them together. They grow better in close proximity to one another because transpiration from the massed leaves increases the overall humidity.

Standing the pots on a gravel tray, or in a container with a layer of gravel on the base, keeps them cool and helps to retain moisture, without the plants becoming waterlogged.

Above *Herbs grouped together on the windowsill are handy for cooking.*

Far left *Scented pelargoniums and lemon verbena grow well as houseplants.*

Left *Culinary herbs in separate pots, standing in an outer container of gravel.*

Herbs in the Greenhouse

It is perfectly possible to grow many herbs without any form of winter protection or artificial heat. But in colder regions a small, frost-free greenhouse is a great help in extending both the season of growth and the range of plants it is possible to grow.

It is often easier to raise plants from seed sown in trays. Under controlled conditions, the success rate is usually higher. With a greenhouse you can start sowing much earlier than if you had to wait for the right outdoor conditions. But remember that young plants, grown on from seedlings, must be acclimatized gradually to being outside, before they are finally planted in the garden. Do this by standing them outside in the daytime for a short period, or transferring them to a cold frame.

Parsley is a good candidate for sowing under glass. Although it is reasonably hardy, it needs heat to germinate (about 18°C, 65°F), which is why it takes so long to emerge when planted straight into the garden early in the year before the soil has warmed up. Germination will be much quicker and more reliable if the seeds are started in trays in the greenhouse, with a view to transplanting outside once grown.

Basil is almost impossible to raise from seed in temperate regions without the benefit of glass. But it is not difficult to get good results if you follow a few guidelines:
• Do not start too early in the year; allow spring to get well under way first, when it will be easier to supply a temperature of 15–18°C (60–65°F).
• Scatter seeds as sparsely as possible, so that little thinning-out is required later and root disturbance minimized.
• Provide the seedlings with adequate ventilation and do not overwater to reduce risk of "damping-off" disease.
• Grow plants on in a large container, rather than planting them directly into the soil. They can then be kept outside or moved into a greenhouse, according to current weather conditions.

Above Capsicum frutescens *'Gipsy', in flower, in a greenhouse.*

Summer Herbs

Unless the summer is exceptionally cool and wet, sweet basil (*Ocimum basilicum*) will usually grow well in a pot outside, but the purple-leafed kinds seldom reach their full potential unless kept under glass.

Chilli peppers (*Capsicum* spp.) also need to be grown in the greenhouse in cooler climates if they are to produce mature, ripe fruits. In parts of the United States chilli peppers can be grown outside. Other herbs to try are the popular Japanese salad plants known as shiso (*Perilla frutescens* and *P. frutescens* 'Crispa') and the culinary flavouring plant, lemon grass, much used in Thai cookery (*Cymbopogon citratus*).

Adequate shading and copious watering are necessary for plants grown under glass in the summer.

Winter Protection

For container-grown plants that are not fully frost-hardy, such as bay, lemon verbena and myrtle, as well as more tender subjects such as scented pelargoniums, a cold greenhouse, provided it is frost-free, gives enough protection to keep them alive through the winter. In the summer months they can stand outside in the garden, as long as they are moved under cover before the first winter frosts.

Many of these plants will lose their leaves, even if they remain evergreen in warm climates. Once they have been moved into the greenhouse in the autumn, cut them back or trim lightly, according to individual requirements. Over the succeeding winter months give them a minimal amount of water and no fertilizer to ensure dormancy.

Growing Herbs

Once the design and overall style have been chosen, it is time to turn them into reality. Practical guidance is included in this chapter on how to do so, through the stages of planning and preparing the site, laying out paths and hard surfaces, to putting in the plants themselves. There are tips on successful propagation and how to train plants into standards or over frames. There is advice on maintenance and seasonal tasks, with a final section on dealing with pests and diseases.

Above *Tools of the trade in an old-style potting shed.*

Left *A supply of freshly cut material for recipes is one of the rewards of growing your own herbs.*

Planning Your Planting

Many of the most familiar herbs are Mediterranean in origin and grow best where there is plenty of sun. Bear this in mind when deciding on the location for your herb garden. Choose an area that has the sun for most of the day and where there is little dense or permanent shade. Take the time to watch the movement of the sun, so that you know exactly where shadows fall. This will help with planning the planting, allocating the right areas for herbs needing sun, shade or semi-shade and deciding where to site features such as a sundial, arbour, fountain or a seat. If you are at the survey stage in winter when the trees have no leaves, don't forget to take into account the deep shade cast by summer foliage.

Shelter is also important. Chilly winds, particularly in winter, can be devastating to many shrubby herbs such as thyme and rosemary. You may be able to make good use of an existing boundary wall to act as a windbreak. Consider putting in hedges, trelliswork or wicker fences to provide a sheltered, secluded environment, but remember that they will cause some shade and loss of light to plants. It may be better to install them on one or two sides only, according to prevailing wind direction, leaving other sides open or with low balustrade fencing.

If productivity is the main objective it is best not to overdo the number of low hedges, central features and dividing pathways, all of which will diminish the amount of space available for cultivation. Nevertheless, the plot can still achieve considerable charm if the production is arranged in an orderly fashion and by building in a feature or two that will add overall interest.

Top *A carefully planned bed, with silvery spokes of* Santolina chamaecyparissus *in a wheel of block planting.*

Right *Herbs flourish in a garden sheltered by a high brick wall.*

Soil and Site Preparation

Time spent preparing the site by improving the soil and eliminating weeds will be repaid many times over. This is not as daunting as it might seem. Improving the texture of the soil (though not weed elimination) applies only to the planting areas and does not have to be carried out where paths and hard surface areas are to be laid.

A light, free-draining soil is best for most herbs. It warms up quickly in spring and does not become as cold and waterlogged as heavy soil in winter. But if it is too porous, moisture and nutrients will be quickly leached away, resulting in a soil so poor and dry that few plants will flourish. Forking in organic matter – garden compost or leaf mould – will ensure better results. On heavy soil, if areas are inclined to become water-logged it is worth digging out trenches and filling them with rubble to form land drains. Chalk and sand both drain rapidly whilst clay retains moisture. The ideal is a crumbly loam which retains the right degree of water and nutrients.

Many herbs, including lavender, do not grow well in a heavy clay soil. One way to overcome the problem is to put

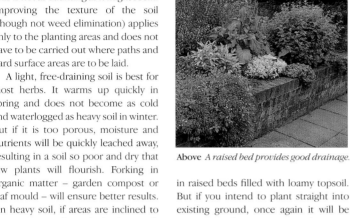

Above *A raised bed provides good drainage.*

in raised beds filled with loamy topsoil. But if you intend to plant straight into existing ground, once again it will be necessary to incorporate organic matter.

For a very heavy soil, the addition of plenty of coarse grit helps to open up the texture further. Double digging, though hard work, is the way to do this most effectively. Take out a trench to the depth of two spades at one end of the plot, turning it straight into a wheelbarrow and removing it to the other end of the area to be treated. Add a layer of grit and

compost to the first trench, covering it with soil from the next section. Continue in this pattern until the whole area has been dug over and organic matter incorporated. When the last trench is reached fill this with the soil from the first trench. After digging, tread down the soil lightly to ensure that no air pockets remain and that the soil does not subsequently settle unevenly. Rake over in several different directions until the surface is level and leave it for a week or so before planting.

Beware of overmanuring ground where herbs are to grow. The object of digging in bulky organic matter is to improve texture and drainage. For the majority of herbs, heavy feeding with rich farmyard manure or artificial fertilizers encourages soft growth, reduces aroma, and lays the plants open to attack by pests and diseases.

Another factor to consider is the alkaline or acid content of the soil, measured by the pH factor. A figure of seven is taken as neutral – anything higher is alkaline, anything lower is on the acid side. An inexpensive soil-testing kit will tell you what you have. Herbs are a disparate group, but as a rule most will grow in a neutral soil.

Weeding

Eliminating perennial weeds as thoroughly as possible before putting in plants pays great dividends. Another advantage of double digging is that you can take out deep roots and every speck of greenery you see as you go along. Fork out all weeds as painstakingly as possible. For stubborn or dense weed growth, cover the area for a full season with a layer of thick black polythene (plastic). Once this is removed, all but the most persistent weeds will be obliterated.

If you would rather get started on the planting immediately, put down a layer of black polythene (plastic), cut with holes for planting pockets, making sure these are completely weed free. Then put in the plants and cover the surface of the polythene with a mulch of gravel or bark chippings.

Above *Double digging eliminates weeds and improves soil texture.*

Above *Forking out weeds.*

Above *Removing all trace of roots helps keep the soil clear for longer.*

Laying Out a Garden

The first thing to do is to make a plan to fit your plot and requirements. You can take it from an existing design in a book, but you will need to tailor it to fit your own site. Check that you have the space to carry out your chosen scheme, that it will complement its surroundings and not be too cramped. Then measure the site and note the position of any existing walls, trees or other features that are to be kept.

Decide on a scale and draw up the plan on graph paper, but remember that it is all too easy to put in too much, too close together. It may look good on paper but will not work in reality. Keep checking as you go along that the layout you have drawn is feasible on site. The simpler it is and the fewer fussy elements you include, the more impact the finished garden is likely to have.

Marking Out a Garden

Once you have worked out the design and chosen the site, it is time to lay it out on your plot and put in hard surfaces.

Take your paper plan on to the chosen area and mark the key points on the ground with stakes. Designate the boundaries and outline the beds and paths with string and pegs, measuring carefully and ensuring that right angles are accurate with a builder's square. A length of garden hose is useful for marking out curves. At this stage it is possible to check that the proportions

are right, that the whole scheme is well balanced and that other parts of the garden do not intrude or clash with the general concept. An upstairs window is often the best place to get a good overall view. Now is the time to change anything that does not look right – it will be difficult and costly to alter later on. It is best to decide on the order of work before you start:

• Changes of levels or major earthworks, including digging out ponds, need to be done first.
• Construction work, paths, terraces, hard surface areas, herb wheels and raised beds come next.
• Boundaries need to be clearly marked before you start, and, if putting in a wall, you may want to do this first, as well as putting in fence posts. But for ease of access and wheelbarrow movement it usually pays to leave fences till after the hard construction is done. Hedges, too, should be put in at a later stage with the bulk of the planting.
• Features such as pergolas, arbours and fountains may be put in at the same time, or after the hard-surface construction.
• Preparation of the soil in the beds should be done a few days in advance of planting if possible.
• Planting the herbs is practically the last stage.
• Finishing touches include adding container plants to the scheme and movable features such as sundials.

Above *Contrasting coloured stones, in this cobbled surface, pick out a star motif and decorative border.*

Putting in Paths and Hard Surface Areas

All paths and hard surface areas require a firm, level base. This can be done by marking a series of pegs with a line 5 cm (2 in) from the top. Hammer the pegs into the ground across the area to be levelled, tapping them in until the tops are flush with each other (using a spirit level to check). Then level and firm down the soil to the mark on the pegs.

Above *Bricks provide a colourful surface.*

Above *Drawing out the design on paper helps to achieve a successful result.*

Above *A random pattern of paving stones.*

Gravel is a relatively inexpensive, quickly laid surface. It comes in a range of colours and in two main types: crushed stone from quarries and pea shingle (pea stone) from gravel pits. It should be laid on a level, well-compacted base of soil covered with a layer of dry concrete, eight parts ballast (gravel) mixed with one part cement, which has been left to dry off for several days. Hessian mesh (burlap), laid over the path before the gravel is spread, prevents weeds.

Stone slabs are a good surface for a terrace or large paved area. They are also useful for using as stepping stones in a wide border and for a mixed surface path of gravel and paving slabs. Bed them into mortar on a hardcore base (stones and broken bricks), as for the brick path, below.

Cobblestones are an attractive finish for a small scale area. They can be used to fill in round shrubs and trees or to lay in conjunction with other hard-surface

materials. Pack them together as closely as possible, set in a bed of mortar on a hardcore base.

Bricks must be hard, impermeable and resistant to frost. Reclaimed bricks, from specialist merchants, have the best mellow colour. They must be laid on a firm, hardcore surface or they will expand and lift with the moisture in the soil and form an uneven path. For a path with less heavy wear a sand base without hardcore is sufficient.

To lay a main brick path

This construction will be suitable for main paths in a herb garden and should withstand average domestic use and weather conditions.

1 *Dig out soil for the path to a depth of one brick plus 10 cm (4 in) for the base. Tread it down till level. Put in an edging of timber boards, held in place with hammered-in pegs, with their upper edges at the level of the finished path. Spread a 7.5 cm (3 in) layer of hardcore, rolling it in until firmly compacted.*

2 *Cover the hardcore base with a dry mix of eight parts ballast to one part cement, approximately 2.5 cm (1 in) thick, lightly tamp it with the head of the rake to fill in any gaps in the hardcore, and then rake to a loose, level surface.*

3 *Lay the bricks into the ballast and cement base, arranging them in a staggered pattern so that you don't have a line of joints. Tap each one down with a mallet, butting it as close to its neighbour as possible; check with a spirit level that the path is even in all directions as you go.*

4 *When all the bricks are in place, spread more ballast and cement over the surface, brushing it repeatedly into the joints to fill them, before cleaning off the surplus. Moisture from the soil will set the cement, but a light spray of water may be applied to hasten the process.*

5 *Before the cement hardens, ease sand from the joints to create pockets for prostrate herbs, then fill in with a little topsoil and sow seeds or plant divisions from established plants.*

Planting the Garden

Once you have a stock of established perennials you will be able to increase them by propagation, and many annuals and biennials will conveniently seed themselves. But you are sure to need to buy some plants in order to get your herb garden started.

Buying Plants

Specialist herb nurseries should have many of the more unusual varieties, but many garden centres now offer a reasonable selection. As you will require several of each species for a good show, the initial outlay could be considerable, so make sure you buy only strong, healthy specimens and follow these tips to get the most for your money:

• Check that a plant has not been too recently potted and whether it lacks a strong root system, or conversely that it has not been too long in the pot and the roots have become congested. Make sure there are no weeds, algae or moss.

• Examine the plant carefully for pests – red spider mite and whitefly may not be obvious at first glance.

• Don't buy anything with discoloured, wilting or blotched leaves – it could be diseased.

• Never assume that a stunted, straggly and overgrown or poor and sickly specimen will improve once planted out. It won't.

• Resist the temptation to buy annuals potted up singly. Many do not transplant well and seed quickly in hot, dry weather – these include coriander (cilantro), chervil, dill and borage. Grow them yourself from seed. Once established they often self-seed.

• Look for annual flowering herbs, such as pot marigolds and nasturtiums, sold as bedding plants in trays, rather than in single pots – or grow them yourself from seed.

• It will probably be necessary to thin seedlings to give them room to develop; and keep them well weeded to prevent competition for moisture and nutrients.

Planting the Design

If you have drawn in the herbs on your plan, this can be very useful as a guideline. A pre-designed scheme helps to group plants effectively for colour, texture, height and so on. However, it is not always easy to visualize on paper how it will look on the ground. Standing the plants in their pots on the soil, and shifting them around as necessary, helps with spacing and final decisions on position which often leads to a happier end result. It cannot be stressed enough that plants always look best in groups, rather than being scattered about singly. A whole bed of purple sage makes a

Above *One healthy and one poor container-grown vervain plant.*

Top *A well-stocked herb garden.*

much more dramatic statement than one little clump lost in a mass of competing colour. A broad sweep of catmint or borage is a sight to savour.

The same principle applies to climbers grown over an arched walkway. With several different plants the result can be very haphazard. One variety will have impact.

Invasive Herbs

Be careful where you put invasive plants. Comfrey, horseradish, sweet cicely and other herbs with strong tap roots can be very difficult to eradicate if you later want to change the planting scheme.

Some herbs, particularly those with creeping roots, encroach on their neighbours. Mint is a well-known culprit; soapwort and tansy can also prove overpowering. It is best to confine them with divisions in the bed: bricks or tiles buried in the soil work very well for shallow-rooting invasive herbs.

Another way to curtail them is to grow them in a large container buried in the soil – but make sure it has adequate drainage holes, or the base removed, if the plants are not to become choked.

Planting a herb garden

1 *When you have put in all the hard surfaces in your garden and prepared the soil as necessary (see Soil and site preparation) it is time to plant up the scheme. Fork in a little organic fertilizer first, to give your herbs a good start, but avoid heavy manure.*

2 *Always water plants well in their pots first, as plants never take up moisture as well after planting if put in dry. Add water until it trickles out of the base of the pot – this is important for trees, shrubs and larger specimens, which may look damp on top but are dry at the rootball.*

3 *Mark your planting positions with sand. Tap each herb out of its pot, make a hole with a trowel, and put in the plant, firming the soil lightly around it afterwards. Water in well. Under very dry conditions it helps if you fill the planting hole with water first.*

4 *Keep the area free of weeds so that the newly set out herbs do not have to compete for moisture and nutrients.*

YOU WILL NEED
Garden fork; organic fertilizer;
a selection of herbs; watering can;
trowel; sand

Right *Recently planted aromatic herbs, set out in a knot pattern, surround a dwarf standard tree.*

Propagation

Propagating your own herbs is a rewarding occupation and the best way to replace plants and to stock your garden economically. The basic techniques are not difficult, but, as herbs are such a disparate range of plants, their requirements and the degree of difficulty in raising them varies. Some are much easier to propagate than others. Many respond better to one method than another so check for the optimum propagation method for each plant.

Raising from Seed

Many herbs are easy to grow from seed. Spring is generally the best time for sowing, but do not start too early: seeds sown when air and soil temperatures are warmer and light levels higher will grow into stronger plants. Some seeds are sown in autumn, as indicated here.

Annuals: All annuals – plants whose life cycle is completed in one year – can be grown from seed sown in spring. Hardy annuals, such as chervil (*Anthriscus cerefolium*), coriander (cilantro) (*Coriandrum sativum*) and pot marigold (*Calendula officinalis*) may also be sown in autumn to give them an early start the following spring. Half-hardy annuals, such as nasturtiums (*Tropaeolum* spp.), should not be sown until late spring or early summer in areas where there is frost. Basil (*Ocimum basilicum)* is tender and should be sown in seed trays under glass in late spring to early summer.

Biennials: These are planted in the late summer or early autumn of one year, to flower the following year – though some of them go into a third year, their life cycle is over once they have flowered. Although parsley is a biennial, it is worth sowing seed every year because the stems coarsen and it does not produce such good leaf in its second year. Biennials include angelica (*Angelica archangelica*), caraway (*Carum carvi*), clary sage (*Salvia sclarea*) and evening primrose (*Oenothera biennis)*.

Perennials: These live for a number of years and many perennial herbs can be successfully raised from seed. But not all of them produce seed, such as French tarragon (*Artemisia dracunculus*) and the non-flowering golden sage (*Salvia officinalis* 'Icterina'). Many hybrids and cultivars do not come "true" from seed, which means they may vary considerably from the parent plant. This includes all the mints, most lavenders and ornamental thymes. These must be vegetatively propagated.

Vernalization: A few herb seeds need to be subjected to a period of intense cold before they will germinate. In the wild, this ensures their survival where winters are cold. To reproduce these conditions artificially, in a process known as "vernalization" or "stratification", put the seeds in a polythene (plastic) bag of moist sand and leave in a refrigerator or freezer for 4–6 weeks before sowing.

This is necessary for: aconitum or monkshood (*Aconitum napellus*), arnica (*Arnica montana*), agrimony (*Agrimonia eupatoria*), juniper (*Juniperus communis*), hawthorn (*Crataegus laevigata*), *Primula* spp., *Rosa* spp., sweet cicely (*Myrrhis odorata*), sweet woodruff (*Galium odoratum*) and sweet violet (*Viola odorata*).

Scarification: Some hard-coated seeds, such as those of legumes, which include broom, clovers and vetches, will germinate more readily if first rubbed with fine sandpaper. This breaks up the outer coating and allows moisture to penetrate, which all seeds require before they will germinate.

Left *Careful labelling prevents mis-identification when new seedlings emerge.*

Sowing in seed trays

The success rate for seeds sown in trays under controlled conditions is higher than for seeds sown outdoors. It is the best method for very fine seeds, such as parsley, and essential for raising tender plants, such as basil. It is also a good way to give many plants an earlier start.

YOU WILL NEED

Cellular seed tray; soilless seed and cuttings compost (soil mix); watering can; herb seeds; garden sieve; label; polythene (plastic) dome or plastic bag; 7.5 cm (3 in) pots

---

1 *Fill a seed tray with soilless growing medium. A tray divided into cells makes it easier to sow thinly and to pot up seedlings with minimum root disturbance. Water first, then scatter two or three seeds in each compartment.*

2 *Cover the tray with a layer of sieved compost (soil mix). Never bury seeds too deeply, especially small ones such as parsley. Water again and don't forget to label the tray (tiny seedlings look similar).*

3 *Put a polythene (plastic) dome over the tray, or enclose it in a plastic bag, to retain moisture. Put the tray on a windowsill or in the greenhouse until the seedlings emerge.*

4 *When the seedlings come through remove the cover and put the tray in a light place out of direct sunlight. Keep moist, but never waterlogged.*

5 *As soon as the seedlings are large enough to handle, pot them up in 7.5 cm (3 in) pots filled with fresh potting compost (soil mix). When strong and bushy they can be planted out.*

Sowing Outdoors

Many seeds can be sown outdoors directly into the soil where they are to grow, or in nursery beds for later transplantation. It is also the sensible way to raise herbs that do not respond well to being transplanted. These include coriander (cilantro), chervil and dill. It is as well to remember that there is a higher failure rate for seeds sown outdoors, rather than in a tray in the greenhouse, due to unexpected adverse weather conditions or the unwanted attention of birds or rodents. On the other hand it saves time and energy in pricking out, potting up and hardening off, and plants raised this way are often sturdier. For a good chance of success with outdoor seeds:

• It is best not to start too early in spring, if still cold. But to speed things up cover the area with cloches for a week or two in advance of sowing to warm up the soil.

• First weed the area thoroughly and rake it to a fine texture and level surface.

• Next make a shallow depression with a stake, or rake handle, in the soil and sprinkle in seeds as thinly as possible. Larger seeds, like nasturtiums or coriander (cilantro) can be placed individually rather than scattered.

• Cover seeds with a thin layer of soil, patting it down lightly, but beware of burying them too deeply.

• Don't forget to mark the area planted clearly. Sowing in straight lines, as appropriate for producing some culinary herbs, makes it easier to distinguish seedlings from weeds.

• Water well after planting and keep the area moist until the seedlings appear.

Above Calendula officinalis *grown from seed.*

Germination Requirements

For seeds to germinate successfully they require:

Moisture: The surface of the growing medium in seed trays must not be allowed to dry out, and outdoor seeds need frequent watering in dry spells.

Warmth: Most seeds need some degree of warmth to germinate, though temperature requirements can vary considerably. Most plants native to northern Europe and North America germinate at 10–13°C (50–55°F); plants from tropical and southern latitudes 15–21°C (60–70°F). Those herbs with special requirements include: lavender, exceptionally low at 4–10°C (40–50°F), parsley, 18–21°C (65–70°F), and rosemary, especially high at 27–32°C (80–90°F).

Light: Seeds should not be sown too deeply, in order that light may penetrate the soil and waken the seed into growth. This is particularly important for fine seeds – larger ones can be buried a little deeper. Light is crucial for thyme (*Thymus vulgaris*), winter savory (*Satureja montana*), poppies (*Papaver* spp.) and also sweet marjoram (*Origanum majorana*).

Air: A peat-based (or peat-substitute) growing medium is best for seeds, as the open texture allows air to circulate and oxygen to reach the developing plant. This is why breaking up the soil to a fine tilth is necessary for outdoor sowing and why seeds fail in compacted, water-logged soil.

Vegetative Propagation

Many perennial herbs are best propagated vegetatively, rather than by seed. This includes those that do not flower and set seed.

Above *Mint (in pot) grown from cuttings.*

Taking cuttings from the stems during the growing season is an effective method for many. Softwood cuttings are taken from soft, new growth in spring through to midsummer. They root quickly with warmth and humidity. Suitable for: *Origanum* spp., *Pelargonium* spp., *Santolina* spp., *Tanacetum* spp., *Mentha* spp. and *Salvia elegans*.

Semi-ripe cuttings are taken from harder, half-ripened wood in mid to late summer and can be taken from many shrubby herbs, including *Buxus* spp., *Citrus* spp., *Helichrysum italicum*, *Rosmarinus officinalis*, *Thymus* spp., *Lavandula* spp. and *Myrtus* spp. Some plants, including *Salvia elegans* and *Artemisia abrotanum*, root from stem cuttings taken at any time during the growing season.

Hardwood cuttings are taken from mature wood in mid to late autumn. They are slow to root (up to 12 months), and are usually kept in a cold frame over winter. This is suitable for trees, shrubs and roses.

Stem cuttings

Many herbs, such as rosemary and southernwood, are best propagated from cuttings. It is also the only way to perpetuate a special flower colour, such as pink-flowered hyssop, or a leaf variation, such as variegated rue. Stem cuttings are all taken in the same way. Do not cram in too many cuttings or put one in the middle of the pot.

YOU WILL NEED

Plants; sharp knife or secateurs (pruners); polythene bag; hormone rooting powder; 15 cm (6 in) pot; cuttings compost (growing medium); dibber (dibble), pencil or stick; plastic dome or bag

1 *Collect only a small amount of material at a time and be sure to keep in the shade in a polythene bag, to minimize water loss. Choose sturdy, non-flowering stems, with lots of leaves. Cut a section about 10 cm (4 in) just below a leaf joint and remove all but the top two or three leaves. These are necessary to supply the plant with nutrients as the root system develops.*

2 *Dip the cuttings into hormone rooting powder, tapping off any excess, and insert them into holes made with a dibber (dibble) round the edge of a pot filled with moist cuttings compost (growing medium). Water lightly and cover with a plastic dome or polythene bag held over a wire frame and sealed at the bottom – this is to maintain maximum humidity.*

3 *Once the cuttings have rooted – 2–4 weeks for softwood cuttings, 4–6 weeks for semi-ripe cuttings – repot into new compost and harden them off gradually before planting out.*

Root cuttings

A method of increasing herbs with creeping roots, such as mint (*Mentha* spp.), soapwort (*Saponaria officinalis*), bergamot (*Monarda didyma*) and herbs with taproots such as horseradish (*Armoracia rusticana*).

1 *Lift a root of mint and cut it into 4 cm (1½ in) pieces. Try to cut at a point where there is a small bud from which a new plant can grow.*

2 *Fill a seed tray with cuttings compost. Lay the pieces of root on the surface, press them in and cover with a further layer of compost. Water and leave in a shady place. There is no need to cover the tray or enclose it in polythene, but do keep it moist.*

3 *Once there are plenty of leaves showing through, divide the new plants and grow them on in bigger pots or plant them out in the open ground.*

YOU WILL NEED

Garden fork; mint, or other suitable plant; secateurs (pruners); seed tray; cuttings or all-purpose compost (growing medium); watering can

Division of roots

Herbs with fibrous or fleshy taproots are very easy to propagate by division. These include: chives (*Allium schoenoprasum*), oregano (*Origanum* spp.), lemon balm (*Melissa officinalis*), lovage (*Levisticum officinale*) and comfrey (*Symphytum* spp).

1 *Dig up a clump of chives. Divide it into several new pieces, pulling it apart with your hands or the aid of a small fork if necessary.*

2 *Cut off some of the top growth. Replant in open ground or firm each new piece into a pot filled with all-purpose compost.*

3 *Keep the new plants well watered. They will soon grow strongly to provide plenty of fresh leaf.*

Layering

A useful method of propagation for shrubby herbs such as bay, rosemary and sage. It works by inducing a side stem to develop new roots while still attached to the parent plant. Mound layering is particularly suitable for thymes, which become straggly after a few years. Pile gritty loam in a mound over the lower, leafless stems, leaving the crown of the plant showing. This stimulates new roots to develop at the base, when they can be separated and then planted in a different position.

1 *Trim the lower leaves from a side stem, attached to the shrub. Bend it over and bed into soil beside the plant.*

2 *Fasten it down with a staple or peg. Water in and leave for several months until roots have formed. Divide the new plant from the parent and replant it.*

Maintenance

Herbs are easy-going plants. Most are not difficult to grow, coming up year after year, or self-seeding exuberantly; but a herb garden, like any other garden, needs regular care and maintenance to keep it looking at its best. Keeping paths and gravel areas free of weeds makes all the difference to the overall appearance, especially in formal gardens, which depend on symmetry and orderliness for effect. If you don't like using weedkiller, there is nothing for it but to hoe out offenders as soon as you see them. Try not to let weeds seed or else the problem will be compounded.

Mulching is a good way to keep beds and borders weed-free. Use well-rotted garden compost, mushroom compost, leaf mould or bark chippings and pile it on thickly round plants. Weeds that come up through the mulch will be weak and easy to pull out. Gravel is also a suitable mulch and weed suppressant for thymes and many shrubby herbs. Grass clippings are useful for mulching round fruit bushes and the base of trees – they can be used fresh, added in a thick layer and allowed to rot down. For weeds with persistent roots, spreading heavy-duty black polythene (plastic) over the area for a full season helps to eradicate them by depriving the seedlings of light and air.

Deciding which plants are un-desirable is not always straightforward, as plenty of herbs are wild plants and often described as "weeds". You may decide to keep some self-sown plants, either leaving them in situ or transplanting to a more convenient spot, and this can add to the interest of the garden. The main thing is to be in control and not to let unwanted plants take over and dominate the scheme.

Clipping

In a formal scheme keeping plants clipped is all-important. Some will need cutting only twice a year, but others may require more frequent light trims to keep them in shape.

Many herbs grow prolifically, if left to themselves, and need frequent cutting back if the garden is not to become untidy and overgrown. Pruned plants can often be harvested for culinary or household use and any spares should be added to the compost heap. Spring is a good time to do some initial tidying and trimming, but many plants will need further cutting back during the summer months or in autumn.

Watering

It should not be necessary to give extra water to fully grown herbs planted out in the garden, except under severe drought conditions. Many of the shrubby herbs of Mediterranean origin are resistant to a shortage of water – rosemary flourishes in the driest of summers. But moisture-lovers, such as angelica, bergamot and mint, may need some help at these times. And of course it is essential in dry spells to water newly-planted young herbs until they are well-established.

Mulching often helps to conserve moisture, but if it is to be effective for this purpose it must be added early in the season before the soil dries out.

The main task is to water container-grown herbs throughout the growing season. In their dormant period, during winter, they should be kept barely moist, or root rot may ensue.

Feeding

Although it is important to keep the soil "in good heart" with the addition of garden compost, heavy manuring and fertilizing with high-nitrogen inorganic products is to be avoided. It results in soft, sappy growth which is susceptible to blackfly infestation and will not withstand the stress of droughts or extreme cold. Worst of all the herbs will lack fragrance and aroma.

A slow-release organic fertilizer, such as blood, fish and bone, forked into the soil, helps to get new plants off to a good start. And any fruit and vegetables in the herb garden will require extra nourish-ment in the form of liquid seaweed or a comfrey fertilizer. Container-grown plants benefit from regular liquid feeds throughout the growing season, especially older plants that have been in the same pot for some time.

Above *A standard bay in a tub needs regular clipping with secateurs (pruners) and feeding.*

Opposite *A rotting compost heap.*

Above *A meticulously maintained garden.*

Comfrey Fertilizer

Comfrey is invaluable as a herb garden fertilizer, containing all the nutrients necessary for healthy plant growth in digestible form. It has a high potash content and is also a source of nitrogen, phosphorus and many other elements. Use it in the following ways:

• As a mulch by spreading freshly cut comfrey leaves round plants (black-currants and other fruit bushes benefit particularly). Topping the comfrey with a layer of lawn mowings adds bulk and speeds decay.

• Add comfrey leaves to the compost heap in thin layers – it doesn't add to the humus content, but works as an "activator", encouraging the breakdown of other plant material. Be careful to avoid adding roots and flowering stems, which will regenerate and form un-wanted plants.

• As a liquid fertilizer, by filling a bucket to the halfway mark with comfrey leaves, fill it with water and cover with a lid – to exclude insects. Leave for 4–5 weeks, then strain off the liquid (which will be very smelly) and use it undiluted as an organic fertilizer for container plants, tomatoes and general garden use.

• A more concentrated version may be made by standing a bucket with a hole in the bottom over another container, filling the bucket with comfrey leaves and pressing them down with a weighted board. The bucket should then be covered with a lid and the leaves left to rot down for several weeks, until a black, tarry liquid seeps out. This should be diluted in water before use.

Above *A variety of garden clippings and fresh vegetable material is added to the heap, for a good supply of garden compost.*

Making a Compost Heap

A good supply of garden compost is always needed in the herb garden for improving the structure and fertility of the soil and as a mulch material.

Containers: There are many types of manufactured compost bins available in plastic, wood and other materials, suitable for gardens of varying sizes, but you can easily make your own. Build the heap straight on to the earth, with a surround of wire mesh, or timber boards to contain it. If using boards, leave airspaces between them.

Materials: Any plant material is suitable, such as, leaves, flowers, lawn clippings, straw, vegetable peelings. Woody stems should be included only if they have been mechanically shredded. Do not add difficult-to-eradicate perennial weeds, especially with their roots or main flowering stems attached. Annual weeds are best avoided if there is any chance of their seeding.

Construction: Build up the heap in layers, alternating lawn clippings with leaves and open-textured material – a variety of materials leads to a better texture. Add an activator every two or three layers – a sprinkling of chicken manure, seaweed meal, blood, fish, and bone, or comfrey leaves.

Processing: Covering up the heap with polythene (plastic), or a manufactured lid helps conserve moisture, so that the heap rots more rapidly. It is not usually necessary to "turn" the heap if it has been well constructed, but it does help to break up material added in clumps, such as lawn mowings. It will take 3–6 months to achieve a dark colour and moist crumbly texture.

Management: Have at least two heaps simultaneously at different stages of decay – one being for current use and one under construction. Dig out the compost from the bottom so that the old material is used first.

Spring Tasks

Propagating and planting are key tasks in what is the busiest and probably most exciting time of the year in the herb garden, with everything burgeoning into new growth. But the timing of "spring" varies greatly from one area to another and from one year to the next, so always take local conditions into account when carrying out suggested tasks.

Propagating

Early spring is the time for sowing seeds of hardy annuals in trays in a cold greenhouse, including borage, summer savory and pot marigold. You can also sow parsley if you can provide constant heat for germination; and perennials that are easy to raise by this method include fennel, sage (*Salvia officinalis* only), pot marjoram, winter savory and horehound. Of the thymes, only common thyme (*Thymus vulgaris*) and wild thyme (*T. serpyllum*) can be grown from seed. Others, which are cultivars, have to be vegetatively propagated.

Leave annuals such as basil, sweet marjoram and nasturtium until late spring, when they can be grown on outside without danger of frost. Seeds of herbs that dislike being transplanted should be sown outside, where they are to grow, including dill, chervil and coriander (cilantro).

Hardy annuals and perennials that are easy to raise from seed should not be sown outdoors until later in spring, when the soil has warmed up.

Now is the time to take root cuttings of mint, tarragon, bergamot and chamomile. There is no need to provide any extra heat.

To layer herbs, mound up earth around straggly thymes and sages, to encourage new shoots, or bed a single branch into soil until it roots to form a new plant.

Fibrous-rooted herbs and herbaceous plants can now be divided throughout the spring months to make vigorous new plants.

Care of Seedlings

Seedlings raised in trays will have to be pricked out and potted up into 7.5 cm (3 in) pots, to develop and harden off before they are finally planted out in the garden.

Outdoor seedlings need thinning out, so that the plants left have enough space to grow and thrive. This is the best time, once the weather has warmed up a little and the soil is still moist, for planting out pot-grown herbs bought from the nursery.

Weeding

Hoe weeds and unwanted plants out of paths and beds immediately as they appear. They will be much easier to control if they are not allowed to set seed or grow too big, especially those with strong taproots. Spread mulch now to suppress weeds and conserve moisture. A mulch is most effective when soil is damp.

Preparing Soil

Prepare beds for planting by forking over and incorporating garden compost or slow-release fertilizer. In heavy soils dig in manure or bulky organic material.

Pruning

Be careful not to start pruning hard too early in spring when frosts are still likely. This is because it will stimulate plants into new growth, which will be susceptible to frost injury. As soon as the weather is suitable and all risk of frost is over, prune shrubs and silvery herbs that have suffered winter damage back to new shoots. Cut out dead and straggly growth on sages and thymes, but trim thymes only lightly, after flowering, as they do not respond well to heavy pruning. Rosemary can be cut back quite hard, but leave it until it has flowered. Trim box hedges, bays and all formal topiary shapes.

Containers

Trim out any dead or old growth on container-grown plants and start to give them more water and a liquid feed. Replant if necessary into a large pot with fresh growing medium.

Above *Lemon balm (*Melissa officinalis*) ready for dividing and replanting.*

Above *Clipping a santolina hedge.*

Above *Seedlings and overwintered cuttings.*

Summer Tasks

Now is the time to enjoy the garden, when plants are in bloom and looking their best. It is also the time for harvesting and making use of the bounty available.

Propagating

Stem cuttings can be taken from many plants, starting with softwood cuttings from late spring to midsummer and continuing with semi-ripe cuttings from late summer to early autumn.

Above *Taking cuttings of purple sage.*

Collect seeds of annuals as they ripen, for use, or for sowing to produce a new crop, such as poppies, pot marigolds, nasturtiums, sunflowers, dill and coriander (cilantro); and of biennials and perennials, including angelica, caraway, sweet cicely (*Myrrhis odorata*), fennel and lovage. Clean the seeds, removing the seed husks, and store in clearly marked paper envelopes. Do not store in polythene (plastic), as moisture will form and they will rot or start into growth. Seeds should be sown within a year of collection, and angelica must be sown within a few months as the seed soon loses viability.

Weeding and Watering

Continue a routine of diligent weeding, to prevent anything undesirable becoming established. Allow plants to self-seed as appropriate; some can always be transplanted. Top up mulches as necessary. Water newly-planted herbs well and any moisture-lovers that may be suffering from drought. Water containers daily.

Above *Nasturtium seeds are collected for drying and replanting the following year.*

Harvesting and Pruning

Summer is the time to make maximum use of fresh-cut herbs in the kitchen and to harvest leaves for drying for winter use, as it is best to cut them before they come into flower. Leafy herbs, such as lovage and mint, should be cut down to ground level in early summer to midsummer, before they start to seed, in order to ensure a second crop. In very dry spells, watering may be needed to achieve this. Cut back chive flowers and stems for new leafy growth and dead-head roses and annuals to encourage new blooms. Cut aromatic foliage and flowers for drying to make pot-pourri.

For plants with variegations, such as variegated lemon balm, cutting out any stems that have reverted to all green helps to prevent the whole plant reverting. Variegated plants are mutants and less prolific in habit than the common version from which they were derived and if left alone the stronger-growing plain foliage will soon take over the whole plant.

Trim fast-growing herbal hedges, such as wall germander (*Teucrium chamaedrys*) and cotton lavender (*Santolina chamaecyparissus*), as often as necessary to keep them in shape during the growing season.

Above *If planting young herbs in summer, choose a damp spell and water well.*

Autumn Tasks

This is the season for clearing up and cutting back, preparing plants for dormancy and planning their protection through the colder months of winter. But there is still propagation to be done, too, if next year's garden is to fulfil its potential.

Propagating

Sow seeds of biennials, including angelica, clary sage (*Salvia sclarea*), anise and caraway in pots to keep in a cold frame or in a cold greenhouse over the winter. Seeds that require vernalization before they will germinate should be sown outdoors, either in pots or in the ground, including sweet cicely (*Myrrhis odorata*), aconite (*Aconitum napellus),* primrose (*Primula* spp.) and sweet violet (*Viola odorata)*. The advantage of sowing in pots is that the seeds are less likely to disappear than if they were sown into the ground to be eaten by birds or to be washed away. Finish collecting seed heads for saving, as they ripen.

Above *Pot up French tarragon to encourage new shoots to appear in spring.*

Many perennials may be divided in autumn for replanting in the border or for starting off as new plants in pots. Dig up French tarragon, put it into a large pot and leave in the cold greenhouse over the winter, for dividing into new plants in spring.

Above *Hardwood rose cuttings.*

Hardwood cuttings of fully mature wood may be taken from shrubs and trees suitable for propagation by this method, including roses, blackcurrants and willow.

Clearing

Cut back dead top growth of hardy herbaceous perennials, which do not need winter protection, such as mint, lemon balm and pot marjoram. If left until spring, new growth is likely to come through before the old stems have been cut back, by which time it is difficult to cut them low enough without clipping into fresh, new foliage. Dig up and compost annuals, including pot marigold, borage, summer savory, sweet marjoram, and biennials in their second year, such as parsley and caraway.

Remove fallen leaves (to make compost or leaf mould) and garden debris – decaying material left lying on plants encourages fungal diseases.

Above *Remove annuals that have finished flowering.*

Pruning

In early autumn, well before the onset of frosts, give box hedges and formally clipped topiary a last trim. Many deciduous shrubs are pruned when they lose their leaves in late autumn to early winter. Common elder (*Sambucus nigra*) and its ornamental cultivars benefit from hard pruning at this time to encourage bushy new growth for the next season and to help retain a neat and controlled shape.

Soil Preparation

For new plantings, dig heavy soils and spread with manure to be broken down by winter frosts.

Above *Double digging the soil.*

Containers

Bring in tender and half-hardy container-grown plants before frosts begin. Cut back excess top growth and give them a minimal amount of water.

Plant Protection

Protect the crowns of French tarragon left in the ground, and other garden-grown plants that are not fully frost-hardy, with agricultural fleece or a coat of straw or bracken.

Dig up at least one tarragon root, to ensure its survival, and also tricolour sage and other less than hardy plants. Pot them up in John Innes compost (soil mix) or similar, and put to spend the winter in a cool greenhouse.

Winter Tasks

During the cold months, when there is less to do outside, take stock of current schemes and plan for the year ahead. In many ways this is the start of the gardening year. Cleaning equipment ready for the new season will be instrumental when it comes to getting an early start on the springtime propagating programme. Order new seed catalogues in good time and plan new garden layouts.

Above *Order seed catalogues and choose seeds for the next season.*

Propagating

If you have a greenhouse, even an unheated one, it is possible to force some herbs for an early crop. Mint and chives are ideal for this treatment. Dig up the roots in late autumn to early winter, divide and replant in a peaty growing medium in quite large pots. Tarragon will need some heat to bring it on early, but may be treated the same way. Plant trees, bare-rooted roses and hedges, such as hawthorn, during their dormant period, and plant garlic bulbs.

Above *Planting a beech hedge.*

Cleaning

Thoroughly wash and clean pots, seed trays and equipment for propagation, getting rid of scum and tidemarks (water stains). Clean out the greenhouse, wash the glass, and do not leave old bags of potting compost (soil mix) around to harbour pests and diseases. Oil and clean garden tools and equipment.

Above *Thoroughly clean pots before storing them until the spring.*

Construction

Provided the weather is not too severe, new paths, terraces or hard surface areas may be constructed, garden schemes laid out and beds prepared for planting. But heavy rain and frosts are not conducive to this work, so local conditions must be taken into account.

Containers

Protect terracotta and stone pots that have not been put under cover against severe temperatures by wrapping them in fleece or hessian. Roots of even relatively hardy plants are more vulnerable if grown in a container, and if the soil freezes it will expand, which is likely to crack the pot.

Give indoor container-grown plants the minimum of water, just enough to ensure the compost (soil mix) does not dry out completely, and do not feed.

Plant Protection

Check that outdoor-grown perennials, which are not totally hardy, such as lemon verbena (*Aloysia triphylla*) are adequately protected with fleece. Some of the ornamental thymes, such as *Thymus vulgaris* 'Silver Posie', will also benefit greatly from a light covering as they dislike cold winds and water-logged roots.

Above *Tying in branches to protect them from the weight of the snow.*

Above *Protecting a plant for the winter.*

Above *A polythene (plastic) plant cover.*

Topiary and Training

Shrubs and trees clipped into geometric shapes have been a garden feature since Roman times. They introduce an appearance of order and formality to the herb garden and provide a contrast for the exuberant growth of many of the other plants. Grown in a pot as a standard, one plant alone makes an interesting focal point, and several placed at strategic intervals lend unity to a scheme. Standards may also be planted in the soil of a parterre (rather than being container-grown) to add height and punctuate the design. Lower-growing herbs clipped into mounds as path edgings or to infill beds emphasize the structure of the design.

Above *Mounds of clipped box*.

Herbs for Topiary

Shrubs or trees with small leaves and a tight habit of growth make ideal subjects for topiary work.

Buxus sempervirens – Box, easy to shape, is the favourite for taller standard trees, cones, spirals and pyramids. Also comes in gold- and silver-leafed varieties.
Buxus sempervirens 'Suffruticosa' – Dwarf box is best for miniature standards and small globes.
Juniperus communis – Juniper, for tall cones and pyramids. Prune in autumn and winter to prevent bleeding of sap.

Above *An imposing display of topiary.*

J. c. 'Compressa' – A dwarf form of juniper that is suitable for lower topiary shapes.
Laurus nobilis – Bay, traditional herb-garden centrepiece as a "lollipop" or standard "mophead".
Myrtus communis – Myrtle responds well to clipping for all topiary shapes. Trim after flowering and give winter protection as it is not fully hardy.
M. c. subsp. *tarentina* – A dwarf form of myrtle ideal for compact globes and low mounds.
Rosmarinus officinalis – Rosemary, for training over wire shapes and clipping into formal hedges.
Ruta graveolens – Rue, effective clipped into mounds.
Santolina chamaecyparissus – Cotton lavender, much used in knot-garden work, also good for clipping into mounds and edges.
Satureja montana – Winter savory responds well to being clipped into low mounds or trained over a frame.
Taxus baccata – Yew, a traditional topiary tree and a favourite for hedging.
Teucrium chamaedrys – Wall germander, for knot gardens and central mounds.

Cones, Pyramids and Spheres

These are relatively simple to achieve as they require no complicated training and pruning, though it helps to have a good "eye" for the job and to stand back frequently, as you clip, to assess progress. Box is the most rewarding to work with as it produces a clean outline and is easy to shape. For a cone, start with a bushy young plant and clip it roughly to shape by eye in its first year. Feed and water it well so that it puts on new growth. In the second year, trim it into a more pronounced cone, using a tripod of canes, encircled with wires as a guide. Keep the shape by trimming twice a year in late spring and early autumn.

Above *Training rosemary over a frame.*

Wire-framed Globes

Plants with flexible stems can be trained to grow over a balloon-shaped wire frame. This works well for rosemary, curry plant (*Helichrysum italicum*), ivies, scented-leaf pelargoniums and climbers such as jasmine. Start with a young plant which has developed a reasonable length of stem. Repot it, cut out any middle growth and push the spiked end of the wire frame into the growing medium. Then tie the stems to the wire frame with twine, avoiding tight knots, which will damage the plant and impede its growth. Clip straggly stems to shape two or three times a year during the growing season.

Standards

Free-form standards: Lemon verbena (*Aloysia triphylla*) can be grown as a free-flowing standard, in contrast to formally clipped box and bay. It is more appropriate in an informal scheme where height and a structural element are required.

Select a young plant with a strong central leader. Remove any competing leaders and strong side stems, leaving higher shoots and some lower laterals to provide food, but shortening the lower laterals by half. Stake the stem to keep it straight. As the plant grows, the shortened laterals can be removed to leave a bare stem. As top laterals develop, pinch out the tips to encourage bushiness. When the plant has reached the desired height and developed a thick head of foliage, pinch out the leading shoot.

Rose standards: Old-fashioned roses trained as weeping standards make a romantic focal point in any scheme and lend colour and contrast to the strict pattern of a potager. Train them over a plastic-covered metal frame shaped like an umbrella for a more formal effect.

Aftercare

Topiary trees in containers all need regular watering and feeding throughout the whole summer to keep them healthy and growing actively. The roots of pot-grown plants are more vulnerable in cold weather than those grown in the soil, so wrap them in hessian (burlap) during frosty spells if they are hardy plants and if less than hardy move them to the protection of a cold greenhouse. Myrtle, bay, rosemary and lemon verbena are all best kept under cover during the winter months.

A mophead bay with a twisted stem

This shows how to make a standard bay with a twisted stem. For a version with a straight stem, simply cut off all side growth to leave one strong central leader, instead of three. Feed regularly throughout the growing season. Replace the top 5 cm (2 in) with fresh compost (soil mix) annually.

YOU WILL NEED

Large pot; multipurpose compost (soil mix); coarse grit (gravel); fertilizer granules; watering can; bay tree; secateurs (pruners); ratchet secateurs or pruning saw

1 *Fill a pot with free-draining, multipurpose growing compost (soil mix), and add a few handfuls of grit (gravel) and a handful of slow release fertilizer.*

2 *Repot a sturdy bay tree with plenty of straight, flexible growth. Clip off side growth to leave three straight stems.*

3 *Using ratchet secateurs or a pruning saw remove lower shoots up to about two-thirds of the overall height.*

4 *Bend over the stems, twisting them carefully, to form a plait.*

5 *Clip the crown to your preferred shape during subsequent years with secateurs (pruners).*

Pests and Diseases

Herbs in general do not suffer greatly from pests and diseases. As predominantly wild plants, they have health and vigour and many are highly aromatic, which gives them inherent protection from insects, which do not like the strong smell. But bacterial and fungal diseases do occasionally strike and no garden is without its share of insect pests. They are, after all, part of a chain, providing food for predators: hedgehogs, birds, mice and other insects.

Pests

Aphids: Blackfly and greenfly, which suck the sap of a plant, weakening it, checking growth and often transmitting viral diseases. Greenfly are attracted to roses and the various species of black aphid to the new soft growth of many green plants. Encourage natural predators such as ladybirds (ladybugs), spray with soapy water, hose with plain water, or spray with derris dust or rotenone. (Black aphids, commonly known as blackfly, should not be confused with American bloodsucking black flies, which are a true fly, rather than an aphid.)

Whitefly: These are small winged insects which usually live on brassicas but can be a problem in the greenhouse. Spray with soft soap, hang up sticky traps (yellow attracts whitefly) or introduce *Encarsia formosa*, a parasitic wasp.

Above *Damage from red spider mites.*

Red spider mite: Flourishes in hot, dry conditions, especially the greenhouse in summer. Difficult to detect without a magnifying glass – watch for bronzed or withered leaves and a fine cobweb mesh on the plants. Cut off badly affected leaves, hose off with plenty of water and spray with soft soap, or introduce a biological predator, another even smaller mite *Phytoseiulus persimilis*.

Scale insects: Flat, brownish insects which attach themselves to the undersides of leaves, suck the sap and spread a sticky substance, followed by a sooty mould. Bay is especially prone to attack. Cut off affected leaves and burn them, spray with insecticidal soap or introduce predatory wasp, *Metaphycus helvolus*, as a control.

Slugs: These do most damage in early spring and appear in the evenings. Pick them off by hand or sink jars filled with beer into the soil to attract and trap them.

Top *Scale insect on a bay leaf.*

Above *The damage caused by a scale insect.*

Diseases

Powdery mildew: A fungal disease which thrives in high humidity. Bergamot, *Monarda didyma*, is prone to it. Don't overwater or overfertilize plants. Spray with Bordeaux mixture.

Botrytis: A fungus which attacks many plants, especially if grown under glass, including tomatoes, strawberries, roses and sunflowers. Seen as a grey mould, it thrives in high humidity. Spray with Bordeaux mixture, following the manufacturer's instructions.

Rust: Brownish-red pustules appear on the leaves and the plant wilts. It affects mint. Dig up and destroy plants if severely affected. Dust with a proprietary sulphur powder following manufacturer's instructions.

Damping-off disease: A fungal disease, it affects seedlings grown under glass. Prevention is best – sow seeds thinly, as overcrowding will encourage the condition, do not overwater, and provide adequate ventilation.

Above *Greenfly suck the sap of a rose.*

Above *Caterpillars on* Polygonatum odoratum.

Prevention

Healthy plants depend on good gardening practice. They should not be overcrowded, which deprives them of light and air. Keep them free of weeds and prune regularly – always using clean secateurs (pruners) and other cutting tools so that you do not pass diseases from one plant to another by mistake.

Vigilance is important – try to remove insect infestations before they build up, and cut out diseased leaves as soon as you see them and burn them. Overfeeding plants with chemical fertilizers will only weaken them and make for fresh, sappy growth which attracts insect pests, but an organic seaweed fertilizer, applied as a spray, helps to build up their resistance.

Correct watering, especially for greenhouse and indoor plants, is also a vital factor. Overwatering tends to lead to rotting plants and inadequate ventilation encourages mildews and botrytis.

Beneficial Insects

Lacewings, ladybirds (ladybugs) and the larvae of the hoverfly all prey on aphids. Grow plants to attract them.

Lacewings: These are attracted by yarrow (*Achillea millefolium*), golden rod (*Solidago virgaurea*) and chamomile (*Chamaemelum nobile*).

Ladybirds (ladybugs): These are attracted by yarrow (*Achillea millefolium*) and pot marigolds (*Calendula officinalis*).

Hoverflies: These are attracted by yarrow (*Achillea millefolium*), lovage (*Levisticum officinale*), dill (*Anethum graveolens*), sweet cicely (*Myrrhis odorata*), fennel (*Foeniculum officinale*), golden rod (*Solidago virgaurea*) and centaury (*Centaurium erythraea*).

Other insects which prey on specific pests can be bought in.

Encarsia formosa: Small parasitic wasps that control whitefly infestations.

Phytoseiulus persimilis: A Chilean mite smaller than its red spider mite prey.

Metaphycus helvolus: Predatory wasp for scale insects.

Aphidoletes aphidimyza: A parasitic midge which preys on aphids.

Above *Yellow sticky traps used for catching whitefly in a commercial greenhouse.*

Organic Pesticides

Sometimes sprays are the only way to control a situation. But the problem with chemical sprays is that they destroy all the beneficial insects as well as pests. They also upset the balance of nature as the predatory insects are less numerous, multiply less enthusiastically than their prey and do not recover. Therefore, the next generation of pests multiplies unchecked and the problem is compounded.

It is best to use organic sprays where possible, but the most effective of these destroy beneficial insects, not just pests.

Soap is the least harmful method. A household liquid soap is suitable. Horticultural insecticidal soaps are even more effective. Derris is made from a tropical plant, and available in liquid or powder form. It kills beneficial insects as well as pests so use with great discretion. Bordeaux mixture is an inorganic chemical fungicide, but not harmful to human or animal life.

Companion Planting

The insect-repellent properties of many herbs, owing to the high concentration of aromatic oils they contain, makes them ideal companions for protecting vulnerable plants such as roses, fruit and vegetables from insect attack. Plant them in a potager garden. Rue (*Ruta graveolens*), cotton lavender (*Santolina chamaecyparissus*), curry plant (*Helichrysum angustifolia*), tansy (*Tanacetum vulgare*) and southernwood (*Artemisia abrotanum*) are all strongly aromatic and can discourage many types of pests.

Chives and garlic are beneficial to roses. They give off an odour which discourages aphids and may help cut the incidence of the disease, blackspot.

Chamomile, once known as "the plants' physician", has a reputation for improving the health and vigour of those plants and herbs surrounding it.

Pennyroyal (*Mentha pulegium*) helps to keep ants away, planted among paving. Summer savory (*Satureja hortensis*), planted in rows next to broad beans (fava beans), provides some protection from blackfly.

French marigolds, *Tagetes*, are excellent at discouraging whitefly, especially in the greenhouse.

Nicotiana sylvestris works on a trap principle. It attracts whitefly, which are then caught by the sticky stems and leaves and can be disposed of.

Directory of Herbs

This botanical A–Z directory of herbs covers over 250 individually photographed plants, giving specific details about their classification and an in-depth description of their appearance to enable precise identification. A brief history describes the traditions and stories behind the herbs, and practical information about their habitats, growth, medicinal uses and related species ensure safe and successful cultivation, growth and usage.

Above *Chives with herb Robert*

Left *Field-grown herbs at the National Herb Centre, England, including from left, white foxgloves, wall germander and santolina.*

Growth Prefers moist but well-drained, slightly acid soil and does not flourish in polluted air. It may be propagated from seed, sown in late autumn or winter, with a period of stratification to aid germination.

Parts used *A. alba,* leaves, resin tapped from mature trees. *A. balsamea,* leaves, oleo-resin collected from blisters on the trunk. Essential oil from resin of both species.

USES Medicinal *A. alba* and *A. balsamea* have aromatic, antiseptic properties, stimulate circulation and increase blood flow and are expectorant and diuretic in action. They are common ingredients of proprietary remedies for coughs and colds, bath preparations, liniments and rubs for rheumatism and neuralgia. Oleo-resin from *A. balsamea* is used in North American traditional medicine for chest infections, cuts, burns, skin eruptions and venereal disease.
Cosmetic The essential oil is an ingredient of cosmetics, perfumes and soaps.

PINACEAE
Abies alba
Silver fir

History and traditions The silver fir was the source of "Strasbourg Turpentine", as described by the French doctor and botanist Pierre Belon in *De Arboribus Coniferis*, 1553, and listed in the London *Pharmacopoeia* until 1788. Its manufacture is covered in the famous work on distillation techniques, *Liber De Arte Distillandi* by the Strasbourg physician Hieronymus Braunschweig, 1450–1534. Turpentine is now more usually made from a selection of several different species of pine, but both *Abies alba* and *A. balsamea* still have a place in many herbal medicines and modern pharmaceutical preparations.
Description It grows from 25–45m/80–150ft and has glossy, dark green needles, silver underneath. It is monoecious – that is, the small male cones and much larger female cones, which are reddish brown when ripe and up to 15cm/6in long, are produced on the same tree.
Related species *A. balsamea* has smooth grey bark, studded with resin blisters, and is strongly scented with balsam.
Habitat/distribution Native to mountainous regions of central and southern Europe, also found in North and Central America.

Above *The leaves of a silver fir are fine and needle-like.*

> **CAUTION** Silver fir is an irritant, which can cause skin reaction in sensitive subjects.

LEGUMINOSAE/MIMOSACEAE
Acacia senegal
Gum Arabic

History and traditions The ancient Egyptians imported what appears to be acacia gum, and it was referred to in the writings of the Greek physician, Theophrastus, in the 4th century BC. Gum arabic is mentioned in many old herbals as an ingredient of pomanders and medicines.
Description *A. senegal*, which produces gum arabic, reaches 6m/19ft tall, has grey bark, pale green pinnate leaves and small pale yellow balls of flowers. There are over 1,000 species in the *Acacia* genus, often called wattles, many of which produce gums for commerce. *A. nilotica* (above) is the source of an inferior gum arabic.
Habitat/distribution The genus is found in dry areas in tropical to warm-temperate zones of Africa, Asia, Australia, Central and South America.
Growth *A. senegal* is tender, requiring a minimum temperature about 15°C/60°F. It needs a slightly acid, well-drained soil and full sun and is propagated by seed, germinated at 21°C/70°F.
Parts used Resin of *A. senegal* (it dissolves in water to form a mucilage which makes a bonding agent).

USES Medicinal Gum arabic is a demulcent, soothes inflamed tissues and is used in pastilles, lotions and pharmaceutical preparations.
Culinary Although it has no place in the domestic kitchen it is used in the food industry in a wide range of products, including confectionery and chewing gum.

> **CAUTION** There are statutory restrictions on the cultivation of wattles in some places.

COMPOSITAE/ASTERACEAE
Achillea millefolium

Yarrow

History and traditions The Latin name honours the legendary Achilles, whose soldiers are said to have staunched their wounds with this plant in the Trojan War, and it has a long tradition as a wound herb. *Millefolium* refers to the many segments of the finely divided leaves. This herb has attracted a wealth of folklore over the centuries, as its common names reveal.

Description A pungent perennial with flat, creamy-white to pinkish flower heads rising on tough stalks 15–30cm/6–12in above a mat of greyish-green, finely-divided leaves. With its creeping roots and efficient self-seeding it is extremely invasive.

Related species There are many ornamental cultivars of *A. millefolium* including 'Moonshine', with light yellow flowers, and the rich crimson 'Fire King'. *A. ageratum* (formerly *A. decolorans*), English mace, is a little-known culinary herb with a mildly spicy flavour, used to flavour chicken dishes, soups, stews and sauces.

Habitat/distribution Widespread in temperate zones, found in grasslands, waste ground and by roadsides. Native of Europe and western Asia, naturalized in North America, Australia and New Zealand.

Growth Propagated by division of roots. The wild species is invasive and when grown as a garden plant it is advisable to keep it in a container or to restrict the roots by surrounding with tiles pushed into the soil.

Yarrow folklore

As "devil's nettle" or "devil's plaything", yarrow was thought to be dedicated to Satan and widely used in charms and spells. It had a place in Druid ceremonies and was made into herbal amulets or strewn on the threshold of houses against witches and evil forces. A bunch hung on the door, and tied to the baby's cradle for good measure on Midsummer's Eve, was hoped to ensure an illness-free year ahead.

Several claims are made for yarrow's supernatural powers in the 15th-century "Book of Secrets", attributed to Albertus Magnus. If put to the nose it will protect "from all feare and fatansye or vysion" and rather more wildly, if the juice is smeared on the hands, when plunged into water they will act as magnets for fish.

Yarrow features in many traditional rhymes connected with finding true love:

> *Yarrow, yarrow, long and narrow,*
> *Tell unto me by tomorrow,*
> *Who my husband is to be.*

Another rhyme, attributed to the county of Suffolk in England and to eastern Europe, refers to yarrow's propensity to cause a nosebleed:

> *Green 'arrow, green*
> *'arrow, you bears a*
> *white blow,*
> *If my love loves me my*
> *nose will bleed now.*

And if eaten at the wedding feast, it was claimed that bride and groom would remain in love for seven years.

As well as its role as a wound herb, reflected in the names soldier's woundwort, herb militaris and carpenter's weed, it was credited with both stopping a nosebleed or bringing one on (a supposed way of relieving migraine), as occasion demanded. It has a pungent smell and, as "old man's pepper", was made into snuff.

Parts used The whole plant, fresh or dried.

USES Medicinal The essential oil contains azulene, which has anti-inflammatory properties. It increases perspiration and is taken internally, as a tea, for colds and feverish conditions, and applied externally for wounds, ulcers and nosebleeds. It is also thought to lower blood pressure and to relieve indigestion.

Cosmetic A weak infusion of the flowering tops in distilled water makes a cleanser or refreshing toner for oily skins.

Other names Soldier's woundwort, herb militaris, carpenter's weed, old man's pepper, nose bleed, devil's nettle, milfoil and also thousand leaf.

Above right *The divided leaves of* Achillea millefolium, *also known as thousand leaf.*

Right Achillea ageratum, *English mace.*

CAUTION Large does can cause headaches. Allergic rashes and skin sensitivity to sunlight may result from prolonged use.

RANUNCULACEAE

Aconitum napellus
Aconite

History and traditions The generic name is from the Greek for a dart (*akontion*) in recognition of its erstwhile use as an arrow poison, but the species name, *napellus*, meaning "little turnip", is supposedly for the shape of the roots, and gives no hint of the deadly nature of this plant. The popular name, monkshood, describes the curious shape of the flowers, while the common name for *A. lycoctonum,* wolf's bane, is a reference to its ability to despatch this once much-feared animal by sprinkling the juice over raw meat as bait. Stories of the dangers of aconite abound in herbals through the ages, such as Gerard's account of the "ignorant persons" of Antwerp who were taken with "most cruel symptoms and so died" when served the leaves in a salad as a "lamentable experiment".
Description The helmet-shaped, inky-blue flowers give this hardy herbaceous perennial a slightly sinister appearance appropriate to its properties. It has tuberous roots and delphinium-like foliage from which the flowering stems rise to a height of 1.5m/5ft.
Related species There are about 100 species, all of which are highly poisonous. *A. lycoctonum* has yellow, sometimes purple, flowers and *A. carmichaelii,* syn. *A. fischeri*, is sometimes used in Chinese medicine as a painkiller.

Habitat/distribution Widespread in Europe and in northern temperate regions, in damp woodlands, meadows and mountainous areas.
Growth Plant in moist, fertile soil and part-shade. Propagation is by division of roots in the autumn for flowering in the second year. Seeds sown in spring will not flower for 2–3 years.
Parts used Dried root tubers.
Other name Monkshood.

USES Medicinal The alkaloid, aconite, gives it toxicity. As a strong sedative and painkiller, it should be used only by qualified practitioners. A very small dose causes numbness of lips, tongue and extremeties and can lead to vomiting, coma and death.

> **CAUTION** The whole plant is highly toxic and if ingested can kill. Contact with skin may cause allergic reactions – always handle with gloves. Subject to legal restrictions in some countries.

ACORACEAE

Acorus calamus
Calamus

History and traditions The first specimens to reach Europe were imported from Asia by the botanical garden in Vienna in the 16th century. Calamus, which means "reed" in Greek, then became popular as a scented strewing herb. Cardinal Wolsey used it extensively for this purpose in Hampton Court Palace. This was yet another example of his extravagance in the eyes of his contemporaries, due to its comparative rarity – at the time calamus was grown only on the Norfolk Broads some distance away. It was also one of the ingredients in Moses's instructions to make "an ointment compound after the art of the apothecary" as a holy anointing oil (Exodus 30:25).
Description A pleasantly aromatic perennial with a thick much-branched rhizome, it has similar-shaped leaves to the irises, although is not botanically related to them. The flower head is a spadix, emerging from the side of the leaf, but it is not usually fertile in Europe and cool northern climates, owing to lack of appropriate insects for pollination.
Related species *A. gramineus*, native to the Far East, is a miniature species, used in Chinese

medicine. Its compact size makes it suitable for growing in ornamental ponds.
Habitat/distribution *A. calamus* (above) is indigenous to central Asia and eastern Europe, and is now widespread in marshy areas and by shallow waterways of northern temperate zones.
Growth Vigorous and easy to propagate, it must have moist soil and plenty of water. Grows best by water margins. Propagate in spring or autumn by cutting rhizomes in small pieces, each with 2–3 buds, and planting in muddy ground.
Parts used Rhizomes, essential oil.

USES Medicinal Used for digestive problems and to dispel intestinal worms. It is slightly sedative to the central nervous system and is traditionally used in Ayurvedic medicine following strokes, and also for bronchial complaints. Externally it is used as an alcohol rub for aching muscles.
Aromatic The essential oil, separated by steam distillation, is a perfumery ingredient. Herbalists of old called it "*calamus aromaticus*", and the ground root was added to potpourris, scented sachets, tooth and hair powders.
Household In Asia it is sometimes used as an insecticide powder to deter ants.
Other names Sweet flag, sweet rush and myrtle grass.

> **CAUTION** Excessive doses can cause adverse reactions, including vomiting.

UMBELLIFERAE/APIACEAE

Aegopodium podagraria
Ground elder

History and traditions The specific name comes from the Latin word for gout, *podagra*, and it was grown in monastery gardens in medieval times as a cure for that disease. The name bishops' weed could be a reference to an episcopal tendency to gout, due to high living and a rich diet of meat and alcohol, or to the plant's prevalence around ecclesiastical sites. It is dedicated to St Gerard, the patron saint of gout sufferers.

Description A herbaceous perennial with a creeping root system, it spreads rapidly, smothering other plants and self-seeds. Umbels of white flowers rise on long stems to 90cm/36in above the leaves in summer.

Related species *A. podagraria* 'Variegatum' is a variegated cultivar with cream patterning at the leaf margins. It is not as invasive as the common variety and makes a pretty border, especially when grown with white lilies or tulips.

Habitat/distribution Native to Europe, naturalized in North America; found in woodlands and wasteground.

Growth Ground elder is a rampant weed that grows in any soil and is almost impossible to eradicate once established. This plant is definitely not suitable for cultivation as it will take over.

Parts used Leaves, stems.

USES Medicinal An anti-inflammatory herb with astringent properties, it has a long tradition as a treatment for gout, sciatica and rheumatism. It can be taken internally as an infusion, and is applied externally for stings and burns.

Culinary Though fairly unpleasant in taste, the young leaves and shoots can be added to salads, or cooked like spinach.

Other names Goutweed, bishops' weed and herb Gerard.

Above Aegopodium podagraria *'Variegatum' (Variegated ground elder) in the foreground with white, lily-flowered tulips.*

HIPPOCASTANACEAE

Aesculus hippocastanum
Horse chestnut

History and traditions This spectacular tree was introduced to western Europe in the mid-16th century, when it was grown in Vienna from seeds brought from Istanbul by the botanist Clusius (Charles de L'Ecluse), although it does not seem to have been widely used for medicinal purposes until the late 19th century. The origins of the name are confused, but are all tied to the use of this tree as animal fodder. *Hippocastanum* is the Latin for "horse chestnut", which the Romans supposedly fed to their livestock.

Description A stately, deciduous tree, 30–40m/98–130ft in height, it has palmate leaves, sticky resinous buds and candelabras of white or pink-tinged flowers in spring. The spiny, globular, green fruit contains glossy reddish-brown seeds (conkers, also called chestnuts).

Habitat/distribution Occurs in eastern Europe, eastern Asia and North America, introduced to Britain and western Europe.

Growth Propagate by seeds, sown in autumn. Often self-seeds and grows rapidly in any soil.

Parts used Bark, seeds.

USES Medicinal Effective in the treatment of oedema and varicose veins. The plant may be used internally and externally and has the following actions: venotonic, anti-inflammatory, antieccymotic (against bruises). Use as a cream to help varicose veins.

CAUTION The whole fruit is mildly toxic and should never be eaten. Only for use by qualified practitioners. Should not be applied to broken skin because saponins in the plant could be an irritant.

LABIATAE/LAMIACEAE
Agastache foeniculum
Anise hyssop

History and traditions A traditional medicinal herb of Native Americans, it became popular with colonists as a bee plant for the distinctive aniseed flavour it gave to honey.
Description A hardy, short-lived perennial with soft, ovate leaves, strongly scented with aniseed. Bold purple flower spikes last all summer. Clumps are 60–90cm/24–36in in height.
Related species *A. rugosa,* known as Korean mint, or wrinkled giant hyssop, is also a hardy perennial, 1m/3ft high, with pointed, mint-scented leaves and mauve flower spikes.
Habitat/distribution *A. foeniculum* is native to North and Central America, and *A. rugosa* comes from eastern Asia.
Growth Grows best in rich moist soil in full sun. Although reasonably hardy, *A. foeniculum* will not stand prolonged frost or temperatures below -6°C/20°F. Propagate by division or softwood cuttings in spring.
Parts used Leaves, flowers – fresh or dried.

USES Medicinal The leaves have antibacterial properties and are taken as an infusion to alleviate coughs and colds, or as a digestive.
Culinary The leaves of both *A. foeniculum* and *A. rugosa* make refreshing tea with a minty flavour. They can be floated in soft drinks and fruit cups to add piquancy. Add a few leaves to a salad to boost flavour and goodness. The dried or fresh leaves may be added to cooked meat dishes and go well with pork.

RUTACEAE
Agathosma betulina
Buchu

History and traditions A prized medicinal plant of the indigenous people of South Africa, its virtues were discovered by colonists of the Cape who introduced it to Europe at the end of the 18th century. In the 1820s the dried leaves were exported in some quantity to Britain and thence to North America, to be included in proprietary medicines and used to flavour cordials. John Lindley in his *Flora Medica*, 1838, records that several species of *Agathosma*, collected as 'bucku', were "found to be an excellent aromatic stomachic and very efficacious as a diuretic. The infusion is much praised as a remedy in chronic inflammations of the bladder and urethra and in chronic rheumatism." All of these uses remain valid in herbal medicine today.
Description A tender, evergreen shrub, 1–2m/3–6ft in height, it has glossy, yellowish-green leaves, which are leathery in texture and studded with oil glands which smell of blackcurrants. White flowers appear in spring. A member of the rue family, it is highly aromatic, scenting the air wherever it grows in quantity.
Related species Several species are used, all indiscriminately termed buchu, or "buka", meaning powder in the local language.

A. betulina is held to be the most effective for medicinal purposes, *A. crenulata,* oval buchu, has ovate leaves and *A. serratifolia*, long buchu, serrated, lance-shaped foliage. These plants were once classified as "barosma" and the term "barosma powder" for buchu is still sometimes used.
Habitat/distribution Dry hillsides of Cape Province, South Africa.
Growth Grown as a conservatory plant in temperate zones, a minimum temperature of 5°C/41°F is required. Pot in ericaceous (lime-free) compost. It must not be overwatered, which can lead to rot, and should be cut back hard in spring to keep it in shape and control size. It grows outside in warm, frost-free regions, and needs well-drained, acid soil and full sun.
Parts used Leaves, which are harvested when the plant is in flower, and dried.

USES Medicinal A strong urinary antiseptic. Used internally to treat urinary infections, especially cystitis, coughs and colds, rheumatism, arthritis and digestive disorders. Applied externally for bruises and sprains.
Culinary Gives a blackcurrant taste to soft drinks and cordials and is used to flavour a local liquor "buchu brandy".
Household Made into a powder to deter ants and other insects.
Other name Round buchu.

AGAVACEAE
Agave americana
Agave

History and traditions Agave comes from the Greek for admirable. It gained the name "century plant" from the mistaken belief that it flowers only after a hundred years – but most bloom after ten years.

Description A tender succulent whose rosettes of spiky grey-green leaves are 1–2m/3–6ft high with a spread of 2–3m/6–10ft. The tall bell-shaped flower spikes, resembling small trees, rise to 8m/26ft. Agaves should not be confused with aloes, and are not botanically related.

Related species *A. americana* 'Variegata' is a cultivar with yellow margins to the leaves.

Habitat/distribution Originally from tropical zones of the Americas, especially Mexico, this plant is now naturalized in southern Europe, India, and Central and South Africa.

Growth Needs well-drained soil, full sun and a minimum temperature of 5°C/41°F. Propagate by offsets. In cool climates it can be grown as a conservatory plant but takes up a lot of space.

Parts used Leaves, roots, sap.

USES Medicinal The sap has anti-inflammatory properties, and is applied externally for burns, bites and stings, by breaking open a leaf.

General The root has cleansing properties and is used for washing clothes and in commercial soap production. Fibres are woven into rope. The powdered leaf makes snuff and the whole plant is much employed as a stock-proof fence.

> **CAUTION** Can provoke a reaction in those with a history of skin problems.

ROSACEAE
Agrimonia eupatoria
Agrimony

History and traditions The species name is from Mithradates Eupator, King of Pontus, who died in 64BC. He practised magic, was a great believer in herbal potions and was thought to have rendered himself immune to injury by saturating his body with lethal poisons. The Anglo-Saxons attributed magical powers to agrimony, including it in charms and dubious preparations of blood and pounded frogs. A sprig under the pillow supposedly brought oblivion, until removed. It was also credited with healing wounds, internal haemorrhages, snake bites, charming away warts and mending bad backs. Retaining its reputation through the centuries, it became the principal ingredient of *eau d'arquebusade*, a lotion for treating the wounds inflicted by the arquebus, a 16th-century firearm and forerunner of the musket. It was an essential ingredient of a springtime drink, still taken by country folk into the early years of this century as a "blood purifier".

Description A perennial with compound pointed leaves, covered in soft hairs. In summer and autumn it has small yellow flower spikes with a hint of an apricot scent. It grows to a height of 30–60cm/1–2ft.

Habitat/distribution Found on waste grounds and roadsides throughout Europe, Asia and North America.

Growth A wild plant which tolerates poor, dry soil, it can be propagated by seed sown in spring or by root division in autumn.

Above *Agrimony in flower.*

Parts used Dried flowering plant.

USES Medicinal Has anti-inflammatory, anti-bacterial and astringent properties and is taken internally for sore throats, catarrh, diarrhoea, cystitis and urinary infections. Applied externally as a lotion for wounds.

Household Yields a yellow dye.

Other names Church steeples, sticklewort and cockleburr.

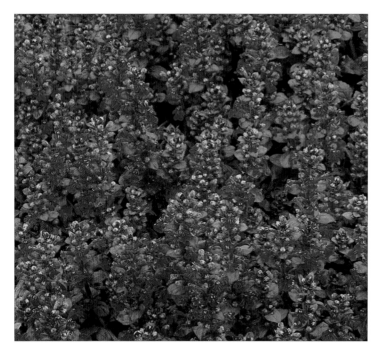

Above Aguja reptans 'Atropurpurea'.

Below Aguja reptans 'Multicolor'.

LABIATAE/LAMIACEAE

Ajuga reptans
Bugle

History and traditions The apothecaries knew it as "bugula" and along with self-heal, *Prunella vulgaris,* it was valued for many centuries as a wound herb. Culpeper thought highly of it: "If the virtues of it make you fall in love with it (as they will if you be wise) keep a syrup of it to take inwardly, and an ointment and plaster of it to use outwardly, always by you". He recommended it for all kinds of sores, gangrene and fistulas. Gerard, who found many specimens growing "in a moist ground upon Black Heath, near London", backs him up, expressing the view that it is common knowledge in France "how he needs neither physician nor surgeon that hath Bugle and Sanicle".

Description A hardy perennial, 10–30cm/ 4–12in high, growing on a creeping rootstock, it has attractive blue flower spikes in spring or early summer, growing from rosettes of basal leaves. White or pink-flowered mutants occasionally occur.

Related species Cultivars with richly coloured foliage make rewarding subjects for the herb garden. *A. r.* 'Atropurpurea' has purple-bronze leaves, *A. r.* 'Multicolor' has colourful variegated foliage of pink, crimson and cream with a hint of green, and *A. r.* 'Variegata' has greyish-green leaves with creamy margins.

Habitat/distribution In damp ground in woodlands and meadows. Native to Europe and introduced elsewhere, it is also found in northern Africa and parts of the Middle East.

Growth Ajugas make excellent ground cover and are easy to propagate by separating and replanting the leafy runners at any time of the year, but preferably in spring or autumn when sufficient moisture can be provided. They do need a moist soil to flourish well, and sun or partial shade.

Parts used Whole plant.

USES Medicinal Its reputation, sadly, has not stood the test of time and bugle is no longer widely used in herbal medicine today. But it is said to be mildly astringent and is sometimes still recommended, in the form of a lotion or ointment, for treating cuts and bruises.

Other names Carpenter's herb and sicklewort.

Habitat/distribution Found in mountainous areas, meadows, pasture lands and on rock ledges in Europe and throughout northern temperate regions.

Growth Grows in any soil in sun or partial shade. Self-seeds prolifically but germination of seed sown artificially is erratic. The easiest way to propagate is by division in spring or autumn. Species planted together hybridize readily.

Parts used Leaves.

USES Medicinal A herb traditionally used in gynaecology to treat menstrual irregularities and some symptoms of menopausal change. Applied externally for vaginal itching, as a lotion for sores and skin irritation, or as a mouthwash.

Culinary The leaves are edible and sometimes shredded and added to salads, but their slightly bitter, undistinguished taste hardly warrants this treatment.

Other names Lion's foot, bear's foot and leontopodium (in French, it is called Pied-de-Lion and in German, Frauenmantle).

ROSACEAE
Alchemilla vulgaris
Lady's mantle

History and traditions This herb was unknown to the writers of the ancient classical world, but was a popular "magic" plant in northern Europe from earliest times, rising to prominence during the Middle Ages for its connections with alchemy. It was also sometimes associated with the Virgin Mary and dubbed Our Lady's mantle, subsequently shortened to lady's mantle, the scalloped leaves supposedly resembling a sculptured cloak. It was traditionally prescribed for infertility and "women's troubles" and was said to regulate the menstrual cycle and ease menopausal symptoms – as it still is prescribed by herbalists today.

Description A perennial 40–50cm/16–20in, it has hairy, branched stems and deeply lobed leaves (seven or nine lobes) with serrated edges and a froth of yellowish-green flowers in late spring and throughout summer.

Related species *A. alpina*, another medicinal species, is lower-growing at 10–20cm/4–8in, with star-shaped leaves. *A. mollis*, from the Carpathian mountains and known as "the garden variety", is the most attractive of the three with paler green, scalloped leaves and a more luxurious show of greeny-yellow flowers. It is widely grown in herb gardens, but has less medicinal value.

Above right Alchemilla mollis *has a froth of greeny-yellow flowers throughout summer.*

Right *The concave shape of* Alchemilla xanthochlora *and* A. mollis *leaves forms a dip where drops of moisture collect.*

The alchemy connection

The magic of lady's mantle lies in its ability to hold moisture drops, often dew, trapped in the central dips of the leaves and by their waxy surface. Dew was a much-prized ingredient in the recipes of the alchemists of old and here was an accessible source. So the herb was named "Alchemilla" – the little alchemist.

In its narrowest and best-known sense, the primary concern of alchemy was the transformation of base metal into gold, but its wider significance is that it marked the beginnings of systematic chemistry. Leading alchemists of the 13th century were Albertus Magnus, Roger Bacon and Arnold de Villeneuve, who wrote widely on the subject. Although they believed in the "philosopher's stone" (the instrument

capable of transmuting metals into gold), they were also pre-occupied with the discovery of a divine water, or elixir of life, capable of healing all maladies – with the purest dew as a necessary component.

In the 16th century, the Swiss physician, Paracelsus, took up some of the tenets of alchemy, including the concept of the "prima materia" and the "quinta essentia", the primary essence of a substance, but gave it a new direction. The chief objective was the making of medicines, dependent on a study of the properties of plants and their effects on the body.

LILIACEAE/ALLIACEAE

Allium

The onion genus provides us with some of the most useful medicinal and culinary herbs. The characteristic strong smell is a result of the sulphur compounds contained within, which are beneficial to the circulatory and respiratory systems and have antibacterial properties. It also makes them among the most popular and powerful flavouring agents in worldwide cuisine.

History and traditions The use of onions and garlic can be traced back to the ancient civilizations of Babylonia, Egypt, Greece and Rome. One variety of onion was accorded divine honours in Egypt, and the pyramid builders are said to have been sustained by doses of garlic.

Many of the old writers on herbs, from Pliny onwards, refer to the medicinal properties of garlic, but not everybody was unanimous in its praise. Horace made the outrageous claim that it is "more poisonous than hemlock", when he was ill following a meal containing garlic. And, in 16th-century Britain, the herbalist Gerard remained doubtful of its virtues. In this he was unusual, as the pungent smell of both onions and garlic ensured a widespread belief that their juice protected from infection and in times of plague they were much in demand. One old recipe book gives water distilled from onions as a treatment for the bites of a rabid dog. The smell of garlic is particularly lingering and all-pervasive and may well be responsible for superstitions about its capacity to ward off vampires and the devil.

Allium cepa
Onion

Description Single bulbs at the base of each stem form the familiar culinary onion.
Related species There are numerous cultivars. *Allium cepa* Proliferum Group is the attractive tree onion, whose flowers produce large bulbils with leaves attached.
Habitat/distribution Origins unknown but probably originated in Central Asia, now grown worldwide.
Growth Propagate from sets in early summer or seed sown in spring or autumn. Plant in well-drained soil, rich in nutrients. Bend over tops in late summer to speed ripening, and dry bulbs before storing.
Parts used Fresh bulb.

USES Medicinal See box opposite.
Culinary Popular vegetable and flavouring agent.

Allium fistulosum
Welsh onion

Description Evergreen hardy perennial 60–90cm/2–3ft tall, with hollow stems and leaves. Tightly packed greenish-white globes form the flowers in spring.
Habitat/distribution Native of Siberia, China and Japan. Widely grown elsewhere.
Growth Grow in well-drained, reasonably rich soil and divide clumps every three years. Seeds can be sown directly into the ground after frost.
Parts used Leaves, bulbs.

USES Medicinal The Welsh onion shares the decongestant, antibacterial properties of garlic and onions, but it is thought to be less concentrated and efficacious.
Culinary Pull the whole plant to make use of the bulb at the root, or cut the leaves and snip into salads and stir-fries.

Avoiding garlic breath

Chewing fresh parsley helps to disguise the smell of garlic on the breath. If you do not like the taste of garlic, but want to benefit from its healthy attributes, it can be taken in capsule form (available from good health stores or pharmacies).

Right Allium cepa *Proliferum Group produces bulbs on its stems.*

Garlic bread

2–3 garlic cloves, peeled
25g/1oz/2 tbsp butter
1 tsp fresh parsley, finely chopped
1 tsp lemon juice
4 slices of bread, cut from a baguette

Using a garlic press, crush the garlic cloves into a small bowl. Beat the crushed garlic with the butter, parsley and lemon juice until softened and evenly combined. Spread it evenly over the slices of bread. Toast under a hot grill, or put on a baking tray in a hot oven, until browned.

Allium sativum
Garlic

Description A hardy perennial, it is often cultivated as an annual. Bulbs are made up of cloves, or bulblets, in a papery, white, or pinkish-white casing. The clump of flat leaves grows to 60cm/2ft. Flowers are greenish white.

Habitat/distribution Originally from India or Central Asia, now grown worldwide, but does not flourish in cold, northern climates.

Growth Plant bulbs in autumn or winter in rich soil and a sunny position. Lift in late summer and dry in the sun before storing. Increase by dividing bulbs and replanting.

Parts used Bulbs, separated into cloves.

USES Medicinal See box below.
Culinary Popular flavouring agent.

Allium schoenoprasum
Chives

Description A hardy perennial with clumps of cylindrical leaves growing from small bulblets to 30cm/12in. The leaves do not withstand very cold winters. Purple flower globes appear in early summer. There are both fine and broad-leafed cultivars.

Habitat/distribution Native to cool regions of Europe, naturalized in North America. Found in dry and damp, rocky areas, grasslands and woods.

Parts used Leaves, flowers.

USES Culinary A prime culinary herb, with no medical applications, it has a milder flavour than its onion cousin, *Allium cepa*. Snip leaves into salads, sauces and soups. Flowers can be used as a garnish.

Allium tuberosum
Garlic chives

Description A perennial with sheaths of coarse, flattened leaves growing from a rhizome (modified stem) to a height of 50cm/20in. Star-shaped white flowers appear in late summer.

Parts used Fresh leaves.

USES Culinary Use as chives.

Right Allium schoenoprasum *makes an attractive addition to the flower garden.*

Medicinal use of garlic and onions

Above *Regularly eating garlic helps to keep your heart healthy.*

Helps lower blood pressure and blood cholesterol
Both garlic and onions may help to lower blood pressure and blood cholesterol. They are also thought to raise levels of beneficial high-density lipoproteins in the blood – these are molecules which play a part in clearing cholesterol from body tissues.

Helps prevent blood clotting
Research studies have also found that eating onions and garlic inhibits blood clotting and helps prevent circulatory diseases such as coronary heart disease, thrombosis and strokes. Studies using animals revealed that a garlic compound, allyl disulphide, helped prevent growth of malignant tumours – but

the case for garlic as a cancer preventive in humans is as yet unproven.

Acts as a decongestant
Garlic and onions reduce nasal congestion and ease cold symptoms, especially when eaten raw, as volatile components are lost in cooking.

Has antiviral and antibacterial properties
The juice of a freshly-cut onion is a useful first-aid measure to relieve insect bites, bee stings and the itching of chilblains.

CAUTION Garlic can interact with anti-coagulant drugs such as warfarin.

ALOEACEAE

Aloe vera syn. *A. barbadensis*

Aloe vera

History and traditions The medicinal value of this plant was recognized by the Egyptians and used as an embalming ingredient. One story goes that Aristotle tried to persuade Alexander the Great to conquer the Indian Ocean island of Socotra (near the Gulf of Aden), for its aloes, being the only known place where they grew at the time. The plant was introduced to Europe in the 10th century and became established over the centuries as an important ingredient in proprietary medicines.

Description A tender succulent, 60–40cm/ 2–3ft tall, with clusters of elongated, very fleshy, greeny-grey leaves, spiked at the edges, and tubular yellow flowers.

Related species Of the 300 species of aloes only a few have medicinal properties, including *A. perryi* and the South African *A. ferox,* which has red spikes at the leaf edges. But *A. vera* is the most potent.

Habitat/distribution Origins are uncertain, but it is widespread in tropical and subtropical regions in dry, sunny areas.

Growth It needs a well-drained soil, full sun and a minimum temperature of 5°C/41°F. In cold climates it can be successfully grown as a conservatory or house plant. Pot up in gritty compost (soil mix), do not overwater, and allow to dry out completely between waterings.

Parts used Leaves, sap. The leaves are cut and the sap is used fresh, preserved and bottled or dried to a brown crystalline solid for use in creams, lotions and medicinal preparations.

USES Medicinal It is the mix of constituents in this plant that gives it exceptional healing properties. Aloe gel and resin may be used. Aloe resin has laxative and anti-inflammatory activity. The gel is immune-enhancing, anti-viral, anti-inflammatory, demulcent and emollient. It contains minerals; antioxidant vitamins C, E, B$_{12}$, beta-carotene and lignin. *A. vera* gel from the leaf is applied externally to promote healing of wounds, burns, sunburn, eczema and skin irritations. It is taken internally for digestive tract problems and there is also some evidence that it may help conditions where the immune system is not functioning well. It has laxative properties and "bitter aloes" is the name for the strong, purgative medicine that is made from the leaves.

Cosmetic It is an ingredient of many commercial cosmetic products.

Other names Aloes, Barbados aloe, Cape aloe and Curaçao aloe.

> **CAUTION** Only to be taken internally with professional healthcare advice. Not to be taken internally if pregnant or in large doses. Subject to legal restrictions in some countries.

VERBENACEAE

Aloysia triphylla syn. *Aloysia citriodora*

Lemon verbena

History and traditions This lemon-scented shrub from South America was introduced to Europe in the 1790s. It is said to be named after Maria Louisa, wife of Carlos IV of Spain, Aloysia being a corruption of Louisa. The Victorians liked it for its long-lasting lemon fragrance, calling it "the lemon plant", and dried it for use in scented sachets.

Description Frost- to half-hardy deciduous shrub with rough-textured, strongly lemon-scented, spear-shaped leaves, dotted on the underside with oil glands. Racemes of tiny mauve-white flowers appear in late summer. In warm climates, where no frost occurs, it grows to 4.5m/15ft, but in cooler regions it is unlikely to grow to more than 1.5m/5ft. It is closely related to the *Lippia* genus, with which it was once classified.

Habitat/distribution Native to Chile and Argentina, it is widely grown in tropical and subtropical zones of the world, in Australia, New Zealand and temperate regions of Europe.

Growth It will usually survive a minimum temperature of -5°C/23°F, provided it is grown in a sheltered, south-facing site in well-drained soil. It will not tolerate prolonged cold and frost, especially if grown in a heavy soil. May be grown as a pot plant if given winter protection.

Above *Lemon verbena has a strong sherbert lemon scent.*

Right *Lemon verbena in flower – it keeps its scent well when dried.*

New leaves do not appear until late spring or early summer. Cut back hard in spring, when it will regenerate from old wood. It is propagated from cuttings, taken in late summer, but needs heat to produce roots and during development of the seedlings.

Parts used Leaves, essential oil.

USES Culinary The leaves (fresh or dry) make a refreshing tea. If used with great discretion, as the taste is strong, they can be included in savoury stuffings and sauces, or used to flavour cakes and ice cream.

Aromatic The benefit of this herb is that the leaves retain their lemon scent, when dried, for several years. They help to deter insects and are ideal for sachets and making potpourri. The essential oil was widely used in perfumery, but has been discovered to sensitize the skin to sunlight.

Lemon verbena potpourri

dried peel of 1 lemon
2 cups dried lemon verbena leaves
1 cup dried chamomile flowers
15cm/6in cinnamon stick, crushed
1 cup dried pot marigold petals
5ml/1 tsp orris root powder
2–3 drops essential oil of lemon verbena (optional)

To dry the lemon peel, scrape it off the fruit with a vegetable peeler, spread on paper and put in a warm place (such as an airing cupboard) for about two weeks, until crisp.

Mix the dried lemon peel, dried lemon verbena leaves, dried chamomile flowers, crushed cinnamon, dried pot marigold petals, orris root powder and oils together. Seal in a tin and put in a warm place for 2–3 weeks, shaking occasionally. Put in a bowl to scent the room, covering when not in use to retain the scent, or in drawstring sachets to hang in a wardrobe.

Lemon verbena essential oil will give the potpourri a stronger fragrance. It is also useful for adding zest to the mixture at a later date, as it will lose strength when constantly exposed to light and air.

ZINGIBERACEAE
Alpinia officinarum
Galangal

History and traditions Very similar to ginger, this plant has a long history as a spice and medicinal plant and has been used in Ayurvedic and Chinese medicine since ancient times. 'Galangal' comes from the Arabic word *Khalanjan*, which could in turn be derived from a Chinese word meaning "mild ginger". Known in Europe since the 9th century, it was probably introduced by Arab or Greek physicians.

Description A tropical evergreen with tall clumps of ovate to lanceolate leaves growing from ginger-scented rhizomes to a height of 1.2m/4ft. Flowers are pale green and white. *A. officinarum*, lesser galangal, is the more important species for both medicinal and culinary purposes.

Related species *A. galanga*, greater galangal, is a larger plant, growing to 2m/6ft, and has a less marked ginger aroma.

Habitat/distribution Found in tropical rainforest and grassland areas of southeast Asia and Australia.

Growth It can be grown only in climates with high humidity and minimum temperatures of 15–18°C/59–64°F. Needs well-drained soil and partial shade. Propagated by division of the rhizomes when new shoots appear.

Parts used Rhizome, oil.

USES Medicinal A good digestive aid. It has antibacterial and antifungal properties, is used for feverish illnesses and fungal infections. *A. galanga* is considered less effective medicinally.

Culinary Both species are used as a ginger-like flavouring in Thai and southeast Asian cookery.

Growth Prefers moist to wet soil and a sunny situation. Propagated by division in autumn or by seed sown in late summer, though germination is often erratic.

Parts used Leaves, roots, flowers.

USES Medicinal The herb contains a demulcent mucilage and is anti-inflammatory in action. *Althaea* is used primarily to influence the digestive and pulmonary systems. It may also be applied locally to ulcers, boils, inflammation of the skin and insect bites.

Culinary At one time the young roots and leaves were boiled, then fried with onions as a spring vegetable, or added to salads – but neither is very palatable.

MALVACEAE
Althaea officinalis
Marshmallow

History and traditions The generic name comes from the Greek, *altho*, meaning "to cure". The family name, Malvaceae, is also of Greek derivation, from *malake*, meaning soft, indicating the emollient, healing properties of this plant, which have long been recognized. Pliny remarked: "Whosoever shall take a spoonful of Mallows shall that day be free from all diseases that may come to him." Early recorded uses include poultices to reduce inflammation and spongy lozenges to soothe coughs and sore throats. It is from this the modern confectionery is descended, though it no longer contains any of the herb. Marshmallow root was eaten as a vegetable by the Romans and in many Middle Eastern and European countries was a standby in times of famine when food was scarce. In more recent times it was a springtime country tradition to eat the young shoots, or make them into a syrup, to "purify the blood".

Description A hardy perennial with soft, downy leaves and pale pink flowers in summer, it reaches 1–1.2m/3–4ft in height. It has large, fleshy taproots.

Habitat/distribution Found in salt marshes, near sea coasts and in moist inland areas, throughout Europe, in temperate regions of Asia, North America and Australia.

Below All parts of
Althaea officinalis *have medicinal properties.*

Below left and right Alcea rosea, *the garden hollyhock, has racemes of single blooms in pink, purple and white. There are also many cultivars with double flowers.*

Related species

MALVACEAE
Alcea rosea formerly *Althaea rosea*
Hollyhock

This spectacular biennial, which first came to Europe from China in the 16th century, is closely related to *Althaea officinalis* and used to be classified in the same genus. It too has soothing properties and the flowers were once used to make cough syrups and to treat chest complaints, but the medicinal properties of its less showy relative are now considered superior. It is still worth its place in the herb garden for its old-fashioned grace and large colourful blooms (pink, purple, yellow or white) on towering spikes. It is easy to grow in well-drained soil and a sunny position from seeds sown *in situ* in spring or late summer.

ANACARDIACEAE
Anacardium occidentale
Cashew nut

History and traditions A native of South and Central America and the Caribbean islands, this well-known nut tree was introduced to India from Brazil by Portuguese colonists in the 16th century, who originally planted it to prevent soil erosion on hillsides in Goa.

Description An evergreen tree, reaching 12m/40ft, it has dark green, rounded, oval leaves. Panicles of pinkish-green flowers are followed by the fleshy fruit, known as the cashew apple, each of which has a kidney-shaped nut suspended from its base, containing a white seed.

Habitat/distribution Naturalized and cultivated in tropical zones worldwide.

Growth Tender trees which need well-drained, sandy soil, periodic high rainfall and a minimum temperature of 18°C/64°F.

Parts used Leaves, bark, fruits, seeds.

USES Medicinal The bark and leaves are used in traditional herbal medicine in Africa to treat malaria.

Culinary The nut, or kernel, is a good source of fibre and protein. It is rich in minerals and mono-unsaturated fat, making it a healthy choice of snack when eaten in moderation. Juice from the fruit is made into soft drinks and distilled to produce spirits.

Other The outer shell of the nut produces a thick, tarry black oil used in engineering, and as a timber preservative to protect against insects.

CAUTION Oil from the cashew nut shell is an irritant and can cause painful skin blistering.

UMBELLIFERAE/APIACEAE
Anethum graveolens
Dill

History and traditions An ancient herb known in biblical times and described both by Pliny, AD23–79, and by the Greek physician Dioscorides, AD40–90, in *De Materia Medica*. It appears in the 10th-century writings of Alfric, Archbishop of Canterbury, and was a favourite herb in Anglo-Saxon charms against witchcraft, at which time it was also burned "to disperse thunder clouds and sulphurous air". The common name is likely to have come from the Saxon word *dillan*, to lull, for its ability to soothe colicky babies and for the ancient Greek tradition of covering the head with dill leaves to induce sleep. The culinary connection with cucumber goes back a long way. Charles I's cook, Joseph Cooper, records a recipe for pickling cucumbers in dill in his book of 1640. It has a long tradition of use in India and Eastern countries as a medicinal and culinary herb.

Description An aromatic annual, 1m/3ft tall, with a single stem and feathery leaves. It has terminal umbels of tiny yellow flowers in midsummer and elliptic, flattened fruits. Resembles fennel, but is shorter and has a subtler, less strongly aniseed flavour.

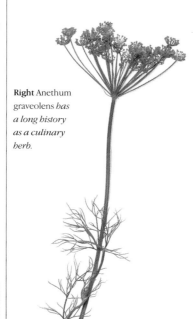

Right Anethum graveolens *has a long history as a culinary herb.*

Related species Indian dill is known as sowa. It is usually classified as *A. sowa*, but this is either a subspecies of *A. graveolens* or very closely related.

Habitat/distribution Originated in southern Europe and Asia, now widely grown in herb gardens worldwide.

Growth Plant dill in well-drained but nutrient-rich soil, in full sun. Requires adequate moisture as it bolts (runs quickly to seed) in poor, dry soil. Best propagated from seed sown in spring, straight into the ground where it is to grow, as it does not take well to being transplanted. Should not be grown near fennel as the two plants crosspollinate.

Parts used Leaves, seeds.

USES Medicinal A cooling, soothing herb which aids digestion, prevents constipation and is an ingredient of "gripe water" given to babies for indigestion. In Indian herbal medicine dill and fenugreek seeds are included in preparations for diarrhoea and dysentery. Poultices of the leaves are applied to boils and to reduce swelling and joint pains. Seeds are chewed to cure bad breath.

Culinary Leaves and seeds add a caraway-like flavour to fish, seafood and egg dishes and go well with bland-tasting vegetables, especially cucumber and potatoes. Widely used in Scandinavian cuisine. In Indian cookery, it is added to curries, rice dishes, soups, pickles and chutneys.

UMBELLIFERAE/APIACEAE
Angelica archangelica

Angelica

History and traditions According to legend, this herb took its name from the angel who revealed its virtues to a monk during a plague epidemic. It was thought to give protection from infection. It is also variously connected with the archangel Gabriel who is said to have appeared to the Virgin Mary at the Annunciation, and the archangel Michael, whose feast day is in May. In all northern European folklore it has an ancient reputation for its powers against witchcraft and evil spirits. In Lapland poets wore crowns of angelica, supposedly to gain inspiration from its scent. John Parkinson in his *Theatre of Plants*, 1640, wrote of it: "The whole plante, both leafe, roote and seede, is of an excellent comfortable scent, savour and taste."

Description Angelica is a statuesque biennial, though it often lives for three years. The whole plant is subtly aromatic. Standing 1.2–2.4m/ 4–8ft high, it has hollow stems, large, deeply divided pale green leaves and globular umbels of green flowers in early summer, followed by flat, oval seeds.

Related species *A. atropurpurea*, American angelica, has red stems. *A. sylvestris* is the wild European angelica.

Habitat/distribution Native to Europe and parts of Asia. Introduced in other parts of the world.
Growth Prefers a rich, damp soil but tolerates most conditions, provided it is not too dry. Plant in sun or partial shade. Self-seeds freely. Propagate by seed sown in autumn, in situ or in pots; seed remains viable for 6–12 months.
Parts used Leaves, stems, roots, seeds.

USES Medicinal Has anti-inflammatory properties, lowers fevers and acts as an expectorant. Infusions of the root are used to aid digestive disorders and bowel complaints. Furocoumarin content increases skin photosensitivity and may cause skin irritation in susceptible people.
Culinary In Europe young stems are candied, cooked with rhubarb, tart fruits and berries to reduce acidity. It can be added to jams or marmalade (ginger and angelica make a good combination), seeds are added to biscuits (cookies). Seeds and roots are constituents of Benedictine, Chartreuse and other liqueurs.
Aromatic Leaves and seeds are dried and added to potpourri.

> **CAUTION** Not to be taken in pregnancy, during heavy menstrual flow, or if taking anti-coagulant medication, such as aspirin. May increase skin photosensitivity.

Far left Angelica atropurpurea *is a North American species with red stems.*
Left *A seed head of angelica.*

Culinary angelica

Angelica and rhubarb
Angelica has a pleasantly aromatic, slightly sweet taste, which enhances the flavour of rhubarb and reduces its acidity, so that less sugar is necessary. Only the very young leaf stems should be used, as older ones are coarse and stringy. Allow two or three 15cm/6in pieces for each 450g/1lb of rhubarb sticks. Cut them into small pieces and add to your favourite rhubarb pie or crumble recipe. Angelica is also excellent puréed with rhubarb to make a fool.
Candied angelica
Old recipe books contain instructions for candying leaves and roots, as well as stems of angelica.
"Boil the stalks of Angelica in water till they are tender; then peel them and cover with other warm water. Let them stand over a gentle fire till they become very green; then lay them on a cloth to dry; take their weight in fine sugar with a little Rose-water and boil it to a Candy height. Then put in your Angelica and boil them up quick; then take them out and dry them for use."

UMBELLIFERAE/APIACEAE
Anthriscus cerefolium
Chervil

History and traditions The Romans were very fond of chervil and it is listed in 15th-century manuscripts as an essential kitchen herb. Confusion sometimes arises, however, as at that time both *A. cerefolium* and sweet cicely, *Myrrhis odorata*, were known as "chervil", sometimes distinguished as "sweet chervil" and "common chervil". John Parkinson, who wrote during the 17th-century in England, indicates: "Common chervil is much used of the French and Dutch people to bee boiled or stewed in a pipkin either by itself or with other herbs, whereof they make a Loblolly and so eate it. Sweete chervil gathered while it is young and put among other herbs for a sallet addeth a marvellous good relish to all the reste."

Description A hardy annual, 30–60cm/1–2ft high, with bright green, finely divided feathery leaves and flat umbels of small white flowers in early summer.

Habitat/distribution Native to the Middle East and southern Russia. Widely cultivated elsewhere in warm and temperate climates.

Growth Chervil prefers light, moist soil and a sunny situation. Propagate from seed sown successionally for a continuous supply. It does not transplant well and runs to seed quickly, but can be sown where it is to grow, or cropped straight from the seed tray.

Parts used Leaves, preferably fresh, cut just before flowering.

USES Medicinal Although it has mild digestive properties, and is sometimes taken as a tea for this purpose, its chief use is culinary.

Culinary The delicate taste, which is more distinctive than parsley, complements most dishes. It brings out the flavour of other herbs and is an essential ingredient, along with parsley, tarragon and chives, of the classic French combination, *fines herbes*. It is best used raw or in a very short cooking process, if the subtle flavour is to be retained.

Left Chervil's light aniseed flavour makes it a culinary herb of distinction.

ROSACEAE
Aphanes arvensis
Parsley piert

History and traditions The common name comes from this herb's vague resemblance to parsley and from the French name for it, *perce-pierre*, meaning to pierce or break a stone. Breakstone is an alternative country name in English also and refers to its traditional use in treating kidney stones. Culpeper lists as its chief use that "it provokes urine, and breaks the stone", and it is still used for the treatment of kidney stones in herbal medicine today.

Description A prostrate annual with small fan-shaped leaves and inconspicuous green flowers in summer.

Habitat/distribution Found in dry places and wastelands, it is native to Britain and widely distributed throughout the world.

Growth As a wild plant, it grows best in well-drained soil, in sun or partial shade, and tolerates gravelly, stony soils. Propagated by seed sown in spring.

Parts used Leaves.

USES Medicinal A diuretic which also soothes irritated and inflamed tissues. It is used to ease painful urination and in the treatment of kidney and bladder stones.

Culinary It was a popular salad herb during the 16th century, but the taste is uninteresting and it is seldom eaten today.

UMBELLIFERAE/APIACEAE

Apium graveolens
Wild celery

History and traditions Although rather bitter in flavour, it was the only celery known until the 17th century, when the cultivated variety we enjoy today, *A. g.* var. *dulce*, was developed.

Description An aromatic biennial with a bulbous, fleshy root. Grooved stems grow from 30–90cm/1–3ft high in the second year. It has pointed, divided leaves (similar in shape to cultivated celery) and umbels of sparse, greenish-white flowers in late summer, followed by small, ridged seeds.

Habitat/distribution Found in marshy, often salty ground in Europe, Asia, northern Africa, North and South America.

Growth It prefers rich, damp soil, sun or partial shade and tolerates saline conditions. Does best in a sheltered position, and bears flowers for seed production in warm climates. It is propagated by seed sown in spring, but needs a temperature of 13–16°C/55–61°F to germinate.

Parts used Roots, stems, leaves, seeds.

USES Medicinal Used in the treatment of arthritis and rheumatism and in Ayurvedic medicine as a nerve tonic.

Culinary The plant is toxic in large quantities. A few seeds may be used for flavouring.

> **CAUTION** Seeds should not be taken if pregnant, or where there is kidney disease or damage. May cause allergic reactions.

COMPOSITAE/ASTERACEAE

Arctium lappa
Greater burdock

History and traditions This plant's names relate to the clinging nature of the burs which follow the flowers. *Arctium* comes from *arktos*, Greek for a bear (supposed to indicate the plant's roughness), and *lappa* from a word meaning to seize, though some authorities also connect the species name with the Celtic word for hand, *llap*. The English common name is a little more obvious in derivation, "bur" referring to the prickles and "dock" to the shape of the large leaves. Culpeper lists its popular names as "Personata", "Happy-Major" and "Clot-bur".

Description A biennial, or short-lived perennial, which grows to 1.5m/5ft tall. It has long, ovate leaves covered in down and thick, hairy stems. Purple thistle-like flowers appear in mid to late summer, followed by fruits (seed heads) made up of hooked spines or burs.

Related species *A. minus,* lesser burdock, has similar properties. *A. lappa* 'Gobo' is a culinary cultivar grown in Japan.

Habitat/distribution Greater burdock is native to temperate regions of Asia and widely distributed throughout Europe and North America, found on roadsides, waste ground and in nitrogen-rich soil.

Growth It is usually collected from the wild, but a cultivated species is grown in Japan. Prefers a moist soil, sun or partial shade and it self-seeds quite freely.

Parts used Roots, stems, seeds, leaves (rarely).

> **CAUTION** Contact dermatitis is possible in those who are sensitive. May increase severity of existing symptoms. Only to be taken on the advice of a herbal or medical practitioner.

Below *Arctium lappa*

Right *Close up of leaf.*

USES Medicinal It has antibacterial and fungicidal properties and is used as a decoction or poultice for inflamed skin, sores, boils and disorders such as eczema and psoriasis. It is also taken for gastric ulcers and is said to increase resistance to infection. Used in traditional Chinese medicine.

Culinary It is cultivated in Japan for the roots, which are eaten as a vegetable. The stalks, before flowering, can be chopped and added to salads, or cooked as a celery-like vegetable. In the past, they were sometimes candied, in the same way as angelica.

Cosmetic An infusion of the leaves, or decoction of the roots, makes a tonic skin freshener or hair rinse for dandruff.

Other names Lappa and beggar's buttons.

ERICACEAE
Arctostaphylos uva-ursi
Bearberry

History and traditions The generic name from the Greek, *arcton staphyle*, and the specific, *uva-ursi*, from the Latin, both mean "bear's grapes", perhaps because bears enjoyed the fruit, or maybe the sour taste of this plant was only thought fit for consumption by bears? It is listed in 13th-century herbal manuscripts and was described in detail by the 16th-century Dutch botanist Clusius (Charles de L'Ecluse). In the 17th century John Josslyn discovered this herb growing in North America, where many of the Native American tribes made use of its medicinal properties and added it to smoking mixtures. He found it to be highly effective against scurvy. It was considered medicinally important in 18th-century Europe, and remained so into the 20th century, appearing in the British *Pharmacopoeia*.

Description A creeping, evergreen shrub, growing to 15cm/6in, with dark green, leathery, small, oval leaves. Terminal clusters of tiny, white or pink, bell-shaped flowers appear in summer, followed by red fruit.

Habitat/distribution Found in rocky moorland and woodland, in northern Europe, Scandinavia and Russia, northern Asia, Japan, North America and cool, northern hemisphere regions.

Growth Needs moist, sandy or peaty soil. Ericaceous compost (soil mix) must be used if container-grown and for propagating, which can be done from seed, by layering in spring or from cuttings, taken with a heel, in summer.

Parts used Leaves – usually dried. For commercial use they are collected from the wild, mostly in Scandinavia and Russia, field cultivation having proved too costly.

USES Culinary Although the berries are edible, they taste extremely sharp, and are more suitable as "grouse feed", (a use given in one herbal). The leaves were at one time a popular tea in Russia.

Medicinal Constituents include arbutin and methylarbutin, which have been established as effectively antibacterial, especially against urinary infections, such as cystitis. Avoid long-term use due to high tannin content.

General The leaves have a high tannin content and have been used in the past in leather tanning and to produce a dark grey dye.

Other names Mountain box and uva-ursi.

> **CAUTION** Bearberry should not be taken by women during pregnancy, by children, or where there is kidney disease.

PALMAE/ARECACEAE
Areca catechu
Betel nut

History and traditions The Chinese discovered the medicinal properties of this tree by 140BC, when they brought it back from their conquests of the Malayan archipelago. It is the main ingredient of paan or "betel nut", a mixture of areca nut, lime and spices, wrapped in betel leaf, *Piper betle*, and it is widely chewed throughout the Middle East and Asia. It induces mild euphoria and is supposed to increase sexual virility.

Description A tall palm, reaching 20m/65ft in height, with numerous feathery leaflets making up its 2m/6ft long leaves. The pale yellow flowers appear when the tree is about 6–8 years old, followed by bunches of up to 100 round, orange fruits.

Habitat/distribution A native of Malaysia, and found throughout India, the Far East and eastern Africa, usually on coastal sites. Introduced in American tropical zones.

Parts used Fruit, rind, seeds.

USES Medicinal Stimulates the flow of saliva, and accelerates heart and perspiration rates. Chewed to sweeten breath, strengthen gums, improve digestion, and suppress intestinal worms – but permanently stains teeth red. Research is being carried out in America on this tree as a source of a potential anti-cancer drug. However, excessive chewing can lead to cancer of the mouth.

> **CAUTION** Toxic in large doses, excess causes vomiting and stupor. Legal restrictions are in force in some countries.

CRUCIFERAE/BRASSICACEAE
Armoracia rusticana

Horseradish

History and traditions Horseradish was valued in the Middle Ages for the medicinal properties of both leaves and root. The great English botanist and herbalist William Turner, writing in 1548, referred to it as 'Red Cole', and it was not commonly called horseradish until so named in England, in Gerard's Herbal of 1597. At that time it was used in Germany and Scandinavia to make the hot and spicy condiment we know today, but this did not become popular in Britain until well into the 17th century. John Parkinson, in 1640, describes its use as a sauce in Germany, adding, "and in our own land also", but he considered it "too strong for tender and gentle stomaches". In 1657, William Coles reiterated that it was the practice in Germany for "the root, sliced thin and mixed with vinegar (to be) eaten as a sauce with meat".

Description A perennial, with a deep, fleshy taproot and large bright green, oblong to ovate leaves, with serrated margins, sprouting from the base to a height of 60cm/2ft. Racemes of tiny, white flowers on drooping stems, up to 1.2m/4ft long, appear in summer.

Habitat/distribution In the wild it is found in dampish soils in Europe and western Asia. Now naturalized in many parts of the world.

Growth In theory it prefers a moist soil, but in practice flourishes in most conditions. It can be propagated by seed in spring, or by root cuttings in spring or autumn. It grows vigorously and,

once established, is nearly impossible to eradicate as it regenerates from the tiniest scrap of root left in the soil.

Parts used Leaves, roots.

USES Medicinal The root may be taken in the form of a syrup for bronchial infections, catarrh and coughs and as a general tonic for debility. Horseradish is known as a "central" or "circulatory" stimulant (meaning it increases activity) for the heart and circulation.

Culinary The young, fresh leaves have a milder flavour than the pungent root and can be added to salads or chopped into smoked-fish pâtés. The fresh root is shredded to make a strong-flavoured, creamy-textured horseradish sauce, traditionally served with beef, but also excellent as an accompaniment to cold, especially smoked, meat and fish, hard-boiled eggs and stuffed aubergines (eggplants). For a milder flavour, grated apple, sprinkled with lemon juice and vinegar, can be mixed with horseradish.

To make horseradish sauce

2–3 pieces of fresh horseradish root
10ml/2 tbsp cider vinegar
115g/4oz fromage frais (farmers'
cheese)
salt, pepper and a pinch of sugar
10ml/2 tsp fresh, chopped dill

Scrub the horseradish root, grate it finely, and cover with the vinegar. Or, for a smoother texture, mix the horseradish and vinegar in an electric blender till pulped. Mix in the fromage frais, season with salt, pepper, sugar and dill.

Left
Horseradish root has a strong scent that can irritate the eyes.

CAUTION May provoke allergic reactions. Large internal doses may cause vomiting. Should not be taken if suffering from stomach ulcers or thyroid problems.

Above *Digging up roots of established plants to make horseradish sauce.*

Above *Leaving some behind will ensure an ongoing supply of material.*

Above *Home-grown horseradish roots make a pungent sauce.*

COMPOSITAE/ASTERACEAE

Arnica montana

Arnica

History and traditions Pier Andrea Mattioli, a household name in herbs in the 16th century, and physician at the Court of the Holy Roman Emperor Ferdinand I, in Prague, rated arnica highly. It became fashionable when he wrote about it in his standard work, *Commentarii*, a version of which appeared in Venice in 1544. It was widely used in the folk medicine of other European countries, principally Germany and Austria, where it has remained an important medicinal herb to this day. Arnica was used by Native Americans to treat muscular injury and back pain.

Description An alpine perennial with a creeping rootstock, it has a basal rosette of small, ovate, downy leaves and flowering stems growing to 30–60cm/1–2ft. The daisy-like flowers are golden yellow and borne in midsummer.

Related species *A. fulgens* is a North American species said to be even more medically powerful.

Habitat/distribution Found in mountainous regions of central and northern Europe and North America. *A. montana* is becoming rare in the wild and is protected in many countries.

Growth It prefers a sandy soil, enriched with humus, and a sunny position. As an alpine plant it needs a cool climate, and does not thrive in wet, waterlogged soil – grow arnica in containers or raised beds if necessary.

Parts used Flowers – dried, for use in pharmaceutical preparations.

USES Medicinal Recent research has established both the therapeutic value of this herb and its toxicity. It has a stimulating effect on the heart muscle and the circulatory system, but effects are rapid and correct doses crucial, with a high risk of overdose. It has antiseptic, anti-inflammatory properites when applied externally and is available as a pharmaceutical ointment for bruises. It is also used in homeopathy, for a range of conditions, including sprains, aching muscles, sore throats and sea sickness. In Britain it is legal only for external use and in the United States it is considered unsafe.

Other names Leopard's bane, mountain arnica, mountain daisy and mountain tobacco.

> **CAUTION** Highly toxic and should not be taken internally, except in homeopathic remedies when the dosage is very small. It may cause dermatitis when used externally – do not apply to broken skin. Legally restricted in some countries. Use with advice from qualified medical practitioners.

Above *Flowers of* Arnica montana.

Right *Golden arnica flowers and pink* Mimulus lewisii *cover a hillside in bloom in Glacier National Park, United States.*

COMPOSITAE/ASTERACEAE

Artemisia

This genus of some 300 species, containing many garden ornamentals, supplies four of the best-known herbs. These include one of the most popular culinary herbs, tarragon, which is the exception of the four in character and uses.

Artemisia abrotanum
Southernwood

History and traditions A native of southern Europe, southernwood was introduced to Britain in about 1548, where the popular name, southernwood, directly described its origins as a woody plant from the south. It soon became established as a cottage garden favourite, attracting new names and associations. 'Lad's love' and 'old man' came about because smearing its ashes in an ointment base was supposed to make pimply youths sprout virile beards and bring new growth to bald heads. Other authorities claim that boys in love wore it in their hats, or gave sprigs as love tokens to the objects of their affections. The French name "garde-robe" refers to the habit of including this herb in sachets to protect clothes from insect infestation. It was also thought to protect from infection and was included in nosegays carried

for the purpose.

Description A shrubby semi-evergreen (it loses foliage in winter in cold climates and as the plants age), it grows to 1m/3ft tall and has feathery, grey-green leaves with a clean, lemony scent. It seldom flowers in northern climates, but in warmer southern regions small yellow flowers appear in summer.

Habitat/distribution Southernwood is native to southern Europe and parts of Asia, introduced and widespread in temperate zones and naturalized in North America.

Growth Prefers a light soil, full sun and tolerates drought. It is easy to propagate from softwood cuttings throughout summer, or heeled cuttings from old wood in autumn. Needs clipping back hard in late spring to prevent straggly, woody growth. Plants are best replaced after 6–8 years.

Parts used Leaves.

USES Medicinal Southernwood tea is said to stimulate the appetite and digestion. It is also prescribed for menstrual problems. At one time it was given to children to rid them of their threadworms.

Culinary Although there is some evidence of its use in southern European cookery, it is really far too bitter for the purpose.

Aromatic Its insect repellent properties and pleasant smell when dried make it a first choice herb for sachets to keep moths and insects at bay, or to include in potpourri.

Other names Lad's love and old man.

Left *Artemisia abrotanum is easy to propagate from cuttings.*

CAUTION Taken internally, southernwood stimulates the uterus and should never be given to pregnant women.

Artemisia absinthium
Wormwood

History and traditions This bitter herb was once highly valued medicinally, with a reputation for overcoming bodily weakness. As a 15th-century manuscript declares: "Water of worm-wood is gode – Grete Lords among the Saracens usen to drinke hitt." And Sir John Hill, in his *Virtues of British Herbs* (1772), alleging that the Germans have a tendency to overeat, says this is made possible by a habit of washing down each mouthful with a decoction of wormwood.

Description A perennial subshrub, 1m/3ft in height, leaves are silvery grey, downy and finely divided. Flowers are yellowish green, tiny and ball-shaped, borne on bracts in late summer.

Habitat/distribution Found wild in temperate regions of Europe, North and South America, Asia and South Africa. Widely introduced as a garden plant.

Parts used Leaves, flowering tops.

USES Medicinal A strong herb with some toxicity. Has anti-inflammatory properties, expels intestinal worms and stimulates the uterus. Sometimes recommended for digestive problems, poor appetite and general debility. Best taken on professional advice.

Aromatic Strongly insect-repellent, it is dried for inclusion in sachets against moths, fleas and other insects, or made into tinctures and infusions to deter them.

CAUTION It should not be given to children, pregnant or breast-feeding women. Taken habitually, or in excess, it can cause vomiting, convulsions, delirium and hyperacidity.

Artemisia vulgaris
Mugwort

History and traditions Ascribed magical properties by cultures in Europe, China and Asia. It was one of the nine herbs in the Anglo-Saxon charm against flying venom and evil spirits, when it was held to be "Mighty against loathed ones / That through the land rove" (Anglo-Saxon Ms, Harleian Collection). Roman soldiers are said to have put it in their shoes to prevent aching feet on long marches. William Coles in *The Art of Simpling*, 1656, asserted, "If a Footman take mugwort and put it into his shoes in the morning, he may goe forty miles before Noon and not be weary." In Europe it is connected with St John the Baptist.

Description A straggly perennial, 1–1.5m/3–5ft tall. Leaves are grey green with white undersides and slightly downy. In the summer panicles of inconspicuous grey-green flowers appear.

Habitat/distribution A wild plant growing by streams and rivers, in wastelands, hedgerows, field margins in Europe, Asia and North America.

Parts used Leaves.

USES Medicinal As with some of the other artemisias, it is said to have digestive properties, stimulates the appetite and acts as a nerve tonic. It is a diuretic and used in regulating menstruation. Used in Chinese medicine for rheumatism.

Culinary At one time it was included in stuffings and sauces but the slightly bitter, unpalatable taste makes it hardly recommendable.

Aromatic Has insect-repellent properties.

> **CAUTION** Only to be taken on professional advice.

Artemisia dracunculus
French tarragon

History and traditions The species' name, *dracunculus*, is from the Latin meaning "a little dragon" after its supposed ability to cure the bites of serpents and mad dogs. A native of southern Europe, it was first introduced to the royal gardens of Britain in Tudor times. John Evelyn in his *Acetaria* (1699) recommended it as "highly cordial and friendly to the head, heart, and liver" and advised that it "must never be excluded from sallets".

Description A perennial 1m/3ft high, with branched erect stems, and slim, pointed leaves. Flowers are inconspicuous and greyish green but appear only on some plants grown in warm climates – it does not flower at all in cool northern climates. Not to be confused with the subspecies, known as Russian tarragon, a larger, more vigorous plant, with coarser leaves and practically no discernible aroma.

Habitat/distribution A native of southern Europe and Asia, widely distributed in temperate zones worldwide.

Growth It prefers a fairly moist, but well-drained soil and full sun. Tarragon needs protection in winter in colder climates, especially in areas where frost is prolonged or where the ground

Right *French tarragon is a superbly flavoured culinary herb.*

becomes waterlogged. Propagate by division of roots in spring or autumn. It cannot be propagated from seed.

Parts used Fresh or dried leaf.

USES Culinary One of the top culinary herbs for distinction of flavour, it is used in salads, savoury pâté, cooked meat, fish and egg dishes. Well known for its affinity with chicken, it also enhances the flavour of root vegetables such as carrots and parsnips. Vinegar flavoured with tarragon is a classic condiment and it is a main ingredient of sauces and stuffings.

LEGUMINOSAE/PAPILIONACEAE

Aspalathus linearis

Rooibos

History and traditions A traditional tea plant of native South Africans of the Cape, it was adopted by European travellers and colonists in the late 18th century. It has gained popularity in the 20th century for its soothing, medicinal properties and its antioxidant content. It makes a pleasant-tasting tea with a refreshing flavour.

Description A small shrub up to 2m/6ft in height, with bright green, thin, linear leaves, bearing short, leafy shoots in their axils. Small yellow pea flowers are followed by long pods. The leaves turn a reddish brown during processing, which gives the tea its name.

Habitat/distribution Native to dry, mountainous areas of Cape Province, South Africa.

Growth A frost-hardy bush – it cannot tolerate temperatures below –5°C/23°F, or prolonged severe weather. Requires dry, sandy soil and full sun. Propagated by seed sown in spring. Pinch out shoots, as it grows, to encourage bushiness. Commercially cultivated in South Africa.

Parts used Leaves and shoots – sun-dried and fermented to make tea.

USES Medicinal High in vitamin C and mineral salts, it is taken internally for digestive disorders and to relieve allergies and eczema and applied externally for skin irritations.

Culinary Pleasant as an alternative to tea with a low caffeine and tannin level. It is sometimes used as a flavouring herb in sauces and soft drinks and as an ingredient of a local alcoholic liquor.

Other name Red bush tea.

ASPARAGACEAE/LILIACEAE

Asparagus officinalis

Asparagus

History and traditions Appreciated as a delicacy by the ancient Greeks and Romans and mentioned by Pliny in his *Natural History*. The name is originally from a Greek word, the medieval Latin for which was "sparagus", leading to the popular derivation of sparrow-grass. This was once so widely used that a commentator remarked in 1791, "The corruption of the word into *sparrow-grass* is so general that *asparagus* has an air of stiffness and pedantry about it." Gerard recommended its culinary virtues and Culpeper stressed the medicinal properties. His assertion that it clears the sight and eases toothache no longer holds sway, but he also recommended it for sciatica, as do herbalists today.

Description A perennial whose fleshy shoots are eaten as a delicacy. If left uncut it develops feathery leaves to a height of 1–1.5m/3–5ft with small greeny-white flowers followed by red berries.

Habitat/distribution Native to coastal, sandy areas and woodlands of Europe and Asia, now widely cultivated throughout the world.

Growth It requires rich, well-drained loam and a sunny position. Plants may be propagated from seed, but beds are usually established from bought one-year-old crowns. It takes three years to produce the vegetable, but beds then last 10–12 years.

Parts used Young shoots.

USES Medicinal Asparagus has cleansing, restorative properties, combats acidity and is taken for rheumatism, sciatica and gout, as

Right *Feathery foliage of* Asparagus officinalis.

either a food or an infusion. It also has diuretic and laxative properties, and is taken for urinary infections, but it should be avoided where there is kidney disease. An important medicinal herb in India traditionally used in cases of impotence, though no research has been undertaken that supports this.

Culinary High in vitamins A and C and minerals, including calcium, phosphorus and iron. Young shoots, lightly steamed, are served as a vegetable with melted butter or a vinaigrette sauce, or puréed to make soup.

Other name Sparrow-grass.

Above *Asparagus emerging from the soil.*

CAUTION Only to be taken medicinally on professional advice.

CHENOPODIACEAE

Atriplex hortensis

Orache

History and traditions This herb was eaten as a spinach-like vegetable by Native American tribes, and introduced to Britain in 1548. Sixteenth-century herbalists considered it to be effective against gout when applied as a poultice with honey, vinegar and salt.
John Evelyn in his *Acetaria* (1719) refers to its "cooling properties" and recommends it as a salad herb or vegetable, advising that, like lettuce, it should be boiled in its own moisture. Culpeper agreed that it could be eaten as a salad but thought its real virtue lay in the seeds, which he claimed made an effective laxative in the form of an alcohol tincture.

Above Atriplex hortensis *var.* rubra, *red orache, makes a spectacular plant in the border, and the leaves add colour to salads.*

Description An upright annual, growing to 1.2m/4ft, it has spear-shaped green to purple leaves, slightly downy when young, and a mass of yellow-green, sorrel-like flowers, borne on tall spikes, in summer.
Related species *A. hortensis* var. *rubra*, or red orache (above) is a more attractive cultivar, with purple-red foliage and flowers, followed by spectacular seed heads sought after by flower arrangers.
Habitat/distribution Occurs in Asia, North America and Europe, often in coastal areas. It is widely cultivated in temperate and warm regions worldwide.
Growth Flourishes in any soil, tolerates dry conditions but growth is more luxuriant in moister, more fertile soil. Prefers an open, sunny position. Propagated by seed sown *in situ* in spring. Self-seeds prolifically.
Parts used Leaves.

USES Culinary Leaves of red orache add colour and interest to salads, but, despite some recommendations, neither red nor green make very succulent spinach substitutes when cooked as vegetables.
Other name Mountain spinach.

Left *Leaves of* Atriplex hortensis *var.* rubra.

SOLANACEAE

Atropa belladonna

Deadly nightshade

History and traditions In 16th-century Venice this plant was known as *herba bella donna*, and used to dilate the pupils of their eyes by women who sought to beautify themselves. Its potential to cause fatalities was well understood at the time, the apothecaries' name for it being *solatrum mortale*, which translates as "deadly nightshade". Writing at the end of the 16th century, Gerard pontificates on its dangers, advising that a plant "so furious and deadly" should be banished from "your gardens".
Description A bushy perennial, 1–1.5m/3–5ft tall, it has ovate, dull green leaves, bearing single, purple-brown, bell-shaped flowers in the axils in summer, followed by shiny black berries.
Related species Not to be confused with the *Solanum* genus, many of which are poisonous also and include other nightshades – as well as potatoes, aubergines (eggplant) and climbers.
Habitat/distribution Native to Europe and Asia, introduced and naturalized elsewhere.
Growth Grown as a commercial crop (for the pharmaceutical industry) in well-drained, moist soil and full sun – warm, dry conditions increase the alkaloid content.
Parts used Whole plant – dried and processed.

USES Medicinal It contains the alkaloid, atropine, which dilates the pupils of the eye and gives the plant its toxic, sedative properties. A constituent of pharmaceutical drugs, used as pre-medication before surgery and in eyedrops for ophthalmic treatment.

CAUTION Highly poisonous. Do not use internally. Use under professional supervision only.

MELIACEAE
Azadirachta indica
Neem tree

History and traditions A common tree of southern Asia, it has played an important role in Ayurvedic medicine, and in agriculture and domestic life as an insect repellent since earliest times. The first part of the botanical name is from a Persian word meaning "noble tree", reflecting its many useful properties, which remain valid to this day. The Neem Foundation, Bombay, dedicated to its study, was established in 1993 and the tree's potential as a source of a low-cost, environmentally-friendly pesticide for field crops in developing countries is currently being investigated.

Description A large, evergreen tree, 12–15m/ 40–50ft tall, it has dense pinnate leaves. Clusters of small white flowers appear in spring to be followed by long greeny-yellow fruits each containing a seed. The wood secretes resin, and *margosa* or *neem* oil is made from the seeds.

Habitat/distribution Occurs in India, Sri Lanka, Myanmar, southeast Asia and tropical regions of Australia and Africa. Widely planted as shade trees to line the roads.

Growth It will not grow in temperatures below 15°C/59°F. It requires sun and tolerates poor, dry soil.

Parts used Leaves, bark, seeds, oil, resin.

USES Medicinal Neem has anti-inflammatory and insecticidal properties, reduces fever, and acts as a tonic and detoxicant, increasing vitality. Traditionally in Indian herbal medicine, it has been used to treat malaria and leprosy. Also used externally for skin disorders and irritations, especially boils and ulcers, and in eye and ear complaints. Twigs can be used to clean teeth, prevent breath odour and protect from infection.
Cosmetic Reputed to prevent hair loss if a decoction of the leaves is applied as a rinse. The oil is used in hair and skin lotions, toothpaste and soap.
General Makes an effective mosquito and insect repellent, and insecticide for crops. In its countries of origin the dried leaves are used to protect stored clothes or books from insect damage. Although it has been found to be safe and efficient as a sheep dip, this use has not been developed commercially.
Other name Margosa.

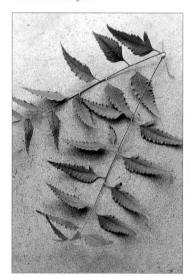

Above Neem leaves have excellent insecticidal properties.

CAUTION Seek medical advice before taking internally. Can interact with pharmaceutical drugs. Not to be taken if pregnant, while breast-feeding or on fertility treatment. Not to be taken long term or in high doses.

BERBERIDACEAE
Berberis vulgaris
Barberry

History and traditions Barberry has been grown since medieval times for medicinal and culinary use and as a dye plant, producing a yellow colour. It was said to be excellent for "hot agues" and all manner of burnings and scaldings. It had a reputation for blighting wheat, now justified, as it is a known host of the disease, wheat rust.

Description A shrub which grows to 2m/6ft, with sharp spines on the stems and small oval leaves. Clusters of yellow flowers in late spring are followed by the shiny red fruits (berries).

Habitat/distribution Found in hedges and woodland in Europe, also in Asia, the Americas and northern Africa.

Growth A wild plant, it grows on any soil in sun or partial shade. It is propagated by layering or by taking cuttings in early autumn and can also be grown from seed.

Parts used Leaves, bark, roots, fruit.

USES Medicinal Barberry can have a strong effect on the liver causing an increase in bile production and a mild to moderate laxative effect. It has a bitter tonic effect and reduces nausea.
Culinary The berries are very bitter, but high in vitamin C. At one time they were made into jams, jellies, preserves and tarts.

CAUTION Only to be taken on the advice of a qualified herbalist or medical practitioner. Not to be taken if pregnant or when breast-feeding.

BORAGINACEAE

Borago officinalis

Borage

History and traditions There are various historical references to the ability of this herb to bring comfort and cheer. Gerard mentions references to it in this context by Pliny and Dioscorides, along with the Latin tag: *"Ego Borago, gaudia semper ago"*, which he translates as "I, Borage, bring alwaies courage". He goes on to advise adding the flowers to salads to "exhilerate and make the mind glad", the leaves to wine to "drive away all sadnesse, dulnesse and melancholy", making a syrup of the flowers to calm a "phrenticke or lunaticke person" or, for even greater force and effect, candying them with sugar. According to John Parkinson, the 16th-century English herbalist, their attractive colour and form made the flowers a favourite motif in needlework.

Description A short-lived hardy annual, 60–90cm/2–3ft high, with a sprawling habit of growth, hollow, hairy stems, downy leaves and blue (sometimes pink) star-shaped flowers with black centres. It is very attractive to bees.

Related species *B. officinalis* 'Alba' is a white-flowered variety.

Habitat/distribution Native to the Mediterranean region from Spain to Turkey. Now naturalized in most of Europe and in many other parts of the world.

Growth Grows in any soil, even if poor and dry, but it makes a lusher, healthier plant, less prone to mildew, given better soil and more moisture. Prefers a sunny position. It is easy to propagate from seed sown in spring or autumn, and despite common advice to the contrary, the seedlings may be successfully transplanted when young, if they are well watered until established. It also self-seeds.

Parts used Leaves, flowers, oil from the seeds.

USES Medicinal A cooling, anti-inflammatory herb with diuretic properties. It is also said to be mildly antidepressant. Used externally to soothe inflamed skin and in mouthwashes and gargles. The seeds contain gamma-linolenic acid, and oil extracted from them is used as an alternative to evening primrose oil for hormonal problems and skin complaints. Borage is grown as a commercial crop for its oil, which is used in pharmaceutical drugs and cosmetic products.

Culinary The leaves have a faint flavour of cucumbers and are added to soft drinks and wine cups. The flowers make a pretty garnish for salads, and are candied or dried as decorations for sweet dishes and cakes.

CAUTION Borage may cause allergic reactions in some people. The leaves, but not the oil, have been found to contain very small amounts of an alkaloid that may cause liver disease. The plant, but not oil extracted from the seeds, is legally restricted in some countries. Use with advice from qualified medical practitioners.

Top left *Borage is grown as a commercial crop for the pharmaceutical and cosmetic industries.*

Top *Borago officinalis 'Alba'.*

Above *Borage flowers make a pretty garnish for salads and drinks.*

BURSERACEAE

Boswellia sacra syn. *B. carteri*

Frankincense

History and traditions Since ancient times, frankincense has been an ingredient of incense, used in the religious ceremonies of the Egyptians, Babylonians, Assyrians, Hebrews, Greeks and Romans, and is still used in religious ritual to this day. It was highly valued by early civilizations as an item of trade, considered as precious as gold, and was one of the gifts said to have been given to Jesus Christ at his birth by the wise men from the east (Matt. 2:11). It is also thought to have been used by Cleopatra as a cosmetic for smoothing skin. In charred form it made *kohl*, the black eyeliner worn by eastern women. Ancient medicinal uses include Pliny's claim that it provided an antidote to hemlock poisoning and Avicenna's recommendations that it should be prescribed for tumours, ulcers, vomiting, dysentery and fevers. There is also some evidence that at one time it was used in China for leprosy.

Description A small deciduous tree, 2–5m/ 6–16ft in height, with papery bark, pinnate leaves and racemes of small greenish-white flowers. The gum is secreted in the wood.

Related species Several species of *Boswellia* produce frankincense – formerly it was mostly derived from *B. sacra* and *B. papyrifera*. Today, *B. carteri* and *B. frereana* are usual sources. *B. serrata* (from India) is grown for timber.

Habitat/distribution *B. sacra* comes from Somalia and southern Arabia, *B. papyrifera* from Nigeria and Ethiopia, *B. carteri* and *B. frereana* from Somalia across to eastern Africa, found in desert scrubland. Many *Boswellia* species are threatened with extinction in the wild, due to over-exploitation and over-grazing.

Growth Grows wild, in shallow, rocky soil.

Parts used Gum resin – obtained by incising the trunk to produce a milky sap, which hardens into yellowish globules. Available in the form of grains or powder.

USES Medicinal Frankincense has anti-inflammatory and anti-arthritic properties. The resin has antiseptic properties and is used in Chinese and Ayurvedic medicine. The essential oil is used in aromatherapy to counteract anxiety.

Aromatic Its chief use is as an ingredient of incenses and fragrant preparations. Also added to commercial cosmetics and is a constituent of an anti-wrinkle face cream.

Other name Olibanum.

CRUCIFERAE/BRASSICACEAE

Brassica nigra

Mustard

History and traditions Mustard has a long history both as a medicinal and as a flavouring herb. The ancient Greeks thought highly of it and Hippocrates recommended that it be taken internally, or as a poultice, for a variety of ailments. It probably came to Britain with the Romans, who mixed the seeds with wine as a condiment and ate the leaves as a vegetable. Gerard describes pounding the seeds with vinegar to make an "excellent sauce" for serving with meat as a digestive and appetite stimulant.

Description An erect annual, 1–1.2m/3–4ft high, with narrow, lobed leaves and racemes of bright yellow flowers, followed by pods containing reddish-brown seeds.

Related species *B. juncea,* or brown mustard, being easier to harvest mechanically, though less pungent, has largely replaced the medicinal *B. nigra*. White mustard (*Synapsis alba,* syn. *Brassica alba*) is grown for commercial production. It is used to make American mustard and is the species sown with cress as a salad.

Growth Requires rich, well-dressed soil and full sun and is propagated by seed sown in spring.

Parts used Leaves, seeds – seedpods are picked before they are fully ripe and dried.

USES Medicinal Mustard has warming and antibiotic properties and is applied externally in poultices, baths or footbaths for rheumatism, aching muscles and chilblains. A mustard footbath is a traditional British remedy for colds.

Culinary The ground seeds, mixed into a paste, make the familiar "hot-flavoured" condiment to serve with a range of dishes. The whole seeds are added to curries, soups, stews, pickles and sauces. Young leaves are eaten with cress, or added to salads.

BUXACEAE

Buxus sempervirens

Box

History and traditions The gardens of ancient Rome featured formally clipped box hedges and topiary, a fashion which was enthusiastically revived in Renaissance Europe, when knot gardens and elaborate parterres dominated designs for gardens. Box foliage has been used to decorate the house for American Thanksgiving and at Christmas time in Europe, when it was made into "kissing boughs" or "Advent crowns" (depending on inclination and piety) – sprigs were tied on to frames and decorated with ribbons, candles and shiny red apples. Sometimes known as "boxwood" for its hard, durable wood, traditionally used to make engraving blocks, wooden tools, musical instruments and fine furniture.

Description Common box is an evergreen shrub, or small tree, growing to about 4.5m/ 14ft, with glossy green, ovate leaves and a strange, rather acrid scent.

Related species There are over 70 species, ranging from tender to hardy. *B. sempervirens* 'Suffruticosa' is a dwarf form – for edging and low hedges: *B. sempervirens* 'Elegantissima' is slow growing with variegated cream and silver-green foliage; *B. sempervirens* 'Latifolia Maculata' has gold leaves; and *B. microphylla* makes low-growing mounds of dark green.

Habitat/distribution Occurs in Europe, Asia, Africa, North and Central America.

Growth Requires well-drained, but not poor, soil, sun or shade. Although hardy, *B. sempervirens* does not thrive in very cold winters and new growth is damaged by frosts – clip after frosts to avoid encouraging vulnerable new shoots. Propagated by semi-ripe cuttings, in late summer.

Parts used Leaves, bark, wood.

USES Medicinal Said to be effective against malaria, but contains toxic alkaloids, and is little used in herbal medicine today. It is currently being researched for its potential as treatments for cancer, HIV and AIDS.

> **CAUTION** Poisonous, can be fatal if taken internally. May cause skin irritations.

Above Buxus sempervirens, *common box.*

Below left to right *Clipped dwarf box,* Buxus sempervirens *'Suffruticosa', the variagated leaves of* B. sempervirens *'Elegantissima' and the compact and very hardy* B. microphylla *var.* koreana.

LABIATAE/LAMIACEAE

Calamintha nepeta

Calamint

History and traditions Now regarded as an ornamental, calamint was once an important medicinal herb, considered to be effective for "hysterical complaints" and "afflictions of the brain", as well as for a range of ailments from leprosy to indigestion. It had a reputation for hindering conception and inducing abortion.

Description A small, bushy perennial, 30–60cm/ 1–2ft high, it has small, ovate leaves and a mass of tubular pinky-mauve flowers in summer.

Related species The medicinal calamint of the apothecaries was *C. officinalis*, now classified as *C. sylvatica*, but *C. nepeta* seems to have been used interchangeably. *C. grandiflora* has larger flowers and *C. grandiflora* 'Variegata' is a cultivar with cream and green variegated foliage.

Habitat/distribution Native to Europe, found in grassland, woodland and chalky uplands of central Asia and northern temperate zones.

Growth Prefers well-drained, not-too-rich soil and a sunny position. The easiest method of propagation is by division in spring.

Parts used Leaves or flowering tops.

USES Medicinal It is taken as a tonic, or for indigestion, in the form of an infusion.

Culinary The young leaves and flowers, fresh or dried, may be infused to make a lightly mint-scented tea or added to salads.

> **CAUTION** Not to be taken during pregnancy, as one of its constituents is pulegone (also found in pennyroyal, *Mentha pulegium),* which stimulates the uterus.

COMPOSITAE/ASTERACEAE
Calendula officinalis
Pot marigold

History and traditions This cheerful, familiar flower was valued for its medicinal, culinary and cosmetic properties in early civilizations of both east and west. Calendula is the diminutive of the Latin *calendulae* and thus "a little calendar or little clock" (*Oxford English Dictionary*). This ties in neatly with its habit of closing its petals when there is no sun as described by Shakespeare in *A Winter's Tale*:

The Marigold that goes to bed wi' the sun
And with him rises weeping.

In medieval England the usual name was simply "golds" – Chaucer refers to a garland of "yellow golds" as an emblem for jealousy and it was only later dubbed "marigold" in honour of the Virgin Mary. Its brightness inspired claims of exceptional virtues from an ability to draw "wicked humours" out of the head (*Macer's Herbal*, 15th century), which makes some sense of a fantastical tale in the *Book of Secrets of Albertus Magnus* (1560) of how an amulet of marigold petals, a bay leaf and a wolf's tooth will ensure that only words of peace will be spoken to the wearer. In Tudor times the petals were dried in huge quantities and sold in grocers' shops to flavour winter stews. They were made into conserves and syrups and also added to salads.
Description A low-growing annual – to 50cm/ 20in – with hairy, slightly sticky leaves and large orange-yellow daisy-like flowers throughout summer into early autumn.

Related species There are a number of hybrids and ornamental cultivars that do not necessarily have the same medicinal value, but may be used for culinary and cosmetic purposes and to add to potpourri. The *Tagetes* genus of marigolds are not related. Many are toxic and should not be used for the same purposes as *Calendula*.
Growth Easy to grow in any soil.
Propagate from seed sown in autumn or spring.

Regular dead-heading ensures a good supply of blooms over a long period. Self-seeds prolifically.
Parts used Flowers – petals can be used fresh or dried.

USES Medicinal Pot marigold or calendula has anti-inflammatory, antiseptic properties and is also antibacterial and antifungal. It makes an excellent ointment for soothing irritated, chapped skin, eczema, insect bites and sunburn. It may also be made into an infused oil, for the same purpose, by steeping petals in warm vegetable oil.
Culinary Once known as "poor man's saffron", the fresh or dried petals add rich colour to rice dishes and salads and may be sprinkled over sweet dishes or baked in buns and biscuits.
Cosmetic Petals are added to beauty creams, or made into an infusion as a lotion for oily skins.
Aromatic Whole dried flowers, or petals, lend colour to a fragrant potpourri.

CAUTION Not to be confused with inedible marigold (*Tagetes*). Occasionally causes allergic reactions.

Pot marigold salad with curried eggs

This dressing has a mild, creamy curry flavour. Serve this salad with baked ham and thick wholemeal (whole-wheat) bread.

Serves 4
4 medium eggs
5ml/1 tsp mild curry powder or paste
75ml/5 tbsp single (light) cream
15ml/1 tbsp chopped parsley
1 bag of mixed salad leaves with light
*   and dark red lettuce*
1 pot marigold head, using the petals only

1 Boil the eggs in a saucepan of boiling water for 4 minutes. Allow to cool. Shell and cut into quarters. Stir together the curry powder or paste, mayonnaise and cream in a mixing bowl.

2 Put the chopped parsley and salad leaves in individual bowls. Add one egg to each bowl, then pour over the curried cream sauce. Add the marigold petals.

CANNABACEAE

Cannabis sativa

Cannabis

History and traditions Cannabis has a long history as a medicinal plant, being mentioned in ancient Chinese and Indian texts dating from the 10th century BC. Herodotus reports that the Scythians (nomadic people of Iranian origin, living between the 7th and 2nd centuries BC) "crept into their huts and threw the seeds onto hot stones". Pliny thought very highly of this plant's medicinal values. Hildegarde of Bingen in AD1150 refers to it as a relief for headaches, and it is mentioned in all the great Renaissance herbals – though its narcotic effects were well understood and it was known as "The Leaf of Delusion". As hemp, it has been grown for its fibre since ancient times, and it provided rope for the hangman in 16th-century Britain (old names are "gallowgrass" and "neckeweed").

Description An annual which grows to 5m/16ft in height, on erect stems with narrow, toothed leaves and panicles of inconspicuous green flowers.

Habitat/distribution Cannabis is native to northern India, southern Siberia, western and central Asia; it can be grown throughout temperate and tropical regions.

Parts used Leaves, flowering tops – processed in various forms, under various names, such as "marijuana", "pot", "dagga", "kif", "ganja", "charas" or "churras", and "bhang".

USES Medicinal Cannabis is widely used as an illegal narcotic drug. It can be addictive, and is weakening and harmful in excess, but there is some evidence of its therapeutic value for diseases such as cancer, multiple sclerosis, cerebral palsy and glaucoma.

General Rope is made from the fibre. Seeds are the source of hempseed oil used in varnishes, foods and cosmetics. Hemp *per se* does not contain appreciable amounts of THC (tetrahdro-cannabinol carboxyli). It is legal in some places.

Other name Hemp.

Below *As a weed cannabis grows with abandon and success in Iowa.*

CAUTION It is illegal in most countries.

CRUCIFERAE/BRASSICACEAE

Capsella bursa-pastoris

Shepherd's purse

History and traditions Most of its names in English, Latin and other European languages refer to the resemblance of the seeds to purses or little pouches. It is of ancient origin, seeds were found at Catal Huyuk, a site dating from 5950BC, and in the stomach of Tollund Man. Following a visit to America, John Josselyn listed it in his herbal in 1672 as one of the plants unknown to the New World before the Pilgrim Fathers went there. Despite being a common weed, it has proved a valid medicinal plant in this century – extracts were used during World War I to treat wounds.

Description An annual, or more usually biennial, plant with a flower stem rising to 50cm/20in from a basal rosette of oval, dentate leaves. It has tiny white flowers, followed by triangular seedpods.

Habitat/distribution Grows worldwide in temperate zones in fields and waysides on gravelly, sandy and nitrogen-rich soils.

Growth A wild plant, it tolerates poor soil. It can be propagated from seed. Self-seeds freely.

Parts used Leaves – fresh, or dried for use in infusions and extracts.

USES Medicinal Contains a glycoside, diosmin, which has blood-clotting effects and is reputed to stop internal haemorrhages and reduce heavy menstruation when taken as an infusion of the dried leaf. Also taken for cystitis and applied externally for eczema and skin complaints.

Culinary The leaves are rich in vitamins A, B and C and, although not very tasty, make a healthy addition to salads.

SOLANACEAE

Capsicum

History and traditions Capsicums were first brought to Europe and the West from Mexico following Columbus's voyage of 1492, when the doctor who accompanied him noted their uses by the Native Americans as pain relievers, toothache remedies and for flavouring food. The Portuguese were responsible for their spread to India and Africa.

Habitat/distribution They are now grown in tropical and subtropical regions worldwide, and under glass in temperate zones. They can be grown outdoors in many areas of North America and in the southern states are a major commercial crop.

Description *Capsicum annuum* var. *annuum* are annuals, sometimes short-lived perennials, and most grow into small bushy plants 60–90cm/2–3ft high; a few may reach 1.5m/ 5ft. They have glossy lance-shaped to ovate leaves and small white flowers followed by conical, or spherical, green, ripening to red, fruits.

Species Most cultivated peppers are of the species *C. annuum* var. *annuum*. There are over 1,000 cultivars grown across the world, with fruit in a wide range of shapes, sizes and degrees of pungency, divided into five main groups:
1. **Cerasiforme Group (cherry peppers)** – with small, very pungent fruits.

2. **Conoides Group (cone peppers)** – with erect, conical fruits.
3. **Fasciculatum Group (red cone peppers)** – slender, red, very pungent fruits.
4. **Grossum Group (bell peppers, sweet peppers, pimento)** – these have large, sweet, bell-shaped fruit, green, then ripening to red or yellow. Rich in vitamin C, they lack the medicinal properties of the hot, pungent peppers.
5. **Longum Group (cayenne peppers, chilli peppers)** – fruits are usually drooping, very pungent and the source of chilli powder, cayenne pepper and hot paprika. *C. frutescens* is a name often used for varieties of *C. annuum* whose fruits are used in Tabasco sauce.

Growth Frost-tender plants, which must be grown under glass in cool temperate climates. Plant in loam-based (John Innes) growing medium (soil mix), water freely, feed with a liquid fertilizer once a week and mist flowers with water daily to ensure that fruit sets. Propagation is from seed, at a temperature of 21°C/70°F in early spring. Outside, they are grown in well-drained, nutrient-rich soil.

Parts used Fruits – eaten ripe or unripe; or dried (ripe only) for powders.

USES Medicinal It is the bitter alkaloid, capsaicin, which gives peppers their hot taste and has been established by modern research as an effective painkiller – it works by depleting the nerve cells of the chemical neurotransmitter which sends pain messages to the brain.

Peppers are antibacterial and also contain vitamins A, C, and mineral salts. Pungent varieties increase blood flow, encourage sweating, stimulate the appetite and help digestion. In tropical countries they are useful food preservatives and help prevent gastric upsets. Taken internally or used as gargles (infusions of the powder) for colds, fevers and sore throats; applied externally (in massage oil or compresses) for rheumatism, arthritis, aching joints and muscles. A pharmaceutical analgesic cream, with capsaicin as active ingredient, has recently been developed for reducing rheumatic pain.

Culinary Sweet red or green peppers make delicious cooked vegetables or raw salad ingredients. Hot chilli peppers are added to pickles and chutneys; dried to make cayenne pepper, chilli powder or paprika (from milder-tasting fruits); added to dishes in Indian, Mexican, Thai and other worldwide cuisines.

Other names Peppers and chilli peppers.

Top centre Capsicum frutescens, *a hot chilli pepper.*

Top right Capsicum annuum *var.* annuum, *Grossum Group, a sweet, bell pepper.*

CAUTION Chillies may cause inflammation and irritation to skin and eyes, so wear gloves when handling them. If taken internally to excess, they may cause digestive disorders.

Carica papaya

Papaya

History and traditions Originally from South and Central America and the West Indies, this tree with its fragrant, fleshy fruit was unknown in Europe before the end of the 17th century. The Spanish took it to Manila and, with the expansion of trade and travel at the beginning of the 18th century, it made its way to Asia and Africa and is now grown in tropical countries around the globe.

Description A small, evergreen tree, up to 6m/ 20ft in height with deeply cut, palmate leaves, forming an umbrella-shaped crown. The large, ovoid fruits have dark green, leathery skin, ripening to yellow, containing sweet orange-yellow flesh and numerous tiny black seeds surrounding a central cavity.

Habitat/distribution Native to South and Central America, occurs widely in tropical zones.

Growth A tender, tropical plant, it will not grow in temperatures below 13°C/55°F. Requires rich, moist soil, and a sunny, humid climate.

Parts used Fruit, seeds, leaves – fresh. Sap, known as "papain", is extracted from the unripe fruits by scarification, and produced in dried or liquid form.

USES Medicinal The fruit is one of the best natural digestives, containing enzymes similar to pepsin. Juice is applied externally to destroy warts and for skin eruptions and irritations. Seeds and papain are used in preparations to expel intestinal worms.

Culinary Fruit is high in vitamin C and minerals, and is eaten fresh, canned or made into ice creams, desserts and soft drinks. Papain is used commercially as a meat tenderizer, and, on a domestic level, the inside of the skin of the fruit and leaves are wrapped round meat for the same purpose. Seeds have a pungent flavour and are sometimes eaten, or used as food flavouring, in countries where it is grown.

Cosmetic Juice smooths skin, removes freckles and reduces sun damage. Papain is included in commercial cosmetic products.

General Papain is used as an insecticide against termites, as an ingredient of chewing gum, to reduce cloudiness in beer and to make woollen and silk fabrics shrinkproof.

Above *Papaya leaves are used to tenderize meat.*

Left *Papaya fruit has excellent digestive properties.*

CAUTION Do not take in large quantities or as a concentrated extract during pregnancy.

Carlina acaulis

Carline thistle

History and traditions In medieval times this thistle was thought to be an antidote to poison and the root was sometimes chewed to relieve toothache. It is said to be named after the Emperor Charlemagne, following a dream that it would cure the plague.

Description A low-growing, short-lived perennial, 5–10cm/2–4in high, with a deep tap root, it has basal rosettes of spiny leaves and large stemless flowers with silvery-white bracts surrounding a brown disc-shaped centre.

Habitat/distribution Native to Europe and Asia, it is found in fields, grasslands and waste ground on poor dry soils in sunny positions.

Growth It grows best in a poor, dry soil. If kept too wet it will rot, and if the soil is too rich it becomes lax, overgrown and loses its neat, stemless habit. Propagated from seed sown in autumn and overwintered in a cold frame.

Parts used Roots – dried for use in decoctions, liquid extracts and tinctures.

USES Medicinal It has antibacterial and diuretic properties. A decoction of the roots is used as a gargle for sore throats, for skin complaints and to clean wounds. It is taken internally for urine retention.

Culinary Claims have been made for the flower centres as substitute artichoke hearts.

CAUTION Large doses taken internally are purgative and emetic.

COMPOSITAE/ASTERACEAE
Carthamus tinctorius
Safflower

History and traditions Cultivated in Egypt, China and India since ancient times, safflower was a valued dye plant – producing a pink dye, used for the original "red tape" of Indian bureaucracy. It was introduced to Europe from the Middle East during the mid-16th century for its medicinal properties, and is now cultivated for the oil extracted from the seeds.

Description A hardy annual, growing to 1m/3ft high, with finely toothed, long, ovate leaves and shaggy, thistle-like, yellow flower heads set in spiny bracts.

Habitat/distribution Native to Asia and Mediterranean regions, widely cultivated for its seeds in many countries, including Asia, India, Africa and Australia.

Growth Grows in any light, well-drained soil and tolerates dry conditions. Propagated by seed, sown in spring.

Parts used Flowers, seeds, oil.

USES Medicinal The oil contains 75 per cent linoleum acid and is a useful source of essential fatty acids. Tea, infused from fresh or dry flowers, is taken to reduce fevers and is mildly laxative. Infusions are applied externally for bruises, skin irritations and inflammations.

Culinary Oil extracted from the seeds is low in cholesterol and has a delicate flavour. The flower petals, which are slightly bitter, have been used as a substitute for saffron in colouring food.

Household Flowers produce a yellow dye with water and red dye with alcohol. They are dried for adding to potpourri and as "everlasting" flowers for dried arrangements.

UMBELLIFERAE/APIACEAE
Carum carvi
Caraway

History and traditions Caraway seeds have been found during archaeological excavations at Neolithic sites in Europe and the plant was well known to the Egyptians, Greeks and Romans. The seeds were a popular culinary flavouring in Tudor England, cooked with fruit and baked in bread and cakes. They were made into sugared "comfits", and frequently served as a side dish with baked apples, as in Shakespeare's *Henry IV* when Falstaff is invited to take "a pippin [apple] and a dish of carraways". This custom is said to have continued into the early 20th century at formal dinners of London livery companies. There is also an old superstition that caraway has retentive powers, and, if sprinkled about, is capable of preventing people and personal belongings from straying.

Description A biennial 45–60cm/18in–2ft tall, it has feathery leaves, with umbels of white flowers appearing in its second year, followed by ridged fruits (popularly known as seeds).

Habitat/distribution Native to Asia and central Europe in meadowlands and waste grounds. Introduced and cultivated elsewhere.

Growth Prefers well-drained soil and a sunny position. Propagated from seed sown in spring, preferably *in situ* as it does not transplant well.

Above Young, tender caraway leaves add flavour to salads.

Parts used Leaves, seeds, essential oil from the seeds.

USES Medicinal Caraway has carminative properties (combats flatulence). A few seeds chewed after a meal or an infusion of the seeds may relieve bloating and excessive wind.

Culinary Seeds are used to flavour cakes, biscuits, bread, cheese, stewed fruit, baked apples, cabbage and meat dishes. Also as a pickling spice and to flavour the liqueur, Kümmel. Young leaves make a garnish and are added to salads.

Aromatic Essential oil (containing over 50% carvone, which gives it its aromatic scent) is used as a flavouring in the food industry and in perfumes and cosmetics.

FAGACEAE
Castanea sativa
Sweet chestnut

History and traditions Sweet chestnut trees
were grown in ancient Greece and Rome.
The Greek physician, Theophrastus, wrote
of their medicinal virtues and the Romans
enjoyed eating them. They were probably
introduced to Britain by the Romans and
there are records of chestnuts grown in the
Forest of Dean being paid as tithes, during
the reign of Henry II, 1154–1189. Writing
in the mid-17th century, Culpeper considered
the "inner skin" of the chestnut would "stop
any flux whatsoever" and that the ground,
dried leaves made into an electuary (medicinal
paste) with honey made "an admirable
remedy for the cough and spitting of blood".
Their culinary diversity was praised by the
17th-century diarist and gourmet, John Evelyn,
as "delicacies for princes and a lusty and
masculine food for rusticks", while he
regretted that all too often they were mere
animal fodder.

Description A deciduous tree, growing to
15m/50ft with dark grey, furrowed bark, and
narrow, glossy, serrated-edged leaves. The small
white flowers, appearing in spring, are followed
by clusters of prickly green spherical fruits,
containing 1–3 edible brown nuts. Trees grown
in cool, northerly regions do not produce the
same quality of large, succulent fruits as those
grown in warmer, Mediterranean climates.

Habitat/distribution Occurs in woodlands of

southern Europe, Asia, North America and
northern Africa.

Growth Grows best in well-drained loam in
sun or partial shade. Propagated by seed
sown in autumn.

Parts used Leaves, seeds (nuts).

USES Medicinal Infusions of the leaves are
taken for coughs and colds and used as a
gargle for sore throats. Also said to be helpful
for rheumatism.

Culinary Chestnuts are equally suited to
savoury and sweet dishes. They are the classic
stuffing ingredient for turkey, other poultry and
game, and make excellent soups, pâtés, and
accompaniments to vegetable and meat dishes.
Sweetened purée forms the basis of desserts,
especially in France, where chestnuts are also
crystallized as "marrons glacés".

Other name Spanish chestnut.

Above *Sweet chestnuts.*

Left *Spiky fruits contain the edible nuts.*

BERBERIDACEAE
Caulophyllum thalictroides
Blue cohosh

History and traditions A herb used in the
traditional medicine of the Native Americans to
facilitate childbirth. Its value being appreciated
by the wider population, it was listed at the end
of the 19th century as an official medicinal herb
in the United States pharmacopoeia. The name
"cohosh" is from a local tribal language.

Description A perennial which grows on
a rhizomatous rootstock. The palmate leaves
develop with, or just after, the yellow-brown
flowers. Fruits split open to reveal spherical
seeds, which turn from green to deep blue
as they ripen.

Habitat/distribution Occurs in moist woodlands in North America.

Growth Requires moist, rich soil, in partial or
deep shade. Divide plants in spring.
Propagation from seed is slow and germination
may often be erratic.

Parts used Rhizomes and roots are dried for
inclusion in powders, liquid extracts and other
medicinal preparations.

USES Medicinal Do not use in pregnancy
unless used under the guidance of a herbalist
or other qualified health professional.
A herb with a long traditional use in
gynaecology. Do not use if you are trying to
conceive, during early pregnancy or lactation.

Other names Squaw root and papoose root.

CAUTION Not to be used without the advice
of a qualified medical practitioner.

LABIATAE/LAMIACEAE

Cedronella canariensis syn
C. triphylla

Balm of Gilead

History and traditions This upstart from the Canary Islands is something of a fraud, sniffily dismissed by Mrs Grieve, in *A Modern Herbal* (1931) as being "called Balm of Gilead for no better reason than that its leaves are fragrant". But it has largely taken over from ancient, more worthy contenders for the name, because it has a similar musky, balsam scent, though not, apparently, any worthwhile medicinal uses. The original Balm of Gilead is usually taken to be *Commiphora opobalsamum*, a rare and protected desert shrub, once valued for its balsam-scented resin. Another source of Balm of Gilead is the balsam poplar, *Populus balsamifera*.

Description A half-hardy shrubby perennial, up to 1m/3ft in height, it has lightly serrated, trifoliate leaves and pink flower clusters, made up of tubular, two-lipped florets.

Habitat/distribution A native of the Canary Islands, where it is found on sunny, rocky slopes. Introduced elsewhere.

Growth Requires well-drained soil and full sun. It does not withstand frost and although it may be grown outside in a sheltered position, in cool climates it needs winter protection. Propagation is easiest from softwood cuttings taken in late spring. Germination from seed is erratic and requires heat.

Parts used Leaves, flowers.

USES Culinary Fresh or dry leaves may be infused to make an invigorating tea.

Aromatic Leaves and flowers are dried for adding to potpourri.

PINACEAE

Cedrus libani

Cedar of Lebanon

History and traditions The ancient Egyptians used oil of cedar for embalming and in their religious rituals. These beautiful, wide-spreading trees, with their head-clearing pine scent, were much prized in biblical times and celebrated in the Song of Solomon ("His countenance is as Lebanon, excellent as the cedars"). And in the Canticles, that evocative Hebrew love poem, also attributed to Solomon, the beloved is compared to many plant fragrances, and told, "The smell of thy garments is like the smell of Lebanon." King Solomon is also alleged to have denuded Lebanon of its cedars to build his massive temple.

Description A tall, 30–40m/100–130ft coniferous tree, with a dark brown or grey, deeply ridged trunk and wide branches bearing whorls of needle-like leaves. It carries both male and female cones, the latter being the larger. They are green at first, turning brown as they ripen over a two-year period, when they break up to release the seeds. Cedars often reach a great age, living for several hundred years.

Related species There are only four species of conifers which are true cedars, all rich in aromatic essential oil. As well as *C. libani*, there is *C. atlantica* (Atlas cedar) and *C. brevifolia* (Cyprus cedar), both classified by some authorities as subspecies of *C. libani*, and *C. deodara*, the Indian cedar.

Habitat/distribution Native to forests of the Mediterranean region from Lebanon to Turkey (*C. libani*), the Atlas Mountains in North Africa (*C. atlantica*), Cyprus (*C. brevifolia*) and the western Himalayas (*C. deodara*).

Growth Fully hardy trees, they grow in any well-drained soil and a sunny position.

Parts used Wood, essential oil.

USES Medicinal The essential oil has antiseptic, fungicide and insect-repellent properties. It is used as a steam inhalation for bronchial and respiratory complaints, to soothe skin irritations, for alopecia, dandruff and other scalp problems. It also has a calming effect for states of anxiety.

Aromatic The oil is added to perfumery, soaps and cosmetics. The wood is used to make furniture and storage chests which, due to its aromatic properties, helps to deter moths and insects.

BOMBACACEAE
Ceiba pentandra
Cotton tree

History and traditions The Ceiba is the national tree of Guatemala and was held sacred by the ancient Mayans of Central America. They believed it grew through the centre of the universe, with its roots in the nine levels of the underworld, its trunk in the thirteen levels of the upperworld and its branches in heaven. The myth still prevails in the area, that this graceful tree is the home of the temptress, Ixtobai, recognizable by her backward-facing feet, who lures unfaithful husbands to disappear with her into the underworld through the trunk.
Description A deciduous, or semi-evergreen, tree growing to 40m/130ft with wide-spreading branches and palmate leaves. The flowers are followed by large pods, containing seeds protected by white, fluffy, silky-textured padding, collected to make kapok.
Habitat/distribution Occurs in rainforests and other damp, wooded areas in tropical North, South and Central America, Africa and Asia.
Growth Requires a temperature of 15°C/59°F. Grown in fertile, moist, but well-drained soil and full sun. Usually propagated by cuttings.
Parts used Leaves, bark, seeds, seed-pod fibre.

USES Medicinal The bark and leaves are made into decoctions, taken internally, for bronchial and respiratory infections, or applied externally in the form of baths. The leaves are boiled in sugar to make cough syrup and applied as a compress for headaches, fevers and sprains.
Culinary The seeds are toxic, but an edible, non-toxic oil is extracted from them which is used locally for cooking.

COMPOSITAE/ASTERACEAE
Centaurea cyanus
Cornflower

History and traditions These pretty blue flowers were once a common sight in cornfields, as their name suggests, but have largely been ousted by the techniques of modern agriculture. In his *Herbal* of 1597, Gerard reports that the Italian name for the cornflower is a reference to blunting sickles, "because it hindereth and annoyeth the reapers, dulling and turning the edges of their sickles" and he includes "hurt-sickle" among its English names of blew-bottle, blew-blow and corne-floure. Although Culpeper found many uses for these flowers, Gerard's view was that there is "no use of them in physic", although they are recommended by some for inflammation of the eye.
Description An annual which grows from 20–80cm/8–32in tall, with grey-green lanceolate leaves and bright blue shaggy flower heads. Cultivated kinds also have pink, purple or white flowers.
Related species *C. montana* is a perennial species, found mainly in mountainous areas of Europe. The wild plant, *C. scabiosa,* is often called knapweed.
Habitat/distribution Native to Europe and the Mediterranean region, naturalized in North America, also found in Asia and Australia. Becoming less common in the wild, widely cultivated and grown in gardens.

Above Cornflowers, once a common weed, are frequently cultivated in gardens for their striking colour and form.

Growth A hardy annual, it is easy to grow from seed sown in spring *in situ*, as it resents being transplanted. May be given an early start by sowing in autumn or very early spring, in plugs, or biodegradable pots, to minimize root disturbance. Plant in well-drained soil and a sunny position.
Parts used Flowers.

USES Medicinal Traditionally used in the past to make eyewashes for tired or strained eyes, but seems to have little place in herbal medicine as practised today.
Aromatic Flowers are dried for potpourris.
Other name Bluebottle.

COMPOSITAE/ASTERACEAE

Chamaemelum nobile

Chamomile

History and traditions "Thys herbe was consecrated by the wyse men of Egypt unto the Sonne and was rekened to be the only remedy for all agues", says William Turner in his *Newe Herball*, 1551, in reference to the veneration of chamomile by the ancient Egyptians. The Greeks called it "earth apple", from which its generic name is derived (*kamai*, meaning "on the ground" and *melon*, apple), and in modern Spanish chamomile is called *"manzanilla"*, meaning "little apple". It does indeed have an apple-like fragrance, especially noticeable after rain or when the plant is lightly crushed. To the Anglo-Saxons it was *"maythen"* and was one of the sacred herbs of Woden. It was featured in the Nine Herbs Lay, a charm against the effects of "flying venom" and "loathed things that over land rove" from the *Lacnunga* in the Harleian manuscript collection, British Museum. Over the centuries chamomile has been celebrated for its soothing properties, and its fragrance heads the list in an anti-stress prescription from *Ram's Little Dodoen*, 1606: "To comfort the braine smel to camomill, eate sage ... wash measurably, sleep reasonably, delight to heare melody and singing".

Description An evergreen perennial with finely divided, feathery leaves growing to 15cm/6in. The white daisy-like flowers, with yellow disc centres, are borne singly on long stems rising to 30cm/1ft.

Related species *C. nobile* 'Flore Pleno' is a cultivar with creamy-coloured double flowers. The whole plant is more compact than the species, about 10cm/4in tall including flower stems, and makes a good edging plant. *C. nobile* 'Treneague' is a non-flowering cultivar which forms a dense carpet useful for lawns and seats and grows to about 6cm/2¹⁄2in.

Habitat/distribution Indigenous to Europe, it is widely grown in North America and many other countries. It is found in the wild on sandy soils in grasslands and waste ground.

Growth Prefers light, sandy soil and a sunny position. It is possible to propagate *C. nobile* from seed sown in spring, but the easier and more usual method is by division of runners or "offsets". *C. n.* 'Flore Pleno' and *C. n.* 'Treneague' must be vegetatively propagated.

Parts used Flowers, essential oil.

USES Medicinal Chamomile has an antiseptic, anti-inflammatory action and is soothing and a relaxant. It is taken as a tea for nausea and indigestion and to help promote sound sleep, and may also be helpful in relieving painful menstruation. It is made into ointments or lotions for skin irritations and insect bites. The true essential oil is very expensive and contains azulene, which gives it a deep blue colour. It is frequently used for skin complaints and eczema (diluted in witch hazel or a pure, mild vegetable oil) and as a steam inhalation for asthma, sinusitis or catarrh.

Cosmetic An infusion of the flowers makes a rinse to give a shine to fair hair, or a skin freshener for sensitive skins. Essential oil or infusions are added to face or hand creams and fresh flowers floated in hot water make a deep-cleansing facial steam treatment.

Aromatic The dried flowers are added to sleep pillows and sachets or put into potpourri.

Other name Roman chamomile.

Above
Chamaemelum
nobile *'Flore Pleno'*.

Top *The double flowers of the dwarf edging plant* C. nobile *'Flore Pleno'*.

CAUTION Despite being such a benevolent herb (when recommended doses and guidelines are followed), if taken internally to excess it may cause vomiting and vertigo. The plant may cause contact dermatitis.

Related species

COMPOSITAE/ASTERACEAE

Matricaria recutita syn.
Chamomilla recutita
Wild chamomile

History and traditions The name *matricaria*
comes from its early gynaecological uses in
herbal medicine.

Description *M. recutita* syn. *M. chamomilla* is
a tall hardy annual which grows to 60cm/2ft.
Although from a different genus (due to
botanical differences), flowers, feathery foliage
and scent are similar in appearance to that of
Chamaemelum nobile. Not to be confused with
the scentless mayweeds, or false chamomiles
Matricaria inodora and *Tripleurosperum
maritimum,* or the almost scentless corn
chamomile (*Anthemis arvensis*).

Habitat/distribution Occurs all over Europe,
Western Asia and India.

Growth Propagated from seed, sown *in situ* in
early spring, it grows easily in any dry, light soil.

Parts used Flowers – they have similar
properties to those of *Chamaemelum nobile.*

USES As for *C. nobile.*

Other names German chamomile and scented
mayweed.

Above Matricaria recutita.

To make oyle of chamomile

Take oyle a pint and halfe, and three
ounces of camomile flowers dryed
one day after they be gathered.
Then put the oyle and the flowers in
a glasse and stop the mouth close
and set it into the sun by the space
of forty days.
The Good Housewife's Handbook, 1588

A chamomile lawn

Chamomile has been popular since
medieval times for scented lawns, paths or
places to sit, all of which still make delightful features in the herb garden.

A chamomile lawn requires regular
hand weeding to keep it looking good
and does not take heavy wear. The trick
is to think small – grow it as a scaled-
down version of a lawn, plant it round a
fountain or sundial, or as a mini lawn
between paving.

• Use rooted cuttings or offsets of non-
flowering *Chamaemelum nobile*
'Treneague', edged (or for a "flowery-
mead" effect, interspersed) with

C. n. 'Flore Pleno'.

• Choose an area with light,
preferably sandy soil,
prepare it well,
eliminating weeds and
removing stones. Rake
in a little peat to
hold water and
help the plants
settle in quickly.

• Set plants 10cm/4in apart, water them in
and keep lightly moist until established.

• To maintain the lawn, weed regularly
and fill in any gaps that appear with
new plants.

Above *A lawn of* C. n. *'Treneague'.*

Above *A brick-built chamomile seat.*

A chamomile seat

These are always attractive and have the
added advantage that the area of
chamomile is small enough to make
maintenance simple of the seat. It is
also a good way to grow chamomile in a
garden with heavy or clay soil, as the
seat forms a raised bed to provide a free-
draining environment.

• The base of the seat may be constructed
with brick, stone or timber, filled with

rubble and a very thick layer of topsoil
for planting.

• It is best to keep to *C. n.* 'Treneague'
only for this, as flowers sticking out of
a bench spoil the effect. Plant as for
the lawn.

• If back and arm rests are required for
the seat, they could be made of the same
material as the base. Clipped box also
looks very effective.

CHENOPODIACEAE

Chenopodium ambrosioides
American wormseed

History and traditions American wormseed was introduced to Europe in the 17th century from Mexico, where it was taken as a tea and used in traditional medicine.

Description An annual, 60cm–1.2m/2–4ft high, it has longer, more lanceolate leaves than those of *C. bonus-henricus* and a strong acrid scent. The tiny, green flowers are followed by small nutlike, one-seeded fruits.

Habitat/distribution Native to tropical Central America, naturalized throughout much of USA and grown in other countries also.

Growth Frost-hardy (to -5°C/23°F), American wormseed grows in any well-drained soil. Propagated by seed sown in spring; in warm climates it often self-seeds freely.

Parts used Flowering stems, essential oil.

USES Medicinal Its chief use has always been to expel intestinal worms. It has also been recommended for nervous disorders, asthma and problems with menstruation. The volatile oil of chenopodium is a powerful insecticide as well as a vermifuge (a medicine that expels intestinal worms), but should never be administered in this concentrated form as it is highly toxic.

> **CAUTION** Poisonous in large doses, it should be taken only under medical supervision and is legally restricted in some countries.

CHENOPODIACEAE

Chenopodium bonus-henricus
Good King Henry

History and traditions According to the 16th-century physician and botanist, Rembert Dodoens, of the Netherlands, this plant was dubbed *bonus henricus*, "good Henry", to distinguish it from a poisonous plant, *malus henricus*, "bad Henry". There is some uncertainty as to who "Henry" was, but one source claims it is a generic term for mischievous elves. "King" appears to have been spin-doctored into the English popular name to give this rather un-attractive plant a spurious connection with King Henry VIII, "Good King Hal". The Latin name *Chenopodium* is derived from the Greek for "goose foot", an eloquent reference to the shape of the leaves.

Description A perennial which grows 60cm/2ft tall and spreads indefinitely, it has fleshy, downy stems, dark green, arrow-shaped leaves and greenish-yellow spikes of sorrel-like flowers in early summer.

Related species *Chenopodium album*, White Goosefoot – also known as allgood and fat hen (because it does a good job of fattening poultry) – as well as pigweed, mutton tops and lamb's quarters. It has long been a staple food of both animals and people. The Iron Age Dane, Tollund Man, made a last meal of it before he was hanged, seeds being found in his stomach.

Habitat/distribution Native to Europe but found worldwide on waste ground and previously cultivated land.

Growth This is an invasive plant which needs no cultivation and thrives in any soil. Said to be of "superior quality" if grown in rich soil, but little difference in taste or texture will be noticed. Tough taproots can make it difficult to eradicate if no longer wanted. Easily propagated from seed, or division, in spring.

Parts used Leaves, stems.

USES Medicinal Once made into ointments and poultices for skin complaints (an old name was "smearwort") but has no known medicinal value currently, apart from being mildly laxative.

Culinary Extravagant claims have been made for this plant as being a spinach-like vegetable (leaves) and asparagus substitute (young stems). Although edible if picked when young and tender, the leaves develop a fibrous texture with age which makes them less palatable. John Evelyn (*Acetaria*, 1719) was right when in reference to one of its names, "blite", from the Greek for insipid, he commented that "it is well-named, being insipid enough". It is rich in vitamins C, B^1, iron and calcium – so it may be a case of "eating up your greens" for the sake of your health.

Other names Goosefoot, allgood, fat hen, English mercury and Lincolnshire asparagus.

Left *The leaves of* Chenopodium bonus-henricus *were thought to resemble goose feet.*

COMPOSITAE/ASTERACEAE
Cichorium intybus
Chicory

History and traditions This herb was cultivated in Egypt over 2,000 years ago, and known to the ancient Greeks and Romans, who used it as a salad ingredient and vegetable. Its use as a coffee substitute is thought to date from 1806 when Napoleon's Continental blockade prevented imports of coffee. It was widely used for the same purpose during the World Wars.

Description A tall, hardy perennial, growing to 1.5m/5ft. It has a deep taproot and thick stem which exudes a milky sap when cut. It has toothed, oval to lanceolate leaves and pale blue flowers appear in summer.

Habitat/distribution Native of the Mediterranean region, western Asia and North Africa, introduced and established worldwide.

Growth For best results grow in rich, but well-drained soil. Propagate from seed sown in spring. Sometimes self-seeds, especially on dry soils.

Parts used Leaves, roots.

USES Medicinal A bitter tonic herb, the dried, crushed root is made into infusions or decoctions for digestive upsets and to improve appetite. It is also a mild stimulant and laxative.

Culinary There are various cultivars whose leaves are added to salads, including red, broad-leafed radicchio types. Blanched heads, or chicons, eaten in salads and cooked as vegetables, are produced by lifting the roots, packing them in boxes in a growing medium, cutting off the leaves and keeping them in complete darkness until white, elongated shoots have sprouted.

RANUNCULACEAE
Cimicifuga racemosa
Black cohosh

History and traditions The root of this herb was used in the medicine of Native Americans for female complaints and it was thought to be an antidote to poison and to rattlesnake venom. The generic name is from the Latin *cimex*, meaning a bug, and *fugere*, to run, in reference to this plant's insect-repellent properties. This genus is sometimes classified as *Actaea*.

Description A tall, clump-forming, aromatic perennial, with a rather unpleasant smell. It makes an attractive plant for the border with spires of creamy-white, bottle-brush flowers, rising to 1.5m/5ft above the three-lobed basal leaves 40cm/16in high.

Habitat/distribution Native to North America, it is grown in northern temperate regions and occurs in moist grassland or woodland.

Growth Fully hardy, it requires moist, fertile soil with plenty of humus and partial shade. It can be propagated by division of roots or by seed, sown in pots in autumn for overwintering in a cold frame for germination the following spring.

Parts used Rhizomes – dried for use in decoctions, tinctures and extracts.

USES Medicinal For arthritis, rheumatism and menstrual and menopausal problems.

> **CAUTION** Large doses may cause liver damage or miscarriage. Not to be taken during pregnancy, while breast-feeding, or by anyone with liver disease. Legally restricted in some countries.

RUBIACEAE
Cinchona officinalis
Cinchona

History and traditions Said to be named after the Countess of Chinchon, wife of the Viceroy of Peru, after she had been cured of a fever (probably malaria) with a cinchona bark medicine in about 1638.

Description Cinchona species are tender, evergreen trees varying in height, according to species and habitat, from 10–25m/30–80ft. The oval leaves are often red-veined and small, crimson flowers are borne in panicles.

Related species There are several species of *Cinchona* of medicinal value, all closely related, including *C. calisaya* and *C. pubescens*.

Habitat/distribution Native to mountainous regions of South America, widely introduced and cultivated in tropical regions worldwide.

Growth In the wild, trees occur in dense, wet forest. Commercial plantations provide well-drained, moist soil and high humidity. Propagated by cuttings.

Parts used Bark – dried and powdered or as a liquid extract.

USES Medicinal Cinchona bark contains the antimalarial alkaloid, quinine, as well as quinidine, which slows the heart rate. It was the major treatment for malaria from the mid-17th century until recently, now largely replaced for this purpose by synthetic drugs. It is still an ingredient of many pharmaceutical preparations for colds and influenza, and of tonic water.

> **CAUTION** For use by medical herbal practitioners only.

LAURACEAE

Cinnamomum zeylanicum

Cinnamon

History and traditions An important aromatic spice since biblical times, cinnamon was an ingredient of the holy ointment made by Moses. It is also cited as amongst the costly merchandise and luxury items available in Babylon, when the fall of that misguided city is predicted in the biblical book, Revelation. The Portuguese occupied Sri Lanka for its cinnamon in 1536. By the 18th century, cinnamon had become such a valuable commodity in Europe, that the Dutch took control of the island and set up a trading monopoly in the spice.

Description A medium-sized evergreen tree, it grows to about 9m/30ft and has brown, papery bark and ovate, leathery green leaves. Creamy-white flowers are borne in short panicles, followed by olive-shaped dark blue fruits.

Habitat/distribution Native to forest areas of Sri Lanka, southern India and Malaysia and widely cultivated in India, the Seychelles, Brazil, the Caribbean and tropical zones.

Growth Cinnamon grows in sandy soils, and needs plenty of rain, sun and a minimum temperature of 15°C/59°F. Young trees are cut to within 30cm/1ft of the ground, stumps covered in mulch to encourage sprouting for re-harvesting within 2–3 years. It is also propagated by seed.

Parts used Inner bark of young stems – dried and wrapped round thin rods to form quills. Essential oil.

USES Medicinal It has digestive properties, dispels nausea, and is taken for colds, sore throats and rheumatic conditions. The essential oil is antibacterial and antifungal, helps deaden the nerve where there is toothache and is added to steam inhalations for colds and upper respiratory tract infections.

Culinary A popular spice for savoury and sweet dishes. It adds flavour to curries, baked goods, stews and meat dishes, savoury and sweet rice and is a traditional ingredient of Christmas puddings, mince pies, mulled wine and hot spiced drinks.

Aromatic Ingredient of potpourri (powdered or whole pieces) and clove-and-orange pomanders. The essential oil is used in perfumery.

Left *Cinnamon sticks are formed from the rolled bark.*

CISTACEAE

Cistus ladanifer

Cistus

History and traditions In his *Relation d'un voyage du Levant,* 1717, French botanist, Pitton de Tournefort, gives an eloquent description of collecting ladanum, a fragrant resin exuded by several species of cistus, by means of dragging a leather-thonged rake (a *ladisteron*) across the plants. He also refers to a method in use since Dioscorides' day, of combing it from the beards of goats allowed to browse on the sticky foliage. It has a perfume reminiscent of ambergris and was one of the main ingredients in the solid, resin-based pomanders popular in the Middle Ages for repelling infection.

Description A hardy evergreen shrub, growing to 2m/6ft, with lanceolate, sticky, dark green leaves. The papery, saucer-shaped white flowers bloom for only one day.

Related species *C. creticus* syn. *C. incanus* subsp. *creticus,* the Cretan rock rose, and also a source of ladanum, is a more compact shrub, growing to 1m/3ft with purplish-pink flowers and yellow stamens.

Habitat/distribution Found in Crete, southern Europe, Turkey, northern Africa and the Canary Islands, on dry, stony soils and sunny hillsides. Introduced and widely grown elsewhere.

Growth Prefers a light, well-drained soil and sheltered site in full sun. It is propagated from seed, sown in containers, in late summer or from softwood cuttings in early summer.

Parts used Dried leaves, oleo-resin – collected from young stems and leaves.

USES Aromatic Used as a fixative in perfumery, and in potpourri and home fragrance products.

RUTACEAE

Citrus

History and traditions The citrus species were unknown to Greek and Roman writers, but they have been cultivated for so long that their origins are hazy. Both oranges and lemons are probably natives of northern India, certainly China, and are thought to have been brought to the West by Arab traders via North Africa, Arabia and Syria, thence to Spain and Sicily. *C. limon*, found in the valleys of Kumaon and Sikkim, in the foothills of the Himalayas, has the Hindustani name *limu* or *nimbu*, which was taken into Arabic as *limun*. *C. aurantium*, the bitter Seville orange, is the species mentioned in a medicinal context by the Arabian physician, Avicenna, 980–1037, practising at Salerno, and was the orange tree planted in Rome by St Dominic in AD1200. These must also have been the oranges which Edward I's Queen, Eleanor of Castile, is purported to have bought from a Spanish ship which called at Portsmouth in 1290 – sweet oranges were not known in the West before the mid-15th century, introduced from the East by the Portuguese. The custom of wearing orange blossom at weddings is said to have originated with the Saracens, who considered it an emblem of fecundity, and the practice was introduced to Europe by returning Crusaders. Essential oil distilled from the flowers of the bitter orange was said to have an "exquisite fragrance" by the Italian Giambattista Porta in his herbal of 1588. It became known as "oil of Neroli" from 1680, because it was favoured by the wife of the Count of Neroli for perfuming gloves.

Habitat/distribution Originated in Asia, cultivated in the Mediterranean region, in southern parts of North America and other countries.

Growth Orange and lemon trees are tender, and must be protected from frost, but they prefer cool rather than hot conditions. If grown in northern climates, with cold, frosty winters, they should be kept outside in summer and in a temperate conservatory or greenhouse in winter. They need a well-drained, not too acid compost – the correct pH value is crucial, 6–6.5 for lemons and 6.5–7 for oranges. *C. aurantium* and *C. limon* may be grown from seed, or from semi-ripe cuttings – but cultivars do not come true from seed.

Citrus limon
Lemon

Description A small evergreen tree, 2–6m/ 6–19ft tall, with light green, oval leaves and thorny stems. Clusters of white flowers, opening from pink-tinted buds, are followed by ovoid, bitter-tasting yellow fruits.

Parts used Fruits, essential oil, expressed from the peel.

USES Medicinal Rich in vitamin C and once used by British seamen to prevent scurvy (limes were also used). Lemons have anti-inflammatory properties and are used in home remedies for colds, frequently in conjunction with honey, which is antiseptic. Applied externally for insect bites and skin irritations.

Culinary The juice and rind are widely used as a flavouring in cooking, and in soft drinks, sauces, pickles, preserves and marinades.

Aromatic The peel is dried for potpourri and home fragrance preparations. The oil is used commercially in perfumery, and to scent soaps and household cleaning products.

Citrus aurantium
Bitter orange

Description An evergreen tree, growing to 8m/26ft high, with shiny, ovate leaves and fragrant white flowers, followed by bitter, orange fruits.

Parts used Leaves, fruits, flowers. Essential oil of neroli, distilled from flowers; essential oil of petitgrain, distilled from leaves and twigs; distilled orange flower water; oil of orange, expressed from the rind.

USES Medicinal Rich in vitamins A, B and C, and has energizing tonic properties. Infusions of leaves and flowers are used for digestive disorders. The essential oil of neroli is an antidepressant and calming. It may also be helpful for insomnia.

Culinary The fruits are used to make Seville orange marmalade and a bitter sauce to complement fatty poultry such as duck and goose. Orange flower water has a delicate fragrance, ideal for flavouring sweet dishes. Oil of orange is a flavouring in commercial food products.

Aromatic Essential oils of neroli and petitgrain are used in perfumery.

Cosmetic Orange rind pounded, mixed with rainwater and applied as a poultice is a traditional Indian remedy for acne. Oil of neroli is soothing for dry, sensitive skins as an ingredient of creams and lotions. Also used in many citrus-based cleaning products.

Other name Seville orange.

Left Citrus limon *'Jambhiri'.*

ASTERACEAE

Cnicus benedictus syn. *Carduus benedictus*

Holy thistle

History and traditions It is known as Holy or Blessed Thistle for much the same reasons as the Carline Thistle (*Carlina acaulis*) is named after Charlemagne – it was all down to visions of this plant as a cure for plague. Considering that it does have antiseptic and antibiotic properties, this may not be as far-fetched as it sounds. One writer of a dissertation on treating plague with this thistle said, "I counsell all that have gardens to nourish it, that they may have it always to their own use, and the use of their neighbours that lacke it."

Description The only plant in the *Cnicus* genus, sometimes classified as *Carduus benedictus*. It is an annual with hairy, branched stems, spiny grey-green leaves and solitary yellow flowers set in prickly bracts.

Habitat/distribution A Mediterranean native, it is widely naturalized throughout Europe and North America.

Growth A wild plant, it grows in any ordinary soil, is easily propagated by seed, and self-seeds. Cultivated commercially in Europe for the pharmaceutical industry.

Parts used Whole plant – leaves and flower tops.

USES Medicinal A very bitter herb with antiseptic, antibiotic properties. Taken in the form of an infusion as a tonic and to stimulate the appetite. It was traditionally used for fevers and is said to be helpful for nursing mothers to improve the supply of milk.

Culinary All parts of the plant are edible and have been eaten cooked or in salads.

BURSERACEAE

Commiphora myrrha syn. *C. molmol*

Myrrh

History and traditions Myrrh has long been valued for its medicinal properties and as an ingredient of incense, perfumes and ointments. A symbol of suffering, myrrh was used in embalming from the Egyptian period, and the name comes from an ancient Hebrew and Arabic word, *mur,* meaning bitter. It was one of the gifts of the Wise Men to Jesus Christ at his birth and was used, along with aloes and spices, to embalm his body following the crucifixion.

Description A small tree or shrub, growing to about 3m/10ft tall, with spiny branches and sparse trifoliate leaves, made up of small oval leaflets. The gum exudes from the bark naturally, and after incisions have been made, when it flows out as a pale yellow liquid and quickly hardens to a reddish-brown resin.

Habitat/distribution Native to Arabia, Somalia and Ethiopia, where it grows in desert scrub.

Growth Grows wild.

Parts used Oleo-gum resin – known as *bdellium.*

USES Medicinal Myrrh has antiseptic, anti-inflammatory properties and encourages healing when applied to wounds, ulcers, boils and bleeding gums. Sometimes added to tooth powders. A preparation is made from the bark for treating skin diseases. In parts of Africa some species are chewed as a source of moisture and used for cleaning teeth.

Aromatic An ingredient of incense. It has fixative properties when used in perfumery, and is added to potpourri, in granule or powdered form, to "fix" the scent.

UMBELLIFERAE/APIACEAE

Conium maculatum

Hemlock

History and traditions Poisoning by hemlock was the official method of state execution in ancient Athens. The philosopher Socrates was its best-known victim. It was also used as a medicinal herb in the classical world, mainly for external application. Dioscorides and Pliny, echoed by Avicenna, recommended it for the treatment of skin diseases and cancerous tumours. It appeared in Anglo-Saxon herbals, and an old English myth associated the splotches on the stems with the mark of Cain.

Description A tall, unpleasant-smelling biennial, 1.5–2.4m/5–8ft in height, with purplish-red speckles towards the base of the stems, finely divided, feathery leaves and large umbels of white flowers in midsummer.

Habitat/distribution Indigenous to Europe and parts of Asia, widely distributed in temperate parts of the world and found in damp, weedy places, waste grounds and waysides.

Growth A wild plant in Australia and other countries, cultivation is legally restricted.

Parts used Leaves, seeds.

USES Medicinal Hemlock contains the highly toxic alkaloid, coniine, in all parts, but especially in the seeds. At one time it was used as a sedative and powerful pain-reliever – but its toxicity made this a risky business and it is not used medicinally today.

> **CAUTION** All parts of the plant are highly poisonous, and may also cause skin irritations on contact.

CONVALLARIACEAE
Convallaria majalis
Lily-of-the-valley

History and traditions This pretty cottage garden plant was known to the Anglo-Saxons for its medicinal properties and appeared in early manuscript herbals, including one written in Latin, attributed to Apuleius, AD400. Many of the 16th- and 17th-century herbalists, from Dodoens to Culpeper, took the line that a distillation of the flowers in wine was good for strengthening the memory and comforting the heart. The specific name is a reference to the month of May, when the flowers bloom – or to Maia, Roman goddess of fertility, if you prefer.

Description A hardy perennial with ribbed ovate to lance-shaped leaves and racemes of fragrant white flowers, hanging like little bells, followed by fruits which are round, red berries.

Habitat/distribution Native to Europe, Asia and North America and found in woodlands and alpine meadows.

Growth Prefers humus-rich, moist soil and partial shade. Propagation is easiest by division of the rhizomes in autumn – keep well watered until established and apply a leaf-mould mulch.

Parts used Leaves, flowers.

USES Medicinal It contains glycosides similar to those of foxgloves (*Digitalis* spp.), which affect the action of the heart. It is considered safer than *Digitalis* by some herbal experts and as having less of a cumulative effect.

> **CAUTION** A poisonous plant which should not be eaten. It should be stressed that it is for use by qualified practitioners only.

UMBELLIFERAE/APIACEAE
Coriandrum sativum
Coriander (Cilantro)

History and traditions Seeds of this herb were found in Tutankhamun's tomb of 1325BC. It was known to the Greeks and Romans and features in many medieval herbals – though the authorities were not always in agreement as to its properties. Galen said it was "warm", Dioscorides and Avicenna took it to be "cold". The *Herbarius Latinus,* printed in Mainz in 1484 by Peter Schoeffer, has much to say on the subject. There are recommendations for mixing the juice with houseleek (*Sempervivum tectorum)* and warm vinegar to put on abscesses, for taking it with vinegar soon after dining heavily to "prohibit vapours from rising to the head", and for mixing it with violets for a hangover. If smelled, sniffed or blown up the nostrils, it is claimed, it will restrain a nosebleed, and is effective against St Anthony's fire (erysipelas) and "in tremors of the heart when its powder is given with borage water". William Turner took the strange line that "Coriander taken out of season doth trouble a man's wit with great jeopardy of madness" (*A Newe Herbal,* 1551). From Tudor times until the beginning of this century coriander seeds coated in sugar (comfits) were a popular sweet.

Description An annual 30–60cm/1–2ft tall, with pungent finely divided leaves – the basal ones are pinnatifid (deeply cleft) and wider than the upper ones, which are linear and feathery. Small umbels of white to mauvish flowers are followed by ridged, spherical, pale brown fruits (seeds). There are related species and numerous cultivars, some developed for leaf quality, others for their seeds. A variety with smaller seeds is grown in temperate zones, and one with larger seeds in warmer climates.

Habitat/distribution Originating in northern Africa and the Mediterranean region, it is widely grown in southwest Asia, North and South America and in temperate regions.

Growth A hardy annual, it is propagated from seed sown in spring, preferably *in situ* as it does not transplant well. It succeeds best grown in a well-drained, fertile soil, with ample water in the early stages followed by warmth and sunshine. Young plants quickly run to seed if attempts are made to transplant them in hot, dry spells.

Parts used Leaves, fruits (seeds), essential oil.

Above *The lower leaves are used in cookery.*

USES Medicinal The leaves and seeds have digestive properties and stimulate appetite. The essential oil has fungicidal, antibacterial properties. Decoctions of the seeds are considered helpful in lowering blood cholesterol levels in Indian herbal medicine. Used as an essential oil in aromatherapy for rheumatism.

Culinary The leaves have a stronger, spicier taste than the seeds, which are milder and sweeter. Both are used in curries, pickles and chutneys and in Middle Eastern, Indian, southeast Asian and South American cuisines. Leaves are added to salads, seeds used in sweet dishes, breads, cakes and to flavour liqueurs.

Aromatic The crushed seeds are added to scented sachets and potpourri. The essential oil has fixative properties.

Commercial The essential oil is used in the pharmaceutical, cosmetic and food industries.

Other name Cilantro.

ROSACEAE

Crataegus laevigata

Hawthorn

History and traditions Many superstitions surround this tree, often known as "may", or "mayblossom", for its time of flowering, associations with May Day celebrations and the return of summer. It was considered an omen of both ill and good fortune – unlucky to bring into the house, yet tied outside as a protection from witches, storms and lightning or to stop milk going sour. The strange perfume, with its overtones of decay, contributed to its reputation as an emblem of death and the plague.

Description A deciduous shrub or small tree, growing to 8m/26ft, with thorny branches and small dark green, lobed, ovate leaves. It is densely covered with clusters of white scented flowers with red anthers in spring, followed by red globe-shaped fruit in autumn.

Related species *C. monogyna* is very similar and hybridizes with *C. laevigata*. There are also many ornamental cultivars, some with pink or red flowers, but they lack therapeutic properties.

Habitat/distribution Native to Europe, northern Africa and western Asia, introduced in temperate regions elsewhere. Occurs in hedges and woodland.

Growth A traditional hedging plant, which grows in any soil in sun or partial shade. Propagated from seed, sown in early spring – stratification is necessary for germination.

Parts used Flowers, leaves, fruits.

USES Medicinal An important medicinal herb in Europe, it acts on the circulatory system, strengthens the heart, regulates its rhythm and lowers blood pessure.

Culinary Leaves, sometimes berries, were once eaten in sandwiches, and young shoots cooked in savoury suet puddings.

Other names May, Mayblossom, quickset and quickthorn.

> **CAUTION** Only to be taken on the advice of a qualified herbalist or medical practitioner. Can interact with medication for high blood pressure and heart disorders.

IRIDACEAE

Crocus sativus

Saffron crocus

History and traditions The Greeks called it *krokos,* the Romans *korkum,* and its common name is derived from the Arabic for yellow, *zafran*. In the classical world saffron was appreciated for its scent, flavour, medicinal properties and above all as a luminous yellow dye. In Greece it was a royal colour and in eastern cultures, too, it was reserved for dyeing the clothing of those of high rank or caste. Originating in Persia, it spread to northern India and the Mediterranean by the 10th century. Its popularity in Europe followed the Crusades and it became a valuable trading commodity. So valuable, indeed, that adulteration was always a temptation – but penalties were high. Regular saffron inspections were held in Nuremberg in the 15th century, and records reveal that at least one man was burned in the market place and three others buried alive for tampering with their saffron. Gerard certainly thought highly of its powers: "For those at death's doore," he wrote, "and almost past breathing, saffron bringeth breath again" (*The Herball,* 1597).

Description A perennial, it has linear leaves, growing from the rounded corm. Fragrant, lilac flowers, with deeper purple veins and yellow anthers, appear in autumn. The saffron spice is produced from the three-branched red style.

Habitat/distribution Occurs in southern Europe, northern Africa, the Middle East and India, with major centres of commercial cultivation in Spain and Kashmir, northern India.

Growth Needs well-drained soil, sun and warm summers in order to flower. Plants are sterile and can be propagated only by offsets.

Parts used Flower pistils – dried. It takes over 4,000 flowers to produce 25g/1oz of dried saffron. Cheap or powdered product is often adulterated – the genuine herb is always expensive and should be a dark reddish-yellow in colour.

USES Medicinal Saffron is known to have digestive properties, improve circulation and help to reduce high blood pressure – its high consumption in Spain has been put forward as an explanation for the low incidence of cardio-vascular disease there. It is also the richest known source of Vitamin B². Externally it is applied as a paste for inflamed skin and sores.
Culinary It is widely used as a flavouring and colorant in Middle Eastern and northern Indian cookery, in rice dishes, such as the classic Spanish paella, and fish soups including bouilla-baisse from France. It is also used in sweets and cakes – especially in eastern cuisine, and the traditional saffron cakes and loaves of Cornwall in England.

Above *The dried threads have medicinal and culinary uses.*

Top Crocus sativus *corms.*

CUCURBITACEAE
Cucumis sativus
Cucumber

History and traditions The cucumber is thought to have originated in northern India, where it has been cultivated for at least 3,000 years. It must have been known in ancient Egypt, as it was one of the luxuries missed by the Israelites after they left Egypt to wander in the desert. It was enjoyed by the Greeks and Romans – the Emperor Tiberius ate it every day, according to Pliny. In Britain it was known from the beginning of the 14th century, but not widely grown there before the 16th century. It features in herbals of the period as being helpful in urinary disorders and was recognized for soothing and cleansing the skin. Gerard believed in its cooling properties and advised eating a cucumber pottage daily for three weeks to "perfectly cure all manner of … copper faces, red and shining fierie noses (as red as Roses) with pimples, pumples, rubies, and such like …" (*The Herball*, 1597).
Description A trailing annual (of the same family as marrows, melons and the creeping wayside plant, bryony, *Bryonia alba*), it has lobed triangular leaves and yellow flowers, followed by the familiar cylindrical fruit with its thick green skin, watery, white flesh and white ovate seeds.
Habitat/distribution Cultivated worldwide.
Growth A tender plant, it must be grown under glass in cool, temperate climates. It is propagated from seed and needs rich, well-drained soil, ample moisture and humidity, with a minimum temperature of 10°C/50°F.
Parts used Fruit, seeds.

USES Medicinal Cucumber is a natural diuretic and laxative and has digestive properties. The seeds are high in potassium and beneficial for diseases associated with excess uric acid, such as arthritis and gout. In traditional Indian medicine, juice from the leaf is combined with coconut milk to restore the electrolyte balance when the body is dehydrated following diarrhoea. When applied externally, the flesh of the cucumber has soothing properties for skin irritations and sunburn.
Culinary The vitamins and minerals (vitamin C, small amounts of vitamin B complex, calcium, phosphorus, iron) which cucumber contains are concentrated in or near the skin, so it should not be peeled. It is also best eaten raw, as cooking destroys the potassium and phosphorus content. A popular salad ingredient, and added to yogurt-based condiments such as the Indian *raita*, Greek *tsatsiki* and Turkish *cacik*.
Cosmetic Soothing and refreshing to the skin, a cucumber face mask helps prevent spots and blackheads. Slices of cucumber, placed over closed eyelids, revive tired eyes.

Cucumber face mask

This recipe doubles up as a lotion to relieve sunburn.
½ cucumber, chopped (but not peeled)
15ml/1 tbsp liquid honey
15ml/1 tbsp rose water
15ml/1 tbsp ground almonds

Liquidize all the ingredients to a pulp in a blender or food processor. Smooth over the face and leave for 15–20 minutes, before wiping off with damp cotton wool (cotton balls).

UMBELLIFERAE/APIACEAE
Cuminum cyminum
Cumin

History and traditions Cumin was grown in Arabia, India and China from earliest times. There are descriptions of how it was cultivated in the Bible (Isaiah 28: vv25–27), and the practice of paying it in tithes (a church tax) is referred to in the New Testament. It is mentioned by the Greek physicians, Hippocrates and Dioscorides, and Pliny reports that the ground seed was taken with bread and water or wine as a remedy for "squeamishness". Cumin was a very popular spice in Britain and Europe during the Middle Ages for its strong taste.

Description A half-hardy annual with finely divided, feathery leaves and umbels of very small white flowers. The fruits (seeds) are yellowish brown and ovoid in shape with a distinctive, warm and spicy lingering aroma. The plant is a little like caraway (*Carum carvi*) in appearance, and occasionally confused with it, but quite different in taste.

Habitat/distribution Indigenous to Egypt and the Mediterranean, it is widely grown in tropical and subtropical regions, including northern Africa, India and North and South America.

Growth Grow in a well-drained to sandy soil. Propagated from seed and should be sown under glass in cool temperate regions and transplanted after all frosts. Although it may flower, it is unlikely that fruits will ripen in cool climates.

Parts used Seeds, essential oil.

USES Medicinal Decoctions or infusions of the seeds are taken for digestive disorders, diarrhoea, colds and feverish illnesses. In Ayurvedic medicine it is also used to treat haemorrhoids and for renal colic. The essential oil has antiseptic and antibacterial properties and is applied externally (diluted) for boils and insect bites.

Culinary Widely used in Indian and Middle Eastern cookery to flavour curries, soups, meat and vegetable dishes, bread, biscuits and cheese; and as an ingredient of spice mixtures, pickles and chutneys. There are several species of cumin which produce seeds of varying colour and strength of flavour.

Right *White cumin seeds.*

Left *Black cumin seeds.*

ZINGIBERACEAE
Curcuma longa
Turmeric

History and traditions Turmeric is mentioned in Sanskrit writings and used in Ayurvedic medicine. A native of southeast Asia, it spread across the Pacific, taken by the Polynesians as far as Hawaii and Easter Island. Used as a dye and food flavouring, the generic name is from the word used in ancient Rome for saffron, *korkum*.

Description A perennial, up to 1.2m/4ft tall, it has shiny, lanceolate leaves and dense spikes of pale yellow flowers, enclosed in a sheathing petiole. Grows on a tuberous rhizome.

Growth A tender, tropical plant, it requires well-drained but moist soil, a humid atmosphere and minimum temperatures of 15–18°C/59–64°F. It is propagated by division of the rhizomes.

Parts used Rhizomes – boiled, skinned, dried and ground into bright yellow powder.

USES Medicinal Has antiseptic properties and is anti-inflammatory, antioxidant and cholesterol reducing. Rich in iron, it is helpful in counteracting anaemia.

Culinary An ingredient of Worcestershire sauce and curry powder, adding colour and a musky flavour to meat, vegetable and savoury dishes.

Cosmetic It makes an excellent skin softener and facial conditioner.

> **CAUTION** Only to be taken on medical advice if taking anti-coagulant drugs, such as warfarin, or other medication. Avoid high doses over long periods and excesive sunlight if using topically.

GRAMINEAE/POACEAE
Cymbopogon citratus
Lemon grass

History and traditions Lemon grass did not come to the attention of the west as a medicinal or culinary plant until the modern era. It is now extensively cultivated, in various tropical countries, mainly for distillation of the essential oil, which is used in commercial products. It has also risen in popularity as a culinary herb.

Description A tall, clump-forming perennial, growing to 1.5m/5ft in height, it has linear, grasslike leaves, strongly scented with lemon.

Habitat/distribution Indigenous to southern India and Sri Lanka, found wild and cultivated in tropical and subtropical zones of Asia, Africa, North and South America.

Growth A tender plant, which is grown in fertile, well-drained soil, but needs plenty of moisture and minimum temperatures of 7–10°C/ 45–50°F. In cool temperate climates it must be grown as a conservatory or warm greenhouse plant, and moved outside in the summer.

Parts used Leaves, young stems, essential oil.

USES Medicinal The essential oil has antiseptic properties and is used externally for rheumatic aches and pains, ringworm and scabies. Internally (in doses of a few drops) it is sometimes taken for indigestion and gastric upsets. The diluted oil is useful to relieve itchy skin.

Culinary The young white stem and leaf base are chopped and used in stir-fry dishes. Leaves may also be infused to make tea.

Aromatic The essential oil is used in home fragrance preparations, in commercial perfumery, soaps and cosmetics and as a flavouring in the food and liquor industries.

COMPOSITAE/ASTERACEAE
Cynara cardunculus Scolymus
Group
Globe artichoke

History and traditions The globe artichoke occurs only in cultivation and was probably developed, by selective breeding in the distant past, from the closely related cardoon (also *Cynara cardunculus*). Both were grown as vegetables by the Greeks and Romans. Medieval Arabian physicians, including Avicenna, knew of its medicinal properties (the common name comes from the Arabic *alkharshuf*), but it does not seem to have been widely grown in Europe before the 16th century, when it was introduced to Britain as a culinary delicacy and ornamental plant. Books of the period abound in recipes for boiling, frying, stewing or potting artichokes and making them into a variety of fancy dishes. Sir Hugh Platt (*Delights for Ladies*, 1594) gives instructions for preserving the stalks in a liquid decoction and for storing the heads (known as apples) throughout the winter.

Description A large perennial, growing to 2m/6ft, with long, greeny-grey, deeply cut leaves, downy on the undersides, ridged stems and large thistle-like flower heads with purple florets and a fleshy receptacle (the heart).

Above *The flower heads are a delicacy.*

Habitat/distribution Native to northern Africa and the Mediterranean, found on light, dry soils. Introduced and widely grown elsewhere.

Growth Tolerates some frost, but does not grow well where temperatures are regularly less than -15°C/5°F, or on heavy, waterlogged soil. Needs humus-rich, well-drained soil and a sunny position. Propagate from seed sown in spring, or by division of sideshoots in spring or autumn.

Parts used Leaves – fresh or dry (medicinal), unopened flowerheads (culinary).

USES Medicinal Artichoke is a bitter tonic, it reduces nausea, and is a diuretic. It is used to influence and protect the liver function, and to treat gout.

Culinary The unopened flower heads are boiled and the tips of the scales eaten, dipped in melted butter or sauce. Hearts are eaten cold with vinaigrette, baked or fried. In Greek, Middle Eastern and Indian cuisines, hearts are eaten raw with lemon juice and pepper.

CAUTION May aggravate conditions such as gallstones. Only to be taken medicinally on professional advice.

LEGUMINOSAE/PAPILIONACEAE

Cytisus scoparius
Broom

History and traditions Known in medieval times as *planta genista*, common broom gave its name to the Plantagenet royal line. It was the adopted emblem of the father of King Henry II of England, Count Geoffrey of Anjou, who wore a sprig in his helmet when going into battle. Broom is mentioned in Anglo-Saxon writings and the earliest printed herbals make much of its medicinal powers. Pickled broom-buds were a popular ingredient of Tudor salads.
Description An upright, deciduous shrub, growing to 1.5m/5ft, it has arching, twiggy branches, small trifoliate leaves and is covered in a mass of bright yellow pea flowers in spring.
Related species There are many hybrids and cultivars that are not suitable for medicinal use.
Habitat/distribution A native of Europe and western Asia, found in heathlands, woods and scrublands. Introduced elsewhere.
Growth Grows in any well-drained soil in a sunny position. Propagation is by seed or semi-ripe cuttings, but seedlings do not transplant as well as established container-grown plants.
Parts used Leaves, flowers.

USES Medicinal A herb containing alkaloids, similar to those in the poison strychnine, which affect respiration and heart action.

> **CAUTION** The whole plant is toxic and if eaten leads to respiratory failure. Subject to legal restriction in some countries. For use by qualified practitioners only. It is under statutory control as a weed in Australia.

SOLANACEAE

Datura stramonium
Datura

History and traditions A native of North and South America, this plant was brought to Europe by the Spaniards in the 16th century. It was named "devil's apple" after European settlers in America discovered its narcotic effects, and "jimson weed" after Jamestown, Virginia, where they first found it growing. Also indigenous to India, datura appears in ancient Hindu literature of the Vedic period, when its intoxicant and healing powers were well understood and the seeds were smoked as a treatment for asthma.
Description A tall, bushy annual, 2m/6ft tall, it has strong-smelling, triangular, lobed leaves and large white, or violet-tinged, trumpet-shaped flowers.
Habitat/distribution Indigenous to the Americas and temperate, hilly regions of India, now widely grown in other countries.
Growth A half-hardy annual, it does not tolerate frost. Grows in any light soil and is propagated by seed sown in spring.
Parts used Leaves, flowers, seeds.

USES Medicinal Of the same family as *Atropa belladonna*, it contains similar poisonous alkaloids, including atropine. It has been found useful in mitigating the symptoms of Parkinson's disease and for treating asthma.

> **CAUTION** All parts of the plant are highly poisonous. Subject to legal restrictions in some countries. For use by qualified practitioners only.

CARYOPHYLLACEAE

Dianthus

History and traditions Pinks are of ancient origin; one species is thought to be represented in the murals at Knossos in Crete and there are records that *D. caryophyllus* was cultivated by the Moors in Valencia in 1460. The Elizabethan name for the pink was gillyflower (or "gillofloure"). This included wild and alpine species and the much-prized clove gillyflower, which seems to have covered any clove-scented pinks. By the 17th century there were many cultivated garden varieties, as featured by Parkinson in his *Paradisi*, 1629, with delightful names like 'Master Tuggie's Princesse', 'Fair Maid of Kent' and 'Lusty Gallant'. Some were known as sops-in-wine after the practice of soaking them in wine to flavour it. Herbals and stillroom books are full of recipes for making

Top Dianthus *'Pink Jewel'*.

Above *An old-fashioned pink* D. *'Mrs Sinkins'.*

syrups and conserves of gillyflowers, pickled and candied gillyflowers and wine. According to Gerard, a conserve of clove gillyflowers and sugar "is exceedingly cordiall, and wonderfully above measure doth comfort the heart, being eaten now and then" (*The Herball,* 1597).

Description The leaves of all *Dianthus* are linear, lance-shaped and blue grey or grey green in colour, with a waxy texture. The flowers are pink, white or purple (some bi-coloured) with short tubular bases and flat heads with double or single layers of petals, some with toothed or fringed margins. Old-fashioned varieties often have fragrant, clove-scented blooms but only one flowering period in early summer. (Modern varieties repeat-flower.) Garden pinks are 25–45cm/10–18in high, and alpine species a more compact 8–10cm/3–4in high. All are fully hardy.

Habitat/distribution Found in mountains and meadows of Europe, Asia and South Africa.

Species There are about 300 species, with more than 30,000 hybrids and cultivars recorded. Pinks traditionally grown in the herb garden include *D. deltoides* (Maiden Pink) with cerise, single flowers with toothed petals (to 20cm/8in high) or the more compact *D. gratia-nopolitanus* syn. *D. caesius,* which has very fragrant single pink flowers (to 15cm/6in high) or any of the fragrant old-fashioned pinks such as *D.* 'Mrs Sinkins', with its highly scented dou-ble white flowers and fringed petals. There are also numerous modern pinks, with an old-fash-ioned look, to choose from, such as *D.* 'Gran's Favourite' or the laced *D.* 'London Delight'.

Growth Pinks need a very well-drained neutral to alkaline soil and full sun. In gardens with heavy, clay soils, they can be grown in raised beds to provide sharp drainage. Easily propagated from cuttings of non-flowering shoots in summer or by division in spring or autumn.

Parts used Flowers – fresh or dried.

USES Medicinal At one time thought to have tonic properties, but they are little used today for medicinal purposes.

Culinary Fresh flowers may be added to salads, floated in drinks or crystallized for garnishing cakes and desserts. Before culinary use, remove the bitter petal base.

Aromatic Flowers are dried for inclusion in potpourri and scented sachets. Flowers should be cut when just fully out, the heads twisted off the stems and dried whole.

Other names Pinks, gillyflower, clove gillyflower and sops-in-wine.

Gillyflower vinegar

"Gilliflowers infused in Vinegar and set in the Sun for certaine dayes, as we do for Rose Vinegar do make a very pleasant and comfortable vinegar, good to be used in time of contagious sickness, and very profitable at all times for such as have feeble spirits."

John Evelyn, *Acetaria,* 1719.

Top left D. gratianopolitanus, *known as the Cheddar pink.*

Top centre D. deltoides, *often called the maiden pink.*

Above *A pink-flowering cultivar of* D. *'Mrs Sinkins'.*

Below *Garden pinks, raised from several wild species of dianthus, are a mainstay of the traditional garden. They thrive on an alkaline soil and dislike damp conditions.*

RUTACEAE

Dictamnus albus

Dittany

History and traditions It is called "burning bush" because the whole plant is rich in volatile oil, which can allegedly be set alight as it evaporates, leaving the foliage intact and undamaged. It has a similar lemony, balsamic scent to that of *Origanum dictamnus*, or dittany of Crete, and both plants are probably named after Mount Dicte in Crete. According to Mrs Grieve (*A Modern Herbal,* 1931), *Dictamnus albus* was an ingredient of a number of exotic pharmaceutical preparations available in the early decades of the 20th century, including "Solomon's Opiate", "Guttète Powder", "Balm of Fioraventi" and "Hyacinth Mixture".

Description A clump-forming, aromatic perennial, 40–90cm/16–36in tall, with pinnate leaves, made up of lance-shaped leaflets, and tall racemes of white flowers.

Related species *D. albus* var. *purpureus* has pale pink flowers, striped with darker pink, and is more commonly grown in gardens than the species, but shares its characteristics.

Habitat/distribution Found from central and southern Europe across to China and Korea in dry grasslands and woodlands.

Growth Dittany grows in any well-drained to dry soil in full sun or partial shade. Propagated by seed sown in late summer, in containers and over-wintered in a cold frame. It does not transplant well and is not easy to establish from division.

Parts used Root – dried and powdered.

USES Medicinal It was once prescribed for nervous complaints and feverish illnesses, but is not widely used in Western herbal medicine today. The root bark of a similar species is used in Chinese medicine for its cooling, antibacterial properties.

Horticultural The chief use of this herb today is as an aromatic ornamental in the border or herb garden.

Other name Burning bush.

Above Dictamnus albus *var.* purpureus.

SCROPHULARIACEAE

Digitalis purpurea

Foxglove

History and traditions The foxglove was given its Latin name by the German botanist, Leonard Fuchs, in 1542 (it does not appear in any classical texts). He called it *digitalis,* for its supposed resemblance to fingers (*digit* = finger), and the common name in German, as in several other European languages, is connected with thimbles. Various ingenious explanations have been put forward for what it has to do with foxes: that they wore the flowers on their feet to muffle their tread when on night-time prowls; that it is really from "folksglove" for the "fairy folk"; or from an Anglo-Saxon word *"foxes-glew"* meaning fox-music, for its resemblance to an ancient musical instrument – you can take your pick. Once used in folk medicine for a variety of disorders (despite occasional fatalities), it was its effectiveness as a diuretic against dropsy which led to the discovery of its action on the heart by a Dr Withering, who published his findings in 1785.

Description A biennial or short-lived perennial, reaching 2m/6ft in height. The plant has a rosette of large, downy leaves and spectacular one-sided flower spikes of purple or pink

tubular flowers, with crimson on the inside.

Related species *D. purpurea* f. *albiflora* is a white-flowering form and *D. lanata* has fawn-coloured flowers with purplish-brown veins. Both *D. purpurea* and *D. lanata* contain the active principles, though *D. lanata* is most commonly grown in Europe for the pharmaceutical industry.

Habitat/distribution Occurs throughout Europe, northern Africa and western Asia, mostly on acid soil in grassland and woodland.

Growth Although it will grow in most conditions, it prefers moist, well-drained soil in partial shade, with a mulch of leaf mould. Propagate from seed sown in autumn and overwinter in a cold frame. Self-seeds.

Parts used Leaves – from which the active principles digitoxin and digoxin are extracted.

USES Medicinal The foxglove contains glycosides, which affect the heartbeat, and is used in orthodox medicine as a heart stimulant. It should never be used for home treatment.

> **CAUTION** Foxgloves are poisonous and should not be eaten or used in any way for self-medication. A prescription drug only. Legal restrictions apply.

COMPOSITAE/ASTERACEAE

Echinacea purpurea

Purple coneflower

History and traditions Coneflowers were used by Native Americans as wound-herbs, to treat snakebite and as a general cure-all. The early settlers took to them as home remedies for coughs, colds and a variety of infections.

Description A hardy perennial, 1.2m/4ft high, with a rhizomatous rootstock and ovate-lanceolate leaves. The purplish-pink daisy-like flowers have raised conical centres, made up of prickly brown scales. There are also white-flowered cultivars.

Related species *E. angustifolia* and *E. pallida* are species with similar properties, which were also used by the Native Americans.

Habitat/distribution Native to Central and eastern North America, found in dry prairies and open woodlands. Introduced and grown in other temperate regions of the world.

Growth It prefers well-drained, humus-rich soil and a sunny position or partial shade. Cut back the stems as the flowers fade to encourage a second blooming. Propagate by seed sown in spring, under glass at a temperature of 13°C/55°F, or by division of roots in late spring or autumn.

Parts used Roots, rhizomes – dried, powdered or made into capsules.

USES Medicinal Recent research has shown that echinacea has a beneficial effect on the immune system and stimulates the production of white blood cells – and has been used in treating aids. It has antiviral, antifungal and antibacterial properties and is taken internally in the form of capsules or tinctures, for respiratory tract infections, kidney infections, skin diseases, boils, abscesses and slow-healing wounds. A decoction of the roots is applied externally for infected wounds and skin complaints.

> **CAUTION** Only to be taken on the advice of a herbal or medical practitioner if taking other medication. May interact with pharmaceutical drugs. Not for long-term use.

Left Echinacea purpurea *boosts the immune system.*

BORAGINACEAE

Echium vulgare
Viper's bugloss

History and traditions Early herbalists thought that the stems, speckled with pustules, looked like snakeskin, the fruits like snakes' heads and the flower stamens like snakes' tongues. So, in line with the medieval Doctrine of Signatures (whereby the appearance of a plant indicates what it can cure) *E. vulgare* was considered an antidote to the bite of an adder, and by extension, to anything else that was poisonous. In the words of William Coles, "a most singular remedy against poyson and the sting of scorpions" (*The Art of Simpling*). It was also widely dispensed against "swooning, sadness and melancholy" (Parkinson). A native of Europe, this attractive but invasive plant spread around the world, and became known as a tiresome weed in many countries, notably Australia and North America – where it is known as "blue devil".

Description A bushy, bristly biennial, 60–90cm/ 2–3ft tall, with narrow lance-shaped leaves, spotted, hairy stems and dense spires of bell-shaped, violet-blue flowers in summer, opening from pinkish buds.

Habitat/distribution Native to Europe and Asia, it occurs on poor, stony soils and semi-dry grassland. Introduced to, and widespread in, many countries worldwide.

Growth Grows in any well-drained soil, in full sun. Propagated from seed sown in spring or early autumn.

Parts used Leaves, flowers and seeds (formerly).

USES Medicinal Not used currently in herbal medicine.

Horticultural Traditionally grown in herb gardens for its historical associations.

Other names Blue weed and blue devil.

Left *The stems of* Echium vulgare *were thought to resemble snakeskin.*

CAUTION May cause stomach upsets if ingested and irritate skin on contact.

ZINGIBERACEAE

Elettaria cardamomum
Cardamom

History and traditions This pungent spice was known to the Greeks and Romans and mentioned by Theophrastus, Dioscorides and other classical writers. It features in Chinese medical texts, dating from AD270, and has long been used in Ayurvedic medicine as a treatment for impotency. Cardamom is a traditional ingredient of eastern aphrodisiacs and mentioned in this context in the *Arabian Nights* stories. *Elettaria* is taken from an Indian name for this plant, *elaichi*.

Description A large perennial, 2–2.4m/6–8ft tall, with a clump of long lanceolate leaves, growing from a fleshy rhizome. Flowers arise from the base of the plant, followed by pale green capsules, which dry to a pale yellow, containing many small, pungent black seeds.

Related species There are various species, including black cardamom, a taller plant with large, dark-brown seed capsules, containing small black seeds with a strong eucalyptus aroma.

Habitat/distribution Native to southern India and Sri Lanka, it is also grown in Thailand, Central and tropical South America.

Above *Green cardamom seed pods.*

Growth It needs a minimum temperature of 18°C/64°F, well-drained, rich soil, partial shade, plenty of rain and high humidity. Propagated by seed or division of the rhizomes.
Parts used Seeds, essential oil.

USES Medicinal A warm, stimulating herb, it acts as a tonic and has antidepressant properties. It is also used as a digestive. Seeds are chewed to freshen the breath. Oil of cardamom is antiseptic.
Culinary A major curry spice, the seeds are also used to flavour hot wine punches, sweet, milky rice puddings and egg custard.
Aromatic The pleasant-smelling essential oil is used in perfumery and pharmaceutical products.

Above *Black cardamom.*

EQUISETACEAE
Equisetum arvense
Horsetail

History and traditions The Latin generic name comes from *equus*, a horse, and *seta*, a bristle. In former times this strange-looking, bottle-brush plant was used to clean pewter vessels and scour wooden kitchen utensils – the stems contain silica, which has a polishing action, as well as being a healing agent. In northern counties of England until the 19th century horsetail was commonly employed by milkmaids for cleaning out their pails. The Swedish botanist, Carl Linnaeus, claims that in his country it was eaten by both cattle and reindeer, though inclined to provoke diarrhoea. There are no records as to whether poor Romans, who were reputed to have eaten it (as an ubiquitous asparagus substitute), were similarly affected. Rich Romans, presumably, did not have to put it to the test. Culpeper lists many medicinal uses for horsetail, and declares that "it solders together the tops of green wounds and cures all ruptures in children".
Description A relic from prehistory, closely related to the vegetation which decayed to form modern coal seams, it is a perennial, which grows on a creeping rhizome to about 50cm/20in in height. Brown stems, topped by cones, release spores and then wither, the method of reproduction of this plant being very similar to that of ferns. The mass of branched green stems, with black-toothed sheaths, are sterile.
Habitat/distribution Occurs throughout Europe from the arctic region to the south, also in Asia and China, and is found in moist waste ground. In some countries, where it has been introduced, it is regarded as a pernicious weed.
Growth A hardy plant, it grows in most conditions, although it prefers moist soil and sun or partial shade. It is propagated by division, but is invasive – and it would be wise to take this into account before introducing it into the garden.
Parts used Stems – fresh or dried.

USES Medicinal It has astringent, diuretic properties and is said to be helpful for prostate problems, cystitis and urinary infections, but it can be an irritant, and self-medication is not advised. It is also said to be beneficial, when applied externally, for haemorrhages and ruptured ligaments.
Other names Bottle-brush and paddock pipes.

CRUCIFERAE/BRASSICACEAE

Eruca vesicaria subsp. *sativa*
Rocket (Arugula)

History and traditions Rocket (arugula) has
been a salad herb since Roman times. Its strong,
mustard-like taste is indicated by the generic
Latin name, which comes from *urere,* to burn.
Various claims were made for it in the past as a
painkiller. William Turner said the seed was
effective "against the bitings of the shrew-
mouse and other venemous beasts". Gerard
made the claim that "whosoever taketh the seed
of Rocket before he be whipt, shall be so hardened that he shall easily endure the paines" (*The
Herball*, 1597). Culpeper declared it to be "celebrated against diseases of the lungs" and that
"the juice is excellent in asthmas … as also
against inveterate coughs". But none of this has
stood the test of time and salad rocket (arugula)
is no longer used medicinally.

Description A frost-hardy
annual, 60–100cm/2–3ft tall,
with dentate, deeply divided
leaves. Small, four-petalled,
white flowers, streaked at
the centre of each petal with
violet, appear in late winter to early
summer. Originally a wild plant, rocket
(arugula) has been cultivated for so long
that it is now classified as a subspecies.

Habitat/distribution Native to the
Mediterranean and Asia, introduced and widely
grown elsewhere.

Growth Propagate from seed, sown
successionally, *in situ*, from late winter to early
summer. When grown on poor, dry soil, with
plenty of sun, it has a more pungent taste than
if grown on moist soil in cooler conditions.

Parts used Leaves.

USES Culinary A pungent herb that lends
interest to lettuce and other bland-tasting leaves
as a salad ingredient.

Other name Salad rocket (arugula).

Below Peppery rocket
(arugula) leaves add
interest to salads.

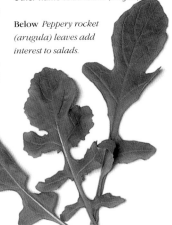

PAPAVERACEAE

Eschscholzia californica
Californian poppy

History and traditions This bright yellow
poppy is the state flower of California. It was
used by Native Americans as a gentle narcotic
and pain reliever, especially against toothache.

Description A hardy annual up to 60cm/2ft
tall, with finely divided, feathery leaves. A mass
of shallow-cupped flowers in orange, yellow,
red and occasionally white appear in early
summer, followed by long curved seedpods.
There is also a wide range of cultivars.

Habitat/distribution Native to western North
America, introduced and widely grown in many
other countries.

Growth Grow this plant in well-drained to poor
soil and full sun. Propagated by seed sown *in
situ* in spring or autumn.

Parts used Whole plant – dried as an
ingredient for infusions and tinctures.

USES Medicinal The Californian poppy is a
sedative herb that relieves pain and it is taken
internally as an infusion, for anxiety, nervous
tension and insomnia. It also has diuretic
properties and promotes perspiration.

CAUTION Only to be taken on professional
advice.

MYRTACEAE
Eucalyptus spp.
Gum tree

History and traditions Eucalyptus trees are native to Australia and were used by the Aborigines in their traditional medicine. They have been widely adopted by other countries, including Africa, the Americas, India and southern Europe, as timber and shade trees, for planting in marshy ground to dry out malaria-inducing swamps, and for their volatile (essential) oil content. Commercial production of eucalyptus essential oils began in Australia in the second half of the 19th century, coinciding with their introduction to the West.

Description Large, fast-growing evergreen trees which grow to considerable heights in warm climates, averaging 70m/230ft, with varying estimates for the record, dating from 1872 between 97m/318ft and 132.5m/434ft. Many have distinctive, rounded juvenile foliage, adult leaves of *E. globulus* and *E. gunnii* are lanceolate, blue grey and studded with oil-bearing glands. Clusters of fluffy cream-coloured flowers appear in summer, followed by globe-shaped fruits.

Species There are over 500 species and all contain antiseptic essential oils, though constituents and properties vary. *E. globulus* (blue gum) has been most widely cultivated around the world and has attractive, juvenile leaves much sought after in floristry. *E. gunnii* is one of the hardiest and most suited to growing in cool temperate regions.

Habitat/distribution: Native to Australia, *E. globulus* is found in moist valleys of New South Wales and Tasmania, *E. gunnii* in Tasmania. All are native to Australia.

Growth *Eucalyptus* spp. vary from tender to fully hardy – but none will stand prolonged low temperatures, especially when immature. *E. globulus* is half-hardy, -5°C/23°F, and *E. gunnii* is frost-hardy, -15°C/5°F. Grow in well-drained soil and full sun. Propagate from seed, sow under cover in spring or autumn.

Parts used Leaves, essential oil.

USES Medicinal Eucalyptus has decongestant, expectorant properties and helps to lower fever. The essential oil is highly antiseptic. Leaf or oil is used in steam inhalations and vapour rubs to ease the symptoms of colds, catarrh, sinusitis and respiratory-tract infections. Essential oil is used in massage oils and compresses for inflammations, rheumatism and painful joints. Used as a tea or tincture to relieve upper respiratory infection.

Above left *Eucalyptus trees are rich in volatile oils.*

Above *Immature foliage of* Eucalyptus gunnii.

Lavender and eucalyptus vapour rub

50g/2oz petroleum jelly
15ml/1 tbsp dried lavender
6 drops eucalyptus essential oil

Melt the petroleum jelly in a bowl over a pan of simmering water. Stir in the lavender and heat for 30 minutes.

Strain the liquid jelly through muslin, leave to cool slightly, then add the eucalyptus oil. Pour into a clean jar and leave to set.

Use as a soothing decongestant rub for throat, chest and back.

COMPOSITAE/ASTERACEAE

Eupatorium

Eupatorium cannabinum
Hemp agrimony

History and traditions The Latin specific name and common name are taken from the words *cannabis* and *hemp*, because of a similarity in the shape of the leaves. Hemp being used for rope fibre, by extension *E. cannabinum* gained the name "holy rope" – a plant with beneficent characteristics was often arbitrarily associated with holiness. But it was never in fact a source of rope and shares none of the properties of *Cannabis sativa*. It has a history of medicinal use as a diuretic, purgative, cure for dropsy, general spring tonic and antiscorbutic (counteracting scurvy). Herbalists in the 17th century also recommended it for healing "fomenting ulcers" and "putrid sores".

Description A woody-based, hardy perennial, up to 1.2m/4ft tall, leaves are opposite and mostly subdivided into 3–5 leaflets. A froth of pinky-white flowers, borne in corymbs (flat-topped flower clusters), appear in midsummer –

giving rise to another of the herb's country names, "raspberries and cream".

Habitat/distribution Indigenous to Europe, found in damp, rich soils, marshy places and fens.

Growth Grow in moist soil, in full sun or partial shade. Propagate by division in spring or sow seed in containers in spring.

Parts used The whole plant – the flowering tops are dried for use in infusions, extracts and other preparations.

USES Medicinal It has long been known for its diuretic properties, as a tonic for debility and a treatment for influenza-like illnesses, but the wider medicinal action of this herb is complex, even contradictory. Recent research suggests that it contains compounds that are capable of stimulating the immune system and combating tumours, but it also contains alkaloids that are potentially dangerous to the liver and in large enough doses could cause liver damage. Externally, it is applied, as in previous times, to ulcers and sores.

Other names Holy rope, St John's herb and ague weed.

Eupatorium perfoliatum
Boneset

History and traditions Boneset was an important herb in the traditional medicine of native Americans, used for fevers, digestive disorders, rheumatism and as a powerful emetic and laxative. It also had magical protective properties assigned to it – infusions were sprinkled to keep evil spirits away. The name has nothing to do with its ability to mend bone fractures, but refers to its efficacy in treating "break bone fever", a virulent flu-like illness, from which the early settlers suffered. It was listed in Dr Griffith's *Universal Formulary* (1859) to be administered in combination with sage and cascarilla bark "for a hectic fever".

Description A tall, hardy perennial, growing to 1.5m/5ft, with lanceolate, rough-textured leaves surrounding the stems (perfoliate), and large clusters of white flowers in late summer.

Habitat/distribution A native of North America in open, marshy regions – introduced in other countries.

Growth Grow in moist soil in full sun or partial shade. Propagate by seed sown in containers in spring or by division in spring or autumn.

Above Boneset in flower.

Parts used Whole plant – dried for use in infusions, extracts and tinctures.

USES Medicinal A popular herb used to manage fevers and infections, taken internally for colds, influenza and bronchitis. It is also thought to stimulate the immune system, as is *E. cannabinum*.

Other names Feverwort, ague weed, thoroughwort, Indian sage, sweating plant.

SCROPHULARIACEAE
Euphrasia officinalis
Eyebright

UMBELLIFERAE/APIACEAE
Ferula assa-foetida
Asafoetida

Eupatorium purpureum
Joe Pye weed

History and traditions Joe Pye is said to have been a traditional healer from New England, with a reputation for successful cures, who swore by *E. purpureum*, using it in his remedies. The name 'gravel root' pertains to the herb's ability to clear urinary stones, for which it is still used today, and the name 'queen of the meadows' is because the massed plants, when in flower, are a truly splendid sight.

Description A handsome hardy perennial which grows to at least 2.1m/7ft tall, with purplish stems, whorls of slender, finely toothed, ovate leaves and dense, domed corymbs of purple-pink flowers in late summer to autumn. It makes a magnificent plant for the border and is often sold as an ornamental.

Habitat/distribution A North American native, found in woodland and grassland on moist or dry soils.

Growth Grows best in moist, well-drained soil in partial shade or sun. Propagated by seed sown in containers in spring, or by division when dormant.

Parts used Rhizomes, roots – dried for use in decoctions and tinctures.

USES Medicinal It has a restorative, cleansing action, mainly used in modern herbal medicine for kidney and urinary disorders, including stone, cystitis and prostate problems. Also used for painful menstruation, rheumatism and gout.

Other names Gravel root, queen of the meadows.

History and traditions The botanical name of this plant comes from the Greek for gladness. It was first introduced as an "eye" herb by Hildegard of Bingen, in 1150. In the 16th century, Fuchs and Dodoens promoted it for eye complaints. The Doctrine of Signatures had a considerable bearing on the matter, as the markings on the little white flower were supposed to resemble a bloodshot eye.

Description An annual semi-parasitic herb, 5–30cm/2–12in in height, it attaches itself to the roots and stems of grasses, absorbing mineral substances from them. Leaves are rounded, toothed and small – 1cm/^{1}/2in long – and the tiny white flowers are double-lipped with yellow throats and dark-purple veins.

Habitat/distribution Native to northern Europe, found also in Siberia and the Himalayas in meadowland and pastures on poor soil.

Growth A wild plant that is difficult to cultivate because of its semi-parasitic habit. If propagation is to be attempted, seeds should be sown near to potential host grasses.

Parts used Whole plant – dried for use in infusions and herbal preparations.

USES Medicinal A herb which reduces inflammation and is said to be helpful, taken as an infusion, for hayfever, allergic rhinitis, catarrh and sinusitis. For external use it is made into washes for sore, itchy eyes and conjunctivitis, or for skin irritations and eczema.

CAUTION May cause eye irritation.

History and traditions The specific name refers to the strong, fetid smell of the gum resin obtained from the roots of this plant. It was valued throughout the Middle Ages as a prophylactic against plague and disease, and a piece was sometimes hung around the neck for this purpose. Asafoetida is still popular in India today as a flavouring and condiment and for its medicinal properties.

Description A herbaceous perennial, growing to 2.3m/7ft, it has a thick, fleshy taproot, finely divided, feathery leaves and yellow flower umbels in summer – and looks like giant fennel.

Habitat/distribution Occurs in western Asia from Iran to Afghanistan and Kashmir, on rocky hillsides and open ground.

Growth It is frost hardy, withstanding temperatures to -5°C/23°F and should be grown in well-drained, reasonably rich soil. Propagated by seed sown in autumn as soon as it is ripe.

Parts used Gum resin – produced from the base of the stems and root crown when the plant is cut down, drying as reddish tears. Sold whole, in powdered form, or as a tincture.

USES Medicinal It has a long tradition of use in Ayurvedic medicine for many complaints, including digestive disorders, respiratory diseases, impotence, painful menstruation, and problems following childbirth, and is said to counteract the effects of opium.

Culinary Despite its strong, sulphurous aroma, when added in small quantities, this herb enhances the flavour of curries and spicy food. The green parts are used as a vegetable.

MORACEAE

Ficus carica

Fig

History and traditions Figs originally came from Caria, a region of modern Turkey, which is the source of the species name. They were widely cultivated in ancient Greece and Rome and there are many references to them in classical writings from Homer to Theophrastus, Dioscorides and Pliny. Greek athletes ate figs to improve their strength and performance and the Romans fed them to their slaves (presumably for similar reasons). In Roman mythology the fig was dedicated to Bacchus and renowned as the tree which gave shelter to the wolf that suckled Romulus and Remus. Figs have been grown in the rest of Europe since they were popularized by the Emperor Charlemagne in the 9th century.

Description A deciduous tree, growing to 10m/33ft with deeply lobed, palmate leaves. The flowers are completely concealed within fleshy receptacles and are followed by small green, pear-shaped fruits, ripening to dark purple, when the flesh surrounding the seeds becomes sweet and juicy.

Habitat/distribution Native to Turkey and southwest Asia, naturalized throughout the Mediterranean region and grown in many warm temperate zones worldwide.

Growth Although fig trees will withstand temperatures to -5°C/23°F, they need some protection from prolonged frost and cold. Warm, sunny summers are necessary to produce good fruit. Grow in well-drained, rich soil in a sunny position, and provide a sheltered place in cool areas. Propagated from semi-ripe cuttings in summer.

Parts used Fruits – fresh or dried.

USES Medicinal Well known for their laxative properties – syrup of figs is a traditional remedy for constipation – they are also highly nutritious, containing vitamins A, C and minerals, including calcium, phosphorus and iron, and are considered restorative and strengthening to the system. The milky juice, or sap, from green figs helps to soften corns and calluses on the skin.

Culinary The fruits are delicious raw, or as a cooked ingredient of sweet pies, pastries, desserts and conserves. Dried figs are stewed, or eaten as they are.

Above *Ficus religiosa.*

Related species

MORACEAE

Ficus religiosa

Peepal

Ficus religiosa is a large, spreading tree with distinctive, broad oval leaves, each tapering to a point. It was while meditating beneath a peepal tree that the Buddha attained enlightenment, and it is revered by both Hindus and Buddhists. In Ayurvedic medicine it is used to treat various diseases, including dysentery and skin disorders.

ROSACEAE

Filipendula ulmaria

Meadowsweet

History and traditions The Dutch named this herb *"reinette"* (little queen) and it is known in several European languages as queen of the meadows. It features in the poetry of Ben Jonson as "meadow's queen" and John Clare celebrates its beauty in his poem "To Summer". It is said to have been Queen Elizabeth I's favourite strewing herb.

Description A herbaceous perennial, on a stout rootstock, 1–1.2m/3–4ft tall, with irregularly pinnate, inversely lance-shaped leaves and dense corymbs of fluffy, creamy flowers in summer. Leaves have a more pleasant, aromatic scent than the sickly, hawthorn-like smell of the flowers.

Habitat/distribution Native to Europe and Asia, introduced and naturalized in North America. Widely grown in temperate regions, in marshlands and meadows, by ponds and streams.

Growth Grow in moist to boggy soil, or by a pond margin, in sun or partial shade – dislikes acid soil. Propagated by seed sown in spring or in autumn and overwintered in a cold frame, or by division in autumn or spring.

Parts used Leaves, flowers – fresh or dried.

USES Medicinal Taken as an infusion for heartburn, excess acidity and gastric ulcers. Also said to be helpful for rheumatism, arthritis and urinary infections.

Aromatic Leaves and flowers, dried, are added to potpourri.

CAUTION Not to be used if allergic to aspirin. May cause gastric upsets.

UMBELLIFERAE/APIACEAE

Foeniculum vulgare

Fennel

History and traditions The Romans enjoyed fennel both as a culinary plant, eating the stems as a vegetable, and for its medicinal properties – Pliny listed it as a remedy for no fewer than 22 complaints. It appears in early Anglo-Saxon texts and European records of the 10th century and was associated with magic and spells, being hung up at doors on Midsummer's Eve to deter witches. It was also used as a slimming aid and to deaden the pangs of hunger. William Coles wrote that it was "much used in drinks and broths for those that are grown fat, to abate their unwieldiness and cause them to grow more gaunt and lank" (*Nature's Paradise* (1650). A use which is still valid today, it may be relevant that the chemical structure of fennel bears certain similarities to that of amphetamines.

Description A graceful aromatic perennial, up to 2m/6ft tall, with erect, hollow stems and mid green, feathery foliage – the leaves are pinnate, with threadlike leaflets. Umbels of yellow flowers are borne in summer, followed by ovoid, ridged, yellow-green seeds. The whole plant is strongly scented with aniseed.

Related species *F. v.* 'Purpureum' has bronze foliage and makes an attractive ornamental. *F. v.* var. *dulce* (Florence fennel, sweet fennel, finocchio) is cultivated for its bulbous, white stem bases.

Habitat/distribution Native to Asia and the Mediterranean, and occurs in much of Europe on wasteland, on dry sunny sites and in coastal areas. Widely naturalized in other countries.

Growth Grow *F. vulgare* and *F. v.* 'Purpureum' in well-drained to sandy soil in a sunny position. Does not always survive severely cold or wet winters, especially if grown on heavy soil. *F. v.* var. *dulce* needs a richer but well-drained soil, and plenty of water to produce the requisite swollen stems, which are blanched by earthing up around them. Propagation is from seed sown in spring.

Parts used Leaves, stems, roots, seeds, essential oil.

USES Medicinal An infusion of the seeds soothes the digestive system, and is said to increase the production of breast milk in nursing mothers as well as being settling for the baby. Also used as a mouthwash for gum disorders and a gargle for sore throats.

Culinary Leaves and seeds go well with fish, especially oily fish, such as mackerel. Seeds lend savour to stir-fry and rice dishes. The bulbous stems of Florence fennel are eaten raw in salads or cooked as a vegetable.

Aromatic The essential oil is used in perfumery, to scent soaps and household products, and as a flavouring in the food industry.

CAUTION Not suitable for pregnant women as in large doses fennel is a uterine stimulant.

Above centre *Fennel foliage.*

Above *F. v.* var. dulce, *florence fennel.*

Fennel tea

Drinking fennel tea can have a good effect when on a slimming regime. Try taking a cup before meals to reduce appetite, or at any time instead of tea or coffee laced with milk and sugar.

250ml/¹⁄₂ pint/1 cup of boiling water
5ml/1 tsp of fennel seeds
¹⁄₂ thin slice of fresh orange

Put the fennel seeds in a cup, crush them lightly and pour over the boiling water. Cover and leave to infuse for 5 minutes. Strain before pouring and add the orange for extra flavour.

Below Wild strawberry leaves are included in blended herbal teas.

ROSACEAE

Fragaria vesca

Wild strawberry

History and traditions The large garden strawberry was not developed until the end of the 18th century by cross-breeding with American species. Until then, wild strawberries were the only kind known, although they were cultivated – when "by diligence of the gardener" the fruits were "as big as the berries of the Bramble in the hedge", as Thomas Hill puts it in *The Gardener's Labyrinth*, 1590. Hill recommended eating them with cream and sugar, or, preferably in his view, with sugar and wine. Old stillroom books give recipes for strawberry teas and cordials, and for beauty aids, such as a face wash of strawberries, tansy and new milk. Culpeper had great faith in the powers of this plant to counteract all manner of disorders, from cooling the liver, blood and spleen, refreshing and comforting fainting spirits and quenching thirst, to washing foul ulcers, fastening loose teeth and healing spongy gums.

Description A low-growing perennial, 25cm/10in tall, which spreads by sending out rooting runners. It has shiny, trifoliate leaves, made up of ovate, toothed leaflets, and small white, yellow-centred flowers, followed by red ovoid fruits with tiny yellow seeds embedded in the surface.

Related species Alpine strawberries are cultivars of the species, *F. vesca*, and have smaller, but more distinctively aromatic fruits.

Habitat/distribution Found in Europe, Asia and North America, in grassland and woodland. Widely grown in temperate and subtropical regions.

Growth Grow in fertile, well-drained soil (on the alkaline side), in sun or partial shade. Propagate by separating and replanting runners – or by seed sown in containers at a temperature of 13–18°C/55–64°F.

Parts used Leaves, roots, fruits.

USES Medicinal Infusions or decoctions of the leaves and root are traditionally recommended for gout, are also taken for digestive disorders and used as a mouthwash to freshen breath. (Leaves of large, garden varieties do not have medicinal properties.) Leaves are diuretic and the fruits are mildly laxative. Preparations made with the fruits can be applied externally for skin inflammations, irritations and sunburn.

Culinary Rich in vitamin C, fruits are eaten fresh or made into desserts, conserves and juices. Dried leaves are included in blended herbal teas to improve taste and aroma.

Cosmetic The wild strawberry fruits have a cleansing, astringent action on the skin and are often added to face masks, skin toners and cleansing lotions.

Strawberry cleansing milk

A soothing lotion suitable for any skin.

225g/8oz fresh, ripe strawberries
150ml/¹/₄ pint/²/₃ cup milk

Mash the strawberries to a pulp and mix with the milk. Pour into a clean bottle and keep in the refrigerator. Apply to the face on pads of cotton wool (cotton balls). Lotion does not keep and should be used within two days.

PAPAVERACEAE
Fumaria officinalis
Fumitory

History and traditions Shakespeare had no high opinion of this plant, referring to it twice as "rank fumitory" – it was one of the "idle weeds" with which King Lear crowned himself when mad, and a plant which grew in "fallow leas", left uncultivated because of war (*Henry V*). *Fumaria* is from the Latin for smoke, *fumus*. Various explanations have been put forward for its application to this plant – from the leaves having a "smoky appearance" to smoke from the plant, when burnt, dispatching evil spirits; or the view, attributed to Pliny, that putting the juice in the eyes makes the tears run to such an extent that it is like being blinded by smoke.

Description An annual herb, 15–30cm/6–12in tall, with trailing stems, small, finely divided grey-green leaves and racemes of tubular, pink flowers from midsummer to autumn.

Habitat/distribution A European native, also found in western Asia and naturalized in North America, occurs on weedy ground, in fields and gardens (once a common cornfield weed).

Growth A wild plant, it will grow in any light soil, in sun or shade. Propagated from seed sown in spring, it also self-seeds readily.

Parts used Whole plant; cut in flower and dried.

USES Medicinal Contains small amounts of similar alkaloids to those found in poppies. Formerly used internally for digestive complaints and externally for eczema, skin disorders and conjunctivitis, but is little used today.

CAUTION Mildly toxic – not for self-medication.

LEGUMINOSAE/PAPILIONACEAE
Galega officinalis
Goat's rue

History and traditions The generic Latin name is said to come from the Greek for milk, *ghala*. The reputation of this herb for increasing the milk supply of cattle and other animals who eat it was established at the end of the 19th century by studies carried out in France. It was, at one time, thought to be helpful in cases of plague and was a favourite choice for fevers.

Culpeper advised that "a bath made of it is very refreshing to the feet of persons tired of over-walking". The common name "goat's rue" is possibly because the crushed leaves have a rank smell.

Description A bushy, hardy perennial, up to 1.5m/5ft tall, with lax stems, pinnately divided leaves and racemes of mauve, white or bi-coloured flowers borne throughout the summer – it makes an attractive plant for the border or herb garden.

Related species *G. offinalis* 'Alba' is a white-flowering cultivar.

Habitat/distribution Native to Europe and western Asia, introduced in other countries, found in moist meadows and pasturelands.

Growth Goat's rue will grow in most soils, but prefers moist conditions, thrives and spreads rapidly in rich, fertile soil. Plant in full sun or partial shade. Propagated from seed sown in spring (soaking seeds overnight, or scarifying them, encourages germination).

Parts used Flowering tops – dried.

USES Medicinal An infusion of the herb is supposed to improve lactation for humans, just as eating the plant does for animals. It also has digestive properties and is said to lower blood-sugar levels, making it helpful for late-onset diabetes.

General High in nitrogen, it makes a useful "green manure" when ploughed into the soil.

Other name French lilac.

Below Galega officinalis *'Alba'*.

RUBIACEAE
Galium

Galium odoratum syn. *Asperula odorata*
Sweet woodruff

History and traditions A strewing herb since medieval times, it is one of many species containing compounds which release coumarin, with its characteristic scent of new-mown hay, as the plant dries. Thomas Tusser called it "sweet grass" and recommended it for making a water to improve the complexion as well as for strewing. Gerard recommended it as a kind of air conditioning: "The flowers are of a very sweet smell as is the rest of the herb, which, being made up into garlands or bundles, and hanged up in houses in the heat of summer, doth very well attemper the air, cool and make fresh the place" (The Herball, 1597). The dried leaves were put into sachet mixtures to deter moths, used to stuff pillows and mattresses and placed between the pages of books.

Description A spreading perennial, growing on a creeping rhizome, about 40cm/16in tall, it has four-angled stems, whorls of rough-textured, lanceolate leaves and a mass of tubular, star-shaped, scented, white flowers in summer.

Habitat/distribution Native to Europe and Asia, also found in northern Africa and naturalized in North America. Found on loamy, nutrient-rich soils in mixed woodland.

Growth Grow in humus-rich soil in partial shade. Propagation is easiest by division of runners in spring or autumn. Can also be grown from seed, sown as soon as ripe in late summer.

Parts used Whole plant – cut when in flower and dried.

USES Medicinal Coumarin gives it sedative properties and infusions are taken for nervous irritability and insomnia. Modern research has found that two of its coumarin molecules join to produce dicoumarol, which prevents blood-clotting and strengthens capillaries, and it is taken internally for varicose veins and thrombo-phlebitis. It is a diuretic and said to improve liver function and have a tonic effect on the system.

Aromatic The coumarin smell intensifies and improves with keeping, so the dried herb is added to potpourri or sachets for the linen cupboard – it helps repel insects.

Galium verum
Ladies' bedstraw

This member of the *Galium* genus has the characteristic four-angled stems and whorls of clinging, bristled leaves, but the flowers are bright yellow and smell of honey. It too emits the sweet, coumarin scent when dry and was much used in the past as a mattress stuffing – hence its popular name. Dioscorides wrote about it as a "milk" plant and it was used in his time and for centuries afterwards as an agent for curdling cheese and colouring it yellow – it does in fact contain a rennin enzyme.

Galium aparine
Goosegrass

This familiar, creeping, clinging plant may look like a tiresome weed (and all too often behave like one) but is not without its uses. It is a traditional springtime tonic in central Europe, taken as an infusion of the fresh green parts, or as a pulped juice, and is said to help eliminate toxins from the system. Some herbalists recommend it for debilitating conditions such as myalgic encephalomyelitis (ME) and glandular fever. It may also be eaten, as a lightly cooked vegetable, as they do in China apparently, and the seeds have even been recommended as a coffee substitute. Gerard's comment was "Women do usually make pottage of cleavers … to cause lanknesse and keepe them from fatnes."

Other name Cleavers.

Above *Ladies' bedstraw.*

ERICACEAE
Gaultheria procumbens
Wintergreen

History and traditions This shrub is the source of the original wintergreen, later extracted from a species of birch, *Betula lenta,* and nowadays mostly produced synthetically. It was used as a tea and medicinally by Canadian Indians for aching muscles and joints. Its Latin name comes from Dr Jean-Francois Gaulthier, who worked in Quebec in the mid-1700s. The leaves were officially in the United States *Pharmacopoeia* until towards the end of the 19th century and wintergreen oil is still listed.

Description A prostrate shrub, 15cm/6in high, it has dark green, glossy, oval leaves and clusters of small, white, drooping, bell-shaped flowers in summer, followed by scarlet berries.

Habitat/distribution A North American native, found in woodlands and mountainous areas.

Growth Grow in a moist soil, on the acid side of neutral, in partial shade. Dividing the rooted suckers is the easiest way to propagate this plant. Semi-ripe cuttings can be taken in summer, or seeds can be sown in containers and overwintered in a cold frame.

Parts used Leaves, essential oil – obtained by distillation of the leaves.

USES Medicinal The leaves contain methyl salicylate, an anti-inflammatory with similar properties to aspirin. The essential oil has anti-septic properties and is used for massaging aches and pains, for rheumatism and arthritis. Infusions of the leaves are used as gargles.

> **CAUTION** The oil is toxic in excess.

GENTIANACEAE
Gentiana lutea
Yellow gentian

History and traditions Gentians are said to be named after a King Gentius of Illyria (an ancient country of the East Adriatic), who was credited by Pliny and Dioscorides as having been the first to recognize its medicinal properties. In the Middle Ages it was popular as a counter-poison and the German physician and botanist Hieronymus Bock in his *Neue Kraüter Buch,* 1539, refers to the use of the roots in dilating wounds. Nicholas Culpeper, inventive as ever, recommends it as a healing decoction for cows unlucky enough to be bitten on the udder by venomous beasts. It is not certain which species were used in former times, but *G. lutea* has proved to be the most important from a medicinal point of view. In former times gentian wine was taken as an aperitif.

Description A hardy herbaceous perennial, it grows on a thick taproot, to a height of 1–2m/3–6ft. Erect stems have fleshy, ribbed leaves in pairs, joined at the base, and bright yellow flowers, with short, tubular petals, borne in clusters in the leaf axils. It usually flowers about three years after planting.

Habitat/distribution Native to Europe and western Asia. Found in mountainous pastures and woodlands.

Growth Grow in well-drained, humus-rich soil, in sun or partial shade, and keep fairly moist – heavy, waterlogged soil is likely to induce root rot. Propagated by division or offshoots in spring, or by seed sown in autumn.

Parts used Roots, rhizomes – dried for use in decoctions, tinctures and other preparations.

USES Medicinal The most bitter of herbs, yellow gentian has been used in tonic medicines for centuries. It is said to be anti-inflammatory and to reduce fevers and is taken internally for digestive complaints and loss of appetite.

General An ingredient of commercially produced tonics and bitter aperitifs.

> **CAUTION** It should not be used without advice from a qualified practitioner, as it could have adverse effects on some gastric disorders. Not to be taken by anyone with high blood pressure, or by pregnant women. Avoid long-term use internally and externally due to high tannin content.

GERANIACEAE
Geranium maculatum
Cranesbill

History and traditions The common name
refers to the beak-like shape of the fruit, and
the generic name is from the Greek word
for a crane, a stork-like bird with a long bill.
The leaves become distinctively speckled as they
age, and the specific name *maculatum* means
spotted. Traditionally used in the folk medicine
of Native Americans, it was at one time listed in
the United States *Pharmacopoeia*.

Description A hardy, clump-forming perennial,
it grows to 75cm/30in and has deeply divided
palmate leaves. Large, round,
purple-pink flowers appear in
the axils in late spring to early
summer, followed by the
beak-shaped fruits.

Left Geranium
sanguineum,
*(Bloody
Cranesbill)*

Related species *G. robertianum* (herb Robert)
is a common wild plant, growing to 50cm/
20in, with a creeping decumbent habit and
soft, downy, reddish stems. Leaves have three
pinnately-lobed leaflets and small five-petalled,
rose-pink flowers, striped in white. It gives off
an unpleasant smell when crushed.

Habitat/distribution *G. maculatum,* native to
North America, and found in a variety of
habitats. Widely grown in temperate regions
elsewhere. *G. robertianum* is native to Europe,
North America, Asia and northern Africa in
poor, dry soils.

Growth *G. maculatum* prefers moist soil and
a sunny position or partial shade. Most easily
propagated by division in early spring or late
winter, seeds may be sown in spring or autumn.
G. robertianum is a wild plant and grows best
in poor, dry soil.

Parts used *G. maculatum* – whole plant, roots
– dried for use in infusions, powders, tinctures
and other preparations.

USES Medicinal *G. maculatum* is an astringent
herb, which is said to control bleeding and
discharges. It was formerly used in the treatment of diarrhoea, dysentery and cholera.
Externally it is applied to wounds and used
as a gargle for sore throats and mouth ulcers.

Other names American cranesbill and
spotted cranesbill.

CAUTION Avoid long-term use.

Above Geranium robertianum.

ROSACEAE
Geum urbanum
Wood avens

History and traditions The medieval
name was *herba benedicta*, or the blessed
herb, for its supposed ability to repel evil
spirits – and the second part of one of its
common names, herb bennet, is a contraction
of *benedicta*. The three-part leaf and the
five petals of the flower supposedly represented
the Holy Trinity and five wounds of Christ,
and it appears as a carved decoration in
13th-century churches. As a medicinal herb,
there were rules laid down as to the time and
season for digging up the root for maximum
efficacy, and it was included in cordials to be
taken as a plague preventive.

Description A rather undistinguished, hardy
perennial plant, growing from 20–60cm/
8–24in, with downy stems, three-lobed leaves
and tiny, yellow, five-petalled flowers in summer,
followed by fruits with brown, hooked bristles.

Habitat/distribution Native to Europe and
found in wasteland, hedgerows and woodlands
on moist, high-nitrogen soils.

Growth A wild plant, it grows best on rich,
moist soils and self-seeds freely.

Parts used Whole plant, roots – the flowering
tops are dried for use in infusions, roots used
fresh or dried in decoctions.

USES Medicinal Another herb with astringent
properties resulting from the high levels of
tannins in the plant. *Geum* is indicated for the
treatment of diarrhoea.

Culinary The roots were formerly used for their
supposed clove-flavouring in soups and ale.

Other name Herb bennet.

ROSACEAE
Gillenia trifoliata
Indian physic

History and traditions A medicinal plant of Native Americans with emetic, purgative properties. Also known as "bowman's root", for its wound-healing effects, and "American ipecacuanha". The early colonists adopted it and it was formerly listed in the United States *Pharmacopoeia*.

Description A graceful hardy perennial, growing to 1m/3ft, with red-tinged, wiry stems, bronze-green, three-palmate leaves and irregularly star-shaped flowers, with narrow white petals and red-tinted calyces.

Habitat/distribution Native to eastern North America, found in moist woodlands, introduced and widely grown as a garden plant in Europe and temperate regions.

Growth Grow in humus-rich, moist soil in partial shade. Propagated by division in spring or autumn, or by seed sown in autumn in containers and overwintered in a cold frame.

Parts used Root bark – dried for use in decoctions and powders.

USES Medicinal It is used as a purgative and expectorant.

Right Gillenia trifoliata.

GINKGOACEAE
Ginkgo biloba
Ginkgo

History and traditions Identical in appearance to tree fossils 200 million years old, ginkgo has always been a sacred tree in China – it was grown for centuries in temples, some specimens reaching a great age, with circumferences up to 9m/29ft. It has been cultivated in Europe since the early 18th century with seeds brought from China or Japan. The seeds have long been used in traditional Chinese medicine, and modern research has discovered constituents in the leaves of potential therapeutic importance, unknown in any other plant species.

Description There is only one species in the genus. A deciduous tree growing to 40m/130ft, it has lobed, fan-shaped leaves (similar in appearance to maidenhair fern foliage, but larger), which turn yellow in autumn. Flowering takes place after 20 years, with male and female flowers and fruits borne on separate trees.

Male trees have an earlier leaf-fall and less spreading form; female fruits have a rancid smell when fallen. Ginkgo is a very robust tree and suffers from few pests, tolerates pollution or a salty atmosphere well.

Habitat/distribution Originating in China and Japan, it is no longer found in the wild, but is cultivated as specimen and shade trees, and now widely grown in other countries.

Growth Fully hardy, it does best in well-drained but fertile soil and a sunny position. Propagated from seed sown in containers in autumn or from cuttings taken in summer. It should not be pruned as this leads to die-back.

Parts used Leaves – picked in autumn and dried. Seeds – used in decoctions.

USES Medicinal The leaves have recently been discovered to contain compounds called ginkgolides. Gingko leaf promotes blood flow and inhibits allergic reactions. The seeds have anti-fungal and antibacterial properties, and are used in Chinese medicine for asthma and coughs.

Culinary Ginkgo nuts (the female fruits with the outer unpleasant layer removed) are roasted and sometimes served in Chinese cuisine.

General Seeds produce oil, which may cause dermatitis in sensitive people, and leaves contain insecticidal compounds.

CAUTION Only to be taken on the advice of a qualified herbalist or medical practitioner. Can interact with pharmaceutical drugs, including anti-coagulants, such as warfarin. May cause headaches and gastric upsets. Not for long-term use.

LEGUMINOSAE/PAPILIONACEAE
Glycyrrhiza glabra
Liquorice

History and traditions Liquorice has been valued for thousands of years for the sweetness of its root (it contains glycosides, including glycyrrhizin, that are 50 times sweeter than sugar) and for its medicinal powers. The generic name is from the Greek *glykys* (sweet) and *rhiza* (a root). This became corrupted to "*gliquiricia*" and thence to "liquorice". The Egyptians put it into funeral jars and some was found in the burial chamber of Tutankhamun. The Chinese believed it was rejuvenating and gave them long life and strength. Roman legionnaires chewed it on the battlefield – a habit taken up by Napoleon, who believed it had a calming effect on the nerves. It did not reach Europe until the 15th century, when it soon became established as a remedy for many ailments, including coughs, chest infections and digestive disorders. In 1760 a Pontefract apothecary, George Dunhill, thought of adding sugar and flour to the liquorice essence to produce the well-known confectionery. Liquorice confectionery is still made from the plant and it is an ingredient of

Above *The dried roots are used in medicinal preparations and to make confectionery.*

many pharmaceutical products, with principal centres of commercial cultivation in Russia, Spain and the Middle East.

Description A hardy perennial, growing up to 1.2m/4ft, the leaves are pinnate, divided into 9–17 oval leaflets; the violet, pea-like flowers are borne in short racemes, followed by long seed pods.

Related species *G. lepidota* is a North American wild species of liquorice, used by Indian tribes to ease childbirth.

Habitat/distribution Originally from the Middle East, Asia and China, it is now cultivated in temperate regions worldwide, including parts of Australia, North and South America.

Growth It requires a deep, rich, moisture-retentive soil and a sunny position. Propagated by division of roots in autumn or spring. Germination from seed is slow. To encourage strong root growth, remove flower heads.

Parts used Roots – lifted in autumn, when plant is 3–4 years old, and dried for use in decoctions, liquid extracts and powders. Roots are boiled to extract the essence used in confectionery.

USES Medicinal An important herb in Ayurvedic medicine for stomach disorders, sore throats, respiratory infections and as first aid for snake or scorpion bites. In Chinese herbal medicine, it is used for sore throats and food poisoning. It has soothing anti-inflammatory properties and is added to proprietary cough mixtures, lozenges and laxatives. Liquorice root should not be used for self-medication.

General As well as being used in confectionery production, liquorice is used to flavour beers and tobacco, and is employed in the manufacture of shoe polish, plastics and fibreboard.

CAUTION Avoid high dosages for prolonged periods without professional advice. Do not use with digoxin, diuretics, laxatives and other drugs that may reduce potassium. Seek help if taking prescribed medication.

HAMAMELIDACEAE
Hamamelis virginiana
Witch hazel

History and traditions Native American tribes used decoctions of the bark to reduce swellings and bruises. Colonists took note and it was listed in the United States *Pharmacopoeia* from 1860 onwards. It was also thought to have supernatural properties and the forked branches were used as divining rods in the search for water and gold.

Description A deciduous tree or shrub, up to 5m/16ft in height, it has smooth brown bark and obovate leaves. Clusters of fragrant, yellow flowers appear in late autumn to early winter.

Habitat/distribution Native to North America, now widely cultivated in other countries as a garden ornamental.

Growth A hardy shrub, it requires moderately fertile, moist but well-drained soil and a sunny or partially shady position. Propagation is from seed sown in containers in autumn.

Parts used Twigs – cut after flowering, to make the distilled extract. Bark – used in tinctures and extracts. Leaves – dried for use in powders, liquid extracts, ointments.

USES Medicinal Distilled witch hazel is available for external use on bruises and sprains. The tincture is much stronger and should be used only under the guidance of a qualified practitioner. Witch hazel extract is a constituent of proprietary haemorrhoid ointments and other pharmaceutical preparations.

COMPOSITAE/ASTERACEAE
Helianthus annuus
Sunflower

History and traditions The sunflower originated in the Americas, probably Mexico. There is evidence that before 1000BC it was grown there for its seeds. It was among the many plants introduced to Europe from the New World in the 16th century, but did not become a major food plant and source of oil until large-scale cultivation began in Russia two centuries later (by the 1970s it was second only to soya bean as an oil crop). At some point it gained a reputation for being antimalarial and was used in Russian folk medicine for reducing fevers. The common name is a translation of the generic term, which is taken from the Greek for sun, *helios*, and flower, *anthos* – both for its sunlike appearance and because it turns its head to follow the sun's direct rays.

Description A tall, impressive annual, up to 3m/10ft in height, with erect stems and oval, hairy leaves. The showy daisy-shaped flower heads, up to 30cm/1ft across, have bright yellow ray florets, and brown disc florets at the centre, followed by the striped black-and-white seeds, about 1,000 per head.

Habitat/distribution Native to Central, North and South America, introduced and widely grown in Europe and other countries in open sunny sites.

Growth A hardy annual which tolerates most soils, as long as reasonably well-drained. Propagate by seed sown in spring.

Parts used Whole plant – cut when flowering begins for use in extracts and tinctures. Seeds are collected when ripe in autumn, and used fresh or pressed to produce a fatty oil.

USES Medicinal Sunflower seeds and oil are a good source of vitamin E, which has anti-oxidant properties. They are high in polyunsaturates, especially linoleic acid, needed for the maintenance of cell membranes – they also help lower blood cholesterol levels. Formerly, preparations made from the seeds were used for treating coughs and bronchial infections, applied externally to bruises and for easing rheumatic pains.

Culinary Seeds are eaten fresh or roasted in salads, bread and bakery products. Oil is used for cooking and in salad dressings. Also a constituent of margarine.

Above Helianthus annuus *'Velvet Queen' is an attractive cultivar.*

COMPOSITAE/ASTERACEAE

Helichrysum italicum syn.

H. angustifolium

Curry plant

History and traditions A native of southern Europe, it seems to have crept into modern herb gardens, where it is now firmly established, because of the popular name, curry plant, relating to its strong smell. But it is not a culinary plant and has nothing to do with curry – or curry leaves (see *Murraya koenigii*). It is one of the "everlasting" flowers (most of which have a papery texture and retain form and colour when dried). It justifies its position as a herb because it is included in potpourri and has insect-repellent properties.

Description An evergreen subshrub, 60cm/ 2ft in height, it has linear, silver-grey leaves and clusters of yellow button-shaped flowers in summer.

Habitat/distribution Native to the Mediterranean and grown throughout Europe, other species occur in Africa and Asia.

Growth Although frost hardy, it does not tolerate prolonged cold, wet winters. Grow in light, well-drained soil in full sun. Propagated by semi-ripe or heel cuttings in summer.

Parts used Leaves, flowers.

USES Aromatic Dried flowers and foliage may be added to potpourri and insect-repellent sachet mixtures. The essential oil is said to be antiviral, but it is not confirmed.

CANNABACEAE

Humulus lupulus

Hops

History and traditions The hop plant was described by Pliny, who named it "*lupus salictarius*", or "willow wolf", for its habit of twining round willow stems and strangling them "as a wolf does a lamb". The Romans ate the young shoots as vegetables. Its major signifi- cance was that it changed the character of beer, acting as a preservative and giving it a bitter flavour. It was first used for this in Flanders in the 14th century, but there was great opposition to it in Britain, where it was thought to "spoil" the traditional ales, so it was not in general use there before the 17th century. Even then John Evelyn wrote, "Hops transmuted our wholesome ale into beer. This one ingredient … preserves the drink indeed, but repays the pleasure in tor- menting diseases and a shorter life" (*Pomona*, 1670). But it did become established as a medi- cinal plant and Culpeper's view was that a "decoction of the tops cleanses the blood, cures the venereal disease, and all kinds of scabs, itch, and other breakings out of the body; as also tetters, ringworms, spreading sores, the morphew, and all discolourings of the skin".

Description A hardy, twining, herbaceous climber, it has clinging hairy stems and 3–7 lobed palmate leaves. Male and female flowers are borne on different plants – the male ones are in small inconspicuous clusters, the female in conelike, pale green inflorescences, which are the hops used in beer making.

Related species *H. lupulus* 'Aureus' has golden-green foliage and it makes an attractive and vigorous ornamental climber for the herb garden.

Habitat/distribution Its country of origin is not certain, but it is found in Europe, western Asia and North America and widely distributed in northern temperate zones. Naturalized in woodland and hedgerows.

Growth Prefers moist, fertile, well-drained soil and a sunny position or partial shade, but is a vigorous plant that grows under most conditions. Propagated by softwood cuttings in spring.

Parts used Female flowers (cone-like) – dried; oil distilled from flowers; fresh young shoots.

USES Medicinal Has sedative, digestive and antibacterial properties. Taken internally in infusions or tinctures for insomnia, nervous tension and anxiety; used externally for skin complaints.

Culinary Young shoots can be cooked and eaten like asparagus.

Aromatic Dried flowers are added to sleep pillows, distilled oil used in perfumes. Thought to help prevent ageing of skin and brittleness of hair. Flowers or essential oil are included in rejuvenating baths and hair treatments.

General Flowers (hops) used to flavour beers and ales, distilled oil and extracts used in the food industry.

CAUTION Avoid in pregnancy and depression.

Above Humulus lupulus *'Aureus', golden hops.*

RANUNCULACEAE

Hydrastis canadensis

Golden seal

History and traditions This was once a very common herb in North America, its orange root being variously used to make a yellow dye, in medicinal remedies for digestive problems, bruises and swellings and also as an insect repellent. Early settlers were impressed by its properties and it was listed in the United States *Pharmacopoeia* from 1831 to 1936. Its continued popularity has led to overexploitation: it is now rare in the wild, from which all trade supplies come (cultivation is difficult).

Description A hardy perennial, 20–30cm/ 8–12in in height, it has a thick, knotted, yellow rhizome, palmate, deeply lobed leaves, and single greenish-white flowers, with no petals, in late spring to early summer. Fruits are red and raspberry-like, but inedible.

Habitat/distribution Native to north-eastern North America, found in damp forests.

Growth It requires moist, humus-rich soil and a shady position. Propagation is by seed sown in autumn, though germination is slow and erratic, or by division in early spring or late autumn. Plants do not establish easily.

Parts used Rhizome – dried for use in tinctures, decoctions and pharmaceutical preparations.

USES Medicinal It has anti-inflammatory properties, helps to check bleeding, is also antibacterial, decongestant and mildly laxative. Popular in North America for boosting the immune system, taken as a tea in combination with other herbs, such as *Echinacea purpurea*.

CAUTION This plant is poisonous in large doses. It should not to be taken if pregnant, breast-feeding, or by anyone with high blood pressure.

SOLANACEAE

Hyoscyamus niger

Henbane

History and traditions This is a poisonous herb with a long history. It appears in the works of Dioscorides, Pliny and other classical writers as a sleep-inducing and pain-relieving drug and is mentioned in Anglo-Saxon herbals under the name of "Henbell". In Greek mythology the dead, consigned to the underworld kingdom of Hades, were crowned with wreaths of henbane. Its narcotic properties, inducing giddiness and stupor, made it a sought-after herb for witches' brews and sorcerers' spells. It is thought to have provided the "leprous distillment" poured into the ear of Hamlet's father as he lay sleeping. Seventeenth-century herbals recognized its deadly nature, recommending it for external use only, and dental practitioners of the time burned seeds of henbane in chafing dishes to produce analgesic fumes as they treated their patients.

Description An annual or biennial, growing to 60–90/cm/2–3ft, it has a rank, unpleasant smell and coarsely toothed, grey-green, sticky leaves. Bell-shaped, creamy-yellow flowers, veined with purple, grow from the leaf axils and appear throughout the summer, followed by fruit capsules containing many seeds.

Habitat/distribution Probably originated in the Mediterranean region, now widely distributed in Europe and Asia, found in sandy waste ground and coastal sites.

Growth Grow in poor, stony or sandy soils. Propagated from seed sown *in situ* in spring, often self-seeds.

Parts used Leaves, flowering tops – dried for use by the pharmaceutical industry.

USES Medicinal It contains toxic alkaloids hyoscyamine, hyoscine and atropine (as in *Atropa bella-donna*) which affect the central nervous system. These constituents are included in some pharmaceutical drugs for asthma and nervous disorders. Also for muscle spasms and tremors as suffered in senility and diseases associated with old age.

Other name Hogbean.

CAUTION All parts are highly poisonous. Henbane is for use by qualified practitioners only and should never be used for self-medication. Legally restricted in some countries.

GUTTIFERAE/CLUSIACEAE

Hypericum perforatum

St John's wort

History and traditions This is a herb that has attracted a wealth of folklore over the centuries and been ascribed many magical and mystical properties. It is named after St John the Baptist, the red pigment, hypericin, which exudes from the crushed flowers signifying his blood. It is in full flower on St John's Day, 24 June, which also coincides with northern hemisphere midsummer rituals, and it was ascribed the power to drive away ghosts and witches and protect from thunderbolts and lightning. Many superstitions surrounded it, including gathering it on St John's Eve with the dew still on it in order to find a husband, or as a childless wife, gathering it naked to ensure a speedy conception. It has, in fact, been discovered recently to be an effective antidepressant, without the side effects of conventional drugs. In Germany it has a medical licence and has been widely prescribed for depressive states, outselling Prozac eight times over. But as with many beneficial plants, there are contra-indications which should be taken into account (see **CAUTION**).

Description It is a hardy perennial, about 30–60cm/1–2ft in height; the stems are erect, woody at the base, with small linear-oval leaves, dotted with glands, which can be seen as little pinpricks when held up to the light. The flowers have five petals, edged with glands.

Habitat/distribution A native of Europe and temperate Asia, found in woodlands, and in hedgerows on semi-dry soils. Naturalized in America and Australia.

Growth Grow in well-drained, dryish soil in full sun or partial shade. Propagation by division is the easiest method; it can also be grown from seed sown in spring or autumn, and spreads rapidly once established.

Parts used Flowering tops – fresh or dried for use in infusions, creams, oils, and as liquid extracts for use in pharmaceutical preparations.

USES Medicinal It is said to have calming properties. Infusions are taken for anxiety and nervous tension. It also has antiseptic and anti-inflammatory properties and promotes healing; creams and infused oils are applied to burns, muscular pain, neuralgia and sciatica.

Above *The flowers of* Hypericum perforatum *contain the active principle hypericin.*

St John's wort oil

To make an infused massage oil to help ease inflammation and joint pain:

25g/1oz flowering tops of St John's wort
600ml/1 pint/2½ cups sunflower oil

Put the flowering tops into a bowl and crush them lightly. Pour in the oil. Stand the bowl over a pan of barely simmering water and heat gently for 1 hour. Strain off the herb by pouring it through muslin fixed over a jug, then transfer to a clean, airtight bottle.

CAUTION May interact with pharmaceutical drugs. Only to be taken on medical advice if on other medication. Can cause sensitivity to sunlight. Harmful if eaten, poisonous to livestock, statutorily controlled in some countries.

LABIATAE/LAMIACEAE

Hyssopus officinalis

Hyssop

History and traditions The name is an ancient one – it is virtually the same in all European languages and comes from the Greek, *hyssopos*. In Hebrew it is *ezob*, meaning a "holy herb", though it is not certain whether the hyssop we know is the plant referred to in the Bible. Hippocrates and Dioscorides rated it highly as a medicinal herb, recommending it for respiratory disorders – as it is still used in herbal medicine today. Its strong, aromatic smell meant it was suitable for strewing in rooms in the house – and is included for this purpose in Thomas Tusser's list (*Five Hundred Points of Good Husbandry,* 1580). It frequently featured in designs for knot gardens of the 17th century, was a popular culinary herb used in "pottages" (soups) and salads, and was taken as a tea, or made into syrups and cordials for coughs and colds. It was one of the original ingredients of the liqueur, Chartreuse.

Description Classed as a semi-evergreen, because it loses some foliage in winter, mainly if weather is severe. It is a bushy perennial, about 60–90cm/2–3ft high. The stems are woody at the base with small, dark green, linear leaves and dense spikes of deep blue flowers in late summer, which are very attractive to bees. There are also forms with pink and white flowers.

Habitat/distribution Native to the Mediterranean region and western Asia, found on dry, rocky soils. Introduced and widely grown throughout Europe and North America.

Growth Grow in well-drained to dry soil in a sunny position. Propagated by seed sown in spring, or by cuttings taken in summer. Prune back hard in spring to prevent it becoming straggly (it will regenerate from the old wood).

Parts used Leaves, flowers – fresh or dried.

Above left *Hyssop flowers add colour to the garden in mid to late summer.*

Above *The leaves have a pungent flavour, popular in Elizabethan culinary dishes.*

USES Medicinal Hyssop has expectorant properties, promotes sweating and is anti-catarrhal and antibacterial. Infusions are taken for coughs, colds and chest infections.

Culinary The leaves have a strong, slightly bitter flavour and may be added to soups and cooked meat and vegetable dishes with discretion. The attractive blue flowers make a pretty garnish for salads.

Old recipes for hyssop

• A Water to Cause an Excellent Colour and Complexion: Drink six spoonfuls of the juice of Hyssop in warm Ale in a Morning and fasting. From *The Receipt Book of John Nott,* cook to the Duke of Bolton, 1723.

• To Make Syrup of Hysop for Colds: Take an handful of Hysop, of Figs, Raysins, Dates, of each an ounce, French Barley one ounce, boyl therein three pintes of fair water to a quart, strain it and clarifie it with two Whites of Eggs, then put in two pound of fine Sugar and boyl it to a Syrup.

The Queen's Closet Opened, W. M., cook to Queen Henrietta Maria, 1655.

COMPOSITAE/ASTERACEAE
Inula helenium
Elecampane

History and traditions It is said to be named after Helen of Troy, who was gathering this herb when abducted by Paris, or, according to another version, it grew from her tears on the same occasion. In any case it is an ancient herb, well known to the Greeks and Romans, who ate it as a bitter vegetable and digestive after a heavy meal. They also appreciated its medicinal properties – Galen recommended it for sciatica and Pliny thought that the root "being chewed fasting, doth fasten teeth". It appears frequently in Anglo-Saxon medical texts and in the writings of Welsh physicians of Myddfai in the 13th century. It remained popular in folk medicine as a cough and asthma remedy over the centuries, and was grown in cottage gardens. The roots were often candied and old herbals contain many recipes for conserves, cough remedies and tonics made of this plant. John Lindley in his *Flora Medica*, 1838, remarks, "The plant is generally kept in rustic gardens, on account of many traditional virtues."

Description A hardy perennial, with tall, erect, softly hairy stems, to 2/m/6ft in height, it has ovate, pointed leaves, toothed at the edges, and terminal yellow flower heads, shaped like shaggy daisies, in late summer.

Habitat/distribution Native to southern Europe and western Asia, naturalized in North America, introduced elsewhere in warm and temperate zones. Found on damp soils, near ruins, in woodland and field edges.

Conserve of elecampane root

Cleanse and scrape the root. Cut them into thin round slices, letting them soke in water over the hot embers … boil them till all the liquor be wasted. Beat them in a stone mortar, very fine. Boyle the whole with a like weighte of honey or sugar two or three times over. All other roots may in like manner be candied … but far pleasanter in the eating if to the confection a quantity of cinnamon be added. Candy the roots in October.
From *The Gardener's Labyrinth*, by Thomas Hill, 1577.

Growth Grow in rich, moist soil in a sunny position. Propagated by division of roots in spring or autumn, or by seed, which may be slow to germinate.

Parts used Roots, flowers – fresh or dried.

USES Medicinal The constituents of this herb include up to 40 per cent insulin. But its chief use in herbal medicine is for coughs, hay fever, asthma, catarrh and respiratory infections, taken as infusions or decoctions (these must be filtered to exclude irritant fibres). Elecampane is also said to have a beneficial effect on the digestion when taken internally. Applied externally it is said to relieve many skin inflammations and irritations and has sometimes been recommended as an embrocation, or rub, for the relief of sciatica and neuralgia.

> **CAUTION** Not to be taken in pregnancy or while breastfeeding. May cause allergic reaction or gastric upsets.

Iris germanica var. *florentina*

Orris

History and traditions Orris, taken directly from the Greek *iris*, is the name for the powdered rhizome of the Florentine iris, which has been valued since ancient Egyptian times for its faint violet scent and fixative properties in perfumery and potpourri. During the 18th century it was incorporated in many cosmetic powders for wigs, hair and teeth. This variety of iris has been associated with Florence, in Italy, since the 13th century, when it was first cultivated there on a large scale, and can still be seen on the city's coat of arms.

Description A hardy perennial, growing on a stout rhizome, 60–90cm/2–3ft tall, with narrow, sword-shaped leaves. Flowers are white, with outer petals mauve-tinged and yellow-bearded, or occasionally pure white.

Habitat/distribution Native to southern Europe, naturalized in central Europe, the Middle East and northern India, introduced elsewhere. Found in sunny, stony, hilly locations.

Growth Grow in well-drained soil in full sun. Propagated by division of rhizomes and offsets in late summer to early autumn.

Parts used Rhizomes – dried and powdered.

USES Aromatic An indispensable ingredient for making potpourri and scented sachet mixtures. It enhances the scent of the other ingredients and gives the whole preparation a more lasting quality. Also used in commercial potpourri products and perfumery.

Cosmetic Occasionally seen as an ingredient of home-made toothpowders. A constituent of commercial dental preparations and scented dusting powders.

Other name Florentine iris.

Above *The rhizome of the Florentine iris is dried to make orris root powder.*

CAUTION All parts of the plant are harmful if eaten – the powdered root causes vomiting. May cause skin irritations.

Isatis tinctoria

Woad

History and traditions Woad was the source of the blue body paint of the ancient Britons, described by Pliny and other Roman writers. Although largely replaced by indigo, from the subtropical *indigofera* species, in the 1630s and then by synthetics at the end of the 19th century, a factory producing dye from woad existed in England until the 1930s.

Description A hardy biennial (or short-lived perennial if flower heads are cut before seeding), it grows on a taproot, from 0.5–1.2m/ 20in–4ft tall. In the first year it produces a rosette of ovate leaves, from which branching stems with lanceolate leaves topped by racemes of yellow flowers grow in summer, followed by pendulous black seeds.

Habitat/distribution Indigenous to Europe and western Asia, introduced elsewhere. Found on chalky (alkaline) soils in sunny, open sites.

Growth Grow in humus-rich, moist but well-drained soil, in full sun. Propagated by seed sown in containers in spring, maintaining a temperature of 13–18°C/55–64°F or in autumn for overwintering in a cold frame. Does not flourish in the same ground for more than a few years.

Parts used Leaves – dried, fermented and also powdered for use as a dye. Leaves and roots – dried for Chinese herbal preparations.

USES Medicinal Traditionally a wound-healing herb, as well as a dye, it has long been used in Chinese herbal medicine and recently discovered to have antiviral properties.

General The leaves yield a very fast blue dye.

JUGLANDACEAE

Juglans regia

Walnut

History and traditions The walnut tree has been valued since ancient Greek times for its medicinal properties and many uses. It was known to the Romans as a fertility symbol and Pliny was the first to give directions for making it into a dye for restoring grey hair to brown – a use which lasted into the 20th century.

Description A variable deciduous tree, growing to about 30m/99ft, it has pinnate leaves, with 7–9 ovate leaflets. Male catkins and female flowers are followed by dark green fruits, each containing a wrinkled brown nut.

Habitat/distribution Native to south eastern Europe, Asia, China and the Himalayas, widely introduced elsewhere.

Growth Walnut trees require deep, rich soil and a sunny position.

Parts used Leaves, bark, fruit, oil.

USES Medicinal Infusions of the leaves are taken internally as a digestive tonic and applied externally for cuts, grazes and skin disorders, such as eczema. Decoctions of the inner bark are used for constipation and of the outer nut rind for diarrhoea.

Culinary The nuts are included in many dishes. Oil from the seeds is popular for salads, especially in France.

Cosmetic An infusion of the nut rind is said to make a hair restorer.

CUPRESSACEAE

Juniperus communis

Juniper

History and traditions From biblical times juniper has symbolized protection, and there are many references to people using it for shelter. "Elijah went a day's journey into the wilderness and came and sat down under a juniper tree" (I Kings 19:4). In medieval Europe a fire of juniper wood was burned to discourage evil spirits and protect from plague – and it was thought that felling a tree would bring a death in the family within a year. Its medicinal properties were recorded by the ancient Greek and Roman physicians. Culpeper recommended it, among many other uses, as "a counter-poison, resister of the pestilence and excellent against the biting of venomous beasts". It is famous as a flavouring ingredient of gin – the English word being an abbreviation of "Holland's Geneva" as gin was first known, from the Dutch word for juniper, *jenever.*

Description A hardy, coniferous, evergreen shrub or small tree, 2–4m/6–13ft tall, of upright or prostrate form with needle-like leaves. The small, spherical fruits, borne on the female plants, are green at first, and take two years to ripen to blue black.

Related species Various junipers were used medicinally by Native Americans, including *J. virginiana*, which produces the extremely toxic red cedar oil. *J. sabina* has poisonous berries and should not be confused with those of *J. communis.*

Habitat/distribution Widely distributed in the northern hemisphere of Europe, Asia and North America on heaths, moors and mountain slopes. Those grown in warmer regions, with longer,

Above *Unripened juniper berries.*

sunnier summers, such as the Mediterranean, have sweeter, more aromatic berries.

Growth Tolerant of most soils. For berry production grow female plants in a sunny position. Propagated by heel cuttings in late summer, or by seed sown in containers under cover in spring or autumn.

Parts used Fruits – collected from wild plants for use fresh, dried or for distillation of the volatile oil.

USES Medicinal The berries have antiseptic, anti-inflammatory and digestive properties and are thought to be helpful for rheumatism, gout, arthritis and colic. This is a strong herb and should only be used for short periods of time.

Culinary Juniper is added to pickles, chutneys, sauces, marinades, meat and game dishes, pâtés and sauerkraut.

General Used to flavour gin. Oil is used in cosmetics and perfumery.

> **CAUTION** The berries are not given to patients with kidney disease, or to pregnant women, as they are a uterine stimulant.

LAURACEAE
Laurus nobilis
Bay

History and traditions This is the plant from which the victor's crown of laurels was made – the Latin name is from *laurus* (praise) and *nobilis* (renowned or noble). It was dedicated to Apollo, Greek god of music, healing, light and truth, and many superstitions arose as to its powers. In the writings of Theophrastus there is a reference to the custom of keeping a bay leaf in the mouth to prevent misfortune and by Roman times it had gained a reputation for preventing lightning strikes – the emperor Tiberius always wore a laurel wreath on his head during thunderstorms as a precaution. Bay trees were also thought to purify the air where they grew. During a plague epidemic, the Roman emperor Claudius moved his court to Laurentium, named after the bay trees that grew there, because of the protection they would provide. Introduced to Britain from the Mediterranean, the sweet bay tree brought its

reputation with it. Writing in the 17th century, Culpeper said of it, "Neither witch nor devil, thunder nor lightning will hurt a man where a bay tree is." A wreath of bay leaves was the traditional garnish for the boar's head, centrepiece of the Yuletide feast.

Description An evergreen shrub, or small tree, 3–15m/10–50ft tall, it has aromatic dark green, glossy ovate leaves. Clusters of small creamy-yellow flowers, opening from tight round buds, appear in spring, followed by purple-black berries.

Related species *L. n.* 'Aurea' is an attractive cultivar with golden-yellow foliage.

Habitat/distribution Native to southern Europe, the Mediterranean and North Africa, introduced and widely grown in other warm temperate regions.

Growth Grow in fertile, reasonably moist but well-drained soil in a sheltered, sunny position. Although frost hardy, it needs winter protection when immature; and foliage is sometimes damaged by severe frosts and cold winds. Propagated by semi-ripe cuttings in summer.

Parts used Leaves – fresh or dried. Essential oil.

USES Medicinal Bay is not widely used in modern herbal medicine. But studies carried out in the late 1980s on the ability of herbs to inhibit bacterial growth showed bay to be one of the most effective.

Culinary A first-rate culinary herb, a bay leaf is always included in a *bouquet garni*, and adds flavour to marinades, casseroles, stews, soups and dishes requiring a long cooking time. Also used to flavour sweet sauces and as a garnish for citrus sorbets.

Above *Bay leaves for culinary use have a more agreeable, less bitter flavour when dried.*

Below *A standard bay tree in a pot.*

Decorative bay

The Romans embellished their houses with branches of bay for the festival of Saturnalia, celebrated between 17th and 23rd December, to coincide with the winter solstice. With Christianity, bay became a symbol of eternal life, as did other evergreens, and was once widely used as a decoration for homes and churches during the Christmas season. The aromatic, dark green leaves make it ideal for festive decorations today.

• Bay leaves make an impressive and welcoming wreath for the front door. Push them into a base of floral foam, in a circular holder, and decorate with fir cones, shiny red apples and ribbon.
• A glass bowl filled with floating candles surrounded by bay leaves makes a spectacular, fragrant table-centre.
• A mophead bay (tree-form standard), studded with baubles, makes an attractive alternative to a fir Christmas tree.

lavender known to the Greeks and Romans. It has short, fat spikes of dark purple flowers, topped by butterfly wing bracts, and grows from 30–90cm/1–3ft.

Habitat/distribution Lavender is native to the Mediterranean and Middle East, introduced and widely grown elsewhere.

Growth Requires a very well-drained soil and plenty of sun. Lavenders hybridize easily; most do not come true from seed and they are best propagated from heel cuttings taken in mid- to late summer. *L. angustifolia* and cultivars are hardy, so are *L.* x *intermedia* and cultivars. *L. stoechas* is frost-hardy. (Some other species of lavender are tender or half-hardy).

Parts used Flowers – fresh or dried, and the essential oil.

USES Medicinal Infusions of the flowers may be applied as a compress to ease headaches, and are sometimes taken internally (made weak) for anxiety and nervous exhaustion. As an embrocation an external stimulant and antiseptic.

LABIATAE/LAMIACEAE

Lavandula

History and traditions The Romans are said to have scented their bathwater with lavender (the Latin name is from *lavare*, to wash) and its inimitable fragrance has ensured its lasting popularity. Its medicinal and insecticidal properties were also recognized early and have been largely vindicated since. In 1387 at the court of Charles VI of France all the cushions were stuffed with lavender both for its pleasant scent and to deter insects. It was an essential ingredient of "Four Thieves' Vinegar", which is supposed to have given immunity to those who robbed the bodies of plague victims, and William Turner had the idea "that the flowers of Lavender quilted in a cap and dayly worne are good for all diseases of the head that come of a cold cause and that they comfort the braine very well" (*A New Herball*, 1551). In the early years of this century, René Gattefosse, one of the founders of aromatherapy, discovered the powers of lavender when his badly burned hand was healed after it had been immersed in undiluted essential oil of lavender. And since then, modern scientific research has established the antiseptic, antibacterial properties of this herb.

Description and species Lavender has been cultivated for so long that accurate identification is not always easy, and most of those grown in gardens are hybrids or cultivars. There are three important groups of lavenders (but this by no means provides a definitive list or complete explanation of lavender nomenclature):

1. *L. angustifolia* (common lavender, English lavender) – Has small purple flowers, grows to 60–90cm/2–3ft, and is said to be effective for medicinal purposes. It has many attractive cultivars, which may not have the same degree of medicinal qualities, but are probably more suitable for fragrant, culinary and decorative purposes. These include *L. a.* 'Hidcote' – with a neat, erect habit and strongly scented, deep violet flowers, 30–60cm/1–2ft. *L. a.* 'Munstead' is more compact, 30–45cm/ 12–18in, with paler, purple flowers. *L. a.* 'Nana Alba' is a dwarf, white-flowered cultivar, 15–30cm/6–12in. There are also some pink-flowered cultivars, such as *L. a.* 'Rosea'.

2. *L.* x *intermedia* 'Grey Hedge' are hybrids of *L. angustifolia* and *L. latifolia* and include *L.* x *intermedia* 'Grappenhall', which has long spikes of lavender-blue flowers, and *L.* x *intermedia* 'Twickel Purple', with shorter, bushier flowers.

3. *L. stoechas* (French or Spanish Lavender) – This is a species that is also considered to have medicinal value – and was probably the type of

Above left Lavandula angustifolia *'Hidcote'*.

Above right Lavandula angustifolia *'Munstead'*.

Left Lavandula stoechas

Essential oil (diluted in a carrier oil) is applied to sunburn, burns and scalds, or used as a massage oil for tension headaches, migraine and muscular aches and pains. Inhaling the fragrance of flowers or oil can be very calming, anti-depressive and may help relieve insomnia. The oil is applied to prevent and relieve insect bites and discourages head lice when applied to the comb.

Culinary Flowers are used to flavour sugar for making cakes, biscuits, meringues, ice creams and desserts. They can be added to vinegar, marmalade or jam, or cooked (tied in a muslin bag) with blackcurrants or soft fruit mixtures.

Cosmetic Infusions of fresh flowers make a fragrant hair rinse, or they can be tied in bags to scent bathwater. Drops of essential oil are also added to baths or included in home-made beauty preparations. Lavender oil is widely used in commercial perfumery.

Aromatic Flowers are dried for potpourri and scented sachets.

Top left Lavandula x intermedia *'Twickle Purple'*.

Top right Lavandula pedunculata *subsp.* pedunculata *with purple sage*.

Centre right Lavandula angustifolia *'Rosea'*.

Above *Dried lavender is a traditional filling for scented sachets.*

Lavender sachets

The flowers of lavender have been used for centuries to scent clothes and deter moths and insects.

• **To dry your own lavender:** Cut the flowers with long stalks, as soon as they are fully open, on a dry day, but before the essential oils evaporate in the sun. Tie with raffia or string, in small bunches and hang up in a warm, dry place, with the heads suspended in paper bags – to keep off dust and catch petals as they fall. When fully dry, this will take about a week, depending on humidity and air temperature, rub the petals off the heads.

• **To make the sachets:** Cut circles of muslin, or any fine see-through fabric, put a small handful of dried lavender in the centre, gather up to form a bundle and fasten at the neck with an elastic band. Finish with a ribbon.

LABIATAE/LAMIACEAE
Leonurus cardiaca
Motherwort

History and traditions In ancient Greece, this herb was given to pregnant women to calm their anxieties. The generic name, *Leonurus,* refers to the plant's supposed resemblance to a lion's tail, but the specific name, *cardiaca,* comes directly from the Greek word for heart because of its widespread use in former times for treating heart palpitations and afflictions. *Macer's Herbal*, 1530 attributes to it supernatural powers against wicked spirits.

Description A tall, hardy, strong-smelling perennial, growing to 1.2m/4ft, it has square, hollow stems, with deeply lobed, prominently veined leaves, set opposite each other. The mauve-pink, double-lipped flowers appear in the upper leaf axils throughout summer. Widely grown in herb gardens for its attractive foliage.

Habitat/distribution Indigenous to Europe and western Asia. Introduced elsewhere. Found on roadsides and waste grounds on light, calcareous soils.

Growth Grow in moist but well-drained soil in a sunny position. Propagated by seed sown in spring, or by division in spring or autumn.

Parts used Flowering tops – dried for use in infusions, liquid extracts and tinctures.

USES Medicinal Research has shown that this herb has a beneficial and calming effect on the heart, and is mildly sedative. It is used to influence the menstrual cycle.

> **CAUTION** Only to be taken on the advice of qualified herbalist or medical practitioner. Not to be taken in pregnancy.

UMBELLIFERAE/APIACEAE
Levisticum officinale
Lovage

History and traditions Lovage has been cultivated since the time of Pliny as a seasoning and digestive herb. The Greeks and Romans chewed the seed to aid digestion, a practice followed by Benedictine monks of the Middle Ages, and Parkinson refers to its "hot, sharpe, biting taste" and culinary usage: "The Germans and other Nations in times past used both the roote and seede instead of Pepper to season their meates and brothes and found them as comfortable and warming" (*Paradisi,* 1629). An earlier writer mentions lovage as a bath herb for its aromatic scent: "This herbe for hys sweete savoure is used in bathe" (*The Gardener's Labyrinth,* 1577). Its former medicinal uses, referred to by many herbalists, included "expelling stone of the kidneys and bladder". All of which remains broadly valid today, though the leaves are used in preference to seeds and roots for culinary purposes.

Description A hardy herbaceous perennial, growing on deep fleshy roots to 2m/6ft in height, it has glossy, deeply divided leaves with a spicy, celery-like scent, and umbels of undistinguished, dull yellow flowers in summer, followed by small seeds.

Habitat/distribution Lovage probably originated in Europe, but has long been widely cultivated throughout the world. Rarely found in the wild, except as a garden escape.

Growth A vigorous, spreading plant, it will grow in most soils (except heavy clay), but thrives best in well-manured, moist but well-drained soil, in sun or partial shade. Propagated from seed sown in spring or by division of the roots in spring or autumn.

Parts used Leaves – fresh or dried for culinary use and infusions; stems – fresh; roots, seeds – dried for use in decoctions and other medicinal preparations; essential oil – distilled from leaves and roots.

USES Medicinal It is taken internally for digestive disorders, colic and flatulence, also for cystitis and kidney stones. Lovage tea was formerly taken for rheumatism. Do not use medicinally during pregnancy.

Culinary Leaves are used to flavour soups, stews, meat, fish or vegetable dishes; young shoots and stems are eaten as a vegetable (like braised celery) and may be candied like angelica; seeds are added to biscuits and bread. Lovage cordial used to be a popular drink.

Aromatic Essential oil is used in perfumery, and as a flavouring in the food and drink industry.

Lilium candidum

Madonna lily

History and traditions *L. candidum* appears in Cretan frescoes dating to 3000BC and has been cultivated since at least 1500BC for its scent and its medicinal properties. The flawless white flowers ensured its place as a symbol of purity and its association with the Virgin Mary and it is frequently featured in religious paintings. Shakespeare makes endless references to the whiteness of the "unsullied lily", the "sweetest and the fairest", and Gerard records that the white lily was known as "Juno's Rose" because it grew from her milk, which had fallen to the ground (*The Herball,* 1597). He also writes of using the bulbs of the white lily, mixed with honey, to heal wounds, but makes it clear that a variety of lilies were used for medicinal purposes. He ascribes many virtues to the "red lily", including its ability to remove facial wrinkles, and reveals that Pliny recommended it as a corn remover. *L. candidum* is little used in modern herbalism, but the flowers are cultivated commercially in some countries for their perfumed essence, and it remains a traditional herb garden ornamental.

Description A perennial, growing from a scaly bulb to 1–1.5m/3–5ft in height, it has stiff, erect stems with small, lance-shaped leaves and racemes of 5–20 fragrant, trumpet-shaped, white flowers, tinged inside with yellow, and with bright yellow anthers. It is the only lily to have overwintering basal leaves.

Habitat/distribution A Mediterranean native, widely cultivated in other countries.

Growth Can be difficult to grow and requires conditions that suit it exactly before it will flourish. All lilies dislike heavy, clay soils.

Parts used Roots, flowers – juice is used fresh in ointments and herbal preparations.

Above *The flawless white blooms of* Lilium candidum *were considered a symbol of purity from earliest times and were closely associated with the Madonna.*

USES Medicinal It has soothing, healing properties and is used externally (but only rarely) for burns, skin inflammations and disorders.

Growing Madonna lilies

Lilium candidum is one of the oldest flowering plants in cultivation and the flowers are strongly fragrant. These beautiful white lilies can be unpredictable to grow, but the following guidelines will help to ensure success:

• Plant bulbs immediately they arrive. If there is a delay, keep it as short as possible, and meanwhile store bulbs in peat in a dark place – if exposed to light, they soften and deteriorate quickly.

• Good drainage is essential. Prepare soil thoroughly. Dig out to two spades' depth, put in a layer of coarse gravel, then replace the top soil, mixing it with sand and leaf mould. Alternatively, plant in containers, putting in a layer of coarse gravel, topped by a gritty, open compost (soil mix).

• Plant in early autumn (preferably at the beginning of September, no later than October, in the northern hemisphere).

• Bulbs should be only just covered – unlike other lilies, which require deeper planting.

• Once planted and established, do not disturb – Madonna lilies resent being moved.

LINACEAE
Linum usitatissimum
Flax

History and traditions Flax has been an important economic crop since 5000BC, valued for its fibre in making linen and for its oil-producing seeds. The Bible has many references to linen woven from flax, and both seeds and cloth have been found in Egyptian tombs. In medieval Europe it was promoted by the Emperor Charlemagne for the health-giving properties of the seeds, and there are detailed descriptions in old herbals of the process of turning flax stems into fibre for making clothing, sheets, sails, fishing nets, thread, rope, sacks, bags and purses. Many superstitions have arisen, especially concerning its cultivation: sitting on the seed bag three times and facing east before planting, ringing church bells on Ascension Day and jumping over midsummer fires were all thought to ensure a good crop – and of course the seeds provided protection from witchcraft. It has also been a valued medicinal herb since Hippocrates recommended it for colds and is still used in herbal medicine.

Description A hardy, slender annual, about 90cm–1.2m/3–4ft in height. It has narrow, lanceolate, greeny-grey leaves and simple, five-petalled, pale blue flowers borne in summer, followed by spherical seed capsules, rich in oil.

Related species *L. usitatissimum* is thought to be a cultivar of *L. bienne* in the distant past. Tall cultivars have been developed for textiles, and shorter ones for the production of seeds for linseed oil. *L. perenne,* grown in Europe and North America, is a perennial species. *L. catharticum* (purging flax) is a white-flowered annual with oval leaves; used homeopathically to treat bronchitis and haemorrhoids.

Habitat/distribution Probably of Middle Eastern origin, it is widely distributed in temperate and subtropical regions of the world and found as a cultivated escape on sunny waste ground and waysides.

Growth Grow in dry, sandy soil in full sun. Propagated from seed sown *in situ* – does not respond well to transplantation. Sow in late spring or early summer.

Parts used Whole plant – used fresh in infusions, cut after flowering for fibre; seeds – collected when ripe – dried for use whole, in infusions and other preparations, or extracted for linseed oil.

USES Medicinal Seeds are used as laxatives, in infusions and macerations for coughs, sore throats and gastric disorders, in poultices for boils and abscesses. Linseed oil contains linolenic essential fatty acids, necessary for many bodily functions, as well as vitamins A, B, D, E, minerals and amino acids. It is said to be helpful for many disorders, including rheumatoid arthritis, menstrual problems and skin complaints. The unripe seeds are toxic.

General Stem varieties are soaked ('retted') in water to release fibres for making linen cloth. Linseed oil from seed varieties is one of the most important commercial drying oils, used in paints, varnishes and putty.

Other name Linseed.

> **CAUTION** Contains traces of prussic acid, but this plant is not thought to be harmful unless taken in very large doses. Some *Linum* species have been suspected of poisoning stock in Australia. Artists' linseed oil should not be taken medicinally.

CAMPANULACEAE
Lobelia inflata
Indian tobacco

History and traditions This North American plant gained its common name from the local tradition of smoking it to relieve chest infections and asthma. It was enthusiastically adopted by early settlers as a cure-all for a wide variety of complaints and promoted in the early 19th century by the herbalist Samuel Thomson, who was charged with murder after one of his patients died from its effects. The generic name *Lobelia* (there are over 350 species) is named after the Flemish botanist Matthias de L'Obel (1538–1616). The specific name is a reference to the inflation of the seed capsule as it ripens.

Description A hardy annual, 20–60cm/ 8–24in, it has hairy stems and ovate leaves, toothed at the edges. Inconspicuous flowers borne in terminal racemes are pale violet, tinged with pink, followed by two-celled, oval capsules.

Habitat/distribution Native to North America.

Growth Grow in rich, moist soil in full sun or partial shade. Propagated by seed.

Parts used Whole plant – cut when flowering.

USES Medicinal It contains alkaloids that increase the rate of respiration and induce vomiting. It is also an expectorant and emetic. In small doses it dilates the bronchioles and is used for conditions such as bronchitis, asthma and pleurisy, but is for use by qualified practitioners only. Used in proprietary cough medicines.

> **CAUTION** Poisonous and can cause fatalities.

CAPRIFOLIACEAE

Lonicera spp
Honeysuckle

History and traditions Various species of honeysuckle have been used since ancient Greek times for their medicinal properties. Dioscorides is quoted by Gerard as recommending the seeds for "removing weariness" and "helping the shortness and difficulty of breathing" and a syrup of the flowers for diseases of lung and spleen. Little used medicinally today, honeysuckle keeps its place in the herb garden as a fragrant climber, memorably described by Shakespeare as the "lush woodbine" and "sweet honeysuckle" which "over-canopied" Titania's bower (*A Midsummer Night's Dream*). The name honeysuckle comes from the old practice of sucking the sweet nectar from the flowers.

Description and species Two species were most often recommended for medicinal purposes: *L. periclymenum* (woodbine, wild or common honeysuckle) has whorls of very fragrant, creamy-white to yellow, tubular two-lipped flowers, followed by red berries; and *L. caprifolium* (Italian, Dutch or perfoliate

honeysuckle) has upper leaves surrounding the stem and creamy-white to pink flowers.
Both are fully hardy, *L. periclymenum* grows to 7m/23ft, *L. caprifolium* to 6m/19ft. *L. japonica* (Japanese honeysuckle) often has violet-tinged white flowers, followed by black berries.

Habitat/distribution Widely distributed in the northern hemisphere, in woodlands, hedgerows and rocky hillsides.

Growth Grow in fertile, well-drained soil in full sun or partial shade. Propagated by seed sown in late summer to autumn in containers and overwintered in a cold frame, or by semi-ripe cuttings taken in summer. Prune out straggly or overgrown branches.

Parts used Flowering stems.

USES Medicinal *L. caprifolium* and *L. periclymenum* were formerly used for their expectorant, laxative properties. *L. japonica* (*jin yin hua*) is used in traditional Chinese medicine for clearing toxins from the system.

> **CAUTION** Honeysuckle berries are poisonous.

Above *The flowers contain sweet nectar.*

Top right *A cultivar of* Lonicera periclymenum.

Growth It grows best in moist to wet soil in sun or partial shade and is propagated by seed or division in autumn or spring. It often self-seeds and spreads rapidly. It is classed as a noxious weed in some countries and imports of the plants and seeds are forbidden.

Parts used The whole flowering plant – it is used fresh or dried in infusions, decoctions and ointments.

USES Medicinal It has been found in modern research to have antibacterial properties and is still recommended by modern herbalists for diarrhoea and dysentery as well as for haemorrhages and excessive menstrual flow. It is said to be soothing, when applied externally, to sores, ulcers, skin irritations and eczema.

LABIATAE/LAMIACEAE

Lycopus europaeus

Gipsyweed

History and traditions This herb is said to have gained its name because gipsies used it to stain their skins darker. It was also effective in dyeing fabrics and at one time was a valuable medicinal plant.

Description A perennial, mint-like herb, but with no aroma, it grows on a creeping root-stock to about 60cm/2ft in height. It has single stems with opposite, deeply toothed, pointed leaves and whorls of small, pale mauve flowers in the leaf axils in late summer.

Related species *L. virginicus* (Virginia bugle weed), also known sometimes as gipsyweed, is native to North America. It is a very similar plant to *L. europaeus* and shares the same properties.

Habitat/distribution *L. europaeus* is a native of Europe and western Asia.

Parts used Whole flowering plant – it can be used fresh or dried.

USES Medicinal Gipsyweed is reputed to have sedative properties. Traditionally it is used to treat hyperthyroidism. Avoid if trying to conceive. Do not take alongside preparation containing thyroid hormone.

General It produces a black or dark grey dye on woollen and linen fabrics.

LYTHRACEAE

Lythrum salicaria

Purple loosestrife

History and traditions The name loosestrife is connected to this herb's old reputation for soothing ill-behaved animals. Gerard, in his *Herball* of 1597, writes of it "appeasing the strife and unruliness which falleth out among oxen at the plough, if it is put about their yokes". As it was also supposed to drive away flies and gnats, perhaps this was the reason for its calming influence. The generic name is from the Greek, *luthron*, meaning blood, a reference to the colour of the flowers, and it was considered by herbalists of old to be effective against internal haemorrhages, excessive menstruation and nosebleeds. John Lindley, in *Flora Medica*, 1838, refers to it as "an astringent, which has been recommended in inveterate cases of diarrhoea," and it was often used in his day to treat outbreaks of cholera.

Description Purple loosestrife is a perennial which grows on a creeping rhizome with erect stems reaching 0.6–1.5m/2–5ft in height. It has long, lanceolate leaves and crimson-purple flowers borne on whorled spikes in mid to late summer.

Habitat/distribution A European native, it occurs widely in Asia, northern Africa, Australia and North America. It is usually found in wet and marshy places.

Above Lythrum salicaria

MALVACEAE
Malva sylvestris
Mallow

History and traditions The common mallow was cultivated by the Romans as a medicinal and culinary herb, the leaves being cooked as a vegetable and seeds added to salads and sauces. By the 16th century it had gained a reputation as a cure-all, commended for its gentle purgative action, a process that was thought to rid the body of disease. But its culinary uses remained paramount, and herbals and household books of the period are full of recipes for cooking the leaves with butter and vinegar, making "suckets" (candy) of the stalks, and, even more imaginatively, cutting and rolling them into balls and passing them off as green peas (*Receipt Book of John Nott,* 1723). The generic name, *Malva,* meaning soft, refers to the downy leaves and soothing properties of the plant.

Description A perennial, growing from 45–90cm/18in–3ft, it has much-branched erect or trailing stems, with 5- to 7-lobed leaves, and pink, five-petalled flowers, streaked with darker veins, borne throughout summer.

Related species *M. moschata* (musk mallow) grows to 90cm/3ft and has purple-spotted stems, heart-shaped basal leaves and narrowly divided upper leaves, both scented faintly with musk. Solitary pale pink flowers are borne in the leaf axils. It is weaker in effect than *M. sylvestris,* but with the same uses. The closely related plant *Althaea officinalis* (marshmallow) is considered more medicinally effective than either of the *Malva.*

Habitat/distribution Native to Europe, western Asia and North America. Found at field edges, embankments and on waste ground, in porous soils and sunny situations.

Growth Grow in well-drained to dry soil, in a sunny position. Propagated by seed sown in the spring or by division of the roots in late autumn or early spring.

Parts used Leaves, flowers – used fresh or dried. Fruits (seed capsules) – picked unripe and used fresh.

USES Medicinal Mallow contains a high proportion of an emollient mucilage, reduces inflammation and calms irritated tissues. Infusions are taken internally for coughs, sore throats and bronchitis. The leaves are applied externally as a poultice for skin complaints, eczema and insect bites. It is also an expectorant herb and large doses can have a laxative effect.

Culinary Young leaves and shoots contain vitamins A, B^1, B^2 and C and can be eaten raw in salads or cooked as vegetables. Unripe fruits are sometimes added to salads.

Other name Common mallow.

Above *A flower of the musk mallow,* Malva moschata.

Above Malva moschata *f.* alba

SOLANACEAE
Mandragora officinarum
Mandrake

History and traditions Mandrake has
attracted more stories and superstitions than
almost any other herb – perhaps because of its
hallucinogenic properties, coupled with its
strange appearance and forked roots, fancifully
thought to resemble the human form.
Closely related to *Atropa belladonna* and
Hyoscyamus niger (henbane), it contains the
toxic alkaloids atropine and hyoscyamine and
has been used since the ancient Greek and
Roman period as a powerful sedative, when it
was first found to deaden the pain of surgery.
An early introduction to Britain, it features in
many Anglo-Saxon medicinal texts and was
mentioned by Turner in 1551 for its anaesthetic
properties. Just holding the fruit (mandrake
apple) in the hand was said to be a cure for
insomnia. At the end of the 19th century it
became an official homeopathic preparation
but is rarely used today and retains its place
as a "herb" because of its historical interest.

Description A low growing perennial, 15cm/
6in in height, it has a basal rosette of broad,
oval, veined and rough-textured leaves, with
wavy margins, which start erect and spread flat
as they grow. Clusters of bell-shaped, greenish-
white flowers, flushed with purple, arise from
the base and are followed by large, spherical
green fruits ripening to yellow.

Habitat/distribution Originated in the
Himalayas and southeast Mediterranean,
introduced into western Europe, Britain and
other countries. Found on sunny sites, in poor,
sandy soil.

Growth Although hardy to -10°C/14°F,
mandrake needs protection from prolonged
cold and wet weather in winter. Grow it in a
sheltered, sunny spot such as at the base of
a wall, or in a rockery, in well-drained,
reasonably fertile soil. It resents disturbance
once properly established and is propagated by
seed in autumn, root cuttings in winter.

Parts used Roots.

USES Medicinal Formerly used as a sedative
and painkiller.

Other name Devil's apples.

> **CAUTION** A dangerously poisonous plant,
> which should not be used internally or
> externally. Can be fatal. Subject to legal
> restrictions in some countries.

Mandrake myths

One of the most popular superstitions
about mandrake was that its unearthly
shrieks, when pulled up, sent people mad
if it did not kill them. As Shakespeare
records: "And shrieks like mandrakes torn
out of the earth/That living mortals hear-
ing them run mad" (*Romeo and Juliet*) or
"Would curses kill as doth the mandrakes
groan" (*Henry VI*, Part 2).

   An ingenious way to avoid death on
digging up the plant was to tie it to a
hungry dog, with a dish of meat just out
of reach, so that he would die instead as
he pulled the root from the ground. Once
dug up it could be handled with impunity.
The fancied resemblance of the roots to

people meant they were sought after as
amulets to protect from witchcraft and
bring prosperity. This led to a lucrative
scam (scathingly described by Turner in his
New Herbal, 1551) of false mandrake
manikins being sculpted out of bryony
roots and sold to the gullible at high
prices. The sensible Gerard, too, dismissed
the mandrake myths with these words:
"There have been many ridiculous tales
brought up of this plant, whether of old
wives or runnegate surgeons, or phisick
mongers, I know not, all which dreames
and old wives tales you shall from hence-
forth cast out your bookes of memorie."
(*The Herball*, 1597).

Above *Mandrake fruits, sometimes known
as the devil's apples.*

LABIATAE/LAMIACEAE

Marrubium vulgare

Horehound

History and traditions This herb has been known since Egyptian times, and is thought to be one of the bitter herbs which the Jews consumed at the Feast of the Passover. The generic name *Marrubium* comes from the Hebrew word *marrob* – a bitter juice. Its reputation as a remedy for coughs and colds goes back to at least Pliny's time. Several 16th-century herbalists, including Gerard, use almost the same words to recommend a syrup of the fresh leaves in sugar as a "most singular remedie against the cough and wheezing of the lungs." Horehound candy was still being made to the old recipes well into the 20th century.

Description A hardy perennial growing to 60cm/2ft, with erect, branched stems and greeny-grey, soft, downy, ovate leaves, bluntly toothed, arranged opposite. Whorls of small, white, tubular flowers appear in the leaf axils in summer.

Related species *Ballota nigra*, although from a different genus, is known as black horehound, and was once used for similar purposes. However, it has an unpleasant smell and is considered less effective and has been superseded by *M. vulgare*.

Habitat/distribution Native to Europe, northern Africa and Asia, introduced elsewhere. Found on dry grassland, pastures and field edges.

Growth Grows in any soil and prefers a sunny situation. Propagated from seed sown in spring, but can be slow to germinate, or by division of roots in spring. (It is under statutory control as a weed in Australia and New Zealand.)

Parts used Flowering stems – fresh or dried.

USES Medicinal Taken as an infusion for coughs, colds and chest infections. Combined with hyssop, sage or thyme to make a gargle for sore throats. Made into cough candy.

Above Marrubium vulgare, *or white horehound.*

Top right and right Ballota nigra *is considered inferior as a medicinal plant.*

Horehound recipes

• **Horehound and ginger tea** – for a cold
15g/¹/₂ oz fresh horehound leaves
5ml/1 tsp powdered ginger
600ml/1 pint/2¹/₂ cups boiling water
honey to taste
Put the roughly chopped leaves into a pot or jug with the ginger, pour in the boiling water, cover and leave to infuse for 5–7 minutes. Strain off the leaves and sweeten with honey to taste before drinking.

• A Recipe for horehound candy from *The Family Herbal* (1810)
Boil some horehound till the juice is extracted. Boil up some sugar to a feather height, add your juice to the sugar, and let it boil till it is again the same height. Stir it till it begins to grow thick, then pour it on to a dish and dust it with sugar and when fairly cool cut into squares. Excellent sweetmeat for colds and coughs.

MYRTACEAE

Melaleuca alternifolia

Tea-tree

History and traditions Tea-tree was named by Captain Cook's crew when, following local custom, they drank it as a tea substitute. The Australian Aborigines used it medicinally, and in World War II tea tree oil, distilled from *M. alternifolia*, was used in Australia as a powerful germicide. It has since gained ground in herbal medicine for its remarkable healing properties.

Description Melaleucas are half-hardy to tender evergreen trees, 15–40m/50–130ft, with thin, peeling, corky bark, narrow, pointed, leathery leaves and bottle-brush-shaped flowers.

Related species Several species of melaleuca are used medicinally. *M. leucadendron* produces distilled cajuput oil, which has similar uses to eucalyptus oil. *M. viridiflora* is the source of niaouli oil used in perfumery.

Habitat/distribution Native to Australia and Malaysia, introduced in other tropical regions. Often found in swampy areas.

Growth *M. alternifolia* is half-hardy, *M. leucadendron* is tender. Grow in moisture-retentive to wet soil, in full sun. They must be grown as conservatory plants in cool, temperate regions. Propagated by seed or by semi-ripe cuttings.

Parts used Essential oil.

USES Medicinal Strongly antiseptic, antibacterial and antifungal, tea-tree oil is used diluted in a carrier oil and applied externally for healing cuts, burns, stings, insect bites, acne, and athlete's foot. It is also said to be effective against warts, verrucas and head lice eggs when used undiluted.

General A constituent of many pharmaceutical and cosmetic industry products.

LEGUMINOSAE/PAPILIONACEAE

Melilotus officinalis

Melilot

History and traditions Once popular as a strewing herb for the haylike scent it develops when drying, due to the coumarin content, the name of the genus means "honey-lotus" for the sweet smell of its nectar and it is very attractive to bees. It was used in the Greek physician Galen's time, AD130–201, as an ingredient of ointments for reducing swellings, tumours and inflammations, and appears in later European herbals for similar purposes. Culpeper adds that "the head often washed with the distilled water of the herb and flowers is good for those who swoon, also to strengthen the memory".

Description An erect, straggly biennial, 0.6m–1.2m/2–4ft high, it has ridged, branched stems with trifoliate leaves and narrow ovate leaflets. The yellow, honey-scented flowers are borne in slender axillary racemes, from midsummer to autumn.

Habitat/distribution Native to Europe and Asia, naturalized in North America. Found in dry, chalky embankments, wastelands and roadsides.

Growth Grow in well-drained to dry soil, in a sunny situation. Propagated by seed sown in spring or autumn.

Parts used: Flowering stems – dried for use in herbal preparations.

USES An aromatic herb with sedative, anti-inflammatory properties, it was formerly taken

Above Melilotus officinalis.

as an infusion or tincture for insomnia, tension headaches and painful menstruation, and applied externally to wounds and skin inflammations. It also has a reputation for helping to prevent thrombosis and has been used for bronchial complaints and catarrh.

Aromatic It has insect-repellent properties and the dried herb is sometimes included in scented sachets for the wardrobe.

Other names Yellow melilot and yellow sweet clover.

> **CAUTION** Dicoumarol, a powerful anticlotting factor, is sometimes produced during the drying process. It is emetic in large doses. Do not use concurrently with warfarin or other anti-coagulants. Harmful to livestock.

LABIATAE/LAMIACEAE
Melissa officinalis
Lemon balm

History and traditions Lemon balm has been cultivated as a bee plant for over 2000 years, bunches being put into empty hives to attract swarms. It is thought that the leaves contain the same terpenoids as found in glands of honey bees. The Arab physicians of the 1st and 2nd centuries are credited with introducing it as an antidepressant medicinal herb. John Parkinson wrote that "the herb without question is an excellent help to comfort the heart" (*Paradisi*, 1629) and many of the old herbalists refer to it as driving away "all melancholy and sadnesse". It has been taken as a calming tea for its gently sedative effects ever since. Unsubstantiated stories of regular drinkers of balm tea living into their hundreds have been perpetuated by modern herbal writers.

Description A vigorous, bushy perennial, 30–80cm/12–32in in height, it has strongly lemon-scented, rough-textured, ovate, toothed leaves. Inconspicuous clusters of pale yellow flowers appear in the leaf axils in late summer.

Related species *M. officinalis* 'Aurea' is a cultivar with bright gold and green variegated leaves. It is inclined to revert as the plant matures, so cut back after flowering to encourage new variegated growth. *M. officinalis* 'All Gold' has bright yellow foliage, but should be planted in partial shade, as it is inclined to scorch in a position where it receives full sun.

Habitat/distribution Native to southern and central Europe, introduced and widely distributed in northern temperate zones. Often found as a garden escape.

Growth Grows in any soil in sun or partial shade. Spreads and self-seeds freely. The easiest method of propagation is by division in spring. The species can be grown from seed, but cultivars must be vegetatively propagated.

Parts used Leaves – best used fresh, as scent and therapeutic properties are lost when dried and stored; essential oil – distilled from leaves.

USES Medicinal Lemon balm has sedative, relaxing, digestive properties and infusions are taken internally for nervous anxiety, depression, tension headaches and indigestion. It also has insect-repellent properties, is antiviral and antibacterial, and is applied externally, in infusions, poultices or ointments, for sores, skin irritations, insect bites and stings. It can be particularly helpful for reducing cold sores (*herpes simplex* virus). The essential oil is used in aromatherapy for anxiety states.

Culinary Fresh leaves add lemon flavour to sweet and savoury dishes as well as drinks.

Above centre Melissa officinalis *'All Gold'*.

Above Melissa officinalis *'Aurea'*.

Recipes for lemon balm

• **Chicken lemon balm**
Use handfuls of the fresh leaves to stuff the body cavity of a chicken, and sit it on a further bed of leaves before roasting it, to keep flesh moist and impart a subtle lemon flavour.

• **Orange and lemon balm salad**
Snip fresh lemon balm over peeled, thinly sliced oranges, sprinkled with a mixture of fresh orange and lemon juice, sweetened with honey.

• **Carmelite cordial**
Lemon balm was one of the chief ingredients of Carmelite water, which also included lemon peel, nutmeg and angelica root – said to be the favourite tipple of the Holy Roman Emperor, Charles V (1500–1558).

LABIATAE/LAMIACEAE

Mentha

History and traditions The Romans made great use of mint for its clean, fresh scent, putting it in their bathwater and making it into perfumes. The poet Ovid describes scouring the boards with "green mint" before setting out food for the gods, and Pliny has been attributed with the view that the smell of mint stirs up the taste buds "to a greedy desire of meat". This conflicts with a modern study, carried out in the United States in 1994, which found that the smell of mint helped alleviate hunger pangs. The Romans introduced spearmint to Britain, where it soon became established. In the late 16th century, Gerard talks of its popularity as a strewing herb "in chambers and places of recreation". It is now one of the most popular herbs.

Habitat/distribution Mints are widely distributed in Europe, Asia and Africa, introduced and naturalized elsewhere, often found in damp or wet soils. Cultivated as a crop in many countries including Europe, North America, the Middle East and Asia.

Species There are 25 species of mint in all, but they are often variable and individual plants can be difficult to identify because mints hybridize readily. The following hardy perennials are top favourites for the herb garden. Most are vigorous, the variegated ones less so, and spread rapidly on creeping rootstocks.

M. x gracilis 'Variegata' (gingermint) – Has gold and green variegated, smooth, ovate leaves, scented with a hint of ginger, and grows 30cm–1m/1–3ft tall. Tiny, pale lilac flowers are borne in whorls in the leaf axils.

M. x piperita (peppermint) – Has dark green (often tinged with purple) lanceolate to ovate, toothed leaves and whorls of pale pink flowers in summer. It grows to 30–90cm/1–3ft tall. Peppermint is a variable hybrid of *M. spicata* and *M. aquatica*, sometimes assigned two different forms as black peppermint, *M. x piperita* f. *rubescens,* and white peppermint, *M. x piperita* f. *pallescens*. It is rich in menthol, which gives it the characteristic cooling, slightly numbing, peppermint taste, but is too dominant for general cookery and is used to flavour sweet foods.

M. x piperita f. *citrata* (eau-de-Cologne mint) (bergamot, lemon or orange mint) – A cultivar with large, toothed, ovate leaves, 30–90cm/ 1–3ft tall. The scent is reminiscent of lavender water with citrus overtones.

M. pulegium (pennyroyal) – There are creeping (to 10cm/4in) and upright (to 40cm/16in) varieties. Both have small, elliptic to ovate, usually smooth-edged leaves, and prolific, distinctive whorls of mauve flowers in the leaf axils. The high concentration of pulegone gives it a pleasantly antiseptic smell, but it is toxic in very large doses and abortifacient.

Mentha requienii (Corsican mint) – A creeping, mat-forming mint, 2.5–10cm/ 1–4in, with very small, smooth and shiny, rounded leaves and tiny, mauve flowers in summer. It makes a good ground cover herb for a damp, shady situation.

M. spicata (spearmint) – This has bright green, wrinkled, finely toothed leaves, with a fresh, uncomplicated, not too overpowering mint scent. White or pale mauve flowers are borne in terminal spikes in mid- to late summer. A popular culinary mint, used since the time of the Romans; 30–90cm/1–3ft tall.

M. suaveolens 'Variegata' (variegated applemint also known as pineapple mint) – This has soft, downy, cream and white variegated leaves and a sweet, apple scent. 30–90cm/1–3ft tall. Pineapple mint makes a very attractive ornamental and container plant.

M x villosa var. *alopecuroides* (Bowles' Mint) – Formerly known as *M. rotundifolia* var. 'Bowles', it is in fact a variety of a sterile hybrid between *M. spicata* and *M. suaveolens*.

The rounded, ovate, toothed leaves are greyish green; soft and downy, lilac-pink flowers are borne in terminal, branched spikes. It is popular for culinary use; the clean mint flavour has overtones of apple.

Growth Mints grow best in rich, damp soil and partial shade. Most do not come true from seed or are sterile hybrids. They are easily propagated by division or by taking root cuttings from early spring throughout the growing season.

Parts used Peppermint, spearmint – leaves, essential oil; pennyroyal, gingermint, Bowles' mint, eau-de-Cologne mint – leaves.

USES Medicinal Peppermint can be taken as a tea for colds and to aid digestion. The essential oil has decongestant, antiseptic, mildly anaesthetic effects and is used externally, often as an inhalant to relieve colds, chest infections, catarrh and asthma. It also has insect-repellent properties. Excess use may cause allergic reactions. Pennyroyal is taken internally as an infusion for indigestion and colic. Stimulates the uterus and should not be given to pregnant or breastfeeding women. Toxic in large doses. An insect-repellent plant, used to deter ants when planted in the garden. Spearmint can be taken as a tea for digestive disorders; it is less pungent than peppermint and a non-irritant.

Culinary Spearmint and Bowles' mint are used in sauces, mint jelly, to flavour yoghurt as a savoury dip or side dish, in salads, rice dishes, meat, fish or vegetable dishes, as a garnish, to flavour herb teas and drinks. Peppermint is used to flavour sweets and chocolates, icings, cakes, desserts, ice creams, cordials and as a tea. Gingermint leaves may be floated in summer drinks. Pennyroyal is traditionally used to flavour black pudding (an old name is pudding grass).

Aromatic Fresh leaves or essential oils are added to baths, cosmetics and fragrant household preparations.

General Essential oils are used in food, pharmaceutical and cosmetic industries.

> **CAUTION** Do not use during pregnancy or when breast-feeding.

Top, from left to right Mentha x gracilis *(gingermint)*; M. x piperita *f.* rubescens *(black peppermint)*; M. x piperita *f.* citrata *(eau-de-Cologne mint)*; M. pulegium *(pennyroyal)*; M. requienii *(Corsican mint)*; M. spicata *(spearmint)*.

Above right M. suaveolens 'Variegata' *(variegated applemint).*

Above Mentha suaveolens, *or applemint.*

LABIATAE/LAMIACEAE
Monarda didyma
Bergamot

History and traditions Native Americans used several monarda species medicinally. *M. didyma* became known as "Oswego tea" after the Oswego river, near Lake Ontario, where it was found growing by European settlers. Its refreshing taste made a good tea substitute. The scent of flowers and leaves is similar to the Bergamot orange, which is how it gained its common name.
Description An aromatic, hardy perennial, 40–90cm/16in–3ft in height, it has soft, downy, greyish-green, ovate leaves, with serrated edges, and red or mauve flowers in solitary terminal whorls in late summer.
Related species: *M. fistulosa* (wild bergamot) is closely related and has purple flowers – also called "Oswego tea". There are many attractive hybrids including 'Cambridge Scarlet' (above) and 'Croftway Pink'.
Habitat/distribution Native of eastern North America, found in damp woodlands, introduced and widely grown elsewhere.
Growth Grow in humus-rich, damp soil. Prefers partial shade, but tolerates full sun if kept moist. Prone to mildew in dry conditions. Propagated by division or by seed sown in spring.
Parts used Leaves, flowers – fresh or dried.

USES Medicinal Taken as a digestive tea. It has expectorant and antiseptic qualities and helps to relieve wind. It is useful as a diluted essential oil for the treatment of shingles.
Culinary Fresh leaves are added to wine cups, fruit drinks and to China tea to give it an "Earl Grey" flavour.
Aromatic Flowers are dried for potpourri.

RUTACEAE
Murraya koenigii
Curry leaves

History and traditions The Indian name for the leaves of this shrub is "curry patta" and they have long been used in southern India and Sri Lanka in local dishes as well as for their medicinal properties. Curry leaves are not widely used in the West because much of the flavour is lost on drying – but they are imported fresh by wholesalers for use in the food industry.
Description An aromatic, more or less deciduous shrub, growing to 6m/20ft in height, it has bright green pinnate leaves, with smooth, ovate leaflets. Clusters of small white flowers are followed by edible berries, which turn from green to purple as they ripen.
Habitat/distribution Native to southern India and Sri Lanka, introduced and grown in all tropical zones, found in rich soils.
Growth A tender, tropical shrub, it is grown in humus-rich, moist but well-drained soil in sun or partial shade. Propagated by seed or cuttings.
Parts used Leaves – picked and used fresh; seeds; essential oil – distilled from leaves.

USES Medicinal Contains alkaloids with anti-fungal activity. The juice of the leaves contains vitamin C and minerals, including calcium, phosphorus and iron and is used as a herbal tonic for digestive disorders. Eating the fresh leaves is reputed by some to help prevent the onset of diabetes and to encourage weight loss. Juice of the crushed berries, mixed with lime juice, is applied to insect bites and stings.
Culinary Used in Indian cookery to flavour a variety of dishes, including curries and chutneys.
General Essential oil used in the soap industry.

MYRICACEAE
Myrica gale
Bog myrtle

History and traditions This was once an indispensable plant in much of northern Europe for its many household uses. It was used as a hops substitute to flavour beer and improve its foaming; the fruits were boiled to produce wax for making candles; it made a yellow dye; and its insect-repellent properties meant it was often put into mattress stuffings, which gave it the former name "flea wood".
Description Hardy, deciduous shrub, growing to 1.5m/5ft, it has narrow, bright green, oval to lanceolate leaves and yellowish-green flowers, borne in dense catkins in late spring to early summer, followed by flattened yellow brown fruits.
Habitat/distribution Native to North America, northwest Europe and northeast Siberia, found in wet heathlands.
Growth Prefers a damp, acid soil (tolerates boggy conditions) and partial shade, but can be grown in full sun. Propagated by separating suckers, by cuttings, or by seed sown in spring or autumn.
Parts used Leaves – dried.

USES Aromatic Strongly insecticidal. Dried leaves can be added to insect-repellent mixtures and sachets.
Other name Sweet gale.

MYRISTICACEAE

Myristica fragrans

Nutmeg / Mace

History and traditions Nutmeg and mace are different parts of the same fruit of the nutmeg tree. The scent of the nutmeg has variously been compared with myrrh and musk. The common name comes from "nut" and the Latin, *muscus,* or old French, *mugue,* meaning musk. Nutmegs were probably introduced to Europe in about the 6th century by Arab or Indian traders, who brought them to the Mediterranean from the Far East. The Portuguese set up a trade monopoly in this valuable spice at the beginning of the 16th century after taking possession of the Moluccan islands where the trees grew. This was taken over by the Dutch, who limited cultivation of nutmeg to the Moluccas and continued the monopoly into the 19th century. Today nutmeg is widely grown in tropical regions, with Indonesia and the West Indies as leading world producers. It has been used over the centuries as a medicinal tonic and culinary spice, its hallucinogenic properties have long been recognized and it acquired a reputation as an effective aphrodisiac.

Description An evergreen dioecious tree, usually 9–12m/29–39ft but occasionally up to 15–20m/49–65ft tall, with glossy, pointed oval leaves and inconspicuous pale yellow flowers, male in clusters with numerous fused stamens, the female solitary or in groups. Brownish-yellow globular fruits each containing an ovoid brown seed (nutmeg), surrounded by a shredded crimson aril (mace), do not appear before the tree is 9–10 years old.

Habitat Indigenous to Molucca (Maluku) and Banda islands, now widely grown in Indonesia, Sri Lanka, India, the West Indies, Brazil and elsewhere in tropical zones, frequently on volcanic soils in areas of high humidity.

Growth A tender, tropical tree, grown in sandy, humus-rich soil. Prefers shade or partial shade. Propagated by seed or cuttings. May be grown as a conservatory or hothouse plant in temperate regions, with a minimum temperature of 18°C/64°F and a humid atmosphere.

Parts used Seed (nutmeg), aril (mace) – dried and used whole or powdered; volatile oil distilled from fruits; fatty oil compressed from mace (nutmeg butter, mace oil).

USES Medicinal Nutmeg is taken internally, in small doses, for digestive disorders, nausea and insomnia. Applied externally for toothache and rheumatic aches and pains.

> **CAUTION** Nutmeg should always be used sparingly. It contains a toxic compound, myristicin, whose chemical structure has similarities with mescaline, and can cause hallucinations and convulsions even in moderate doses.

Above left *Whole nutmeg fruits on the tree.*

Above *The outer shell splits to reveal the nutmeg seed, enclosed in a red aril.*

Culinary Both nutmeg and mace are ground or grated and used in a wide range of sweet and savoury dishes, but mace is less pungent. Added to soups, sauces, milk and cheese dishes, meat and vegetable dishes, biscuits, fruit cakes, puddings and drinks.

General Volatile oil and fatty oil (nutmeg butter) are used in the pharmaceutical and perfumery industries.

Top *Nutmegs with outer covering of mace (dried aril).*

Centre *Ground nutmeg.*

Right *Dried nutmeg seeds.*

UMBELLIFERAE/APIACEAE
Myrrhis odorata
Sweet cicely

History and traditions The Latin name refers
to the sweet aniseed smell of this herb, said to
resemble myrrh – *Myrrhis* comes from the Greek
word for fragrance. It is probable that the "wild
chervil", or "sweet chervil", referred to in old
herbals is the same plant. *The Leech Book of
Bald*, c. AD950, gives a salve of wild chervil
for the treatment of tumours. It was used as
a medieval strewing herb, and the roots and
leaves were cooked as a pot-herb. Recent
scientific research has found that compounds
isolated from *M. odorata* are related in chemical
structure to podophyllotoxin, the highly
poisonous active ingredient of *Podophyllum
peltatum* (American may-apple). However, this
does not mean that *M. odorata* as a whole
plant, or the isolated compounds, have the
same high level of toxicity as *Podophyllum
peltatum*, and it is not thought to be harmful
as a culinary herb.
Description A vigorous, hardy, herbaceous
perennial, with a strong taproot, grows
0.9–1.2m/3–4ft tall, with hollow stems and soft,
downy fernlike leaves. Compound umbels of
white flowers appear in late spring, followed by
large, distinctively beaked and ridged brown
fruit. The whole plant is pleasantly scented.
Habitat/distribution Native to Europe,
introduced and naturalized in other temperate
regions, found in hedgerows and field edges
often in shady positions.
Growth Grows under any conditions, in sun or
shade, but said to prefer moist, humus-rich soil.

Right Myrrhis
odorata

An invasive plant which self-seeds and spreads
rapidly and is virtually impossible to eradicate
once established. Propagated by seed, after
vernalization, or by division of roots in spring.
Parts used Leaves – fresh.

USES Culinary Traditionally used as a
sweetening agent and flavouring for stewed
soft fruits and rhubarb. Leaves also make a
pretty garnish for sweet and savoury dishes.

MYRTACEAE
Myrtus communis
Myrtle

History and traditions This sweet-smelling
shrub from the Mediterranean was dedicated to
Venus, goddess of love. Myrtle has long been
associated with weddings and included in bridal
bouquets. After the ceremony, sprigs were often
planted as cuttings in the garden of the marital
home or beside the front door, to ensure peace
and love within, which happy states would be
lost if the plants died or were dug up.
Description An evergreen shrub, to 3m/10ft
tall, with glossy ovate to lanceolate leaves,
dotted with oil glands. Fragrant white five-
petalled flowers, which appear in early summer,
are followed by blue-black berries.
Related species *M. communis* subsp. *tarentina*
is a compact variant, 0.9–1.5m/3–5ft tall.
Habitat/description Native to the
Mediterranean region and western Asia,
introduced and widely grown elsewhere.
Growth Frost-hardy, but does not tolerate
prolonged cold spells and waterlogged soils.
Propagated by semi-ripe cuttings in late summer.
Parts used Leaves – fresh for culinary use, dried
for infusions; fruits – fresh or dried; volatile oil.

USES Medicinal Myrtle has antiseptic,
decongestant properties and it is taken
internally, in infusions, for colds, chest
infections, sinusitis and for urinary infections.
Culinary The leaves and fruits are used in
Middle Eastern cookery with lamb and game.
General The essential oil is used in perfumery,
cosmetic and soap industries.

VALERIANACEAE

Nardostachys grandiflora

Spikenard

History and traditions This plant was an ingredient of the expensive perfumed unguents of the Romans and ancient Eastern nations, prized for the durability of its scent. It was the "very costly" ointment of spikenard with which Mary wiped the feet of Jesus (John 12:3–5). The Indian name *jatamansi* refers to the bearded appearance of the fibrous rhizomes, or "spikes", which were supposed to resemble ears of corn.

Description An erect perennial, 25–30cm/ 10–12in in height, with a fibrous rootstock, crowned by nearly basal lanceolate leaves and from which stems bearing pale pink flowers in terminal clusters arise.

Habitat/distribution Native to the Himalayas from Kumaon to Sikkim and Bhutan, at altitudes of 3,000–5,000m/9,800–16,400ft, where the atmosphere is cool and moist, on poor, stony soil and rocky ledges.

Growth Fully hardy; grow in gritty, well-drained, poorish soil, in a rockery or similar situation, but provide midday or partial shade and plenty of moisture to keep roots cool.

Parts used Roots – dried for use in decoctions; volatile oil distilled from roots.

USES Medicinal: An important herb in Ayurvedic medicine for over 3,000 years, the root has antiseptic, bitter tonic properties and is soothing to the nervous system. It is used for insomnia and as a gentle tranquillizer, for menopausal problems, respiratory disorders and in the treatment of intestinal worms.

LABIATAE/LAMIACEAE

Nepeta cataria

Catmint

History and traditions This herb often proves irresistible to cats. It is mildly hallucinogenic, which could be the attraction, but another theory is that the plant has overtones of tomcats' urine and is associated with courtship behaviour. It is also said to be hated by rats. Chewing the root is reputed to make humans aggressive, and one old British story recalls that a reluctant hangman used it to give him courage to carry out his duties. There are references to its medicinal properties in old herbals, it was occasionally used for flavouring, and found its way into herbal tobaccos, but it does not seem to be widely used today, except perhaps to make toys for cats.

Description A hardy perennial, 30–90cm/ 1–3ft tall, it has coarse-textured, ovate, grey-green leaves, with serrated edges. Pale mauve flowers in terminal or axillary whorls are borne from midsummer to autumn. The whole plant has a strong, antiseptic, mintlike odour, similar to pennyroyal.

Related species The hybrid *N.* x *faassenii*, commonly known as *N. mussinii*, is a more attractive plant, frequently grown in herb gardens for its prolific, soft-blue flowers, which bloom over a long period. It has no medicinal virtues – but cats have been observed rolling in it.

Habitat/distribution Occurs in Europe, Asia and Africa, introduced and naturalized in North America and temperate zones. Found in moist, calcareous soils, on roadsides, in hedgerows and field edges.

Above Nepeta x faassenii.

Growth Catmint prefers moist soil and a sunny position. Propagated by root division in spring or autumn or by cuttings in summer.

Parts used Leaves and flowering stems – dried or fresh.

USES Medicinal Catmint lowers fever, increases perspiration and is mildly sedative. It is sometimes taken as an infusion for feverish colds, influenza, nervous tension, anxiety and gastric upsets, or applied externally to cuts and bruises.

Culinary It makes a stimulating, minty tea.

Household The dried herb is used to stuff toys for cats.

Other names Catnip and catnep.

Right Nepeta cataria *'Citriodora', a lemon-scented cultivar.*

Left Nepeta cataria

LABIATAE/LAMIACEAE

Ocimum basilicum

Basil

History and traditions A native of India, basil first came to Europe in the 16th century. In India, where it is known as *tulsi*, it is sacred to the god Vishnu. It is thought to protect from misfortune and is planted in temple gardens and offered at Hindu shrines. Traditionally, a basil leaf was placed on the chest of a corpse, after the head had been washed in basil water. In other Eastern cultures it became a funeral herb, planted or scattered on graves. Basil has a mass of conflicting associations. As Culpeper remarked, "This is the herb which all authors are together by the ears about and rail at one another (like lawyers)" (*The English Physician*, 1653). The Greeks and Romans thought it represented hate and misfortune, and that shouting abuse at it encouraged it to grow. In some later European cultures it represented sympathy and the acceptance of love. In Crete, it stood for love washed with tears, taking a middle line. There was no agreement on its properties either, in former times. Some said it was poisonous, others that it was health-inducing. In 16th-century Britain it

was appreciated for its scent. Thomas Tusser listed it as a strewing herb and John Parkinson wrote, "The ordinary Basil is in a manner wholly spent to make sweete or washing waters among other sweete herbs, yet sometimes it is put into nosegays" (*Paradisi*, 1629). Today it is among the most popular and widely grown of culinary herbs.

Description A much-branched half-hardy annual, to 20–60cm/8–24in tall, with soft, ovate, bright green leaves and whorls of small white flowers, borne in terminal racemes in mid to late summer.

Related species Basils are extremely variable. Even within the same species, the pungency and flavour vary considerably, according to the composition of their volatile oils, which depends on soil, climate and growing conditions. They also hybridize easily under cultivation and many that are sold commercially are not recognized as distinct varieties or cultivars by botanists. *O. glabrescens* 'Dark Opal' is a reliable cultivar with purple leaves and bright cerise-pink flowers. *O. g.* 'Purple Ruffles' has large crinkled, purplish leaves with curly edges and makes a vigorous bush. *O. basilicum.* var. *crispum* (curly basil) has coarse, curled, dark green leaves, and is sometimes known as "Neapolitana".

O. b. 'Genovese' has soft but broader leaves than the species, is strongly aromatic, and frequently offered as a culinary variety – popular in pesto sauce. *O. b.* var. *minimum* (bush basil, Greek basil) is very compact and bushy, growing 15–30cm/6–12in tall, and has small, but pungent leaves and tiny white flowers. *O. sanctum* (holy basil, tulsi) is a shrubby perennial, 45–60cm/18–24in, with green, slightly hairy, ovate leaves and thin white to pale mauve flower spikes. Other cultivars with interesting flavours include *O. b.* 'Horapha', often used in oriental cuisines; and *O. b.* 'Cinnamon', which is from Mexico, about 30–60cm/12–24in high, with pink flowers and a distinctive cinnamon scent.

Habitat/distribution Native to India and the Middle East, naturalized in parts of Africa and other tropical and subtropical regions, introduced and widely grown elsewhere.

Growth Basil requires well-drained, moist, medium-rich soil and full sun. It is propagated from seed, which must be sown after any danger of frost in cool regions. In cold, wet, northern summers it may need to be grown on under glass, but flourishes as a container plant and should be kept outside in hot, dry spells to develop the best flavour.

Parts used Leaves – fresh, essential oil.

Top, from left to right Ocimum basilicum; O. glabrescens *'Dark Opal'*; O. g. *'Purple Ruffles'*; O. b. *'Cinnamon'*; O. b. *'Green Ruffles'*; O. b. *'Thai'*.

Right Ocimum basilicum *var.* minimum.

Below right Ocimum sanctum.

USES Medicinal Has antidepressant, antiseptic, soothing properties. The fresh leaves are rubbed on insect bites and stings to relieve itching, made into cough syrups, and taken as an infusion for colds. The leaves or essential oil are used in steam inhalations as a decongestant for colds; diluted essential oil makes an insect repellent or massage oil for depression and anxiety.
Culinary The leaves do not retain their flavour well when dried and are better used fresh. They have an affinity with tomatoes and aubergines (eggplants), and add a distinctive fragrance to tomato-based dishes. Fresh basil should be added towards the end of the cooking process so that its fragrance is not lost. Basil is a good choice for planting in a kitchen herb garden.
Aromatic The essential oil is used in aromatherapy and as a perfumery ingredient.
Other name Sweet basil.

Pesto sauce

The traditional way of making this sauce was to pound the ingredients with a pestle and mortar.

Serves 4
50g/2oz fresh basil leaves
25g/1oz fresh parsley
2–3 cloves of garlic
8 tbsp extra virgin olive oil
25g/1oz grated Parmesan cheese
salt and ground black pepper

Put the basil, parsley, garlic and olive, into a food processor or blender and blend until smooth. Scrape down the mixture from time to time. Decant into a bowl. Stir in the grated Parmesan and season to taste. Keep refrigerated for up to two weeks.

CAUTION Essential oil should not be used during pregnancy. *Ocimum sanctum*, Holy Basil, should only be taken on professional advice and is not to be taken by diabetics.

ONAGRACEAE

Oenothera biennis

Evening primrose

History and traditions An American native, the evening primrose was introduced to Europe in 1619, when seeds were brought to the Padua Botanic Garden in Italy. Although it had some place in the folk medicine of Native Americans, in Europe it was used more as a culinary than a medicinal herb – leaves were put into salads and roots cooked as vegetables. It came to prominence after modern research in the 1980s established that oil from the seeds contains GLA, or gamma-linolenic acid, an unsaturated fatty acid which assists the production of prostaglandins, hormone-like substances, which act as chemical messengers and regulate hormonal systems. It is not related to the primrose (*Primula vulgaris*).

Description An erect biennial, up to 1.5m/ 5ft tall, with a thick, yellowish taproot and a rosette of basal leaves from which the flowering stems arise. These have alternate, lanceolate to ovate leaves, and are topped by bright yellow flowers, which open at night to release their fragrance and are pollinated by moths. Downy pods follow, containing tiny seeds.

Habitat/distribution Originated in North America, introduced and naturalized throughout Europe and in temperate zones. Found on poor, sandy soils, waste ground and embankments, as a garden escapee.

Growth Grow in open, sandy soil in a warm sunny position. This plant self-seeds freely once established. Propagated from seed sown in autumn or spring.

Parts used Seeds – pressed to produce oil.

USES Medicinal The oil is thought to benefit the immune system and regulate hormones. It is taken internally for premenstrual tension, menopausal problems, allergies, skin complaints, such as eczema and acne, and to counteract the effects of excess alcohol. It may also be helpful for high blood pressure, arthritis and multiple sclerosis.

Cosmetic The fresh flowers are often made into face masks to improve skin tone. The oil is an ingredient in commercial cosmetics and pharmaceutical products.

> **CAUTION** Only to be taken on medical advice if other prescribed medication is being taken. Can interact with epilepsy drugs. Not to be taken in pregnancy.

OLEACEAE

Olea europaea

Olive

History and traditions There is evidence that the olive tree has been cultivated north of the Dead Sea since 3700–3600BC. Known to the Egyptians, it was always prized for the quality of the oil from the fruits. The Romans called the tree "*olea*", from *oleum,* meaning oil, the Greek word being *elaio*. The olive branch has been a symbol of peace and reconciliation since the biblical story of the dove returning to Noah's Ark with a sprig of olive in its beak after the flood had subsided.

Description An evergreen tree, 9–12m/ 29–40ft tall, it has pale grey bark and pendulous branches, with smooth, leathery, grey-green, lanceolate to oblong leaves. Creamy-white flowers are borne in short panicles in summer, followed by green, ripening to dark purple fruits, known as drupes.

Habitat/distribution Native to the Mediterranean region, introduced in warm temperate regions of Africa and Asia.

Growth Requires well-drained to dry soil and full sun. Although frost hardy, it can be grown outside successfully only in Mediterranean climates. Propagated by seed sown in autumn or by semi-ripe cuttings in summer.

Parts used Leaves – dried for use in infusions and other herbal preparations; fruits – harvested in autumn and winter, by beating them from

Onopordum acanthium

Scotch thistle

History and traditions This is thought to be the thistle that is the national emblem of Scotland, dating from the time of James III of Scotland (d. 1488). It is also the emblem of the ancient, knightly Order of the Thistle, inaugurated by James V of Scotland, 1513–1542. Some bizarre claims were made for the properties of this plant. Pliny recommended it for baldness and Dioscorides as "a remedy for those that have their bodies drawne backwards".

Description A hardy biennial, growing on a strong taproot, the spiny, toothed, dark green leaves have a striking cobweb-effect pattern of white veins, with purple thistle-head flowers rising on long stems to 1.5m/5ft.

Habitat/distribution Occurs in the Mediterranean, Europe and Asia, introduced and naturalized in other countries.

Growth Grows in most conditions, but flourishes in reasonably fertile, well-drained soil and a sunny position. Propagated by seed sown in autumn or spring.

Parts used Leaves, stems, flowers.

USES Medicinal Scotch thistle is rarely used medicinally currently.

Culinary The whole plant is edible if not very palatable. Young stems can be boiled as a vegetable; flower receptacles are said to be substitutes for artichoke hearts.

Horticultural It is widely grown as a herb garden ornamental.

Other names Cotton thistle and woolly thistle.

---

the trees on to groundsheets; oil – pressed from the fruit. Extra virgin, cold-pressed oil, extracted without heat or chemical solvents, has the best flavour and properties.

USES Medicinal The oil is monounsaturated and its consumption is thought to help lower cholesterol levels and blood pressure, reducing risk of circulatory diseases. Leaves are antiseptic and astringent, taken internally in infusions for nervous tension and high blood pressure and applied externally to cuts and abrasions. The oil

Top The olive tree is slow growing and often attains a great age.

Above An olive grove in Extremadura, Spain.

is thought to be helpful when taken internally for constipation and peptic ulcers.

Culinary The fruits of the olive tree are eaten as appetizers, made into *tapenade* spread, added to salads, sauces, bread, pizzas, pasta and many other dishes. The oil is used in salad dressings, sauces, mayonnaise and as a general cooking oil.

LABIATAE/LAMIACEAE

Origanum

Origanum majorana
Sweet marjoram

Description A half-hardy perennial, often grown as an annual, 60cm/2ft tall, with elliptic pale greyish-green leaves, arranged opposite. The small, white, sometimes pinkish, flowers grow in distinctive knotlike clusters, surrounding the stems, giving it the once popular name "knotted marjoram".

Habitat/distribution *O. majorana* originated in the Mediterranean and Turkey and is widely naturalized in northern Africa, western Asia, parts of India and introduced to many places elsewhere. Found on dryish but often nutrient-rich soils in sunny positions.

Growth Requires well-drained, but not too dry, fertile soil and full sun. Propagated by seed sown in spring, after danger of frost in cool temperate regions.

Parts used Leaves, flowering stems – fresh or dry; essential oil distilled from leaves.

USES Medicinal A warming, relaxing herb with antiseptic properties, taken internally as an infusion for nervous anxiety, insomnia, tension headaches, colds and bronchial complaints, digestive complaints and painful menstruation. Dilute oil is applied externally for muscular aches and pains, sprains and stiff joints.

Culinary It is said to have the most delicate flavour of the marjorams and is widely used in Italian, Greek and Mediterranean cookery, especially in pasta sauces, pizza toppings, tomato sauces, vegetable dishes, and to flavour bread, oil and vinegar.

Aromatic Dried flowering stems add fragrance to potpourri. Essential oil is used in food and cosmetic industries.

History and traditions *Origanum* means "joy of the mountains" from the Greek *oros*, a mountain, and *ganos*, brightness or joy. According to legend, Aphrodite, Greek goddess of love, found this herb in the depths of the ocean and took it to the top of a mountain where it would be close to the sun's rays. Ever since, it has been associated with the return of sunshine and warmth, with love and the banishing of sorrow. It found a place at both weddings and funerals, being used to crown newly married couples and to provide comfort to mourners. The tradition arose that planting *Origanum* on a grave ensured a happy afterlife for the deceased and Gerard recommends it for those "given to over much sighing" (*The Herball*, 1597). It is one of the most versatile herbs, variable in form, and valued through the centuries for its fragrant, medicinal and culinary properties alike.

Species and nomenclature There is often confusion about the difference between oregano and marjoram. Marjoram is the common English name for the *Origanum* species, but *O. vulgare*, or 'wild marjoram', is widely known as 'oregano' and *O. onites* is sometimes called 'Greek oregano'. To complicate

Above Origanum onites, *or pot marjoram, surrounded by Golden marjoram.*

Right Origanum vulgare, *popularly known as oregano, adds flavour to Mediterranean cookery.*

matters further, there are many hybrids among cultivated marjorams, which are difficult to identify and variously named.

Origanum onites
Pot marjoram

Description A hardy to frost-hardy perennial, 60cm/2ft tall, with hairy stems, and ovate-elliptic, bright green, downy leaves. White or purple flowers are borne in dense clusters in mid to late summer.

Habitat/distribution Native to the Mediterranean and the Middle East, introduced and widely grown in other countries. Grows on light, well-drained soils and open hillsides.

Growth Grow in well-drained soil in a sunny position. Propagated by division or by cuttings taken in summer.

Parts used Leaves, flowers – fresh or dried.

USES Culinary The flavour is less delicate than *O. majorana*, and not as pungent and aromatic as most *O. vulgare*, but it makes an acceptable alternative for similar culinary uses.

Aromatic Dried leaves and flowers are added to potpourri.

Right
Origanum
onites

Origanum vulgare
Oregano

Description A variable, bushy, hardy perennial, to 60cm/2ft, with aromatic, ovate, dark green leaves and panicles of pink to purple tubular flowers in summer. It usually has a higher proportion of thymol than *O. majorana*, giving it a more thyme-like scent. The composition of the essential oils and flavour of the plant varies according to soil, sun and general growing conditions. Oregano grown in cooler, wetter regions does not have the same intensity of flavour as that grown in a Mediterranean climate.

Related species There are many attractive, ornamental cultivars of *O. vulgare*, which are not suitable for culinary and medicinal use but are frequently grown in herb gardens, including *O. v.* 'Aureum', a golden marjoram, and *O. v.* 'Polyphant', a variegated marjoram.

Habitat/distribution Native to the Mediterranean, found in dry soils on sunny, open hillsides. Introduced and widely grown in other countries.

Growth Requires well-drained soil and a sunny position. *O. vulgare* is best propagated by division or by cuttings taken in summer – the cultivars must be vegetatively propagated.

Parts used Leaves, flowers – fresh or dried; essential oil distilled from the leaves.

Top Origanum vulgare *'Polyphant'*.

Below Origanum vulgare *'Aureum', an attractive ornamental*.

USES Medicinal Similar uses to *O. majorana*.

Culinary Similar uses to *O. majorana*.

Other name Wild marjoram.

> **CAUTION** Marjorams are only to be taken on medical advice if other prescribed medication is being taken. Can interact with other drugs. Not to be taken in pregnancy.

ARALIACEA

Panax ginseng

Ginseng

History and traditions Used as a tonic and "vital essence" in Chinese medicine for thousands of years. It was so highly prized for its medicinal properties that emperors set up monopolies and wars were fought over the rights to harvest ginseng. First introduced to Europe as early as the 9th century, it did not catch on until the 1950s when scientific studies discovered that its active principles have a "normalizing" effect on various bodily functions. The name *panax* comes from *pan,* all, and *akos,* a remedy. The Chinese name, from which the word ginseng is adapted, means man root, or like a man. *Various Panax* species are cultivated in Asia, China, Russia, Japan, the United States and Britain.

Description A hardy perennial, 70–80cm/ 28–31in tall, it usually has a forked root, erect stems, with fleshy scales at the base and whorls of palmate leaves, with finely serrated leaflets. Insignificant greenish-yellow flowers are followed by bright red berries.

Related species There are several species of ginseng with similar medicinal properties, and as the plants look very alike they are often confused. These include *P. japonicus,* which grows wild in wooded areas of central Japan; *P. quinquefolius* (American ginseng); *Eleutherococcus senticosus* (Siberian ginseng), which has almost identical properties to the Panax species, but is stronger and considered very beneficial. *P. pseudoginseng* refers to several sub-species found in Asia, from the Himalayas to China.

Habitat/distribution The *Panax* species are native to China, Korea and Japan. Found in damp, cool, woodlands. *Eleutherococcus senticosus* is from Siberia.

Growth For successful cultivation, well-drained, sandy loam, with added leaf mould, is essential. Propagation is from seed, but germination is often erratic.

Parts used Roots – processed from 6–7-year-old plants for use in tablets, extracts, tea and medicinal preparations.

USES Medicinal Ginseng is said to stimulate the nervous and immune systems, improve and regulate hormonal secretion, increase general stamina and strength, lower blood sugar and blood cholesterol levels. Modern research has not managed to isolate an active principle in this herb which relates to any one of the specific claims made for it. However, it has been found that the combined action of its many constituents has a general tonic effect on the whole body.

Top left Panax ginseng *roots.*

Top right Panax japonicus.

Centre right Eleutherococcus senticosus.

Right Panax quinquefolius.

CAUTION Should only be taken under medical supervision for short periods. Excess or regular intake may cause headaches, giddiness, nausea, double vision and raised blood pressure. Do not use if you have high blood pressure or in pregnancy.

PAPAVERACEAE

Papaver somniferum

Opium poppy

History and traditions Opium, made by lancing the green seed capsule to extract the milky latex, has been used for medicinal purposes since earliest times, and the Greek authorities Theophrastus and Dioscorides wrote of it in this context. It was probably introduced to Europe by early Arabian physicians, and a cough syrup made from the opium poppy, widely recommended by the Arabian, Mesue, in the 11th century, was adopted as a standard for many centuries following. But as a highly addictive, powerful narcotic, opium caused as many problems as it solved. Opium poppies are now cultivated on a large scale as the source of powerful pain-killing drugs, including morphine and codeine (two of the most important of its 25 alkaloids), as well as to produce the drug heroin (diamorphine). The flowers are frequently grown in herb gardens as ornamentals.

Description A hardy annual, up to 1.5m/5ft tall, it has oblong, deeply lobed, blue-green leaves. Large, lilac, pink or white flowers, with papery petals, borne in early summer, are followed by blue-green seed pods.

Habitat/distribution Native to southeast Europe, the Middle East and Asia. Introduced elsewhere. Grows on shallow, chalky (alkaline) soils in sunny positions.

Growth Prefers well-drained soil and full sun. Propagated by seed sown in spring, often self-seeds once established.

Parts used Fruits, seeds.

USES Medicinal Proprietary drugs and pharmaceutical products are made from the fruits. Not for home remedies or self-treatment.

Culinary The seeds do not contain any of the alkaloids found in the capsules. They are dried for use whole or ground in breads, biscuits, bakery products and as a garnish. Commercially produced seed is from a subspecies of *P. somniferum*, developed for its seed production.

> **CAUTION** Legal restrictions apply to this plant and its products in most countries.

PASSIFLORACEAE

Passiflora incarnata

Passion flower

History and traditions A plant of tropical and subtropical regions of the Americas, it was imaginatively dubbed "Calvary Lesson" by Roman Catholic missionaries in South America, taking the intricate form of its flower to represent Christ's crucifixion. The three styles are for the nails used on the cross; the five anthers for the five wounds; the corona is the crown of thorns; and the ten sepals are for ten of the twelve apostles – leaving out Peter and Judas Iscariot, who betrayed him. The lobed leaves and tendrils symbolize the hands and scourges of Christ's tormentors.

Description A hardy perennial, climbing plant on a woody stem, to 8m/26ft, it clings to its support with axillary tendrils and has deeply lobed leaves and attractive creamy-white to lavender flowers, with purple calyces.

Habitat/distribution Native to tropical regions of North and South America, occurs in Asia and Australia, introduced and grown elsewhere.

Growth Requires well-drained, sandy soil and a sunny position. Propagation is easiest from semi-ripe cuttings taken in summer. Seed requires heat to germinate and can be slow and erratic to grow.

Parts used The whole plant – cut when fruiting and dried for use in infusions and medicinal preparations.

USES Medicinal Has sedative, pain-relieving properties and is taken for nervous conditions and insomnia.

GERANIACEAE

Pelargonium

History and traditions Most scented pelargoniums, often familiarly known as "geraniums", come from South Africa and were introduced to Europe some time in the 17th century. The scented-leafed varieties were very popular in Britain with the Victorians, who grew them as house plants, and in France distilled oil from the "rose-scented" group became an important perfume ingredient in the mid-19th century.

Description and species There are numerous hybrids and cultivars with differing foliage, habits of growth and types of fragrance. It is the leaves that are scented. The flowers, appearing in summer, are virtually unperfumed, smaller and more insignificant than those of regal and zonal pelargoniums, grown as colourful bedding plants. These are some of the most popular scented-leafed pelargoniums:

P. graveolens – An upright shrubby plant, it grows 60–90cm/2–3ft tall, and has deeply cut, triangular, rough-textured, bright green leaves and small pink flowers. It grows vigorously and is slightly hardier than most of the others. This is the original "rose geranium", though the scent is much harsher and more spicy than a true rose fragrance, with strong overtones of lemon.

P. odoratissimum – A low-growing, species – 30cm/1ft – with a trailing habit and little white flowers borne on long stems. The soft, rounded, bright green leaves are wavy at the edges and apple-scented.

P. crispum – Has a neat, upright habit, and grows 60–70cm/24–28in tall. It has pink flowers and clear green, three-lobed, crinkly leaves, which are coarse to the touch and pungently lemon-scented.

P. crispum 'Variegatum' – Is an attractive variegated cultivar, with crisply curled leaves, edged with creamy yellow and the same, strong lemon scent as the species.

P. tomentosum – Is a lovely trailing, or prostrate species, 0.9–1.2m/3–4ft, which makes a good container plant, if grown on a stand and allowed to drape downward. It has small white flowers and soft, downy, grey-green leaves with a strong peppermint fragrance.

P. 'Fragrans' – A small, upright subshrub, 45cm/18in tall, it has clusters of small, greyish-green, rounded leaves, with finely cut, crinkled edges and a smooth, silky texture.

The flowers are white and the foliage pleasantly pine-scented with overtones of nutmeg.

P. 'Lady Plymouth' – An attractive hybrid, 0.6–1.5m/2–5ft tall, it has triangular, deeply lobed, crisp-textured leaves, with a cream and green variegation, little pink flowers and a citrus fragrance with a hint of rose.

Habitat/distribution Most pelargoniums are natives of South Africa; a few come from tropical Africa, the eastern Mediterranean, the Middle East, India, western Asia and Australia. Cultivated in France, northern Africa and Réunion for essential-oil production.

Growth All are tender and must be grown as conservatory plants in cool, temperate regions, though they are best kept outside in the summer months. A few (including *P. graveolens* and *P.* 'Fragrans') may survive a mild winter in a cold greenhouse. They make good container plants and should be given a gritty, loam-based compost. Cut back in autumn and prune lightly in spring to maintain a neat, bushy habit. Pelargoniums grown outside need free-draining soil and a sunny position. They are easily propagated by softwood cuttings taken in summer.

Parts used Leaves, essential oil – distilled from the leaves.

USES Culinary The pungency of the leaves makes them suitable as flavouring agents only – not to be eaten. Leaves of *P. graveolens* and *P. odoratissimum* are best for flavouring ice creams and cakes and fruit punches.

Aromatic Dried leaves and essential oil are added to potpourri and their strong scents make them effective in insect repellent or anti-moth sachets. "Geranium oil" is used as a commercial flavouring and perfume ingredient and used in aromatherapy.

Other name Scented pelargonium.

Opposite page, far left and top right Pelargonium graveolens; below right Pelargonium odoratissimum.

This page, clockwise from top to bottom Pelargonium tomentosum; Pelargonium 'Fragrans'; Pelargonium 'Lady Plymouth' Pelargonium crispum.

LABIATAE/LAMIACEAE

Perilla frutescens

Perilla

History and traditions In China, perilla has been a medicinal herb for centuries and it has long been cultivated in the East, from India to Japan, as a culinary herb and for its many economic uses. The leaves produce a sweet volatile oil, the seeds a pressed oil, which is used in similar ways to linseed oil. It has recently become increasingly popular in the West for its culinary uses and as an ornamental garden plant.

Description A half-hardy annual with broadly ovate, deeply-veined leaves, reddish stems and small spikes of white flowers in summer. There are both green and purple-leaved forms.

Related species *P. frutescens* 'Crispa' (pictured below) is a variety with curly-edged leaves.

Habitat/distribution Occurs from the Himalayas to East Asia, naturalized in parts of Europe and North America.

Growth Grows best in deep, rich, moist but well-drained soil, in sun or partial shade. Propagated by seed sown in spring, after frosts in cool temperate regions. Pinch out tips to encourage and maintain bushy plants.

Parts used Leaves – fresh for culinary use, dried for medicinal infusions and decoctions; seeds – dried for decoctions; volatile oil – from leaves; pressed oil – from seeds.

USES Medicinal Used in Chinese herbal medicine for colds and chest infections, nausea, stomach upsets and allergic reactions.

Culinary Leaves and seeds are a popular ingredient in Japanese cookery and add colour and an unusual spicy flavour to salads, seafood and stir-fry dishes.

General Volatile oil is added to commercial food, confectionery and dental products; oil from seeds is used to waterproof paper for umbrellas, in paints and printing inks.

Other names Beefsteak plant and shiso.

Above *P. frutescens 'Crispa'*.

UMBELLIFERAE/APIACEAE

Petroselinum crispum

Parsley

History and traditions Petroselinum comes from the Greek name given to it by Dioscorides, *petros selinon*. In the Middle Ages this became corrupted to *petrocilium*, ending up in the anglicized version, by a process of "Chinese whispers" as parsley. The Greeks associated it with death and funerals and according to Homer fed it to their chariot horses, but it was the Romans who took to it as a major culinary herb. Pliny complained that every sauce and salad contained it, and it has remained ubiquitous as a sauce, salad and garnishing herb to this day. Parsley has attracted a mass of silly superstitions. Transplanting it, giving it away, picking it when in love and so on, all foretold disaster. Some said it flourished only where the "mistress is master", others that it would grow only for the wicked, or, conversely, for the honest. Its slowness to germinate when soil is cold led to tales that it had gone seven times to the devil and back, and should be sown on Good Friday to outwit him. *A Grete Herball*, 1539, has some ingenious ideas on how to ensure it is well "crisped" or curly: "Before the sowing of them, stuffe a tennis ball with the seedes and beat the same well against the ground, whereby the seedes may be a little bruised. Or when the

parcelye is well come up, go over the bed with a waighty roller whereby it may so presse the leaves down."

Description A frost-hardy biennial, growing on a short, stout taproot to 30–60cm/1–2ft, it has triangular, three-pinnate leaves, curled at the margin. Yellow-green flowers are borne in umbels in its second year.

Related species *Petroselinum crispum* 'Italian', also known as French or flat-leaved parsley, is a larger, hardier plant, growing to 80–90cm/32in–3ft and has smooth, uncurled three-pinnate leaves. *P. c.* var. *tuberosum*, Hamburg parsley, has small, flat leaves, with a celery-like flavour and is grown for its large roots, which are eaten as a vegetable.

Habitat/distribution
The genus is native to the Mediterranean region of Europe, found in fields and on rocky slopes.

P. crispum has been developed under cultivation and is widely grown as a crop in many countries.

Growth Parsley requires rich, moist but well-drained soil and a sunny position, or partial shade. As leaves coarsen in the second, flowering, year, it is often grown as an annual and is propagated by seed, sown in spring. If sown *in situ* before soil has warmed up, germination may be slow or erratic. For best results, sow in containers, maintaining a temperature of 18–21°C/64–70°F until seedlings appear. The young plants can then be hardened off to grow outside at lower temperatures.

Parts used Leaves, stems – best fresh or frozen for culinary use as flavour is lost with drying; roots – of 'Hamburg' variety; essential oil – distilled from leaves and seeds.

Left and right
Flat-leaved parsley.

Above left *'Italian' or flat-leaved parsley.*

Above *Hamburg parsley.*

USES Medicinal Parsley is rich in vitamin A and C, and acts as an antioxidant. It also contains a flavonoid, apigenin, which is an anti-allergen. Although used in herbal medicine for a variety of complaints, including menstrual problems, kidney stones, urinary infections, rheumatism and arthritis, it is not for self-treatment. Tea can be made from leaves or roots used to treat jaundice and coughs.

Culinary The leaves of this herb are added to salads, sauces, salad dressings, butter, stuffings, snipped into meat, fish and vegetable dishes and used as a garnish. The stalks, which have a stronger flavour than the leaves, are essential to a *bouquet garni* for flavouring casseroles and cooked dishes. The roots of *P. tuberosum* are cooked as a vegetable. The essential oil is used in commercial food products.

CAUTION Although parsley is perfectly safe, used whole in culinary dishes, it is toxic in excess, particularly in the form of essential oil. Flat-leaved *Petroselinum* should not be confused with *Aethusa cynapium*, a highly poisonous wild plant. Should not be used medicinally if pregnant.

MONIMIACEAE
Peumus boldus
Boldo

History and traditions The medicinal properties of this small, shrubby tree from Chile were first investigated in Europe by a French doctor in 1869. It was discovered to be effective in stimulating the liver and expelling intestinal worms. In its country of origin it was formerly taken as a tonic tea and digestive, prescribed as a substitute for quinine and made into a powder to take as snuff.

Description An aromatic evergreen tree growing to 6–7m/19–23ft, it is the sole species of its genus. It has light to grey-green, leathery leaves, rich in a balsamic volatile oil. Greenish male and female flowers appear in late summer, borne on separate trees.

Habitat/distribution It is native to Chile, introduced elsewhere. Occurs on sunny slopes of the Andes mountains.

Growth It is frost-hardy, and grows best in sandy, acid soil in a sunny position. Propagated by semi-ripe cuttings in summer, may also be grown from seed sown in spring.

Parts used Leaves – dried for use in infusions and other medicinal preparations; bark – dried for extracts.

USES Medicinal It has mainly been used for liver complaints, urinary infections and to expel intestinal worms. Extracts are included in commercial and pharmaceutical products.

PHYTOLACCACEAE
Phytolacca americana
Pokeweed

History and traditions A poisonous plant, once used by Native Americans as a purgative and powerful treatment for various complaints. They knew it as *pocan*, which is where the name pokeweed comes from. It was adopted by European settlers as a treatment for venereal disease, and for its painkilling and anti-inflammatory properties. In modern times, its complex chemical structure has attracted much scientific interest. It contains compounds that affect cell division and it is currently being investigated as a potential source of drugs to combat AIDS-related diseases and cancers.

Description A large, frost-hardy perennial, 0.9–1.5m/3–5ft tall, with smooth, hollow, purplish stems and ovate to lanceolate leaves. It has racemes of white, sometimes pink-tinged flowers in late summer, followed by large drooping spikes of purple-black berries, which provide a dye to colour ink.

Habitat/distribution A North American native, it has been introduced elsewhere and widely grown in the Mediterranean region of Europe. Occurs in rich soils at field edges.

Growth Grow in rich, moist soil. Propagated by seed sown in spring or autumn or by division.

Parts used Roots and fruits (berries) – collected in autumn and dried for use in decoctions, tinctures and other medicinal preparations.

USES Medicinal Pokeweed has anti-inflammatory, antibacterial, antiviral, antifungal properties and is destructive to many parasitic disease-causing organisms. It is also capable of stimulating the immune and lymphatic systems. Used for many disorders, including auto-immune diseases, skin diseases, bronchitis and arthritis, but is for qualified practitioners only. Despite its toxicity, the leaves of this plant are sometimes boiled as a vegetable, the water being discarded.

CAUTION The whole plant is toxic if eaten, especially roots and berries.

PIPERACEAE
Piper nigrum
Black pepper

History and traditions Black pepper has been a valuable trading commodity since Alaric I, King of the Visigoths, demanded 3,000lb of it as a ransom during his siege of Rome between 410–408BC. Its high price during the Middle Ages was a major incentive for the Portuguese to find a sea route to India, where it came from, although the price fell following the discovery of a passage round the Cape of Good Hope in 1498. As cultivation was extended into Malaysia, the Portuguese retained a lucrative trading monopoly in pepper into the 18th century, and much of the wealth of Venice and Genoa depended on its trade. In Britain it was heavily taxed from the 17th to the 19th centuries. Pepper's virtues as a digestive were early recognized in the West and it has a long tradition of medicinal use in Ayurvedic and Chinese systems of healing.

Description A perennial climber, growing to 6m/20ft, with a strong, woody stem and ovate, prominently-veined, dark green leaves. It has drooping spikes of inconspicuous white flowers, followed by long clusters of spherical green fruits or berries, which redden as they mature. Black pepper is produced from whole fruits, picked and dried just as they start to go red; white pepper is from ripe fruits, with the outer layer removed, and green pepper is from unripe fruits, pickled to prevent it turning dark.

Habitat/distribution Native to southern India and Sri Lanka, introduced and cultivated in Indonesia, Malaysia, Brazil and many tropical regions. In the wild it grows in humus-rich, moist soil. It is cultivated by training it up trees or horizontally along frames.

Growth Pepper requires deep, rich, manured soil, plenty of water, a humid atmosphere and a shady position. It is sometimes grown as a pot plant in temperate climates.

Parts used Fruits (peppercorns).

USES Medicinal A pungent, stimulating digestive, which relieves flatulence. It is used in Ayurvedic medicine for coughs and colds and as a nerve tonic. It also has a reputation as an aphrodisiac.

Culinary Its chief use is as a condiment and flavouring in a wide range of dishes in the cookery of most countries. It is currently the most widely consumed spice in the world.

Below *Mixed peppercorns.*

PLANTAGINACEAE
Plantago major
Plantain

History and traditions The Saxons called it *"waybroad"*, because it was so often found by the wayside. And the story goes that this plant was once a beautiful young girl, who was changed into plantain for refusing to leave the roadway where she expected her lover to appear. As a medicinal herb it was highly rated by Pliny, who attributed to it the ability to fuse together pieces of flesh cooking in a pot, and to cure the madness of dogs – or their bites. It was often recommended as an antidote to poison and in the US it was held to be a remedy for rattle-snake bite by native tribes.

Description A small, undistinguished perennial, 40cm/16in high, it has a basal rosette of ovate leaves and cylindrical spikes of inconspicuous brownish-green flowers.

Habitat/distribution Native to Europe and introduced in other temperate zones worldwide. Occurs widely in cultivated land, garden paths and lawns, fields, wastelands and roadsides.

Growth Said to prefer moist soil, but tolerates any conditions in sun or shade. Self-seeds freely.

Parts used Leaves – fresh or dried.

USES Medicinal Plantain was thought to promote healing and to have antibacterial properties. Mainly used as a poultice or in ointments to be applied externally to wounds, sores, ulcers, bites and stings.

BERBERIDACEAE

Podophyllum peltatum

American mandrake

History and traditions A poisonous herb, *Podophyllum peltatum* was formerly used by Native Americans as a powerful purgative medicine, vermifuge and wart remover. They also made it into an insecticide for potato crops and reputedly took it to commit suicide. It was introduced to Western medicine in the 1780s by a German doctor involved in the American War of Independence and by 1820 was listed in the United States *Pharmacopoeia*. It is called may apple for the juicy fruits, which were sometimes eaten, despite their relative toxicity. The generic name comes from the Greek for *podos*, a foot, and *phyllon*, a leaf, for its supposed resemblance to a bird's webbed foot. The specific term, *peltatum*, means shield-shaped. Despite being called mandrake it is not related to *Mandragora*. In recent years, the active ingredient, podophyllotoxin, has been isolated for use in anti-cancer drugs.

Description A hardy perennial with a creeping rhizome, and usually unbranched stems, it is 30–45cm/12–18in tall. The large leaves are deeply divided into 4–7 wedge-shaped segments, lobed at the tops. Small, drooping white flowers, with yellow centres, are followed by fleshy, lemon-shaped fruits. The whole plant has an unpleasant smell.

Related species *P. hexandrum* (Indian podophyllum) which grows in the Himalayas, has red fruits and is more poisonous, with a higher concentration of podophyllotoxin.

Habitat *P. peltatum* is native to North America, found in damp woods and meadows.

Growth Grow in humus-rich, moist soil in dappled shade. Propagated by division of runners.

Parts used Rhizomes – extracted for commercial drugs.

USES Medicinal It is a component of pharmaceutical drugs for treating certain cancers.

Other name May apple.

> **CAUTION** Although once used in herbal treatments, it is very poisonous and should never be used for self-medication. Subject to legal restrictions in most countries.

POLEMONIACEAE

Polemonium caeruleum

Jacob's ladder

History and traditions This is an ornamental plant, which retains its place in the herb garden through its ancient traditions and associations. Known to the Greeks, it was mentioned by Dioscorides, used for treating dysentery and thought to be effective against the bites of venomous beasts. It was still listed in various European pharmacopoeias into the 19th century. The whole flowering plant and roots were used and it was recommended for venereal disease and the bites of rabid dogs, but it is no longer considered to be of medicinal value. The name Jacob's ladder comes from the ladder-like arrangement of the leaves, and someone thought of associating it with the ladder to heaven of Jacob's dream in the biblical story (Genesis 28:12), with the sky represented by the blue flowers.

Description A hardy, clump-forming perennial, 30–90cm/1–3ft tall, it grows on a creeping rootstock, with pinnate leaves divided into lance-shaped leaflets. The lavender-blue, bell-shaped flowers are borne on erect stems in drooping panicles.

Habitat/distribution Occurs widely in northern and central Europe, North America, and Asia in damp areas and shady woodlands.

Growth Requires rich, moisture-retentive soil and a shady or partially shady position. Propagated by seed sown in spring or by division in autumn.

USES Medicinal Rarely used today.

POLYGONACEAE

Polygonum bistorta
Bistort

History and traditions The generic name comes from the Greek *poly*, many, and *gonu*, knee, for the knotted shape of the stems of many polygonum species. Bistort became known as a medicinal plant in the 16th century, gaining a reputation as a wound-healing herb. It was cited in *The Universal Herbal*, 1832, as a treatment for "intermittent fever", and considered helpful for diabetes into the 20th century.

Description A hardy perennial with a stout, twisted rhizome, it has a clump of broad, ovate basal leaves, from which the pale pink, cylindrical flower spikes arise on erect "jointed" stems to about 50cm/20in.

Habitat/distribution Occurs throughout Europe and Asia, frequently found near streams and waterways in damp meadows, mixed woodlands and on high slopes.

Growth Grows best in rich, moist soil, in sun or partial shade. Easily propagated by division, it is an invasive plant, but can make useful ground cover in damp areas.

Parts used Rhizomes – dried for powders, extracts, decoctions and other medicinal preparations.

USES Medicinal High in tannins so has a strong astringent action. Said to reduce inflammation and promote healing, it is used as a gargle for gum disease, mouth ulcers and sore throats, applied externally to haemorrhoids, cuts and wounds and taken internally for diarrhoea.

PORTULACACEAE

Portulaca oleracea
Purslane

History and traditions A herb of ancient origin, purslane was known to the Egyptians, and grown in India and China for thousands of years. The Romans ate it as a vegetable and it was cultivated in Europe from at least the beginning of the 16th century, though not introduced to Britain until 1582. An important remedy for scurvy, it was one of the herbs that the early settlers thought indispensable and took with them to North America. Although it had some medicinal applications in former times, especially in China, it has always been chiefly valued for its culinary uses. It is still appreciated in France and commercially cultivated there for this purpose.

Description A half-hardy annual, with pink, prostrate, much-branched stems and rounded, fleshy, bright green leaves, it grows to about 30cm/12in. It has very small, yellow flowers in late summer which soon fade to reveal the seed capsules with opening lids and filled with numerous black seeds.

Related species There is a golden-leafed variety, *P. oleracea* var. *aurea*, and the widely cultivated *P. oleracea* var. *sativa*.

Habitat/distribution Native to southern Europe, Asia and China, introduced elsewhere. Occurs on dry, sandy soils in sunny sites.

Growth Grow in light, well-drained soil, but provide plenty of water for good leaf development. Propagated from seed, sown after danger of frosts in cool temperate regions.

Parts used Leaves – fresh, picked before flowering for culinary use, fresh or dried for medicinal use.

USES Medicinal Recent scientific studies have found that *P. oleracea* contains omega-3 fatty acids, thought to be helpful in preventing heart disease and strengthening the immune system. The leaves are also a good source of Vitamin C and contain calcium, iron, carotene, thiamine, riboflavin and niacin. Purslane is also a diuretic and mildly laxative.

Culinary In 18th-century Britain it was a popular salad herb and is still eaten in the Middle East and India as a cooked vegetable and in salads. In France it is used in sorrel soup, helping to reduce the acidity of the sorrel.

Sorrel and purslane soup

Serves 4–6

15ml/1 tbsp olive oil
1 medium onion, chopped
2 cloves garlic, crushed
225g/8oz sorrel leaves
50g/2oz purslane leaves
225g/8oz potatoes, peeled and diced
1.2 litres/2 pints/5 cups water
salt and ground black pepper
a dash of grated nutmeg

Heat the oil in a pan, add the onion and garlic and cook gently for 5 minutes, until soft but not browned. Add the sorrel, purslane and potato and stir over a low heat for 2–3 minutes. Season, and add a little grated nutmeg. Pour in the water, bring to the boil then simmer for about 15 minutes until the potatoes are tender. Cool slightly, then liquidize the soup. Reheat before serving.

PRIMULACEAE
Primula veris
Cowslip

History and traditions Cowslips were
sometimes known as "keyflowers", suggested by
the shape of the flower clusters, which look like
a little bunch of keys. In Norse mythology they
were dedicated to Freya, giving access to her
palace, but in the Christian era became
"St Peter's Keys" or the "Keys to Heaven".
The generic name, *Primula*, comes from *primus*,
first, in recognition that they are among the
earliest flowers of spring. At one time, when
they were plentiful, they were gathered in vast
quantities to make spring tonics and the
gently soporific, pale yellow cowslip wine.
Many medicinal uses were assigned to the
flowers and distilled cowslip water was said
to be good for the memory. The cosmetic
applications were mentioned reprovingly by
William Turner: "Some women we find, sprinkle
ye floures of cowslip with whyte wine and after
still it and wash their faces with that water to
drive wrinkles away and to make them fayre in
the eyes of the worlde rather than in the eyes
of God, Whom they are not afrayd to offend"
(*The New Herball*, 1551).
Description A perennial on a short rhizome
with dense fibrous roots and a rosette of broadly
ovate, rough-textured leaves. Flower stems rise
above the basal leaves, 15–20cm/6–8in, and are
topped by terminal umbels of fragrant, golden-
yellow flowers, with tubular calyces.
Habitat/distribution Native to Europe and
parts of Asia, introduced and sometimes
naturalized elsewhere, found in meadows and
pasture lands. A once common plant, it is now
rare in the wild and a protected species in many
European countries.
Growth Prefers deep, humus-rich, moist soil
and partial shade. Propagated by seed sown in
late summer in containers, left outside through
the winter as a period of stratification, when
they are exposed to frost, is necessary for germination. Easily propagated by division in autumn.
Parts used Flowers – fresh (but must not be
picked from the wild, as they are quite rare).

USES Medicinal Cowslips have sedative,
expectorant properties and contain salicylates
(as in aspirin). They are mildly diuretic and are
taken as a tea for insomnia, anxiety and
respiratory tract infections.
Culinary Flowers may be added to salads.

> **CAUTION** Should not be taken medicinally
> during pregnancy or if sensitive to aspirin.
> May cause allergic skin irritations.

PRIMULACEAE
Primula vulgaris
Primrose

History and traditions The medicinal
properties of the primrose, *P. vulgaris*, are similar
to those of the cowslip (*P. veris*) and have been
listed in old herbals, since Pliny's time, for similar
complaints. The primrose was made into salves
and ointments and considered an important
remedy for paralysis, rheumatic pain and gout.
Its value as a sedative was well known and
Gerard remarks that primrose tea, drunk in the
month of May, "is famous for curing the
phrensie". It was popular in cookery.
Description A low-growing perennial, to
15cm/6in, with a rosette of deeply veined,
softly hairy, broad ovate leaves and clusters of
saucer-shaped, pale yellow, slightly fragrant
flowers in early spring.
Habitat/distribution A European native, found
in northern Asia, introduced elsewhere,
found on rich, damp soils in shady woodlands
and hedgerows. Now becoming rare in the
wild, and a protected species in many countries.
Growth See *P. veris*.
Parts used Flowers (must not be picked from
the wild, as they are becoming very rare).

USES Medicinal Taken as a tea to calm anxiety.
They have similar properties to cowslips.
Culinary Flowers are added to salads and
desserts or candied to decorate cakes.

> **CAUTION** Not be taken during pregnancy or if
> sensitive to aspirin.

Pulmonaria officinalis

Lungwort

History and traditions Both the Latin and common names of this herb point to its principal former use in treating lung complaints. The spotted leaves were thought to resemble lungs and it is often cited as an example of the application of the Doctrine of Signatures, an influential Renaissance philosophy, which held that the medicinal uses of plants were indicated by their correspondence in appearance to the part of the human body affected. It is often grown in herb gardens for its historical associations and attractive foliage and habit.

Description A hardy perennial, growing to 30cm/12in, it has hairy stems and dark green leaves, blotched with creamy-white spots. The tubular flowers, borne in spring, are pink at first, then turn blue.

Habitat/distribution Occurs in Europe, parts of Asia and North America, in woodlands.

Growth Grows best in humus-rich, moist soil and a shady position. Propagated by division, in late spring after flowering, or in autumn. Although it self-seeds in the garden, collected seed seldom germinates satisfactorily.

Parts used Leaves – dried for use in infusions and extracts.

USES Medicinal The herb contains a soothing mucilage and has expectorant properties. It is still sometimes used for bronchial infections and coughs, but it is now thought that it may mirror some of the toxicity discovered in *Symphytum*, to which it is closely related.

LABIATAE/LAMIACEAE

Prunella vulgaris

Selfheal

History and traditions A herb with an ancient history in Chinese herbalism, but apparently unknown to the ancient Greeks and Romans. *Prunella vulgaris* has featured in Chinese medical texts since the end of the previous millennium, where it is said to be mainly associated with "liver energy" disorders. In Europe its common names, "self-heal", "all-heal" and "hook-heal", all indicate its former use as a wound herb and activator of the body's defences, as explained by Culpeper: "Self-heal, whereby when you're hurt you heal yourself." It was held to be "a special remedy for inward and outward wounds" (Culpeper, *The English Physician*, 1653) and commonly taken to have the same virtues as *Ajuga reptans* (bugle). It was taken to North America by settlers, where it soon became established and known as "heart of the earth" and "blue curls". However, unlike *Ajuga* it still has a limited place in modern herbal medicine.

Description An aromatic perennial on a creeping rootstock, it is 50cm/20in in height. Leaves are linear to ovate, and compact spikes of violet, two-lipped florets are borne in the leaf axils from midsummer to mid-autumn.

Habitat/distribution Native to Europe, northern Africa and Asia, naturalized in North America, found on sunny banks, in dry grassland and open woodland.

Growth Grow in light soil in sun or dappled shade; tolerates most conditions. Propagated by seed sown in spring or by division in spring. It is inclined to be invasive.

Parts used Flowering stems – dried for use in infusions and medicinal preparations.

USES Medicinal It has antibacterial properties and is used externally to soothe burns, skin inflammations, bites and bruises, sore throats and inflamed gums.

axils and followed by ovoid fruit, in little "cups" (acorns).

Related species The North American *Q. alba*, the white oak, also has a history of medicinal use, and was said to be effective against gangrene.

Habitat/distribution Native to Europe, occurs widely in the northern hemisphere in forests, open woodland and parkland, often found on clay soils.

Growth Grow in deep, fertile soil. May be propagated from seed, sown in containers in autumn. Very slow-growing.

Parts used Bark – stripped from mature trees and dried for use in decoctions and extracts.

USES Medicinal The oak has astringent, anti-inflammatory, antiseptic properties and is said to control bleeding. Applied externally to cuts, abrasions, ulcers, skin irritations, varicose veins and haemorrhoids. Sometimes recommended to be taken internally for haemorrhage, diarrhoea and gastric upsets. It was formerly used as a substitute for cinchona bark.

Other names Common oak and English oak.

FAGACEAE
Quercus robur
Oak

History and traditions Few plants have been invested with as much magic, mystery and symbolic importance in Britain and much of Europe as the common oak. It was used in Druid ceremonies and thought to protect from lightning strikes – especially if planted near buildings to attract lightning away from them. Carrying an acorn was said to preserve youth, and dew gathered from beneath an oak was a potent ingredient in beauty lotions. They are exceptionally long-lived trees, and individual oaks were attributed characters of their own, complete with their own canon of folklore. They were also greatly valued for the durability of the wood, used in furniture, buildings and ships. The medicinal properties of the bark were well recognized by herbalists in former times. Culpeper lists many uses for it, declaring that it will "assuage inflammation and stop all manner of fluxes in man or woman".

Description A large deciduous tree, growing up to 25m/82ft in height. It has wide spreading branches, rugged grey-brown bark and small dark green ovate leaves, with deep rounded lobes. Male flowers are thin catkins; female flowers are borne in spikes in the leaf

Top *An English oak, Quercus robur, growing in a park in Germany.*

Above *An oak tree.*

Left *The distinctive, lobed dark green leaves of the oak tree feature in decorative carvings through the centuries, as family emblems and on heraldic shields.*

Left Rheum palmatum.

Above R. rhabarbarum.

POLYGONACEAE

Rheum palmatum

Rhubarb

History and traditions Rhubarb has been an important medicinal herb in China for many centuries. It is mentioned in the *Shen Nong Canon of Herbs*, dating from c.100BC, though claims exist that it has been recorded in much earlier Chinese texts, dating from 2700BC. Several species of rhubarb (there are 50 in the genus) were used, but *R. palmatum* is thought to be the main source of Chinese medicinal rhubarb. The plant was first grown in Europe in 1763. *R. officinale*, also medicinal and of Chinese origin,

came to Europe, as a plant, in 1867. However, rhubarb in dried or powdered form had been known for centuries before that in the West. It was imported to ancient Greece, where they called it *rha-barbarum* because it was brought by traders from the barbaric regions beyond the river Rha (Volga). It reached Europe in the 13th century and was in demand as a purgative drug, which lacked the side effects of other more toxic products, remaining popular into the 20th century. Rhubarb powder was a major constituent of the 19th-century proprietary medicine, Gregory powder, named after the Scottish doctor who patented it. In an article in *The Lancet*, 1921, it is cited as a certain, even

"magical", remedy for dysentery, when administered in small, strictly controlled amounts.

Description A large hardy perennial, to 2m/6ft, on a thick rhizome, with a basal clump of palmately lobed leaves. Spires of reddish-green flowers arise on long, hollow stems in summer.

Related species Edible garden rhubarb is from hybrids, developed during the 19th century, of *R. rhabarbarum* syn. *R. rhaponticum*, and there are now many cultivars. It is slightly laxative, but does not have medicinal properties.

Habitat/distribution Native to China and northeast Asia, found on deep, moist soils at altitudes of 3,000–4,000m. Introduced elsewhere in temperate zones.

Growth Requires rich, moist soil and a sunny situation. It is possible to propagate from seed, but division of roots in spring or autumn is the preferable method. Cultivars must be propagated by division.

Parts used Rhizomes – dried for use in decoctions, powders and medicinal preparations.

USES Medicinal Used in very small doses for diarrhoea and gastric upsets, and in larger doses for chronic constipation. Also given for liver and gall bladder complaints.

A 13th-century wonder drug

Rhubarb's reputation as a wonder drug is said to have been established in the 13th century after an Armenian monk staked his life (and won) that rhubarb would cure a lady of the court of the Mongol chieftain Mangu.

Medicinal dried rhubarb all came from China originally but was known by a variety of names after the route it took to reach its customers in Europe. "East India rhubarb" came down the Indus to the Persian Gulf, the Red Sea and Alexandria. "Turkey rhubarb" came overland, to the Turkish ports of Aleppo and Smyrna.

"Chinese rhubarb" came via Moscow, and "Russian" or "Crown rhubarb" was the same product, so named once it had become a Russian monopoly, controlled from the early 18th century by the Kiachta Rhubarb Commission, set up on the Siberian/Mongolian border.

This organization maintained quality and price but prevented international trade until its eventual abolition in 1782. *R. rhabarbarum* (from which edible, garden rhubarb was later developed) comes from Siberia and was grown in the Padua Botanic Gardens from 1608.

CAUTION All rhubarb leaves are toxic. Medicinal rhubarb should not be taken during pregnancy or while breast-feeding.

ROSACEAE

Rosa

History and traditions Roses have been cultivated for thousands of years and were once valued as much for their medicinal and culinary qualities as for their fragrance. Asian species of roses were used in ancient Chinese medicine and roses of Persian origin by the Greeks and Romans. The Greek poet Anacreon referred to their therapeutic value when he wrote, "The rose distils a healing balm, the beating pulse of pain to calm." In AD77 the Roman writer Pliny listed over 30 disorders as responding to treatment with preparations of rose. Medieval herbals contain many entries on the healing and restorative power of the rose, and in *The English Physician*, 1653, Culpeper gives pages of rose

remedies for inflammation of the liver, venereal disease, sores in the mouth and throat, aching joints, "slippery bowels" and a host of other complaints. Red rose petals were listed in the British *Pharmacopoeia* as ingredients for pharmaceutical preparations until the 1930s. Their medicinal, culinary and fragrant uses are celebrated in all the old herbals and stillroom books with a huge range of recipes for ointments, lozenges, syrups, vinegars, conserves, cakes, candies and wafers. There are instructions for making rose water, rose oil and cosmetic lotions. Sir Hugh Platt, in *Delights for Ladies*, 1594, has at least three lengthy entries on different methods of drying rose "leaves" (petals) to best effect.

Description and species

***R. canina* (Dog rose)** – This is the wild rose of English hedgerows, known as the dog rose for its supposed ability, according to Pliny, to cure the bites of mad dogs. Its succulent, but acidic, red hips were made into tarts in the 17th century, and came to be greatly valued in the 20th century for their high vitamin C content. It is a hardy, deciduous climber, 3 x 3m/10 x 10ft, with prickly stems and single flat, white, or pink-tinged flowers, followed by scarlet, ovoid hips.

***R. rubiginosa* (Sweet briar, or Eglantine)** – A vigorous semi-climber, 2.5 x 2.5m/8 x 8ft, it has lovely apple-scented foliage and numerous

single pink flowers, followed by rounded ovoid red hips. This is the rose which appears in the works of Chaucer and is described by Shakespeare as adorning Titania's bower:

With sweet musk roses and with eglantine
There sleeps Titania, sometime of the night
Lull'd in these flowers with dances and delight.

***R. gallica* var. *officinalis* (Apothecary's rose)** – Probably the oldest of garden roses, it was widely grown in medieval times for its medicinal properties (though *R. damascena*, the damask rose, said to have been brought to Europe by the Crusaders in the 11th century, was almost as popular). A hardy deciduous, bushy shrub, 1.2 x 1.2m/4 x 4ft, it has large, very fragrant, semi-double, bright pink blooms and distinctive golden stamens.

***R. gallica* 'Versicolor'** Also known as Rosa Mundi, after the 'Fair Rosamund', mistress of King Henry IV of England, (1367–1413). A sport from *R. g. officinalis*, it has crimson-pink petals, splashed with cream.

Growth Fertile, moist soil and a sunny position are best for producing thriving rose plants with large flowers. However, *R. rubiginosa* does quite well on a poor, dry soil. The most suitable method of propagation is by hardwood cuttings in the autumn.

Parts used Flowers of *R. gallica*, hips of *R. canina*, essential oil, distilled rosewater from various rose species.

USES Medicinal Rose essential oil is used in aromatherapy for depression and nervous anxiety. In its purest form it is said to be the least toxic of the essential oils, safe to use undiluted. But many are adulterated, synthetic or semi-synthetic, and of no therapeutic value. Both hips and flowers are still sometimes recommended by herbalists to be taken internally in various preparations for colds, bronchial infections and gastric upsets and applied externally for sores and skin irritations. Rose hips are used nutritionally for their vitamin C content.

Culinary Hips are used for making vinegar, syrups, preserves and wines. Flower petals are added to salads and desserts, crystallized, made into jellies, jams and conserves. Distilled rose water is used to flavour confectionery and desserts, especially in Middle Eastern dishes.

Aromatic Dried petals and essential oil are added to potpourri, other fragrant articles for the home and beauty preparations, such as hand lotions and masks. Rosebuds and whole flowers are dried for decorative use. Dry roses in a warm, dry room but not in direct sunlight, which will bleach the petals.

Opposite page, clockwise from lower left Rosa rubiginosa; Rosa canina; *and the superb double cultivar* Rosa *'Charles de Mills'*.

This page, clockwise from top left Rosa gallica *'Versicolor'; the hips of* Rosa canina; *a single flower of* Rosa gallica *var.* officinalis – *the famed Apothecary's rose; and the massed blooms of the Apothecary's rose on a bush.*

Rose-petal skin freshener

40g/1¹/₂oz fragrant fresh red rose petals
600ml/1 pint/2¹/₂ cups boiling
  distilled water
15ml/1 tbsp cider vinegar

Put the rose petals in a bowl, pour over the boiling water and add the vinegar. Cover and leave to stand for 2 hours, then strain into a clean bottle. Apply to the face with cotton wool (cotton balls) to tone the skin. Keep chilled or in a refrigerator and use up within 2–3 days.

LABIATAE/LAMIACEAE

Rosmarinus officinalis

Rosemary

History and traditions Rosemary was well
known in ancient Greece and Rome and the
Latin generic name, *Rosmarinus*, means "dew
of the sea", from its coastal habitat and the
appearance of its flowers. It gained an early
reputation for improving memory and uplifting
the spirits, which is referred to in many herbals.
Bancke's Herbal, 1525, includes a long list of
remedies, practical suggestions and superstitions
regarding rosemary, including putting it under
the bed to "be delivered of all evill dreames",
boiling it in wine as a cosmetic face wash,
binding it round the legs against gout, and
drinking it in wine for a cough or for lost
appetite. It was also a major ingredient of
Hungary Water, said to be invented by a hermit
for Queen Elizabeth of Hungary, who was cured
of paralysis after rubbing it on daily. A symbol
of remembrance, it found a place at weddings,
funerals and in Christmas decorations, when it
was often gilded. In Spanish folklore rosemary is
believed to give protection from the evil eye and
to have sheltered the Virgin Mary, during the
flight into Egypt, when the once white flowers
took on the celestial blue of her cloak.
Description A variable evergreen shrub, to 2m/
6ft, it has woody branches and strongly
aromatic, needle-like foliage. A dense covering
of small, tubular, two-lipped flowers, usually
pale blue (but there are dark blue and
occasionally pink variants) appear in spring.
Habitat/distribution Native to the
Mediterranean coast, found on sunny hillsides
and in open situations. It is introduced and
widely grown elsewhere.

Growth Thrives on sharply drained, stony
soils and requires little moisture. Although
R. officinalis is frost hardy (not all species are), it
needs a sunny, sheltered position and protection
in cold winters and periods of prolonged frost.
Easily propagated from semi-ripe cuttings taken
in summer. It becomes straggly unless pruned
hard in summer, after flowering, but must not
be cut back to old wood.
Parts used The leaves and flowering tops are
used fresh or dried for cookery and in medicinal
preparations; essential oil distilled from leaves.

USES Medicinal A restorative, tonic herb, with
antiseptic and antibacterial properties. It is
taken internally as an infusion for colds,
influenza, fatigue and headaches, or as a
tincture for depression and nervous tension; and
applied externally in massage oil for rheumatic
and muscular pain. The essential oil is added to
bath water for aching joints and tiredness.

Above left *Flowers of* Rosmarinus officinalis.

Above Rosmarinus officinalis *'Miss Jessopp's
Upright'.*

Culinary A classic flavouring for lamb, stews
and casseroles, and added to marinades,
vinegar, oil and dressings.
Cosmetic Infusions are used as rinses for dry
hair and dandruff and added to bath lotions
and beauty preparations. Essential oil is used in
perfumery and cosmetic industries.
Aromatic Dried leaves add fragrance to
potpourri and insect-repellent sachets.

> **CAUTION** Not suitable to be taken internally in
> medicinal doses when pregnant, especially
> in the form of essential oil, as excess may
> cause miscarriage. Safe for normal
> culinary use.

Description A hardy perennial, growing up to 1.2m/4ft, with large, pale green, oblong to lanceolate leaves, and large terminal spikes of small disc-shaped reddish-brown flowers on long stalks.

Related species *R. scutatus*, Buckler-leaved, or French Sorrel, is a lower-growing plant, with shield-shaped leaves and less acidity, and is favoured for culinary uses in France.

Habitat/distribution Occurs in Europe and North Asia in grasslands and is frequently found on nitrogen-rich soils.

Growth Grows best and runs to seed less quickly in rich, moist soil, in a sunny or partially shady position. Propagated by seed sown in spring or by division in spring or autumn.

Parts used Leaves – when fresh and young.

USES Culinary Sorrel adds a pleasant, lemony flavour to soups, sauces, salads, egg and cheese dishes. But it is acidic and not recommended for rheumatism and arthritis sufferers. The leaves have the best flavour and texture in spring, before they become coarse and fibrous.

Above left Rumex acetosa – *the leaves are high in vitamin C.*

Above *Sorrel in flower.*

CAUTION Sorrel contains oxalates, also found in spinach and rhubarb, which are toxic in excess.

Right Rumex scutatus, *French sorrel.*

POLYGONACEAE
Rumex acetosa
Sorrel

History and traditions Various species of sorrel were used medicinally from at least the 14th century, but it was always chiefly valued as a culinary herb, especially in France and Belgium, where it was even potted as a preserve for winter use. Recipe books of the 17th and 18th centuries reveal that sorrel was not just made into soup, but frequently served with eggs, put into a sweet tart with orange flowers and cinnamon, as well as being cooked as a spinach-like vegetable. John Evelyn considered that it should never be left out of a salad, lending it sharpness, as a useful substitute for lemons and oranges when they were scarce. He also wrote that it "sharpens appetite ... cools the liver and strengthens the heart" (*Acetaria*, 1719). Culpeper recommended it for many medicinal purposes, including the breaking of plague sores and boils.

Above Ruta graveolens *'Variegata'.*

Left Ruta graveolens *in flower.*

is a widely grown cultivar with steel-blue foliage. There is also a variegated cultivar with cream and grey-green leaves.

Habitat/distribution Native to southern Europe on dry rocky soils, introduced and often naturalized throughout Europe, North America and Australia.

Growth Prefers light, well-drained soil and, although reasonably hardy, requires a sunny, sheltered position in cooler regions. Variegated cultivars are slightly less hardy. Propagated from seed (not cultivars) sown in spring, or from cuttings taken in spring (always wear gloves to handle). Prune in spring, or just after flowering in summer, to maintain a neat shape, but do not cut into old woody stems. It should not be planted at the front of a border where it can be brushed against.

Parts used Leaves.

USES Medicinal Although recommended by some herbalists for various complaints, including painful menstruation, it is a dangerous, toxic herb and there are safer alternative remedies for such conditions.

Aromatic It has insect-repellent properties and leaves may be dried for adding to potpourri.

> **CAUTION** For practitioner use only. Rue is a skin irritant, especially in full sun, and causes severe blistering. Gloves should be worn when handling. Toxic if taken internally in excess, it affects the central nervous system and may be fatal. It is also an abortifacient.

RUTACEAE

Ruta graveolens

Rue

History and traditions Rue has a long tradition as an antidote to poison and defence against disease. The Greek physician Galen (c. AD130–201) took rue and coriander (cilantro), mixed with oil and salt, as a protection against infection, and Dioscorides (c. AD40–90) recommended it against every kind of venom. Most 17th-century herbalists continued the anti-venom theme, as illustrated by William Coles: "The weasell when she is to encounter the serpent arms herselfe with eating of rue" (*The Art of Simpling*, 1656). Rue was an ingredient of the celebrated anti-plague concoction, Four Thieves Vinegar, and always included in the judge's posy, placed in the courtroom to protect him from diseased prisoners and the dreaded jail-fever. The name "herb of grace" is said by some to originate from the practice of sprinkling holy water with a sprig of rue at Sunday mass. Its potent smell and protective attributes ensured its place as a powerful anti-witchcraft and spells herb. Although it is an attractive plant and widely grown in herb gardens, it has few herbal uses today. Far from being a protective, it is now recognized as a toxic irritant.

Description An evergreen, or semi-evergreen, shrubby perennial to 60cm/2ft, it has deeply divided blue-green leaves, with rounded spatulate leaf segments and a mass of small yellow, four-petalled flowers in midsummer.

Related species *R. graveolens* 'Jackman's Blue'

SALICACEAE
Salix alba
Willow

History and traditions The willow contains salicylic acid and is the origin of aspirin (acetylsalicylic acid), which was synthesized from it as early as 1853. The bark had been used in Europe for centuries to reduce pain and fever, and in Native American traditional medicine several willow species were used for the same purposes. Willow branches were popular church decorations in Britain and used as substitute palms (which were not readily available) on Palm Sunday. In Russia, the week leading up to Easter was often called "willow week". The tree was always an emblem of sadness (it was a willow beneath which the "children of Israel" sat down and wept) and garlands of it were worn by the forsaken in love.

Description A spreading, fast-growing deciduous tree, up to 25m/82ft, it has greyish, fissured bark, arching branches and silvery-green, slender lanceolate leaves. Stalkless, yellow male and female catkins are borne in spring.

Related species There are several species of willow with medicinal properties in this large genus, including the North American *S. myrsinifolia* or black willow.

Habitat/distribution *S. alba* occurs widely in Europe and Asia, most often near rivers, streams and waterways.

Growth Requires damp soil and even does well on heavy clay, but dislikes chalk. Propagated by greenwood cuttings in spring, or by hardwood cuttings in winter.

Parts used Bark – collected from 2–3-year-old trees and dried for use in decoctions and other preparations; leaves – are also occasionally used in infusions.

USES Medicinal The salicylic compounds it contains give willow fever-reducing, analgesic, anti-rheumatic properties. Although it has been completely replaced by synthetics in pharmaceutical preparations it is still sometimes used in herbal medicine in baths for rheumatic pain and in ointments and compresses for cuts, burns and skin complaints.

Above right Salix alba *(white willow).*

Right Salix alba *subsp.* vitellina, *coppiced to maintain its ornamental stems.*

LABIATAE/LAMIACEAE

Salvia

Salvia officinalis
Sage

History and traditions The Latin name comes from *salvere*, to save or heal, and this herb has always been connected with good health and a long life – even immortality. An old Arabian proverb asks, "How can a man die who has sage in his garden?" and John Evelyn wrote, 'Tis a plant, indeed, with so many and wonderful properties as that the assiduous use of it is said to render men immortal", (*Acetaria*, 1719). And Sir John Hill in *The Virtues of British Herbs,* 1772, has many anecdotes of people living to improbable ages through regular intake of sage. It is another plant, like rosemary, which is said to thrive where the woman rules the household: "If the sage tree thrives and grows/The master's not master and he knows."

Description An evergreen, highly aromatic, shrubby perennial, growing to 60cm/2ft, it has downy, rough-textured, grey-green, ovate leaves and spikes of tubular, violet-blue flowers in early summer. *S. officinalis* is one of the few hardy plants in this huge genus of around 900 species worldwide.

Related species *S. o.* 'Icterina' (golden sage) has gold and green variegated leaves. It seldom

flowers in cool climates, but in warmer regions sometimes has pale mauve blooms. Although it may be used as a culinary herb it does not have such a good flavour as the species, or as the purple sages. But it does add colour when used in salads. It is reliably variegated, not as prone to revert as many and makes an attractive contrasting foliage plant for the border. *S. o.* Purpurascens Group (purple sage, or red sage) has striking purple, grey and green foliage. Some of its variants produce blue flower spikes. It has a strong flavour, is often used as a culinary herb and widely cultivated for its ornamental value. *S. elegans* (pineapple sage)

is a half-hardy perennial with green, soft, ovate leaves, scented with pineapple, and scarlet, tubular flowers in winter.

Habitat/distribution Sage is native to southern Europe, found on dry, sunny slopes, introduced in cool temperate regions.

Growth Grow in light, well-drained soil in full sun. Although *S. officinalis* is hardy, it does not always withstand prolonged cold below -10°C/14°F, especially in wet conditions. The cultivars are slightly less hardy than the species.
S. officinalis may be propagated from seed; cultivars must be propagated from cuttings or by layering. Prune sage in the spring to keep it

Above Salvia officinalis *Purpurascens Group.*

Above Salvia elegans *in flower.*

in good shape, or just after flowering, but do not cut into old wood. After a few years, sages can become straggly and need to be replaced. Pineapple sage must be protected from frost and kept under cover during the winter. Grow in moist soil, and if container-grown, keep the compost (soil mix) damp. It is very easy to propagate from softwood cuttings taken throughout the summer.

Parts used Leaves – fresh or dried, essential oil.

USES Medicinal An astringent, antiseptic, antibacterial herb, infusions of the leaves are used as a gargle or mouthwash for sore throats, mouth ulcers, gum disease, laryngitis and tonsillitis. Infusions are taken internally as tonics, to aid digestion and for menopausal problems, and applied externally as compresses to help heal wounds.

Culinary Leaves are used to flavour Mediterranean dishes, cheese, sausages, goose, pork and other fatty meat. In Italy it is added to liver dishes. It is also made into stuffings, a classic combination is sage and onion. Leaves of pineapple sage may be floated in drinks.

Aromatic/cosmetic An infusion of the leaves makes a rinse for dark hair and to treat dandruff. The essential oil is used in the perfume and cosmetic industries.

Above Salvia officinalis *in flower.*

Opposite page, bottom left Salvia officinalis; **top left** *A flowering form of* S. o. *Purpurascens Group;* **top right** S. elegans *in leaf.*

This page, top left S. o. *'Icterina';* **top centre** S. o. *'Tricolor'.*

CAUTION Sage, especially the essential oil, is toxic in excess doses, and should not be taken medicinally over long periods, by pregnant or breast-feeding women or by epileptics (the thujone content may trigger fits). It is safe in small amounts in cookery.

Salvia sclarea
Clary sage

History and traditions The specific name, *sclarea*, comes from *clarus*, meaning clear, and is the origin of the common name clary, a corruption of "clear eye" which refers to an old use of clary sage as a lotion for eye inflammations. It has long been a flavouring for alcohol and clary wine is said to have been a 16th-century aphrodisiac. In the 19th century it was sometimes used as a hop substitute, to make beer heady and intoxicating. With elderflowers, it provided German wine producers with a way of adding a muscatel flavour to Rhenish wine.

Description A biennial, up to 1.2m/4ft tall, it has a large basal clump of broadly ovate grey-green leaves, and in its second year a tall, branched, flower spike of silvery, lilac-blue and pink two-lipped florets. The whole plant has an unpleasantly overpowering scent, but it is showy and decorative in the border.

Habitat/distribution Native to southern Europe, found on dry, sandy soils.

Growth Grow in free-draining, but reasonably moist and fertile soil. Propagated by seed sown in spring or autumn. Often self-seeds.

Parts used Leaves – fresh or dried, essential oil.

USES Medicinal Infusions of the leaves are used as lotions for cuts and abrasions, and as a gargle for mouth ulcers. Sometimes recommended to be taken internally in small doses for promoting appetite. The essential oil is used in aromatherapy to treat a range of actions including cystitis and anxiety.

Aromatic Essential oil is used to flavour vermouth and liqueurs, and widely used in commercial soaps, scents and eau-de-Cologne.

CAPRIFOLIACEAE

Sambucus nigra

Elder

History and traditions The elder has been associated since earliest times with myth and magic, witchcraft and spells. At the same time it was always valued for its many practical uses, medicinal, household, culinary and cosmetic. In Norse mythology, hauntings, deaths and harmed babies were the result of upsetting the Elder-Mother and guardian spirit, by not obtaining her permission before cutting down a tree to make furniture or cradles. Christian legends, referred to in English literature from the 14th-century *Piers Plowman* by William Langland to Spenser and Shakespeare, included the story that Judas hanged himself on an elder tree, and that it was the wood used to make the cross of Calvary. From this it became a symbol of sorrow and death and was planted in graveyards. The idea that elders provided protection from witchcraft and evil spirits has ancient roots, and it is cited in Coles's *The Art of Simpling*, 1656, as being planted near cottages and fixed to doors and windows on the last day of April for this purpose. Some years earlier, in 1644, *The Anatomie of the Elder* was published, which celebrated its medicinal properties and asserted its capability of curing all known ills. Old herbals

are full of culinary recipes, too, for the flowers, shoots, buds and berries, and the distilled water was said to ensure a fair complexion. The timber was valued for making fences, skewers, pegs and small household articles and the easily removable core of soft pith made elder prime material for pop-guns (as referred to by Culpeper), penny whistles and musical pipes, a use it has been put to since classical times. The generic name, *Sambucus*, is from the Greek for a musical instrument.

Description A small deciduous tree, up to 10m/33ft tall, it has dull green, pinnate leaves, divided into five elliptic leaflets. Flat umbels of creamy, musk-scented flowers in early summer are followed by pendulous clusters of spherical black fruits on red stalks in early autumn.

Related species There are a few ornamental cultivars which make attractive subjects for the garden but have no medicinal or culinary value.

Habitat/distribution Native to Europe, western Asia and northern Africa. Occurs widely in temperate and subtropical regions in hedgerows, woodlands and roadsides.

Growth Prefers moist but well-drained, humus-rich soil in sun or partial shade. Propagation by suckers or semi-ripe cuttings in summer are the easiest methods. The species, but not cultivars, can also be grown from seed. Elders often self-seed prolifically.

Parts used Leaves – fresh; flowers – fresh or dried; fruits – fresh.

USES Medicinal Has anticatarrhal and anti-inflammatory properties. Infusions of the flowers are taken for colds, sinusitis, influenza and feverish illnesses, and are said to be sooth-ing for hayfever. The fruits (berries) are made into syrups, or "elderberry rob", also for colds.

Culinary Fresh flower heads in batter make elderflower fritters; fresh or dried flowers give a muscatel flavour to gooseberries and stewed fruits, and are added to desserts and sorbets. Flowers and berries are used to make vinegars, cordials and wines.

Cosmetic Fresh or dried flowers are used in skin toners, face creams and other home-made beauty preparations.

General The leaves have insecticidal properties and are boiled in water to make sprays against aphids and garden pests.

Elderflower

To take away the freckles in the face
Wash your face, in the wane of the Moone, with a sponge, morning and evening, with the distilled water of Elder-leaves, letting the same dry into the skinne. Your water must be distilled in May. This from a Traveller, who hath cured himselfe thereby.

Delights for Ladies, 1659

Elderflower skin freshener
A soothing and refreshing lotion for sensitive or sunburned skin. Pour 600ml/1 pint/2½ cups boiling distilled water over 25g/1oz dried elderflowers. Leave to cool, strain off the flowers and apply to the skin on cotton wool (cotton balls). Keep the lotion refrigerated and use within 2–3 days.

CAUTION Leaves contain toxic cyanogenic glycosides and should not be eaten. Berries are harmful if eaten raw.

Top left Sambucus nigra *in flower.*

Left *Elderberries.*

ROSACEAE

Sanguisorba minor
Salad burnet

History and traditions This is a traditional herb-garden plant recommended by Francis Bacon in his essay on the ideal garden (1625), to be planted in "alleys", or walks, along with thyme and water mints, for the pleasant perfume when crushed. The common name is a reference to the fact that this herb often lasted through the winter, providing welcome edible greenery when little else was available. It was also added to wine cups or ale for the cooling effect of the leaves. The generic name, *Sanguisorba*, comes from the Latin for *sanguis*, blood, and *sorbere*, to absorb, as it was formerly used medicinally as a wound herb interchangeably with *S. officinalis*, greater burnet.

Description A clump-forming perennial, 15–40cm/6–16in in height, it has pinnate leaves with numerous pairs of oval, serrated-edged leaflets and long stalks topped by rounded crimson flower heads.

Habitat/distribution It is native to Europe and Asia, naturalized in North America. It is found on chalky soils in grassy meadows and roadsides.

Growth Thrives on chalk (alkaline). Requires reasonably rich, moist soil for good leaf production and a sunny or partially shady position. Propagated by seed sown in spring. Cut it back as soon as the flower buds appear in order to ensure a continuous supply of leaves.

Parts used Leaves – fresh.

USES Culinary The leaves have a mild, cucumber flavour, make a pleasant addition to salads and are floated in drinks or wine punch.

COMPOSITAE/ASTERACEAE

Santolina chamaecyparissus
Cotton lavender

History and traditions Cotton lavender is a native of southern Europe and was well known to the ancient Greeks and Romans and has long been valued as a vermifuge and for its insect-repellent properties. Culpeper recommended it also against poisonous bites and skin irritations (*The English Physician*, 1653). The neat, silvery foliage responds well to close clipping and it was introduced to Britain and northern Europe in the 16th century as hedging for knot gardens.

Description A small highly aromatic shrub, growing to about 60cm/2ft, it has silvery-grey, finely divided, woolly foliage and bright yellow, globular button-shaped flowers.

Related species *S. rosmarinifolia* subsp. *rosmarinifolia* syn. *S. viridis* has bright green foliage and makes an interesting contrast in knot garden work.

Habitat/distribution Cotton lavender is native to the Mediterranean region, introduced and widely cultivated worldwide. Found in fields and wastelands on calcareous soil.

Growth Grow in light, sandy soil and a sunny position. Tolerates drought. Propagated by semi-ripe cuttings in summer. Prune hard in spring to maintain a neat, clipped shape. It will regenerate if cut back to old wood.

Parts used Leaves – dried.

USES Medicinal Formerly used to expel intestinal worms. It is said to have anti-inflammatory properties and is sometimes made into an infusion as a lotion for skin irritations and insect bites, but in general it is little used in herbal medicine today.

Aromatic Dried leaves are added to potpourri and insect-repellent sachets.

Other name Lavender cotton in the US.

Below Santolina chamaecyparissus.

Bottom Santolina rosmarinifolia *subsp.* rosmarinifolia *syn.* S. viridis.

CARYOPHYLLACEAE

Saponaria officinalis

Soapwort

History and traditions Soapwort is indigenous to Europe and the Middle East and has been used there for its cleansing properties for many centuries. Some authorities claim that it was even known to the Assyrians around the 8th century BC. The name *Saponaria* comes from *sapo*, the Latin for soap, and, because of the high saponin content, soapwort roots produce a foamy lather when mixed with water. In Syria it was used for washing woollens, in Switzerland for washing sheep before shearing, and the medieval fullers, who "finished" cloth, used soapwort in the process. The common name, bouncing Bet, is a reference to the activity of plump washerwomen. It had its medicinal uses too. A decoction of the roots was formerly used for a variety of ailments from rheumatism to syphilis. Soapwort has been used until very recently by museums and by the National Trust in Britain, as it was found to be more suitable for cleaning delicate old tapestries and fabrics than most modern detergents.

Description A spreading, hardy perennial, on a creeping rhizomatous rootstock, 60–90cm/2–3ft tall, it has bright green, fleshy, ovate to elliptical leaves, and clusters of pale pink flowers in mid- to late summer.

Habitat/distribution Native to Europe, the Middle East and western Asia, naturalized in North America and widely grown in temperate regions. Found near streams and in wastelands, often as an escapee from gardens.

Growth Prefers moist, loamy soil, but tolerates most conditions and can become invasive. The easiest method of propagation is by division of the runners in spring. It can also be grown successfully from seed.

Parts used Roots, leafy stems – fresh or dried.

USES Medicinal It is seldom used in herbal medicine today.

Cosmetic An infusion or decoction of the roots and leafy stems makes shampoo – the addition of eau-de-Cologne improves the slightly unpleasant smell.

Household Used for cleaning delicate fabrics.

Other name Bouncing Bet.

Above left Saponaria officinalis.

Above right *A decoction of the whole plant makes a gentle shampoo.*

Soapwort shampoo

The gentle cleansing properties of soapwort shampoo are beneficial if you suffer from an itchy scalp or dandruff.

25g/1oz fresh soapwort root, leaves and stem or 15g/¹/₂ oz dried soapwort root
750ml/1¹/₄ pints/3 cups water
lavender water or eau-de-Cologne

Break up the soapwort stems, roughly chop the root and put the whole lot into a pan with the water. Bring to the boil and simmer for 20 minutes. Strain off the herbs and add a dash of lavender water or eau-de-Cologne, as soapwort has a slightly unpleasant scent.

Use like shampoo, rubbing well into the scalp and rinsing.

CAUTION Soapwort should not be taken internally as it can be upsetting to the digestive system and is capable of destroying red blood cells if taken in large quantities.

LABIATAE/LAMIACEAE

Satureja

Satureja hortensis
Summer savory

History and traditions Both summer and winter savory are Mediterranean herbs that were appreciated by the Romans and commonly used in their cuisine. The poet Virgil, 70–19BC, celebrated them as being among the most fragrant of plants suitable for growing near beehives. Shakespeare too, writes of the scent of savory and it is included in Perdita's herbal gift to Polixenes in The Winter's Tale. The savories were among the herbs listed by John Josselyn which were taken to North America by early settlers to remind them of their English gardens. Culpeper promotes both herbs to ease a range of ailments, including asthma, and for expelling "tough phlegm from the chest", with summer savory especially suitable for drying to make conserves and syrups. It has been established by modern scientific studies (carried out in the 1980s) that the savories do have strong antibacterial properties. However, the subtle, spicy flavour (like marjoram, with a hint of thyme) ensures that both summer and winter savory remain first and foremost culinary herbs.

Description A small, bushy, hardy annual, to 38cm/15in high, it has woody, much-branched stems and small, leathery, dark green, linear-lanceolate leaves. Tiny white or pale lilac flowers appear in summer.

Habitat/distribution Mediterranean in origin, introduced and widely grown in warm and temperate regions elsewhere. Occurs on chalky soils (alkaline) and rocky hillsides.

Growth Grow in well-drained soil in full sun. Propagated from seed sown in containers, or *in situ*, in early spring. It may help reduce the incidence of blackfly when grown near beans.

Parts used Leaves, flowering tops – used fresh or dried.

USES Medicinal Has antiseptic, antibacterial properties and is said to improve digestion.

Culinary Summer savory has an affinity with beans and adds a spicy flavour to dried herb mixtures, stuffings, pulses, pâtés and meat dishes. Extracts and essential oil are used in commercial products in the food industry.

> **CAUTION** The savories stimulate the uterus and are not to be given to pregnant women in medicinal doses.

Below *The leaves have a mildly spicy flavour.*

Satureja montana
Winter savory

Description A clump-forming, hardy perennial, to 38cm/15in tall, it is semi-evergreen (does not keep all its leaves in cool temperate regions through the winter, especially if frosts are prolonged). It has dark green, linear-lanceolate, pointed leaves and dense whorls of small white flowers in summer. It has a stronger, coarser fragrance than summer savory, due to the higher proportion of thymol it contains.

Growth Grow in well-drained soil, in full sun. Propagated by seed, by division in spring, or by cuttings in summer. Prune lightly in early summer, after flowering, to maintain a neat shape.

USES It has the same uses as summer savory, but to most tastes has a less refined flavour for culinary purposes.

Above
Satureja
montana

SCROPHULARIACEAE

Scrophularia nodosa

Figwort

History and traditions This herb was used in the past to treat scrofula or "the king's evil", a disease which affected the lymph glands in the neck. It conformed to the Doctrine of Signatures theory because the knots on the rhizome were thought to resemble swollen glands. Culpeper, writing in 1653, called it "Throatwort", adding that "it taketh away all redness, spots and freckles in the face, as also the scurf and any foul deformity therein".

Description A strong-smelling perennial on a stout, knotted rhizome, 40–80cm/16–32in in height, it has ovate to lanceolate leaves and terminal spikes of small, dull pink flowers.

Habitat/distribution Native to Europe and temperate parts of Asia, naturalized in North America. Found in woods and hedgerows.

Growth Grow in very damp soil, in sun or partial shade. Propagated by division in spring, or by seed sown in spring or autumn.

Parts used Rhizomes – dried for use in decoctions and other medicinal preparations; leaves and flowering stems – fresh or dried.

USES Medicinal This has cleansing properties. Infusions of the leaves are taken internally or applied externally in washes or compresses for skin disorders and inflammations. Decoctions of the root are taken internally for throat infections, swollen glands and feverish illnesses.

> **CAUTION** This herb has a stimulating effect on the heart and is not given to patients with heart diseases.

CRASSULACEAE

Sempervivum tectorum

Houseleek

History and traditions In the folklore of most European countries, houseleek is dedicated to Jupiter or Thor and was deemed to provide protection from lightning. It has been planted on thatched roofs or in the crevices of roof tiles ever since the Emperor Charlemagne, 747–814AD, decreed to this effect. The second part of the common name, houseleek, is from the Anglo-Saxon word for plant, *leac*. Its Latin name refers to its ability to withstand any conditions, and comes from *semper*, always, and *vivum*, living or alive. The specific name *tectorum* is a reference to its roof use. This herb has been used since the time of Dioscorides and Pliny as a soothing agent for skin complaints. And Culpeper, writing in the 17th century, suggests a first-aid measure, which is equally valid today: "the leaves being gently rubbed on any place stung with nettles or bees, doth quickly take away the pain".

Description A mat-forming hardy succulent, it has blue-green, rounded leaves with pointed spiny tips, arranged in rosettes. Erect, hairy stems, to a height of 30cm/12in, bear pinkish-red star-shaped flowers in summer.

Habitat/distribution Native to southern Europe and western Asia, found on rocky slopes and in mountainous areas. Introduced and widely grown elsewhere.

Growth Thrives in gritty or stony, sharply drained soil and withstands drought. The easiest method of propagation is by separating and replanting offsets in spring.

Parts used Leaves – fresh.

USES Medicinal The leaves are made into infusions, compresses, lotions and ointments, or cut open to release the sap and applied directly to insect bites and stings, sunburn, skin irritations, warts and corns.

Above *A cultivar of* Sempervivum tectorum *with red-suffused leaves.*

Below *Break open leaves to release the sap.*

COMPOSITAE/ASTERACEAE
Silybum marianum

Milk thistle

History and traditions It is called milk thistle for its milky-white veins, from which it earned its reputation, under the Doctrine of Signatures, as improving the milk supply of nursing mothers. The Latin specific name, *marianum*, associates it with the Virgin Mary, from the tradition that her milk once fell upon its leaves, and the genus name is a corruption of *silybon*, which was Dioscorides' term for this herb. Milk thistles were formerly frequently cultivated as a vegetable and it was decreed by Thomas Tryon (*The Good Housewife*, 1692) that "they are very wholesome and exceed all other greens in taste".

Description A tall annual or biennial, up to 1.2m/4ft in height, it has large, deeply lobed, spiny leaves with white veins and purple thistle flowers in summer.

Habitat/distribution Native to Europe, introduced elsewhere and naturalized in North America and other countries. Found on dry, stony soils, in fields and roadsides.

Growth Grows in any well-drained soil in a sunny position. Propagation is by seed, sown in spring or autumn, and it self-seeds prolifically.

Parts used Leaves and flowering stems – dried for use in infusions or for extractions of the active principle silymarin.

USES Medicinal Taken as an infusion to stimulate appetite and for digestive disorders. Contains compounds, known as silymarin, which are said to be effective as an antidote to toxic substances that cause liver damage.

Other name Marian thistle.

SIMMONDSIACIAE
Simmondsia chinensis

Jojoba

History and traditions The oil from the seeds of this herb was used by Native Americans as a cosmetic and for softening garments made from animal skins. In the 1970s jojoba was discovered to be a valuable replacement for sperm whale oil and large commercial plantations have since been established in Arizona and across wide areas of semi-arid grassland in the United States.

Description A half-hardy shrub, up to 2m/6ft in height, with leathery, ovate leaves, it is the only species in the genus. Pale yellow flowers appear in axillary clusters on male plants, the greenish female flowers are usually solitary and followed by ovoid seed capsules.

Habitat/distribution It is native to south-western North America and Mexico, and is widely grown as a crop in the United States and the Middle East.

Growth Tolerant of drought, it thrives in dry, gravelly soil. A half-hardy plant, it is propagated by seed sown in spring, or by heel cuttings taken in autumn.

Parts used Oil – expressed straight from the ripe seeds.

USES Medicinal Jojoba oil has exceptionally soothing and softening properties and is used in pharmaceutical ointments for dry skins, psoriasis and eczema.

Cosmetic It is also an important ingredient of moisturisers, body lotions and sunscreens.

General The oil is used as an engine lubricant. The shrubs are planted to prevent further encroachment of total desert in arid areas.

APIACEAE
Smyrnium olusatrum

Alexanders

History and traditions Alexanders was valued chiefly as a culinary herb from the days of the ancient Greeks until well into the 19th century. It is high in vitamin C and at one time was recognised as a useful aid against scurvy. It was also thought to have some medicinal properties, chiefly as a diuretic and stomachic. It was taken for asthma and to help menstrual flow, but it is no longer used in herbal medicine.

Description A large perennial, it grows up to 1.5m/5ft tall, with thick ridged stems, dark green, shiny leaves and domed umbels of greenish-yellow flowers, followed by black seeds. It is sometimes confused with angelica, of which it is taken to be a wild species.

Habitat/distribution Native to Europe and the Mediterranean, frequently found on coastal sites.

Growth It grows best in sandy, but moist and reasonably fertile soil, and is propagated by seed sown in spring.

Parts used Leaves, young stems, flower buds, seeds, roots.

USES Culinary The whole plant is edible. Leaves and young stems may be used like celery, the roots cooked as parsnips, the flower buds added to salads and the seeds lightly crushed or ground as a seasoning.

Other name Black lovage.

COMPOSITAE/ASTERACEAE

Solidago virgaurea
Golden rod

History and traditions Most of the nearly 100 species of *Solidago* came from North America, where a number of them were used in traditional Native American medicine for healing wounds, sores, insect bites and stings. In the 17th century the dried herb was imported and sold on the London market for high prices as an exotic cure-all, until one day someone noticed golden rod growing wild on Hampstead Heath in London and the bottom dropped out of the market. As Thomas Fuller put it in his *History of the Worthies of England,* 1662, "When golden rod was brought at great expense from foreign countries, it was highly valued; but it was no sooner discovered to be a native plant, than it was discarded." However, by the 19th century, in Britain, it was firmly established as a popular ornamental, causing William Cobbett to complain in *The American Gardener,* 1816, "A yellow flower called the 'Plain-weed', which is the torment of the neighbouring farmer, has been above all the plants in this world, chosen as the most conspicuous ornament of the front of the King of England's grandest palace, that of Hampton Court."

Description A vigorous hardy perennial, growing to 1m/3ft in height. It has branched stems, lanceolate, finely toothed leaves and terminal panicles of golden-yellow flowers in late summer. It is an invasive plant and spreads very rapidly.

Related species *S. canadensis,* native to Canada and North America, is a taller plant, growing to 1.5m/5ft, often seen in gardens, and also has medicinal properties. Most garden varieties of golden rod are hybrids.

Habitat/distribution *S. virgaurea* is the only native European species, and is found in woodland and grassland on acid and calcareous (alkaline) soils. Many closely-related species are native to North America.

Growth Prefers not too rich soil and an open, sunny position. Propagated by seed sown in spring, or by division in spring and autumn.

Parts used Leaves, flowering tops – dried for use in infusions, powders, ointments and other medicinal preparations.

USES Medicinal Golden rod has antifungal, anti-inflammatory and antiseptic properties. It is applied externally in lotions, ointments and poultices to help heal wounds, skin irritations, bites, stings and ulcers. Used traditionally to treat chronic catarrh.

Above left *A garden hybrid of* Solidago canadensis *and* S. virgaurea *in flower, and in bud* (**above**).

Golden rod superstitions

- Where golden rod grows, secret treasure is buried.
- When it springs up near the door of a house, it brings good fortune.

LABIATAE/LAMIACEAE

Stachys officinalis
Betony

History and traditions Betony was highly prized as a medicinal herb in Roman times, when Antonius Musa, physician to the Emperor Augustus, wrote a treatise on its virtues, assigning 47 remedies to it. It was of great importance to the Anglo-Saxons for its magical as well as its medicinal properties and is mentioned in the 10th-century manuscript herbal, the *Lacnunga.* It was made into amulets to be worn against evil spirits, planted in churchyards and held to be capable of driving away despair. *The Herbal of Apuleius* (c. AD400) describes betony as "good for a man's soul or his body". Betony was much valued throughout Europe, and inspired the Italian proverb "sell your coat and buy betony". It was always associated with treatments for maladies of the head and said to be a certain cure for headaches – a use that it retains today in modern herbal practice. The name betony derives from *vettonica,* as the Romans knew it, which became *betonica* (as it was until recently classified). *Stachys* is from the Greek for a spike or ear of corn and refers to the shape of the flower cluster.

Description A mat-forming, hairy, hardy perennial, it has a basal rosette of wrinkled, ovate leaves with dentate margins. Flower stems rise to 60cm/2ft with smaller opposite leaves and dense, terminal spikes of magenta-pink two-lipped flowers borne in summer.

Above S. byzantina *syn* S. lanata.

Related species *S. byzantina* syn. *S. lanata* is popularly known as "lambs' ears", "lambs' lugs", "lambs' tails" or "lambs' tongues" for its white, woolly foliage. It forms a mat of whitish-green, soft, downy, wrinkled leaves with short mauve flower spikes to 45cm/18in tall. It is grown as a herb garden ornamental.

Habitat/distribution Native to Europe, grows on sandy loam in open woods and grassland.

Growth Grow in ordinary, dry soil in sun or partial shade. Propagated by seed sown in spring or by division during dormancy.

Parts used Leaves, flowering stems – fresh or dried for infusions, ointments and lotions.

USES Medicinal Infusions are taken for headaches, especially if associated with anxiety and nervous tension, often combined with *Hypericum perforatum* and *Lavandula*. Made into lotions or ointments (often in combination with other herbs) for applying to cuts, abrasions and bruises.

Conserve of betony

Betony new and tender one pound, the best sugar three pound, beat them very small in a stone mortar, let the sugar be boyled with two quarts of betony water to the consistency of a syrup, then mix them together by little and little over a small Fire, and so make it into a Conserve and keep it in Glasses [bottles].

The Queen's Closet Opened by W. M., cook to Queen Henrietta Maria, 1655.

CARYOPHYLLACEAE
Stellaria media
Chickweed

History and traditions The common name, chickweed, and the popular names in several other European languages refer to this herb's former usefulness as bird feed. It provided a source of fresh greens and seeds during the winter when other foods were scarce. For the same reason it was much valued as a culinary herb in broths and salads. Although it does not seem to have made its mark in the classical world, it appears in herbals from medieval times usually as an ingredient in a mixed green ointment based on lard, for rubbing on sores and swellings. The Latin name of the genus is from *stella*, a star, for the shape of the flowers.

Description A spreading, mat-forming annual, the much-branched stems grow up to 40cm/16in long, but most are decumbent and creep along the ground. It has small ovate leaves and tiny, white, star-shaped flowers. It propagates quickly, reappearing throughout the year, and is often seen in the winter months.

Habitat/distribution Chickweed is native to Europe but naturalized in many countries throughout the world. Found on moist cultivated land and field edges.

Growth Grows in any reasonably moist soil in sun or partial shade. Self-seeds.

Parts used Leaves – fresh.

USES Medicinal It is rich in mineral salts, including calcium and potassium, and has anti-rheumatic properties when taken internally as a juice or infusion. Applied as a poultice or ointment for eczema, skin irritations and other skin complaints.

Culinary A pleasantly neutral-tasting herb for inclusion in salads or for cooking as a vegetable. It combines well with parsley to make a dip.

Chickweed and parsley dip

25g/1oz fresh chickweed
25g/1oz flat-leaved parsley
225g/8oz fromage frais
15ml/1 tbsp mayonnaise
Salt and ground black pepper

Rinse and pick over the chickweed, and chop it finely with the parsley. Mix well with the fromage frais and mayonnaise. Season to taste.

Serve as a dip with raw carrots, celery, cucumber and peppers.

BORAGINACEAE
Symphytum officinale
Comfrey

History and traditions Comfrey has been known since at least the Middle Ages as a healing agent for fractures. The generic name, *Symphytum*, is from the Greek, *sympho*, "growing together", and *phyton*, a plant. The common English name, comfrey, is derived from the medieval Latin, *confervia*, meaning to heal or "boil together". Gerard wrote that "a salve concocted from the fresh herb will certainly tend to promote the healing of bruised and broken parts" (*The Herball*, 1597), and he and other herbalists of his time advised taking it internally for "inward hurts" as well. The modern history of this herb is a chequered one. In about 1910 it was established that it contained allantoin, a cell-proliferant substance, which promotes healing of bone and bodily tissues. By the 1960s Russian comfrey, *S.* x *uplandicum*, was being promoted as a herbal wonder cure. However, scientific studies of the late 1970s and 1980s, mostly carried out in Australia and Japan, revealed that comfrey also contains pyrrolizidine alkaloids (plant toxins that are most associated with disease in humans and in animals). Levels are higher in the roots than the leaves). These toxins were shown to cause liver damage and tumours in laboratory animals when extracts were injected in large quantities. This has led to a ban on comfrey in many countries, including Australia, New Zealand, Canada and the United States.

Description A vigorous perennial, growing on thick taproots, 0.6–1.2m/2–4ft in height, it has oval, lanceolate leaves, with a rough, hairy texture. Pinkish-purple to violet, tubular flowers are borne in drooping clusters in early to midsummer.

Related species *S.* x *uplandicum* (Russian comfrey) is a larger – to 2m/6ft – and more vigorous hybrid.

Habitat/distribution Native to Europe and the Mediterranean, and also from Siberia to Asia, introduced and naturalized elsewhere. Found in damp meadows, near rivers and streams.

Growth Although it favours damp soil in the wild, comfrey is a vigorous plant, which flourishes under any conditions and grows happily when planted in dry soil, in sun or partial shade. It is easily propagated by division of roots in spring, but is invasive and almost impossible to eradicate once established.

Parts used Leaves – fresh.

USES Medicinal The leaves are made into poultices, compresses and ointments and applied externally to bruises, varicose veins, inflamed muscles and tendons. While external use of the whole leaf is considered safe, it is inadvisable to take comfrey internally.

Horticultural The leaves are high in potash and make a good garden fertilizer, mulch and compost activator.

Other name Knitbone.

Top, from left to right *The flowers of* Symphytum officinale *are usually pink or blue, but there are forms with white or yellow flowers too.*

CAUTION Comfrey is subject to legal restrictions in some countries. Do not use the root internally due to the high levels of pyrrolizidine alkaloids in the plant, which are known to be toxic to the liver.

by seed or cuttings. The cloves (the unopened flower buds) are harvested when the tree is 6–8 years old. The crop can be sporadic: one year heavy and the next light. Cloves are usually hand picked to avoid damage to the branches which would jeopardize subsequent crops.
Parts used Unripe flower buds – sun-dried; essential oil.

USES Medicinal Cloves have digestive properties, help relieve nausea, control vomiting and prevent intestinal worms and parasites. Oil of cloves is still used as a dental antiseptic and analgesic. A cotton bud (cotton swab) soaked in oil of cloves and applied directly to the tooth will ease toothache.
Culinary Widely used as a spice in whole or ground form to add flavour to curries, pickles, preserves, chutneys and meat dishes – especially baked ham. It is also used in baked apples and apple pie, desserts and cakes, and for making mulled wine.
Aromatic Added whole or ground to potpourri and used to make pomanders. Essential oil is used in perfumery, and added to toothpastes, mouthwashes and gargles.

Above *Whole cloves.*

MYRTACEAE
Syzygium aromaticum
Clove tree

History and traditions The medicinal use of cloves is first mentioned in ancient Chinese texts, and it was a custom during the Han dynasty (266BC–AD220) to keep a clove in the mouth when addressing the emperor. Cloves originally came from the Molucca Islands, a group of islands in Indonesia, and were brought to the Mediterranean by Persian and Arab traders. They are mentioned in the writings of Pliny under the name *caryophyllon*, and were widely used in Europe by the 4th century, when their strong fragrance made them popular as ingredients of pomanders and as prevention against plague and infection. During the 17th century there was rivalry between the Dutch and the Portuguese over establishing a trading

monopoly in this valuable spice. But by 1770 the French were growing their own crops in Mauritius, and they were subsequently cultivated in Guiana, Brazil, the West Indies and Zanzibar. The name cloves comes from the French word for nail, *clou*, which they are supposed to resemble.
Description An evergreen tree, 20m/65ft in height, it has soft, grey bark and dark green, ovate leaves, with a shiny, leathery texture. At the beginning of the rainy season, fragrant green buds (cloves) appear at the ends of the branches. They gradually turn red and, if left unpicked, develop into pink or crimson flowers.
Habitat/distribution Native to the Moluccas, introduced and cultivated in other tropical zones.
Growth Tender, tropical trees, grown in fertile soil and requiring high humidity and minimum temperatures of 15–18°C/59–64°F. Propagated

Above *Ground cloves.*

COMPOSITAE/ASTERACEAE

Tanacetum

Tanacetum balsamita
Alecost

History and traditions Alecost came to
Europe from the Middle East during the 16th
century and soon became popular for its
pleasant balsam fragrance. As Culpeper wrote
a century later, "This is so frequently known to
be an inhabitant in almost every garden, that I
suppose it is needless to write a description
thereof." As its common name suggests, it
was used to flavour ale, the second syllable
"cost" is from a Greek word, *kostos*, meaning
fragrant or spicy. In the 17th century it was
taken to America by settlers, where it became
known as Bible-leaf from the custom of using it
as a Bible bookmark and sniffing its revivifying
scent during long sermons. As a medicinal herb
it was frequently recommended for disorders of
the stomach and head, and Culpeper gives
instructions for making it into a salve with
olive oil, thickened with wax, rosin and
turpentine. It is now little used as a
medicinal herb.

Description A hardy perennial, up to 1m/3ft
tall, it has a creeping rhizome and oval, silvery-
green, soft-textured leaves, with a minty
balsamic fragrance. Small, daisy-like flowers
are borne in mid- to late summer. Formerly
classified in the *Chrysanthemum* genus.

Habitat/distribution Native to western Asia,
naturalized in Europe and North America.

Growth Prefers a moisture-retentive but
well-drained soil and a sunny position.
Most easily propagated by division or
cuttings in spring, but can also be
grown from seed.

Parts used Leaves – fresh or dried.

USES Medicinal An infusion of the leaves
helps reduce the pain of insect bites and
stings, and a fresh leaf may be applied
directly to the spot as "first aid".

Culinary Fresh leaves may be added to fruit
cups and drinks; fresh or dried leaves make
an aromatic tea.

Aromatic The dried leaves are added to
potpourri and make fragrant bookmarks.

Other names Costmary and Bible-leaf.

Above *The fresh leaves
of* Tanacetum balsamita
*have a pleasant
minty fragrance.*

Tanacetum parthenium
Feverfew

History and traditions The medicinal
properties of feverfew have long been
recognized. The Greek philosopher, Plutarch,
writing in 1st-century Athens, says that the
plant was named *parthenium* after treatment
with feverfew saved the life of a workman who
fell from the Parthenon. The common name
comes from the Latin *febris*, fever, and *fugure*,
to chase away. In the centuries that followed,
herbalists recommended this herb, usually in a
mixture of honey or sweet wine to disguise its
bitterness, for a range of ills. *Bancke's Herbal*,
1525, advocates it for stomach disorders,
toothache and insect bites, Culpeper
recommends it for 'women's troubles' and as
an antidote to a liberal intake of opium (*The
English Physician*, 1653). But others evidently
recognized its value for the relief of headaches
and migraine. Gerard wrote, "it is very good for
them that are giddie in the head, or which have
the turning called Vertigo, that is, swimming
and turning in the head" (*The Herball*, 1597).
And Sir John Hill, in his *Family Herbal*, 1772,
states clearly, "in the worst headaches, this herb
exceeds whatever else is known." Feverfew
came to prominence in modern times after a
Welsh doctor's wife found relief in 1974 from
both chronic migraine and rheumatism by

Tanacetum vulgare
Tansy

History and traditions Tansy is one of the essential strewing herbs, listed by Thomas Tusser in *One Hundred Points of Good Husbandry*, 1577, doubtless chosen for its insect-repellent properties. Despite the bitter flavour, there is evidence that it was widely used for culinary purposes in the past. It was a popular ingredient of cakes and puddings, made with eggs and cream, traditionally served on Easter Day. William Coles, in *The Art of Simpling*, 1656, refers to the effect of tansy on the constitution after a Lenten diet of salt-fish. Tansy was also a popular substitute for mint in a sauce to accompany lamb. One authority refers to its cosmetic application. "I have heard that if maids will take wild Tansy and lay it to soake in Buttermilk for the space of nine days and wash their faces therewith, it will make them look very faire" (Jerome Braunschwyke, *The Virtuose Boke of Distyllacion*, 1527).

Description A spreading rhizomatous perennial, to 1.2m/4ft in height, it has dark green, feathery, pinnately-divided leaves, which are pungently aromatic, and terminal clusters of button-like bright yellow flowers in summer.

Related species *T. vulgare* var. *crispum* is a more compact plant, with attractive, curly, fern-like leaves.

Growth Grows well in dry, stony soil and prefers a sunny position. Propagated by seed, division or cuttings in spring.

Parts used Leaves.

USES Medicinal This herb is said to have been used in enemas for expelling intestinal worms, but is seldom used in herbal medicine today.

Culinary Despite the wealth of recipes in old books, Tansy is not recommended as a pudding ingredient as it has an unpleasantly bitter taste, although the leaves used to be added to lamb dishes and spring puddings.

Horticultural Tansy is supposed to be an insect repellent and ward off aphids in companion planting.

CAUTION It is unsafe to take internally as a medicinal herb. The volatile oil is extremely toxic and should be avoided. Do not take during pregnancy or while breast-feeding.

eating feverfew leaves. Since then this herb has undergone much scientific study and has been found to be a relatively effective and safe remedy for these complaints.

Description A bushy, hardy perennial, to 1m/3ft, with bright green, pungently aromatic, pinnately-lobed leaves and a mass of white daisy-like flowers, with yellow centres, in early to midsummer.

Related species There are a number of cultivars, including some with golden foliage (as above), or double flowers, which make attractive ornamentals, but do not have the same medicinal properties.

Habitat/distribution It is native to southern Europe, widely introduced elsewhere. Found on dry, stony soils.

Growth Grows in any poor, free-draining soil and tolerates drought. Propagate by seed sown in spring, or by cuttings or division in spring. Self-seeds prolifically.

Parts used Leaves, flowering tops – for eating fresh, or dried for use in tablets and pharmaceutical products.

USES Medicinal Feverfew lowers fever and dilates blood vessels. Fresh leaves are sometimes eaten (usually sweetened with honey, as they are very bitter) to reduce the effects of migraine headaches. It is also taken in tablet form for migraine, rheumatism and menstrual problems.

Above *Golden feverfew does not have the medicinal properties of the species.*

CAUTION Only to be taken on medical advice if on other medication. Can interact with anti-coagulant and other pharmaceutical drugs. Not to be taken in pregnancy or while breast-feeding. Can cause dermatitis, allergic reactions, mouth ulcers and gastric upsets.

Above Tanacetum vulgare.

COMPOSITAE/ASTERACEAE

Taraxacum officinale

Dandelion

History and traditions Although known much earlier in Chinese medicine, the dandelion was first recognized in Europe in the 10th or 11th century, through the influence of the Arabian physicians, then prominent as medical authorities. The name, dandelion, comes from the French *dents de lion*, lion's tooth.

Description A perennial which grows on a stout taproot to 30cm/1ft long, it has a basal rosette of leaves and yellow, solitary flowers followed by spherical, fluffy seed heads.

Habitat/distribution Native to Europe and Asia, and occurs widely in temperate regions of the world, often found on nitrogen-rich soils.

Growth Grows in profusion in the wild and self-seeds. Cultivated dandelions are grown in moist, fertile soil. Propagated from seed.

Parts used Leaves, flowers – fresh for culinary use, fresh or dried for medicinal preparations; roots – dried.

USES Medicinal An effective diuretic, it is taken internally for urinary infections and diseases of the liver and gall bladder. Considered beneficial for rheumatic complaints and gout. Also said to improve appetite and digestion. Of great benefit nutritionally, high in vitamins A and C and a rich source of iron, magnesium, potassium and calcium.

Culinary Young leaves of dandelions are added to salads, often blanched first to reduce bitterness, or cooked, like spinach, as a vegetable. Flowers are made into wine. The roasted root makes a palatable, soothing, caffeine-free substitute for coffee.

TAXACEAE

Taxus baccata

Yew

History and traditions Yews were sacred to the Druids and used in their ceremonies. They have also been grown in churchyards from the beginning of the Christian era. As evergreens and exceptionally long-lived trees (1,000–2,000 years), they were a life symbol and often used to decorate the church or to scatter in graves. *Taxus* is from the Greek word *taxon*, a bow, and the flexible, close-grained wood was the traditional material for longbows. Yew is from the Anglo-Saxon name for the tree. There are rare references to its former medicinal uses, in treating snakebite and rabies for example, but its poisonous nature was always recognized and it was known to kill cattle at a stroke. It has sometimes been used in homeopathy. In recent

times yews have come to prominence as a source of taxol, used in the treatment of ovarian cancer.

Description *T. baccata* is a spreading, evergreen tree, growing to about 15m/50ft, with a rounded crown and reddish-brown scaly bark. The leaves are dark green, flattened needles, arranged alternately. It is a dioecious tree, and the male flowers are small globular cones, which release clouds of pollen in very early spring; the female flower is a small green bud, followed by the fruit, a highly poisonous seed, partially enclosed in a fleshy, red, non-poisonous aril.

Related species *T. brevifolia*, the Pacific yew, has the highest taxol content, mostly in the bark, and is the main source of the drug, but six trees are needed to make one dose and wild stocks have been grossly over-exploited. *T. baccata*, the common yew, contains less significant levels of taxol-yielding compounds, found in the leaves, but is now used in taxol synthesis.

Above Taxus brevifolia.

Top Taxus baccata *'Fruco-luteo', a cultivar with yellow fruits.*

Left Taxus baccata *'Fastigiata', the Irish yew.*

Habitat/distribution *T. baccata* is native to Europe, Asia and northern Africa and *T. brevifolia* is found in north-western North America to the south-west of Canada.

Growth Yews will grow in any soil, including chalk. Propagated by seed, sown in early spring, or by cuttings in September. *T. baccata* responds well to close clipping and is frequently used as a hedge, or in topiary work.

Parts used Leaves, bark – for extraction of taxol.

USES Medicinal Extracts of yew are used in drugs for treatment of cancers, mainly ovarian, breast and lung cancer.

> **CAUTION** All parts of yew are poisonous and it should never be used for self-medication.

LABIATAE/LAMIACEAE
Teucrium chamaedrys
Wall germander

History and traditions *T. chamaedrys* is said to be named after Teucer, son of Scamander, King of Troy, who, according to Greek mythology, was the first to recognize the medicinal properties of this herb. It is mentioned in the works of Dioscorides and developed a reputation over the centuries for being an effective treatment for gout. It was also taken in powdered form for catarrh and as a herbal snuff. Germander comes from the Latin form, *gamandrea*, of the Greek *khamaidrys*, and means "ground-oak", from *khamai*, on the ground, and *drus*, oak, a reference to the shape of the leaves.

Description A shrubby, evergreen perennial, 10–30cm/4–12in in height, it has creeping roots and dark green, glossy foliage, shaped like miniature oak leaves. Tubular, rose-purple flowers are borne in dense terminal spikes.

Habitat/distribution It is native to Europe and western Asia, widely introduced elsewhere and found in rocky areas, on old walls and in dry woodlands.

Growth Flourishes in light, dry, stony soils. Easily propagated by semi-ripe cuttings taken in early summer. Although the branches are erect to start with, it is inclined to sprawl, especially if allowed to flower. Clip hard in late spring or early autumn to maintain a neat shape.

Parts used Leaves, flowering stems.

USES Medicinal Although it is said to have some medicinal uses and digestive properties, it may cause liver damage and is best avoided.

LABIATAE/LAMIACEAE
Teucrium scorodonia
Wood sage

History and traditions A bitter-tasting herb, wood sage is one of the many plants said to have been used at one time for flavouring beer before hops became common for this purpose. One old story tells that hinds, wounded in the chase, sought it out for its healing properties. In past times it was used, like *Teucrium chamaedrys*, to treat gout and rheumatism and as a poultice or lotion for "moist ulcers and sores" (Culpeper). Its specific name, *scorodonia*, is from a Greek word for garlic, and if the leaves are crushed, it is possible with a little imagination, to detect a faint garlic odour.

Description: A hardy perennial, 30–60cm/1–2ft tall, it has ovate to heart-shaped, pale green, soft-textured leaves and inconspicuous greenish-yellow flowers in summer. *T. scorodonia* 'Crispum' has attractive, curly-edged foliage.

Habitat/distribution Native to Europe, naturalized in many northern temperate regions. Found in dry, shady woodland areas.

Growth It will grow in most conditions, but prefers a light, gravelly soil and partial shade.

Parts used Leaves (formerly).

USES Its herbal uses are now obsolete, but it makes an attractive traditional herb-garden plant – especially the curly-leaved form.

LABIATAE/LAMIACEAE

Thymus

History and traditions To the Greeks, thyme was an emblem of courage, to the Romans a remedy for melancholy, and appreciated by both for its scent. To tell someone they smelled of thyme was a compliment in ancient Greece, and Gerard refers to a description by the 3rd-century Roman writer, Aelianus, of the houses of a newly taken city being strewn with roses and thyme to sweeten them. *Thymus* is the original Greek name, used by Dioscorides. The scent of thyme is irresistible to bees, and the finest-flavoured honey comes from its nectar. The image of bees hovering over thyme was a frequent embroidery motif in former times. Its medicinal virtues were well known to the 16th- and 17th-century herbalists. Gerard recommended it to treat "the bitings of any venomous beast, either taken in drinke, or outwardly applied" and for Culpeper it was "a noble strengthener of the lungs". In modern times its antiseptic, antibacterial credentials have been fully established.

Description and species There are some 350 species of thyme, many hybrids and cultivars. The classification of them is complex and there are many synonyms and invalid names. For medicinal purposes, *T. vulgaris* and *T. serpyllum* are the main ones. For cookery, *T. vulgaris* and *T.* x *citriodorus* have the best flavour, though most of the others may also be used.

T. serpyllum (wild thyme) – Also sometimes called the "mother of thyme" and "creeping thyme", has a prostrate habit, growing to about 7.5cm/3in, and has tiny, ovate leaves and clusters of mauve to pink flowers in early summer, but is very variable in form. It is found throughout Europe and Asia on well-drained, stony or sandy soils and on sunny slopes.

T. vulgaris (common thyme) – Is a variable sub-shrub, 30–45cm/12–18in tall, with gnarled, woody stems, dark green to grey-green leaves and white, sometimes mauve, flowers. Native to southern Europe and the Mediterranean region, introduced elsewhere.

T. x *citriodorus* (lemon thyme) – A variable hybrid, 25–30cm/10–12in tall, with bright green, ovate to lanceolate, lemon-scented leaves and pale mauve flowers in early summer. Cultivated worldwide.

T. x *citriodorus* 'Aureus' (golden lemon thyme) – Is a cultivar with golden foliage, which may be used interchangeably with *T.* x *citriodorus*.

Of the many ornamental thymes, these are some of the most attractive:

T. serpyllum 'Pink Chintz' – Is a creeping thyme with grey-green woolly foliage and striking, bright pink flowers. First selected as a cultivar, at the Royal Horticultural Society gardens at Wisley in 1939.

T. serpyllum 'Coccineus' – Is a favourite prostrate variety for the depth of colour of its crimson-pink flowers and the attractive form of dark green foliage.

Above far left Thymus vulgaris *in flower with* T. x citriodorus; **above left** Thymus serpyllum.

Above Thymus serpyllum *'Pink Chintz'.*

Below Thymus serpyllum *var. 'Coccineus'.*

T. vulgaris, 'Silver Posie', and *T.* x *citriodorus*, 'Silver Queen' – Are grown for their variegated silver foliage, useful for giving contrast to an ornamental scheme.

T. pseudolanuginosus (woolly thyme) – Is a prostrate form with grey-green woolly leaves and pale pink flowers.

Growth All thymes require very free-draining, gritty soil and a sunny position. Though the

Above Thymus x citriodorus *'Silver Queen'*.

Right A decorative thyme pot.

Below left Thymus pulegioides *'Broad-leafed thyme'*; **below right** Thymus pseudolanuginosus.

Thyme and the ageing process

Research carried out by Dr Stanley Deans at the Scottish Agricultural College, Ayr, during the 1990s, in conjunction with Semmelweiss Medical University in Budapest, has found that laboratory animals fed with thyme oil aged much slower than animals that did not receive it. Thyme oil apparently delayed the onset of age-related conditions such as deterioration of the retina, loss of brain function and wasted muscles.

A key factor was the high level of antioxidants present in thyme oil, which helped prevent a decline in PUFAs (polyunsaturated fatty acids), important components of every living cell which help keep cell membranes fluid and strong.

ones mentioned are hardy to at least -10°C/14°F, in cool temperate climates they may need some protection in winter, as they are vulnerable to cold winds, especially if soil becomes too wet. Propagated by layering in spring, or by cuttings in summer. *T. vulgaris* and *T. serpyllum* can be propagated by seed sown in spring.

Parts used Leaves – fresh or dry for culinary use; leaves, flowering tops – fresh or dried for infusions and medicinal preparations; essential oil – distilled from leaves and flowering tops.

USES Medicinal A strongly antiseptic, anti-bacterial and antifungal herb. Infusions are taken for coughs, colds, chest infections and digestive upsets. Made into syrups for coughs, and gargles for sore throats. The diluted essential oil is used as as a rub for chest infections, as a massage oil for rheumatic pain and has been found to be effective against head lice.

Culinary Widely used as a culinary flavouring in marinades, meat, soups, stews and casseroles.

CAUTION Avoid medicinal doses of thyme, and especially of thyme oil during pregnancy, as it is a uterine stimulant.

LEGUMINOSAE/PAPILIONACEAE

Trifolium pratense
Red clover

History and traditions Red clover has been an important agricultural and animal fodder crop since ancient times. But it was seldom used medicinally until its early introduction to the United States, where Native American tribes discovered its therapeutic properties. They used it to treat cancerous tumours and skin complaints, took it during pregnancy and childbirth and as a general purification for bodily systems. It found its way into British herbal medicine sometime during the 19th century.

Description A short-lived perennial, it is decumbent to erect, 20–60cm/8in–2ft in height. The leaves are trifoliate and the flowers rose purple to white.

Habitat/distribution It is native to Europe, found across Asia to Afghanistan, and naturalized in North America and Australia.

Growth It requires moist, well-drained soil and is propagated from seed.

Parts used Flowering tops.

USES Medicinal Red clover blossoms are taken internally for skin complaints such as eczema and psoriasis, and applied externally for ulcers, sores and burns. Infusions were at one time thought to be helpful for bronchial complaints and the herb is also said to be effective in balancing blood sugar levels. Red clover is used by women to reduce the incidence and severity of menopausal hot sweats.

CAUTION Not to be taken in pregnancy or while breast-feeding. Can cause allergy.

TILIACEAE
Tilia cordata
Lime

History and traditions Linden tea, made from the flowers of *T. cordata*, has always been popular in Europe, especially in France, where it is called "tilleul" – as a soothing drink and for its medicinal properties. An infusion of the leaves as a complexion wash is an old prescription for a "fair" skin. The tree has been valued over the centuries for its many economic uses. The white, close-grained wood was used to make household articles, piano keys and carvings (notably by Grinling Gibbons, 1648–1721, at Windsor Castle and Chatsworth House, England). The inner bark produced fibre for matting and baskets; the sap provided a sweetener and the foliage animal fodder.

Description A hardy, deciduous tree, to 25m/82ft in height, with a large rounded crown, it has smooth, silver-grey bark and heart-shaped leaves, dark green above and greyish below. The five-petalled, fluffy, pale yellow flowers have a honey scent and appear in clusters in midsummer, followed by globe-shaped fruits.

Related species *T. cordata* is the small-leaved lime. Flowers of *T. platyphyllos*, the large-leaved lime, and of hybrids, such as *T.* x *europaea*, are also collected for tea. *T. tomentosa* (silver lime) and *T. americana* (American lime) do not have the same concentrations of active principles.

Habitat/distribution *T. cordata* occurs in Europe and western Asia.

Growth Prefers moist, well-drained soil in full sun or partial shade. Propagated from seed, which needs a long period of stratification (at least three months) to germinate.

Parts used Flowers – collected when they first open and dried for teas.

USES Medicinal A soothing herb, which increases perspiration and is said to help lower blood pressure, the flowers are taken as an infusion, often sweetened with honey and flavoured with lemon, for colds, catarrh and feverish illnesses, for anxiety and as a digestive.

Other name Linden.

Above *The flowers of* Tilia cordata, *the small-leaved lime, are collected for tea.*

LEGUMINOSAE/PAPILIONACEAE
Trigonella foenum-graecum
Fenugreek

History and traditions A herb with an ancient history, fenugreek has been cultivated since the time of the Assyrians and its seeds were found in Tutankhamun's tomb, c.1325BC. In Europe it was one of the many herbs promoted by the Emperor Charlemagne, c. AD742–814, and the seeds were sold for medicinal uses by the 16th- and 17th-century druggists and apothecaries. In Chinese medicine they have a history as a tonic and in Ayurvedic medicine are renowned for their exceptional ability to cleanse the system of impurities. They also have a reputation as an aphrodisiac. *Trigonella*, meaning triangle, refers to the leaf shape and the specific name, *foenum-graecum*, translates as "Greek hay", a reference to its long use as horse fodder. In recent times it has aroused interest for components of the seeds: the alkaloid, trigonelline, for its anti-cancer potential and a steroidal saponin diosgenin for its contraceptive effects.

Description A hardy annual, 60cm/2ft tall, it has an erect, branched stem and trifoliate leaves. Pale yellow pea-flowers appear in the upper leaf axils in summer followed by the fruit, a curved pod with a pointed "beak", containing up to 20 light brown, aromatic seeds.

Habitat/distribution Native to southern Europe and Asia, widely cultivated in the Middle East, India and northern Africa.

Growth Grow fenugreek in well-drained, fertile soil in a sunny position. Propagated by seed, sown in spring.

Parts used Leaves – fresh for culinary use; seeds – dried for cookery or for making infusions, decoctions, powders or extracts.

USES Medicinal The seeds are rich in a softening mucilage and are used in compresses or ointments to ease swellings, inflammations, ulcers and boils. They are taken in infusions to reduce fevers, have digestive properties and are said to rid the body of toxins, dispelling bad breath and body odour. Fenugreek is also thought to control blood sugar levels in cases of diabetes.

Culinary Leaves, which have a high vitamin, mineral and iron content, are cooked as vegetables, mainly in India. Seeds are sprouted as salad vegetables, and used as a flavouring and condiment in northern African, Ethiopian, Middle Eastern, Egyptian and Indian cookery.

> **CAUTION** Only to be taken on medical advice if taking other medication. Can interact with anti-coagulant and diabetes medicines. Can cause gastric upsets.

Above *Fresh fenugreek leaves.*

TRILLIACEAE
Trillium erectum
Bethroot

History and traditions Bethroot – the name is a corruption of birthroot – was traditionally used by Native Americans to control bleeding after childbirth and for soothing the sore nipples of nursing mothers. It was taken up by the Shaker community for the same purposes, for easing excessive menstruation and for haemorrhages in general. Sniffing the unpleasant smell of the flowers, which has been likened to rotting meat, was said to stop a nosebleed. The generic name comes from the triple arrangement of all its parts.

Description A variable perennial, 25–38cm/ 10–15in tall, it has broadly rhomboid three-sectioned leaves and solitary three-petalled flowers, ranging from crimson purple to white.

Habitat/distribution Native to north-eastern North America and the Himalayan region of Asia and found in damp, shady woodland.

Growth Trilliums require moist, humus-rich soil and partial shade. Propagation by division in the dormant period is the easiest method, as growing from seed is slow and erratic.

Parts used Rhizomes – dried for use in decoctions and extracts.

USES Medicinal An antiseptic, astringent herb, it is said to be helpful to the female reproductive system and to control bleeding. Poultices are applied for skin diseases and the roots were at one time boiled in milk to be taken for diarrhoea and dysentery.

TROPAEOLACEAE

Tropaeolum majus

Nasturtium

History and traditions The garden nasturtium comes from South America. It was introduced to Spain, from Peru, in the 16th century and originally known as *Nasturtium indicum*, or Indian cress, for the spicy flavour of its leaves. Leaves and flowers were popular 17th-century salad ingredients. As nasturtiums are high in vitamin C, they were useful for preventing scurvy. The generic name *Tropaeolum* comes from *tropalon*, the Greek word for a trophy, as the round leaves were thought to resemble the trophy-bearing shields of the classical world.

Description In South America it is a perennial, but in Europe and cool temperate regions it is a half-hardy annual. It has trailing stems, to about 3m/10ft, and circular leaves with a radiating pattern of veins. The yellow or orange flowers grow on stalks arising singly from the leaf axils, and have prominently spurred calyces. They are followed by the globular fruits. There are many low-growing and climbing cultivars.

Habitat/distribution Native to South America, now widely grown throughout the world.

Growth Grow in relatively poor soil for the best production of flowers, but supply plenty of moisture. Easily propagated from seed sown in containers, or *in situ*, in spring.

Parts used Leaves, flowers, seeds – used fresh.

USES Medicinal The seeds have antiseptic, antibacterial properties and are taken in infusions for urinary and upper respiratory tract infections.

Culinary The leaves are added to salads for their peppery taste and the flowers for their colour. Flowers are also used as a flavouring for vinegar. Seeds, when still green, are pickled as a substitute for capers.

Other name Indian cress.

Above *The flowers and leaves make colourful and nutritious additions to a summer salad.*

Above Tropaeolum majus

An old recipe for pickled nasturtium seeds

Gather your little knobs quickly after your blossoms are off; put them in cold water and salt for three days, shifting them once a day; then make a pickle (but do not boil it at all) of some white wine, shallot, horse-radish, pepper, salt, cloves, and mace whole and nutmeg quartered; then put in your seeds and stop them close; they are to be eaten as capers.

The Complete Housewife, 1736.

A simple modern version

Collect the nasturtium seeds while they are still green, until you have about 50g/2oz. Stir 25g/1oz salt into 300ml/½ pint/ 1¼ cups water, add the nasturtium seeds and leave for 24 hours. Then strain them and rinse well in fresh water. Put the seeds into a jar with a muslin bag filled with mixed pickling spice, top up with malt vinegar and seal with an airtight lid. Leave for 3–4 weeks before eating.

Growth It is an invasive plant that needs no cultivation. Propagated from seed or by division.
Parts used Leaves, flowers – fresh or dried.

USES Medicinal Coltsfoot is said to have tonic effects and contain mucilage, which is soothing to the mucous membranes. It is still recommended by herbalists to be taken in infusions for coughs and applied externally as a wash or compress, or as fresh leaves mixed in a paste of honey, for sores, ulcers, skin inflammation and insect bites.
Culinary Traditionally, leaves were added to springtime salads and soups.

Above *The leaves of* Tussilago farfara *appear after the flowers have faded.*

COMPOSITAE/ASTERACEAE
Tussilago farfara
Coltsfoot

History and traditions Known since the days of Dioscorides and Pliny as a herb to relieve coughs, often taken in the form of a smoking mixture, it is still a basic ingredient of herbal tobaccos. The generic name comes from *tussis*, a cough (from which we get the word tussive), and *agere*, to take away. In the Middle Ages it was sometimes known as *Filius ante patrem* (son before father), because the flowers appear before the leaves. Although still used in herbal medicine for cough remedies, recent tests have revealed that it contains low quantities of pyrrolizidine alkaloids, which are carcinogenic in high doses. (Also found in *Symphytum officinale* – comfrey).
Description A small perennial, on a creeping rhizome, 15–20cm/ 6–8in in height. The bright yellow, dandelion-like flowers, borne singly, appear before the rosette of toothed heart-shaped leaves.
Habitat/distribution Native to Europe, western Asia and northern Africa, introduced elsewhere including North America. Found on roadsides, wastelands, fields and hedgerows, in moist, loamy soil.

Above Tussilago farfara

ULMACEAE
Ulmus rubra syn. *Ulmus fulva*
Slippery elm

History and traditions The common name is taken from the slippery texture of the inner bark when moistened. It was a traditional medicine of Native Americans, used mainly for gastric problems and for healing wounds, and was taken up by early settlers, who made the powdered bark into a nutritious gruel for invalids with weak digestions.
Description A deciduous tree 15–20m/50–65ft in height, it has dark brown, rough bark, and obovate, toothed, deeply-veined leaves. Inconspicuous clusters of red-stamened flowers are followed by reddish-brown, winged fruits.
Habitat/distribution Native to eastern and central North America and eastern Canada. It is found in moist woodlands.
Growth This tree grows well in poorish soil and is propagated by seed or cuttings. It is liable to Dutch elm disease.
Parts used Inner bark – dried and ground into powder. (Bark should not be stripped from wild trees, which are becoming rare, only from those cultivated for the purpose.)
USES Medicinal Rich in mucilage, slippery elm powder is taken for stomach and bowel disorders, gastric ulcers, cystitis and urinary complaints. It is soothing to sore throats and applied in poultices for skin inflammations, boils, abscesses and ulcers and to encourage the healing of wounds.
Other name Red elm.

> **CAUTION** Subject to legal restrictions in some countries, especially as whole bark.

Left Urtica dioica

URTICACEAE
Urtica dioica
Stinging nettle

History and traditions The common stinging nettle may be an unpopular weed, but over the centuries it has been put to many practical uses, remaining an important nutritious and medicinal herb. It was named *Urtica* by Pliny, from *urere*, to burn. Roman legionaries are said to have flailed themselves with nettles against the bone-chilling cold of a northern British winter. They even brought their own seeds, in case no plants grew locally. Whipping with nettles later became an established cure for rheumatism. The nettle was a common source of fibre (similar to that of flax and hemp) in many northern European nations. One of Hans Andersen's fairy-tales tells of the Princess who wove nettle coats for her brothers. Above all, in former times, it made a valuable springtime pot-herb, tonic and antiscorbutic after the deprivations of winter and was made into all manner of soups, puddings and porridges, as well as nettle beer.
Description A tough, spreading perennial, the erect stems grow to 1.5m/5ft tall, on creeping roots. The stems and ovate, toothed, dull green leaves are covered in stinging hairs. Inconspicuous greenish-yellow flowers (male and female on separate plants) appear in mid to late summer.
Related species *U. urens* is a small, annual nettle, found in cool, northern temperate regions. *U. pilulifera* (Roman nettle) originates in southern Europe.
Habitat/distribution Found in waste ground, grassland, field edges, gardens, near human habitation or ruins, in nitrogen-rich soil.
Growth Cultivation is usually unnecessary for domestic use as nettles are plentiful in wild and semi-wild areas and can be invasive in the garden. Grown as a crop they require moist, nitrogen-rich soil. Cut back before flowering to ensure a second crop of young leaves.
Parts used Leafy stems – cut in spring, before flowering, fresh for cookery, fresh or dried for infusions, extracts, lotions and ointments. Roots – fresh or dried for decoctions for hair use.

USES Medicinal Constituents include histamine and formic acid, which causes the sting, vitamins A, B, C, iron and other minerals. The high vitamin C content ensures proper absorption of iron and the juice is taken for anaemia. Its diuretic properties help rid the body of uric acid and it is taken as an infusion for rheumatism, arthritis and gout, or applied as a compress to ease pain. It also stimulates the circulation and is said to lower blood pressure. Decoctions of the root and leaves are applied for dry scalp, dandruff and are said to help prevent baldness.
Culinary Only fresh young leaves should be used, cooked as a spinach-like vegetable or made into soup. Leaves should not be eaten raw as they are highly irritant in this state.

VALERIANACEAE
Valeriana officinalis
Valerian

History and traditions This is thought to be the same plant known to the medical authorities of ancient Greece as *phu*, for the offensive odour of its roots, and recommended by them for its diuretic properties. The name *Valeriana* dates from about the 10th century and is said to be from the Latin *valere*, to be in good health. It was promoted by the Arabian physicians of this era, appears in Anglo-Saxon leech-books of the 11th century and became known in medieval Europe as "All-heal" for its supposed therapeutic powers. It was appreciated in the 16th century and Turner's *Herbal*, 1568, describes laying the aromatic dried roots among linen. In fact it has a musky scent, similar to *Nardostachys jatamansi* (once classified as a valerian), and the essential oil is a perfumery ingredient to this day. It is

Above *Flowers of* Centranthus ruber.

also attractive to cats and rats.

Description A tall, hardy perennial, growing to 1.5m/5ft, it has grooved stems and pinnate leaves with lanceolate, toothed leaflets. The white, sometimes pinkish, flowers are borne in terminal clusters in summer. *V. officinalis* should not be confused with red valerian, *Centranthus ruber*, which has no medicinal value, but is grown as a herb garden ornamental.

Habitat/distribution Native to Europe and western Asia, introduced to many temperate regions and naturalized in North America. Found in damp meadows and ditches, often near streams.

Growth Grow in damp, fertile soil in a sunny position. Propagated by seed sown in spring, or by division in spring or autumn. It is inclined to be invasive.

Parts used Roots – dried for use in decoctions, medicinal preparations and extracts; essential oil – distilled from roots.

USES Medicinal It has sedative properties and is taken as a tea for insomnia, nervous tension, anxiety, headaches and indigestion. Also said to lower blood pressure.

Aromatic The essential oil is used in perfumery, and extracts as a flavouring in the food industry.

CAUTION Only to be taken on medical advice if on other medication. Can interact with epilepsy drugs. Excess doses are harmful and may cause headaches or a racing heart. Should not be taken long term or where there is liver disease.

SCROPHULARIACEAE

Verbascum thapsus

Mullein

History and traditions "Candlewick plant" and "hag's taper" are two of the many country names for this plant and refer to its former use, when dried, as a lamp wick or taper. The tall flower spires also look like giant candles, as described by Henry Lyte: "the whole toppe, with its pleasant yellow floures sheweth like to a wax candle or taper cunningly wrought" (*The Niewe Herball*, 1578). As a medicinal herb, it was taken for colds, in the form of "mullein tea", as indeed it still is, and was sometimes smoked as a tobacco for coughs and asthma (which must have made things worse). It also made a yellow hair dye. Throughout Europe and Asia mullein had an ancient reputation as a magic plant, capable of driving away evil spirits.

Description A tall, hardy biennial, growing to 2m/6ft, it has a basal rosette of soft, downy, blue-grey leaves, broadly ovate in shape, in the first year. Yellow flowers are borne on tall spikes in the second year.

Habitat/distribution Native to Europe, Asia and northern Africa, found on shallow, stony soils in grassland and wasteland.

Growth Thrives in dry, stony or gravelly soil and a sunny position. Propagated by seed sown in autumn. Often self-seeds.

Parts used Leaves – dried for use in infusions and liquid extracts; flowers – fresh or dried for infusions. Preparations must be carefully strained to eliminate irritating fine particles.

USES Medicinal It has antiseptic properties and is rich in soothing mucilage. Its main use is for coughs, colds, influenza and respiratory infections, when it is taken as an infusion. It is sometimes recommended for colic, digestive upsets, nervous tension and insomnia. An infused oil, made of the flowers, has been applied to sores, chapped skin and to relieve earache.

Other name Aaron's rod.

Above *The tall flower spikes of* Verbascum thapsus *appear in the second year.*

VERBENACEAE
Verbena officinalis

Vervain

History and traditions This unspectacular plant has a long history as a magical herb of exceptional powers and features widely in the folklore of Celtic and northern European cultures. It was venerated by the Romans, who scattered it on their temple altars and whose soldiers carried sprigs to protect them. A story began that it grew at the site of Christ's crucifixion and was used to staunch his wounds on the cross. It was called *herba sacra*, a holy herb, when used in religious ceremonies, and *herba veneris* for its supposed aphrodisiac powers. In Anglo-Saxon and medieval times it was worn as an amulet to protect against plague, snakebites and evil in general. And, with so much going for it, by the 16th century it became an "official" herb of the apothecaries, used for at least 30 complaints. Although it had largely fallen from favour by the early 19th century, it does have a place in herbal medicine today and in traditional Chinese medicine.

Related species Many of the ornamental verbenas grown in gardens come from Brazil and South America. Others with medicinal properties include a West Indian species and *V. hastata*, with blue flowers, which is indigenous to eastern North America.

Description A hardy, rather straggly perennial, with an erect, branched stem, it has ovate, deeply lobed, sometimes pinnate, leaves, which are dull green and slightly hairy. Small, pale lilac flowers are sparsely arranged in terminal spikes.

Habitat/distribution Native to Europe, western Asia and northern Africa, found in waste places and roadsides, usually in a sheltered, sunny position.

Growth Grow in well-drained but moist soil in full sun. Propagated by seed sown in spring.

Parts used Leaves, flowering stems – dried for use in infusions, ointments, liquid extracts and other medicinal preparations.

USES Medicinal Not to be taken internally without medical advice. Vervain has mildly sedative properties and is taken as infusions for nervous exhaustion, anxiety, insomnia, tension headaches and migraine. Also for disorders associated with the stomach, kidneys, liver and gall bladder. Externally it is used in compresses and lotions for skin complaints and as a gargle for sore gums and mouth ulcers.

Left Verbena
officinalis

GRAMINEAE/POACEAE
Vetiveria zizanioides

Vetiver

History and traditions A large coarse grass with many economic uses in the East, it was at one time planted on Sri Lankan tea estates to control erosion. An Indian name for it is *khus-khus*, and it has been used since the time of the Moghul Emperors to make scented screens, popularly known as "*khus-khus* tatties" which were sprinkled with water to keep buildings cool before the days of air conditioning, and which deterred insects as well. It is now widely cultivated for the volatile oil contained in its roots, especially in Réunion, which produces more than 35 tons annually.

Description A clump-forming grass, which grows to about 1.5m/5ft, with aromatic, rhizomatous roots, it has linear spears of leaves and brownish flowers produced on long stalks.

Habitat/distribution Grows wild in tropical Asia, eastern Africa and Central America and is widely cultivated there as well; also in Java, Réunion, the Seychelles, New Guinea and Brazil.

Growth A tender, tropical plant. Propagated by division or layering.

Parts used Roots – distilled for essential oil.

USES Aromatic The essential oil has a woody, musky odour, is strongly insect-repellent and antiseptic, and has sedative properties. It is used as a fixative for perfumes and as an ingredient of soaps and cosmetics.

APOCYNACEAE

Vinca major
Greater periwinkle

History and traditions The periwinkle is mentioned by Pliny and was woven into garlands in ancient Greece and Rome to decorate rooms, or to wear at celebratory banquets. An old name for it is "sorcerer's violet" and it has a long tradition in early herbal literature as an anti-witchcraft herb. *Macer's Herbal*, dating from the 11th century, writes of its power against "wykked spirits", and the *Herbal of Apuleius* recommends it "against devil sickness and demoniacal possession". The always imaginative 14th-century *Boke of Secrets of Albertus Magnus* tells of a recipe for wrapping it in earthworms, reducing it to a powder and mixing it with houseleek, to be eaten with a meal for inducing love between man and wife. In European cultures it has variously been seen as a flower of death, of immortality and of friendship. The generic term *Vinca* is from the Latin, *vincire*, to bind, a reference to the plant's twining stems. The name periwinkle is derived from the full Latin version of the name, *pervinca*.

Description A trailing evergreen perennial, to 45cm/18in, it has prostrate stems which root at the nodes, and glossy, ovate, dark green leaves. Five-petalled, violet-blue flowers appear in the axils of the upper leaves in summer.

Related species *V. minor* is quite similar in appearance, but lower-growing and with smaller flowers; it also has similar medicinal properties. The Madagascan periwinkle, *Catharanthus roseus*, formerly *Vinca rosea*, contains the toxic alkaloids vincristine and vinblastine. These are isolated to make drugs used in the treatment of certain cancers.

Habitat/distribution Periwinkle is native to Europe, found on loamy calcareous (alkaline) soils, often in woodland.

Growth Tolerates dry conditions, but prefers moist soil and shade or partial shade. It is propagated by division throughout the dormant

Above left Vinca major *is often used as a climber, scrambling through shrubs and hedges. It retains its glossy green leaves throughout the winter and produces bright blue flowers in early spring.*

Above Vinca major *'Variegata' looks good against dark hedges.*

period. Periwinkle makes useful ground cover, but can be invasive. Cut back hard in autumn to restrict its spread.

Parts used Leaves, flowering stems – processed for extraction of alkaloids.

USES Medicinal Both *V. major* and *V. minor* contain the alkaloid vincamine, which dilates blood vessels and reduces blood pressure, and is used in pharmaceutical preparations for cardiovascular disorders.

> **CAUTION** All parts of the plant are poisonous if eaten. Do not take internally or use for self-treatment.

VIOLACEAE
Viola odorata
Sweet violet

History and traditions Violets were greatly esteemed in the classical world and are mentioned by Theophrastus (400 BC) as well as appearing in the works of Horace, Pliny and Juvenal. The Greek word for violet is *io* and in Greek mythology Io, daughter of the King of Argos, was ravished by Zeus and then turned into a heifer so that his wife Hera wouldn't find him out. But at least he had the decency to provide sweet-scented flowers (later named after her) for Io in heifer-form to eat. Violet was the favourite perfume of Josephine and the flowers became the emblem of the Bonapartes after Napoleon became sentimentally attached to them. Despite its elusive scent, the violet has long been an emblem of constancy. Many medicinal uses are listed in old herbals and syrup of violets was a gentle laxative, still in use at the beginning of the 20th century. Household recipe books from the 16th to the 19th centuries give many examples of violet flower syrups, honey, conserve, cakes and vinegar.

Description A low-growing, hardy perennial, 15cm/6in tall, with a short rhizome and creeping stolons that root at the tips. The toothed, heart-shaped leaves form a basal rosette from which the solitary, drooping, purple or white flowers arise on long stalks, in spring.

Related species *V. tricolor*, heartsease, or wild pansy, is a hardy annual or perennial, which has branched stems and alternately arranged, lobed or toothed, ovate to lanceolate leaves. The flowers, like small pansies, are in combinations of yellow, white, purple or mauve borne on leafless stems sprouting from the leaf axils. Medicinal uses are similar to those of *V. odorata*. Strong doses may cause vomiting and allergic skin reactions. The common dog violet and wood violets are unscented and have no herbal value.

Habitat/distribution Native to Europe, Asia and northern Africa, introduced elsewhere. Found on damp soils in shady woodland.

Growth Grow in humus-rich, moist but well-drained soil, in sun or partial shade. The easiest method of propagation is by division during autumn. Also grown from seed sown in spring or autumn.

Parts used Flowers – fresh for culinary use; leaves, flowers, rhizomes – fresh or dried for use in infusions and medicinal preparations; essential oil – extracted from flowers.

USES Medicinal A healing, anti-inflammatory herb with expectorant, diuretic properties, it is taken internally as a tea for coughs, colds and rheumatism. Applied externally in compresses and lotions for skin complaints, swellings and ulcers and in gargles for mouth and throat infections. The essential oil is used in aromatherapy. *V. tricolor* is known to be a heart tonic, used to treat high blood pressure, colds and indigestion.

Culinary The flowers are candied, made into jellies, jams, conserves and vinegars, or added fresh to salads and desserts.

Aromatic The essential oil is used in perfumery.

> **CAUTION** Not to be taken in pregnancy. *Viola tricolor* is toxic in high doses.

Top Viola tricolor *(beartsease or wild pansy) has some medicinal value, but the flowers are not scented.*

Centre Viola tricolor *with golden feverfew leaves.*

Above *Leaves of* Viola cornuta, *the borned violet, which has lightly scented flowers.*

Right *Fresh ginger root and crystallized ginger.*

VERBENACEAE

Vitex agnus-castus
Chaste tree

History and traditions The association of this tree with chastity probably stems from its former use as a pepper substitute (made from the dried, powdered fruits) said to have been served in monasteries to suppress libido. It was used in earlier times to relieve aches and pains.

Description A hardy deciduous shrub or small tree, to 5m/16ft tall; it has palmate leaves, dull green on the upper surfaces, downy and greyish beneath, with long spikes of fragrant lilac flowers in summer, followed by small black fruits.

Habitat/distribution Originates in southern Europe and western Asia, also found in North and South America. Found on dry coastal sites.

Growth Grows in most soils and tolerates dry conditions. Propagated by seed or by semi-ripe cuttings taken in summer.

Parts used Fruits.

USES Medicinal Traditionally usd for gynaecological complaints, chaste tree has also been researched for treating menstrual problems.

> **CAUTION** Only to be taken on medical advice if on other medication. Can interact with other drugs, especially the contraceptive pill, HRT and fertility treatment. Not to be taken in pregnancy. May cause headaches, dizziness and gastric upsets.

ZINGIBERACEAE

Zingiber officinale
Ginger

History and traditions Ginger has been known in China and India since earliest times, valued for its medicinal properties and as a potent culinary flavouring. It was imported by the Greeks and Romans from the East. During the Middle Ages it was an important trading commodity, appearing on import-duty tariffs at European ports from 1170 onwards. It is frequently referred to in Anglo-Saxon leech-books, and in the 13th and 14th centuries it was second only to pepper as an imported spice. At the start of the 16th century, ginger was taken by the Spaniards from the East Indies to the Americas and West Indies, where it soon became established and was exported to Europe in large quantities. Ginger is one of the most popular culinary flavourings worldwide. It is an important ingredient in Chinese and Ayurvedic medicine, known in the latter as *maha-aushadi*, "the great medicine", and has an eastern tradition as an aphrodisiac, probably because it stimulates circulation and increases blood flow.

Description A perennial reed-like plant, it has thick, branching rhizomes and grows 1–1.2m/3–4ft tall, with bright green, lanceolate, alternately arranged leaves, on short, sheathed stems. The yellow-green flowers are borne in dense cones on separate stalks from the leaves.

Habitat/distribution Native to southeast Asia, introduced and widely grown in tropical zones.

Growth A tender, tropical plant, grown in fertile, humus-rich, well-drained soil with plenty of moisture and humidity. It is usually treated as an annual crop. Propagated by division.

Parts used Rhizomes – fresh, or dried, whole or ground.

USES Medicinal Ginger has antiseptic, expectorant properties, promotes sweating and is taken in decoctions for colds, chills and feverish infections. It is taken in tablet form or as a tincture for nausea, travel sickness, indigestion, stomach upsets and menstrual pain. The essential oil is taken in drops on sugar lumps for fevers, nausea and digestive upsets, and added to massage oil to ease rheumatic pain and aching joints. It reduces wind and enhances peripheral circulation.

Culinary Fresh ginger is grated and added to stir-fry dishes, and widely used, fresh or dried, in Chinese and Thai cuisines. Dried ground ginger is an ingredient of curry powder, pickles and chutneys and used in Western cookery in biscuits, cakes and desserts. Whole fresh ginger is crystallized in sugar syrup and made into chocolates and confectionery.

Aromatic The essential oil is used in perfumery and as a flavouring in the food industry.

> **CAUTION** Not to be taken in pregnancy or if on anti-coagulants without medical supervision. Not to be taken in high doses.

The Herb Kitchen

For centuries, herbs have been prized for their remarkable seasoning qualities. This section celebrates those special characteristics, which can transform simple dishes into something quite delicious. It also contains a veritable cornucopia of enticing recipes that encompass every type of dish, from soups, salads and fish to poultry, cakes and desserts, all of which have been enhanced by the addition of a wide range of different herbs.

Above, clockwise from top left *A mezzaluna is useful for chopping herbs; Grilled Red Mullet with Rosemary; Lavender jellies; Red Onion and Rosemary Focaccia.*

Left *Freshly picked herbs have a wonderful texture, flavour and aroma and can be used in any number of delicious dishes.*

Using Herbs

This chapter covers when and how to harvest your herbs, with guidelines on successful drying and storing for culinary and other uses. There is a short section on essential oils; what they are and how they are produced, their history and current uses, with some practical suggestions for making the most of them. Suggestions for different ways of preserving herbs in oil, vinegar, sugar and honey are given, as well as a wide range of culinary uses.

Above *Aromatic resins, frankincense and benzoin from the styrax tree*

Left *Dried herbs, pot marigold and lemon verbena, with cocoa butter (at centre) and other ingredients for making herbal preparations*

HARVESTING HERBS

Harvesting the herbs you have grown is a continuous process rather than a one-off annual event. Once established, most will grow strongly enough to allow plenty of repeat picking, which in itself encourages new growth in healthy, well-cared-for plants. It makes sense not to denude small, immature plants before they have much foliage, but many annuals and herbaceous perennials, such as lovage (*Levisticum officinale*), will produce a second crop once they have flowered, if they are cut back almost to the ground. When cutting perennial, shrubby herbs think of it as pruning and aim to improve the overall shape of the plant.

The optimum time for harvesting plant material to preserve it for later use depends on the growth pattern of the individual herb and the part of it that is required – leaf, flower, seed or root. Usually it will be during the growing season, but a few herbs, such as thyme, rosemary and sage, may be lightly picked when dormant, although they will not have such a full flavour. Whether harvesting herbs to dry for culinary use, cosmetics and pot-pourri or for home remedies, the following guidelines will ensure good results:

• Choose a fine, sunny day for picking, so that the essential oil content, which gives the plant its flavour and scent, is at its best. Wait until any dew or residual raindrops have evaporated – herbs tend to go mouldy before the drying process is complete if picked when wet – but try to finish picking in the morning before volatile oils have been drawn to the surface of the leaf by the heat, and then dissipated.

• Use only sharp scissors or secateurs (pruners) so as not to damage the plant and limit further cropping. Make sure that your equipment is clean and that sticky blades do not pass pest or disease problems from one plant to another.

• Pick only prime material from plants that are at their peak – avoid anything damaged, discoloured, diseased or spent with age.

• Pick herbs in small quantities, only as much as you can deal with at one time. Herbs should not be left in heaps, waiting to be processed, as even quite a small pile encourages heat and deterioration sets in. The idea is to preserve the plant before the active constituents start to break down and lose viability.

• Flowers and foliage must be wiped clean and be insect free before they are processed: they can be lightly sponged and patted dry with a paper towel, but do not wash them as this will impede drying.

Above: Cutting a head of angelica to collect the seeds.

Left: A freshly gathered harvest of garden herbs, ready to be preserved and stored in containers for future use.

Leaves: Most should be picked before they come into flower, when leaf flavour and texture are at their best. Pick small-leafed plants on the stem for stripping later – larger leaves may be picked individually. Shrubby perennials which last through the winter should not be cut severely late in the season, as this will leave them weak and vulnerable to frost damage.

Flowers: These should be cut soon after they have opened when they are at their best, and not left to drop their petals, when colour and scent will be minimal. Pick single blooms or flower heads as appropriate and strip off petals or florets when spreading them to dry. Lavender should be picked with a long stem, and flowers such as borage, where only the tiny blue "star" is required, need careful individual collection.

Seeds: The pods or seed heads must be picked as soon as they are ripe, when they are no longer green, but before they fall. Watch them carefully, as they can ripen and disperse very quickly.

Roots and rhizomes: These are usually collected during their dormant period in autumn or winter. When digging them up, try to leave some portion of the root so that the plant can regenerate. With some herbs, such as horseradish, this is not difficult, as it will regrow vigorously from the tiniest portion of root. Wash roots and rhizomes thoroughly with plenty of cold water and cut into pieces before processing.

Bulbs: These include garlic and onions. Dig them up in late summer to early autumn.

Bark: Bark should not be stripped from very young trees. They must never be ring-barked (stripped of bark all round the circumference of the trunk), nor should too much be taken in one year as this could kill the tree. Tools should be clean and sharp, and the lowest cut made at 1 m (3 ft) above ground level. Endangered or protected species should not be harvested at all.

Wild plants: Wild plants should be picked with the utmost caution, both for safety reasons and for the sake of the environment. Many wild plants are protected by law (check if this applies),

and should not be touched – in any case none should be uprooted or overpicked, especially if they are less than common. Any wild plants that grow near crops should be treated with suspicion, as they may contain pesticide residues, and of course you must be confident of correct identification before using. If you are not sure, leave them alone.

Right: Fresh sage leaves tied up in small bunches for drying.

Harvesting marjoram

1 Cut bunches of healthy material at mid-morning on a dry day.

2 Strip off the lower leaves, which may otherwise become damaged.

3 Twist an elastic (rubber) band around the stems to hold them tightly together.

4 Gather as many bunches of marjoram as you think you will need, then the bunches can be hung in a dry, well-ventilated place where they are protected from light.

DRYING

Successful drying depends on removing the moisture in the fresh material without sacrificing the volatile oil content. The process has to be completed quickly so that oils are not lost through a natural process of decay, but not so quickly that they are destroyed by heat. The key to success is creating an environment with the right temperature and low humidity.

An average temperature for commercially dried herbs is 38°C (99°F), but this would be difficult to provide at home without special equipment. Between 20–32°C (68–90°F) works well and can be found in an airing cupboard, or a cupboard near a hot-water heater. A spare room, with an electric heater (not directed straight at petals or loose material), could also be used.

The place chosen should be dry and well ventilated (garages are not really suitable, but a clean shed may be ideal) and, for better colour preservation, dark. Sun drying is a traditional method in climates where air temperatures are high and the humidity is low, but it does lead to colour loss and there is also a greater risk of contamination than when the herbs are dried in an indoor, controlled environment.

Oven drying is generally too fierce for flowers and foliage, even when the oven is used at its lowest setting. It is, however, suitable for roots. Microwaving is not ideal as it is necessary to include a small container of water to prevent arcing, and this makes for humidity, which is counterproductive.

Green Herbs
Small-leaved green herbs may be dried on the stem and larger leaves dried individually. Spread them on slatted trays, or on fine netting stretched over a frame so that air can circulate beneath, and put them in a warm, dark place with some ventilation.

Leave the herbs until they are crackly-dry to the touch. The length of time will depend on the thickness and moisture content of the leaf, the level of heat provided and humidity in the air. The process takes from 3–4 days to a week at the most. Once dried, strip leaves off the stems, or crumble larger ones into small pieces ready to store. Wearing cotton gloves makes the job easier on the hands.

Herbs may also be tied in bunches with raffia or string and hung up in a clean, airy place to dry.

Above: Drying lavender commercially on a custom-built, movable frame.

Flowers
Twist off heads of large blooms, such as roses, and spread out the petals on paper on slatted trays. Put in a warm place and leave them until they are papery dry.

Pot marigold (*Calendula officinalis*) flowers are easier to dry whole, then twist off the petals afterwards if required.

Lavender is best hung up in bunches, tied loosely with string or raffia, and with the heads in paper bags to exclude dust and catch petals that may fall as they dry.

Once the flowers are dried, they may be left whole, according to their intended use, or stripped from the stems in the same way as green herbs.

Chive flowers, or rosebuds that are required for decorative purposes, will keep a good shape if dried upright, with stems pushed through wire cake trays.

Specially treated dry sand or silica gel may also be used for drying flowers, and give a good colour and perfect shape. Place a flower on a thin layer of sand, sift more sand gently over it until it is completely covered and leave for three weeks in a warm, dry place. Uncover carefully.

Above: Herbs drying in a dark, clean and well-ventilated shed.

Above: Lavender, tied in bunches to dry, is well spaced to allow air to circulate.

Seeds

A good way to dry seeds is to pick the seed heads with stems attached. Tie them in bunches, insert the heads into paper bags and hang them up in a warm, airy place. When completely dry, clean off the pods or husks before storing in clearly marked envelopes. Seeds should not be stored in polythene (plastic), which encourages moisture.

Roots

Roots require a higher temperature than flowers and leaves for successful drying from 50–60°C (120–140°F). An oven, at a very low setting, with the door left open is suitable. Make sure the roots are scrubbed clean, then cut them in pieces and spread on baking trays. Put them in a cool oven and turn at intervals to ensure even heat. Leave until brittle, but test frequently as they should not become shrivelled and overbrown – length of time depends on the size and moisture content of root pieces.

Storing

Dried herbs and flowers deteriorate quickly, losing aroma and colour, if left exposed to light and air. Always store them in the dark and keep in a dry place. Flowers and foliage required for pot-pourri can be kept in paper bags, airtight tins or glass jars.

Above: Dried herbs retain colour and flavour stored in opaque containers.

Above: Dried bay leaves in a jar.

Right: Pot-pourri ingredients, stored in glass, are best kept in a dark cupboard.

HERBAL ESSENTIAL OILS

What are essential oils? The essential, or volatile, oil in a plant is the substance that gives the plant its scent. Despite the name, essential oils are not oily – a drop applied to paper does not usually leave any mark. They are volatile liquids, which evaporate at normal air temperatures and which are secreted from minute glands and hairs in the leaves, stems, flowers, seeds, fruit, roots or bark of plants and trees.

Some plants, such as roses, contain their essential oil mainly in the flowers; others, such as lemon balm (*Melissa officinalis*) mainly in the leaves. The orange tree (*Citrus aurantium*) contains three differently-named essential oils, in the flowers (neroli), the leaves petitgrain) and the rind of the fruit (orange oil).

The organic chemical structure of plant essential oils is extremely complex. Analysis by gas liquid chromatography (GLC) reveals that peppermint oil, whose 50 per cent menthol content provides its minty smell, has 98 other constituents. Flower essential oils have as many as several hundred components. For this reason it is impossible to chemically reproduce an exact copy of a naturally occurring essential oil in the laboratory.

Above: The leaves of Melissa officinalis *are distilled to produce a cheering, tonic essential oil.*

Above right: Essential oils have long been valued for their therapeutic properties.

Production

Essential oils are soluble in fats, vegetable and mineral oils and in alcohol. For the most part they do not dissolve in water, though some of their constituents may do so. The main fragrance molecules of roses and orange flowers, for example, are soluble in water. Steam distillation is the most frequent method of extraction, and volatile solvents and alcohol are some-times used in the process. A few fragile flower fragrances are still obtained by the centuries-old method of macerating the petals in trays of fat, and volatile oil from orange rind is extracted by expression: that is by pressing it out, nowadays by machine, but formerly pressed by hand. Quality is affected by varying soils, climates and harvesting conditions. Some oils may have been diluted or adulterated. It is not easy to tell, so look for a reliable source.

Using Essential Oils

Plant essential oils and extracts are widely used in the pharmaceutical, cosmetic and food industries. In the home they are used therapeutically in aromatherapy and herbal medicine, by taking them internally, by inhaling them in vaporizers and in fragrance products such as pot-pourri, by massaging them into the skin, by applying them in compresses, or by putting them in the bath. They are sometimes used in a domestic context to flavour food, but only in very small quantities, the whole plant being safer and usually more satisfactory for culinary use.

The important thing to remember is that, as extracts of the active principles of plants, essential oils are concentrated substances and should be taken internally only in controlled, drop-sized doses. When applied externally they must be diluted in a carrier oil.

Essential Oils in History

The origin of the name "essential oils" derives from the *quinta essentia*, or quintessence, a term coined by a Swiss physician Paracelsus, 1493–1541. He took the medieval theory of alchemy, which sought to isolate the *prima materia*, or elemental matter, of a substance, and applied it specifically to plants. His goal was to divide the "essential matter" of a plant from its "non-essential" components.

In ancient times, extracting plant fragrance by macerating it in oil or fat was common, and a technique of destructive distillation, such as that which produces oil of turpentine, was also known. At the beginning of the 11th century, steam distillation as a means of making plant-scented waters was discovered, usually credited to the physician, Avicenna, 980–1037, author of the *Canon of Medicine*. Arnald de Villanova, d. 1311, a Spanish doctor, further popularized the use of distilled herb waters for medicinal purposes.

Distillation was seen at the time as a means of refining plant material to its purest form, through fire, and alcohol was widely used in the process as producing the best results. But it was not until the mid-16th century that the nature of essential oils was understood and the process of separating them from the distillate put into practice.

By the beginning of the 17th century plant essential oils were available from professional pharmacies, as well as being produced on a domestic scale in the stillrooms of grand houses. Many herbals and old recipe books contained detailed instructions.

Inhaling Essential Oils

Breathing in the fragrance of essential oils has an immediate effect on mood and can be immensely therapeutic. An essential oil burner or vaporizer is one of the best ways to do this. You could also put a few drops of oil on a handkerchief to tuck under a pillow, or mix some into a pot-pourri of flowers and herbs.

To lift depression, anxiety and nervous tension try essential oil of frankincense, jasmine, neroli, rose or sandalwood. Sedative oils for insomnia include chamomile, juniper, lavender and marjoram. For stress and shock there is cedarwood, melissa or peppermint, and for mental fatigue and lethargy use basil, black pepper, cardamom or pine.

Bath Oils

Adding essential oil in drops to the bath water is another way to benefit from the fragrance. To make a bath oil for dry skins, mix about 20 drops of essential oil into a 10 ml (2 tsp) bottle of almond or sunflower oil which has first been infused with fresh flowers or herbs, such as chamomile or lavender.

A lavender bath is deeply relaxing, mildly antiseptic and helps to heal tiny cuts and scratches, bites or swellings. It is also soothing when you have a cold.

Right: A bath oil including essential oil of chamomile is soothing to sensitive skins.

Below: Lavender, mixed with a light oil for massage, releases an aroma which will help ease stress headaches and promote calm and restful sleep. It also helps muscular aches and pains. To release the scent, warm the oil slightly before you begin.

Insect Repellent Oils

Essential oil of lavender makes an effective insect repellent. Good quality and pure lavender and tea-tree oils are two of the few oils that may be applied directly to the skin. But if you are not sure of its provenance, or are likely to suffer from allergies, dilute it in a carrier (such as sunflower) oil first. Candles scented with citronella or eucalyptus help deter midges and flying insects.

PREPARING LEAFY HERBS

There are several different ways of preparing leafy herbs. The technique used depends on the individual characteristic of the herb, its culinary use and whether it is fresh or dried.

Washing and Drying

Leafy herbs must be carefully washed and dried before use. Wash them under cold running water to dislodge any dirt or insects then shake them as dry as possible. To dry them completely place the leaves flat on a paper towel, cover with another one, then press gently. Alternatively leave them to dry on a wire rack.

Stripping Herbs from their Stems

For woody-stemmed herbs, the leaves can be stripped from the stems before use. Hold the sprig at the tip and strip off the leaves with a fork. This technique can also be used to remove the leaves from dried herb sprigs. Strip large leaves from the stems using your fingers. Discard the stems.

COOK'S TIP

If you are not ready to use a freshly picked herb immediately, submerge the cut ends in cold water and store in a cool place. Alternatively, you can wrap the leaves loosely in a plastic bag and chill in the refrigerator.

Above: A mezzaluna is useful for chopping large quantities of herbs.

Snipping

To prepare chives, snip (chop) them into a container using kitchen scissors.

Tearing

Herbs with soft, fragrant leaves, such as basil, should always be removed from the stalks and torn directly into the dish when used for salads, dressings and sauces. Basil should never be chopped with a knife or cut with scissors – this will bruise the leaves, removing the essential oils and will make the flavour of the herb bitter. Tearing will maintain the beautiful colour of the leaves, whereas chopping will blacken them. Pick the leaves from the plant at the last minute and add them to the dish just before serving so that none of the delicious, fresh flavour is lost.

Chopping

Herbs can be chopped coarsely or finely depending on personal preference, and according to the dish they are to be used in. Remove any coarse stalks and gather the herbs into a tight clump with one hand while you chop with the other. Then chop with both hands on the knife until they are sufficiently fine.

Slicing

Large, soft-leafed herbs like lovage, sorrel, basil and rocket (arugula) can be finely sliced, either for garnishing or so that their flavours can be readily released into dishes such as salads, soups and sauces. Wash the leaves if necessary, pat them dry and remove the stalks. Stack them on top of one another and roll up tightly. Slice finely using a chopping knife.

Crumbling Dried Leaves

Once thoroughly dried and ready for storing, herbs should crumble readily between the fingers. Work over a sheet of paper or a small bowl. If the herbs are coarse, use a food processor, or put them in a small plastic bag and crush them with a rolling pin. Store the crumbled herbs in a dark container with a sealed lid. Keep in a cool place away from moisture.

Bruising

To release the flavour of any herbs into dishes that are cooked quickly, the herbs can be bruised first. Use a mortar and pestle to lightly crush the whole leaves or sprigs just before adding them to a dish.

Making a Bouquet Garni

A bouquet garni is useful when you want the flavour of the herbs but do not want them to show in the finished dish. A classic bouquet garni comprises parsley stalks, a sprig of thyme and a bay leaf tied together with string, although you can tailor the contents to suit your personal preference or the dish you are cooking, omitting some ingredients and adding more of others. Other vegetables or herbs you may like to include are a piece of celery stick for poultry dishes; a rosemary sprig for beef or lamb; or a piece of fennel or leek, or a strip of lemon zest, to flavour fish dishes.

1 Bundle the selection of fresh herbs or flavourings together and tie them firmly with string.

Garnishing

Small sprigs, cut at the last minute from the tips of the herbs make pretty garnishes. Alternatively, pick the small whole leaves from herbs such as mint, basil and parsley and scatter over the dish just before serving.

Once it has been used to flavour a soup, stew or casserole, fish it out with a spoon.

2 Another way to make a bouquet garni is to wrap the herbs in squares of muslin (cheesecloth). This is a good choice where the herbs may be dried or crumble easily.

3 Break or tear the herbs into small pieces and place in the centre of a 10–13 cm (4–5 in) square of clean muslin. Bring the edges up over the herbs and tie firmly into a bag with a length of string.

4 Use the string to tie the bundle to the pan handle, making it easy to remove. Make muslin bundles in batches so that they are readily at hand for cooking.

PREPARING VEGETABLE HERBS AND BULBS

The definition of what constitutes a herb is broad and wide-ranging. It is not just green leafy herbs such as parsley, rosemary, bay and thyme that we readily acknowledge as being herbs that fit the definition. It may be surprising to know that many vegetables such as cucumbers, peppers and artichokes, bulbs such as onions and garlic, flowers like marigolds, cowslip and lavender, seeds such as sunflower and poppy, and fruits such as fig and lemon, also fit under the broad umbrella of a herb. Paramount among these are members of the allium family – onions, shallots, garlic, spring onions (scallions) – and the capsicum family, notably (bell) peppers and chillies. Knowing how to prepare these commonly used ingredients will ensure the best results.

Seeding Chillies

Slit the chilli lengthways, open it out then scoop out and discard the seeds. Raw chillies contain volatile oils which irritate sensitive skin such as lips and the area around the eyes, so take care when handling them. Either use protective gloves or make sure you wash your hands thoroughly afterwards. Alternatively, slice the chilli into fine rings and scatter over the dish.

Roasting Peppers

Peppers are such a versatile vegetable. They can be eaten raw in salads (washed, sliced and with the seeds removed), or cooked in many different ways, such as stuffed with a delicious filling of rice and vegetables. Roasting (broiling) peppers under the grill (broiler) brings out their natural sweet flavour more than any other method of cooking.

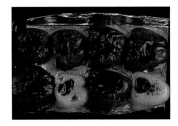

Cut the bell peppers in half and remove the seeds, membrane and stalk. Place on a baking sheet skin-side up and either cook under a hot grill, or in the oven until the skins are blackened. Remove from the heat.

USING GARLIC

Part of the allium family, garlic adds an unmistakable and delicious, pungent flavour to foods. It can also be eaten cooked or raw, although a little goes a long way. Most recipes call for just one or two cloves from the bulb to be used.

To break up the bulb, push the tip of a knife through the outer papery layer of the bulb between two cloves. Use the opening to lever the bulb apart. The cloves will come away easily.

Peeling Garlic Cloves

Each clove of garlic has a fine skin that must be removed. The easiest way to peel garlic is to place it on a chopping board and use the flat side of a wide-bladed knife to crush the clove. Place the blade flat on the clove and press it down firmly with your fist or the heel of your hand, breaking the skin of the garlic. The skin will then peel off easily. This also bruises the garlic, which allows the flavour to come out.

Chopping and Crushing Garlic

1 For a mild flavour, cut the garlic into thin slices, across the clove, or chop the clove roughly.

2 For a stronger flavour, crush the garlic rather than chop it. To make a paste you can use a mortar and pestle or a garlic press, or you can simply crush the garlic with the flat blade of a knife.

Roasting Garlic

Garlic can be roasted in much the same way as peppers, either by placing the whole bulb under a heat source or by placing the individual cloves under the heat. Roasting reduces the strength of flavour of the herb, leaving a sweetly aromatic herb. Once roasted, squeeze the garlic out of the skins for a delicious purée to add to salsas, dressings and dips.

Peeling Shallots

If you are peeling a lot of shallots, it is easier if you blanch them first in boiling water. Cut off the neck of each shallot and cut a thin slice off the bottom, but leave the root base intact. Place in a bowl and add enough boiling water to cover. Leave for about 3 minutes, drain, then slip the shallots out of their skins.

Peeling Onions

The easiest way to peel an onion is to cut off the top and bottom. Slit the skin and peel it off in one go.

Chopping Onions

Onions can be tricky to cut as they can slip about if you are not careful. First, slice the onion in half from top to bottom and place it cut-side down on a board. Slice across the onion, leaving a small section uncut at the root end, then slice down through the onion at right angles to these cuts from neck to root.

Minty Fresh Breath
To stop your breath smelling after eating onions, try rubbing the soles of your feet with pure peppermint oil. Within 30 minutes your breath should smell of mint.

Above: To remove the smell of garlic from your hands, sprinkle them with salt, then rinse in cold water before washing them with hot water and soap.

Leave the root end uncut to prevent the onion falling apart. Slice across the onion at right angles to the second set of cuts.

Watering Eyes
Chopping onions makes you cry because this action releases the volatile chemicals that give onions their strength. An old wives' tale suggests that if you bite on a crust of bread while preparing onions, then you won't cry. Perhaps the crust forms a barrier to prevent the onion's water vapour from reaching your nose and eyes.

COOK'S TIP
It is unwise to prepare any members of the onion family too far in advance. Raw alliums can develop "off-flavours" due to sulphur compounds that are released when their cell walls are broken.

PREPARING AROMATIC INGREDIENTS

Aromatic spices, leafy herbs, seeds, flower petals, fruits and nuts all have their own distinct flavours that will add colour, texture, and vital flavour to food.

PREPARING SEEDS, SPICES AND NUTS

The seeds of many herbs are used in food preparation either whole, lightly crushed or ground into powder. They can also be gently roasted or dry-fried to enhance their flavour. Similarly, most nuts are available whole, chopped or ground, or, in the case of almonds, flaked (sliced), and they too can be roasted to emphasize their flavours.

Roasting Seeds

Seeds like coriander, mustard, fennel, cumin and caraway can be lightly roasted before crushing and using, to bring out their flavours. Heat a small, heavy pan over a moderate heat for about 1 minute. Add the seeds and dry-fry them, shaking the pan constantly for a couple of minutes until the aroma starts to rise. Watch the pan, as the seeds will soon start to burn.

Grinding Seeds and Nuts

Although most herb and spice seeds can be purchased ready ground as powder, there is nothing quite so fragrant as the aroma of freshly ground

seeds. Small, easily ground seeds such as cumin, fennel and caraway can be crushed using a pestle and mortar. Place a small amount, about a tablespoon or two, in the mortar and grind in a circular motion. Some harder seeds, such as coriander, can be ground in a spice or pepper mill. Some people prefer to use a coffee grinder; grind the seeds in short bursts.

Grating Nutmeg

Nutmeg is widely available, both whole and ground, but as the flavour of the powder deteriorates quickly, it is worth buying a whole one and storing it in an airtight container. Grate the amount needed using a fine grater.

Chopping Nuts

Nuts are widely sold whole, chopped or ground and there is probably not much need to process them yourself. But if you do have a fresh supply and want to chop or grind them, do this in a food processor. The flavour will be so much better than commercially packed ones.

Roasting Nuts

Nuts, like seeds, can be roasted to accentuate their flavour. Place them in a pan over a moderate heat until lightly browned.

Infusing Saffron

Saffron threads are always infused in warm water before use to release their wonderful aroma and yellow colour. Warm a little water, add the saffron and leave to infuse (steep) for about 5 minutes. You can use both the strands and the liquid in the recipe.

Infusing Vanilla

Vanilla pods (beans) impart a sweet aromatic flavour to foods. They are generally used whole and most commonly in milk or sugar. To flavour sugar for use in custards and desserts, simply pour sugar into a clean, dry screwtop jar. Add a whole pod, then seal the jar. Leave for a few weeks before using.

To flavour milk and cream for use in ice creams and custards, add a whole vanilla pod to a pan of milk. Heat the milk with the vanilla pod until just boiling, then remove from the heat. (To intensify the flavour split the pod lengthways.) Cover and infuse for 10 minutes. Remove and discard the pod.

Savoury sauces can be infused in the same way, using herbs that complement the main ingredient – parsley sauce is the best known, although the herb remains in the sauce.

Preparing Fresh Root Ginger

This spice is one of the oldest cultivated and most popular medicinal herbs. Its unmistakable hot, fragrant and peppery taste is used in a huge variety of sweet and savoury dishes, such as tisanes, soups, stir-fries, curries, grains, desserts and cakes. More often than not it is ground ginger that is used in recipes, but finely grated ginger can also be used.

1 Fresh root ginger is most easily peeled using a vegetable peeler or a small, sharp paring knife.

2 Chop ginger using a sharp knife to the size specified in the recipe.

3 Grate ginger finely – a box grater works well. Freshly grated ginger can also be squeezed to release the juice.

FLOWERS

Many flowers add delicate flavour and beautiful colour to summer salads, desserts and cakes. Harvest herb flowers carefully as they tend to be delicate and only pick when dry or they will collapse. Gently pull the flowers from the stems.

Above: Lavender flowers are one of the most versatile herbs.

Infusing Floral Herbs

Lavender flowers can be added to sugar in the same way as vanilla pods, or heated with liquid to impart their essential aroma.

HERB OILS AND VINEGARS

Flavouring culinary oils and vinegars with fresh herbs is an easy yet wonderful way to enjoy their flavours right through the winter months. They also make perfect gifts, presented in attractive bottles or jars. After making up bottles of oil, store in a cool place for at least a couple of weeks before use so that the herby flavours are absorbed, after which the flowers should be removed. Drain the oil through muslin (cheesecloth), and pour the liquid into clean bottles, after which it will be good for three to six months. Herb oils are delicious for cooking chicken and fish, flavouring soups and breads and drizzling on to pizzas and roasted vegetables, while the vinegars add a refreshing tang to sauces, salad dressings and syrupy desserts.

VARIATIONS

Mixed Herb Oils Try combining several herbs in one bottle. Rosemary, bay, thyme, marjoram and oregano are delicious together. Lemon, orange or lime slices add a refreshing tang to any of the combinations.

Spiced Herb Oils For a spicy flavour, add any of the following – cinnamon sticks, dried chillies, whole cloves, mace blades, cardamom pods, coriander seeds or peppercorns.

Garlic-infused Herb Oils Used sparingly, garlic adds a delicious flavour to oil. Peel several cloves, put in a small pan and just cover with the oil you are using for bottling. Poach very gently for about 25 minutes. Leave to cool then drain the garlic. Fill clean, dry bottles with the infused oil.

WARNING

There is some evidence that oils containing fresh herbs and spices can grow harmful moulds, especially once the bottle has been opened and the contents are not fully covered by the oil. To protect against this, it is recommended that the herbs and spices are removed once their flavour has passed to the oil.

HERB OILS

Strongly flavoured herbs such as thyme, bay, basil, rosemary, marjoram, oregano, sage and tarragon are particularly suited to flavouring oils, and in some cases the flowers work well too. Use a single herb or a mixture of two or more and add additional ingredients like garlic and chilli for a more robust flavour. Choose oils, like light olive oils, sunflower oil and grapeseed oil, that will not overpower the herbs. The paler the colour of the oil, the more the herbs will show through – worth bearing in mind if giving as presents. Once made for a couple of weeks, check the intensity of the flavour. If too indistinct (remember it will be further diluted once used in cooking) remove the sprigs and add fresh ones to the jar.

Aromatic Herb Oil

Use your favourite herb to flavour this delicious oil for use in salad dressings or for cooking.

MAKES ABOUT 600ML/1 PINT/2½ CUPS

INGREDIENTS
    Several large sprigs of rosemary, thyme, oregano, tarragon or sage
    4 bay leaves
    about 600ml/1 pint/2½ cups light olive oil or sunflower oil, or a mixture of the two

1 Wash the herbs and pat dry, discarding any damaged parts. Push the herbs down into clean, dry bottles so the tips face upwards. Don't cram too many into a small space.

2 Fill the bottles up to the necks with the oil and cover with the cork.

Basil Oil

When making basil oil the leaves can be lightly bruised to bring out the flavour. If you like, use garlic-infused (steeped) oil instead of natural olive oil for a delicious Mediterranean flavour.

MAKES 450ML/¾ PINT/ SCANT 2 CUPS

INGREDIENTS
    handful of basil leaves, about 15g/½ oz/½ cup
    450ml/¾ pint/scant 2 cups olive oil

1 Bruise the basil leaves lightly using a mortar and pestle, then stir in a little of the oil.

2 Transfer the mixture to a clean, dry bottle and pour over the remaining oil. Cover with a lid or cork and store in a cool place for 2–3 weeks.

3 To remove the basil leaves, line a sieve (strainer) with muslin (cheesecloth) and drain the oil into a jug (pitcher). Allow all the oil to soak through before removing the leaves from the sieve.

4 Discard and pour the oil back into the jar. Add fresh leaves. Cover with a lid or cork and store in a cool place.

Marjoram Flower Oil

Use this fragrant oil to cook an aromatic, vegetable-filled omelette or mix with breadcrumbs and garlic to top baked vegetables.

MAKES 450ML/¾ PINT/SCANT 2 CUPS

INGREDIENTS
  30–40 marjoram flower clusters, clean, dry and free of insects
  450ml/¾ pint/scant 2 cups olive oil

1 Fill a large, clean, dry jam jar with the flower clusters (do not worry about removing any small leaves).

2 Cover with the olive oil, making sure the flowers are submerged.

3 Cover with a lid and leave in a warm place for two weeks, shaking the jar occasionally.

4 Line a small sieve (strainer) with clean muslin (cheesecloth) and position over a jug (pitcher). Strain the oil.

5 Pour the oil into a cleaned, attractive bottle with a 450ml/¾ pint/ scant 2 cups capacity. Cover with a lid or cork and store in a cool, dry place for 3–6 months.

Above: For very strong herbs such as chillies and garlic, use rich nut oils. For more delicate ones use light olive oil.

Below: Try any flowers that you have an abundance of. Thyme, rosemary, lavender, mint and basil are all delicious.

HERB VINEGARS

Many herbs and their flowers make delicious vinegars as their flavours are very readily absorbed. Basil, rosemary, thyme, bay, tarragon, dill, mint and even rose petals give good results. Red or white wine vinegar, sherry or cider vinegars all work equally well although a richly coloured, red wine vinegar might obscure the sprigs of herbs in the bottles. Do not use an untreated aluminium pan for heating the vinegar as it might impart a metallic taste.

Aromatic Vinegar

Garlic, lemon, bay and a good-quality vinegar provide a well-flavoured base for your choice of herb.

MAKES 600ML/1 PINT/2½ CUPS

INGREDIENTS
15ml/1 tbsp mixed peppercorns
2 lemon slices
4 garlic cloves, peeled
small handful of basil, rosemary, thyme or tarragon sprigs
3 bay leaves
600ml/1 pint/2½ cups good-quality vinegar

1 Put the peppercorns, lemon slices and garlic cloves into a clean, dry bottle with a capacity of about 600ml/1 pint/2½ cups. (Alternatively use two smaller bottles.)

2 Push herb sprigs into the bottles with the tips facing upwards. Add the bay leaves.

3 Fill the bottles up to the necks with the vinegar. Cover with a lid or cork and store in a cool place for 2 weeks, then remove the herbs.

Rosemary-infused Vinegar

Heating the vinegar for infusing (steeping) the herbs makes a strong-flavoured herb vinegar that is ready for almost immediate use.

MAKES 600ML/1 PINT/2½ CUPS

INGREDIENTS
600ml/1pint/2½ cups white wine or cider vinegar
90ml/6 tbsp chopped fresh rosemary, plus several whole sprigs

1 Bring the vinegar just to the boil in a large pan. Pour over the chopped rosemary in a bowl. Cover and leave to infuse (steep) for 3 days.

2 Strain the vinegar through a muslin-(cheesecloth-) lined sieve (strainer) into a large jug (pitcher). Pour into a 600ml/1 pint/2½ cup clean, dry bottle or two smaller bottles. Push several sprigs of rosemary, tips facing uppermost, into the bottle. Fit with a stopper or cork. Use immediately if you keep the herbs in the vinegar or store for up to 6 months without the herbs.

Below: Rosemary is one of the most useful culinary herbs.

Mint Flower Vinegar

This makes a lovely vinegar for a summery salad dressing.

MAKES 450ML/¾ PINT/SCANT 2 CUPS

INGREDIENTS
large handful of mint flowers with stems and leaves attached
450ml/¾pint/scant 2 cups white wine or cider vinegar
extra mint flowers for decoration

1 Put the flowers in a large, clean jar or a wide-necked bottle. Bring the vinegar to the boil, then pour over the flowers.

2 Cover and leave for 3 to 4 weeks. Remove the flowers and pour the vinegar into a clean 450ml/¾pint/scant 2 cup jar or bottle.

3 Fit with a lid or stopper and store in a cool place.

VARIATION
Spiced Herb Vinegar
Use a mixture of spices such as cinnamon sticks, allspice berries, mace blades, cardamom pods and coriander or cumin seeds.

Thyme and Raspberry Vinegar

Fruit and herbs always make a delicious marriage of flavours. This rich, sweet and fragrant vinegar gives a summery freshness to fruity salads and can be used to deglaze the pan when making game and poultry dishes.

MAKES 750ML/1¼ PINTS/3 CUPS

INGREDIENTS
  600ml/1 pint/2½ cups red
    wine vinegar
  15ml/1 tbsp pickling spice
  450g/1lb/2⅔ cups fresh raspberries
  small handful of fresh thyme sprigs,
    preferably lemon thyme

1 Put the vinegar and pickling spice into a pan and heat gently for 5 minutes. Put the raspberries in a bowl.

2 Pour the vinegar over the raspberries. Stir in the thyme, then cover and leave in a cool place to infuse (steep) for 2 days, stirring occasionally.

3 Remove the thyme sprigs and strain the vinegar through a large plastic sieve (strainer) into a large jug (pitcher).

4 Pour into clean, dry bottles and seal with a stopper or cork.

Rose-petal Vinegar

Use this delicately rose-flavoured vinegar in a dressing for light summer salads.

MAKES 300ML/½ PINT/1¼ CUPS

INGREDIENTS
  4 large red or pink unsprayed roses
  300ml/½ pint/1¼ cups white wine or
    cider vinegar
  rose petals, for decoration (optional)

1 Choose an unblemished rose, then gently pull the rose petals from the flower-heads. Scald the vinegar by bringing it almost to boiling point. Allow to cool.

Below: Rose-petal vinegar.

2 Chop off any damaged parts of the petals and put the petals in a large, clean, dry glass jar or bottle. Add the cooled vinegar, cover with a stopper or cork and store in a sunny position for about three weeks before using.

3 Strain the vinegar into a clean jar and discard the petals.

HERB TEAS AND TISANES

Well before the arrival of tea from China, people had discovered that infusing (steeping) the leaves, fruit and flowers of almost any edible plant in boiling water produced a refreshing, flavoursome drink which was easy, quick, free and in most cases beneficial to their health. These herbal drinks, or "tisanes", have enjoyed a remarkable revival as both supermarkets and tea specialists cater to our desire to experiment with an ever-increasing range of healthy alternatives to coffee and traditional tea.

Almost any herbs and herb flowers can be used, and the technique is generally the same. Several sprigs of the freshly picked herb are steeped in a cup of hot, but not boiling water, and left for several minutes to infuse. Remove the leaves by straining through a sieve. Serve hot or cold with honey, lemon or sugar, if you like.

MEDICINAL TISANES

Many tisanes are used as much for their therapeutic qualities as they are for their refreshing flavour. Rosemary is said to stimulate the circulation and alleviate migraine. Lavender, hyssop, thyme and marjoram infused together in a pot are taken as a remedy for cold symptoms, and hops, chamomile and lime flower are used to help beat insomnia. Peppermint is an excellent aid to digestion.

Above: Lavender tisane has an uplifting, sweet scent.

Left: Lime-blossom tisane will ensure a good night's sleep.

Lavender Tisanes

Put three sprigs of lavender flower-heads in a heatproof glass cup or mug and pour boiling water over. Leave to infuse (steep) for about 4 minutes, stirring the sprigs frequently, then remove them and serve warm or cold, sweetened with a little honey, if you like.

To make a soothing brew to relieve a headache, mix 2.5ml/½ tsp of dried lavender with 5ml/1 tsp of wood betony. Top up with hot water and leave to infuse for 10 minutes. Strain and drink.

Rose-petal Tea

A mixture of dried rose petals and China tea makes a highly scented and refreshing drink. It looks lovely served unstrained in small glasses so the petals can be seen in the base.

MAKES 130G/4½OZ

INGREDIENTS
    15g/½oz dried, scented red or pink
      unsprayed rose petals
    115g/4oz oolong or other mild- to
      medium-strength China tea

1 Mix the rose petals with the tea and store in an airtight container.

2 Make as for ordinary tea, and serve without milk.

Below: Mix dried rose petals with oolong tea and store in an airtight container in a dark place.

Left: Rose petals add a distinctive scent to tea.

Iced Apple-mint Tea

A jug (pitcher) of iced tea can be stored overnight in the refrigerator for a refreshing, summery thirst quencher.

MAKES 900ML/1½ PINTS/3¾ CUPS

INGREDIENTS
    15ml/1 tbsp Indian tea
    60ml/4 tbsp chopped fresh mint
    15ml/1 tbsp caster (superfine) sugar
    300ml/½ pint/1¼ cups clear
      apple juice
    ice cubes and sprigs of mint to serve

1 Put the tea and chopped mint in a pot or large jug and add 750ml/1½ pints/ 3 cups boiling water. Leave to infuse (steep) for 5 minutes.

2 Strain into a jug and stir in the sugar. Leave to cool. Add the apple juice and chill until ready to serve.

3 Serve in tall glasses with ice cubes and sprigs of mint.

Below: Chamomile, with its pretty, daisy-like flowers, is one of the better-known herbs. Taken in tea, it helps to assist digestion and settle nerves and anxiety leading to peaceful sleep.

VARIATIONS

Chamomile Tisane Infuse (steep) three or four flower-heads in hot but not boiling water as for Lavender Tisane. Do not infuse them for too long as the drink might become bitter.

Hyssop Tisane Make as above, using one sprig of flowering hyssop.

Lemon Verbena Tisane Take a flowering spray of lemon verbena and a couple of leaves and infuse.

Lime-blossom Tisane Use lime flowers as they begin to open. Steep five or six flowers for each cup and add hot, but not boiling water.

Peppermint Tisane Make as above, infusing one large sprig of peppermint leaves and flowers.

Chamomile and Peppermint Tisane Mix together 75g/3oz dried chamomile flowers and 25g/1oz dried peppermint leaves. Store and use as Rose-petal Tea.

Lemon Balm and Ceylon Tea Mix together 25g/1oz dried lemon balm and 115g/4oz Ceylon tea. Store and use as for Rose-petal Tea.

Marigold and Verbena Tisane Mix together 50g/2oz dried marigold petals and 25g/1oz dried lemon verbena leaves. Store and use as for Rose-petal Tea.

HERB CORDIALS AND DRINKS

From fragrant and Sparkling Elderflower Drink to smooth, tangy Rosehip Cordial, herbs and flowers can be used as a base for an interesting assortment of drinks, and as a lively addition to various fruit, vegetable and dairy-based drinks. Fruit and herbs can be infused (steeped) in alcohol to create an irresistibly punchy tipple, or steeped in syrups to make fresh-tasting, vibrant cordials that keep for months. Many herbs, particularly those in flower, make stunning additions to fruit punches, for summer parties and barbecues.

CORDIALS

Home-made cordials have a fresh, intense flavour that can rarely be bought in a shop. They can be lavished on to scoops of fruit or vanilla ice cream, swirled into fruit compotes or salads or simply served topped up with ice-cold water or lemonade as a thirst-quenching drink.

Rosehip Cordial

Collect rosehips from the hedgerows for this delightful cordial. It makes a wonderful autumn and winter drink.

MAKES 1.75 LITRES/3 PINTS/7½ CUPS

INGREDIENTS
1kg/2¼lb rosehips
granulated sugar

1 Put 1.75 litres/3 pints/7½ cups water in a large, heavy pan and bring to the boil. Meanwhile blend the rosehips in a food processor until finely chopped. Add to the boiling water and return to the boil. Cover with a lid and simmer very gently for 10 minutes. Turn off the heat and leave for 15 minutes.

2 Sterilize a jelly bag by immersing it in boiling water for 2 minutes. Drain and suspend the jelly bag over a large bowl. Strain the rosehips through the jelly bag and leave overnight until the juices stop dripping through.

COOK'S TIP
Cordials can be stored, chilled in the refrigerator, for 3 weeks. Sterilize bottles before use.

3 Measure the juice and return to the pan. Add 350g/12oz/1¾ cups sugar for every 600ml/1 pint/2½ cups syrup. Heat gently, stirring until the sugar has dissolved. Bring to the boil and boil for 5 minutes, or until syrupy. Pour into thoroughly cleaned bottles and cover with stoppers or corks. Store in the refrigerator.

Below: Rosehip cordial is a healthy drink, high in vitamin C.

Rosemary, Redcurrant and Orange Cordial

Redcurrants and oranges combine with a subtle hint of rosemary to make a tangy, summery cordial.

MAKES ABOUT 900ML/1½ PINTS/3¾ CUPS

INGREDIENTS
    900g/2lb/8 cups fresh redcurrants
    8 large sprigs of rosemary
    finely grated rind and juice of
        2 oranges
    granulated sugar

1 Strip the redcurrants from their stems, put in a pan and mash lightly using a potato masher. Add the rosemary, orange rind and 300ml/½ pint/1¼ cups water. Bring just to the boil, then remove from the heat and leave to cool. Stir in the orange juice.

2 Sterilize a jelly bag by immersing it in boiling water for 2 minutes. Suspend the jelly bag over a large bowl. Strain the fruit and juices through the bag overnight until the mixture is dry.

3 Put the juice in a pan adding 350g/12oz/1¾ cups sugar for every 600ml/1 pint/2½ cups syrup. Heat gently until the sugar has dissolved then bring to the boil and boil for 5 minutes, or until syrupy. Pour into thoroughly cleaned bottles and cover with stoppers or corks. Store in the refrigerator.

Lemon Barley and Bay Syrup

Despite its image as a remedy for minor ailments, chilled lemon barley juice is both delicious and invigorating. The gentle earthiness of the bay leaves blend perfectly with the tangy flavour of the lemons.

MAKES 750ML/1¼ PINTS/3 CUPS

INGREDIENTS
    75g/3oz/½ cup pearl barley
    3 lemons
    4 bay leaves
    75g/3oz/6 tbsp granulated sugar
    ice cubes, lemon slices and sprigs of
        lemon balm, to decorate

Above: Fragrant herbal cordials are cool and refreshing in summer. Serve with decorative, floral ice cubes.

1 Put the pearl barley in a bowl and cover with boiling water. Stir well then rinse thoroughly until the water runs clear. Put in a pan with 1 litre/1¾ pints/4 cups boiling water. Bring to the boil, cover with a lid and simmer gently for 45 minutes.

2 Scrub the lemons and pare off the rind with a sharp knife. Squeeze the juice and reserve. Put the pared rind in a bowl with the bay leaves and sugar.

3 Strain the hot barley water over the sugar mixture and stir until the sugar has dissolved. Cover and leave overnight.

4 Add the lemon juice and transfer to a jug (pitcher). Chill for up to two weeks. Serve undiluted with ice, lemon slices and sprigs of lemon balm to decorate.

Basil, Tabasco and Tomato Juice

Drinks that combine herbs, fruit and vegetables are renowned for boosting health and vitality. Serve any time.

MAKES 1 GLASS

INGREDIENTS
    small handful fresh basil leaves
    5cm/2in length cucumber, roughly
        chopped
    3 vine-ripened tomatoes, roughly
        chopped
    ½ red (bell) pepper, deseeded and
        roughly chopped
    60ml/4 tbsp freshly squeezed
        orange juice
    few drops Tabasco sauce, to taste

1 Put all the ingredients, except the Tabasco in a food processor or blender and process until smooth, scraping the mixture from around the sides of the bowl.

2 Pour into a tall glass and add Tabasco to taste. Serve with ice cubes if you like.

Mint Cup

Sweet, tangy and irresistibly minty, this summer cup is perfect for *al fresco* eating and drinking.

SERVES 4–6

INGREDIENTS
    large handful fresh mint leaves
    30ml/2 tbsp caster (superfine) sugar
    plenty of crushed ice
    30ml/2 tbsp freshly squeezed
      lemon juice
    175ml/6fl oz/¾ cup freshly squeezed
      grapefruit juice
    600ml/1 pint/2½ cups tonic
      water, chilled
    mint sprigs and lemon slices,
      to decorate

1 Crush the mint leaves with the sugar using a mortar and pestle, or a small bowl and the back of a spoon.

2 Transfer the mixture to a serving jug (pitcher) and fill the jug with plenty of crushed ice.

3 Add the lemon juice, grapefruit juice and tonic water. Stir gently and serve decorated with sprigs of mint and lemon slices.

VARIATION
Lemon Balm, Chilli and Lime Crush
For an evening dinner party, substitute lemon balm instead of the mint leaves and use lime juice instead of the lemon. Add a few drops of chilli oil with the grapefruit juice. A splash of Tequila can be added for extra kick!

Summer Punch

Borage, cucumber and mint give a subtle but essential fragrance to a classic Pimm's drink. Let all the ingredients chill together in the jug before topping up with the alcohol at the last minute, if you have time.

SERVES 4–6

INGREDIENTS
    several sprigs of
      borage flowers
    ¼ cucumber
    1 orange, scrubbed
    ice cubes
    ¼ bottle Pimm's, chilled
    several sprigs of mint
      or lemon balm
    chilled lemonade
      for topping up
    extra borage flowers, to decorate

1 Remove each of the borage flower-heads from the green calyx by gently easing it out.

Above: It would not be summer without a jug (pitcher) of refreshing punch, topped with fruit and chilled with ice.

2 Halve the cucumber lengthways and cut into thin slices. Chop the orange into small chunks leaving the skin on.

3 Put the cucumber and orange in a large jug and add the ice cubes, Pimm's, mint or lemon balm and borage.

4 Top up with lemonade, mix well to combine and serve decorated with extra borage flowers.

Above: Sparkling elderflower drink is light and refreshing, just perfect for summer, and will make an unusual addition to a special occasion.

Sparkling Elderflower Drink

Made simply from elderflowers, sugar, lemons and white wine vinegar, this sparkling drink is surprisingly potent, perfect for country weddings and other summer celebrations.

MAKES 4.5 LITRES/8 PINTS/20 CUPS

INGREDIENTS
    12 elderflower heads
    juice and finely grated rind of
        1 lemon
    30ml/2 tbsp white wine vinegar
    700g/1½ lb/3½ cups caster
        (superfine) sugar

1 Strip the elderflower heads from the stalks and put in a very large bowl with the lemon rind, juice, vinegar, sugar and 4.5 litres/8 pints/20 cups water. Cover with muslin and leave for 24 hours.

2 Strain through a fresh piece of muslin (cheesecloth) into sterilized bottles, using a funnel. Cork the bottles and leave in a cool place for 2 weeks before drinking undiluted.

Strawberry and Lavender Gin

Flavouring gin with fruits is an ancient tradition. Lavender makes a delicate, fragrant addition.

MAKES ABOUT 750ML/1¼ PINTS/3 CUPS

INGREDIENTS
    400g/14oz/3½ cups ripe but still
        firm strawberries, thickly sliced
    175g/6oz/scant 1 cup caster
        (superfine) sugar
    8 large lavender flowers
    750ml/1¼ pints/3 cups gin

1 Place all the ingredients in a large, wide-necked jar. Cover with the lid. Leave in a cool place for one week, shaking the jar gently each day.

2 Strain the gin and return to the bottle. Chill for up to 4 months. Serve over ice or with chilled tonic water.

Mint Flower Yogurt Drink

The familiar combination of yogurt and mint are blended here with beautifully scented raspberries. Enjoy this cooling drink on a hot summer's day.

SERVES 2

INGREDIENTS
    250ml/8fl oz/1 cup natural (plain)
        yogurt
    75g/3oz/½ cup fresh raspberries
    50g/2oz/¼ cup caster (superfine) sugar
    2 sprigs flowering mint, plus extra,
        to decorate

Put all the ingredients in a food processor or blender with 120ml/4fl oz/½ cup chilled water. Blend until smooth. Pour into glasses and serve decorated with sprigs of flowering mint.

Above: Enjoy mint flower yogurt drink on a hot summer day, or for a refreshingly fruity breakfast drink, substitute a fresh ripe peach instead of the raspberries.

HERB PICKLES AND PRESERVES

Above: Fruits and vegetables made into savoury preserves taste better if they are left to mature.

From bottled fruits and vegetables to sweet jellies and jams, most preserves benefit from the feast of flavours provided by the herb garden. Presentation plays an important role in the making of pickles and preserves as they are frequently given as gifts. An assortment of different bottles and jars is worth collecting, if you have enough space, and saves you rooting around at the last minute looking for suitable containers.

COOK'S TIPS

• All jars and bottles should be thoroughly sterilized before being used for storing preserves. Wash the container in hot soapy soapy water and remove any old labels. Rinse them in hot water, dry them with a clean dish towel and put them in the oven set at 150°C/300°C/Gas 2 for 15 minutes before filling.
• Cellophane jam-pot covers are ideal for all preserves except pickles as the vinegar will gradually evaporate through them and spoil the top of the pickle.
• Many preserving bottles and jars have attached lids with rubber seals. Remove the seals before sterilizing.

Spiced Pears with Ginger

Use any firm pears for this tangy, spiced preserve. It is particularly good with cold meats such as ham, gammon or smoked chicken or turkey.

MAKES 1KG/2¼LB

INGREDIENTS
  600ml/1 pint/2½ cups red wine vinegar
  rind of 1 lemon
  4cm/1½in length fresh root ginger,
    peeled and sliced
  1 cinnamon stick
  10ml/2 tsp whole allspice berries
  2 bay leaves
  450g/1lb/2¼ cups granulated sugar
  1kg/2¼lb pears
  cloves

1 Put all the ingredients except the pears and cloves in a large pan and heat gently until the sugar dissolves, stirring frequently.

2 Peel the pears, leaving them whole, and stud a clove into each one. Add to the vinegar and simmer very gently, covered with a lid, until the pears are very tender, about 25–30 minutes. Lift out the pears and transfer them to hot jars. Boil the syrup until slightly thickened and pour over the pears. Seal the jars immediately.

Bottled Cherry Tomatoes with Basil

Other small, well-flavoured tomatoes can be used instead of cherry tomatoes but these look particularly pretty.

MAKES 1KG/2¼LB

INGREDIENTS
  1kg/2¼lb cherry tomatoes
  5ml/1 tsp salt per 1 litre/1¾ pint/
    4 cup jar
  5ml/1 tsp sugar per 1 litre/1¾ pint/
    4 cup jar
  handful of fresh basil
  4 garlic cloves per jar

1 Preheat the oven to 120°C/250°F/ Gas ½. Prick each tomato with a wooden cocktail stick (toothpick), then pack tightly into sterilized jars with heatproof lids, adding salt and sugar.

2 Fill the jars to within 2cm/¾in of the tops, tucking the basil and garlic in among the tomatoes. Rest the lids on the jars but do not seal. Stand the jars on a baking sheet lined with newspaper.

3 Place the filled jars in the oven and cook for about 45 minutes, or until the juices start simmering. Remove from the oven and seal immediately. Store and use within 6 months.

Dill Pickle

Use a glut supply of dill to make this classic preserve, delicious with both cheese and cold meats.

MAKES 3 LITRES/5¼ PINTS/12 CUPS

INGREDIENTS
675g/1½lb ridge cucumbers
large bunch fresh dill
5 garlic cloves, peeled and sliced
900ml/1½ pints/3¾ cups white
  wine vinegar
45ml/3 tbsp coarse salt
10ml/2 tsp mixed peppercorns
3 bay leaves
2 star anise

1 Trim the ends off the cucumbers and cut into 5cm/2in pieces. Place in a bowl of cold water and chill for 24 hours.

2 Drain and pierce the cucumber pieces in several places with a wooden cocktail stick.

COOK'S TIP
Add 45ml/3 tbsp sugar to the vinegar for a sweeter flavour.

3 Pack into sterilized jars with plenty of dill and the garlic. Put the vinegar in a pan with 375ml/13fl oz/scant 1⅔ cups water. Add the salt, peppercorns, bay leaves and star anise. Bring to the boil and boil for 5 minutes. Pour over the cucumbers and seal immediately.

Kashmir Chutney

Ginger, cayenne, coriander and garlic are used to flavour this traditional family recipe for chutney. Enjoy it with a cheese ploughman's or hot or cold grilled (broiled) sausages and meats.

MAKES ABOUT 2.75KG/6LB

INGREDIENTS
1kg/2¼lb green apples
15g/½ oz garlic cloves
1 litre/1¾ pints/4 cups malt vinegar
450g/1lb/3¼ cups fresh or semi-
  dried dates
115g/4oz stem ginger
450g/1lb/3¼ cups seedless raisins
450g/1lb/2 cups light muscovado
  (brown) sugar
2.5ml/½ tsp cayenne pepper
20g/¾ oz salt
large handful fresh coriander (cilantro)

1 Core and coarsely chop the apples.

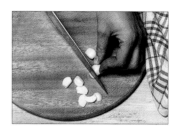

2 Peel and chop the garlic. Put the apples and garlic in a large, heavy pan with enough vinegar to cover them.

3 Boil until the apples are softened. Add the remaining ingredients, except the coriander, to the pan. Cook for 45 minutes, stirring frequently, until thickened and pulpy. Chop the coriander, stir in and cook for 2 minutes. Spoon into sterilized jars and seal immediately.

Left: Pickles add flavour to plain food.

VARIATION
Dry-fry 30ml/2 tbsp mustard seeds in a small pan until they start to pop. Use instead of the star anise.

Tomato Ketchup

Use really ripe tomatoes to give maximum flavour to this spicy sauce.

MAKES 2.75KG/6LB

INGREDIENTS
2.25kg/5lb ripe tomatoes, peeled
1 onion, peeled
8 cloves
6 allspice berries
6 black peppercorns
several sprigs fresh rosemary
3 bay leaves
25g/1oz fresh root ginger, peeled
  and sliced
1 celery heart
30ml/2 tbsp dark brown sugar
65ml/4½ tbsp raspberry or red
  wine vinegar
3 garlic cloves, peeled
15ml/1 tbsp salt

1 Halve the tomatoes and scoop out the seeds. Place the flesh in a large, heavy pan. Stud the onion with cloves and tie in a double-thickness layer of muslin (cheesecloth) with the allspice, peppercorns, rosemary, bay and ginger.

2 Chop the celery and add to the pan with the bag of spices, sugar, vinegar, garlic and salt. Bring to the boil, reduce the heat and simmer, uncovered, stirring frequently for about 1½ hours.

3 Remove the muslin bag, squeezing out the juices, and blend the tomato mixture in a food processor or blender until smooth.

4 Return to the pan and simmer for 5 minutes. Transfer to jars and store in the refrigerator for up to 2 weeks.

Mint Sauce

Home-made mint sauce is far superior to store-bought and keeps for several months in the refrigerator. To make a 250ml/8fl oz/1 cup quantity, finely chop 1 large bunch fresh mint and put in a large bowl. Add 105ml/7 tbsp boiling water and leave to infuse (steep). When cooled to lukewarm, add 150ml/ ¼ pint/⅔ cup white wine vinegar and 30–45ml/2–3 tbsp caster (superfine) sugar to taste. Pour into a clean bottle or jar and store in the refrigerator.

Papaya and Lemon Relish

Although this relish makes a small quantity, its flavour is strong and a little goes a long way.

MAKES ABOUT 450G/1LB

INGREDIENTS
1 large unripe papaya
1 onion, thinly sliced
40g/1½ oz/⅓ cup raisins
250ml/8fl oz/1 cup red wine vinegar
juice of 2 lemons
150ml/¼ pint/⅔ cup elderflower
  cordial
165g/5½ oz/generous ¾ cup golden
  granulated sugar
1 cinnamon stick
2 bay leaves
5ml/1 tsp paprika
2.5ml/½ tsp salt

Left: Tomato Ketchup and Mint Sauce.

1 Peel the papaya, halve lengthways and scoop out the seeds. Roughly chop the flesh and put in a heavy pan.

2 Add the onion, raisins and vinegar. Bring to the boil and simmer gently for 10 minutes. Add the remaining ingredients and bring to the boil, stirring. Reduce the heat and simmer gently for 50–60 minutes.

3 Transfer to sterilized jars, cover and store for at least 1 week before using. Chill once opened.

VARIATION
Mango and Lemon Relish Use a large, firm mango instead of the papaya.

Lavender Jelly

This pretty jelly really captures the essence of summer. Serve it with roast lamb, chicken or duck, or even with warmed scones or croissants. Do not worry about peeling and coring the apples as the mixture is strained through a jelly bag.

MAKES ABOUT 1.8KG/4LB

INGREDIENTS
1.8kg/4lb cooking apples, washed and roughly chopped
105ml/7 tbsp lavender flowers, chopped
about 1.3kg/3lb/6¾ cups sugar

1 Put the apples in a pan with 75ml/ 5 tbsp of the lavender flowers and 1.75 litres/3 pints/7½ cups water. Simmer gently for about 25 minutes, or until the apples are soft and mushy.

2 Sterilize a jelly bag by immersing it in boiling water for 2 minutes. Drain and suspend the jelly bag securely over a large bowl.

3 Strain the apple mixture through the bag and leave overnight until the juices stop dripping through.

4 Measure the juice and return to the pan, adding 450g/1lb/2¼ cups sugar for every 600ml/1 pint/2½ cups juice. Heat gently, stirring until the sugar has dissolved. Bring to the boil and boil until setting point is reached (see Cook's Tip).

5 Leave to cool for 15 minutes then stir in the remaining lavender flowers. Transfer to dry, sterilized jars and cover with a lid. Store in a cool place for up to 6 months.

> **VARIATION**
> **Apple, Strawberry and Rosemary Jelly**
> Use chopped rosemary instead of the lavender and substitute 900g/ 2lb/8 cups whole strawberries for half the apples, adding them for the final 5 minutes' cooking time.

Pickled Plums de Provence

These savoury plums are transformed into an unusual accompaniment for cold roast meats by adding aromatic herbs, including rosemary, garlic and sweet lavender.

MAKES ABOUT 1.3KG/3LB

INGREDIENTS
1.3kg/3lb firm plums
4 sprigs rosemary
4 bay leaves
4 lavender flowers
2 thyme sprigs
4 unpeeled garlic cloves
900ml/1½ pints/3¾ cups white wine vinegar
500g/1¼ lb/2¾ cups granulated sugar

1 Prick over the plums with a wooden cocktail stick and pack them into 1 medium and 1 small Kilner jar, tucking in the herb sprigs and garlic.

2 Put the vinegar and sugar in a pan and heat gently until the sugar dissolves. Bring to the boil and boil for 5 minutes, or until syrupy. Allow to cool, then remove the herb sprigs.

3 Pour over the plums, making sure they are completely covered. Seal tightly and store in a cool place for at least 1 month before using.

COOK'S TIP
To check if jelly or jam is at setting point, put a small amount on a saucer – if it holds its shape it is ready.

Left: Lavender jelly is an unusual addition to the store cupboard (pantry).

HERB SAUCES

A well-flavoured sauce, mayonnaise or dip makes an imaginative accompaniment to serve with a variety of dishes. Tasty combinations of herbs, such as dill and capers, rosemary and onion; parsley and bay, or garlic and mixed herbs, are ideal additions to sauces to serve with plain foods.

White Sauce

This classic white sauce is an essential part of many savoury dishes. A good sauce, which is smooth, glossy and buttery, makes the perfect base to which herbs, spices and other flavours can be added (see variations).

MAKES ABOUT 600ML/1 PINT/2½ CUPS

INGREDIENTS
    40g/1½ oz/3 tbsp butter
    40g/1½ oz/⅓ cup plain
      (all-purpose) flour
    600ml/1pint/2½ cups milk
    good pinch of freshly grated nutmeg
    30–45ml/2–3 tbsp double (heavy)
      cream (optional)
    salt and ground black pepper

1 Melt the butter in a heavy pan over a moderate heat. Remove from the heat and stir in the flour.

2 Gradually whisk in about a quarter of the milk until completely smooth, then whisk in the remainder. Set the pan over a moderate heat and bring to the boil, whisking continuously.

3 When the sauce starts to thicken, reduce the heat to its lowest setting and cook gently, stirring frequently until smooth and glossy. Stir in the nutmeg, cream, if using, and seasoning to taste.

VARIATIONS

Cheese Sauce Add 50g/2oz/½ cup finely grated Cheddar cheese, 5ml/1 tsp finely chopped fresh thyme and 2.5ml/½ tsp Dijon mustard at step 3 of the White Sauce recipe.

Dill and Caper Sauce Finely chop 30ml/2 tbsp capers and add to the sauce at step 3 with 30ml/2 tbsp finely chopped dill.

Egg and Chive Sauce Shell and finely chop 2 hard-boiled eggs. Add to the sauce at step 3 with 45ml/3 tbsp chopped chives.

Parsley Sauce Heat the milk in a pan with 1 bay leaf, 1 whole peeled onion and 12 black peppercorns and bring almost to the boil. Remove from the heat and leave to infuse (steep) for 20 minutes. Strain and make the white sauce as before. Stir in 60ml/4 tbsp finely chopped parsley at step 3.

Rosemary and Onion Sauce Finely chop 1 onion and sauté gently in the butter before adding the flour. Add 15ml/1 tbsp finely chopped rosemary at step 3.

COOK'S TIPS

• A white sauce can be made ahead and reheated. Transfer to a bowl, add a dot of butter and let it melt over the surface to prevent a skin forming. Leave to cool. Refrigerate for up to 2 days and reheat before serving. Alternatively place a circle of baking parchment over the surface of the sauce.
• The recipe for White Sauce gives a consistency that is suitable for pastry and pie fillings or as a topping for lasagne and crêpes.
• To make an accompanying sauce to meat, fish and vegetables use 15g/½ oz/2 tbsp butter and 15g/½ oz/2 tbsp flour.
• For a thicker sauce for use as a soufflé base or to bind ingredients together, use 50g/2oz/¼ cup butter and 50g/2oz/½ cup flour.

Bread Sauce

Bread sauce flavoured with cloves and bay leaves makes a comforting, wintry accompaniment to roast game, turkey, chicken and lamb.

SERVES 6–8

INGREDIENTS
    1 onion, peeled
    8 whole cloves
    2 bay leaves
    600ml/1 pint/2½ cups milk
    115g/4oz/2 cups fresh breadcrumbs
    15g/½ oz/1 tbsp butter
    45ml/3 tbsp single (light) cream
    salt and ground black pepper

1 Stud the onion with cloves and put in a pan with the bay leaves and milk. Bring to the boil, then remove from the heat and leave to infuse (steep) for 15 minutes.

2 Remove the onion and bay leaves and stir in the breadcrumbs. Simmer gently for about 10 minutes, or until thickened. Stir in the butter, cream and seasoning.

Below: Richly flavoured bread sauce.

Herby Onion Gravy

The sage, thyme and parsley make this gravy delicious with roasts, sausages, liver and bacon. Make sure you really caramelize the onions in the oil before adding the other ingredients.

MAKES ABOUT 900ML/1½ PINTS/3¾ CUPS

INGREDIENTS
  30ml/2 tbsp vegetable oil
  3 onions, finely sliced
  2.5ml/½ tsp caster (superfine) sugar
  10ml/2 tsp plain (all-purpose) flour
  2 sprigs each of sage, thyme
    and parsley
  900ml/1½ pints/3¾ cups chicken or
    vegetable stock
  10ml/2 tsp dark soy sauce
  salt and ground black pepper

1 Heat the oil in a frying pan. Add the onions and sugar and sauté gently for about 10 minutes, or until the onions are just beginning to turn golden. Sprinkle on the flour and cook, stirring for 1 minute.

2 Add the herbs, stock and soy sauce and bring to the boil. Reduce the heat and simmer gently, uncovered, for 5 minutes, or until slightly thickened. Season to taste.

Rich Tomato Sauce

Generously flavoured with Mediterranean herbs, this intensely flavoured sauce keeps well in the refrigerator for several days and makes a lovely sauce for pasta, grilled (broiled) meats and barbecues, or as a pizza topping.

SERVES 4–6

INGREDIENTS
  45ml/3 tbsp olive oil
  2 celery sticks, finely chopped
  1 onion, finely chopped
  3 garlic cloves, crushed
  small handful of chopped mixed
    herbs, such as parsley, thyme,
    marjoram, oregano, basil
  1 bay leaf
  675g/1½lb ripe tomatoes, peeled
    and chopped
  30ml/2 tbsp sun-dried tomato paste
  150ml/¼ pint/⅔ cup vegetable stock
  salt and ground black pepper

1 Heat the oil in a pan. Add the celery and onion and fry gently for 5 minutes. Add the garlic and herbs, and fry for 2 minutes.

Above: Herby onion gravy is irresistible.

2 Add the tomatoes, tomato paste and stock, and bring to the boil. Reduce the heat and simmer gently for about 20 minutes, or until thickened and pulpy. Season to taste and serve hot.

Sauce Vierge

This quick sauce adds interest to fried or grilled meat and fish. Heat 60ml/ 4 tbsp extra virgin olive oil in a small pan. Add 1.5ml/¼ tsp crushed coriander seeds and fry for 1 minute. Add 5 ripe, skinned and seeded tomatoes, a small handful of chopped parsley, tarragon and chervil and a little seasoning. Cook for 30 seconds before serving.

HERBS IN SALSAS, MAYONNAISE AND DIPS

Due largely to healthy and delicious Mediterranean ingredients, such as herbs, richly flavoured olive oils and other flavourings, we have a fabulous selection of chilled, olive-oil-based sauces to choose from. Those fresh, summery tastes, from the classic mayonnaise and all its variations to thick, aromatic olive oil dressings, will quickly enliven even the simplest meat, fish and vegetable dishes. Serve them freshly made if convenient, or store in the refrigerator, covered tightly for up to 2 days.

Salsa Verde

Nothing quite epitomizes the wonderfully aromatic, intense flavour of herbs better than a freshly blended Salsa Verde. Excellent with roast or grilled (broiled) meats as well as pan-fried fish and vegetable dishes.

SERVES 4

INGREDIENTS
    2 garlic cloves, chopped
    25g/1oz/1 cup flat leaf parsley
    15g/½ oz/½ cup fresh basil, mint or
       coriander (cilantro), or a mixture
       of herbs
    15ml/1 tbsp chopped chives
    15ml/1 tbsp capers, rinsed
    120ml/4fl oz/½ cup extra virgin
       olive oil
    5 anchovy fillets, rinsed
    10ml/2 tsp French mustard
    a little finely grated lemon rind
       and juice
    salt and ground black pepper

Above: Salsa verde, one of the best known and flavoursome salsas.

1 Put the first five ingredients and 15ml/1 tbsp of the oil in a blender or food processor and process lightly.

2 Gradually add the remaining oil to the food processor in a thin stream with the motor running until the mixture becomes a thick sauce.

VARIATIONS
• For a creamier flavour whisk in 45ml/3 tbsp crème fraîche.
• Substitute herbs such as chervil, tarragon, dill or fennel for a sauce that goes particularly well with fish, shellfish or chicken.

3 Transfer the herb mixture to a bowl and add the lemon rind and juice, and seasoning to taste. (You might not need additional salt as the anchovies and capers are very salty.) Serve immediately or chill until required.

Fresh Mayonnaise

Mayonnaise is definitely worth making, provided you have a little time and patience. Store in the refrigerator, covered tightly for up to 1 week. Use the freshest possible eggs. Infants, the elderly and those with compromised immune systems shold avoid eating foods containing uncooked eggs.

MAKES ABOUT 350ML/12FL OZ/1½ CUPS

INGREDIENTS
　　2 egg yolks
　　350ml/12fl oz/1½ cups olive oil
　　15–30ml/1–2 tbsp lemon juice or
　　　white wine vinegar
　　5–10ml/1–2 tsp Dijon mustard
　　salt and ground black pepper

COOK'S TIP
• Mayonnaise can be made successfully in a food processor. Make exactly as above, pouring in the oil while the motor is running. If it separates beat another egg yolk. Gradually whisk in the curdled mixture as before.

1 Put the egg yolks in a bowl with a pinch of salt, and beat well.

2 Add the oil, a little at a time, beating constantly with an electric mixer or balloon whisk.

3 When a quarter of the oil has been added, beat in 5–10ml/1–2 tsp of the lemon juice or vinegar.

4 Continue beating in the oil in a thin, steady stream. As the mayonnaise thickens, add a little more lemon juice or vinegar.

5 When all the oil has been added, stir in the mustard, seasoning and a little more lemon juice or vinegar, if necessary. (If the mayonnaise is too thick, stir in a spoonful of water.) Store covered with plastic film or in an airtight container in the refrigerator.

VARIATIONS
Basil and Garlic Mayonnaise Tear a small handful each of green and opal basil leaves into small pieces and stir into the mayonnaise with 2 crushed garlic cloves.
Cucumber and Dill Mayonnaise Halve and scoop out the seeds from a 7.5cm/3in length of cucumber. Finely chop the flesh and add to the mayonnaise with 30ml/2 tbsp chopped dill.
Green Mayonnaise Add 25g/1oz/ ½ cup each of finely chopped parsley and watercress, 1 crushed garlic clove and 3 finely chopped spring onions (scallions).
Tartare Sauce Add 30ml/2 tbsp each of chopped tarragon and parsley, 15ml/1 tbsp each of chopped capers and gherkins and a dash of lemon juice or vinegar.

Left: Complete a fresh prawn salad with a creamy home-made mayonnaise.

DIPS

The simplest dips can be made by folding chopped herbs into mayonnaise, fromage frais or thick yogurt. You can also pep them up with garlic, lemon, ginger, spices and other aromatic ingredients. Serve with colourful crudités, interesting breads, or crisps.

Mellow Garlic Dip

Baking garlic until it is soft and succulent mellows its fiery, raw flavour, leaving it sweet and delicious.

SERVES 4

INGREDIENTS

    2 whole garlic heads
    15ml/1 tbsp olive oil
    60ml/4 tbsp mayonnaise
    75ml/5 tbsp natural (plain) yogurt
    5ml/1 tsp grainy mustard
    salt and ground black pepper

1 Brush the garlic heads with olive oil and wrap them tightly in kitchen foil. Bake at 200°C/400°F/Gas 6 for about 40 minutes, until soft to the touch. When cool enough to handle, separate the garlic cloves and remove their skins. Sprinkle the cloves with salt and mash on the chopping board with a knife, until puréed.

COOK'S TIPS

• The foil-wrapped garlic heads can also be cooked around the edges of a barbecue. Allow about 25 minutes, turning occasionally.
• Leftover dip will keep, well covered, in the refrigerator for 3–4 days. Use as a topping for baked potatoes, in sandwiches or serve with pan-fried meat or fish.

2 Put the garlic in a bowl and stir in the mayonnaise, yogurt and mustard. Beat well.

3 Check the seasoning, adding more salt and pepper to taste. Transfer to a serving bowl, cover and chill until ready to serve.

VARIATIONS

Garlic, Lovage and Apple Dip Make as above using 1 garlic head. Add 15ml/1 tbsp chopped lovage and 1 peeled and grated dessert apple.

Tarragon, Walnut and Roquefort Dip Make as above increasing the yogurt to 150g/5oz. Add 30ml/2 tbsp chopped tarragon, 25g/1oz/¼ cup finely chopped walnuts and 40g/1½oz crumbled Roquefort cheese.

Sage Flower and Garlic Dip Pull the sage flowers from the stems until you have a small handful. Add to the garlic dip with 30ml/2 tbsp chopped flat leaf parsley.

Anchovy, Olive and Basil Dip Make as above using 1 garlic head. Add 4 drained and chopped canned anchovy fillets, 10 pitted and sliced black olives and shredded basil leaves. Omit the salt.

Aubergine and Mint Dip Chop half a small aubergine (eggplant) and fry it in olive oil until tender. Leave to cool. Fold the aubergine into the dip omitting the mustard and add 45ml/3 tbsp chopped mint.

Saffron Dip

This herb and saffron dip is made with fromage frais or thick yogurt for a light, refreshing texture. Substitute half the fromage frais for mayonnaise for a fuller flavour. Add more or less herbs depending on your taste.

SERVES 4

INGREDIENTS
  small pinch saffron threads
  200g/7oz/scant 1 cup fromage frais
    or thick yogurt
  10 chives
  10 large basil leaves
  salt and ground black pepper

COOK'S TIP
Saffron has a unique flavour that cannot be substituted. Although expensive, a small pinch of the threads goes a long way, particularly if you chill the dip for a couple of hours before serving to let the flavours mingle.

Below: Herbs add subtle flavour and texture to dips.

1 Put 15ml/1 tbsp boiling water into a bowl and add the saffron threads. Leave to infuse (steep) for 5 minutes.

2 Beat the fromage frais or yogurt in a large bowl until smooth. Stir in the infused saffron and liquid.

3 Chop the chives into the dip. Tear the basil leaves into small pieces and stir them in. Mix well. Season with salt and black pepper to taste. Transfer the saffron dip to a serving bowl, cover and refrigerate until ready to serve.

> **VARIATIONS**
> **Ginger and Saffron Dip** Finely grate a 2.5cm/1in length fresh root ginger. Stir the ginger into a little of the fromage frais or thick yogurt, then add the rest. Add 30ml/2 tbsp chopped coriander (cilantro) instead of basil.
> **Apricot, Saffron and Almond Dip** Finely chop 50g/2oz/¼ cup no-soak dried apricots and 40g/1½oz/⅓ cup lightly toasted flaked (sliced) almonds. Stir into the fromage frais or thick yogurt with the saffron and add 15ml/1 tbsp chopped flat leaf parsley and 15ml/1 tbsp chopped coriander (cilantro) instead of chives and basil.
> **Mascarpone and Rocket Dip** Omit the saffron and make the dip as above, beating 115g/4oz/½ cup mascarpone into the fromage frais or thick yogurt. Add a small handful of torn rocket (arugula) leaves (preferably wild rocket) with the herbs.
> **Saffron and Rosemary Dip** Add 15ml/1 tbsp chopped rosemary to the saffron when you are infusing it in boiling water. Finish the dip as above, substituting 15ml/1 tbsp grainy mustard and a small handful of rosemary flowers, if available, for the chives and basil.

BUTTERS, CREAMS AND CHEESES

Dairy produce is subtle in flavour, and cream and butter in particular are often bland, making them ideal ingredients that will carry the flavour of aromatic herbs and spices.

FLAVOURED BUTTERS

A pat of herb butter, melting over steak, fish or vegetables, turns a fairly ordinary dish into something far more interesting. Almost any herbs can be used, the butters freeze well and have infinite uses: try them spread on to warm, crusty bread, scones and sandwiches or swirled into soups and sauces.

Simple Herb Butters

To add interest to plain cooked meat, fish and vegetables, make a herb butter using a herb with a natural affinity to the main ingredient.

SERVES 4

INGREDIENTS
115g/4oz/½ cup softened butter
45ml/3 tbsp chopped herbs e.g.
    parsley, thyme, rosemary, tarragon,
    chives, basil, marjoram or coriander
    (cilantro), or a mixture of
    several herbs
finely grated rind of ½ lemon
good pinch cayenne pepper
salt and ground black pepper

1 Beat the butter until creamy, then beat in the herbs, lemon rind, cayenne and a little seasoning. Transfer to a small bowl and chill until required.

COOK'S TIP
Use herbs singly such as garlic, or make up a combination of herbs.

2 Alternatively, shape while still soft as follows:

Butter Slices Transfer the butter to a piece of baking parchment and shape into a neat roll. Wrap and chill. Cut into slices.

Butter Shapes Put the butter on to a sheet of baking parchment and flatten to about 5mm/¼in thick with a metal spatula. Chill and stamp out shapes using a cutter.

Below: Herb butter balls make a visually attractive accompaniment to food.

HERB CREAMS AND CHEESES

Because of their intense, aromatic flavour, herbs are great for infusing in cream or milk to create some of the simplest dessert ideas. Infuse sweet herbs such as rosemary, bay, thyme, rose geranium and lavender in the milk or cream before making ice creams, custard and rice pudding, to add a fragrant depth to the finished dish. Sprigs of herbs make lovely garnishes.

Rosemary and Ratafia Cream

Make and chill this almond-flavoured cream in advance and serve with a platter of fresh summer fruits.

SERVES 6

INGREDIENTS
300ml/½ pint/1¼ cups double (heavy) cream
several sprigs of rosemary
25g/1oz/½ cup ratafia biscuits (almond macaroons), crushed

Bring the cream to the boil. Remove from the heat and add the rosemary. Leave to cool, then chill. Strain into a bowl and whisk until it holds its shape. Fold in the biscuits and chill.

VARIATIONS
Bay and Lemon Ratafia Cream Use 3 bay leaves instead of rosemary and add the finely grated rind of 1 lemon when whisking.
Rose Geranium and Cointreau Cream Use 10 rose-geranium leaves instead of rosemary. Omit the ratafia biscuits. Add 15ml/1 tbsp Cointreau.

Above: Rosemary and ratafia-flavoured cream is ideal with summer berries.

HERB CREAMS

A platter of herb-flavoured cheeses makes a delicious finale to a light lunch. They also make delicious gifts. Use soft cheeses with a creamy consistency for best results. Store in a wrapping of waxed or baking parchment for up to 3 days.

Dill and Pink Peppercorn Cheese Finely chop several sprigs of dill and mix with 2.5ml/½ tsp crushed pink peppercorns. Using a teaspoon, spoon the mixture over the top and sides of a 150g/5oz medium-fat goat's cheese.
Thyme and Garlic Cheese Strip the leaves from several thyme stems adding any of the small flowers. Mix with a finely chopped garlic clove. Press the mixture over a 90g/3½oz round of full-fat goat's cheese.
Minted Feta Cheese Finely chop a small bunch of mint. Drain 200g/7oz feta cheese, cut into dice and roll in the mint until coated.
Tarragon and Lemon Cheese Cut a 200g/7oz pack of low-fat cream cheese into two. Tear the leaves off some tarragon and finely chop. Grate the rind of half a lemon. Mix with the tarragon and coat the cheese.

Below: Herb cheeses are delicious served with savoury biscuits or crackers.

HERB CONDIMENTS AND SUGARS

Flavouring salt, pepper, mustard and sugar with fresh herbs adds yet another dimension to their vast range of culinary uses. Many specialist shops and supermarkets stock a supply of ready-mixed herb and spice blends, but nothing can beat the fresh, vibrant flavour of home-made versions, a selection of which can add variety and interest to all aspects of cooking. The wealth of different herbs and spices around us provides plenty of scope for experimentation. This will inevitably lead to discovering some firm favourites which can be remade each season to take you through the winter.

Herby Salt

Allow time to dry the herbs before making herb salts.

MAKES ABOUT 300G/11OZ

INGREDIENTS
  6 dried bay leaves
  90ml/6 tbsp mixed dried herbs, such
    as thyme, rosemary, oregano,
    tarragon, dill, fennel
  300g/11oz coarse salt

1 Crumble all the herbs together in a large mortar. Add the salt and crush with a pestle until the herbs are finely distributed in the salt.

2 Transfer to an airtight container and store in a cool, dry place.

COOK'S TIP
Uses for Herby Salt
• Stir into tomato juice as an alternative to Tabasco or Worcester sauce.
• Rub into meat, poultry or fish as a dry marinade before roasting or grilling (broiling). Chill for an hour in the salt if you have time.
• Stir into soups, stews, casseroles and sauces.
• Sprinkle over chips and home-made crisps.
• Use as a seasoning for boiled eggs or quail's eggs.
• Use in salad dressings.

Right: Salt infused with herb layers.

Lemon Verbena Seasoning

This delicious blend of lemony flavours makes a wonderful dry marinade for chicken, lamb or pork.

MAKES ABOUT 50G/2OZ

INGREDIENTS
  2 lemons
  30ml/2 tbsp lemon thyme, chopped
  15ml/1 tbsp lemon verbena, chopped
  15ml/1 tbsp lemon grass, chopped

1 Pare fine strips of rind from the lemons, taking care not to remove too much of the white pith. Dry the rind and herbs on a rack in a warm place, such as an airing cupboard for 24–48 hours.

2 When thoroughly dry, pound the lemon rind using a mortar and pestle. Add the remaining ingredients and crush finely. Alternatively, use the small section of a food processor to blend the ingredients together.

3 Pack into small jars or fabric bags and store in a cool, dry place.

VARIATIONS
Herb Seasoning for Fish Use one or more of the following herbs: dill, parsley, chervil, tarragon and fennel, adding crushed dill or fennel seeds and lemon or ordinary pepper.
Herb Seasoning for Meat Use a mixture of rosemary, thyme, oregano, sage, parsley and chives, adding crushed black or white mustard seeds.
Lime and Herb Pepper Home-dried lime rind gives pepper extra bite and flavour. Finely grate the rind of 3 limes and leave to dry out on a tray for 24 hours. Grind with 115g/4oz black pepper and 60ml/4 tbsp dried rosemary, parsley or tarragon.
Spicy Salt Combine 15ml/1 tbsp each of cumin seeds, coriander seeds, black peppercorns and cardamom pods with a teaspoon each of ground cloves, chilli powder and ginger. Blend with the salt.

HERB MUSTARDS

Making mustard is surprisingly easy and produces really aromatic results. Use white mustard seeds for a mild flavour and the black seeds for extra heat.

Tarragon and Champagne Mustard

Enjoy this mustard, delicately flavoured with tarragon and champagne, with cold seafood or chicken.

MAKES ABOUT 250G/9OZ

INGREDIENTS
  30ml/2 tbsp mustard seeds
  75ml/5 tbsp champagne or white
    wine vinegar
  115g/4oz dry mustard powder
  115g/4oz/½ cup brown sugar
  2.5ml/½ tsp salt
  50ml/3½ tbsp olive oil
  60ml/4 tbsp chopped tarragon

1 Soak the mustard seeds overnight in the vinegar.

2 Pour the mixture into the bowl of a blender or small section of a food processor. Add the mustard powder, sugar and salt, and blend until smooth. Slowly add the oil while blending. Stir in the tarragon and pour into small, thoroughly clean jars. Store in a cool place for up to 6 weeks.

Horseradish Mustard

Traditionally associated with roast beef, fresh horseradish has a character-istically strong flavour with none of the taste of a store-bought brand. In this delicious recipe it blends with mustard to make a tangy relish for cold meats, smoked fish or cheese.

MAKES ABOUT 400G/14OZ

INGREDIENTS
  25g/1oz mustard seeds
  115g/4oz dry mustard powder
  115g/4oz/½ cup light muscovado
    (brown) sugar
  120ml/4fl oz/½ cup white wine
    vinegar or cider vinegar
  50ml/2fl oz/¼ cup olive oil
  5ml/1 tsp lemon juice
  45ml/3 tbsp freshly grated
    horseradish

1 Put the mustard seeds in a bowl and pour over 250ml/8fl oz/1 cup boiling water. Leave for 1 hour.

2 Drain the seeds, discarding the liquid, and place in a food processor or blender with the remaining ingredients. Blend until smooth.

3 Spoon into clean jars, and store in the refrigerator. Use fresh.

HERB, FLOWER AND SPICE SUGARS

The same technique that is used to flavour sugar with a vanilla pod (bean) works equally well with herbs, flowers and spices. Rose petals, rose-geranium leaves, lavender sprigs, cloves, cinnamon, ginger, cardamom and dried orange and lemon peel all make delicious flavourings, used either individually or in simple combinations. Once infused (steeped) for two weeks they can be used as a ready-made flavouring for creamy desserts, fruit salads, ice creams and custards, or sprinkled on to sponge cakes and pastries.

Making Infused Sugars

Ensure that flower petals are clean and dry, and break larger spices, such as cinnamon sticks, into smaller pieces. Layer up in small jars with caster (superfine) or granulated sugar and store in a cool, dry place. The greater the ratio of flavourings to sugar the more intense the final result.

  Do not combine more than two or three different flavourings in each sugar or they might detract from each other. Combinations like rose petal, cardamom and ginger, or lavender and orange blend really well.

Below: Many aromatic ingredients can be used to infuse flavour.

HERBAL AND FLORAL DECORATIONS

Herbs and their romantic petite flowers can be used to make some of the prettiest culinary decorations. Crystallizing edible flowers – coating them in a fine dusting of caster (superfine) sugar – both enhances their delicate flavours and makes a simple and effective way of preserving them for later use. Once dry they can be stored in an airtight container for up to a week, ready to decorate special occasion cakes and summer desserts.

Freezing fresh herb flowers in ice cubes also prolongs the enjoyment of these stunning flowers, but most impressive of all is a classic "ice-bowl".

COOK'S TIPS

• Use any herb flowers or edible flowers such as mint, sweet cicely, sage, pansy, nasturtium, marigold, viola, rosemary, lavender, borage and rosebuds or small roses. Large roses can be used if separated into petals. You can use a mixture of colours but sometimes the bowls look more delicate if just one colour is used.
• Do not pack in too many herbs and flowers or the bowl will lose its clear icy look.
• Do not worry if you hear ice-cracking sounds when releasing the ice bowl. It will not fall apart!
• Do not be tempted to leave the bowls in hot water for too long as the ice will quickly melt and become fragile. Be cautious, even if it means redipping the bowl once or twice.
• For convenience, fill the bowl with ice cream or sorbet and return to the freezer so that it is ready and waiting for you. Serve on a plate, preferably glass, with a shallow rim to catch the melting ice.
• For a special occasion, ice bowls also look stunning filled with chilled water and floating candles.

Right: Ice bowls will retain their shape for many hours before melting, although keep out of the sun where possible. For a colour co-ordinated centrepiece, why not choose herbs and flowers that complement the taste or colours of the intended contents?

Herb-flower Ice Bowl

Easy to make, this stunning flower ice bowl provides a perfect container for ice creams and sorbets.

MAKES 1 BOWL

INGREDIENTS
    ice cubes
    freshly picked herb sprigs and their
        flowers (see Cook's Tips)
    freshly picked flowers
    water

1 Find two bowls, either glass or plastic, which will fit inside one another leaving a gap of about 2cm/¾in between them. Put some ice cubes in the base of the larger bowl and tuck some herb sprigs and flowers around them.

2 Position the smaller bowl inside it and tape the bowls together across the tops so that the smaller bowl is centred. Pour cold water into the large bowl until the level starts to come up the sides. Freeze for 2–3 hours until firm.

3 Tuck more herb sprigs and flowers between the two bowls using a skewer to arrange them so that they look attractive through the sides of the bowl. Fill the large bowl with water until it comes to the rim. Carefully transfer to the freezer and freeze overnight.

4 Peel off the tape. Half-fill a washing-up bowl with hot water, sit the frozen bowls in it and pour a little hot water into the smaller bowl. Count to 30 then remove the bowls and pour the water out of the small bowl. Use a thin knife to loosen the ice from the edges of the bowls.

Making Floral Ice Cubes

Use small herb flowers that will tuck easily into ice-cube compartments, or separate larger flowers into petals. Small summer fruits such as red and white currants or raspberries can be tucked in with the flowers. Use the ice cubes in punches, cordials, sparkling table water or to decorate a platter of summer fruits.

INGREDIENTS
  a selection of freshly picked edible
    flowers
  cold water

1 Pour water into ice-cube trays until they are half full.

2 Position the flowers using tweezers, if easier to handle. Freeze for about 1 hour, or until firm. Add more water to fill the trays and refreeze until firm.

Below: Floral ice cubes make an attractive addition to a glass of summer punch or herb-flavoured cordial.

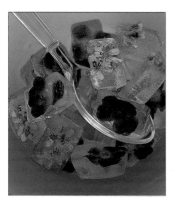

Crystallized Flowers

Pick flowers for crystallization when they are perfectly dry, and check that they are free of insects. Most herb flowers can be crystallized (candied), although some, like rosemary and thyme flowers are too fiddly to bother with. Borage, sage, nasturtium, sweet cicely fronds and rose petals work really well, as do other edible flowers like violas, violets, pansies, primroses, cowslips and pinks.

INGREDIENTS
  1 egg white
  caster (superfine) sugar
  plenty of fresh flowers or petals

1 Put the egg white into a small bowl and lightly whisk until it is broken up.

2 Coat a flower with egg white, using a paintbrush. Sprinkle the flower with sugar and shake off the excess. Transfer to a sheet of baking parchment and leave in a warm place until dry. Store in a sealed container for up to a week until ready to use.

COOK'S TIP

If you want the crystallized flowers to keep for more than a week it is best to use gum arabic (available from a chemist) instead of egg white. Dissolve 5ml/1 tsp in 25ml/1½ tbsp water or a colourless spirit such as gin or vodka and follow the recipe for the remaining steps. Gum arabic will make the petals very hard and brittle, so keep in a cool place away from any source of moisture.

Crystallized Roses

Coat all the petals in egg white and sugar as before, then push one end of a 15cm/6in length of fine floristry wire through the flower base. Bend and hook the other end of the wire over the rim of a tall glass or bowl so the rose is suspended. Leave until dry.

Below: Fresh roses dusted with sugar are stylish and sophisticated and deceptively simple to make.

Soups

The fresh flavours of herbs are emphasized in chilled soups – perfect for a hot summer's day. Piquant fusions such as sorrel, fennel and dill, or fragrant combinations of basil, thyme and marjoram transform summery dishes into elegant feasts. When the weather is cooler, hot soups make ideas lunches or first courses. Golden saffron, warming garlic and pungent fennel seeds are some of the ingredients used here to create satisfying dishes.

Above *Potato and Fennel Soup*

Left *Tomato, Ciabatta and Basil Oil Soup*

MELON AND BASIL SOUP

BASIL AND LIME GIVE ZEST TO SWEET MELON IN THIS CHILLED SUMMER SOUP. SIMPLE TO PREPARE, BUT STRIKINGLY UNUSUAL, IT MAKES A PERFECT START TO A SUMMER MEAL.

3 Place the sugar, water and lime rind in a small pan over a low heat. Stir until dissolved, then bring to the boil and simmer for 2–3 minutes.

4 Remove the pan from the heat and leave to cool slightly. Pour half the mixture into the food processor or blender with the melon flesh.

5 Blend the mixture until smooth, adding the remaining syrup and lime juice to taste.

6 Pour the mixture into a bowl, then stir in the basil.

7 Cover the bowl with clear film and transfer to the refrigerator to chill for 2–3 hours.

8 When ready to serve, pour the soup into individual bowls and serve garnished with basil leaves and melon balls.

COOK'S TIP
Add the syrup in two stages, as the amount of sugar needed will depend on the sweetness of the melon.

SERVES 4–6

INGREDIENTS
2 Charentais or cantaloupe melons
75g/3oz/6 tbsp caster
  (superfine) sugar
175ml/6fl oz/¾ cup water
finely grated rind and juice of
  1 lime
45ml/3 tbsp finely chopped
  fresh basil
fresh basil leaves, to garnish

1 Cut the melons in half across the middle. Scrape out the seeds with a spoon and discard.

2 Using a melon baller, scoop out 20–24 balls and set aside for the garnish. Scoop out the remaining flesh and place in the bowl of a food processor or blender.

Energy 75Kcal/317kJ; Protein 1.1g; Carbohydrate 18.2g, of which sugars 17.7g; Fat 0.2g, of which saturates 0g; Cholesterol 0mg; Calcium 46mg; Fibre 1.2g; Sodium 10mg.

SORREL, SPINACH AND DILL SOUP

THE WARM FLAVOUR OF HORSERADISH AND THE ANISEED FLAVOUR OF DILL MELD WITH SORREL AND SPINACH TO MAKE THIS UNUSUAL RUSSIAN SOUP. AN EXCELLENT SUMMER SOUP, SERVED CHILLED.

SERVES 6

INGREDIENTS
25g/1oz/2 tbsp butter
225g/8oz sorrel,
   stalks removed
225g/8oz young spinach,
   stalks removed
25g/1oz fresh horseradish,
   grated
750ml/1¼ pints/3 cups cider
1 pickled cucumber,
   finely chopped
30ml/2 tbsp chopped fresh dill
225g/8oz cooked fish, such as
   pike, perch or salmon, skinned
   and boned
salt and ground black pepper
sprig of dill, to garnish

1 Melt the butter in a large pan. Add the prepared sorrel and spinach leaves, together with the grated fresh horseradish. Mix well.

2 Cover the pan with a lid and allow the mixture to cook gently for 3–4 minutes, or until the sorrel and spinach leaves have wilted.

3 Tip into a food processor or blender and process to a fine purée (paste). Ladle into a tureen or bowl and stir in the cider, cucumber and dill.

4 Chop the fish into bitesize pieces. Add to the soup, then season well. Chill for at least 3 hours before serving, garnished with a sprig of dill.

Energy 163Kcal/680kJ; Protein 9.8g; Carbohydrate 4.6g, of which sugars 4.5g; Fat 8.2g, of which saturates 3g; Cholesterol 28mg; Calcium 153mg; Fibre 1.7g; Sodium 162mg.

ROASTED PEPPER SOUP <u>WITH</u> CHIVES <u>AND</u> PARMESAN TOAST

THE SECRET OF THIS SOUP IS TO SERVE IT JUST COLD, NOT OVER-CHILLED, TOPPED WITH HOT PARMESAN TOAST DRIPPING WITH CHEESE AND MELTED BUTTER.

SERVES 4

INGREDIENTS

1 onion, quartered
4 garlic cloves, unpeeled
2 red (bell) peppers, seeded
  and quartered
2 yellow (bell) peppers, seeded
  and quartered
30–45ml/2–3 tbsp olive oil
grated rind and juice of 1 orange
200g/7oz can chopped tomatoes
600ml/1 pint/2½ cups cold water
salt and ground black pepper
30ml/2 tbsp chopped fresh chives,
  to garnish (optional)
For the hot Parmesan toast
1 medium baguette
50g/2oz/¼ cup butter
175g/6oz Parmesan cheese

COOK'S TIP
If you don't have a champignon, then use the bottom of a large ladle or the back of a wooden spoon instead.

1 Preheat the oven to 200°C/400°F/ Gas 6. Put the onion, garlic and peppers in a roasting tin (pan). Drizzle the oil over the vegetables and mix well, then turn the pieces of pepper skin sides up.

2 Roast for 25–30 minutes, until slightly charred, then allow to cool slightly.

3 Squeeze the garlic flesh out of the skins into a food processor or blender. Add the roasted vegetables, orange rind and juice, tomatoes and water. Process until smooth.

4 Press through a sieve (strainer) into a bowl using a champignon. Season well and chill for 30 minutes.

5 Make the Parmesan toasts when you are ready to serve the soup. Preheat the grill (broiler) to high. Tear the baguette in half lengthways, then tear or cut it across to give four large pieces. Spread the pieces of bread with butter.

6 Pare most of the Parmesan into thin slices or shavings using a swivel-bladed vegetable knife or a small paring knife, then finely grate the remainder.

7 Arrange the sliced Parmesan on the toasts, then dredge with the grated cheese. Transfer to a large baking sheet and toast under the grill (broiler) for a few minutes until well browned.

8 Ladle the chilled soup into large, shallow bowls and sprinkle with chopped fresh chives, if using, and plenty of freshly ground black pepper. Serve the craggy hot Parmesan toast with the chilled soup.

Energy 124Kcal/516kJ; Protein 2.4g; Carbohydrate 15g, of which sugars 14.2g; Fat 6.4g, of which saturates 1g; Cholesterol 0mg; Calcium 23mg; Fibre 3.5g; Sodium 13mg.

CHILLED GARLIC <u>AND</u> ALMOND SOUP <u>WITH</u> GRAPES

USE PLUMP GARLIC CLOVES FOR THIS RICHLY FLAVOURED AND CREAMY CHILLED SOUP, WHICH IS BASED ON AN ANCIENT MOORISH RECIPE FROM ANDALUSIA IN SOUTHERN SPAIN.

SERVES 6

INGREDIENTS
75g/3oz/½ cup blanched almonds
50g/2oz/½ cup pine nuts
6 large garlic cloves, peeled but
  left whole
200g/7oz good-quality day-old
  bread, crusts removed
900ml–1 litre/1½–1¾ pints/
  3¾–4 cups still mineral
  water, chilled
120ml/4fl oz/½ cup extra virgin
  olive oil, plus extra to serve
15ml/1 tbsp sherry vinegar
30–45ml/2–3 tbsp dry sherry
250g/9oz grapes, peeled, halved
  and seeded
salt and ground white pepper
ice cubes and chopped fresh chives,
  to garnish

1 Stirring continuously, roast the almonds and pine nuts together in a dry pan over a moderate heat until they are very lightly browned.

2 Allow the nuts to cool, then grind them to a powder.

3 Blanch the peeled garlic cloves in boiling water for 3 minutes, then drain and rinse.

COOK'S TIPS
• Blanching the garlic softens its flavour.
• Toasting the nuts slightly accentuates their flavour, but you can omit this step if you prefer a paler soup.

4 Soak the bread in 300ml/½ pint/ 1¼ cups of the water for 10 minutes, then squeeze it dry. Process the garlic, bread, nuts and 5ml/1 tsp salt in a food processor or blender until it forms a paste.

5 Gradually blend in the olive oil and sherry vinegar, followed by sufficient water to make a smooth soup with a creamy consistency.

6 Stir in 30ml/2 tbsp of the sherry. Adjust the seasoning and add more dry sherry to taste.

7 Chill the soup for at least 3 hours, then adjust the seasoning again and stir in a little more iced water if the soup has thickened.

8 Reserve a few of the grapes for the garnish and stir the remainder into the soup.

9 Ladle the soup into bowls (glass bowls look good) and garnish with ice cubes, the reserved grapes and chopped chives.

10 Serve with additional extra virgin olive oil for drizzling to taste over the soup just before it is eaten.

Energy 355Kcal/1481kJ; Protein 6.8g; Carbohydrate 24.1g, of which sugars 8.2g; Fat 25.9g, of which saturates 2.7g; Cholesterol 0mg; Calcium 73mg; Fibre 1.9g; Sodium 177mg.

CUCUMBER AND GARLIC SOUP WITH WALNUTS

YOGURT AND CUCUMBER MAKE REFRESHING PARTNERS FOR CHILLED SOUP. HERE, THE FAMILIAR COMBINATION IS GIVEN A RICHER DIMENSION USING PUNGENT GARLIC AND DILL.

4 Add the walnut or sunflower oil slowly, and use the pestle to combine the mixture well.

5 Transfer the mixture into a large bowl and beat in the yogurt and the diced cucumber flesh.

SERVES 5–6

INGREDIENTS
½ cucumber
4 garlic cloves, peeled but left whole
2.5ml/½ tsp salt
75g/3oz/¾ cup walnut pieces
40g/1½oz day-old bread, torn
 into pieces
30ml/2 tbsp walnut or sunflower oil
400ml/14fl oz/1⅔ cups natural
 (plain) yogurt
120ml/4fl oz/½ cup cold water or
 chilled still mineral water
5–10ml/1–2 tsp lemon juice
For the garnish
40g/1½oz/scant ⅓ cup coarsely
 chopped walnuts
25ml/1½ tbsp olive oil
sprigs of fresh dill

1 Dice the cucumber flesh and set aside.

2 Using a large mortar and pestle, crush the garlic cloves and salt together.

3 Add the walnut and bread pieces and crush everything together until the consistency is smooth.

6 Add the cold water or mineral water and lemon juice to taste, then pour the soup into chilled bowls to serve. Garnish with the coarsely chopped walnuts, a little olive oil drizzled over the nuts and sprigs of fresh dill.

COOK'S TIP
If you prefer your soup to be smooth, purée it in a food processor or blender before serving.

Energy 209Kcal/864kJ; Protein 3.6g; Carbohydrate 4.4g, of which sugars 1.1g; Fat 19.8g, of which saturates 1.9g; Cholesterol 0mg; Calcium 31mg; Fibre 1g; Sodium 37mg.

GARLIC AND CORIANDER SOUP

THIS RECIPE IS BASED ON THE WONDERFUL BREAD SOUPS OR ACORDAS OF PORTUGAL. USING THE BEST-QUALITY INGREDIENTS WILL ENSURE THIS SIMPLE SOUP IS A SUCCESS.

SERVES 6

INGREDIENTS
25g/1oz/1 cup fresh coriander
  (cilantro), leaves and stalks
  chopped separately
1.5 litres/2½ pints/6¼ cups
  vegetable or chicken stock, or water
5–6 plump garlic cloves, peeled
6 eggs
275g/10oz day-old bread, with most
  of the crust removed, torn into
  bitesize pieces
90ml/6 tbsp extra virgin olive oil,
  plus extra to serve
salt and ground black pepper

1 Place the coriander stalks in a pan. Add the stock or water and bring to the boil. Lower the heat and simmer for 10 minutes, then process in a food processor or blender. Sieve the soup and return it to the pan.

2 Crush the garlic with 5ml/1 tsp salt, then stir in 120ml/4fl oz/½ cup of the hot soup. Return the mixture to the rest of the soup in the pan.

3 Meanwhile, poach the eggs in a frying pan of simmering water for 3–4 minutes, or until just set.

4 Use a draining spoon to remove them from the pan and transfer to a warmed plate. Trim off any untidy bits of white.

5 Meanwhile, bring the soup back to the boil and add seasoning to taste. Stir in the chopped coriander leaves and remove from the heat.

6 Place the bread in six soup plates or bowls and drizzle the oil over it. Ladle in the soup and stir. Add a poached egg to each bowl and serve immediately, offering olive oil at the table so that it can be drizzled over the soup as desired.

Energy 288Kcal/1206kJ; Protein 10.8g; Carbohydrate 24g, of which sugars 1.3g; Fat 17.5g, of which saturates 3.1g; Cholesterol 190mg; Calcium 81mg; Fibre 1g; Sodium 309mg.

TOMATO AND FRESH BASIL SOUP

FRESH BASIL AND FULL-FLAVOURED TOMATOES ARE A FAVOURITE COMBINATION OF FLAVOURS. MAKE THIS DELICIOUS, SIMPLE ITALIAN SOUP IN LATE SUMMER WHEN TOMATOES ARE AT THEIR BEST AND THERE IS STILL PLENTY OF FRESH BASIL TO BE PICKED.

2 Stir in the chopped tomatoes and garlic, then add the stock, white wine and tomato purée, with seasoning to taste. Bring to the boil, then reduce the heat, half-cover the pan and simmer for 20 minutes, stirring occasionally.

3 Purée the soup with the chopped basil in a food processor or blender, then press through a sieve into a clean pan. Discard the residue in the sieve.

SERVES 4

INGREDIENTS
    15ml/1 tbsp olive oil
    1 onion, finely chopped
    900g/2lb ripe Italian plum tomatoes,
        roughly chopped
    1 garlic clove, roughly chopped
    about 750ml/1¼ pints/3 cups
        chicken or vegetable stock
    120ml/4fl oz/½ cup dry white wine
    30ml/2 tbsp sun-dried tomato
        purée (paste)
    30ml/2 tbsp chopped fresh basil,
        plus a few whole leaves to garnish
    30ml/2 tbsp single (light) cream
    salt and ground black pepper

1 Heat the olive oil in a large pan over a medium heat. Add the chopped onion and cook it gently for about 5 minutes, stirring frequently with a wooden spoon, until it is softened but not brown.

4 Add the cream and heat through, stirring. Do not allow the soup to boil. Check the consistency and add more hot stock if necessary, then add the seasoning. Pour into bowls and garnish with basil leaves. Serve immediately.

Energy 108Kcal/455kJ; Protein 2.4g; Carbohydrate 9.6g, of which sugars 9.2g; Fat 4.9g, of which saturates 1.5g; Cholesterol 4mg; Calcium 32mg; Fibre 2.7g; Sodium 42mg.

TOMATO, CIABATTA AND BASIL OIL SOUP

THROUGHOUT EUROPE, BREAD IS A POPULAR INGREDIENT FOR THICKENING SOUP, AND THIS RECIPE SHOWS HOW WONDERFULLY QUICK AND EASY THIS METHOD CAN BE. THE ADDITION OF HOME-MADE BASIL OIL SUBTLY ENHANCES THE FLAVOUR OF THE TOMATOES.

SERVES 4

INGREDIENTS

45ml/3 tbsp olive oil
1 red onion, chopped
6 garlic cloves, chopped
300ml/½ pint/1¼ cups white wine
150ml/¼ pint/⅔ cup water
12 plum tomatoes, quartered
2 x 400g/14oz cans plum tomatoes
2.5ml/½ tsp sugar
½ ciabatta loaf
salt and ground black pepper
basil leaves, to garnish
For the basil oil
115g/4oz basil leaves
120ml/4fl oz/½ cup olive oil

1 For the basil oil, process the basil and oil in a food processor or blender to make a paste. Line a bowl with muslin (cheesecloth) and scrape the paste into it. Gather up the muslin and squeeze firmly to extract all the oil. Set aside.

2 Heat the oil in a large pan and cook the onion and garlic for 4–5 minutes until softened.

3 Add the wine, water, fresh and canned tomatoes. Bring to the boil, reduce the heat and cover the pan, then simmer for 3–4 minutes. Add the sugar and season well with salt and black pepper.

4 Break the bread into bite sized pieces and stir into the soup.

5 Ladle the soup into bowls. Garnish with basil and drizzle the basil oil over each portion.

Energy 332Kcal/1396kJ; Protein 7.8g; Carbohydrate 35.4g, of which sugars 16.3g; Fat 13.4g, of which saturates 2g; Cholesterol 0mg; Calcium 98mg; Fibre 5g; Sodium 306mg.

BABY CHERRY TOMATO SOUP
WITH ROCKET PESTO

FOR THEIR SIZE, BABY TOMATOES ARE A POWERHOUSE OF SWEETNESS AND FLAVOUR. HERE THEY ARE COMPLEMENTED BEAUTIFULLY BY A RICH PASTE OF PEPPERY ROCKET.

SERVES 4

INGREDIENTS
225g/8oz baby cherry
  tomatoes, halved
225g/8oz baby plum tomatoes, halved
225g/8oz vine-ripened
  tomatoes, halved
2 shallots, roughly chopped
25ml/1½ tbsp sun-dried
  tomato paste
600ml/1 pint/2½ cups
  vegetable stock
salt and ground black pepper
ice cubes, to serve

For the pesto
15g/½oz rocket
  (arugula) leaves
75ml/5 tbsp olive oil
15g/½oz/2 tbsp pine nuts
1 garlic clove
25g/1oz/⅓ cup freshly
  grated Parmesan cheese

1 Purée all the tomatoes and the shallots in a food processor or blender.

2 Add the sun-dried tomato paste and process until smooth. Press the purée through a sieve (strainer) into a pan.

3 Add the vegetable stock, bring to the boil and simmer gently for 4–5 minutes.

4 Season well with salt and black pepper. Leave to cool, then chill in the refrigerator for at least 4 hours.

5 To make the pesto, purée the rocket, oil, pine nuts and garlic using a mortar and pestle. Alternatively, use a food processor.

6 Stir the Parmesan cheese into the pesto mix, grinding it well.

7 Ladle the soup into bowls and add a few ice cubes to each. Spoon some of the rocket pesto into the centre of each portion and serve.

VARIATION
The pesto can be made with other soft-leaved herbs in place of rocket. Try fresh basil, coriander (cilantro) or mint, or use a mixture of herb leaves, if you like. Parsley and mint are a good flavour combination and make delicious pesto.

Energy 197Kcal/819kJ; Protein 4.9g; Carbohydrate 7.9g, of which sugars 7.6g; Fat 16.5g, of which saturates 3.3g; Cholesterol 6mg; Calcium 101mg; Fibre 2.4g; Sodium 105mg.

SUMMER HERB SOUP <u>WITH</u> CHARGRILLED RADICCHIO

THE SWEETNESS OF SHALLOTS AND LEEKS IN THIS SOUP IS BALANCED BEAUTIFULLY BY THE SLIGHTLY ACIDIC SORREL WITH ITS HINT OF LEMON, AND A BOUQUET OF SUMMER HERBS.

SERVES 4–6

INGREDIENTS
 30ml/2 tbsp dry white wine
 2 shallots, finely chopped
 1 garlic clove, crushed
 2 leeks, sliced
 1 large potato, about 225g/8oz,
  roughly chopped
 2 courgettes (zucchini), chopped
 600ml/1 pint/2½ cups water
 115g/4oz sorrel, torn
 large handful of fresh chervil
 large handful of fresh flat leaf parsley
 large handful of fresh mint
 1 round (butterhead) lettuce,
  separated into leaves
 600ml/1 pint/2½ cups
  vegetable stock
 1 small head of radicchio
 5ml/1 tsp groundnut (peanut) oil
 salt and ground black pepper

1 Put the wine, shallots and garlic into a heavy-based pan and bring to the boil. Cook for 2–3 minutes, until softened.

2 Add the leeks, potato and courgette with enough of the water to come about halfway up the vegetables. Lay a wetted piece of greaseproof paper over the vegetables and put a lid on the pan, then cook for 10–15 minutes, until soft.

3 Remove the paper and add the fresh herbs and lettuce. Cook for 1–2 minutes, or until wilted.

4 Pour in the remaining water and the vegetable stock and simmer for 10–12 minutes. Cool the soup slightly, then process it in a food processor or blender until smooth. Return the soup to the rinsed-out pan and season well.

5 Cut the radicchio into thin wedges that hold together, then brush the cut sides with the oil. Heat a ridged griddle or frying pan until very hot and add the radicchio wedges.

6 Cook the radicchio for 1 minute on each side until slightly charred. Reheat the soup over a low heat, then ladle it into warmed shallow bowls. Serve a wedge of charred radicchio on top.

Energy 102Kcal/428kJ; Protein 5g; Carbohydrate 15.1g, of which sugars 5.7g; Fat 2.2g, of which saturates 0.4g; Cholesterol 0mg; Calcium 135mg; Fibre 4.9g; Sodium 57mg.

CAULIFLOWER AND BEAN SOUP WITH FENNEL SEED AND PARSLEY

FENNEL SEEDS SAUTÉED WITH GARLIC AND ONION GIVE A DELICIOUS EDGE TO THE MILD FLAVOURS OF CAULIFLOWER AND FLAGEOLET BEANS IN THIS SUBSTANTIAL AND WARMING SOUP.

SERVES 4–6

INGREDIENTS

  15ml/1 tbsp olive oil
  1 garlic clove, crushed
  1 onion, chopped
  10ml/2 tsp fennel seeds
  1 cauliflower, cut into small florets
  2 × 400g/14oz cans flageolet or
    cannellini beans, drained and rinsed
  1.2 litres/2 pints/5 cups vegetable
    stock or water
  60–90ml/4–6 tbsp chopped fresh
    parsley
  salt and ground black pepper
  toasted slices of French bread,
    to serve

1 Heat the olive oil in a large, flameproof casserole or heavy pan.

2 Add the garlic, onion and fennel seeds and cook them gently for 5 minutes, or until they are softened.

3 Add the cauliflower florets and half of the flageolet beans and pour in the stock or water.

4 Bring to the boil. Reduce the heat and simmer for 10 minutes, or until the cauliflower is tender.

5 Pour the soup into a food processor or blender and blend until smooth. Return to the pan, and stir in the remaining flageolet beans. Season to taste.

6 Reheat the soup and pour into bowls. Sprinkle with chopped parsley and serve with toasted slices of French bread.

Energy 145Kcal/611kJ; Protein 9.6g; Carbohydrate 20.8g, of which sugars 6g; Fat 3.1g, of which saturates 0.5g; Cholesterol 0mg; Calcium 101mg; Fibre 7.9g; Sodium 399mg.

CREAM OF MUSHROOM AND PARSLEY SOUP

A HANDFUL OF PARSLEY HARMONIZES WITH WHOLESOME FIELD MUSHROOMS, ENHANCING WITHOUT DOMINEERING THEIR FLAVOUR. SERVE WITH CRUSTY BREAD ON COLD AUTUMN DAYS.

SERVES 8

INGREDIENTS
- 75g/3oz/6 tbsp unsalted (sweet) butter
- 2 onions, roughly chopped
- 600ml/1 pint/2½ cups milk
- 900g/2lb field (portobello) mushrooms, sliced
- 8 slices white bread
- 60ml/4 tbsp chopped fresh parsley, plus extra to garnish
- 300ml/½ pint/1¼ cups double (heavy) cream
- salt and ground black pepper

COOK'S TIP
Use fresh flat leaf parsley in this soup. It has a superior flavour to the curly variety.

1 Melt the butter and sauté the chopped onion for about 5 minutes, or until it is soft but not coloured. Add the milk.

2 Add the sliced mushrooms to the pan and continue cooking for a further 5 minutes.

3 Tear the bread into pieces, drop them into the soup and leave to soak for 15 minutes. Purée the soup and return it to the pan. Add the chopped parsley, cream and salt and pepper to taste. Reheat gently, but do not allow the soup to boil. Serve at once, garnished with extra chopped parsley.

Energy 382Kcal/1587kJ; Protein 8g; Carbohydrate 20.9g, of which sugars 7.3g; Fat 30.3g, of which saturates 18.3g; Cholesterol 76mg; Calcium 156mg; Fibre 2.2g; Sodium 245mg.

SHERRIED ONION AND SAFFRON SOUP

THE SPANISH COMBINATION OF ONIONS, GARLIC, SAFFRON AND SHERRY GIVES THIS PALE YELLOW SOUP A BEGUILING FLAVOUR THAT MAKES IT THE PERFECT OPENING COURSE FOR A SPECIAL MEAL.

3 Add the saffron threads and cook, uncovered, for 3–4 minutes, then add the ground almonds and continue to cook, stirring constantly, for another 2–3 minutes.

4 Pour in the chicken or vegetable stock and sherry and stir in 5ml/1 tsp salt. Season with plenty of black pepper and mix well.

5 Bring the mixture to the boil, then lower the heat and simmer gently for about 10 minutes.

6 Process the soup in a food processor or blender until smooth, then return it to the rinsed pan.

7 Reheat the soup slowly, without allowing it to boil, stirring occasionally.

8 Taste the soup for seasoning, adding more salt and ground black pepper if you like.

9 Ladle the soup into four heated bowls, then garnish with the toasted flaked almonds and chopped fresh parsley, and serve immediately.

SERVES 4

INGREDIENTS
40g/1½oz/3 tbsp butter
2 large yellow onions, thinly sliced
1 small garlic clove, finely chopped
good pinch of saffron threads
(about 12 threads)
50g/2oz/⅓ cup blanched almonds,
toasted and finely ground
750ml/1¼ pints/3 cups good chicken
or vegetable stock
45ml/3 tbsp dry sherry
salt and ground black pepper
30ml/2 tbsp toasted flaked (sliced)
almonds and chopped fresh parsley,
to garnish

1 Melt the butter in a pan over a low heat. Add the onions and garlic, stirring to coat them thoroughly in the butter.

2 Cover the pan and cook the mixture very gently, stirring frequently, for 15–20 minutes, or until the onions are soft and golden yellow.

COOK'S TIP

This soup is also delicious served chilled. Add a little more chicken or vegetable stock to make a slightly thinner soup, then leave to cool and chill for at least 4 hours (or overnight). Just before serving, taste for seasoning. Float one or two ice cubes in each bowl.

Energy 200Kcal/827kJ; Protein 3.9g; Carbohydrate 9g, of which sugars 6.4g; Fat 15.4g, of which saturates 5.8g; Cholesterol 21mg; Calcium 58mg; Fibre 2.3g; Sodium 67mg.

LEEK, POTATO AND ROCKET SOUP

ROCKET ADDS ITS DISTINCTIVE, PEPPERY TASTE TO THIS WONDERFULLY SATISFYING SOUP. SERVE IT HOT, GARNISHED WITH A GENEROUS SPRINKLING OF TASTY CIABATTA CROÛTONS.

SERVES 4–6

INGREDIENTS

50g/2oz/¼ cup butter
1 onion, chopped
3 leeks, chopped
2 medium floury potatoes, diced
900ml/1½ pints/3¾ cups light
  chicken stock or water
2 large handfuls of rocket (arugula),
  roughly chopped
150ml/¼ pint/⅔ cup double
  (heavy) cream
salt and ground black pepper
garlic-flavoured ciabatta croûtons,
  to serve (see Cook's Tip)

1 Melt the butter in a large, heavy pan then add the chopped onion and leeks and the diced potatoes. Stir until the vegetables are coated in melted butter. Heat the ingredients until they are sizzling then reduce the heat to low.

2 Cover and sweat the vegetables for 15 minutes. Pour in the chicken stock or water and bring to the boil then reduce the heat, cover again and allow to simmer for 20 minutes, or until the vegetables are tender.

3 Press the soup through a sieve (strainer) or pass through a food mill and return to the rinsed-out pan. (When puréeing the soup, don't use a food processor or blender, as these will give the soup a gluey texture.) Add the chopped rocket to the pan.

4 Allow the soup to cook gently, uncovered, for 5 minutes.

5 Stir in the cream, then season to taste and reheat gently. Ladle into warmed bowls and serve with a scattering of garlic-flavoured ciabatta croûtons.

COOK'S TIP
For the croûtons, cut 1cm/½in cubes of ciabatta bread. Heat a peeled garlic clove in 60ml/4 tbsp olive oil. Remove, then fry the croûtons until golden.

Energy 246Kcal/1019kJ; Protein 3.1g; Carbohydrate 12g, of which sugars 3.7g; Fat 21g, of which saturates 12.8g; Cholesterol 52mg; Calcium 54mg; Fibre 2.7g; Sodium 75mg.

POTATO AND FENNEL SOUP

THE SIMPLE FLAVOURS IN THIS FINE SOUP ARE ENHANCED BY THE DELICATE PERFUME OF HERB FLOWERS, AND COMPLEMENTED BY WARM ROSEMARY-SEASONED SCONES.

SERVES 4

INGREDIENTS
75g/3oz/6 tbsp butter
2 onions, chopped
5ml/1 tsp fennel seeds, crushed
3 fennel bulbs, coarsely chopped
900g/2lb potatoes, thinly sliced
1.2 litres/2 pints/5 cups
  chicken stock
150ml/¼ pint/⅔ cup double
  (heavy) cream
salt and ground black pepper
fresh herb flowers and 15ml/
  1 tbsp chopped fresh chives,
  to garnish

For the rosemary scones
225g/8oz/2 cups self-raising
  (self-rising) flour
2.5ml/½ tsp salt
5ml/1 tsp baking powder
10ml/2 tsp chopped fresh
  rosemary
50g/2oz/¼ cup butter
150ml/¼ pint/⅔ cup milk
1 egg, beaten, to glaze

1 Melt the butter in a pan. Add the onions and cook gently for 10 minutes, stirring occasionally, until very soft. Add the fennel seeds and cook for 2–3 minutes. Stir in the fennel and potatoes.

2 Cover the vegetables with a sheet of wet baking parchment and put a lid on the pan. Cook gently for 10 minutes until very soft.

3 Remove the parchment. Pour in the stock, bring to the boil, cover and simmer for 35 minutes.

4 Meanwhile, make the scones. Preheat the oven to 230°C/450°F/Gas 8 and grease a baking tray.

5 Sift the flour, salt and baking powder into a bowl. Stir in the rosemary, then rub in the butter. Add the milk and mix to a soft dough.

6 Knead very lightly on a floured surface. Roll out to 2cm/¾in thick. Stamp out 12 rounds with a cutter.

7 Brush with the egg and bake on the prepared baking tray for 8–10 minutes, until risen and golden. Cool on a wire rack until warm.

8 Leave the soup to cool slightly, then purée it in a food processor or blender until smooth. Press through a sieve (strainer) into the rinsed pan.

9 Stir in the cream with seasoning to taste. Reheat gently but do not boil.

10 Ladle the soup into four warmed soup bowls and scatter a few herb flowers and chopped chives over each.

11 Serve immediately with the warm rosemary scones.

Energy 797Kcal/3332kJ; Protein 12.3g; Carbohydrate 84.1g, of which sugars 8.8g; Fat 48.1g, of which saturates 29.6g; Cholesterol 120mg; Calcium 316mg; Fibre 7.6g; Sodium 703mg.

PUMPKIN AND CINNAMON SOUP WITH RICE

PUMPKIN IS SO FULL OF COLOUR AND FLAVOUR THAT IT INSPIRES YOU TO BUY IT, GO HOME AND START COOKING THIS DELICIOUS WINTER SOUP.

SERVES 4

INGREDIENTS
  1.1kg/2lb 7oz pumpkin
  750ml/1¼ pints/3 cups
    chicken stock
  750ml/1¼ pints/3 cups semi-
    skimmed (low-fat) milk
  10–15ml/2–3 tsp sugar
  75g/3oz/½ cup cooked white rice
  salt and ground black pepper
  5ml/1 tsp ground cinnamon,
    to serve

1 Remove the seeds from the pumpkin, cut off the peel and chop the flesh.

2 Place in a pan and add the stock, milk, sugar and seasoning. Bring to the boil, then reduce the heat and simmer for about 20 minutes, or until the pumpkin is tender. Drain the pumpkin, reserving the liquid, and purée it in a food processor, then return it to the pan with the liquid.

3 Bring the soup back to the boil, throw in the rice and simmer for a few minutes. Check the seasoning, pour into bowls and dust with cinnamon.

Energy 202Kcal/856kJ; Protein 9.7g; Carbohydrate 33.1g, of which sugars 15.6g; Fat 4.4g, of which saturates 2.5g; Cholesterol 11mg; Calcium 315mg; Fibre 2.8g; Sodium 82mg.

Italian Pea and Basil Soup with Parmesan

The pungent flavour of basil lifts this appetizing Italian soup of petits pois, while the onion and garlic give depth. Serve it with good crusty bread to enjoy it at its best.

2 Add the peas and stock to the pan and bring to the boil.

3 Reduce the heat, add the basil and seasoning, then simmer for 10 minutes.

4 Spoon the soup into a food processor or blender (you may have to do this in batches) and process until the soup is smooth.

5 Return the soup to the rinsed pan and reheat gently until piping hot.

6 Ladle the soup into warm bowls, sprinkle with shaved Parmesan and garnish with basil.

SERVES 4

INGREDIENTS
75ml/5 tbsp olive oil
2 large onions, chopped
1 celery stick, chopped
1 carrot, chopped
1 garlic clove, finely chopped
400g/14oz/3½ cups frozen
   petits pois (baby peas)
900ml/1½ pints/3¾ cups
   vegetable stock
25g/1oz/1 cup fresh basil leaves,
   roughly torn, plus extra to garnish
salt and ground black pepper
shaved Parmesan cheese,
   to serve

1 Heat the oil in a large pan and add the onions, celery, carrot and garlic. Cover the pan and cook over a low heat for 45 minutes, or until the vegetables are soft, stirring occasionally to prevent the vegetables sticking.

VARIATION
You can also use mint or a mixture of parsley, mint and chives in place of the basil, if you like.

Energy 263Kcal/1087kJ; Protein 8.9g; Carbohydrate 23.1g, of which sugars 11.1g; Fat 15.7g, of which saturates 2.3g; Cholesterol 0mg; Calcium 85mg; Fibre 7.6g; Sodium 18mg.

AUBERGINE SOUP WITH MOZZARELLA AND HERBY GREMOLATA

GREMOLATA, A CLASSIC ITALIAN MIXTURE OF GARLIC, LEMON AND PARSLEY, ADDS A FLOURISH OF FRESH FLAVOUR TO THIS RICH CREAM SOUP.

SERVES 6

INGREDIENTS
  30ml/2 tbsp olive oil
  2 shallots, chopped
  2 garlic cloves, chopped
  1kg/2¼lb aubergines (eggplants),
    trimmed and roughly chopped
  1 litre/1¾ pints/4 cups
    chicken stock
  150ml/¼ pint/⅔ cup double
    (heavy) cream
  30ml/2 tbsp chopped
    fresh parsley
  175g/6oz buffalo mozzarella,
    thinly sliced
  salt and ground black pepper

For the gremolata
  2 garlic cloves, finely chopped
  grated rind of 2 lemons
  15ml/1 tbsp chopped fresh parsley

1 Heat the oil in a large pan and add the shallots and garlic. Cook for 4–5 minutes, until soft. Add the aubergines and cook for about 25 minutes, stirring occasionally, until soft and browned.

2 Pour in the stock and cook for about 5 minutes. Leave the soup to cool slightly, then purée in a food processor or blender until smooth. Return to the rinsed pan and season. Add the cream and parsley and bring to the boil.

3 Mix the ingredients for the gremolata in a small bowl.

4 Ladle the soup into bowls and lay the mozzarella on top. Sprinkle with gremolata and serve.

Energy 261Kcal/1079kJ; Protein 7.5g; Carbohydrate 4.9g, of which sugars 4.3g; Fat 23.7g, of which saturates 13.1g; Cholesterol 51mg; Calcium 137mg; Fibre 3.5g; Sodium 124mg.

Salads

Salads are the perfect way to fully appreciate the flavours and textures of herbs, as well as their versatility. Here herbs are paired with vibrant vegetables, creamy cheeses and satisfying lentils and grains to produce a feast of flavours. From basil, dill and parsley to cumin, purslane and thyme, herbs are used to emphasize and complement a wide range of mouthwatering appetizers, accompaniments and warm and cold main course salads.

Above *Potato and Mussel Salad with Shallot and Chive Dressing*

Left *Wild Rocket and Cos Lettuce Salad with Herbs*

ORANGE AND RED ONION SALAD WITH CUMIN

THIS SALAD COMBINES ORANGES, THINLY SLICED RED ONIONS AND BLACK OLIVES, AND IS FLAVOURED WITH TWO POPULAR MIDDLE EASTERN INGREDIENTS – CUMIN SEEDS AND MINT. IT IS AN IDEAL SALAD TO MAKE IN THE WINTER, WHEN OTHER SALAD INGREDIENTS MAY BE IN SHORT SUPPLY, AND IT IS DELICIOUS EITHER ON ITS OWN AS AN APPETIZER OR AS A SIDE DISH.

SERVES 6

INGREDIENTS
  6 oranges
  2 red onions
  15ml/1 tbsp cumin seeds
  5ml/1 tsp coarsely ground
    black pepper
  15ml/1 tbsp chopped fresh mint
  90ml/6 tbsp olive oil
  salt
  fresh mint sprigs and black olives,
    to garnish

COOK'S TIP
It is important to let the salad stand before serving. This allows the flavours to develop and the pungent taste of the onion to soften slightly.

1 Using a sharp knife, slice the oranges thinly, working over a bowl to catch any juice. Then, holding each orange slice in turn over the bowl, cut round the middle fleshy section with scissors to remove the peel and pith. Reserve the juice. Slice the two red onions thinly and separate the rings.

2 Arrange the orange and onion slices in layers in a shallow dish, sprinkling each layer with cumin seeds, pepper, mint, olive oil and salt. Pour in the reserved orange juice. Leave to marinate in a cool place for about 2 hours. Just before serving, scatter with the mint sprigs and black olives.

MIXED SALAD WITH OLIVES AND CAPERS

THIS COLOURFUL AND FLAVOURSOME SALAD MAKES AN IDEAL APPETIZER. SIMPLY PLACE THE BOWL IN THE CENTRE OF THE TABLE AND LET EVERYONE HELP THEMSELVES, WITH A FORK.

SERVES 4

INGREDIENTS
  4 large tomatoes
  ½ cucumber
  1 bunch spring onions (scallions)
  1 bunch watercress or rocket
    (arugula), washed
  8 pimiento-stuffed olives
  30ml/2 tbsp drained
    pickled capers
For the dressing
  1 garlic clove, finely chopped
  30ml/2 tbsp red wine vinegar
  5ml/1 tsp paprika
  2.5ml/½ tsp ground cumin
  75ml/5 tbsp virgin olive oil
  salt and ground black pepper

COOK'S TIP
Try to use tomatoes when red and ripe. Firm ones should be used in salads and soft ones in sauces.

1 To peel the tomatoes, place them in a heatproof bowl, pour over boiling water to cover and leave to stand for 1 minute. Lift out with a slotted spoon and plunge into a bowl of cold water. Leave for 1 minute, then drain. Slip off the skins and dice the flesh finely. Put in a salad bowl.

2 Peel the cucumber, dice finely and add to the tomatoes. Trim and chop half the spring onions, and add to the bowl.

3 Toss the vegetables together, then break the watercress or rocket into small sprigs. Add to the tomato mixture, with the olives and capers.

4 Make the dressing. Crush the garlic to a paste with a little salt, using the flat of a knife. Put in a bowl and mix in the vinegar and spices. Whisk in the oil and taste for seasoning. Dress the salad, and serve garnished with the remaining spring onions.

Energy 169Kcal/702kJ; Protein 2.3g; Carbohydrate 15.5g, of which sugars 14.3g; Fat 11.3g, of which saturates 1.6g; Cholesterol 0mg; Calcium 89mg; Fibre 3.3g; Sodium 10mg.
Energy 183Kcal/759kJ; Protein 3.1g; Carbohydrate 7.7g, of which sugars 7.6g; Fat 15.8g, of which saturates 2.4g; Cholesterol 0mg; Calcium 84mg; Fibre 3.4g; Sodium 280mg.

WILD ROCKET AND COS LETTUCE SALAD WITH HERBS

THE OFTEN QUITE BITTER FLAVOUR OF COS LETTUCE IS PAIRED WITH PEPPERY WILD ROCKET IN THIS SIMPLE YET STUNNING GREEN SALAD. CHOPPED PARSLEY AND DILL AND PLENTY OF FRESH LEMON JUICE LIFT THE FLAVOURS TO PRODUCE A REALLY FRAGRANT COMBINATION THAT IS PERFECT AS A LIGHT APPETIZER OR AS AN ACCOMPANIMENT TO A HOT MEAL.

SERVES 4

INGREDIENTS
  a large handful of rocket
    (arugula) leaves
  2 cos or romaine lettuce hearts
  3 or 4 fresh flat leaf parsley sprigs,
    coarsely chopped
  30–45ml/2–3 tbsp finely
    chopped fresh dill
  75ml/5 tbsp extra virgin olive oil
  15–30ml/1–2 tbsp lemon juice
  salt

COOK'S TIP
It is important to balance the bitterness of the rocket and the sweetness of the cos or romaine lettuce, and the best way to find this out is by taste.

1 If the rocket leaves are young and tender they can be left whole, but older ones should be trimmed of thick stalks and then sliced coarsely. Discard any tough stalks.

2 Slice the cos or romaine lettuce hearts into thin ribbons and place these in a bowl, then add the rocket and the chopped fresh parsley and dill.

3 Make a dressing by whisking the extra virgin olive oil and lemon juice with salt to taste in a bowl until the mixture emulsifies and thickens. Just before serving, pour over the dressing and toss lightly to coat everything in the glistening oil. Serve with crusty bread and a cheese or fish dish.

SUN-RIPENED TOMATO AND FETA SALAD WITH PURSLANE

PURSLANE IS A HERB OF ANCIENT ORIGIN THAT DATES BACK TO ANCIENT EGYPTIAN TIMES, AND DURING THE 16TH CENTURY IT WAS USED AS A REMEDY FOR SCURVY. TODAY IT IS APPRECIATED FOR ITS FLAVOUR AS MUCH AS ITS MEDICINAL QUALITIES, AND HERE IT ADDS AN INTERESTING TWIST TO A TRADITIONAL COMBINATION OF TOMATO, PEPPER, CUCUMBER, FETA AND OLIVES.

SERVES 4

INGREDIENTS
  225g/8oz tomatoes
  1 red onion, thinly sliced
  1 green (bell) pepper, cored and
  sliced in thin ribbons
  1 piece of cucumber, about 15cm/
  6in in length, peeled and sliced
  in rounds
  150g/5oz feta cheese, cubed
  a large handful of fresh purslane,
  trimmed of thick stalks
  8–10 black olives
  90–105ml/6–7 tbsp extra virgin
  olive oil
  15ml/1 tbsp lemon juice
  1.5ml/¼ tsp dried oregano
  salt and ground black pepper

1 Cut the tomatoes in quarters and place them in a salad bowl. Add the onion, green pepper, cucumber, feta, purslane and olives.

COOK'S TP
If purslane is not available, you can use rocket (arugula) instead.

2 Sprinkle the extra virgin olive oil, lemon juice and oregano on top. Add salt and ground black pepper to taste, then toss to coat everything in the olive oil and lemon, and to amalgamate the flavours. If possible, let the salad stand for 10–15 minutes at room temperature before serving.

Energy 283Kcal/1,168kJ; Protein 7.2g; Carbohydrate 6.8g, of which sugars 6.3g; Fat 25.4g, of which saturates 7.7g; Cholesterol 26mg; Calcium 158mg; Fibre 1.9g; Sodium 717mg.

ROASTED TOMATO AND MOZZARELLA SALAD WITH BASIL DRESSING

FRESH BASIL MAKES AN APPETIZING AND VIVIDLY COLOURED OIL THAT IS PERFECT FOR SERVING WITH MOZZARELLA AND TOMATOES. ROASTING THE TOMATOES BRINGS OUT THEIR FLAVOUR AND ADDS A NEW DIMENSION TO THIS SIMPLE AND COLOURFUL SALAD.

SERVES 4

INGREDIENTS
    olive oil, for brushing
    6 large plum tomatoes
    2 balls fresh mozzarella cheese,
      cut into 8–12 slices
    salt and ground black pepper
    basil leaves, to garnish
For the basil oil
    25 basil leaves
    60ml/4 tbsp extra virgin olive oil
    1 garlic clove, crushed

COOK'S TIP
Make the basil oil just before serving to
retain its fresh flavour and bright colour.

1 Preheat the oven to 200°C/400°F/
Gas 6 and oil a baking tray. Cut the
tomatoes in half lengthways and remove
the seeds. Place skin-side down on the
baking tray and roast for 20 minutes, or
until the tomatoes are tender but still
retain their shape.

2 Meanwhile, make the basil oil. Place
the basil leaves, olive oil and garlic in a
food processor or blender and process
until smooth. Transfer to a bowl and
chill until required.

3 For each serving, place the tomato
halves on top of two or three slices of
mozzarella and drizzle over the oil.

4 Season well. Garnish with basil leaves
and serve at once.

COOK'S TIP
The best mozzarella to use for this
salad is the traditional kind made
from buffalo's milk, which has the
best flavour.

MIXED HERB SALAD WITH TOASTED SUNFLOWER AND PUMPKIN SEEDS

THE FUSION OF CORIANDER, PARSLEY, BASIL AND ROCKET WITH SUNFLOWER AND PUMPKIN SEEDS GIVES THIS SALAD ITS CRUNCHY AND CRISPY TEXTURES.

SERVES 4

INGREDIENTS
    25g/1oz/3 tbsp pumpkin seeds
    25g/1oz/3 tbsp sunflower seeds
    90g/3½oz mixed
      salad leaves
    50g/2oz/2 cups mixed
      salad herbs, such as coriander
      (cilantro), parsley, basil
      and rocket (arugula)
For the dressing
    60ml/4 tbsp extra virgin
      olive oil
    15ml/1 tbsp balsamic vinegar
    2.5ml/½ tsp Dijon mustard
    salt and ground black pepper

COOK'S TIP
Use your hands to toss the salad to avoid
bruising the leaves.

1 To make the dressing, combine the
ingredients in a bowl or screw-top jar,
and shake or mix with a small whisk or
fork until combined.

2 Toast the pumpkin and sunflower
seeds in a dry frying pan over a
medium heat for 2 minutes, or until
golden, tossing frequently to prevent
them burning. Allow to cool slightly.

3 Put the salad and herb leaves in a
large bowl and then sprinkle with the
cooled seeds.

4 Pour the dressing over the salad and
toss carefully until the leaves are well
coated, then serve.

Energy 285Kcal/1183kJ; Protein 12.7g; Carbohydrate 4.7g, of which sugars 4.7g; Fat 24.1g, of which saturates 10.3g; Cholesterol 36mg; Calcium 237mg; Fibre 1.5g; Sodium 261mg.
Energy 177Kcal/729kJ; Protein 2.8g; Carbohydrate 2.9g, of which sugars 0.8g; Fat 17.1g, of which saturates 2.2g; Cholesterol 0mg; Calcium 24mg; Fibre 1.1g; Sodium 2mg.

Salad of Fresh Ceps with Parsley and Walnut Dressing

The distinctive flavour of walnuts is a natural partner to all types of mushrooms.
Here, wild mushrooms and walnuts meld with Parmesan cheese, French mustard, lemon,
parsley and nut oils in a richly flavoured salad.

SERVES 4

INGREDIENTS

   350g/12oz/4¾ cups fresh small
     cep mushrooms
   50g/2oz/½ cup broken
     walnut pieces
   175g/6oz mixed salad leaves, to
     include Batavia, young spinach
     and frisée
   50g/2oz/⅔ cup freshly shaved
     Parmesan cheese
   salt and ground black pepper
For the dressing
   2 egg yolks
   2.5ml/½ tsp French mustard
   75ml/5 tbsp groundnut
     (peanut) oil
   45ml/3 tbsp walnut oil
   30ml/2 tbsp lemon juice
   30ml/2 tbsp chopped
     fresh parsley
   1 pinch caster
     (superfine) sugar

1 To make the dressing, place the egg yolks in a screw-top jar with the mustard, groundnut and walnut oils, lemon juice, parsley and sugar.

2 Screw the lid on to the jar and shake vigorously to mix the dressing ingredients thoroughly.

VARIATION
For special occasions, two or three drops of truffle oil will impart a deep and mysterious flavour.

3 Slice the mushrooms thinly with a sharp knife, keeping the slices intact if you can.

4 Transfer the sliced mushrooms to a large bowl and combine with the dressing. Set aside for 10–15 minutes to allow the flavours to mingle.

5 Meanwhile, preheat the grill (broiler) to medium-hot, place the walnut pieces in a grill (broiling) pan and toast for about a minute, shaking the pan to ensure that they toast evenly. Alternatively, dry-fry them on a griddle until they turn golden brown.

6 Wash and spin the mixed salad leaves, then add to the mushrooms in the bowl and toss with spoons to combine.

7 To serve, spoon the salad and mushroom mixture on to four large serving plates.

8 Season well then sprinkle with the toasted walnuts and shavings of Parmesan cheese.

COOK'S TIP
• If fresh ceps are unavailable, this salad can also be made with a range of other fresh mushrooms. Chestnut mushrooms, fresh shiitake mushrooms and even the familiar button (white) mushrooms would all work well.
• The dressing for this salad uses raw egg yolks. Be sure to use only the freshest eggs from a reputable supplier. Pregnant women, young children and the elderly are advised not to eat raw egg yolks. This dressing can be made without the egg yolks if necessary.

Energy 392Kcal/1620kJ; Protein 10.2g; Carbohydrate 2.6g, of which sugars 2.3g; Fat 38g, of which saturates 7.5g; Cholesterol 113mg; Calcium 192mg; Fibre 1.8g; Sodium 148mg.

GRIDDLED FENNEL AND HERB SALAD WITH SPICY TOMATO DRESSING

THIS IS AN EXCELLENT SALAD TO MAKE IN THE EARLY AUTUMN WHEN DELICATELY SWEET FENNEL AND YOUNG LEEKS ARE AT THEIR BEST. THYME, BAY LEAVES, SHALLOTS, OLIVES AND A DASH OF CHILLI COMPLETE THE FUSION OF FLAVOURS. SERVE WITH GRILLED FISH OR SIMPLY WITH BREAD.

SERVES 6 AS A FIRST COURSE

INGREDIENTS

675g/1½lb leeks
2 large fennel bulbs
120ml/4fl oz/½ cup extra virgin
   olive oil
2 shallots, chopped
150ml/¼ pint/⅔ cup dry white wine
   or white vermouth
5ml/1 tsp fennel seeds, crushed
6 fresh thyme sprigs
2–3 bay leaves
good pinch of dried red chilli flakes
350g/12oz tomatoes, peeled, seeded
   and diced
5ml/1 tsp sun-dried tomato
   paste (optional)
good pinch of sugar (optional)
75g/3oz/½ cup small black olives
salt and ground black pepper

2 Trim the fennel bulbs with a sharp knife, reserving any feathery tops for the garnish and cut the bulbs either into thin slices or into thicker wedges, according to taste.

3 Cook the fennel in the reserved cooking water for about 5 minutes, then drain thoroughly and toss with 30ml/ 2 tbsp of the olive oil. Season to taste with black pepper.

6 Add the diced tomatoes to the pan and cook briskly over a high heat for 5–8 minutes, or until the mixture has reduced and thickened.

7 Add the tomato paste, if using, and adjust the seasoning, adding a good pinch of sugar, if you think the dressing needs it.

1 Cook the leeks in a pan of boiling salted water for 4–5 minutes. Use a draining spoon to remove the leeks, place them in a colander to drain thoroughly and cool. Reserve the cooking water in the pan. Then squeeze out excess water and cut the leeks into 7.5cm/3in lengths.

COOK'S TIP

When buying fennel, look for rounded bulbs; flatter ones are immature. The flesh should be crisp and white, with no signs of bruising. Avoid specimens with broken leaves or that appear to be either soggy or dried out.

4 Heat a ridged cast-iron griddle. Arrange the leeks and fennel slices or wedges on the griddle and cook until they are tinged deep brown. Remove the vegetables from the griddle, place in a large, shallow dish and set aside.

5 Place the remaining olive oil in a large pan with the shallots, white wine or vermouth, crushed fennel seeds, thyme, bay leaves and chilli flakes, and bring to the boil over a medium heat. Lower the heat and simmer for 10 minutes.

8 Pour the dressing over the leeks and fennel, toss to mix and leave to cool.

9 The salad may be made several hours in advance and kept in the refrigerator, but bring it back to room temperature before serving.

10 When you are ready to serve, spoon the salad into bowls and sprinkle the black olives and chopped fennel tops over the top.

VARIATION

If you prefer, the black olives can be served in a separate bowl, so that guests can help themselves if they wish.

Energy 192Kcal/796kJ; Protein 3.1g; Carbohydrate 7.2g, of which sugars 6.1g; Fat 15.6g, of which saturates 2.3g; Cholesterol 0mg; Calcium 59mg; Fibre 5.2g; Sodium 297mg.

FENNEL AND EGG TABBOULEH WITH HERBS

TABBOULEH IS A MIDDLE EASTERN SALAD OF BULGUR WHEAT, FLAVOURED WITH LOTS OF PARSLEY, MINT, LEMON JUICE AND GARLIC. HERE, THE SALAD ALSO INCLUDES FENNEL AND BLACK OLIVES.

SERVES 4

INGREDIENTS
  250g/9oz/1⅓ cups bulgur wheat
  4 small eggs
  1 fennel bulb
  1 bunch of spring onions (scallions),
    chopped
  25g/1oz/½ cup drained sun-dried
    tomatoes in oil, sliced
  45ml/3 tbsp chopped fresh parsley
  30ml/2 tbsp chopped fresh mint
  75g/3oz/½ cup black olives
  60ml/4 tbsp olive oil
  30ml/2 tbsp garlic oil
  30ml/2 tbsp lemon juice
  50g/2oz/½ cup chopped hazelnuts,
    toasted
  1 open-textured loaf or 4 pitta
    breads, warmed
  salt and ground black pepper

1 In a bowl, pour boiling water over the bulgur wheat, and leave to soak for about 15 minutes.

2 Drain the bulgur wheat in a metal sieve (strainer), and place the sieve over a pan of boiling water. Cover and steam for about 10 minutes. Fluff up the grains with a fork and spread out on a metal tray. Set aside to cool.

3 Hard-boil the eggs for 8 minutes. Cool under running water, then peel and quarter.

4 Halve and finely slice the fennel. Boil in salted water for 6 minutes, then drain and cool under running water.

5 Combine the eggs, fennel, spring onions, sun-dried tomatoes, parsley, mint and olives with the bulgur wheat. Dress with olive oil, garlic oil and lemon juice, then add the nuts. Season well, then tear the bread into pieces and add to the salad. Serve immediately.

COOK'S TIP
If you are short of time, simply soak the bulgur wheat in boiling water for about 20 minutes. Drain and rinse under cold water to cool, then drain thoroughly.

Energy 515Kcal/2139kJ; Protein 15.8g; Carbohydrate 51.3g, of which sugars 3.2g; Fat 28.1g, of which saturates 4.1g; Cholesterol 190mg; Calcium 134mg; Fibre 4.2g; Sodium 511mg.

LENTIL AND SPINACH SALAD WITH ONION, CUMIN AND GARLIC

THIS EARTHY SALAD IS A BLEND OF HERBY FLAVOURS. PUY LENTILS ARE TOSSED WITH ONIONS, BAY, THYME, PARSLEY AND CUMIN AND THEN DRESSED IN A MEDLEY OF MUSTARD, GARLIC AND LEMON.

SERVES 6

INGREDIENTS
225g/8oz/1 cup Puy lentils
1 fresh bay leaf
1 celery stick
fresh thyme sprig
30ml/2 tbsp olive oil
1 onion or 3–4 shallots, finely chopped
10ml/2 tsp crushed toasted
   cumin seeds
400g/14oz young spinach
30–45ml/2–3 tbsp chopped
   fresh parsley
toasted French bread, to serve
salt and ground black pepper
For the dressing
75ml/5 tbsp extra virgin olive oil
5ml/1 tsp Dijon mustard
15–25ml/1–1½ tbsp red wine vinegar
1 small garlic clove, finely chopped
2.5ml/½ tsp finely grated
   lemon rind

1 Rinse the lentils and place them in a large pan. Add plenty of water to cover. Tie the bay leaf, celery and thyme into a bundle and add to the pan, then bring to the boil. Reduce the heat so that the water just boils steadily. Cook the lentils for 30–45 minutes, or until just tender. Do not add salt at this stage, as it toughens the lentils.

2 Meanwhile, to make the dressing, mix the oil, mustard and 15ml/1 tbsp vinegar with the garlic and lemon rind, and season well with salt and pepper.

3 Thoroughly drain the lentils and turn them into a bowl. Add most of the dressing and toss well, then set the lentils aside, stirring occasionally.

COOK'S TIP
Named after Puy in France, these small, greyish-green lentils are considered to have the best and most distinctive flavour. They keep both their shape and colour well when cooked.

4 Heat the olive oil in a pan or deep frying pan and sauté the chopped onion or shallots over a low heat for 4–5 minutes, or until they are beginning to soften. Add the cumin and cook for a further 1 minute.

5 Add the spinach and season to taste, then cover and cook for 2 minutes. Stir and cook again briefly until wilted.

6 Stir the spinach into the lentils and leave the salad to cool. Bring back to room temperature, if necessary. Stir in the remaining dressing and chopped parsley. Adjust the seasoning, and add extra red wine vinegar, if necessary.

7 Turn the salad on to a serving platter and serve with slices of toasted French bread.

Energy 252Kcal/1052kJ; Protein 10.8g; Carbohydrate 22.2g, of which sugars 2g; Fat 13.9g, of which saturates 2g; Cholesterol 0mg; Calcium 135mg; Fibre 3.3g; Sodium 110mg.

POTATO AND MUSSEL SALAD WITH SHALLOT AND CHIVE DRESSING

SHALLOT AND CHIVES IN A CREAMY DRESSING ADD BITE TO THIS SALAD OF POTATO AND SWEET MUSSELS AND PARSLEY. SERVE WITH FULL-FLAVOURED WATERCRESS AND PLENTY OF WHOLEMEAL BREAD.

SERVES 4

INGREDIENTS
  675g/1½lb salad potatoes
  1kg/2¼lb mussels, scrubbed and
    beards removed
  200ml/7fl oz/scant 1 cup dry
    white wine
  15g/½oz/¼ cup chopped flat
    leaf parsley
  salt and ground black pepper
  chopped fresh chives or chive
    flowers, to garnish
For the dressing
  105ml/7 tbsp mild olive oil
  15–30ml/1–2 tbsp white
    wine vinegar
  5ml/1 tsp Dijon mustard
  1 large shallot, very finely chopped
  15ml/1 tbsp chopped fresh chives
  45ml/3 tbsp double (heavy) cream
  pinch of caster (superfine) sugar

1 Boil the potatoes in boiling, salted water for 15–20 minutes. Drain, cool, peel, then slice into a bowl and toss with 30ml/2 tbsp of the oil for the dressing.

2 Discard any open mussels that do not close when sharply tapped. Bring the white wine to the boil in a large, heavy pan. Add the mussels, cover and boil shaking occasionally, for 3–4 minutes, or until the mussels have opened.

3 Discard any mussels which have not opened after 5 minutes' cooking.

4 Drain and shell the mussels, reserving the cooking liquid.

5 Boil the reserved cooking liquid until reduced to about 45ml/3 tbsp.

6 Strain through a fine sieve (strainer) over the potatoes and toss to mix.

7 For the dressing, whisk together the remaining oil, 15ml/1 tbsp vinegar, the mustard, shallot and chives.

8 Add the cream and whisk again to form a thick dressing.

9 Adjust the seasoning, adding more vinegar and a pinch of sugar to taste.

10 Toss the mussels with the potatoes, then mix in the dressing and chopped parsley and combine thoroughly.

11 Serve sprinkled with chopped chives or chive flowers separated into florets.

COOK'S TIP
Potato salads, such as this one, should not be chilled if at all possible as the cold alters the texture of the potatoes and of the creamy dressing. For the best flavour and texture, serve this salad soon after it is cooked, when it is just cool or at room temperature, rather than making it ahead and storing it in the refrigerator until ready to serve.

Energy 451Kcal/1882kJ; Protein 16.3g; Carbohydrate 28.9g, of which sugars 3.5g; Fat 27.3g, of which saturates 6.9g; Cholesterol 45mg; Calcium 172mg; Fibre 1.9g; Sodium 181mg

SCENTED FISH SALAD <u>WITH</u> CHILLI <u>AND</u> CORIANDER

THIS THAI FISH SALAD COMBINES THE DELICATE FLESH OF FISH WITH FRESH FRUIT AND THE POWERFUL FLAVOURS OF CHILLI, CORIANDER, CUMIN, FENNEL AND LIME.

SERVES 4

INGREDIENTS
350g/12oz fillet of red mullet,
   sea bream or snapper
1 cos or romaine lettuce, washed
   and dried
1 papaya or mango, peeled
   and sliced
1 pitaya, peeled and sliced
1 large ripe tomato, cut into wedges
½ cucumber, peeled and cut
   into batons
3 spring onions (scallions), sliced
salt
For the marinade
   5ml/1 tsp coriander seeds
   5ml/1 tsp fennel seeds
   2.5ml/½ tsp cumin seeds
   5ml/1 tsp caster (superfine) sugar
   2.5ml/½ tsp hot chilli sauce
   30ml/2 tbsp garlic oil
For the dressing
   15ml/1 tbsp creamed coconut
   or 60ml/4 tbsp coconut cream
   pinch of salt
   60ml/4 tbsp groundnut (peanut) oil
   finely grated rind and juice of 1 lime
   1 fresh red chilli, seeded and
   finely chopped
   5ml/1 tsp granulated sugar
   45ml/3 tbsp chopped fresh
   coriander (cilantro)

1 Cut the fish fillets into fairly thin, even strips, removing any stray bones wtih your fingers. Set aside on a plate.

2 Make the marinade. Put the coriander, fennel and cumin seeds in a mortar. Add the sugar and crush with a pestle. Stir in the chilli sauce and garlic oil, then add salt to taste and mix to a smooth paste.

3 Spread the paste over the fish strips, cover with clear film (plastic wrap) and leave to marinate in a cool place for at least 20 minutes.

4 Make the dressing. If using creamed coconut, mix with 45ml/3 tbsp boiling water in a screw-top jar. Add the rest of the dressing ingredients (including coconut cream if using instead of creamed coconut), and shake well.

5 Mix the papaya or mango, pitaya, tomato, cucumber and spring onions with the dressing and toss well to coat.

6 Heat a large non-stick frying pan, add the fish and cook for 5 minutes, turning once. Add the cooked fish to the salad, toss lightly and serve immediately.

COOK'S TIP
You can make the dressing in advance, but do not add the coriander until just before serving and shake vigorously before pouring over the salad.

Energy 227Kcal/995kJ; Protein 18.0g; Carbohydrate 16.3g, of which sugars 1.2g; Fat 10.0g, of which saturates 1.1g; Cholesterol 15mg; Calcium 100mg; Fibre 2.3g; Sodium 178mg.

CHICKEN AND CORIANDER SALAD

SERVE THIS SUBSTANTIAL SUMMER SALAD WARM TO MAKE THE MOST OF THE WONDERFUL FLAVOURS OF CHICKEN AND CORIANDER. THE CHICKEN CAN BE GRILLED OR COOKED ON A BARBECUE.

2 Cook the mangetouts for 2 minutes in boiling water, then refresh in cold water. Tear the lettuces into small pieces and mix all the salad ingredients and the bacon together. Arrange the salad in individual dishes.

3 Season the chicken breast fillets with salt and pepper, then grill (broil) them on medium heat for 10–15 minutes, or cook on a medium barbecue. Baste with the marinade and turn once during cooking, until cooked through.

4 Slice the chicken into thin pieces. Divide among the bowls of salad and add some of the dressing to each dish. Combine and sprinkle some fresh coriander over each bowl, to garnish.

SERVES 6

INGREDIENTS
  4 medium chicken breast fillets, skinned and boned
  225g/8oz mangetouts (snow peas)
  2 heads decorative lettuce such as lollo rosso or feuille de chêne
  3 carrots, cut into matchsticks
  175g/6oz/2⅓ cups sliced button (white) mushrooms
  6 bacon rashers (strips), fried and chopped
  salt and ground black pepper
  60ml/4 tbsp fresh coriander (cilantro) leaves
For the coriander dressing
  120ml/4fl oz/½ cup lemon juice
  30ml/2 tbsp wholegrain mustard
  250ml/8fl oz/1 cup olive oil
  75ml/2½fl oz/⅓ cup sesame oil
  5ml/1 tsp coriander seeds, crushed

1 Mix all the dressing ingredients in a bowl. Place the prepared chicken breast fillets in a shallow dish and pour over half the dressing. Leave to marinate overnight in the refrigerator. Chill the remaining dressing.

COOK'S TIP
Use any of your favourite herbs in this dish, basil, parsley and thyme all work well.

Energy 568Kcal/2360kJ; Protein 40.5g; Carbohydrate 2.9g, of which sugars 2.5g; Fat 43.9g, of which saturates 8g; Cholesterol 113mg; Calcium 43mg; Fibre 1.7g; Sodium 662mg.

CHICKEN SALAD WITH HERBS AND LAVENDER

*THE DELIGHTFUL SCENT OF LAVENDER HAS A NATURAL AFFINITY WITH GARLIC, THYME, MARJORAM
AND ORANGE, AND THE POLENTA OR CORNMEAL MAKES THIS SALAD BOTH FILLING AND DELICIOUS.*

SERVES 4

INGREDIENTS
    4 skinless chicken breast fillets
    900ml/1½ pints/3¾ cups light
        chicken stock
    175g/6oz/1½ cups fine polenta
        or cornmeal
    50g/2oz/¼ cup butter, plus extra
        for greasing
    450g/1lb young spinach
    175g/6oz lamb's lettuce
    8 small tomatoes, halved
    salt and ground black pepper
    8 sprigs fresh lavender,
        to garnish
For the marinade
    6 fresh lavender flowers
    10ml/2 tsp finely grated orange rind
    2 garlic cloves, crushed
    10ml/2 tsp clear honey
    30ml/2 tbsp olive oil
    10ml/2 tsp chopped fresh thyme
    10ml/2 tsp chopped fresh marjoram
    salt

1 To make the marinade, strip the
lavender flowers from the stems and
combine them with the orange rind,
garlic, honey and salt. Add the oil and
herbs and mix well.

2 Slash the chicken deeply, spread the
mixture over and leave to marinate in
the refrigerator for 20 minutes.

3 To make the polenta, bring the
chicken stock to the boil in a pan.
Add the polenta or cornmeal in a steady
stream, stirring all the time until the
mixture is thick.

4 Turn the cooked polenta or cornmeal
out on to a shallow, buttered tray and
leave to cool.

COOK'S TIP
When preparing the spinach, tear the
leaves into smaller pieces just before you
are ready to serve. Do not cut them with
a knife, as this tends to make the edges
turn brown.

5 Cook the chicken on a medium
barbecue or under the grill (broiler) for
15 minutes, basting with the marinade
and turning once, until cooked through.

6 Cut the polenta into 2.5cm/1in cubes
using a wet knife.

7 Heat the butter in a large frying pan
and fry the polenta until it is golden.

8 Divide the spinach and lamb's lettuce
among four dinner plates. Slice each
chicken breast fillet and arrange among
the salad. Add the polenta and tomato
halves to each plate.

9 Season each salad with salt and
ground black pepper and garnish with
sprigs of lavender. Serve immediately.

Energy 555Kcal/2318kJ; Protein 56.6g; Carbohydrate 34.6g, of which sugars 2.4g; Fat 20.7g, of which saturates 8.1g; Cholesterol 167mg; Calcium 279mg; Fibre 4.3g; Sodium 415mg.

BEEF AND GRILLED SWEET POTATO SALAD WITH SHALLOT AND HERB DRESSING

THIS SALAD MAKES A GOOD MAIN DISH FOR A SUMMER BUFFET AND IT IS ABSOLUTELY DELICIOUS WITH A SIMPLE POTATO SALAD AND SOME PEPPERY LEAVES, SUCH AS WATERCRESS, MIZUNA OR ROCKET.

4 Remove the beef from the oven, and cover with foil, then leave to rest for 10–15 minutes.

5 Meanwhile, preheat the grill (broiler). Cut the sweet potatoes into 1cm/½in slices. Brush with the remaining olive oil, season to taste with salt and pepper, and grill (broil) for about 5–6 minutes on each side, until tender and browned. Cut the sweet potato slices into strips and place them in a bowl.

6 Cut the beef into slices or strips and toss with the sweet potato.

7 For the dressing, process the garlic, parsley, coriander, capers, chilli, mustard and 10ml/2 tsp of the vinegar in a food processor or blender until chopped. With the motor still running, gradually pour in the oil to make a smooth dressing.

8 Season the dressing with salt and pepper and add more vinegar, to taste. Stir in the shallots.

9 Toss the dressing into the sweet potatoes and beef and leave to stand for up to 2 hours before serving.

SERVES 6–8

INGREDIENTS
800g/1¾lb fillet (tenderloin) of beef
5ml/1 tsp black peppercorns, crushed
10ml/2 tsp chopped fresh thyme
60ml/4 tbsp olive oil
450g/1lb orange-fleshed sweet
  potato, peeled
salt and ground black pepper
For the dressing
1 garlic clove, chopped
15g/½oz/⅓ cup flat leaf parsley
30ml/2 tbsp chopped fresh
  coriander (cilantro)
15ml/1 tbsp salted capers, rinsed
½–1 fresh green chilli, seeded
  and chopped
10ml/2 tsp Dijon mustard
10–15ml/2–3 tsp white wine vinegar
75ml/5 tbsp extra virgin olive oil
2 shallots, finely chopped

1 Roll the beef fillet in the crushed peppercorns and thyme, then set aside to marinate for a few hours. Preheat the oven to 200°C/400°F/Gas 6.

2 Heat half the olive oil in a heavy frying pan. Add the beef and brown it all over, turning frequently, to seal it.

3 Place on a baking tray and cook in the oven for 10–15 minutes.

COOK'S TIP
Not only do orange-fleshed sweet potatoes look more appetizing than white ones, but they are also better for you, as they contain antioxidant vitamins that help protect against disease.

Energy 400Kcal/1670kJ; Protein 29.2g; Carbohydrate 16g, of which sugars 4.3g; Fat 24.9g, of which saturates 6.2g; Cholesterol 81mg; Calcium 23mg; Fibre 1.8g; Sodium 89mg.

GRILLED BEEF SALAD ᵂᴵᵀᴴ MUSHROOMS ᴬᴺᴰ CORIANDER

THIS FRAGRANT SALAD COMBINES THIN STRIPS OF TENDER STEAK, EARTHY MUSHROOMS AND FIERY CHILLIES WITH CRISP SALAD LEAVES AND THE DISTINCTIVE FLAVOUR OF CORIANDER.

SERVES 4

INGREDIENTS
675g/1½lb fillet steak
    (beef tenderloin)
30ml/2 tbsp olive oil
2 small mild red chillies, seeded
    and sliced
225g/8oz/3¼ cups shiitake
    mushrooms, sliced
For the dressing
3 spring onions (scallions), chopped
2 garlic cloves, finely chopped
juice of 1 lime
15–30ml/1–2 tbsp fish or oyster
    sauce, to taste
5ml/1 tsp soft light brown sugar
30ml/2 tbsp chopped fresh
    coriander (cilantro)
To serve
1 cos or romaine lettuce, torn
    into strips
175g/6oz cherry tomatoes, halved
5cm/2in piece cucumber, peeled,
    halved and thinly sliced
45ml/3 tbsp toasted sesame seeds

1 Preheat the grill (broiler), then cook the steak for 2–4 minutes on each side depending on how well done you like steak. Leave to cool.

2 Slice the meat as thinly as possible and place the slices in a bowl.

VARIATION
If you can find them, yellow chillies make a colourful addition to this dish. Substitute one for one of the red chillies.

3 Heat the olive oil in a small frying pan. Add the seeded and sliced red chillies and the sliced mushrooms and cook for 5 minutes, stirring occasionally. Turn off the heat and add the grilled (broiled) steak slices to the pan, then stir well to coat the slices in the chilli and mushroom mixture.

4 Stir all the ingredients for the dressing together, then pour it over the meat mixture and toss gently.

5 Arrange the salad ingredients on a serving plate. Spoon the warm steak mixture into the centre and sprinkle the sesame seeds over, then serve.

Energy 381Kcal/1591kJ; Protein 39.8g; Carbohydrate 4.1g, of which sugars 3.8g; Fat 23g, of which saturates 6.6g; Cholesterol 103mg; Calcium 105mg; Fibre 2.5g; Sodium 352mg.

Light Meals

Enjoy the variety of flavours herbs bring to brunches, light lunches or suppers. Serve light toasted brioche stuffed with scrambled egg and chives, or appreciate the creaminess of roasted garlic with crisp toast. Frittatas feature here, as well as pasta dishes, making use of onion, garlic, bell peppers and stunning combinations of aromatic herbs. Or, for a delicate touch, the flowers and leaves of sweet cicely add scent to roasted peppers for a special meal.

Above *Roasted Peppers with Sweet Cicely*

Left *Vermicelli with Herb Frittata*

CHIVE SCRAMBLED EGGS IN BRIOCHE

DELICIOUSLY CREAMY SCRAMBLED EGG WITH A HINT OF CHIVES CONCEALS A LAYER OF WARM MUSHROOMS IN THESE SATISFYING BRIOCHE BASKETS. SERVE FOR A LIGHT LUNCH OR AS A DELIGHTFULLY INDULGENT WEEKEND BREAKFAST.

SERVES 4

INGREDIENTS
115g/4oz/½ cup unsalted
  (sweet) butter
75g/3oz/1¼ cups finely sliced brown
  cap (cremini) mushrooms
4 individual brioches
8 eggs
15ml/1 tbsp chopped fresh chives,
  plus extra to garnish
salt and ground black pepper

1 Preheat the oven to 180°C/350°F/ Gas 4. Melt 25g/1oz of the butter in a frying pan. Fry the mushrooms for about 3 minutes, until soft, then set aside and keep warm.

COOK'S TIP
Do not cook the eggs for too long or over a high heat or the mixture will become dry and crumbly.

2 Slice the tops off the brioches, then scoop out the centres and discard. Put the brioches and lids on a baking sheet and bake for 5 minutes.

3 Meanwhile, beat the eggs lightly and season to taste with salt and ground black pepper. Melt the remaining butter in a heavy pan over a gentle heat. When the butter is foaming slightly, add the eggs. Stir constantly, to ensure the egg does not stick to the pan.

4 Continue to stir gently until about three-quarters of the egg is semi-solid and creamy – this process should take 2–3 minutes. Remove from the heat, then stir in the chopped chives.

5 To serve, spoon a little of the mushrooms into the bottom of each brioche and top with the scrambled eggs. Sprinkle with extra chives, balance the brioche lids on top and serve immediately.

QUAIL'S EGGS AND FOCACCIA WITH HERBS

ITALIAN FOCACCIA BREAD IS TRANSFORMED WITH A SIMPLE TOPPING OF FRESH MIXED HERBS AND GARLIC AND IS THE PERFECT PARTNER FOR QUAIL'S EGGS. A MAYONNAISE DIP FLAVOURED WITH CAPERS AND SHALLOTS PROVIDES CONTRASTING TEXTURE TO THE SPRING ONIONS AND BEETROOT.

SERVES 6

INGREDIENTS
    1 large Italian focaccia or 2–3 Indian
      parathas or other flatbreads
    olive oil, for brushing and dipping
    1 large garlic clove, finely chopped
    small handful of fresh mixed herbs,
      such as coriander (cilantro), mint,
      parsley and oregano, chopped
    18–24 quail's eggs
    30ml/2 tbsp home-made mayonnaise
    30ml/2 tbsp sour cream
    5ml/1 tsp chopped capers
    5ml/1 tsp finely chopped shallot
    225g/8oz fresh beetroot (beet),
      cooked in water, peeled and sliced
    ½ bunch spring onions (scallions),
      halved lengthways
    60ml/4 tbsp red onion chutney
    salt and ground black pepper
    coarse salt and mixed peppercorns,
      roughly ground, to serve

1 Preheat the oven to 190°C/375°F/ Gas 5. Brush the bread with olive oil, sprinkle with garlic, mixed herbs and seasoning, and bake for 10–15 minutes, or until golden. Keep warm.

2 Put the quail's eggs into a pan of cold water. Bring the water to the boil and cook for 5 minutes. Carefully lift the eggs out of the pan, using a slotted spoon, and place in a bowl of cold water. Leave to cool.

3 To make the mayonnaise dip, mix together the mayonnaise, sour cream, capers, shallot and seasoning. Peel the eggs and arrange in a serving dish.

4 Cut the bread into wedges and serve with the eggs and mayonnaise dip, along with dishes of beetroot, spring onions and chutney.

5 Serve with bowls of salt, ground peppercorns and olive oil for dipping.

Energy 361Kcal/1515kJ; Protein 12.7g; Carbohydrate 35.3g, of which sugars 6.7g; Fat 20g, of which saturates 2.8g; Cholesterol 197mg; Calcium 102mg; Fibre 3.6g; Sodium 241mg.

SPICED ONION PAKORAS WITH CUMIN, CORIANDER AND TURMERIC

CORIANDER, CUMIN, TURMERIC AND CHILLIES CREATE THE TRADITIONAL FLAVOURING FOR THESE INDIAN ONION FRITTERS. CHICKPEA FLOUR IS AVAILABLE FROM SUPERMARKETS AND INDIAN STORES.

SERVES 4–5

INGREDIENTS

675g/1½lb onions, halved and
  thinly sliced
5ml/1 tsp salt
5ml/1 tsp ground coriander seeds
5ml/1 tsp ground cumin
2.5ml/½ tsp ground turmeric
1–2 fresh green chillies, seeded and
  finely chopped
45ml/3 tbsp chopped fresh
  coriander (cilantro)
90g/3½oz/scant ¾ cup chickpea flour
2.5ml/½ tsp baking powder
vegetable oil, for deep-frying
To serve
  lemon wedges
  fresh coriander (cilantro) sprigs
  yogurt and herb dip or yogurt and
    cucumber dip (see Cook's Tips)

1 Place the onions in a colander, add the salt and toss well. Stand the colander on a plate for 45 minutes, tossing once or twice. Rinse, then squeeze out excess moisture.

2 Place in a bowl. Add the ground coriander, cumin, turmeric, chillies and fresh coriander. Mix well.

COOK'S TIPS
• To make a yogurt and herb dip, stir 30ml/2 tbsp each of chopped fresh coriander and mint into about 250ml/8fl oz/1 cup set yogurt. Season with salt, ground toasted cumin seeds and a pinch of muscovado (molasses) sugar.
• For a cucumber dip, stir half a diced cucumber and one seeded and chopped green chilli into 250ml/8fl oz/1 cup set yogurt. Season with salt and cumin.

3 Add the chickpea flour and baking powder to the onion mixture, then use your hand to combine the ingredients.

4 Shape the mixture by hand into 12–15 pakoras, which should be about the size of golf balls.

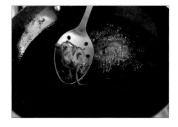

5 Heat the oil for deep-frying to 180–190°C/350–375°F or until a cube of day-old bread browns in 30–45 seconds. Fry the pakoras, four to five at a time, until deep golden brown all over. Drain each batch on kitchen paper and keep warm until all the pakoras are cooked. Serve with lemon wedges, coriander sprigs and a yogurt dip.

Energy 207Kcal/861kJ; Protein 5.4g; Carbohydrate 19.8g, of which sugars 8.2g; Fat 12.3g, of which saturates 1.4g; Cholesterol 0mg; Calcium 84mg; Fibre 4.3g; Sodium 14mg.

LITTLE ONIONS <u>WITH</u> CORIANDER, WINE <u>AND</u> OLIVE OIL

CHILLIES AND TOASTED CORIANDER SEEDS ADD PIQUANCY TO THE SMALL ONIONS USED HERE. BAY, GARLIC, THYME, OREGANO, LEMON AND PARSLEY PROVIDE AN UNMISTAKABLY MEDITERRANEAN KICK.

SERVES 6

INGREDIENTS

105ml/7 tbsp olive oil
675g/1½lb small onions, peeled
150ml/¼ pint/⅔ cup dry white wine
2 bay leaves
2 garlic cloves, bruised
1–2 small dried red chillies
15ml/1 tbsp coriander seeds, toasted
  and lightly crushed
2.5ml/½ tsp sugar
a few fresh thyme sprigs
30ml/2 tbsp currants
10ml/2 tsp chopped fresh oregano
  or marjoram
5ml/1 tsp grated lemon rind
15ml/1 tbsp chopped fresh flat
  leaf parsley
30–45ml/2–3 tbsp pine nuts, toasted
salt and ground black pepper

1 Place 30ml/2 tbsp of the olive oil in a wide pan. Add the onions, place over a medium heat and cook gently for about 5 minutes, or until the onions begin to colour. Use a draining spoon to remove from the pan and set aside.

2 Add the remaining oil, the wine, bay leaves, garlic, chillies, coriander seeds, sugar and thyme to the pan.

3 Bring to the boil and cook briskly for 5 minutes. Return the onions to the pan. Add the currants, reduce the heat and cook gently for 15–20 minutes, or until the onions are tender but not falling apart.

4 Use a slotted spoon to transfer the onions to a serving dish, then boil the liquid vigorously over a high heat until it reduces considerably.

5 Taste and adjust the seasoning, if necessary, then pour the liquid over the onions.

6 Sprinkle the chopped oregano or marjoram over the onions in the dish, then cool and chill them.

7 Just before you are ready to serve the onions, stir in the grated lemon rind, chopped flat leaf parsley and toasted pine nuts.

COOK'S TIP
You might like to serve this dish as part of a mixed hors d'oeuvre – an antipasto – perhaps accompanied by mild mayonnaise-dressed celeriac salad and some thinly sliced prosciutto or other air-dried ham.

Energy 226Kcal/933kJ; Protein 2.4g; Carbohydrate 12.9g, of which sugars 10.2g; Fat 16.6g, of which saturates 2.1g; Cholesterol 0mg; Calcium 51mg; Fibre 2.1g; Sodium 8mg.

ROASTED GARLIC TOASTS

*GARLIC ROASTED OR COOKED ON A BARBECUE IN ITS SKIN BECOMES A SOFT, AROMATIC PURÉE WITH
A SWEET, NUTTY FLAVOUR, WHICH IS PERFECTLY COMPLEMENTED BY AROMATIC ROSEMARY. SPREAD ON
CRISP TOAST TO MAKE A DELICIOUS APPETIZER OR ACCOMPANIMENT TO MEAT OR VEGETABLE DISHES.*

SERVES 4

INGREDIENTS

2 whole garlic heads
extra virgin olive oil, for
  brushing and drizzling
fresh rosemary sprigs
ciabatta loaf or thick baguette
chopped fresh rosemary
salt and ground
  black pepper

1 Preheat the oven to 200°C/400°F/
Gas 6 or light the barbecue, if using.

2 Remove the tops from both of the
whole heads of garlic, by slicing them
with a sharp kitchen knife.

3 Brush the garlic heads with olive oil
and add a few sprigs of fresh rosemary,
before wrapping in kitchen foil.

4 Bake in the oven for 25–30 minutes,
or until the garlic is soft. Alternatively,
cook the parcels on a medium-hot
barbecue, turning them occasionally.

5 Slice the ciabatta or baguette and
brush each slice generously with olive
oil. Toast the slices until they are crisp
and golden, turning once.

6 Squeeze the garlic cloves from their
skins on to the toasts. Sprinkle with the
chopped fresh rosemary and olive oil,
and add salt and black pepper to taste.

Energy 337Kcal/1427kJ; Protein 11g; Carbohydrate 60.2g, of which sugars 3.2g; Fat 7.6g, of which saturates 1.2g; Cholesterol 0mg; Calcium 126mg; Fibre 3.4g; Sodium 617mg.

VEGETABLES <u>WITH</u> TAPENADE <u>AND</u> HERB AIOLI

*THE DELICATE BUT DISTINCTIVE FLAVOURS OF CHERVIL, TARRAGON AND PARSLEY ARE COMBINED WITH
GARLIC FOR THIS HERB AIOLI. HERE, IT ACCOMPANIES A FULL-FLAVOURED TAPENADE AND IS SERVED
WITH A PLATTER OF SUMMER VEGETABLES AND QUAIL'S EGGS.*

SERVES 6

INGREDIENTS
   2 red (bell) peppers, cut into
     wide strips
   30ml/2 tbsp olive oil
   225g/8oz new potatoes
   115g/4oz green beans
   225g/8oz baby carrots
   225g/8oz young asparagus
   12 quail's eggs
   fresh herbs, to garnish
   coarse salt, for sprinkling
For the tapenade
   175g/6oz/1½ cups pitted
     black olives
   50g/2oz can anchovy fillets, drained
   30ml/2 tbsp capers
   about 120ml/4fl oz/½ cup olive oil
   finely grated rind of 1 lemon
   15ml/1 tbsp brandy (optional)
For the herb aioli
   5 garlic cloves, crushed
   2 egg yolks
   5ml/1 tsp Dijon mustard
   about 10ml/2 tsp white
     wine vinegar
   250ml/8fl oz/1 cup light olive oil
   45ml/3 tbsp chopped mixed fresh
     herbs, such as chervil, parsley
     and tarragon
   30ml/2 tbsp chopped watercress
   salt and ground black pepper

1 To make the tapenade, finely chop
the olives, anchovies and capers and
beat together with the oil, lemon rind
and brandy, if using. (Alternatively,
lightly process the ingredients in a
blender or food processor.)

2 Season the tapenade with pepper
and blend in a little more oil if the
mixture seems very dry. Transfer to
a serving dish.

3 To make the aioli, beat together the
garlic, egg yolks, mustard and vinegar.
Gradually blend in the olive oil, a drop
at a time, whisking the mixture well
until thick and smooth.

4 Stir in the mixed herbs and chopped
watercress. Season with salt and pepper
to taste, adding a little more vinegar if
necessary. Cover with clear film (plastic
wrap) and chill until ready to serve.

5 Brush the peppers with oil, and place
on a hot barbecue or under a hot grill
(broiler) until they begin to char.

6 Cook the potatoes in a large pan of
boiling, salted water until tender. Add
the beans and carrots and blanch for
1 minute. Add the asparagus and cook
for a further 30 seconds. Drain the
vegetables. Cook the quail's eggs in
boiling water for 2 minutes.

7 Arrange all the vegetables, eggs and
sauces on a serving platter. Garnish
with fresh herbs and serve with coarse
salt, for sprinkling.

COOK'S TIPS
• Stir any leftover tapenade into pasta
or spread on to warm toast.
• If you are making this dish as part of
a picnic, allow the vegetables to cool
before packing in an airtight container.
Pack the quail's eggs in the original box.

Energy 583Kcal/2408kJ; Protein 10.7g; Carbohydrate 14.6g, of which sugars 8g; Fat 54g, of which saturates 8.6g; Cholesterol 199mg; Calcium 104mg; Fibre 4.3g; Sodium 1050mg.

ROASTED PEPPERS WITH SWEET CICELY

THE SWEET ANISEED FLAVOURS OF SWEET CICELY AND FENNEL COMBINE BEAUTIFULLY WITH THE
SUCCULENT TASTES OF THE PEPPERS AND TOMATOES AND THE PIQUANCY OF CAPERS. THIS DISH CAN
BE SERVED AS A LIGHT LUNCH OR AS AN UNUSUAL FIRST COURSE FOR A DINNER PARTY.

3 Position a whole small or half
a medium tomato in each half of a
pepper cavity.

4 Sprinkle the tomatoes and peppers
with the semi-ripe sweet cicely seeds,
fennel seeds and capers and about half
the sweet cicely flowers. Drizzle the
olive oil all over.

5 Bake in the top of the oven for 1 hour.
Remove from the oven and add the rest
of the flowers.

6 Transfer to serving plates, allowing
two pepper halves per person.

7 Garnish with fresh sweet cicely
leaves and flowers, and serve with lots
of fresh crusty bread to soak up the
delicious juices.

VARIATION
If sweet cicely is not available, this
dish can also be made with a range of
different herbs, although they will all
impart a distinctive flavour. Celery
leaves, chervil and lovage are some
you might like to try.

SERVES 4

INGREDIENTS
  4 red (bell) peppers
  8 small or 4 medium tomatoes
  15ml/1 tbsp semi-ripe sweet
    cicely seeds
  15ml/1 tbsp fennel seeds
  15ml/1 tbsp capers
  8 sweet cicely flowers, newly
    opened, stems removed
  60ml/4 tbsp olive oil
For the garnish
  a few small sweet
    cicely leaves
  8 more flowers

1 Preheat the oven to 180°C/350°F/
Gas 4. Halve and deseed the red
peppers, then place the halves in
a large ovenproof dish and set aside.

2 To skin the tomatoes, cut a cross at
the base, then pour over boiling water
and leave them to stand for 30 seconds
to 1 minute. Cut them in half if they are
of medium size.

COOK'S TIP
Try adding the stems from the sweet
cicely to the water in which fruit is
stewed. They will add a delightful flavour
and reduce the need for sugar.

Energy 172Kcal/714kJ; Protein 2.5g; Carbohydrate 14.3g, of which sugars 13.8g; Fat 12g, of which saturates 1.9g; Cholesterol 0mg; Calcium 21mg; Fibre 3.8g; Sodium 16mg.

FRIED PEPPERS WITH CHEESE AND PARSLEY

TANGY FETA CHEESE GOES PARTICULARLY WELL WITH PARSLEY AND A HINT OF CHILLI, AND IS USED HERE AS A FILLING FOR SWEET, RIPE PEPPERS IN THIS TRADITIONAL BULGARIAN DISH. RED, GREEN OR YELLOW PEPPERS ARE EQUALLY DELICIOUS SERVED THIS WAY.

SERVES 2–4

INGREDIENTS

    4 red (bell) peppers
    50g/2oz/½ cup plain (all-purpose)
      flour, seasoned
    1 egg, beaten
    olive oil, for shallow frying
    cucumber and tomato salad, to serve
For the filling
    1 egg
    90g/3½oz feta cheese, finely
      crumbled
    30ml/2 tbsp chopped fresh parsley
    1 small fresh chilli, seeded and
      finely chopped

1 Slit open the peppers lengthways and scoop out the seeds using a spoon. Remove the cores, leaving the peppers in one piece.

2 Carefully open out the peppers and place under a preheated grill (broiler), skin side uppermost.

3 Cook until the skin is charred and blackened. Place the peppers on a plate, cover with clear film (plastic wrap) and leave for 10 minutes.

4 Using a sharp knife, carefully peel away the skin from the peppers.

COOK'S TIP
Feta cheese is traditionally made from ewe's or goat's milk, although it is now sometimes made from cow's milk. It keeps well if stored in an airtight jar in the refrigerator.

5 In a bowl, thoroughly mix all the filling ingredients together. Divide evenly among the four peppers.

6 Reshape the peppers to look whole. Dip them into the seasoned flour, then the egg, then the flour again.

7 Fry the peppers gently in a little olive oil for 6–8 minutes, turning once, or until golden brown and the filling is set.

8 Drain the peppers on kitchen paper before serving with a cucumber and tomato salad.

Energy 261Kcal/1081kJ; Protein 8.7g; Carbohydrate 14.7g, of which sugars 11.3g; Fat 18.9g, of which saturates 5.5g; Cholesterol 101mg; Calcium 133mg; Fibre 3.4g; Sodium 366mg.

STUFFED PROVENÇAL THYME MUSHROOMS WITH GARLIC

THYME FLOWERS ARE NOT ONLY PRETTY, BUT THEY ALSO HAVE A ZINGY, OFTEN LEMONY, FLAVOUR AND ADD REAL PUNCH TO YOUR COOKING. HERE, THEY COMBINE WITH BREADCRUMBS, THYME LEAVES AND GARLIC TO MAKE A DELICIOUS MUSHROOM STUFFING.

SERVES 8

INGREDIENTS
   8 flat or field (portobello) mushrooms
   25g/1oz/½ cup white breadcrumbs
   30ml/2 tbsp thyme leaves
   2 garlic cloves
   45ml/3 tbsp olive oil
   30ml/2 tbsp thyme flowers
   coarse salt and ground
      black pepper

1 Preheat the oven to 200°C/400°F/ Gas 6. Clean and skin the mushrooms. Remove the stalks.

2 Finely slice the stalks and set aside. Place the mushrooms cup-side up in a large ovenproof dish.

3 Blend the breadcrumbs, mushroom stalks, thyme leaves and garlic in a food processor. Add salt and pepper to taste, and 15ml/1 tbsp olive oil.

4 Pulse briefly to mix, then stir in 15ml/1 tbsp thyme flowers.

5 Divide the stuffing mixture among the mushrooms, filling each with a generous amount, and drizzle over the remaining olive oil.

6 Cook in the oven until the mushrooms are soft and the breadcrumbs lightly browned. Sprinkle over the remaining flowers just before serving.

Energy 66Kcal/274kJ; Protein 1.6g; Carbohydrate 5.1g, of which sugars 0.3g; Fat 4.5g, of which saturates 0.6g; Cholesterol 0mg; Calcium 11mg; Fibre 0.7g; Sodium 50mg.

STUFFED GARLIC MUSHROOMS WITH PROSCIUTTO AND HERBS

LARGE FIELD MUSHROOMS, WITH THEIR RICH, EARTHY FLAVOUR, ARE EXCELLENT STUFFED AND BAKED. THE STUFFING USED HERE COMBINES ONION, GARLIC, PARSLEY AND THYME WITH STRONGLY FLAVOURED WILD MUSHROOMS, AND IS SIMPLY MOUTHWATERING.

SERVES 4

INGREDIENTS
1 onion, chopped
75g/3oz/6 tbsp unsalted (sweet) butter
8 flat or field (portobello) mushrooms
15g/½oz/¼ cup dried porcini mushrooms, soaked in warm water for 20 minutes
1 garlic clove, crushed
75g/3oz/2½ cups fresh breadcrumbs
1 egg
75ml/5 tbsp chopped fresh parsley
15ml/1 tbsp chopped fresh thyme
115g/4oz prosciutto, thinly sliced
salt and ground black pepper
fresh parsley, to garnish

1 Preheat the oven to 190°C/375°F/ Gas 5. Fry the onion gently in half the butter for 6–8 minutes, or until soft but not coloured.

2 Meanwhile, break off the stems of the field mushrooms, setting the caps aside.

3 Drain the porcini mushrooms and chop these and the stems of the field mushrooms finely. Add to the onion together with the garlic and cook for a further 2–3 minutes.

4 Transfer the mixture to a bowl, add the breadcrumbs, egg, herbs and seasoning. Melt the remaining butter and brush over the mushroom caps.

5 Arrange the mushrooms on a baking sheet and spoon in the filling.

6 Bake the mushrooms in the preheated oven for 20–25 minutes, or until the filling is well browned.

7 Top each filled mushroom cap with a strip of prosciutto, garnish with fresh parsley and serve.

VARIATION
For a vegetarian version of this dish, omit the prosciutto and top the mushrooms with sun-dried tomatoes instead.

COOK'S TIPS
• These stuffed garlic mushrooms can be easily prepared in advance ready to go into the oven.
• Do not discard the porcini soaking water. Strain it, then use it for thinning sauces or for adding flavour to vegetable stock or soups.

Energy 292Kcal/1218kJ; Protein 13.4g; Carbohydrate 17.5g, of which sugars 2.4g; Fat 19.3g, of which saturates 10.7g; Cholesterol 104mg; Calcium 78mg; Fibre 3.5g; Sodium 633mg.

FALAFEL <u>WITH</u> TAHINI <u>AND</u> MINT YOGURT DIP

THESE SPICY PATTIES HAVE A CRUNCHY COATING OF SESAME SEEDS. SERVE WITH THE MINT-FLAVOURED TAHINI YOGURT DIP AND WARM PITTA BREAD AS A LIGHT LUNCH OR SUPPER DISH.

SERVES 4

INGREDIENTS
250g/9oz/1⅓ cups dried chickpeas
2 garlic cloves, crushed
1 red chilli, seeded and
  finely sliced
5ml/1 tsp ground
  coriander seeds
5ml/1 tsp ground cumin
15ml/1 tbsp chopped
  fresh mint
15ml/1 tbsp chopped
  fresh parsley
2 spring onions (scallions),
  finely chopped
1 large egg, beaten
sesame seeds,
  for coating
sunflower oil,
  for frying
salt and ground
  black pepper

For the tahini yogurt dip
  30ml/2 tbsp light tahini
  200g/7oz/scant 1 cup natural
    (plain) yogurt
  5ml/1 tsp cayenne pepper,
    plus extra for sprinkling
  15ml/1 tbsp chopped fresh mint
  1 spring onion (scallion),
    finely sliced

1 Place the chickpeas in a bowl, cover with cold water and soak overnight.

2 Drain and rinse them, then place in a pan and cover with cold water.

3 Bring to the boil and boil rapidly for 10 minutes, reduce the heat and simmer for 1½–2 hours. Drain.

4 To make the tahini yogurt dip, mix together the tahini, yogurt, cayenne pepper and mint in a small bowl. Sprinkle the spring onion and extra cayenne on top, and chill until required.

5 Combine the chickpeas with the garlic, chilli, ground spices, herbs, spring onions and seasoning, then mix in the egg.

6 Place in a food processor and blend until the mixture forms a coarse paste. If the paste seems too soft, chill it for 30 minutes.

7 Form the chilled chickpea paste into 12 patties with your hands, then roll in the sesame seeds to coat thoroughly.

8 Heat enough oil to cover the base of a frying pan. Fry the falafel for 6 minutes, turning once. Serve with the yogurt dip.

Energy 412Kcal/1725kJ; Protein 20.6g; Carbohydrate 35.2g, of which sugars 5.7g; Fat 22.2g, of which saturates 3.3g; Cholesterol 96mg; Calcium 271mg; Fibre 7.6g; Sodium 104mg.

BAKED FENNEL WITH A CRUMB CRUST

GARLIC AND PARSLEY BLEND PERFECTLY WITH THE DELICATE, ANISEED FLAVOUR OF FENNEL IN THIS TASTY GRATIN. IT GOES WELL WITH PASTA DISHES AND RISOTTOS.

SERVES 4

INGREDIENTS
    3 fennel bulbs, cut lengthways
        into quarters
    30ml/2 tbsp olive oil
    1 garlic clove, chopped
    50g/2oz/1 cup day-old wholemeal
        (whole-wheat) breadcrumbs
    30ml/2 tbsp chopped fresh flat
        leaf parsley
    salt and ground black pepper
    fennel leaves, to garnish (optional)

VARIATION
To make a cheese-topped version of this dish, simply add 60ml/4 tbsp finely grated strong-flavoured cheese, such as mature Cheddar, Red Leicester or Parmesan, to the breadcrumb mixture in step 4. Sprinkle the mixture over the fennel as described.

1 Cook the fennel in a pan of boiling salted water for 10 minutes, or until just tender.

2 Drain the fennel quarters and place them in a baking dish or roasting pan, then brush them all over with half of the olive oil.

3 Preheat the oven to 190°C/375°F/ Gas 5.

4 In a small bowl, mix together the garlic, breadcrumbs and parsley with the rest of the oil. Sprinkle the mixture evenly over the fennel, then season well with salt and pepper.

5 Bake for 30 minutes, or until the fennel is tender and the breadcrumbs are crisp and golden. Serve hot, garnished with a few fennel leaves, if you wish.

Energy 123Kcal/515kJ; Protein 3.7g; Carbohydrate 14g, of which sugars 4.3g; Fat 6.3g, of which saturates 0.8g; Cholesterol 0mg; Calcium 85mg; Fibre 6.1g; Sodium 122mg.

LEMON AND HERB RISOTTO BAKE

CHIVES AND PARSLEY COMBINE WITH THE RIND OF LEMON TO FLAVOUR THIS UNUSUAL MOZZARELLA
AND RICE DISH. IT CAN BE SERVED AS A MAIN COURSE WITH SALAD, OR AS A SATISFYING SIDE DISH.
IT'S ALSO GOOD SERVED COLD, AND PACKS WELL FOR PICNICS.

2 Cook the leek in a large pan with 45ml/3 tbsp stock, stirring over a moderate heat, until softened. Add the rice and the remaining stock.

3 Bring the liquid to the boil over a high heat, then lower the temperature to a moderate heat.

4 Cover the pan and simmer gently, stirring occasionally, for 20 minutes, or until all the liquid is absorbed.

5 Stir in the lemon rind, herbs, cheese and seasoning.

6 Spoon the mixture into the tin, cover with foil and bake for 30–35 minutes, or until lightly browned.

7 Turn the cake out and serve in slices, garnished with chopped parsley and lemon wedges.

COOK'S TIP
The best type of rice to choose for this recipe is the Italian round-grain arborio rice, but if it is not available, use pudding rice instead.

SERVES 4

INGREDIENTS
oil, for greasing
1 small leek, thinly sliced
600ml/1 pint/2½ cups chicken stock
225g/8oz/generous 1 cup risotto rice
finely grated rind of 1 lemon
30ml/2 tbsp chopped fresh chives
30ml/2 tbsp chopped fresh parsley
75g/3oz/¾ cup grated
  mozzarella cheese
salt and ground black pepper
parsley and lemon wedges,
  to garnish

1 Preheat the oven to 200°C/400°F/ Gas 6. Use a pastry brush to lightly oil the base and sides of a 21cm/8½in round, loose-bottomed cake tin (pan).

Energy 264Kcal/1103kJ; Protein 8.7g; Carbohydrate 46.5g, of which sugars 1.3g; Fat 4.5g, of which saturates 2.6g; Cholesterol 11mg; Calcium 114mg; Fibre 1.6g; Sodium 79mg.

ONION, FENNEL AND LAVENDER TARTS

FRAGRANT LAVENDER COMBINES PERFECTLY WITH THE AROMATIC FLAVOUR OF FENNEL AND MILDLY FLAVOURED SPANISH ONION. THESE UNUSUAL AND MOUTHWATERING TARTLETS MAKE AN APPEALING LIGHT SUMMER MEAL SERVED WITH A SIMPLE GREEN SALAD.

SERVES 4

INGREDIENTS
    75g/3oz/6 tbsp butter
    1 large Spanish onion, finely sliced
    1 fennel bulb, trimmed and sliced
    30ml/2 tbsp fresh lavender florets or
        15ml/1 tbsp roughly chopped dried
        culinary lavender
    2 egg yolks
    150ml/¼ pint/⅔ cup crème fraîche
    salt and ground black pepper
    fresh lavender florets, to garnish
        (optional)
For the pastry
    115g/4oz/1 cup plain (all-purpose)
        flour
    pinch of salt
    50g/2oz/¼ cup chilled butter, cut
        into cubes
    10ml/2 tsp cold water

1 To make the pastry, sift the flour and salt together. Rub the butter into the flour until the mixture resembles breadcrumbs. Stir in the water and bring the dough together to form a ball.

2 Roll the pastry out on a lightly floured surface to line four 7.5cm/3in round, loose-based flan tins (quiche pans). Prick the bases with a fork and chill. Preheat the oven to 200°C/400°F/Gas 6.

3 Melt the butter in a shallow pan and add the sliced onion and fennel and the chopped lavender. Reduce the heat to low. Cover the pan with wet greaseproof (waxed) paper and cook gently for 15 minutes, or until golden.

4 Line the pastry cases with greaseproof paper and bake blind for 5 minutes. Remove the paper, return to the oven and bake for a further 4 minutes.

5 Reduce the oven temperature to 180°C/350°F/Gas 4. Mix the egg yolks, crème fraîche and seasoning together.

6 Spoon the onion mixture into the pastry cases. Spoon the crème fraîche mixture on top and bake for 10–15 minutes, or until the mixture has set and the filling is puffed up and golden.

7 Sprinkle a little extra lavender on top, if you like, and serve warm or cold.

Energy 539Kcal/2233kJ; Protein 6.8g; Carbohydrate 30.7g, of which sugars 6.9g; Fat 44.1g, of which saturates 27.3g; Cholesterol 210mg; Calcium 116mg; Fibre 3.8g; Sodium 214mg.

LIVER PÂTÉ PIE <u>WITH</u> MUSTARD, KIRSCH <u>AND</u> PARSLEY

A PORK AND HAM PÂTÉ IS FLAVOURED WITH ONION, MUSTARD, PARSLEY AND KIRSCH IN THIS RICH AND SATISFYING PIE. DELICIOUS SERVED FOR LUNCH WITH A GLASS OF PILSNER BEER.

SERVES 10

INGREDIENTS
675g/1½lb minced
  (ground) pork
350g/12oz pork liver
350g/12oz/2 cups diced
  cooked ham
1 small onion, finely chopped
30ml/2 tbsp chopped
  fresh parsley
5ml/1 tsp German mustard
30ml/2 tbsp Kirsch
salt and ground black pepper
beaten egg, for sealing
  and glazing
25g/1oz sachet aspic jelly
250ml/8fl oz/1 cup boiling water
mustard, bread and dill pickles,
  to serve

For the pastry
  450g/1lb/4 cups plain (all-purpose)
    flour, plus extra for dusting
  pinch of salt
  275g/10oz/1¼ cups butter
  2 eggs and 1 egg yolk
  30ml/2 tbsp water

1 Preheat the oven to 200°C/400°F/
Gas 6. To make the pastry, sift the flour
and salt and rub in the butter. Beat the
eggs, egg yolk and water, add to the dry
ingredients and mix.

2 Knead the dough briefly until it is
smooth. Roll out two-thirds on a lightly
floured surface and use it to line a
10 × 25cm/4 × 10in loaf tin (pan).
Trim away any excess dough to give
a neat finish.

3 Process half the minced pork and
the liver until fairly smooth. Stir in the
remaining pork, ham, onion, parsley,
mustard, Kirsch and seasoning. Spoon
the filling into the tin, smoothing it down
and levelling the surface.

4 Roll out the remaining pastry and use
it to top the pie, sealing the edges with
some of the beaten egg. Decorate with
the pastry trimmings and glaze with the
remaining beaten egg. Using a fork,
make three or four holes in the top.

5 Bake for 40 minutes, then reduce the
oven temperature to 180°C/350°F/Gas 4
and cook for a further 1 hour. Cover
with tin foil if the top starts to brown
too much. Allow to cool in the tin.

6 Make up the aspic jelly, using the
boiling water. Stir to dissolve. When it is
cool, make a small hole near the edge
of the pie with a skewer, then pour in
the aspic through a baking-parchment
funnel. Chill for at least 2 hours before
serving the pie in slices with mustard,
bread and dill pickles.

Energy 575Kcal/2404kJ; Protein 32.9g; Carbohydrate 36g, of which sugars 1.5g; Fat 33.7g, of which saturates 18.1g; Cholesterol 273mg; Calcium 86mg; Fibre 1.5g; Sodium 676mg.

ROAST GARLIC WITH GOAT'S CHEESE, WALNUT AND HERB PÂTÉ

THE COMBINATION OF SWEET ROASTED GARLIC AND GOAT'S CHEESE IS A CLASSIC ONE. THE PÂTÉ IS PARTICULARLY GOOD MADE WITH FRESH THYME AND PARSLEY, AND THE NEW SEASON'S WALNUTS.

SERVES 4

INGREDIENTS
    4 large garlic bulbs
    4 fresh rosemary sprigs
    8 fresh thyme sprigs
    60ml/4 tbsp olive oil
    coarse salt and ground
        black pepper
For the pâté
    175g/6oz/¾ cup soft
        goat's cheese
    5ml/1 tsp finely chopped
        fresh thyme
    15ml/1 tbsp finely chopped
        fresh parsley
    50g/2oz/½ cup chopped
        shelled walnuts
    15ml/1 tbsp walnut
    oil (optional)
To serve
    4–8 slices sourdough bread
    shelled walnuts

1 Preheat the oven to 180°C/350°F/ Gas 4. Strip the papery outer skin from the garlic bulbs. Place them in an ovenproof dish large enough to hold them snugly.

2 Tuck the rosemary and thyme sprigs between the garlic bulbs, drizzle the oil over and season to taste with coarse salt and black pepper.

VARIATION
If you prefer, the pâté can also be made with other kinds of chopped nuts, such as hazelnuts and cashews.

3 Cover the garlic closely with foil and bake for 50–60 minutes, basting once. Leave to cool.

4 Preheat the grill (broiler). To make the pâté, cream the cheese with the thyme, parsley and chopped walnuts. Beat in 15ml/1 tbsp of the cooking oil from the garlic and season to taste, then transfer the pâté to a serving bowl.

5 Brush the sourdough bread with the remaining cooking oil from the garlic, then grill (broil) until toasted.

6 Drizzle the walnut oil, if using, over the pâté and grind some black pepper over it. Place a bulb of garlic on each plate and serve with the pâté and toasted bread. Serve with a few shelled walnuts and a little coarse salt.

Energy 350Kcal/1445kJ; Protein 13.1g; Carbohydrate 4.9g, of which sugars 1.2g; Fat 31g, of which saturates 10.1g; Cholesterol 41mg; Calcium 75mg; Fibre 1.5g; Sodium 265mg.

MINTED POTATO AND RED PEPPER FRITTATA

FRESH MINT TASTES WONDERFUL WITH NEW POTATOES. IN THIS ITALIAN-STYLE OMELETTE IT COMBINES WITH GARLIC, ONION AND BRIGHT RED PEPPERS TO MAKE A TEMPTING LUNCH DISH.

SERVES 3–4

INGREDIENTS
450g/1lb small new or
 salad potatoes
6 eggs
30ml/2 tbsp chopped fresh mint
30ml/2 tbsp olive oil
1 onion, chopped
2 garlic cloves, crushed
2 red (bell) peppers, seeded and
 roughly chopped
salt and ground black pepper
mint sprigs, to garnish

1 Cook the potatoes in their skins in boiling salted water until just tender. Drain, cool slightly, then slice thickly.

2 Whisk together the eggs, chopped fresh mint and seasoning in a bowl, then set aside.

3 Heat the olive oil in a large frying pan that is suitable for use under the grill (broiler).

4 Add the onion, garlic, peppers and potatoes to the pan and cook, stirring occasionally, for 5 minutes.

5 Pour the egg mixture over the vegetables in the frying pan and stir gently with a wooden spoon to ensure the egg is evenly distributed.

6 Push the mixture towards the centre of the pan as it cooks to allow the liquid egg to run on to the base and cook. Meanwhile preheat the grill.

7 When the frittata is lightly set, place the frying pan under the hot grill for 2–3 minutes until the top of the frittata is a light golden brown colour.

8 Serve the frittata hot or cold, cut into wedges. Garnish with extra sprigs of mint.

Energy 267Kcal/1115kJ; Protein 12.2g; Carbohydrate 23.7g, of which sugars 6.8g; Fat 14.5g, of which saturates 3.3g; Cholesterol 285mg; Calcium 57mg; Fibre 2.5g; Sodium 121mg.

VERMICELLI WITH HERB FRITTATA

HERE, ROASTED RED PEPPER, BASIL, PARSLEY, GARLIC AND ONION CREATE A FULL AND FRESH FLAVOUR.
IT MAKES A SUBSTANTIAL AND TASTY LUNCHEON DISH AND IS ALSO EXCELLENT FOR PICNICS.

SERVES 4–6

INGREDIENTS

50g/2oz dried vermicelli
6 eggs
60ml/4 tbsp double (heavy) cream
1 handful fresh basil
  leaves, chopped
1 handful fresh flat leaf
  parsley, chopped
75g/3oz/1 cup freshly grated
  Parmesan cheese
25g/1oz/2 tbsp butter
15ml/1 tbsp olive oil
1 onion, finely sliced
3 large pieces bottled roasted red
  (bell) pepper, drained, rinsed,
  dried and cut into strips
1 garlic clove, crushed
salt and ground black pepper
rocket (arugula) leaves, to serve

1 Preheat the oven to 190°C/375°F/
Gas 5. Cook the pasta in a pan
of boiling salted water for 8 minutes.

2 Meanwhile, break the eggs into a bowl
and add the cream and herbs. Whisk in
about two-thirds of the grated Parmesan
and add salt and pepper to taste.

3 Drain the pasta well and allow to cool;
snip it into short lengths with scissors.
Add to the egg mixture and whisk again.

4 Melt the butter in the oil in a large,
ovenproof, non-stick frying pan. Add
the onion and cook gently, stirring
frequently, until softened. Add the
pepper and garlic.

5 Pour the egg and pasta mixture into
the pan and stir well. Cook over a low
to medium heat, without stirring, for
3–5 minutes, or until the frittata is just
set underneath.

6 Sprinkle over the remaining Parmesan
and bake in the oven for 5 minutes or
until set.

7 Before serving, leave to stand for at
least 5 minutes. Cut into wedges and
serve warm or cold, accompanied by
rocket leaves.

Energy 222Kcal/923kJ; Protein 12.6g; Carbohydrate 9.3g, of which sugars 2.5g; Fat 15.2g, of which saturates 6.6g; Cholesterol 212mg; Calcium 203mg; Fibre 1g; Sodium 236mg.

TAGLIATELLE <u>WITH</u> HERBS

IN SUMMER, WHEN HERBS ARE PLENTIFUL, ENJOY THIS SIMPLE PASTA DISH THAT IS SO FULL OF FLAVOUR. ROSEMARY, PARSLEY, MINT, SAGE, BASIL, BAY AND GARLIC ARE ALL HERE, MERGING TOGETHER TO CREATE A LIGHT AND TASTY MEAL.

SERVES 6

INGREDIENTS
3 rosemary sprigs
1 small handful fresh
  flat leaf parsley
5–6 fresh mint leaves
5–6 fresh sage leaves
8–10 large fresh basil leaves
30ml/2 tbsp extra virgin olive oil
50g/2oz/¼ cup butter
1 shallot, finely chopped
2 garlic cloves, finely chopped
pinch of chilli powder, to taste
400g/14oz fresh egg tagliatelle
1 bay leaf
120ml/4fl oz/½ cup dry white wine
90–120ml/6–8 tbsp vegetable stock
salt and ground black pepper
basil leaves, to garnish

1 Strip the rosemary and parsley leaves from their stalks and chop them together with the other fresh herbs.

2 Heat the oil and half the butter in a large pan. Add the shallot, garlic and chilli powder. Cook on a very low heat, stirring frequently, for 2–3 minutes.

3 Cook the fresh pasta in a large pan of boiling salted water according to the packet instructions.

4 Add the chopped herbs and the bay leaf to the shallot mixture and stir for 2–3 minutes, then add the wine and increase the heat. Boil rapidly for 1–2 minutes, or until reduced. Lower the heat, add the stock and simmer gently for 1–2 minutes. Season.

5 Drain the pasta and add it to the herb mixture. Toss well to mix and remove and discard the bay leaf.

6 Put the remaining butter in a warmed large bowl, tip the dressed pasta into it and toss well to mix. Serve immediately, garnished with basil.

Energy 289Kcal/1223kJ; Protein 8.5g; Carbohydrate 50.7g, of which sugars 3.2g; Fat 5.8g, of which saturates 2.5g; Cholesterol 9mg; Calcium 47mg; Fibre 2.7g; Sodium 33mg.

LINGUINE WITH ROCKET

THIS IS A FIRST COURSE THAT YOU WILL FIND IN MANY A FASHIONABLE RESTAURANT IN ITALY. THE DISTINCTIVE PEPPERY FLAVOUR OF ROCKET IS WELL DEFINED IN THIS QUICK AND EASY-TO-PREPARE DISH, WHICH COULD ALSO BE MADE WITH SPAGHETTI.

SERVES 4

INGREDIENTS

350g/12oz fresh or dried linguine
120ml/4fl oz/½ cup extra virgin olive oil
150g/5oz rocket (arugula)
75g/3oz/1 cup freshly grated
  Parmesan cheese
salt and ground black pepper

1 Cook the pasta in a large pan of boiling salted water, then drain.

2 Heat about 60ml/4 tbsp of the olive oil in the pasta pan, then add the drained pasta, then the rocket. Toss over a medium to high heat for 1–2 minutes or until the rocket is just wilted, then remove from the heat.

3 Tip the pasta and rocket into a warmed large bowl. Add half the freshly grated Parmesan and the remaining olive oil. Add a little salt and black pepper to taste.

4 Toss the mixture quickly to mix. Serve immediately, sprinkled with the remaining Parmesan.

COOK'S TIP
Buy rocket by the bunch from the greengrocer. The type sold in small cellophane packets in supermarkets is very expensive for this kind of dish. Always check when buying rocket that all the leaves are bright green. In hot weather, rocket quickly turns yellow.

Energy 632Kcal/2647kJ; Protein 28.8g; Carbohydrate 71.1g, of which sugars 8.8g; Fat 27.6g, of which saturates 6.8g; Cholesterol 19mg; Calcium 910mg; Fibre 10.7g; Sodium 753mg

PENNE WITH ROCKET AND MOZZARELLA

LIKE A WARM SALAD, THIS PASTA DISH IS VERY QUICK AND EASY TO MAKE — PERFECT FOR AN AL FRESCO SUMMER LUNCH. CRISP ROCKET, CREAMY MOZZARELLA AND GOOD-QUALITY, FRESH AND RIPE TOMATOES PROVIDE THE ESSENTIAL FLAVOURINGS HERE.

SERVES 4

INGREDIENTS
400g/14oz/3½ cups fresh or
   dried penne
6 ripe plum tomatoes,
   peeled, seeded and diced
2 × 150g/5oz packets mozzarella
   cheese, drained and diced
2 large handfuls of
   rocket (arugula), total
   weight about 150g/5oz
75ml/5 tbsp extra virgin
   olive oil
salt and ground
   black pepper

VARIATION
For a change, a combination of fresh,
torn basil and rocket leaves also works
very well.

1 Cook the fresh or dried pasta in
a large pan of boiling salted water
according to the packet instructions
until it is *al dente*.

2 Meanwhile, put the diced tomatoes,
mozzarella, rocket and olive oil into a
large bowl with a little salt and ground
black pepper to taste and toss
everything together well to mix.

3 Drain the cooked pasta and tip it into
the bowl with the other ingredients.
Toss together well to mix thoroughly
and serve immediately.

COOK'S TIP
To keep the pasta shapes separate, stir
it frequently during cooking. This is
especially important at the start of the
cooking process.

FUSILLI WITH BASIL AND PEPPERS

CHARGRILLED PEPPERS HAVE A WONDERFUL, SMOKY FLAVOUR THAT MARRIES WELL WITH GARLIC, OLIVES, BASIL AND TOMATOES IN THIS DELECTABLE PASTA DISH.

SERVES 4

INGREDIENTS
3 large (bell) peppers (red,
   yellow and orange)
350g/12oz/3 cups fresh or
   dried fusilli
60ml/4 tbsp extra virgin
   olive oil
1–2 garlic cloves, to taste,
   finely chopped
4 ripe plum tomatoes,
   peeled, seeded and diced
50g/2oz/½ cup pitted black olives,
   halved or quartered lengthways
1 handful of fresh basil leaves
salt and ground black pepper

VARIATION
Add a few slivers of bottled or canned
anchovy fillets at step 5.

1 Put the whole peppers under a hot
grill (broiler) and grill (broil) for about
10 minutes, turning frequently until
charred on all sides.

2 Put the hot peppers in a plastic bag,
seal the bag and set aside until the
peppers are cold.

3 Remove the peppers from the bag
and hold them, one at a time, under
cold running water.

4 Peel off the charred skins with your
fingers, split the peppers open and pull
out the cores. Rub off all the seeds
under the running water, then pat the
peppers dry on kitchen paper.

5 Cook the pasta in salted boiling water
until *al dente*.

6 Meanwhile, thinly slice the peppers
and place them in a large bowl with
the olive oil, garlic, tomatoes, olives
and basil. Season with salt and pepper
to taste.

7 Drain the cooked pasta and tip it into
the bowl with the other ingredients.
Toss together well to mix thoroughly
and serve immediately.

Energy 693Kcal/2913kJ; Protein 28.1g; Carbohydrate 79.4g, of which sugars 8.5g; Fat 31.5g, of which saturates 12.7g; Cholesterol 44mg; Calcium 371mg; Fibre 5.2g; Sodium 365mg.
Energy 476Kcal/2007kJ; Protein 12.8g; Carbohydrate 77.5g, of which sugars 15.2g; Fat 14.9g, of which saturates 2.2g; Cholesterol 0mg; Calcium 49mg; Fibre 6.3g; Sodium 299mg.

ORECCHIETTE <u>WITH</u> ROCKET <u>AND</u> OREGANO

GARLIC AND TOMATOES ARE FREQUENT PARTNERS IN ITALIAN COOKING. IN THIS HEARTY DISH FROM
PUGLIA IN SOUTH-EAST ITALY, ROCKET ADDS A PEPPERY DEFINITION TO A PASTA SAUCE.

SERVES 4–6

INGREDIENTS

45ml/3 tbsp olive oil
1 small onion, finely chopped
300g/11oz canned chopped
  Italian plum tomatoes or passata
  (bottled strained tomatoes)
2.5ml/½ tsp dried oregano
pinch of chilli powder or
  cayenne pepper
30ml/2 tbsp red or white wine
2 potatoes, total weight about
  200g/7oz, diced
300g/11oz/2¾ cups dried orecchiette
2 garlic cloves, finely chopped
150g/5oz rocket (arugula) leaves,
  stalks removed
90g/3½oz/scant ½ cup ricotta cheese
salt and ground black pepper
freshly grated Pecorino cheese,
  to serve

1 Heat 15ml/1 tbsp of the olive oil in a medium pan, add half the finely chopped onion and cook gently, stirring frequently, for about 5 minutes, or until softened. Add the canned tomatoes or passata, oregano and chilli powder or cayenne pepper to the onion. Pour the wine over, and add a little salt and pepper to taste. Cover the pan and simmer for about 15 minutes, stirring the mixture occasionally.

2 Bring a large pan of salted water to the boil. Add the potatoes and pasta. Stir well and let the water return to the boil. Lower the heat and simmer for 15 minutes, or according to the instructions on the packet, until the pasta is cooked.

3 Heat the remaining oil in a large pan, add the rest of the onion and the garlic and fry for 2–3 minutes, stirring occasionally. Add the rocket, toss over the heat for about 2 minutes, or until wilted, then stir in the tomato sauce and the ricotta. Mix well.

4 Drain the pasta and potatoes, add them both to the pan of sauce and toss to mix. Taste the sauce for seasoning and then serve immediately in warmed bowls, with grated Pecorino offered separately.

Energy 269Kcal/1133kJ; Protein 9.3g; Carbohydrate 42.2g, of which sugars 5.1g; Fat 8g, of which saturates 1.8g; Cholesterol 4mg; Calcium 80mg; Fibre 2.9g; Sodium 113mg.

PASTA SALAD <u>WITH</u> PRAWNS <u>AND</u> HERBS

THIS PRAWN AND PASTA SALAD IS ENLIVENED WITH A LEMON, BASIL AND CORIANDER DRESSING, SPIKED WITH A LITTLE RED CHILLI. IT MAKES A DELICIOUS LUNCH SERVED WITH WARM CIABATTA BREAD.

SERVES 4

INGREDIENTS

225g/8oz/2 cups dried farfalle
juice of ½ lemon
1 small fresh red chilli, seeded and
  very finely chopped
60ml/4 tbsp chopped fresh basil
30ml/2 tbsp chopped fresh
  coriander (cilantro)
60ml/4 tbsp extra virgin olive oil
15ml/1 tbsp mayonnaise
250g/9oz/1½ cups peeled cooked
  prawns (shrimp)
1 avocado
salt and ground black pepper

1 Cook the pasta in a large pan of boiling salted water until *al dente*.

2 Meanwhile, put the lemon juice and chilli in a bowl with half the basil and coriander, and salt and pepper to taste. Whisk well to mix, then whisk in the oil and mayonnaise until thick.

3 Add the prawns and gently stir to coat them with the dressing.

4 Drain the pasta into a colander, and rinse under cold running water until cold. Leave to drain and dry, shaking the colander occasionally.

5 Halve, stone (pit) and peel the avocado, then cut the flesh into neat dice. Add to the prawns and dressing with the pasta, toss to mix and taste for seasoning. Serve immediately, sprinkled with the remaining basil and coriander.

COOK'S TIP
This pasta salad can be made several hours ahead of time, without the avocado. Cover the bowl with clear film and chill. Prepare the avocado and add it to the salad just before serving, or it will discolour.

Energy 416Kcal/1743kJ; Protein 18.6g; Carbohydrate 42.5g, of which sugars 2.3g; Fat 20.2g, of which saturates 3.2g; Cholesterol 125mg; Calcium 87mg; Fibre 3g; Sodium 142mg.

PANSOTTI WITH HERBS AND CHEESE

HERB-FLAVOURED PASTA ENCLOSES A FILLING OF RICOTTA CHEESE, BASIL, PARSLEY, MARJORAM AND GARLIC. THE PANSOTTI ARE THEN SERVED WITH A RICH AND SATISFYING WALNUT SAUCE — HEAVENLY.

SERVES 6–8

INGREDIENTS

For the herb-flavoured pasta
  300g/11oz/2¾ cups flour
  3 eggs
  5ml/1 tsp salt
  3 small handfuls of fresh herbs,
    finely chopped
  flour, for dusting
  50g/2oz/¼ cup butter
  freshly grated Parmesan cheese,
    to serve

For the filling
  250g/9oz/generous 1 cup ricotta cheese
  150g/5oz/1⅔ cups freshly grated
    Parmesan cheese
  1 large handful fresh basil leaves,
    finely chopped
  1 large handful fresh flat leaf parsley,
    finely chopped
  a few sprigs fresh marjoram or
    oregano, leaves removed and
    finely chopped
  1 garlic clove, crushed
  1 small egg
  salt and ground black pepper

For the sauce
  90g/3½oz/½ cup shelled walnuts
  1 garlic clove
  60ml/4 tbsp extra virgin olive oil
  120ml/4fl oz/½ cup double
    (heavy) cream

1 Mound the flour on the work surface and make a deep well in the centre.

2 Crack the eggs into the well, then add the salt and herbs. With a table knife, mix the eggs, salt and herbs together, then start incorporating the flour from the sides of the well.

3 As soon as the mixture is no longer liquid dip your fingers in the flour and use them to work the ingredients into a sticky dough. Press the dough into a ball and knead it as you would bread, for 10 minutes until smooth and elastic. Wrap in clear film and leave to rest at room temperature for 20 minutes.

4 To make the filling, put the ricotta, Parmesan, herbs, garlic and egg in a bowl with salt and pepper to taste and beat well to mix.

5 To make the sauce, put the walnuts, garlic clove and olive oil in a food processor and process to a paste, adding up to 120ml/4fl oz/½ cup warm water through the feeder tube to lighten the consistency.

6 Spoon the mixture into a large bowl and add the cream. Beat well to mix, then add salt and pepper to taste.

7 Using a pasta machine, roll out one-quarter of the pasta into a 90cm/36in strip.

8 Cut the strip with a sharp knife into two 45cm/18in lengths (you can do this during rolling if the strip gets too long to manage).

9 Using a 5cm/2in square ravioli cutter, cut eight or nine squares from one of the pasta strips. Using a teaspoon, put a mound of filling in the centre of each square.

10 Brush a little water around the edge of each square, then fold the square diagonally in half over the filling to make a triangular shape. Press the edges gently to seal.

11 Spread out the pansotti on clean, floured dish towels, sprinkle lightly with flour and leave to dry. Repeat the process with the remaining dough to make 64–80 pansotti altogether.

12 Cook the pansotti in a large pan of salted boiling water for 4–5 minutes. Meanwhile, put the walnut sauce in a large, warmed bowl and add a ladleful of the pasta cooking water to thin it down. Melt the butter in a small pan until sizzling.

13 Drain the pansotti and tip them into the bowl of walnut sauce. Drizzle the butter over them, toss well, then sprinkle with Parmesan.

14 Alternatively, toss the pansotti in the melted butter, spoon into warmed individual bowls and drizzle over the sauce. Serve immediately, with more Parmesan offered separately.

Energy 541Kcal/2249kJ; Protein 20.8g; Carbohydrate 31.1g, of which sugars 2.4g; Fat 38.4g, of which saturates 16g; Cholesterol 155mg; Calcium 360mg; Fibre 1.9g; Sodium 421mg.

Fish and Shellfish

There are so many ways to complement or contrast the delicate taste of fish using fresh herbs. Try sealing in the flavours by baking "en papillote", for example. Gently enhance the flavour of grilled fish by adding rosemary or thyme and garlic, or add fragrance with a melting herb butter. Herby salsas, sauces and crispy crusts are combined with baked, poached, grilled and pan-fried fish to create a taste sensation.

Above *Fillets of Sea Bream with Sorrel in Filo Pastry*

Left *Oven-baked Salt Cod with Mediterranean Herbs*

PAN-FRIED COD WITH CREAMY VERMOUTH AND HERB SAUCE

Chunky cod is teamed with a quick pan sauce of vermouth, creamy goat's cheese, parsley and chervil. Grilled plum tomatoes make the perfect accompaniment.

SERVES 4

INGREDIENTS

4 pieces of cod fillet, about
  150g/5oz each, skinned
30ml/2 tbsp olive oil
4 spring onions (scallions), chopped
150ml/¼ pint/⅔ cup dry vermouth,
  preferably Noilly Prat
300ml/½ pint/1¼ cups fish stock
45ml/3 tbsp crème fraîche or
  double (heavy) cream
65g/2½oz goat's cheese, rind
  removed, and chopped
30ml/2 tbsp chopped fresh parsley
15ml/1 tbsp chopped fresh chervil
salt and ground black pepper
flat leaf parsley, to garnish
grilled plum tomatoes, to serve

1 Remove any stray bones from the cod fillets. Rinse the fish under cold running water and pat dry with kitchen paper. Place on a plate and season well.

COOK'S TIP
The cooking time may change according to the thickness of the fish fillets.

2 Heat a non-stick frying pan, then add 15ml/1 tbsp of the oil, swirling it around to coat the bottom. Add the pieces of cod and cook, without turning or moving them, for 4 minutes, or until nicely caramelized.

3 Turn each piece over and cook the other side for a further 3 minutes, or until just firm. Remove it to a serving plate and keep hot.

4 Heat the remaining oil and stir-fry the spring onions for 1 minute. Add the vermouth and cook until reduced by half. Add the stock and cook again until reduced by half.

5 Stir in the crème fraîche or cream and goat's cheese and simmer for 3 minutes. Add salt and pepper, stir in the herbs and spoon over the fish. Garnish with parsley and serve with grilled tomatoes.

VARIATION
Instead of cod you could use salmon, haddock or plaice.

Energy 307Kcal/1280kJ; Protein 31.4g; Carbohydrate 1.9g, of which sugars 1.8g; Fat 15.3g, of which saturates 6.9g; Cholesterol 97mg; Calcium 48mg; Fibre 0.2g; Sodium 195mg.

BAKED COD <small>WITH</small> HORSERADISH SAUCE <small>AND</small> PARSLEY

FISH KEEPS MOIST WHEN BAKED IN A SAUCE. IN THIS UKRAINIAN RECIPE, A CREAMY HORSERADISH SAUCE IS SERVED ALONGSIDE, FOR ADDED FLAVOUR.

SERVES 4

INGREDIENTS
4 thick cod fillets
  or steaks
15ml/1 tbsp lemon juice
25g/1oz/2 tbsp butter
25g/1oz/¼ cup plain
  (all-purpose) flour, sifted
150ml/¼pint/⅔ cup milk
150ml/¼pint/⅔ cup fish stock
salt and ground
  black pepper
sprigs of flat leaf parsley,
  to garnish
potato wedges and fried
  sliced leeks, to serve
For the horseradish sauce
30ml/2 tbsp tomato
  purée (paste)
30ml/2 tbsp grated
  fresh horseradish
150ml/¼pint/⅔ cup sour cream

1 Preheat the oven to 180°C/350°F/ Gas 4.

2 Place the fish in a buttered ovenproof dish in a single layer. Sprinkle with lemon juice.

3 Melt the butter in a small, heavy pan. Stir in the flour and mix thoroughly to form a paste.

4 Cook for 3–4 minutes, or until the mixture is lightly golden. Stir to stop the flour sticking to the pan. Remove from the heat.

5 Gradually whisk the milk, and then the fish stock, into the flour mixture. Season with salt and ground black pepper. Bring to the boil, stirring, and simmer for 3 minutes, still stirring.

6 Pour the sauce over the fish and bake for 20–25 minutes, depending on the thickness of the fish. Check by inserting a knife into the thickest part: the flesh should be opaque.

7 For the horseradish sauce, blend the tomato purée and horseradish with the sour cream in a small pan. Slowly bring to the boil, stirring, then simmer for 1 minute.

8 Pour the sauce into a serving bowl and serve alongside the baked fish. Serve the fish immediately. Garnish with the parsley sprigs and serve with potato wedges and fried sliced leeks.

Energy 292Kcal/1219kJ; Protein 31.2g; Carbohydrate 9.5g, of which sugars 4.7g; Fat 14.6g, of which saturates 8.5g; Cholesterol 107mg; Calcium 131mg; Fibre 1g; Sodium 182mg.

OVEN-BAKED SALT COD WITH MEDITERRANEAN HERBS

THIS WARMING, COLOURFUL DISH COMBINES THE MEATY FLESH OF SALT COD WITH THE ROBUST FLAVOURS OF THE MEDITERRANEAN: TOMATOES, GARLIC, OLIVES AND PLENTY OF FRESH HERBS.

SERVES 4

INGREDIENTS
675g/1½lb salt cod
800g/1¾lb potatoes, cut into wedges
1 large onion, finely chopped
2 or 3 garlic cloves, chopped
leaves from 1 fresh rosemary sprig
30ml/2 tbsp chopped fresh parsley
120ml/4fl oz/½ cup olive oil
400g/14oz can chopped tomatoes
15ml/1 tbsp tomato purée (paste)
300ml/½ pint/1¼ cups hot water
5ml/1 tsp dried oregano
12 black olives
ground black pepper

1 Soak the cod in cold water overnight, changing the water as often as possible. The cod does not have to be skinned for this dish, but you may prefer to remove the skin. You should remove any obvious fins or bones.

2 After soaking, drain the cod and cut it into 7cm/2¾in squares.

3 Preheat the oven to 180°C/350°F/Gas 4. Mix the potatoes, onion, garlic, rosemary and parsley in a large roasting pan with plenty of black pepper. Add the olive oil and toss until coated.

4 Arrange the pieces of cod between the coated vegetables and spread the tomatoes over the surface.

5 Stir the tomato purée into the hot water until dissolved, then pour over the contents of the pan. Sprinkle the oregano on top. Bake for 1 hour, basting occasionally with the pan juices.

6 Remove the roasting pan from the oven, sprinkle the olives on top, and then cook for 30 minutes more, adding a little more hot water if the mixture seems to be drying out. Garnish with fresh parsley. Serve hot or cold.

COOK'S TIP
Salt cod can often be bought from Italian and Spanish groceries, as well as from Greek food stores. It is often sold in small squares, ready for soaking and draining. If you buy it in one piece, cut it into 7cm/2¾in squares; it will shrink slightly with cooking so it is rarely used in smaller pieces than this. Larger chunks may take longer to cook.

Energy 624Kcal/2,624kJ; Protein 61g; Carbohydrate 45.6g, of which sugars 12.9g; Fat 23.3g, of which saturates 3.5g; Cholesterol 100mg; Calcium 98mg; Fibre 4.8g; Sodium 918mg.

GRILLED SWORDFISH SKEWERS <u>WITH</u> GARLIC <u>AND</u> OREGANO

DRIED OREGANO HAS A DISTINCTIVE FLAVOUR AND IT IS THE PERFECT PARTNER TO CRUNCHY ONION, JUICY PEPPER AND TENDER FRESH SWORDFISH IN THESE SIMPLE SKEWERS.

SERVES 4

INGREDIENTS
    2 red onions, quartered
    2 red or green (bell) peppers,
        quartered and seeded
    20–24 thick cubes of swordfish,
        675–800g/1½–1¾lb in total
    75ml/5 tbsp extra virgin olive oil
    1 garlic clove, crushed
    large pinch of dried oregano
    salt and ground black pepper
    lemon wedges, to garnish

1 Carefully separate the onion quarters in pieces, each composed of two or three layers.

2 Slice each pepper quarter in half widthways, or into thirds if you have very large peppers.

3 Construct the skewers by threading five or six pieces of swordfish on to each of four long metal skewers, alternating with pieces of the pepper and onion.

4 Lay the skewers across a grill (broiler) pan or roasting tray and set aside while you make the basting sauce.

5 Whisk the olive oil, crushed garlic and oregano in a bowl. Add salt and pepper, and whisk again. Brush the skewers generously on all sides with the basting sauce.

6 Preheat the grill to the highest setting, or prepare a barbecue. Slide the grill pan or roasting tray underneath the grill or transfer the skewers to the barbecue, making sure that they are not too close to the heat and that the heat is evenly distributed throughout.

7 Cook for 8–10 minutes, turning the skewers several times, until the fish is cooked and the peppers and onions have begun to scorch around the edges.

8 Every time you turn the skewers, brush them with the basting sauce to increase the flavours.

9 Serve immediately, garnished with wedges of lemon and a salad of cucumber, red onion and fresh olives.

COOK'S TIP
Many fishmongers will prepare the swordfish for you. But if you prefer to do this yourself, or you are buying the swordfish whole, you will need approximately 800g/1¾lb swordfish. The cubes should be fairly big – about 5cm/2in square, as they shrink in size as they are cooking. Larger cubes may need a longer cooking time.

Energy 363Kcal/1,511kJ; Protein 32.2g; Carbohydrate 11.5g, of which sugars 9.6g; Fat 21.2g, of which saturates 3.6g; Cholesterol 69mg; Calcium 33mg; Fibre 2.5g; Sodium 225mg.

GRILLED RED MULLET <u>WITH</u> BAY LEAVES

WHOLE RED MULLET ARE VERY SIMPLE TO COOK ON A BARBECUE OR UNDER A GRILL, AND THE SUCCULENT FLESH TASTES FABULOUS WHEN IT IS SUBTLY FLAVOURED WITH BAY LEAVES AND A GENEROUS DRIBBLE OF TANGY DRESSING INSTEAD OF A MARINADE.

3 To make the dressing, heat the olive oil in a small pan and fry the chopped garlic with the dried chilli.

4 Add the lemon juice and strain the dressing into a small jug (pitcher). Add the parsley and stir to combine.

5 Serve the mullet on warmed plates, drizzled with the dressing.

COOK'S TIPS
• Nicknamed the woodcock of the sea, red mullet are one of the fish that are classically cooked uncleaned to give them extra flavour. In this recipe, however, the fish are cleaned and herbs are used to add extra flavour to the fish.
• If cooking on a barbecue, light the barbecue well in advance. Before cooking, the charcoal or wood should be grey, with no flames.

SERVES 4

INGREDIENTS
   4 red mullet or snapper, about
      225–275g/8–10oz each, cleaned
      and descaled if cooking under a
      grill (broiler)
   olive oil, for brushing
   fresh herb sprigs, such as fennel,
      dill, parsley, or thyme
   2–3 dozen fresh or dried bay leaves
For the dressing
   90ml/6 tbsp olive oil
   6 garlic cloves, finely chopped
   ½ dried chilli, seeded and chopped
   juice of ½ lemon
   15ml/1 tbsp parsley

COOK'S TIP
If you are cooking on the barbecue, the fish do not need to be scaled.

1 Prepare the barbecue or preheat the grill (broiler) with the shelf 15cm/6in from the heat source.

2 Brush each fish with oil and stuff the cavities with the herb sprigs. Brush the grill pan with oil and lay bay leaves across the cooking rack. Place the fish on top and cook for 15–20 minutes until cooked through, turning once.

Energy 307Kcal/1279kJ; Protein 25.4g; Carbohydrate 2.4g, of which sugars 0.5g; Fat 22g, of which saturates 2.4g; Cholesterol 0mg; Calcium 118mg; Fibre 1.1g; Sodium 130mg.

GRILLED RED MULLET WITH ROSEMARY

THIS RECIPE IS VERY QUICK AND SIMPLE — THE TASTE OF GRILLED RED MULLET IS SO GOOD IN ITSELF THAT IT NEEDS VERY LITTLE TO BRING OUT THE FLAVOUR: FRESH GARLIC, LEMON AND JUST A HINT OF ROSEMARY ARE ALL THAT ARE NEEDED.

SERVES 4

INGREDIENTS

4 red mullet or snapper, about
    275g/10oz each, cleaned
4 garlic cloves, cut lengthways
    into thin slivers
75ml/5 tbsp olive oil
30ml/2 tbsp balsamic vinegar
10ml/2 tsp very finely chopped fresh
    rosemary or 5ml/1 tsp dried
ground black pepper
fresh rosemary sprigs and lemon
    wedges, to garnish
coarse salt, to serve

COOK'S TIP
Red mullet are extra delicious cooked on the barbecue. If possible, enclose them in a basket grill so that they are easy to turn over.

1 Cut three diagonal slits in both sides of each fish with a sharp kitchen knife. Push the garlic slivers into the slits in the fish.

2 Place the fish in a single layer in a shallow dish. Make a marinade by whisking the olive oil, balsamic vinegar and rosemary with ground black pepper to taste.

3 Pour the liquid over the fish, cover with clear film (plastic wrap) and leave to marinate in the refrigerator for at least 1 hour. Grill (broil) for 5–6 minutes on each side, turning once and brushing with the marinade.

4 Serve hot, sprinkled with coarse salt and garnished with fresh rosemary sprigs and lemon wedges.

Energy 297Kcal/1237kJ; Protein 27.8g; Carbohydrate 2.4g, of which sugars 0.5g; Fat 19.8g, of which saturates 2g; Cholesterol 0mg; Calcium 127mg; Fibre 1.1g; Sodium 142mg.

BAKED TUNA WITH A CORIANDER CRUST

FRESH TUNA IS VERY MEATY AND FILLING AND TASTES DELICIOUS WHEN IT IS ACCOMPANIED BY A LIGHT SALSA OF MANGO AND LIME WITH JUST A DASH OF CHILLI. TOPPING THE FISH WITH A FRESH CORIANDER AND LEMON CRUST ADDS A TASTY CRISPNESS.

2 Mix together the lemon rind, black peppercorns, chopped onion and fresh coriander in a mortar and pestle to make a coarse paste.

3 Spread the paste on to one side of each tuna steak, pressing on well to ensure it sticks.

SERVES 4

INGREDIENTS

   finely grated rind of 1 lemon
   5ml/1 tsp black peppercorns
   ½ small onion, finely chopped
   30ml/2 tbsp chopped fresh
     coriander (cilantro)
   4 fresh tuna steaks, about
     175g/6oz each
   120ml/4fl oz/½ cup olive oil
For the salsa
   1 mango
   finely grated rind and juice
     of 1 lime
   ½ red chilli, deseeded
     and chopped

1 To make the mango salsa, peel the mango, remove the stone (pit) and chop the flesh into small pieces. Mix the mango flesh, lime rind and juice, and chilli in a bowl and leave to marinate for at least 1 hour.

4 Heat the olive oil in a heavy frying pan until it begins to smoke. Add the tuna, paste-side down, and fry until a crust forms. Lower the heat and turn the steaks to cook for 1 minute more.

5 Pat off any excess oil on to absorbent kitchen paper, and serve with the mango salsa.

Energy 264Kcal/1112kJ; Protein 42.1g; Carbohydrate 5.6g, of which sugars 5.5g; Fat 8.3g, of which saturates 2.2g; Cholesterol 49mg; Calcium 58mg; Fibre 1.6g; Sodium 87mg.

SARDINES WITH WARM HERB SALSA

PLAIN GRILLING OR COOKING ON A BARBECUE ARE THE BEST WAYS TO COOK FRESH SARDINES. SERVED WITH THIS LUSCIOUS SALSA OF PARSLEY, CHIVES AND BASIL, THE ONLY OTHER ESSENTIAL INGREDIENT IS FRESH, CRUSTY BREAD, TO MOP UP THE TASTY JUICES.

SERVES 4

INGREDIENTS
    12–16 fresh sardines
    oil for brushing
    juice of 1 lemon
    crusty bread, to serve
For the salsa
    15ml/1 tbsp butter
    4 spring onions
      (scallions), chopped
    1 garlic clove, finely chopped
    rind of 1 lemon
    30ml/2 tbsp finely chopped
      fresh parsley
    30ml/2 tbsp finely chopped
      fresh chives
    30ml/2 tbsp finely chopped
      fresh basil
    30ml/2 tbsp green olive paste
    10ml/2 tsp balsamic vinegar
    salt and ground
      black pepper

3 Add the lemon rind and remaining salsa ingredients to the onions and garlic in the pan and keep warm, stirring occasionally. Do not allow the mixture to boil.

4 Brush the sardines lightly with oil and sprinkle with lemon juice and seasoning. Cook for about 2 minutes on each side, on a barbecue or under a moderate grill. Serve with the salsa and bread.

1 To clean the sardines, use a pair of small kitchen scissors to slit the fish along the belly and pull out the innards. Wipe the fish with kitchen paper, and then arrange on a grill (broiler) rack.

2 To make the salsa, melt the butter in a small pan and gently sauté the spring onions and garlic for about 2 minutes, shaking the pan occasionally, until softened but not browned.

COOK'S TIP
It is important to remove the innards as soon as possible, or they will start to taint the surrounding flesh.

Energy 194Kcal/806kJ; Protein 20g; Carbohydrate 0.7g, of which sugars 0.6g; Fat 12.3g, of which saturates 4.4g; Cholesterol 8mg; Calcium 131mg; Fibre 1.1g; Sodium 359mg.

SEA BASS IN A SALT CRUST WITH HERBS

BAKING FISH IN A CRUST OF SEA SALT KEEPS IN THE FLAVOURS, ENHANCING THE NATURAL TASTE OF THE FISH AND THE HERBS THAT ARE STUFFED IN ITS CAVITY. ANY FIRM FISH CAN BE COOKED WITH A SALT CRUST. BREAK IT OPEN AT THE TABLE TO RELEASE THE GLORIOUS AROMA.

SERVES 4

INGREDIENTS
    1 sea bass, about 1kg/2¼lb,
      cleaned and scaled
    1 sprig fresh fennel
    1 sprig fresh rosemary
    1 sprig fresh thyme
    2kg/4½lb coarse sea salt
    mixed peppercorns
    seaweed or samphire, blanched,
      to garnish
    lemon slices,
      to serve

1 Preheat the oven to 240°C/475°F/ Gas 9. Make sure that you leave enough time for the oven to heat up properly as a cooler oven will not be able to set the salt crust. Spread half the salt on a shallow baking tray (ideally oval or rectangular).

2 Wash out the fish and dry any excess moisture with kitchen paper. Open the fish and lightly season the insides with salt and freshly ground black pepper. Open the fish out and then fill the cavity of the fish with all the herbs.

3 Do not worry if the fish does not close properly as the herbs will become more compact as soon as they have been heated through and cooked.

4 Lay the sea bass on the salt. Cover the fish with a 1cm/½in layer of salt, pressing it down firmly. Moisten the salt lightly by spraying with water from an atomizer. Bake the fish in the hot oven for 30–40 minutes, or until the salt crust is just beginning to colour.

5 Garnish with seaweed or samphire and use a sharp knife to break open the crust. Serve with lemon slices.

Energy 150Kcal/632kJ; Protein 29g; Carbohydrate 0g, of which sugars 0g; Fat 3.8g, of which saturates 0.6g; Cholesterol 120mg; Calcium 195mg; Fibre 0g; Sodium 595mg.

GRILLED SEA BASS <u>WITH</u> FENNEL

FENNEL HAS A DISTINCTIVE ANISEED FLAVOUR AND MAKE A TASTY ADDITION TO MANY FISH DISHES.
THE ANISEED-FLAVOURED PASTIS ADDS FURTHER WARMTH AND RICHNESS TO THE GRILLED SEA BASS,
COMPLEMENTING THE FLAVOUR OF THE FENNEL.

SERVES 6–8

INGREDIENTS
  1 sea bass, weighing 1.8kg/
    4–4½lb, cleaned
  60–90ml/4–6 tbsp extra virgin
    olive oil
  10–15ml/2–3 tsp fennel seeds
  2 large fennel bulbs, trimmed
    and thinly sliced (reserve
    any fronds)
  60ml/4 tbsp pastis (such as
    Pernod or Ricard)
  salt and ground black pepper

VARIATION
If you have access to it, use traditional
Greek ouzo instead of pastis. It has a
similar aniseed flavour and is frequently
used in Greek cooking to enhance the
taste of fish and shellfish. You can buy it
in Greek stores and it is sometimes also
available in Turkish stores.

1 With a sharp knife, make three or
four deep cuts in both sides of the
fish, more if the fish is large. Brush the
fish with extra virgin olive oil and season
with salt and freshly ground black
pepper, both inside and outside.

2 Sprinkle the fennel seeds into the
stomach cavity and push deep down
into each of the cuts. Cover loosely
and set aside in a cool place while
you prepare and cook the fennel.

3 Preheat the grill (broiler) to a medium
heat. Put the slices of fennel in a
flameproof dish or on the grill rack and
brush with extra virgin olive oil. Grill
(broil) for 4 minutes on each side until
tender. Transfer to a platter and spread
evenly to cover the base, loosely cover
to keep warm and set aside.

4 Place the fish on the oiled grill rack
and position about 10–13cm/4–5in
away from a medium heat. Grill
for 10–12 minutes on each side,
brushing occasionally with extra
virgin olive oil.

5 Transfer the fish to the platter, on top
of the fennel. Garnish with chopped and
whole fennel fronds.

6 Heat the pastis in a small pan, light it
and pour it, flaming, over the fish. Serve
immediately.

Energy 296Kcal/1,238kJ; Protein 39.2g; Carbohydrate 1.2g, of which sugars 1.1g; Fat 12.5g, of which saturates 1.9g; Cholesterol 160mg; Calcium 276mg; Fibre 1.6g; Sodium 145mg.

COD, BASIL, TOMATO AND POTATO PIE

FRESH AND SMOKED FISH MAKE A GREAT COMBINATION, ESPECIALLY WITH THE HINT OF TOMATO AND BASIL. SERVED WITH A GREEN SALAD, THIS MAKES AN IDEAL DISH FOR LUNCH OR A FAMILY SUPPER.

3 Melt 75g/3oz/6 tbsp of the butter in a large pan, add the onion and cook for about 5 minutes, until softened and tender but not browned. Sprinkle over the flour and half the chopped basil.

4 Gradually add the reserved fish cooking liquid, adding a little more milk if necessary to make a fairly thin sauce, stirring constantly to make a smooth consistency. Bring to the boil, season with salt and pepper, and add the remaining basil.

5 Remove the pan from the heat, then add the fish and tomatoes and stir gently to combine. Pour into an ovenproof dish.

SERVES 8

INGREDIENTS

1kg/2¼lb smoked cod fillets
1kg/2¼lb fresh cod fillets
900ml/1½ pint/3¾ cups milk
1.2litres/2 pints/5 cups water
2 fresh basil sprigs
1 fresh lemon thyme sprig
150g/5oz/⅔ cup butter
1 onion, chopped
75g/3oz/⅔ cup plain
  (all-purpose) flour
30ml/2 tbsp chopped
  fresh basil
4 firm plum tomatoes, peeled
  and chopped
12 medium floury potatoes
salt and ground black pepper
crushed black peppercorns,
  to garnish
lettuce leaves, to serve

1 Place both kinds of fish in a roasting pan with 600ml/1 pint/2½ cups of the milk, the water and the herb sprigs.

2 Bring to a simmer and cook gently for about 3–4 minutes. Remove from the heat and leave the fish to cool in the liquid for about 20 minutes. Drain the fish, reserving the cooking liquid for use in the sauce. Flake the fish, removing the skin and any remaining bones.

6 Preheat the oven to 180°C/350°F/Gas 4. Cook the potatoes in boiling water until tender. Drain then add the remaining butter and milk and mash.

7 Season to taste and spoon over the fish mixture, using a fork to create a pattern. You can freeze the pie at this stage. Bake for 30 minutes until the top is golden. Sprinkle with the crushed peppercorns and serve hot with lettuce.

Energy 474Kcal/1989kJ; Protein 49.6g; Carbohydrate 30.7g, of which sugars 4.6g; Fat 17.8g, of which saturates 10.2g; Cholesterol 155mg; Calcium 62mg; Fibre 2.5g; Sodium 1672mg

HERBY FISH PIE WITH MUSHROOMS

THIS SIMPLE DISH CAN BE VARIED TO SUIT YOUR TASTE AND POCKET. YOU COULD ADD PRAWNS OR HARD-BOILED EGGS, OR MIX THE POTATO TOPPING WITH SPRING ONIONS OR FRESH PARSLEY.

SERVES 4

INGREDIENTS
450g/1lb cod or haddock fillets
225g/8oz smoked cod fillets
300ml/½ pint/1¼ cups milk
½ lemon, sliced
1 bay leaf
1 fresh thyme sprig
4–5 black peppercorns
50g/2oz/¼ cup butter
25g/1oz/¼ cup plain (all-purpose) flour
30ml/2 tbsp chopped fresh parsley
5ml/1 tsp anchovy extract
150g/5oz/2 cups sliced mushrooms
salt, ground black pepper and cayenne pepper
For the topping
450g/1lb potatoes, cooked and mashed with milk
50g/2oz/¼ cup butter
2 tomatoes, sliced
25g/1oz/¼ cup grated Cheddar cheese (optional)

1 Put the fish, skin side down, in a shallow pan. Add the milk, lemon slices, bay leaf, thyme and peppercorns. Bring to the boil, then lower the heat and poach gently for about 5 minutes, until just cooked. Strain off and reserve the milk. Remove the fish skin and flake the flesh, discarding any bones.

2 Melt half the butter in a small pan, stir in the flour and cook gently, stirring, for 1 minute. Add the milk and boil, whisking, until smooth and creamy. Stir in the parsley and anchovy essence and season to taste.

3 Heat the remaining butter in a frying pan, add the sliced mushrooms and sauté until tender. Season and add to the flaked fish. Mix the sauce into the fish and stir gently to combine. Transfer the mixture to an ovenproof dish.

4 Preheat the oven to 200°C/400°F/ Gas 6. Beat the mashed potato with the butter until very creamy. Season, then spread the topping evenly over the fish. Fork up the surface and arrange the sliced tomatoes around the edge. Sprinkle the exposed topping with the grated cheese, if using.

5 Bake for 20–25 minutes, until the topping is lightly browned. If you prefer, finish browning under a grill (broiler).

VARIATION
Instead of using plain mashed potatoes, try a mixture of mashed potato and mashed swede (rutabaga) or celeriac.

Energy 382Kcal/1600kJ; Protein 34.8g; Carbohydrate 24.3g, of which sugars 3.1g; Fat 16.8g, of which saturates 9.9g; Cholesterol 118mg; Calcium 62mg; Fibre 2.7g; Sodium 859mg.

SMOKED HADDOCK WITH PARSLEY SAUCE

A GOOD, STRONG, FRESH PARSLEY SAUCE IS GREAT WITH FULL-FLAVOURED SMOKED HADDOCK.
THIS RECIPE IS QUICK TO PREPARE AND MAKES A TASTY MIDWEEK MEAL.

SERVES 4

INGREDIENTS
 4 smoked haddock fillets,
  about 225g/8oz each
 75g/3oz/6 tbsp butter, softened
 25g/1oz/¼ cup plain
  (all-purpose) flour
 300ml/½ pint/1¼ cups milk
 60ml/4 tbsp chopped
  fresh parsley
 salt and ground black pepper
 parsley sprigs, to garnish

1 Smear the fish on both sides with 50g/2oz/¼ cup butter.

2 Preheat the grill (broiler). Beat the remaining 25g/1oz butter and flour together in a small bowl with a wooden spoon to make a thick and smooth paste.

3 Grill (broil) the fish over a medium high heat for 10–15 minutes, turning when necessary.

4 Meanwhile, heat the milk until just below boiling point.

5 Add the flour mixture in small knobs, whisking constantly over the heat. Continue until smooth and thick.

6 Stir in the seasoning and parsley, and serve poured over the fillets, or in a serving jug (pitcher). Serve immediately, garnished with parsley and your choice of vegetables.

Energy 382Kcal/1604kJ; Protein 46.4g; Carbohydrate 8.8g, of which sugars 4g; Fat 18.3g, of which saturates 10.8g; Cholesterol 125mg; Calcium 177mg; Fibre 0.8g; Sodium 1860mg.

HAKE AND CLAMS WITH SALSA VERDE

SALSA VERDE, A FRAGRANT SAUCE MADE FROM FRESH PARSLEY, OLIVE OIL AND GARLIC, MAKES A DELICIOUS ACCOMPANIMENT TO A MIXTURE OF HAKE AND CLAMS.

SERVES 4

INGREDIENTS

    4 hake steaks, about 2cm/¾in thick
    50g/2oz/½ cup plain
      (all-purpose) flour, for dusting,
      plus 30ml/2 tbsp
    60ml/4 tbsp olive oil
    1 small onion, finely chopped
    4 garlic cloves, finely chopped
    150ml/¼ pint/⅔ cup fish stock
    150ml/¼ pint/⅔ cup white wine
    90ml/6 tbsp chopped fresh parsley
    75g/3oz/¾ cup frozen petits pois
      (baby peas)
    16 fresh clams, cleaned
    salt and ground black pepper

COOK'S TIP
To make fish stock, put 450g/1lb fish bones, head and skin in a large pan with 1 sliced onion, 1 sliced carrot, ½ sliced celery stalk, 3–4 thick parsley stalks, snapped in places, 1 bay leaf, 10ml/ 2 tsp lemon juice or wine vinegar and 175ml/ 6fl oz/¾ cup dry white wine or vermouth. Bring to the boil, then reduce the heat and simmer for 30 minutes. Strain. If you can't buy fish bits, collect fish leftovers in the freezer: prawn (shrimp) heads, the spines from cooked fish, poaching water from a salmon, and mussel or clam stock from opening the shellfish. It is also worth buying a small whole fish to add to the stock.

1 Preheat the oven to 180°C/350°F/ Gas 4. Season the fish, then dust with flour.

2 Heat half the oil in a large pan, add the fish and fry for 1 minute on each side. Transfer to an ovenproof dish.

3 Heat the remaining oil in a clean pan and fry the onion and garlic, stirring, until soft. Stir in the 30ml/2 tbsp flour and cook for about 1 minute.

4 Slowly add the stock and wine to the pan, stirring until the mixture has thickened.

5 Add 75ml/5 tbsp of the parsley and the petits pois to the sauce and season with plenty of salt and pepper.

6 Pour the sauce over the fish, and bake for 15–20 minutes, adding the clams 3–4 minutes before the end of the cooking time.

7 Discard any clams that do not open once they are cooked, then sprinkle the fish with the remaining parsley and serve immediately.

VARIATION
For a change, you can include fresh young asparagus tips as well as peas. Simply replace half the peas with asparagus tips.

Energy 389Kcal/1627kJ; Protein 42g; Carbohydrate 13.9g, of which sugars 1.9g; Fat 16.1g, of which saturates 2.3g; Cholesterol 59mg; Calcium 91mg; Fibre 2g; Sodium 431mg.

FILLETS OF SEA BREAM WITH SORREL IN FILO PASTRY

EACH AROMATIC LITTLE PARCEL IS A MEAL IN ITSELF AND CAN BE PREPARED SEVERAL HOURS IN ADVANCE, WHICH MAKES THIS AN IDEAL RECIPE FOR ENTERTAINING. IF YOU LIKE, SERVE THE PASTRIES WITH FENNEL BRAISED WITH ORANGE JUICE OR A MIXED LEAF SALAD.

SERVES 4

INGREDIENTS

8 small waxy salad potatoes,
  preferably red-skinned
200g/7oz sorrel, stalks removed
30ml/2 tbsp extra virgin olive oil
16 filo pastry sheets, thawed if frozen
4 sea bream fillets, about 175g/6oz
  each, scaled but not skinned
50g/2oz/¼ cup butter, melted
120ml/4fl oz/½ cup fish stock
250ml/8fl oz/1 cup whipping cream
salt and ground black pepper
finely diced red (bell) pepper,
  to garnish

VARIATION
If sorrel isn't available, small spinach
leaves or baby chard leaves make a very
good substitute.

1 Cook the potatoes in a pan of lightly salted boiling water for about 15–20 minutes, or until just tender. Drain and leave to cool. Preheat the oven to 200°C/400°F/Gas 6. Set about half the sorrel leaves aside. Shred the remaining leaves by piling up 6 or 8 at a time, rolling them up like a fat cigar and then slicing them with a sharp knife. Thinly slice the potatoes lengthways.

2 Brush a baking sheet with a little oil. Lay a sheet of filo pastry on the sheet, brush with oil, then lay a second sheet crossways over the first. Repeat with two more sheets. Arrange a quarter of the potatoes in the centre, season and add a quarter of the sorrel. Lay a bream fillet on top, skin side up. Season with salt and ground black pepper.

3 Loosely fold the filo pastry up and over to make a neat parcel. Make three more parcels; place on the baking sheet. Brush with half the butter. Bake for about 20 minutes, or until the filo is puffed up and golden brown.

4 Meanwhile, make the sorrel sauce. Heat the remaining butter in a pan, add the reserved sorrel and cook gently for 3 minutes, stirring, until it wilts. Stir in the stock and cream. Heat almost to boiling point, stirring so that the sorrel breaks down. Season to taste and keep hot until the fish parcels are ready. Serve garnished with red pepper. Hand round the sauce separately.

Energy 651Kcal/2,710kJ; Protein 35.8g; Carbohydrate 23.2g, of which sugars 3.3g; Fat 46.8g, of which saturates 23.2g; Cholesterol 159mg; Calcium 222mg; Fibre 2g; Sodium 359mg.

SALMON EN PAPILLOTE WITH CHILLIES AND CHIVES

COOKING FISH "EN PAPILLOTE" ENSURES THAT THE AROMATIC INGREDIENTS RETAIN THEIR FLAVOUR, AND THAT THE SALMON REMAINS MOIST AND SUCCULENT. IT IS ALSO EXCELLENT WHEN ENTERTAINING, AS THE PARCELS MAY BE PREPARED AHEAD OF COOKING.

SERVES 6

INGREDIENTS
25ml/1½ tbsp groundnut (peanut) oil
2 yellow (bell) peppers, seeded and thinly sliced
4cm/1½in fresh root ginger, peeled and finely grated
1 large fennel bulb, finely sliced, feathery tops chopped and reserved
1 fresh green chilli, seeded and finely sliced
2 large leeks, cut into 10cm/4in lengths and sliced lengthways
60ml/4 tbsp chopped chives
10ml/2 tsp light soy sauce
6 portions salmon fillet, about 175g/6oz each, skinned
10ml/2 tsp toasted sesame oil
salt and ground black pepper

1 Heat the oil in a large, non-stick frying pan and cook the peppers, ginger and fennel for 5–6 minutes, or until they are softened but not browned. Add the chilli and leeks and cook for a further 2–3 minutes. Stir in half the chives and the soy sauce with seasoning to taste. Set aside to cool.

2 Preheat the oven to 190°C/375°F/ Gas 5. Cut six 35cm/14in circles of baking parchment or foil. Divide the vegetable mixture among the circles and place a portion of salmon on top. Drizzle with sesame oil and sprinkle with the remaining chives and the chopped fennel tops. Season to taste.

3 Fold the paper or foil over to enclose the fish, rolling and twisting the edges together to seal the parcels.

4 Place the fish parcels on a baking tray and bake in the centre of the oven for 15–20 minutes, or until the parcels are puffed up and, if made with paper, lightly browned.

5 Carefully transfer the fish parcels to warmed individual plates and serve immediately.

COOK'S TIP
This dish is excellent served with a simple accompaniment such as buttered new potatoes or plain egg noodles.

Energy 394Kcal/1640kJ; Protein 39.1g; Carbohydrate 6.5g, of which sugars 5.8g; Fat 23.6g, of which saturates 4g; Cholesterol 92mg; Calcium 70mg; Fibre 3.4g; Sodium 210mg.

SALMON RISOTTO <u>WITH</u> CUCUMBER <u>AND</u> TARRAGON

THE SUBTLE FLAVOUR OF CUCUMBER IS A FAMILIAR COMPANION FOR SALMON. IN THIS SIMPLE RISOTTO FRESH TARRAGON ADDS ITS UNMISTAKABLE, DELICATE AROMA AND FLAVOUR.

3 Stir in the risotto rice, then pour in the stock and white wine. Bring to the boil, then lower the heat and allow to simmer, uncovered, for 10 minutes, stirring occasionally.

4 Stir in the diced salmon and then season to taste with salt and ground black pepper.

5 Continue cooking for a further 5 minutes, stirring occasionally to avoid sticking, then remove from the heat.

6 Cover the pan and leave the risotto to stand for 5 minutes.

7 Remove the lid, add the chopped fresh tarragon and mix lightly.

8 Spoon the risotto into a warmed bowl and serve immediately.

COOK'S TIP
Carnaroli risotto rice would be an excellent choice for this risotto, although, if it is not available, arborio rice can be used instead.

<u>SERVES 4</u>

INGREDIENTS
25g/1oz/2 tbsp butter
small bunch of spring onions
(scallions), white parts only,
chopped
½ cucumber, peeled, seeded
and chopped
350g/12oz/1¾ cups risotto rice
1.2 litres/2 pints/5 cups hot chicken
or fish stock
150ml/¼ pint/⅔ cup dry white wine
450g/1lb salmon fillet, skinned
and diced
45ml/3 tbsp chopped fresh tarragon
salt and ground black pepper

1 Heat the butter in a large pan and mix in the spring onions and cucumber.

2 Cook for 2–3 minutes, stirring occasionally. Do not let the spring onions colour.

Energy 591Kcal/2465kJ; Protein 29.5g; Carbohydrate 70.5g, of which sugars 0.6g; Fat 18g, of which saturates 5.4g; Cholesterol 70mg; Calcium 50mg; Fibre 0.2g; Sodium 91mg.

GREEN FISH CURRY WITH THAI HERBS, CHILLI AND COCONUT MILK

ANY FIRM-FLESHED FISH, SUCH AS COD, MAHI-MAHI, HOKI OR SWORDFISH, CAN BE USED FOR THIS DELICIOUS CURRY, WHICH GAINS ITS RICH COLOUR FROM A MIXTURE OF FRESH HERBS.

SERVES 4

INGREDIENTS

4 garlic cloves, coarsely chopped
5cm/2in piece fresh root ginger, peeled and coarsely chopped
2 fresh green chillies, seeded and coarsely chopped
grated rind and juice of 1 lime
5–10ml/1–2 tsp shrimp paste
5ml/1 tsp coriander seeds
5ml/1 tsp five-spice powder
75ml/5 tbsp sesame oil
2 red onions, finely chopped
900g/2lb hoki fillets, skinned
400ml/14fl oz/1⅔ cups coconut milk
45ml/3 tbsp Thai fish sauce
50g/2oz fresh coriander (cilantro) leaves
50g/2oz fresh mint leaves
50g/2oz fresh basil leaves
6 spring onions (scallions), chopped
150ml/¼ pint/⅔ cup sunflower oil
sliced fresh green chilli and finely chopped fresh coriander (cilantro), to garnish
cooked rice and lime wedges, to serve

1 First make the curry paste. Combine the garlic, fresh root ginger, green chillies, the lime juice and shrimp paste in a food processor. Add the coriander seeds and five-spice powder, with half the sesame oil. Process to a fine paste, then set aside until required.

COOK'S TIP
Shrimp paste, also known as blachan or terasi, is available in Asian food stores.

2 Heat a wok or large shallow pan and pour in the remaining sesame oil. When it is hot, stir-fry the red onions over a high heat for 2 minutes. Add the fish and stir-fry for 1–2 minutes to seal the fillets on all sides.

3 Lift out the red onions and fish and put them on a plate. Add the curry paste to the wok or pan and cook for 1 minute, stirring. Return the fish and red onions to the wok or pan, pour in the coconut milk and bring to the boil. Lower the heat, add the Thai fish sauce and simmer for 5–7 minutes, until the fish is cooked through.

4 Meanwhile, process the herbs, spring onions, lime rind and oil in a food processor to a coarse paste. Stir into the fish curry. Garnish with chilli and coriander and serve with rice and lime wedges.

Energy 575Kcal/2390kJ; Protein 40g; Carbohydrate 6.2g, of which sugars 4.9g; Fat 43.5g, of which saturates 5.9g; Cholesterol 6mg; Calcium 132mg; Fibre 0g; Sodium 362mg.

PISSALADIÈRE WITH HERBS AND ANCHOVIES

*GENTLY COOKED, SWEET SPANISH ONIONS FLAVOURED WITH GARLIC, THYME AND ROSEMARY MAKE A
MELLOW BACKDROP TO THE ANCHOVIES AND OLIVES IN THIS DISH. IT CAN BE MADE USING EITHER
SHORTCRUST PASTRY OR, AS HERE, YEASTED DOUGH, SIMILAR TO A PIZZA BASE.*

SERVES 6

INGREDIENTS
    250g/9oz/2¼ cups strong white
        bread flour, plus extra
        for dusting
    50g/2oz/½ cup fine polenta
        or semolina
    5ml/1 tsp salt
    175ml/6fl oz/¾ cup lukewarm water
    5ml/1 tsp dried yeast
    5ml/1 tsp caster (superfine) sugar
    30ml/2 tbsp extra virgin olive oil,
        plus extra for greasing
For the topping
    60–75ml/4–5 tbsp extra virgin olive oil
    6 large sweet onions, thinly sliced
    2 large garlic cloves, thinly sliced
    5ml/1 tsp chopped fresh thyme, plus
        several sprigs
    1 fresh rosemary sprig
    1–2 × 50g/2oz cans anchovies in
        olive oil
    50–75g/2–3oz/⅓–½ cup small
        black olives, preferably small
        Niçoise olives
    salt and ground black pepper

1 Mix the flour, polenta or semolina and salt in a large mixing bowl. Pour half the water into a bowl. Add the yeast and sugar, then leave in a warm place for 10 minutes, or until frothy. Pour the yeast mixture into the flour mixture with the remaining water and the olive oil.

2 Using your hands, mix all the ingredients together to form a dough, then turn out and knead for 5 minutes, or until smooth, springy and elastic.

3 Return the dough to the clean, floured bowl and place it in a plastic bag or cover with oiled clear film, then set the dough aside at room temperature for 30–60 minutes to rise and double in bulk.

4 Meanwhile, start to prepare the topping. Heat 45ml/3 tbsp of the olive oil in a large, heavy pan and add the sliced onions in the oil, then cover the pan and cook over a very low heat, stirring occasionally, for 20–30 minutes. (Use a heat-diffuser mat to keep the heat low, if possible.)

5 Add a little salt to taste and the garlic, chopped thyme and rosemary sprig. Stir well and continue cooking for another 15–25 minutes, or until the onions are soft and deep golden yellow but not browned.

6 Uncover the pan for the last 5–10 minutes if the onions seem very wet.

7 Remove and discard the rosemary. Set the onions aside to cool.

8 Preheat the oven to 220°C/425°F/ Gas 7. Roll out the dough and use to line a large baking sheet, about 30 × 23cm/ 12 × 9in. Taste the onions for seasoning before spreading them over the dough.

9 Drain the anchovies, cut them in half lengthways and arrange them in a lattice pattern over the onions.

10 Sprinkle the olives and thyme sprigs over the top of the pissaladière and drizzle with the remaining olive oil. Bake for about 20–25 minutes, or until the dough is browned and cooked. Season with pepper and serve warm, cut into slices.

VARIATIONS
• Shortcrust pastry can be used instead of yeast dough as a base: bake it blind for 10–15 minutes at 200°C/400°F/ Gas 6 before adding the filling.
• With either base, if you are fond of anchovies, try spreading about 60ml/ 4 tbsp anchovy purée (paste) (anchoïade) over the base before adding the onions. Alternatively, spread black olive paste over the base.

Energy 335Kcal/1402kJ; Protein 8.1g; Carbohydrate 47.1g, of which sugars 6.9g; Fat 13.8g, of which saturates 1.9g; Cholesterol 5mg; Calcium 114mg; Fibre 3.1g; Sodium 519mg.

MUSTARD AND PARSLEY CRAB CAKES

UNLIKE FISH CAKES, CRAB CAKES ARE BOUND WITH EGG AND MAYONNAISE OR TARTARE SAUCE INSTEAD OF POTATOES, WHICH MAKES THEM LIGHT IN TEXTURE. IF YOU PREFER, THEY CAN BE GRILLED INSTEAD OF FRIED; BRUSH WITH A LITTLE OIL FIRST.

SERVES 4

INGREDIENTS

450g/1lb mixed brown and white
  crab meat
30ml/2 tbsp mayonnaise or
  tartare sauce
2.5–5ml/½–1 tsp mustard powder
1 egg, lightly beaten
Tabasco sauce
45ml/3 tbsp chopped
  fresh parsley
4 spring onions (scallions), finely
  chopped (optional)
50–75g/2–3oz/½–¾ cup dried
  breadcrumbs, preferably home-made
sunflower oil, for frying
salt, ground black pepper and
  cayenne pepper
chopped spring onions (scallions),
  to garnish
red onion marmalade,
  to serve

1 Put the crab meat in a bowl and stir in the mayonnaise or tartare sauce, with the mustard and egg. Season with Tabasco, salt, pepper and cayenne.

2 Stir in the parsley, spring onions, if using, and 50g/2oz/½ cup of the breadcrumbs. The mixture should be just firm enough to hold together; depending on how much brown crab meat there is, you may need to add some more breadcrumbs.

3 Divide the mixture into eight portions, roll each into a ball and flatten slightly to make a thick flat disc. Spread out the crab cakes on a platter and put in the refrigerator for 30 minutes before frying.

4 Pour the oil into a shallow pan to a depth of about 5mm/¼in. Cook the crab cakes, in two batches, until golden brown all over. Drain on kitchen paper and keep hot. Serve with a spring onion garnish and red onion marmalade.

Energy 310Kcal/1292kJ; Protein 24g; Carbohydrate 10.4g, of which sugars 0.9g; Fat 19.5g, of which saturates 2.7g; Cholesterol 134mg; Calcium 183mg; Fibre 0.9g; Sodium 769mg.

MUSSELS WITH PROVENÇAL HERBS

THESE DELECTABLE MUSSELS ARE SERVED WITH A ROBUST HERBY TOMATO SAUCE. HAND ROUND PLENTY OF CRUSTY FRENCH BREAD FOR MOPPING UP THE JUICES AND DON'T FORGET FINGERBOWLS OF WARM WATER AND A PLATE FOR DISCARDED SHELLS.

SERVES 4

INGREDIENTS

30ml/2 tbsp olive oil
200g/7oz rindless unsmoked streaky (fatty) bacon, cubed
1 onion, finely chopped
3 garlic cloves, finely chopped
1 bay leaf
15ml/1 tbsp chopped fresh mixed Provençal herbs, such as thyme, marjoram, basil, oregano and savory
15–30ml/1–2 tbsp sun-dried tomatoes in oil, chopped
4 large, very ripe tomatoes, peeled, seeded and chopped
50g/2oz/½ cup pitted black olives, chopped
105ml/7 tbsp dry white wine
2.25kg/5–5¼lb fresh mussels, scrubbed and bearded
salt and ground black pepper
60ml/4 tbsp coarsely chopped fresh parsley, to garnish

1 Heat the oil in a large pan. Cook the bacon until golden and crisp. Remove with a slotted spoon; set aside. Add the onion and garlic to the pan and cook gently until softened. Add the herbs, with both types of tomatoes. Cook gently for 5 minutes, stirring frequently. Stir in the olives and season.

2 Put the wine and mussels in another pan. Cover and shake over a high heat for 5 minutes, until the mussels open. Discard any that remain closed.

3 Strain the mussel cooking liquid into the pan containing the tomato sauce through a sieve (strainer) lined with muslin (cheesecloth) and boil until the mixture is reduced by about one-third. Add the mussels and stir to coat them thoroughly with the sauce. Remove and discard the bay leaf.

4 Divide the mussels and sauce among four heated dishes. Sprinkle over the fried bacon and chopped parsley and serve piping hot.

Energy 392Kcal/1643kJ; Protein 38.6g; Carbohydrate 5.5g, of which sugars 5.2g; Fat 22.4g, of which saturates 5.8g; Cholesterol 100mg; Calcium 358mg; Fibre 1.8g; Sodium 1294mg.

PAN-STEAMED MUSSELS <u>WITH</u> FRAGRANT THAI HERBS

LIKE SO MANY THAI DISHES, THIS IS VERY EASY TO PREPARE. THE LEMON GRASS AND KAFFIR LIME LEAVES ADD A REFRESHING TANG TO THE MUSSELS.

SERVES 4–6

INGREDIENTS

- 1kg/2¼lb fresh mussels
- 2 lemon grass stalks, finely chopped
- 4 shallots, chopped
- 4 kaffir lime leaves, coarsely torn
- 2 fresh red chillies, sliced
- 15ml/1 tbsp Thai fish sauce
- 30ml/2 tbsp fresh lime juice
- thinly sliced spring onions (scallions) and coriander (cilantro) leaves, to garnish

1 Clean the mussels by pulling off the beards, scrubbing the shells well and removing any barnacles. Discard any mussels that are broken or which do not close when tapped sharply.

2 Place the mussels in a large, heavy pan and add the lemon grass, shallots, kaffir lime leaves, chillies, fish sauce and lime juice. Mix well. Cover the pan tightly and steam the mussels over a high heat, shaking the pan occasionally, for 5–7 minutes, until the shells have opened.

3 Using a slotted spoon, transfer the cooked mussels to a warmed serving dish or individual bowls. Discard any mussels that have failed to open.

4 Garnish the mussels with the thinly sliced spring onions and coriander leaves. Serve immediately.

Energy 48Kcal/206kJ; Protein 8.9g; Carbohydrate 1.1g, of which sugars 0.8g; Fat 1g, of which saturates 0.2g; Cholesterol 20mg; Calcium 102mg; Fibre 0.2g; Sodium 283mg.

MUSSELS AND CLAMS WITH LEMON GRASS AND COCONUT CREAM

LEMON GRASS HAS AN INCOMPARABLE AROMATIC FLAVOUR AND IS WIDELY USED WITH ALL KINDS OF SEAFOOD IN THAILAND AS THE FLAVOURS MARRY SO PERFECTLY.

SERVES 6

INGREDIENTS

1.8kg/4lb fresh mussels
450g/1lb baby clams
120ml/4fl oz/½ cup dry white wine
1 bunch spring onions
   (scallions), chopped
2 lemon grass stalks, chopped
6 kaffir lime leaves, chopped
10ml/2 tsp Thai green curry paste
200ml/7fl oz/scant 1 cup
   coconut cream
30ml/2 tbsp chopped fresh
   coriander (cilantro)
salt and ground black pepper
garlic chives, to garnish

1 Clean the mussels by pulling off the beards, scrubbing the shells well and scraping off any barnacles with the blade of a knife. Scrub the clams. Discard any mussels or clams that are damaged or broken or which do not close immediately when tapped sharply.

2 Put the wine in a large pan with the spring onions, lemon grass and lime leaves. Stir in the curry paste. Simmer until the wine has almost evaporated.

COOK'S TIPS
• Buy shellfish from fish stores rather than gathering them yourself, as store-bought ones will have either been farmed or have undergone a purging process to clean them.
• If you can't buy clams, use a few extra mussels instead.

3 Add the mussels and clams to the pan and increase the heat to high. Cover tightly and steam the shellfish for 5–6 minutes, until they open.

4 Using a slotted spoon, transfer the mussels and clams to a heated serving bowl, cover and keep hot. Discard any shellfish that remain closed. Strain the cooking liquid into a clean pan through a sieve (strainer) lined with muslin (cheesecloth) and simmer briefly to reduce to about 250ml/8fl oz/1 cup.

5 Stir the coconut cream and chopped coriander into the sauce and season with salt and pepper to taste. Heat through. Pour the sauce over the mussels and clams, garnish with the garlic chives and serve immediately.

Energy 223Kcal/932kJ; Protein 19.5g; Carbohydrate 1.8g, of which sugars 1.5g; Fat 14g, of which saturates 10.3g; Cholesterol 47mg; Calcium 212mg; Fibre 0.4g; Sodium 398mg.

OCTOPUS STEW WITH TOMATOES AND HERBS

IN THIS SPANISH RECIPE OCTOPUS IS STEWED WITH TOMATOES, POTATOES AND LOTS OF HERBS, TO MAKE A SUBSTANTIAL MAIN COURSE. SERVE WITH WARM CRUSTY BREAD AND SALAD.

SERVES 4–6

INGREDIENTS

1kg/2¼lb octopus, cleaned
45ml/3 tbsp olive oil
1 large red onion, chopped
3 garlic cloves, finely chopped
30ml/2 tbsp brandy
300ml/½ pint/1¼ cups dry
  white wine
800g/1¾lb ripe plum tomatoes,
  peeled and chopped or 2 × 400g/
  14oz cans chopped tomatoes
1 dried red chilli, seeded
  and chopped
1.5ml/¼ tsp paprika
450g/1lb small
  new potatoes
15ml/1 tbsp chopped
  fresh rosemary
15ml/1 tbsp fresh thyme leaves
1.2 litres/2 pints/5 cups fish stock
30ml/2 tbsp chopped fresh
  flat leaf parsley leaves
salt and ground black pepper
rosemary sprigs, to garnish
salad leaves and French bread,
  to serve

3 Pour the brandy over the octopus and ignite it. When the flames have died down, add the wine, bring to the boil and bubble gently for about 5 minutes.

4 Stir in the chopped tomatoes, with the chilli and paprika, then add the potatoes, rosemary and thyme. Simmer gently for 5 minutes.

5 Pour in the fish stock and season. Cover and simmer for 20–30 minutes, stirring occasionally, until the octopus and potatoes are tender and the sauce has thickened slightly.

6 To serve, check the seasoning and stir in the parsley. Garnish with rosemary and accompany with salad and bread.

COOK'S TIPS

• Octopus skin can be removed with salted fingers. Large octopus often have scaly rings inside the suckers. Run your fingers down the tentacles to pop the rings out.
• You can make this dish the day before. Simply leave to cool, then chill. To serve, reheat gently, then check the seasoning and stir in the parsley.

1 Cut the octopus into large pieces, put in a pan and pour over enough cold water to cover. Season with salt, bring to the boil, then lower the heat and simmer for 30 minutes to tenderize it. Drain and cut into bitesize pieces.

2 Heat the oil in a large shallow pan. Fry the onion until lightly coloured, then add the garlic and fry for 1 minute. Add the octopus and fry for 2–3 minutes, stirring, until coloured.

Energy 325Kcal/1369kJ; Protein 32.7g; Carbohydrate 20.5g, of which sugars 8.2g; Fat 8.4g, of which saturates 1.5g; Cholesterol 80mg; Calcium 86mg; Fibre 2.8g; Sodium 24mg.

SCALLOPS WITH PARSLEY, GARLIC AND TOMATO

IN THIS DELECTABLE DISH, FLAMED SCALLOPS ARE COVERED IN A RICH HERB AND TOMATO SAUCE AND ARE SERVED HOT IN THE CURVED SHELL, WITH CRISP BREADCRUMBS ON TOP.

SERVES 4

INGREDIENTS

30ml/2 tbsp olive oil
1 onion, finely chopped
2 garlic cloves, finely chopped
200g/7oz can tomatoes
pinch of cayenne pepper
45ml/3 tbsp finely chopped
 fresh parsley
50ml/2fl oz/¼ cup orange juice
50g/2oz/4 tbsp butter
450g/1lb large shelled scallops,
 or 8–12 large ones on the shell,
 detached and cleaned
30ml/2 tbsp anis spirit, such as
 Ricard or Pernod
90ml/6 tbsp stale breadcrumbs
salt and ground
 black pepper

1 Heat the oil in a pan and fry the onion and garlic over a gentle heat. Add the tomatoes and cook for 10–15 minutes, stirring occasionally. Season with a little salt and cayenne pepper.

2 Transfer the tomato mixture to a small food processor or blender, add 30ml/ 2 tbsp of the parsley and the orange juice and blend to form a smooth purée.

3 Preheat the grill (broiler) with the shelf at its highest. Arrange four curved scallop shells, or flameproof ramekin dishes, on a baking tray.

4 Heat 25g/1oz/2 tbsp of the butter in a small frying pan and fry the scallops gently, for about 2 minutes, or until sealed but not totally cooked through.

5 Pour the anis spirit into a ladle and set light to it. Pour over the scallops and shake the pan gently until the flames die down. Divide the scallops among the prepared shells (or dishes) and salt them lightly. Add the pan juices to the tomato sauce.

6 Pour the tomato sauce over the scallops. Mix together the breadcrumbs and the remaining parsley, season very lightly and sprinkle over the top.

7 Melt the remaining butter in a small pan and drizzle over the breadcrumbs. Grill (broil) the scallops for about 1 minute to colour the tops and heat through. Serve immediately.

COOK'S TIP
If you can lay your hands on the curved shells of scallops, wash and keep them after use. Fresh scallops are usually sold on the flat shell so the second shell, which can be used as a little dish, is now quite a rarity.

Energy 393Kcal/1648kJ; Protein 29.6g; Carbohydrate 25.4g, of which sugars 4.4g; Fat 18.1g, of which saturates 7.8g; Cholesterol 80mg; Calcium 90mg; Fibre 1.7g; Sodium 458mg.

SEARED SCALLOPS WITH CHIVE SAUCE ON LEEK AND CARROT RICE

THE SWEET FLESH OF SCALLOPS PAIRS SUPERBLY WITH THE DELICATE FLAVOUR OF CHIVES. SERVED ON A BED OF WILD AND WHITE RICE WITH LEEKS, CARROTS AND CHERVIL, THIS IS AN IMPRESSIVE DISH.

SERVES 4

INGREDIENTS
    12–16 shelled scallops
    45ml/3 tbsp olive oil
    50g/2oz/⅓ cup wild rice
    65g/2½oz/5 tbsp butter
    4 carrots, cut into long, thin strips
    2 leeks, cut into thick diagonal slices
    1 small onion, finely chopped
    90g/3½oz/½ cup long grain rice
    1 fresh bay leaf
    200ml/7fl oz/scant 1 cup white wine
    450ml/¾ pint/scant 2 cups well-
      flavoured fish stock
    60ml/4 tbsp double (heavy) cream
    a little lemon juice
    25ml/1½ tbsp chopped fresh chives
    30ml/2 tbsp chopped fresh chervil
    salt and ground black pepper

1 Lightly season the scallops, brush with 15ml/1 tbsp of the olive oil and set aside.

2 Cook the wild rice in plenty of boiling water for about 30 minutes, until tender, then drain.

3 Melt half the butter in a small frying pan and sauté the carrots fairly gently for 4–5 minutes. Add the leeks and fry for another 2 minutes.

4 Season to taste and add 30–45ml/2–3 tbsp water, then cover and cook for a few minutes. Uncover and cook until the liquid evaporates. Set aside off the heat.

5 Melt half the rest of the butter with 15ml/1 tbsp of the remaining oil in a heavy pan. Add the onion and fry for 3–4 minutes, or until softened but not browned.

6 Add the long grain rice and bay leaf and cook, stirring constantly, until the rice looks translucent and the grains are coated with oil.

7 Pour in half the wine and half the stock. Season with 2.5ml/½ tsp salt and bring to the boil. Stir, then cover and cook very gently for 15 minutes, or until the liquid is absorbed and the rice is cooked and tender.

8 Reheat the carrots and leeks gently, then stir them into the long grain rice with the wild rice. Add seasoning to taste, if necessary.

9 Meanwhile, pour the remaining wine and stock into a small pan and boil rapidly until the liquid has reduced by about half.

COOK'S TIP
To shell a fresh scallop, hold it firmly with the flat-side up, and insert a strong knife blade between the shells to cut the top muscle. Separate the two shells. Slide the knife blade under the skirt to cut the second muscle. Remove the scallop. The edible part is the round white part and the coral, or roe, if present. Discard the beard-like fringe and intestinal thread.

10 Heat a heavy frying pan over a high heat. Add the remaining butter and olive oil. Sear the scallops for 1–2 minutes each side, or until browned, then remove and keep warm.

11 Pour the reduced stock into the frying pan and heat until bubbling, then add the double cream and boil until the mixture is thickened. Season with lemon juice, salt and black pepper. Stir in the chopped chives.

12 Stir the chervil into the rice and vegetable mixture and pile it on to plates. Arrange the scallops on top and spoon the sauce over the rice.

Energy 598Kcal/2489kJ; Protein 30.8g; Carbohydrate 38.9g, of which sugars 6.3g; Fat 32g, of which saturates 15.3g; Cholesterol 108mg; Calcium 88mg; Fibre 3.1g; Sodium 321mg.

Poultry and Meat

Enrich the flavour of meat using herbs. Add the subtle fragrance of lemon grass or lavender to pork or lamb, or permeate tender chicken with garlic for a pronounced flavour. Use herbs for sauces or for dressings, or to flavour accompaniments, such as sage and onion stuffing, horseradish dumplings or coriander yogurt. Whether roasting, braising, cooking on a barbecue or frying, herbs will give your meat a whole new dimension.

Above *Stir-fried Chicken with Basil and Chilli*

Left *Veal Escalopes in a Herby White Wine Sauce*

CHICKEN WITH FORTY CLOVES OF GARLIC

This dish does not have to be mathematically exact — the important thing is that there should be lots of garlic. The smell that emanates from the oven is truly delicious.

4 Sprinkle in 5ml/1 tsp flour and cook for 1 minute. Add the port or wine. Tuck in the whole heads of garlic and the peeled cloves with the herb sprigs. Pour over the remaining oil and season to taste with salt and pepper.

5 Mix the main batch of flour with sufficient water to make a firm dough. Roll it out into a long sausage and press it around the rim of the casserole, then press on the lid, folding the dough up and over the lid to create a tight seal. Cook in the oven for 1½ hours.

6 To serve, break the seal and remove the chicken and whole garlic to a serving platter and keep warm.

7 Remove and discard the herb sprigs, then place the casserole on the hob and whisk the contents to combine the garlic with the juices.

8 Add the crème fraîche, if using, and a little lemon juice to taste, if liked. Process the sauce in a food processor or blender or press it through a sieve (strainer) for a smoother result. Serve the garlic purée with the chicken.

SERVES 4–5

INGREDIENTS
5–6 whole heads of garlic
15g/½oz/1 tbsp butter
45ml/3 tbsp olive oil
1.8–2kg/4–4½lb chicken
150g/5oz/1¼ cups plain (all-purpose)
   flour, plus 5ml/1 tsp
75ml/5 tbsp white port, Pineau
   de Charentes or other white,
   fortified wine
2–3 fresh tarragon or rosemary sprigs
30ml/2 tbsp crème fraîche (optional)
few drops of lemon juice (optional)
salt and ground black pepper

1 Separate three of the heads of garlic into cloves and peel them. Remove the first layer of papery skin from the remaining heads of garlic and cut off the tops to expose the cloves, but leave them whole. Preheat the oven to 180°C/350°F/Gas 4.

2 Heat the butter and 15ml/1 tbsp of the olive oil in a flameproof casserole which is just large enough to take the chicken and garlic.

3 Add the chicken and cook over a medium heat, turning frequently, for 10–15 minutes.

Energy 474Kcal/1976kJ; Protein 25.5g; Carbohydrate 31.6g, of which sugars 2.9g; Fat 26.2g, of which saturates 7.4g; Cholesterol 109mg; Calcium 59mg; Fibre 2.6g; Sodium 101mg.

CHICKEN WITH FRESH HERBS AND GARLIC

THYME, SAGE, GARLIC AND LEMON COMBINE TO GIVE ROAST CHICKEN A SUMMERY FLAVOUR.
IF YOU PREFER, COOK THE CHICKEN ON A SPIT ON THE BARBECUE.

SERVES 4

INGREDIENTS

2kg/4½lb chicken
finely grated rind and juice of
  1 lemon
1 garlic clove, crushed
30ml/2 tbsp olive oil
2 fresh thyme sprigs
2 fresh sage sprigs
90ml/6 tbsp unsalted (sweet)
  butter, softened
salt and ground black pepper

COOK'S TIP
If you are roasting a chicken to serve
cold, cooking it in foil helps to keep it
succulent – open the foil for the last
20 minutes to brown the skin, then close
it as the chicken cools.

1 Season the chicken well and place in
a shallow non-metallic dish.

2 Mix the lemon rind and juice, crushed
garlic and olive oil together and pour
them over the chicken. Leave to
marinate in the refrigerator for at least
2 hours. Preheat the oven to 230°C/
450°F/Gas 8.

3 Place the herbs in the cavity of the
bird and smear the butter over the skin.
Roast in the oven for 1½–1¾ hours,
reducing the heat to 190°C/375°F/Gas 5
after the first 10 minutes. Baste with
marinade during cooking. The chicken
is cooked when the juices run clear
when the thigh is pierced with a skewer.
Leave for 15 minutes before carving.

Energy 427Kcal/1768kJ; Protein 30.9g; Carbohydrate 0.3g, of which sugars 0.3g; Fat 33.5g, of which saturates 9.6g; Cholesterol 165mg; Calcium 36mg; Fibre 0.6g; Sodium 144mg.

BAKED CHICKEN <u>WITH</u> SHALLOTS, GARLIC <u>AND</u> FENNEL

LEAVE THE CHICKEN TO MARINATE FOR A FEW HOURS BEFORE BAKING SO THAT THE COMPLEMENTARY FLAVOURS OF GARLIC, SHALLOTS AND FENNEL SEEDS CAN REALLY PERMEATE THE FLESH IN THIS DISH.

SERVES 4

INGREDIENTS

1.6–1.8kg/3½–4lb chicken, cut into
  8 pieces or 8 chicken joints
250g/9oz shallots, chopped
1 head garlic, separated into cloves
  and peeled
60ml/4 tbsp extra virgin olive oil
45ml/3 tbsp tarragon vinegar
45ml/3 tbsp white wine
5ml/1 tsp fennel seeds, crushed
2 bulbs fennel, cut into wedges,
  feathery tops reserved
150ml/¼ pint/⅔ cup double
  (heavy) cream
5ml/1 tsp redcurrant jelly
15ml/1 tbsp tarragon mustard
caster (superfine) sugar (optional)
30ml/2 tbsp chopped fresh flat
  leaf parsley
salt and ground black pepper

1 Place the chicken, shallots and all but one of the garlic cloves in a flameproof dish or roasting pan. Add the oil, vinegar, wine and fennel seeds. Season with pepper and mix well, then marinate for 2–3 hours.

2 Preheat the oven to 190°C/375°F/ Gas 5. Add the fennel to the chicken, season with salt, and mix. Cook for 50–60 minutes, stirring once or twice.

3 Transfer the chicken and vegetables to a serving dish and keep warm. Skim off some of the fat and bring the juices to the boil, then pour in the cream.

4 Stir, then whisk in the redcurrant jelly and mustard. Check the seasoning, adding a little sugar, if you like.

5 Chop the remaining garlic with the reserved fennel tops and mix with the chopped parsley. Pour the sauce over the chicken and sprinkle the chopped garlic and herb mixture over the top. Serve immediately.

COOK'S TIPS
• If possible, use the fresh new season's garlic for this dish, as it is plump, moist and full of flavour. Purple-skinned garlic is considered to have the best flavour.
• The cut surfaces of fennel tend to discolour quickly, so try not to prepare it much in advance of using it. If you must, then put the wedges into a bowl of cold water that has been acidulated with a little lemon juice.

Energy 568Kcal/2349kJ; Protein 24.3g; Carbohydrate 6.5g, of which sugars 5.3g; Fat 49.6g, of which saturates 19.4g; Cholesterol 163mg; Calcium 76mg; Fibre 2.9g; Sodium 112mg.

CHICKEN CASSEROLE <u>WITH</u> LAVENDER <u>AND</u> THYME FLOWERS

HERE, LAVENDER FLOWERS ARE USED TO PERFUME AND FLAVOUR CHICKEN COOKED IN A LARGE CASSEROLE WITH RED WINE, ORANGE AND THYME.

SERVES 4

INGREDIENTS
  4 chicken portions
  15ml/1 tbsp butter
  15ml/1 tbsp olive oil
  8 shallots
  30ml/2 tbsp plain
    (all-purpose) flour
  250ml/8fl oz/1 cup red wine
  250ml/8fl oz/1 cup chicken stock
  4 sprigs thyme
  10ml/2 tsp thyme flowers, removed
    from the stalk
  10ml/2 tsp lavender flowers
  grated rind and juice of
    1 orange
  salt and ground black pepper
For the garnish
  1 orange, divided into segments
  12 lavender sprigs
  20ml/4 tsp lavender flowers

1 Cut each chicken portion into two using a large, sharp knife. Heat the butter and olive oil in a heavy pan and add the chicken pieces.

2 Cook for about 5 minutes, or until they are browned all over, then transfer to a large, flameproof casserole. Add the shallots to the frying pan and cook for 2 minutes. Add to the casserole.

3 Add the flour to the frying pan, and cook for 2 minutes, stirring continuously. Pour in enough of the wine and stock to make a thin sauce. Bring to the boil, stirring all the time, and season to taste.

4 Stir in the thyme sprigs, thyme and lavender flowers, orange rind and juice. Pour the sauce over the chicken in the casserole.

5 Cover the casserole and simmer for 30–40 minutes, or until the chicken is tender.

6 Remove the thyme sprigs before serving. Serve the stew garnished with orange segments, and fresh lavender sprigs and flowers.

VARIATION
• This recipe works equally well using turkey portions in place of chicken.
• If you don't want to include the red wine, simply substitute chicken stock in its place.

Energy 322Kcal/1354kJ; Protein 49.4g; Carbohydrate 10.9g, of which sugars 4g; Fat 9.3g, of which saturates 3.1g; Cholesterol 148mg; Calcium 35mg; Fibre 1g; Sodium 146mg.

STIR-FRIED CHICKEN WITH BASIL AND CHILLI

THIS QUICK AND EASY CHICKEN DISH MAKES AN EXCELLENT SUPPER DISH. THAI BASIL, WHICH IS SOMETIMES KNOWN AS HOLY BASIL, HAS A UNIQUE, PUNGENT FLAVOUR THAT IS BOTH SPICY AND SHARP. DEEP-FRYING THE LEAVES ADDS ANOTHER DIMENSION TO THIS DISH.

SERVES 4–6

INGREDIENTS

45ml/3 tbsp vegetable oil
4 garlic cloves, thinly sliced
2–4 fresh red chillies, seeded and
  finely chopped
450g/1lb skinless boneless chicken
  breast portions, cut into
  bitesize pieces
45ml/3 tbsp Thai fish sauce
10ml/2 tsp dark soy sauce
5ml/1 tsp granulated sugar
10–12 fresh Thai basil leaves
2 fresh red chillies, seeded and
  finely chopped, and about 20 deep-
  fried Thai basil leaves, to garnish

1 Heat the oil in a wok or large, heavy frying pan. Add the garlic and chillies and stir-fry over a medium heat for 1–2 minutes until the garlic is golden. Take care not to let the garlic burn, otherwise it will taste bitter.

2 Add the pieces of chicken to the wok or pan, in batches if necessary, and stir-fry until the chicken changes colour.

3 Stir in the fish sauce, soy sauce and sugar. Continue to stir-fry the mixture for 3–4 minutes, or until the chicken is fully cooked and golden brown.

4 Stir in the fresh Thai basil leaves. Spoon the mixture on to a warm platter, or into individual dishes. Garnish with the chopped chillies and deep-fried Thai basil and serve immediately.

COOK'S TIP
To deep-fry Thai basil leaves, first make sure that the leaves are completely dry or they will splutter when added to the oil. Heat vegetable or groundnut (peanut) oil in a wok or deep-fryer to 190°C/375°F or until a cube of bread, added to the oil, browns in about 45 seconds. Add the leaves and deep-fry them briefly until they are crisp and translucent – this will take only about 30–40 seconds. Lift out the leaves using a slotted spoon or wire basket and leave them to drain on kitchen paper before using.

Energy 136Kcal/568kJ; Protein 18.3g; Carbohydrate 1.5g, of which sugars 1.4g; Fat 6.3g, of which saturates 0.9g; Cholesterol 53mg; Calcium 6mg; Fibre 0g; Sodium 698mg.

GRILLED CHICKEN <u>WITH</u> CORIANDER SAUCE

SUCCULENT CHICKEN BREAST FILLETS ARE FLAVOURED WITH THAI HERBS AND SPICES IN THIS SIMPLE DISH. IF YOU HAVE TIME, PREPARE THE CHICKEN IN ADVANCE AND LEAVE IT TO MARINATE IN THE REFRIGERATOR FOR SEVERAL HOURS — OR EVEN OVERNIGHT — UNTIL READY TO COOK.

SERVES 4

INGREDIENTS
450g/1lb chicken breast fillets,
   with the skin on
30ml/2 tbsp sesame oil
2 garlic cloves, crushed
2 coriander (cilantro) roots,
   finely chopped
2 small fresh red chillies, seeded
   and finely chopped
30ml/2 tbsp Thai fish sauce
5ml/1 tsp sugar
cooked rice, to serve
lime wedges, to garnish
For the sauce
90ml/6 tbsp rice vinegar
60ml/4 tbsp sugar
2.5ml/½ tsp salt
2 garlic cloves, crushed
1 small fresh red chilli, seeded
   and finely chopped
115g/4oz/4 cups fresh coriander
   (cilantro), finely chopped

1 Lay the chicken breast fillets between two sheets of clear film (plastic wrap), and beat with the side of a rolling pin or the flat side of a meat tenderizer until the meat is about half its original thickness. Place in a large, shallow dish.

2 Mix together the sesame oil, garlic, coriander roots, red chillies, fish sauce and sugar in a jug (pitcher), stirring until the sugar has dissolved. Pour the mixture over the chicken and turn to coat. Cover with clear film and set aside to marinate in a cool place for at least 20 minutes. Meanwhile, make the sauce.

3 Heat the vinegar in a small pan, add the sugar and stir until dissolved. Add the salt and stir until the mixture begins to thicken. Add the remaining sauce ingredients, stir well, then spoon the sauce into a serving bowl.

4 Preheat the grill (broiler) and cook the chicken for 5 minutes. Turn and baste with the marinade, then cook for 5 minutes more, or until cooked through and golden. Serve with rice and the sauce, garnished with lime wedges.

Energy 226Kcal/952kJ; Protein 28.2g; Carbohydrate 13.1g, of which sugars 12.9g; Fat 7.1g, of which saturates 1.2g; Cholesterol 79mg; Calcium 71mg; Fibre 1.5g; Sodium 790mg.

PAN-FRIED PORK <u>WITH</u> THYME <u>AND</u> GARLIC RISOTTO

LEAN PORK CHOPS ARE DELICIOUS MARINATED IN GARLIC AND LEMON. SERVED WITH A CREAMY AND ROBUST RISOTTO, VIBRANTLY FLAVOURED WITH GARLIC AND THYME, THEY MAKE A TASTY MEAL.

3 To make the risotto, heat the butter with the oil in a large, heavy pan until foaming. Sauté the chopped shallots and garlic gently until the shallots are softened, but not coloured.

4 Add the rice and thyme and stir until the grains are well coated.

5 Add a ladleful of boiling stock and cook gently, stirring occasionally. When all the stock is absorbed, add another ladleful. Continue cooking in this way until all the stock is absorbed. Keep the stock simmering and do not add too much at a time. This should take 25–30 minutes. Season to taste.

SERVES 4

INGREDIENTS

4 large pork chump or loin chops, each weighing about 175g/6oz, rind removed
1 garlic clove, finely chopped
juice of ½ lemon
5ml/1 tsp soft light brown sugar
25g/1oz/2 tbsp butter
fresh thyme sprigs, to garnish

For the risotto

25g/1oz/2 tbsp butter
15ml/1 tbsp olive oil
2 shallots, chopped
2 garlic cloves, finely chopped
250g/9oz/1⅓ cups risotto rice
15ml/1 tbsp fresh thyme leaves
900ml/1½ pints/3¾ cups boiling pork or chicken stock
salt and ground black pepper

1 Put the chops in a shallow dish and sprinkle the garlic over. To make the marinade, mix the lemon juice and soft light brown sugar together, and drizzle this over the chops.

2 Turn the chops to coat both sides with the lemon mixture, then cover the dish and leave them to marinate in the refrigerator while making the risotto.

6 Cook the chops when the risotto is half cooked. Melt the butter in a large, heavy frying pan. Remove the chops from the marinade, allowing the lemon juice to drip off, and fry them for 3–4 minutes on each side.

7 Divide the risotto among four plates and arrange the chops on top. Serve immediately, garnished with fresh thyme.

Energy 747Kcal/3116kJ; Protein 61.4g; Carbohydrate 52.2g, of which sugars 2g; Fat 32.1g, of which saturates 13.6g; Cholesterol 219mg; Calcium 34mg; Fibre 0.2g; Sodium 223mg.

ROLLED ROAST PORK <u>WITH</u> SAGE <u>AND</u> ONION STUFFING

*SAGE AND ONION MAKE A CLASSIC STUFFING FOR ROAST PORK, DUCK AND TURKEY, WITH THE SAGE
COUNTERACTING THE FATTINESS OF THE RICH MEATS. SERVE WITH APPLE SAUCE AND ROAST POTATOES.*

SERVES 6–8

INGREDIENTS
1.3–1.6kg/3–3½lb boneless loin of pork
60ml/4 tbsp fine, dry breadcrumbs
10ml/2 tsp chopped fresh sage
25ml/1½ tbsp plain (all-
   purpose) flour
300ml/½ pint/1¼ cups (hard) cider
150ml/¼ pint/⅔ cup water
5–10ml/1–2 tsp crab apple or
   redcurrant jelly
salt and ground black pepper
fresh thyme sprigs, to garnish
For the stuffing
25g/1oz/2 tbsp butter
50g/2oz bacon, finely chopped
2 large onions, finely chopped
75g/3oz/1½ cups fresh
   white breadcrumbs
30ml/2 tbsp chopped fresh sage
5ml/1 tsp chopped fresh thyme
10ml/2 tsp finely grated lemon rind
1 small (US medium)
   egg, beaten

1 Preheat the oven to 220°C/425°F/
Gas 7. To make the stuffing, melt the
butter in a pan and cook the bacon
until it begins to brown, then add the
onions and cook gently until softened.

2 Mix with the breadcrumbs, sage,
thyme, lemon rind and egg. Season well.

3 Cut the rind off the piece of pork in
one piece and score it well. Cooking the
rind separately makes crisper crackling
than leaving it on the pork.

4 Place the pork fat side down, and
season. Add a layer of stuffing, then
roll up and tie neatly.

5 Lay the rind over the pork and rub in
5ml/1 tsp salt. Roast for 2–2½ hours,
basting with the pork fat once or twice.
Reduce the temperature to 190°C/
375°F/Gas 5 after 20 minutes. Shape
the remaining stuffing into balls and
add to the roasting pan for the last
30 minutes of the cooking time.

6 Remove the rind from the pork.
Increase the oven temperature to
220°C/425°F/Gas 7 and roast the rind
for a further 20–25 minutes, until crisp.

7 Mix the dry breadcrumbs and sage
and press them into the fat. Cook the
pork for 10 minutes, then cover and set
aside in a warm place for 15–20 minutes.

8 Remove all but 30–45ml/2–3 tbsp of
the fat from the roasting pan and place
it on the hob (stovetop). Stir in the flour,
followed by the cider and water. Bring
to the boil and then cook gently for
10 minutes. Strain the gravy into a
clean pan, add the crab apple or
redcurrant jelly, and cook for another
5 minutes. Adjust the seasoning.

9 Serve the pork cut into thick slices and
the crisp crackling cut into strips with the
cider gravy, garnished with thyme.

Energy 446Kcal/1872kJ; Protein 53.6g; Carbohydrate 21.1g, of which sugars 5g; Fat 15.8g, of which saturates 6.1g; Cholesterol 161mg; Calcium 66mg; Fibre 1.2g; Sodium 356mg.

PORK BELLY WITH FIVE SPICES

THIS FRAGRANT FUSION DISH COMBINES CHINESE SPICES AND SUCCULENT PORK WITH LOTS OF FRESH CORIANDER AND A RICH TOMATO SAUCE TO MAKE AN INTERESTING AND DELICIOUS MEAL.

SERVES 4

INGREDIENTS

1 large bunch fresh coriander
  (cilantro) with roots
30ml/2 tbsp vegetable oil
1 garlic clove, crushed
30ml/2 tbsp five-spice powder
500g/1¼lb pork belly, cut into
  2.5cm/1in pieces
400g/14oz can chopped tomatoes
150ml/¼ pint/⅔ cup hot water
30ml/2 tbsp dark soy sauce
45ml/3 tbsp Thai fish sauce
30ml/2 tbsp granulated sugar
1 lime, halved

COOK'S TIP
Make sure that you buy Chinese five-spice powder, as the Indian variety is made up from quite different spices.

1 Cut off the coriander roots. Chop five of them finely and freeze the remainder for another occasion. Chop the coriander stalks and leaves and set them aside. Keep the roots separate.

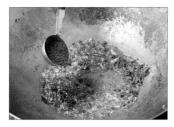

2 Heat the oil in a large pan and cook the garlic until golden brown. Stirring constantly, add the chopped coriander roots and then the five-spice powder.

3 Add the pork and stir-fry until the meat is thoroughly coated in spices and has browned. Add the tomatoes and hot water. Bring to the boil, then stir in the soy sauce, fish sauce and sugar.

4 Reduce the heat, cover the pan and simmer for 30 minutes. Stir in the chopped coriander stalks and leaves, squeeze over the lime juice and serve.

Energy 582Kcal/2409kJ; Protein 20.6g; Carbohydrate 12.2g, of which sugars 12g; Fat 50.4g, of which saturates 17.1g; Cholesterol 90mg; Calcium 53mg; Fibre 1.8g; Sodium 818mg.

PORK <u>ON</u> LEMON GRASS STICKS

THIS SIMPLE RECIPE MAKES A SUBSTANTIAL SNACK, AND THE LEMON GRASS STICKS NOT ONLY ADD A SUBTLE FLAVOUR BUT ALSO MAKE A GOOD TALKING POINT.

SERVES 4

INGREDIENTS
    300g/11oz minced (ground) pork
    4 garlic cloves, crushed
    4 fresh coriander (cilantro) roots,
        finely chopped
    2.5ml/½ tsp granulated sugar
    15ml/1 tbsp soy sauce
    salt and ground black pepper
    8 x 10cm/4in lengths of lemon
        grass stalk
    sweet chilli sauce,
        to serve

VARIATION
Slimmer versions of these pork sticks are perfect for parties. The mixture will be enough for 12 lemon grass sticks if you use it sparingly.

1 Place the minced pork, crushed garlic, chopped coriander root, sugar and soy sauce in a large bowl. Season with salt and pepper to taste and mix well.

2 Divide into eight portions and mould each one into a ball. It may help to dampen your hands before shaping the mixture to prevent it from sticking.

3 Stick a length of lemon grass halfway into each ball, then press the meat mixture around the lemon grass to make a shape like a chicken leg.

4 Cook the pork sticks under a hot grill (broiler) for 3–4 minutes on each side, until golden and cooked through. Serve with the chilli sauce for dipping.

Energy 129Kcal/538kJ; Protein 14.5g; Carbohydrate 1.4g, of which sugars 1.3g; Fat 7.3g, of which saturates 2.7g; Cholesterol 50mg; Calcium 7mg; Fibre 0g; Sodium 317mg.

HERB-CRUSTED RACK OF LAMB WITH PUY LENTILS

THIS ROAST IS QUICK AND EASY TO PREPARE, YET IMPRESSIVE WHEN SERVED: THE PERFECT CHOICE WHEN ENTERTAINING. BOILED OR STEAMED NEW POTATOES AND LIGHTLY COOKED BROCCOLI OR SUGAR SNAP PEAS ARE SUITABLE ACCOMPANIMENTS FOR THE LAMB. SERVE WITH A LIGHT RED WINE.

SERVES 4

INGREDIENTS
  2 x 6-bone racks of lamb, chined
  50g/2oz/1 cup fresh white
    breadcrumbs
  2 large garlic cloves, crushed
  90ml/6 tbsp chopped mixed fresh
    herbs, such as rosemary, thyme, flat
    leaf parsley and marjoram, plus
    extra sprigs to garnish
  50g/2oz ¼ cup butter, melted
  salt and ground black pepper
For the Puy lentils
  1 red onion, chopped
  30ml/2 tbsp olive oil
  400g/14oz can Puy or green lentils,
    rinsed and drained
  400g/14oz can chopped tomatoes
  30ml/2 tbsp chopped fresh parsley

1 Preheat the oven to 220°C/425°F/ Gas 7. Trim any excess fat from the lamb, season and place in a roasting tin.

2 Mix together the breadcrumbs, garlic, chopped herbs and butter. Press the mixture on to the fat-sides of the lamb. Roast for 25 minutes. Cover with foil and stand for 5 minutes before carving.

3 Cook the onion in the olive oil until softened. Add the lentils and tomatoes and cook gently for 5 minutes, or until the lentils are piping hot. Stir in the parsley and season to taste.

4 Cut each rack of lamb in half and serve with the lentils and new potatoes. Garnish with herb sprigs.

Energy 639Kcal/2673kJ; Protein 51.5g; Carbohydrate 28.2g, of which sugars 1.9g; Fat 36.4g, of which saturates 16.7g; Cholesterol 171mg; Calcium 89mg; Fibre 4.9g; Sodium 294mg.

LAMB STEAKS MARINATED <u>WITH</u> MINT <u>AND</u> LEMON

USE THIS SIMPLE AND TRADITIONAL MARINADE TO MAKE THE MOST OF FINE-QUALITY LAMB LEG STEAKS. THE COMBINATION OF LEMON AND FRESH MINT GOES EXTREMELY WELL WITH THE FLAVOUR OF THE MEAT, ESPECIALLY WHEN IT HAS BEEN COOKED ON A BARBECUE OR UNDER A GRILL.

SERVES 4

INGREDIENTS
   4 lamb steaks, about 225g/8oz each
   5ml/1 tsp finely chopped fresh mint
   fresh mint leaves, to garnish
For the marinade
   grated rind and juice of ½ lemon
   1 garlic clove, crushed
   1 spring onion (scallion),
     finely chopped
   30ml/2 tbsp extra virgin olive oil
   salt and ground black pepper

1 Mix all the ingredients for the marinade and season to taste with salt and ground black pepper.

2 Place the lamb steaks in a shallow dish and add the marinade and mint, ensuring that all the meat is coated. Cover with clear film and leave the lamb to marinate in the refrigerator for several hours or overnight if possible.

3 Drain the lamb and cook under a medium-hot grill (broiler), or on a barbecue, for 10–15 minutes, or until just cooked, basting with marinade occasionally and turning once. Garnish with the fresh mint leaves.

Energy 502Kcal/2099kJ; Protein 66.3g; Carbohydrate 0.9g, of which sugars 0.2g; Fat 25.9g, of which saturates 8.9g; Cholesterol 236mg; Calcium 74mg; Fibre 0.1g; Sodium 160mg.

SKEWERED LAMB WITH CORIANDER YOGURT

TENDER CHUNKS OF LEAN LAMB ARE MARINATED WITH THE AROMATIC FLAVOURS OF ONION, BAY AND ROSEMARY, AND SERVED WITH A FRESH MINT AND CORIANDER YOGURT.

SERVES 4

INGREDIENTS
900g/2lb lean boneless lamb
1 large onion, grated
3 bay leaves
5 rosemary or thyme sprigs
grated rind and juice of 1 lemon
2.5ml/½ tsp caster (superfine) sugar
75ml/2½fl oz/⅓ cup olive oil
salt and ground black pepper
sprigs of fresh rosemary, to garnish
lemon wedges, to serve
For the coriander yogurt
150ml/¼ pint/⅔ cup thick natural (plain) yogurt
15ml/1 tbsp chopped fresh mint
15ml/1 tbsp chopped fresh coriander (cilantro)
10ml/2 tsp grated onion

1 To make the coriander yogurt, mix together the natural yogurt, chopped fresh mint, chopped fresh coriander and grated onion. Transfer the mixture to a serving bowl.

2 To make the kebabs, cut the lamb into 2.5cm/1in cubes with a sharp knife and put in a bowl.

3 Mix together the onion, herbs, lemon rind and juice, sugar and oil, then season to taste.

4 Pour the marinade over the meat in the bowl and stir to ensure the meat is thoroughly covered.

5 Cover with clear film (plastic wrap) and leave to marinate for several hours.

6 Drain the meat and thread on to metal skewers. Cook under a hot grill (broiler), or on a barbecue, for about 10 minutes.

7 Garnish with rosemary and serve with lemon wedges and the coriander yogurt (cook the lemon wedges as well, if you like).

COOK'S TIP
If possible, try to use real Greek (US strained plain) yogurt for the coriander yogurt in this recipe. Made from either sheep's or cow's milk, it is deliciously thick and creamy, and is also much less acidic than skimmed milk natural (plain) yogurt. American readers need to strain natural yogurt to thicken it up.

Energy 548Kcal/2282kJ; Protein 46.6g; Carbohydrate 4.9g, of which sugars 4.5g; Fat 38.3g, of which saturates 13.7g; Cholesterol 172mg; Calcium 118mg; Fibre 0.8g; Sodium 229mg.

LAMB WITH LAVENDER BALSAMIC MARINADE

FRAGRANT LAVENDER IS AN UNUSUAL FLAVOUR TO USE WITH MEAT, BUT ITS HEADY, SUMMERY SCENT WORKS WELL WITH TENDER LAMB CUTLETS. IF YOU PREFER, ROSEMARY CAN TAKE ITS PLACE.

SERVES 4

INGREDIENTS

    4 racks of lamb, with
      3–4 cutlets on each
    1 shallot, finely chopped
    45ml/3 tbsp chopped
      fresh lavender florets, plus
      extra to garnish
    15ml/1 tbsp balsamic vinegar
    30ml/2 tbsp olive oil
    15ml/1 tbsp lemon juice
    salt and ground
      black pepper
    handful of lavender sprigs

1 Place the racks of lamb in a large mixing bowl or wide dish and sprinkle over the chopped shallot.

2 Sprinkle the chopped fresh lavender over the racks of lamb.

3 Beat together the balsamic vinegar, olive oil and lemon juice and pour them over the lamb.

4 Season well with salt and ground black pepper and then turn the meat to coat it evenly.

5 Sprinkle a few of the lavender sprigs over the grill (broiler) or on the coals of a medium-hot barbecue.

6 Cook the lamb for about 15–20 minutes, turning once and basting with any remaining marinade.

7 Serve the lamb while it is still slightly pink in the centre, garnished with the remaining lavender.

COOK'S TIP
If you have time or want to prepare in advance, you can cover the bowl containing the meat and flavourings with clear film (plastic wrap) and leave it to marinade in the refrigerator overnight.

Energy 565Kcal/2363kJ; Protein 61.5g; Carbohydrate 1.5g, of which sugars 1.1g; Fat 34.9g, of which saturates 14.7g; Cholesterol 216mg; Calcium 58mg; Fibre 0.8g; Sodium 178mg.

HERB-STUDDED GIGOT BOULANGÈRE

*THIS DISH COMBINES LAMB, GARLIC AND SPRIGS OF ROSEMARY OF THYME, AND IS A TROUBLE-FREE
AND DELICIOUS CHOICE FOR SUNDAY LUNCH.*

4 Pour in the hot stock and add a little hot water, if necessary, to bring the liquid to just below the level of the potatoes. Dot with the remaining butter, cover with foil and cook in the oven for 40 minutes. Increase the oven temperature to 200°C/400°F/Gas 6.

5 Meanwhile, cut the rest of the garlic into slivers. Make slits all over the lamb and insert slivers of garlic and sprigs of thyme or rosemary into the slits. Season the lamb well with salt and pepper.

SERVES 6

INGREDIENTS
   50g/2oz/¼ cup butter, plus extra
      for greasing
   4–6 garlic cloves
   2 yellow onions, thinly sliced
   12–18 small fresh thyme or
      rosemary sprigs
   2 fresh bay leaves
   1.8kg/4lb red potatoes, thinly sliced
   450ml/¾ pint/scant 2 cups hot lamb
      or vegetable stock
   2kg/4½lb leg of lamb
   30ml/2 tbsp olive oil
   salt and ground black pepper

1 Preheat the oven to 190°C/375°F/ Gas 5. Use a little butter to grease a large ovenproof dish, about 6cm/2½in deep. Finely chop half the garlic and sprinkle a little over the prepared dish.

2 Cook the onions in 25g/1oz/2 tbsp of the butter for 5–8 minutes, until softened. Coarsely chop half the thyme or rosemary and crush the bay leaves.

3 Arrange a layer of potatoes in the dish, season and sprinkle with half the remaining chopped garlic, rosemary or thyme, 1 bay leaf and the onions. Add the remaining potatoes, chopped garlic and herbs.

6 Uncover the potatoes and sprinkle a few rosemary or thyme sprigs over them. Rest a roasting rack or ovenproof cooling rack over the dish and place the lamb on it. Rub the olive oil over the meat, then return the dish to the oven.

7 Cook, turning the lamb once or twice, for 1½–1¾ hours, depending on how well done you prefer lamb.

8 Leave the lamb to rest for 20 minutes in a warm place (in the switched-off oven, for example) before carving.

Energy 1006Kcal/4228kJ; Protein 105g; Carbohydrate 53.6g, of which sugars 7.7g; Fat 42.9g, of which saturates 17.8g; Cholesterol 351mg; Calcium 60mg; Fibre 3.9g; Sodium 296mg.

ROAST LEG OF LAMB WITH PESTO

THIS WOULD BE A WONDERFUL CHOICE FOR A CELEBRATORY SUNDAY LUNCH, AS IT LOOKS, TASTES AND SMELLS FABULOUS AND A WHOLE LEG OF LAMB WILL SERVE QUITE A LARGE GATHERING.

SERVES 6–8

INGREDIENTS
50g/2oz/2 cups fresh basil leaves
4 garlic cloves, coarsely chopped
45ml/3 tbsp pine nuts
150ml/¼ pint/⅔ cup olive oil
50g/2oz/⅔ cup freshly grated
  Parmesan cheese
5ml/1 tsp salt
2.25–2.75kg/5–6lb leg of lamb
cooked baby vegetables and
  miniature roast potatoes, to serve

1 To make the pesto, combine the basil, garlic and pine nuts in a food processor, and process until finely chopped. With the motor running, gradually add the oil in a steady stream.

2 Scrape the mixture into a bowl. Stir in the Parmesan and salt.

3 Place the lamb in a roasting pan. Make several slits in the meat with a sharp knife and spoon some of the pesto into each slit.

4 Rub more pesto evenly over the surface of the lamb.

5 Continue patting on the pesto in a thick, even layer. Cover and leave to stand for 2 hours at room temperature or in the refrigerator overnight.

6 Bring the lamb back to room temperature 30 minutes before roasting. Preheat the oven to 180°C/350°F/Gas 4. Place the lamb in the oven and roast, allowing about 20 minutes per 450g/1lb for rare meat or 25 minutes per 450g/1lb for medium-rare. Turn the lamb occasionally during roasting.

7 Remove the leg of lamb from the oven, cover it loosely with foil and leave to rest for about 15 minutes before carving into slices and serving with a selection of baby vegetables and miniature roast potatoes.

Energy 755Kcal/3158kJ; Protein 87.1g; Carbohydrate 1g, of which sugars 0.8g; Fat 44.9g, of which saturates 14g; Cholesterol 288mg; Calcium 110mg; Fibre 0.5g; Sodium 493mg.

BEEF STROGANOFF <u>WITH</u> PARSLEY

THE COMBINATION OF STRIPS OF LEAN BEEF IN A SOUR CREAM SAUCE FLAVOURED WITH BRANDY AND HERBS IS PERFECT FOR A COLD WINTER'S EVENING. SERVE THIS RICH DISH WITH PLAIN BOILED RICE AND A SIMPLE GREEN SALAD OR STEAMED GREEN VEGETABLES.

SERVES 8

INGREDIENTS

  1.2kg/2½lb fillet (tenderloin) of beef
  30ml/2 tbsp plain (all-purpose) flour
  large pinch each of cayenne pepper
    and paprika
  75ml/5 tbsp sunflower oil
  1 large onion, chopped
  3 garlic cloves, finely chopped
  450g/1lb/6½ cups chestnut
    mushrooms, sliced
  75ml/5 tbsp brandy
  300ml/½ pint/1¼ cups beef stock
    or consommé
  300ml/½ pint/1¼ cups sour cream
  45ml/3 tbsp chopped fresh flat
    leaf parsley
  salt and ground black pepper

1 Thinly slice the fillet of beef across the grain, then cut it into fine strips. Season the flour with the cayenne pepper and paprika.

2 Heat half the oil in a large frying pan, add the onion and garlic and cook gently until the onion has softened.

3 Add the mushrooms and stir-fry over a high heat. Transfer the vegetables and their juices to a dish and set aside.

4 Wipe the pan, then add and heat the remaining oil. Coat a batch of meat with flour, then stir-fry over a high heat until browned. Remove from the pan, then coat and stir-fry another batch.

5 When the last batch of steak is cooked, replace all the meat and vegetables. Add the brandy and simmer until it has almost evaporated.

6 Stir in the stock or consommé and seasoning and cook for 10–15 minutes, stirring frequently, or until the meat is tender and the sauce is thick and glossy.

7 Add the sour cream and sprinkle with chopped parsley. Serve with rice and a simple salad.

COOK'S TIP
If you do not have a very large pan, it may be easier to cook the meat and vegetables in two separate pans. A large flameproof casserole may be used.

Energy 392Kcal/1630kJ; Protein 35g; Carbohydrate 9.5g, of which sugars 5.1g; Fat 23.9g, of which saturates 9.8g; Cholesterol 114mg; Calcium 65mg; Fibre 1.6g; Sodium 86mg.

STEAK BÉARNAISE

BÉARNAISE, AFTER BÉARN IN SOUTH-WEST FRANCE, IS A CREAMY EGG AND BUTTER SAUCE FLAVOURED WITH FRESH TARRAGON. IT IS A CLASSIC COMPLEMENT TO GRIDDLED, GRILLED OR PAN-FRIED STEAK AND IS ALSO EXCELLENT WITH ROAST BEEF. ROASTED VEGETABLES MAKE A GOOD ACCOMPANIMENT.

SERVES 4

INGREDIENTS

4 sirloin steaks, each weighing
    about 225g/8oz, trimmed
15ml/1 tbsp sunflower oil (optional)
salt and ground black pepper
For the Béarnaise sauce
    90ml/6 tbsp white wine vinegar
    12 black peppercorns
    2 bay leaves
    2 shallots, finely chopped
    4 fresh tarragon sprigs
    4 egg yolks
    225g/8oz/1 cup unsalted (sweet)
      butter at room temperature, diced
    30ml/2 tbsp chopped fresh tarragon
    ground white pepper

1 Start by making the sauce. Put the vinegar, peppercorns, bay leaves, shallots and tarragon sprigs in a small pan and simmer until reduced to 30ml/2 tbsp. Strain the vinegar through a fine sieve (strainer).

2 Beat the egg yolks with salt and freshly ground white pepper in a small, heatproof bowl. Stand the bowl over a pan of very gently simmering water, then gradually beat the strained vinegar into the yolks.

3 Gradually beat in the butter, one piece at a time, allowing each addition to melt before adding the next. Do not allow the water to heat beyond a gentle simmer or the sauce will overheat and curdle.

4 While cooking the sauce, heat a griddle or grill until very hot.

COOK'S TIP
If you are confident about preparing egg and butter sauces, the best method is to reduce the flavoured vinegar before cooking the steak, then finish the sauce while the steak is cooking. This way, the sauce does not have to be kept hot and there is less risk of overheating it or allowing it to become too thick.

5 Beat the chopped fresh tarragon into the sauce and remove the pan from the heat. The sauce should be smooth, thick and glossy.

6 Cover the surface of the sauce with clear film (plastic wrap) or dampened baking parchment to prevent a skin forming and leave over the pan of hot water, still off the heat, to keep hot while you cook the steak.

7 Season the steaks with salt and plenty freshly ground black pepper.

8 A pan is not usually oiled before cooking steak, but if it is essential to grease the pan, add only the minimum oil. Cook the steaks for 2–4 minutes on each side. The cooking time depends on the thickness of the steaks and the extent to which you want to cook them. As a guide, 2–4 minutes will give a medium-rare result.

9 Serve the steaks on warmed plates. Peel the clear film or dampened baking parchment off the sauce and stir it lightly, then spoon it over the steaks.

Energy 789Kcal/3269kJ; Protein 56.3g; Carbohydrate 1.5g, of which sugars 1.2g; Fat 61.9g, of which saturates 35.4g; Cholesterol 436mg; Calcium 49mg; Fibre 0.2g; Sodium 508mg.

SPAGHETTI WITH MEATBALLS AND PARSLEY

FOR A GREAT INTRODUCTION TO THE CHARM OF CHILLIES, THIS SIMPLE PASTA DISH IS HARD TO BEAT. CHILDREN LOVE THE GENTLE HEAT OF THE SWEET AND SPICY TOMATO SAUCE.

SERVES 6–8

INGREDIENTS
  350g/12oz minced (ground) beef
  1 egg
  60ml/4 tbsp roughly chopped fresh
    flat leaf parsley
  2.5ml/½ tsp crushed dried
    red chillies
  1 thick slice white bread,
    crusts removed
  30ml/2 tbsp milk
  about 30ml/2 tbsp olive oil
  300ml/½ pint/1¼ cups passata
    (bottled strained tomatoes)
  400ml/14fl oz/1⅔ cups
    vegetable stock
  5ml/1 tsp granulated sugar
  350–450g/12oz–1lb fresh or
    dried spaghetti
  salt and ground black pepper
  shavings of Parmesan cheese,
    to serve

1 Put the beef in a large bowl. Add the egg, with half the parsley and half the crushed chillies. Season with plenty of salt and pepper.

2 Tear the bread into small pieces and place these in a small bowl. Moisten with the milk. Leave to soak for a few minutes, then squeeze out the excess milk and crumble the bread over the meat mixture. Mix everything together with a wooden spoon, then use your hands to squeeze and knead the mixture so that it becomes smooth and quite sticky.

3 Wash your hands, rinse them under the cold tap, then pick up small pieces of the mixture and roll them between your palms to make about 30 small balls. Place the meatballs on a tray and chill for 30 minutes.

4 Heat the oil in a large non-stick frying pan. Cook the meatballs in batches until browned on all sides. Pour the passata and stock into a large pan. Heat gently, then add the remaining chillies and the sugar, and season. Add the meatballs and bring to the boil. Reduce the heat, and simmer for 20 minutes.

5 Bring a large pan of lightly salted water to the boil and cook the pasta until it is just tender, following the instructions on the packet. Drain and tip it into a large heated bowl. Pour over the sauce and toss gently. Sprinkle with the remaining parsley and shavings of Parmesan cheese. Serve immediately.

Energy 275Kcal/1161kJ; Protein 15.3g; Carbohydrate 36g, of which sugars 3.4g; Fat 8.8g, of which saturates 3.4g; Cholesterol 50mg; Calcium 30mg; Fibre 1.7g; Sodium 68mg.

CHILLI BEEF WITH BASIL

THIS IS A VERY EASY DISH THAT CHILLI LOVERS WILL ENJOY COOKING AND EATING. USE BIRD'S EYE CHILLIES IF YOU CAN AND FRAGRANT THAI JASMINE RICE TO SERVE WITH IT.

SERVES 2

INGREDIENTS

16–20 large fresh basil leaves,
    plus 30ml/2 tbsp finely
    chopped basil
about 90ml/6 tbsp groundnut
    (peanut) oil
275g/10oz rump (round) steak
30ml/2 tbsp Thai fish sauce
5ml/1 tsp soft dark brown sugar
2 fresh red chillies, sliced into rings
3 garlic cloves, chopped
5ml/1 tsp chopped fresh root ginger
1 shallot, thinly sliced
squeeze of lemon juice
salt and ground black pepper
Thai jasmine rice, to serve

1 Dry the basil leaves thoroughly, if necessary. Heat the oil in a wok. When it is hot, add the basil leaves and fry for about 1 minute until crisp and golden.

2 Scoop out and drain on kitchen paper. Remove the wok from the heat and carefully pour off all but 30ml/2 tbsp of the oil.

3 Cut the steak across the grain into thin strips. In a bowl, mix together the fish sauce and sugar. Add the beef, mix well, then cover and set aside to marinate for about 30 minutes.

COOK'S TIP
Groundnut oil is widely used in Chinese cooking. Its ability to be heated to a high temperature without burning makes it ideal for stir-frying. It has a mild, pleasant taste.

4 Reheat the oil until hot, add the chillies, garlic, ginger and shallot, and stir-fry for 30 seconds. Add the beef and chopped basil, and stir-fry for about 3 minutes more. Flavour with lemon juice and add salt and pepper to taste.

5 Transfer to a warmed serving platter, arrange the fried basil leaves over the top and serve immediately with rice. Good accompaniments would be lightly steamed green vegetables or a crisp green salad to provide contrast.

Energy 494Kcal/2049kJ; Protein 31.1g; Carbohydrate 5.7g, of which sugars 4.9g; Fat 38.7g, of which saturates 6.2g; Cholesterol 81mg; Calcium 17mg; Fibre 0.4g; Sodium 1152mg.

PROVENÇAL BEEF AND OLIVE DAUBE WITH HERBS

A DAUBE IS A FRENCH METHOD OF BRAISING MEAT WITH WINE AND HERBS. THIS VERSION FROM THE NICE AREA IN THE SOUTH OF FRANCE ALSO INCLUDES BLACK OLIVES AND TOMATOES.

SERVES 6

INGREDIENTS

1.3–1.6kg/3–3½lb topside (pot roast) of beef
225g/8oz lardons, or thick streaky (fatty) bacon cut into strips
225g/8oz carrots, thickly sliced
1 bay leaf
1 fresh thyme sprig
2 fresh parsley stalks
3 garlic cloves
225g/8oz/2 cups pitted black olives
400g/14oz can chopped tomatoes
crusty bread, flageolet or cannellini beans or pasta, to serve

For the marinade

120ml/4fl oz/½ cup extra virgin olive oil or other mild oil
1 onion, sliced
4 shallots, sliced
1 celery stick, sliced
1 carrot, sliced
150ml/¼ pint/⅔ cup red wine
6 whole black peppercorns
2 garlic cloves, sliced
1 bay leaf
1 fresh thyme sprig
2 fresh parsley stalks
salt and ground black pepper

VARIATIONS
• This dish can be varied quite easily. Simply keep the main ingredients the same and change the herbs: instead of thyme and parsley, try rosemary.
• If you prefer, use chicken instead of beef and make the marinade with white wine.
• You could vary this dish further by choosing sweet white wine or adding some extra sugar, and leaving out the olives and herbs in favour of Chinese five-spice powder. This will give the dish a more exotic flavour.
• If you don't have any chopped tomatoes, you could chop canned whole tomatoes yourself, but these tend to be rather more watery.

1 To make the marinade, gently heat the oil in a large, shallow pan. Add the sliced onion, shallots, celery and carrot, then cook for 2 minutes.

2 Lower the heat and wait until the ingredients have cooled slightly, then add the red wine, peppercorns, garlic, bay leaf, thyme and parsley stalks. Season with a little salt, then cover and simmer over a gentle heat for 15–20 minutes, stirring occasionally. Set the pan aside.

3 Place the beef in a large glass or earthenware dish and pour over the cooled marinade from the frying pan.

4 Cover the dish with a dishtowel, clear film (plastic wrap) or baking parchment and leave the beef to marinate in a cool place for several hours or in the refrigerator overnight. Turn the meat every few hours if possible, but turn it at least once during this time.

5 Preheat the oven to 160°C/325°F/ Gas 3. Lift the meat out of the marinade and fit snugly into a casserole. Add the lardons or bacon and carrots, along with the herbs and garlic.

6 Strain in all the marinade. Cover the casserole with greaseproof paper, then the lid and cook in the oven for 2½ hours.

7 Remove the casserole from the oven, blot the surface of the liquid with kitchen paper to remove the surplus fat, or use a spoon to skim it off, then stir in the olives and tomatoes.

8 Re-cover the casserole, return to the oven and cook for a further 30 minutes. Carve the meat into thick slices and serve with crusty bread, plain boiled flageolet or cannellini beans or pasta.

COOK'S TIP
For those with an alcohol sensitivity, red grape juice and a squeeze of lemon juice can be substituted for the wine.

Energy 551Kcal/2302kJ; Protein 56.9g; Carbohydrate 5.9g, of which sugars 5.5g; Fat 31.7g, of which saturates 8g; Cholesterol 133mg; Calcium 57mg; Fibre 2.8g; Sodium 1501mg.

ROAST VEAL WITH PARSLEY STUFFING

COOKING THIS LOIN OF VEAL, WITH ITS FRAGRANT PARSLEY AND LEEK STUFFING, IN A ROASTING BAG MAKES SURE THAT IT IS SUCCULENT AND FULL FLAVOURED WHEN SERVED.

SERVES 6

INGREDIENTS
  25g/1oz/2 tbsp butter
  15ml/1 tbsp sunflower oil
  1 leek, finely chopped
  1 celery stick, finely chopped
  50g/2oz/1 cup fresh
    white breadcrumbs
  50g/2oz/½ cup chopped fresh flat
    leaf parsley
  900g/2lb boned loin
    of veal
  salt and ground
    black pepper

VARIATION
Other mild herbs can be used in the stuffing instead of parsley. Try tarragon, chervil and chives, but avoid strong-flavoured herbs, such as marjoram, oregano and thyme, which tend to overpower the delicate flavour of veal.

1 Preheat the oven to 180°C/350°F/ Gas 4. Heat the butter and oil in a frying pan until foaming. Cook the leek and celery until they are just starting to colour, then remove the pan from the heat and stir in the breadcrumbs, parsley and seasoning.

2 Lay the loin of veal out flat. Spread the stuffing over the meat, then roll it up carefully and tie the roll at regular intervals to secure it in a neat shape.

3 Place the veal in a roasting bag and close the bag with an ovenproof tie, then place it in a roasting pan. Roast the veal for 1¼ hours.

4 Pierce the meat with a metal skewer to check whether it is cooked: when cooked the meat juices will run clear. Leave the veal to stand for about 10–15 minutes, then carve it into thick slices and serve with gravy, sautéed potatoes, asparagus and sugar snaps.

ESCALOPES OF VEAL WITH TARRAGON SAUCE

THIS QUICK DISH COMBINES VEAL WITH A HERBY CREAM SAUCE AND IS DELICIOUS SERVED WITH BUTTERED TAGLIATELLE AND LIGHTLY STEAMED GREEN VEGETABLES.

SERVES 4

INGREDIENTS
  15ml/1 tbsp plain (all-purpose) flour
  4 veal escalopes (US scallops), each
    weighing about 75–115g/3–4oz
  30ml/2 tbsp sunflower oil
  1 shallot, chopped
  150g/5oz/2 cups oyster
    mushrooms, sliced
  30ml/2 tbsp Marsala or
    medium-dry sherry
  200ml/7fl oz/scant 1 cup
    crème fraîche
  30ml/2 tbsp chopped fresh tarragon
  salt and ground black pepper

COOK'S TIP
If the sauce seems to be too thick, add 30ml/2 tbsp water.

1 Season the flour and use to dust the veal escalopes, then set aside.

2 Heat the oil in a large frying pan and cook the shallot and mushrooms for 5 minutes. Add the escalopes and cook over a high heat for about 1½ minutes on each side. Pour in the Marsala or sherry and cook until reduced by half.

3 Use a spatula to remove the veal escalopes from the pan. Stir the crème fraîche, tarragon and seasoning into the juices remaining in the pan and simmer gently for 3–5 minutes, or until the sauce is thick and creamy.

4 Return the escalopes to the pan and heat through for 1 minute before serving.

Energy 415Kcal/1737kJ; Protein 49.1g; Carbohydrate 7.6g, of which sugars 1.1g; Fat 21.1g, of which saturates 7.8g; Cholesterol 241mg; Calcium 56mg; Fibre 1.3g; Sodium 238mg.
Energy 371Kcal/1542kJ; Protein 24.8g; Carbohydrate 4.7g, of which sugars 1.6g; Fat 27.4g, of which saturates 14.9g; Cholesterol 108mg; Calcium 41mg; Fibre 0.5g; Sodium 74mg.

VEAL ESCALOPES IN A HERBY WHITE WINE SAUCE

SAGE AND PARSLEY ADD FLAVOUR AND TEXTURE TO THE RICH WHITE WINE SAUCE THAT ACCOMPANIES THE SUCCULENT ESCALOPES OF VEAL IN THIS DELICIOUS DISH. THE RECIPE COMES FROM THE ISLAND OF CORFU, WHERE ITALIAN INFLUENCES ARE STILL STRONG.

SERVES 4

INGREDIENTS

675g/1½lb thin veal
  escalopes (US scallops)
40g/1½oz/⅓ cup plain
  (all-purpose) flour
90ml/6 tbsp extra virgin
  olive oil
1 small onion, thinly sliced
3 garlic cloves, finely chopped
2 or 3 fresh sage leaves,
  finely chopped
175ml/6fl oz/¾ cup white wine
juice of ½ lemon
450ml/¾ pint/scant 2 cups beef
  or chicken stock
30ml/2 tbsp finely chopped fresh
  flat leaf parsley
salt and ground black pepper

1 Sprinkle the veal escalopes with a little salt and pepper, then coat them lightly in the flour.

2 Heat the olive oil in a large frying pan over a medium heat. Add the veal escalopes and cook until they are lightly browned on both sides. Remove from the pan and transfer them to a wide flameproof casserole.

3 Add the sliced onion to the oil remaining in the frying pan and sauté the slices until translucent, then stir in the chopped garlic and sage. As soon as the garlic becomes aromatic, add the white wine and the lemon juice.

4 Raise the heat to high and cook for 10 minutes, stirring constantly and scraping the base to incorporate any sediment into the pan juices.

5 Pour the pan juices over the meat and add the stock. Sprinkle over salt and freshly ground black pepper to taste, then add the finely chopped flat leaf parsley.

6 Bring to the boil, lower the heat, cover and simmer for 45–50 minutes, or until the meat is tender and the sauce is a velvety consistency.

7 Transfer to a serving platter or dish and serve immediately while it is still piping hot. Garnish with salad leaves, such as rocket (arugula), cos or romaine lettuce, and accompany with new potatoes tossed in extra virgin olive oil, or fresh crusty bread.

COOK'S TIP

Escalopes are thin slices of veal that are cut from the leg. If they are a bit thick, place them between sheets of clear film (plastic wrap) and beat them with a meat mallet. Thin slices of pork can be cooked in the same way.

Energy 398Kcal/1,666kJ; Protein 39.7g; Carbohydrate 9.4g, of which sugars 1.4g; Fat 19.6g, of which saturates 3.4g; Cholesterol 88mg; Calcium 44mg; Fibre 0.9g; Sodium 105mg.

MEDALLIONS OF VENISON WITH HERBY HORSERADISH DUMPLINGS

VENISON IS LEAN AND FULL-FLAVOURED AND IS ESPECIALLY DELICIOUS SERVED WITH THESE HORSERADISH AND HERB DUMPLINGS. THIS RECIPE MAKES A SPECTACULAR MAIN COURSE TO SERVE AT A DINNER PARTY AND IS ACTUALLY VERY EASY TO PREPARE.

SERVES 4

INGREDIENTS

600ml/1 pint/2½ cups venison stock
120ml/4fl oz/½ cup port
15ml/1 tbsp sunflower oil
4 medallions of venison, about
  175g/6oz each
chopped parsley, to garnish
steamed baby vegetables, such as
  carrots, courgettes (zucchini) and
  turnips, to serve
For the dumplings
  75g/3oz/⅔ cup self-raising
  (self-rising) flour
  40g/1½oz beef suet (US chilled,
  grated shortening)
  15ml/1 tbsp chopped fresh mixed herbs
  5ml/1 tsp creamed horseradish
  45–60ml/3–4 tbsp water
  salt and ground black pepper

1 To make the dumplings, mix together the flour, beef suet, mixed herbs and seasoning, and make a well in the middle. Add the creamed horseradish and water, then mix to make a soft but not sticky dough.

2 Shape the dough into walnut-size balls and chill for up to 1 hour.

3 Boil the venison stock in a pan until reduced by half. Add the port and continue boiling until reduced again by half, then pour the reduced stock into a large frying pan.

4 Heat the stock until it is simmering and add the dumplings. Poach gently for 5–10 minutes, or until risen and cooked through. Use a draining spoon to remove the dumplings from the pan.

5 Smear the oil over a non-stick griddle and heat until very hot. Add the venison medallions and cook them for 2–3 minutes on each side. Remove from the pan. Place them on warm serving plates and pour the sauce over.

6 Serve with the dumplings and the baby vegetables, garnished with chopped parsley.

Energy 402Kcal/1691kJ; Protein 40.9g; Carbohydrate 19.5g, of which sugars 4.3g; Fat 16.1g, of which saturates 6.8g; Cholesterol 96mg; Calcium 99mg; Fibre 1.2g; Sodium 180mg.

Vegetarian Dishes

Make vegetarian dishes even more tempting by adding herbs to them. Enrich chickpeas with coriander, turmeric, chilli and creamy ground cashew nuts, or top grilled polenta with caramelized sweet onions. For entertaining, serve a delicate flan made with creamy ricotta and summer herbs, a flavoursome onion tart, or a vegetable curry enlivened with chilli, lemon grass and Thai spices. Here is a wealth of vegetarian ideas that is sure to please, whatever your preference.

Above *Baked Vegetables with Thyme and Parmesan Cheese*

Left *Garlic and Chive Risotto*

RISOTTO WITH FOUR CHEESES AND PARSLEY

Fresh parsley lifts this very rich dish. It is the perfect choice for a dinner party with an Italian theme, served with a light, dry sparkling white wine.

SERVES 4

INGREDIENTS

40g/1½oz/3 tbsp butter
1 small onion, finely chopped
1.2 litres/2 pints/5 cups vegetable
  stock, preferably home-made
350g/12oz/1¾ cups risotto rice
200ml/7fl oz/scant 1 cup dry
  white wine
50g/2oz/½ cup grated Gruyère cheese
50g/2oz/½ cup diced Taleggio cheese
50g/2oz/½ cup diced
  Gorgonzola cheese
50g/2oz/⅔ cup freshly grated
  Parmesan cheese
salt and ground black pepper
chopped fresh flat leaf parsley,
  to garnish

1 Melt the butter in a large, heavy pan or deep frying pan and cook the onion over a low heat, stirring frequently, for about 4–5 minutes, until softened and lightly browned.

2 Meanwhile, pour the stock into another pan and heat until simmering.

3 Add the rice to the onion mixture, stir until the grains start to swell and burst, then add the wine. Stir until it stops sizzling and most of it has been absorbed by the rice, then pour in a little of the hot stock.

4 Season to taste. Stir over a low heat until the stock has been absorbed.

5 Gradually add the remaining stock, a little at a time, allowing the rice to absorb the liquid before adding more, and stirring constantly. After about 20–25 minutes the rice will be *al dente* and the risotto creamy.

6 Turn off the heat under the pan, then add the Gruyère, Taleggio, Gorgonzola and 30ml/2 tbsp of the Parmesan cheese.

7 Stir gently until the cheeses have melted, then taste and adjust the seasoning, if necessary.

8 Spoon the risotto into a warm serving bowl and garnish with parsley. Serve immediately, handing the remaining grated Parmesan separately.

Energy 640Kcal/2662kJ; Protein 22.1g; Carbohydrate 67.1g, of which sugars 1.2g; Fat 26g, of which saturates 15.9g; Cholesterol 70mg; Calcium 451mg; Fibre 0.2g; Sodium 473mg.

RISOTTO WITH RICOTTA AND BASIL

THIS IS A WELL-FLAVOURED RISOTTO, WHICH BENEFITS FROM THE ADDITION OF DISTINCTIVELY PUNGENT BASIL, AND IS MELLOWED WITH SMOOTH RICOTTA.

SERVES 3–4

INGREDIENTS
45ml/3 tbsp olive oil
1 onion, finely chopped
275g/10oz/1½ cups risotto rice
1 litre/1¾ pints/4 cups hot
  vegetable stock
175g/6oz/¾ cup ricotta cheese
50g/2oz/2 cups fresh
  basil leaves, finely chopped,
  plus extra to garnish
75g/3oz/1 cup freshly grated
  Parmesan cheese
salt and ground black pepper

1 Heat the oil in a large pan or flameproof casserole and cook the onion over a low heat until soft. Do not allow the onion to brown.

2 Tip the rice into the pan containing the onions. Cook for a few minutes, stirring constantly, until the rice grains are well coated with oil and have become slightly translucent.

3 Pour in a quarter of the stock. Cook, stirring, until all the stock has been absorbed, then add another ladleful.

4 Continue in this manner, adding more stock when the previous ladleful has been absorbed, until the risotto has been cooking for about 20 minutes and the rice is just tender.

5 Spoon the ricotta into a bowl and break it up a little with a fork.

6 Gently stir the ricotta into the risotto, then mix in the chopped basil and grated Parmesan.

7 Taste and adjust the seasoning, if necessary, then cover and leave to stand for 2–3 minutes before serving, garnished with basil leaves.

Energy 715Kcal/2975kJ; Protein 22.4g; Carbohydrate 72.6g, of which sugars 2.8g; Fat 36.2g, of which saturates 16.4g; Cholesterol 70mg; Calcium 382mg; Fibre 0.7g; Sodium 442mg.

GARLIC AND CHIVE RISOTTO

GARLIC, ONIONS AND CHIVES BELONG TO THE ALLIUM FAMILY OF PLANTS. FIRSTLY, THE ONIONS ARE GENTLY COOKED IN BUTTER — AS IN ALL CLASSIC RISOTTOS — THEN THE GARLIC AND CHIVES ARE ADDED. THE RISOTTO IS TOPPED WITH A FINAL SPRINKLING OF DELICIOUS, CRISP FRIED ONIONS.

SERVES 4

INGREDIENTS

75g/3oz/6 tbsp butter
15ml/1 tbsp olive oil, plus extra for
  shallow frying
1 onion, finely chopped
4 garlic cloves, finely chopped
350g/12oz/1⅔ cups risotto rice
150ml/¼ pint/⅔ cup dry white wine
pinch of saffron threads (about
  12 threads)
about 1.2 litres/2 pints/5 cups
  simmering vegetable stock
1 large yellow onion, thinly sliced
15g/½oz chopped fresh chives
75g/3oz/1 cup freshly grated
Parmesan cheese, plus extra to taste
salt and ground black pepper

1 Melt half the butter with the oil in a large, deep frying pan or heavy pan.

2 Add the onion with a pinch of salt and cook over a very low heat, stirring frequently, for 10–15 minutes, or until softened and just turning golden. Do not allow the onion to brown.

3 Add the garlic and rice and cook, stirring constantly, for 3–4 minutes, or until the rice is coated and looks translucent. Season with a little salt and ground black pepper.

4 Pour in the wine and stir in the saffron with a ladleful of hot stock. Cook slowly, stirring frequently, until all the liquid has been absorbed.

5 Continue cooking the risotto for 18–20 minutes, adding one or two ladlefuls of stock at a time, until the rice is swollen and tender outside, but still *al dente* on the inside.

6 Keep the heat low and stir frequently. The finished risotto should be moist, but not like soup.

7 Separate the slices of yellow onion into rings while the risotto is cooking. Heat a shallow layer of oil in a frying pan. Cook the onion rings slowly at first until they are soft, then increase the heat and fry them briskly until they are brown and crisp. Drain them thoroughly on kitchen paper.

8 Beat the chopped chives, the remaining butter and half the Parmesan into the risotto until it looks creamy. Taste and add salt and ground black pepper, if necessary.

9 Serve the risotto in warmed bowls, topped with the crisp fried onions. Add more grated Parmesan to taste at the table.

Energy 600Kcal/2495kJ; Protein 15.4g; Carbohydrate 77.4g, of which sugars 5.5g; Fat 25.1g, of which saturates 14g; Cholesterol 59mg; Calcium 293mg; Fibre 1.9g; Sodium 325mg.

FRESH HERB RISOTTO

HERE IS A RISOTTO TO CELEBRATE AN ABUNDANCE OF SUMMER HERBS. AN AROMATIC BLEND OF
OREGANO, CHIVES, PARSLEY AND BASIL COMBINES WITH A MIXTURE OF WILD AND ARBORIO RICE AND
PARMESAN CHEESE TO MAKE A RICH, CREAMY AND SATISFYING MEAL.

SERVES 4

INGREDIENTS
  90g/3½oz/½ cup wild rice
  15ml/1 tbsp butter
  15ml/1 tbsp olive oil
  1 small onion, finely chopped
  450g/1lb/2¼ cups arborio rice
  300ml/½ pint/1¼ cups dry
    white wine
  1.2 litres/2 pints/5 cups simmering
    vegetable stock
  45ml/3 tbsp chopped fresh oregano
  45ml/3 tbsp chopped fresh chives
  60ml/4 tbsp chopped fresh flat
    leaf parsley
  60ml/4 tbsp chopped fresh basil
  75g/3oz/1 cup freshly grated
    Parmesan cheese
  salt and ground black pepper

1 Cook the wild rice in boiling salted water according to the instructions on the packet.

2 Heat the butter and oil in a large, heavy pan. When the butter has melted, add the onion and cook for 3 minutes.

3 Add the arborio rice and cook for 2 minutes, stirring to coat.

COOK'S TIPS
• Risotto rice is essential to achieve the correct creamy texture in this dish. Other types of rice simply will not do.
• Fresh herbs are also a must, but you can use tarragon, chervil, marjoram or thyme instead of the ones listed here, if you prefer.

4 Pour in the dry white wine and bring to the boil. Reduce the heat and cook for 10 minutes, or until all the wine has been absorbed.

5 Add the hot vegetable stock, a little at a time, waiting for each quantity to be absorbed before adding more, and stirring continuously.

6 After 25 minutes the rice should be tender and creamy. Season well with salt and pepper to taste. Add the herbs and wild rice; heat for 2 minutes, stirring frequently.

7 Stir in two-thirds of the Parmesan and cook until melted. Serve sprinkled with the remaining Parmesan.

Energy 681Kcal/2843kJ; Protein 18g; Carbohydrate 109.7g, of which sugars 1.6g; Fat 12.8g, of which saturates 6.2g; Cholesterol 27mg; Calcium 287mg; Fibre 0.8g; Sodium 235mg.

ROSEMARY RISOTTO ~~WITH~~ BORLOTTI BEANS

THIS IS A CLASSIC RISOTTO WITH A SUBTLE AND COMPLEX TASTE, FROM THE HEADY FLAVOURS OF ROSEMARY TO THE SAVOURY BEANS AND THE FRUITY-SWEET TASTES OF MASCARPONE AND PARMESAN.

3 Heat the olive oil in a large pan and gently fry the onion and garlic for 6–8 minutes, or until very soft. Add the rice and cook over a medium heat for a few minutes, stirring constantly, until the grains are thoroughly coated in oil and are slightly translucent.

4 Pour in the wine. Cook over a medium heat for 2–3 minutes, stirring all the time, until the wine has been absorbed. Add the stock gradually, a ladleful at a time, waiting for each quantity to be absorbed before adding more, and continuing to stir.

5 When the rice is about three-quarters cooked, stir in the bean purée (paste). Continue to cook the risotto, adding any stock that remains, until it has reached a creamy consistency and the rice is tender but still has a bit of "bite".

SERVES 3–4

INGREDIENTS
  400g/14oz can borlotti beans
  30ml/2 tbsp olive oil
  1 onion, chopped
  2 garlic cloves, crushed
  275g/10oz/1½ cups risotto rice
  175ml/6fl oz/¾ cup dry white wine
  900ml–1 litre/1½–1¾ pints/
    3¾–4 cups simmering
    vegetable stock
  60ml/4 tbsp mascarpone cheese
  65g/2½oz/¾ cup freshly grated
    Parmesan cheese, plus extra
    to serve (optional)
  5ml/1 tsp chopped fresh rosemary
  salt and ground black pepper

1 Drain the canned borlotti beans, rinse them well under plenty of cold water and drain again.

2 Purée about two-thirds of the beans fairly coarsely in a food processor or blender. Set the remainder aside.

6 Add the reserved beans, with the mascarpone, Parmesan and rosemary, then season to taste.

7 Stir thoroughly, then cover and leave to stand for about 5 minutes so that the risotto absorbs the flavours fully and the rice finishes cooking. Serve with extra Parmesan, if you like.

VARIATION
Fresh thyme or marjoram could be used for this risotto instead of rosemary, if preferred. One of the great virtues of risotto is that it lends itself well to a range of equally tasty variations. Experiment with different herbs to make your own speciality dish.

Energy 531Kcal/2220kJ; Protein 20g; Carbohydrate 74.6g, of which sugars 5.2g; Fat 14g, of which saturates 5.6g; Cholesterol 23mg; Calcium 287mg; Fibre 6.4g; Sodium 569mg.

RICE WITH DILL AND BROAD BEANS

THIS IS A FAVOURITE RICE DISH IN IRAN, WHERE IT IS CALLED BAGHALI POLO. THE COMBINATION OF BROAD BEANS, DILL, WARM CINNAMON AND CUMIN WORKS VERY WELL.

SERVES 4

INGREDIENTS

275g/10oz/1½ cups basmati
  rice, soaked
750ml/1¼ pints/3 cups water
40g/1½oz/3 tbsp butter
175g/6oz/1½ cups frozen baby broad
  (fava) beans, thawed and peeled
90ml/6 tbsp finely chopped fresh
  dill, plus 1 fresh dill sprig,
  to garnish
5ml/1 tsp ground cinnamon
5ml/1 tsp ground cumin
2–3 saffron threads, soaked in
  15ml/1 tbsp boiling water
salt

1 Drain the rice, tip it into a pan and pour in the water. Add a little salt. Bring to the boil, then lower the heat and simmer very gently for 5 minutes. Drain, rinse well in warm water and then drain once again.

2 Melt the butter gently over a low heat in a non-stick pan. Pour two-thirds of the melted butter into a small jug (pitcher) and set aside.

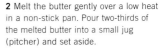

3 Spoon enough rice into the pan to cover the base. Add a quarter of the beans and a little dill. Spread over another layer of rice, then a layer of beans and dill. Repeat the layers until all the beans and dill have been used up, ending with a layer of rice. Cook over a gentle heat for 8 minutes until the rice and beans are nearly tender.

4 Pour the reserved melted butter over the rice. Sprinkle with the ground cinnamon and cumin. Cover the pan with a clean dish towel and a tight-fitting lid, lifting the corners of the cloth back over the lid. Cook over a low heat for 25–30 minutes.

5 Spoon about 45ml/3 tbsp of the cooked rice into the bowl of saffron water; mix well. Mound the remaining rice mixture on a large serving plate and spoon the saffron rice on one side to decorate. Serve at once, decorated with the sprig of dill.

Energy 364Kcal/1521kJ; Protein 9.3g; Carbohydrate 60.7g, of which sugars 1.2g; Fat 9.1g, of which saturates 5.3g; Cholesterol 21mg; Calcium 84mg; Fibre 4g; Sodium 72mg.

THAI VEGETABLE AND CORIANDER CURRY WITH LEMON GRASS JASMINE RICE

AN ARRAY OF THAI SEASONINGS GIVES THIS RICH CURRY ITS MARVELLOUS FLAVOUR. LEMON GRASS ADDS ITS DELICATE SCENT TO THE CURRY AND THE JASMINE RICE ACCOMPANIMENT.

SERVES 4

INGREDIENTS

10ml/2 tsp vegetable oil
400ml/14fl oz/1⅔ cups coconut milk
300ml/½ pint/1¼ cups good-quality
  vegetable stock
225g/8oz new potatoes, halved or
  quartered, if large
130g/4½oz baby corn cobs
5ml/1 tsp golden caster (superfine)
  sugar
185g/6½oz broccoli florets
1 red (bell) pepper, seeded and
  sliced lengthways
115g/4oz spinach, tough stalks
  removed and finely sliced
30ml/2 tbsp chopped fresh
  coriander (cilantro)
salt and ground black pepper

For the spice paste
1 red chilli, seeded and chopped
3 green chillies, seeded and chopped
1 lemon grass stalk, outer leaves
  removed and lower 5cm/2in
  finely chopped
2 shallots, chopped
finely grated rind of 1 lime
2 garlic cloves, chopped
5ml/1 tsp ground coriander
2.5ml/½ tsp ground cumin
1cm/½in fresh galangal, finely
  chopped or 2.5ml/½ tsp dried
  (optional)
45ml/3 tbsp chopped fresh coriander
  (cilantro)

For the rice
225g/8oz/generous 1 cup jasmine
  rice, rinsed
1 lemon grass stalk, outer leaves
  removed and cut into
  three pieces
6 cardamom pods, bruised

COOK'S TIP
Galangal is the pungent, aromatic root
of an Asian plant. It can usually be
found, in either fresh or dried form,
in good Asian supermarkets.

1 Begin by making the spice paste.
Place all the ingredients together in a
food processor or blender and blend to
a coarse paste.

2 Heat the oil in a large, heavy pan
and fry the spice paste for 1–2 minutes,
stirring constantly. Add the coconut milk
and stock, and bring to the boil.

3 Reduce the heat, add the potatoes,
and simmer for 15 minutes. Add the
baby corn and seasoning, then cook for
2 minutes.

4 Stir in the sugar, broccoli and
red pepper, mix well, and cook for
2 minutes more, or until the vegetables
are tender.

5 Stir in the finely sliced spinach and
15ml/1 tbsp of the chopped fresh
coriander. Cook for a further 2 minutes.

VARIATION
Try substituting other vegetables for the
ones used here. Mushrooms and carrots
would both work well.

6 Meanwhile, prepare the rice. Tip the
rinsed rice into a large pan and add the
pieces of lemon grass stalk and the
cardamom pods. Pour over 475ml/
16fl oz/2 cups water.

7 Bring to the boil, then reduce the
heat, cover the pan and allow to cook
for 10–15 minutes, or until the water is
absorbed and the rice is tender and
slightly sticky. Season with salt, leave to
stand for 10 minutes, then fluff up the
rice with a fork.

8 Remove the spices and serve the rice
with the curry, sprinkled with the
remaining fresh coriander.

Energy 330Kcal/1384kJ; Protein 10.3g; Carbohydrate 65g, of which sugars 11g; Fat 3.4g, of which saturates 0.6g; Cholesterol 0mg; Calcium 153mg; Fibre 4.1g; Sodium 554mg.

CORIANDER OMELETTE PARCELS WITH ASIAN VEGETABLES

PIQUANT, STIR-FRIED VEGETABLES WITH GINGER, CHILLIES AND BLACK BEAN SAUCE ARE WRAPPED IN A LIGHT CORIANDER OMELETTE. THEY MAKE AN ATTRACTIVE AND FLAVOURSOME LUNCH.

SERVES 4

INGREDIENTS
130g/4½oz broccoli, cut into
  small florets
30ml/2 tbsp groundnut
  (peanut) oil
1cm/½in piece fresh
  root ginger, finely grated
1 large garlic clove, crushed
2 fresh red chillies, seeded
  and finely sliced
4 spring onions (scallions),
  sliced diagonally
175g/6oz/3 cups shredded
  pak choi (bok choy)
50g/2oz/2 cups fresh coriander
  (cilantro) leaves, plus extra
  to garnish
115g/4oz/½ cup beansprouts
45ml/3 tbsp black
  bean sauce
4 eggs
salt and ground black pepper

1 Blanch the broccoli in boiling salted water for 2 minutes, drain, then refresh under cold running water.

2 Meanwhile, heat 15ml/1 tbsp of the oil in a frying pan or wok. Add the ginger, garlic and half the chilli and stir-fry for 1 minute.

3 Add the spring onions, broccoli and pak choi to the frying pan or wok, and stir-fry for 2 minutes more, tossing the vegetables continuously to prevent sticking and to cook them evenly.

4 Chop three-quarters of the coriander and add to the frying pan or wok. Add the beansprouts, stir-fry for 1 minute, then add the black bean sauce and heat through for 1 minute more. Remove the pan from the heat and keep warm.

5 Mix the eggs lightly with a fork and season them well. Heat a little of the remaining oil in a small frying pan and add a quarter of the beaten egg.

6 Swirl the egg until it covers the base of the pan, then sprinkle over a quarter of the reserved coriander leaves. Cook until set, then turn out the omelette on to a plate and keep warm while you make three more omelettes, adding more oil, when necessary.

7 Spoon the vegetable stir-fry on to the omelettes and roll up. Cut in half crossways and serve garnished with coriander leaves and the remaining sliced chilli.

Energy 174Kcal/722kJ; Protein 10.6g; Carbohydrate 6.4g, of which sugars 5.5g; Fat 12.1g, of which saturates 2.7g; Cholesterol 190mg; Calcium 158mg; Fibre 3.1g; Sodium 324mg.

FRITTATA <u>WITH</u> TOMATOES <u>AND</u> THYME

A FRITTATA IS AN ITALIAN OMELETTE THAT IS COOKED UNTIL FIRM ENOUGH TO BE CUT INTO WEDGES.
SUN-DRIED TOMATOES AND A HINT OF THYME GIVE THIS FRITTATA A DISTINCTIVE FLAVOUR.

3 Heat the oil in a large, non-stick frying pan. Stir in the chopped onion and cook for 5–6 minutes, or until softened and golden.

4 Stir in the sun-dried tomatoes and thyme, and cook over a moderate heat for a further 2–3 minutes, stirring from time to time. Season with salt and ground black pepper.

5 Break the eggs into a bowl and beat lightly. Stir in 45ml/3 tbsp of the tomato soaking water and the Parmesan. Raise the heat under the pan. When the oil is sizzling, add the eggs. Mix quickly into the other ingredients, then stop stirring. Lower the heat to moderate and cook for 4–5 minutes, or until the base is golden and the top puffed.

SERVES 3–4

INGREDIENTS
6 sun-dried tomatoes
60ml/4 tbsp olive oil
1 small onion, finely chopped
60ml/4 tbsp fresh thyme leaves
6 eggs
50g/2oz/⅔ cup freshly grated
  Parmesan cheese
salt and ground black pepper
sprigs of thyme, to garnish
shavings of Parmesan, to serve

COOK'S TIP
If you find it difficult to slide the frittata on to a plate, simply place the pan under a hot grill to brown the top, protecting the handle if necessary.

1 Place the tomatoes in a small bowl and pour on enough hot water just to cover them. Leave to soak for about 15 minutes.

2 Lift out of the water and pat dry on kitchen paper. Reserve the soaking water. Cut the tomatoes into thin strips.

6 Take a large plate, place it upside down over the pan and, holding it firmly with oven gloves, turn the pan and the frittata over on to it. Slide the frittata back into the pan, and continue cooking for 3–4 minutes, or until golden on the second side. Remove from the heat. Cut into wedges, garnish with thyme and serve with Parmesan.

Energy 170Kcal/705kJ; Protein 5.7g; Carbohydrate 3g, of which sugars 2.6g; Fat 15.2g, of which saturates 4.1g; Cholesterol 13mg; Calcium 158mg; Fibre 0.6g; Sodium 167mg.

BAKED HERB CRÊPES

ADD FRESH HERBS TO MAKE CRÊPES SOMETHING SPECIAL, THEN FILL WITH SPINACH, PINE NUTS AND RICOTTA CHEESE FLAVOURED WITH BASIL. DELICIOUS SERVED WITH A GARLIC AND TOMATO SAUCE.

SERVES 4

INGREDIENTS
  25g/1oz/½ cup chopped fresh herbs
  15ml/1 tbsp sunflower oil,
    plus extra for frying
  120ml/4fl oz/½ cup milk
  3 eggs
  25g/1oz/¼ cup plain
    (all-purpose) flour
  pinch of salt
  oil, for greasing
For the sauce
  30ml/2 tbsp olive oil
  1 small onion, chopped
  2 garlic cloves, crushed
  400g/14oz can chopped tomatoes
  pinch of soft light brown sugar
For the filling
  450g/1lb fresh spinach, cooked
    and drained
  175g/6oz/¾ cup ricotta cheese
  25g/1oz/¼ cup pine nuts, toasted
  5 sun-dried tomato halves in olive
    oil, drained and chopped
  30ml/2 tbsp chopped fresh basil
  salt, nutmeg and ground
    black pepper
  4 egg whites

1 To make the crêpes, place the herbs and oil in a food processor and blend until smooth. Add the milk, eggs, flour and salt and process again until smooth. Leave to rest for 30 minutes.

2 Heat a small, non-stick frying pan and add a small amount of oil. Add a ladleful of batter. Swirl around to cover the base. Cook for 2 minutes, turn and cook for 2 minutes. Make seven more crêpes.

3 To make the sauce, heat the oil in a small pan, add the onion and garlic and cook gently for 5 minutes. Add the tomatoes and sugar and cook for about 10 minutes, or until thickened. Purée in a blender, then sieve and set aside.

4 To make the filling, mix together the spinach with the ricotta, pine nuts, tomatoes and basil. Season with salt, nutmeg and pepper.

5 Preheat the oven to 190°C/375°F/ Gas 5. Whisk the egg whites until stiff. Fold one-third into the spinach mixture, then gently fold in the rest.

6 Place one crêpe at a time on a lightly oiled baking sheet, add a spoonful of filling and fold into quarters. Bake for 12 minutes until set. Reheat the sauce and serve with the crêpes.

Energy 434Kcal/1800kJ; Protein 14.9g; Carbohydrate 15.1g, of which sugars 9.8g; Fat 35.4g, of which saturates 8.3g; Cholesterol 161mg; Calcium 251mg; Fibre 5g; Sodium 229mg

COURGETTE <u>AND</u> DILL TART

THE SUBTLE FLAVOUR OF COURGETTES IS LIFTED DRAMATICALLY BY THE ADDITION OF FRESH DILL IN THIS TART. TAKE TIME TO ARRANGE THE COURGETTE LAYERS TO CREATE AN EYE-CATCHING DISH.

SERVES 4

INGREDIENTS

15ml/1 tbsp sunflower oil
3 courgettes (zucchini), thinly sliced
2 egg yolks
150ml/¼pint/⅔ cup double
  (heavy) cream
1 garlic clove, crushed
15ml/1 tbsp finely chopped fresh dill
salt and ground black pepper

For the pastry
115g/4oz/1 cup wholemeal
  (whole-wheat) flour
115g/4oz/1 cup self-raising
  (self-rising) flour
pinch of salt
115g/4oz/½ cup butter, chilled
  and diced
75ml/5 tbsp chilled water

1 To make the pastry, sift the flours into a bowl, tipping the bran into the bowl, then place in a food processor. Add the salt and diced butter and process using the pulse button until the mixture resembles fine breadcrumbs.

2 With the motor running, gradually add the water until the mixture forms a dough. Do not over-process. Wrap the pastry and chill for 30 minutes.

3 Preheat the oven to 200°C/400°F/ Gas 6 and grease a 20cm/8in flan tin (quiche pan).

COOK'S TIP
The smaller and skinnier courgettes are, the better they taste. Choose ones that have glossy green skins and feel firm.

4 Roll out the pastry and ease it into the tin. Prick the base, trim the edges and bake blind for 10–15 minutes.

5 Meanwhile, heat the oil in a frying pan, add the courgettes and sauté for 2–3 minutes until lightly browned, turning occasionally.

6 Mix the egg yolks, cream, garlic and dill in a small bowl. Season with salt and pepper.

7 Line the pastry case with courgettes and pour over the cream mixture.

8 Return to the oven for 25–30 minutes and bake until firm. Cool the tart in the tin, then remove and serve.

Energy 666Kcal/2767kJ; Protein 11.1g; Carbohydrate 43.6g, of which sugars 4.3g; Fat 50.9g, of which saturates 28.9g; Cholesterol 214mg; Calcium 184mg; Fibre 4.8g; Sodium 293mg.

ONION TART <u>WITH</u> NUTMEG

THIS CLASSIC ONION TART, FLAVOURED WITH NUTMEG, COMES FROM ALSACE IN EASTERN FRANCE.
IT MAKES A DELICIOUS WARM MAIN COURSE WHEN ACCOMPANIED BY A GREEN SALAD.

SERVES 4–6

INGREDIENTS
175g/6oz/1½ cups plain
  (all-purpose) flour
75g/3oz/6 tbsp butter, chilled
30–45ml/2–3 tbsp iced water
For the filling
50g/2oz/¼ cup butter
900g/2lb Spanish onions, sliced
1 egg plus 2 egg yolks
250ml/8fl oz/1 cup double
  (heavy) cream
1.5ml/¼ tsp freshly grated nutmeg
salt and ground black pepper

1 Process the flour, a pinch of salt and the butter in a food processor until reduced to fine crumbs. Alternatively, rub the fat into the flour using the finger-tips. Add the water and process, or knead, briefly to form a dough.

2 Gather the dough into a ball, wrap in clear film (plastic wrap) and chill in the refirgerator for 40 minutes.

3 Meanwhile, start the filling. Melt the butter in a large pan and add the onions and a pinch of salt. Turn them in the butter.

4 Cover and cook gently over a low heat, stirring frequently, for 30–40 minutes, or until golden. Cool slightly.

VARIATIONS
There are endless variations on this classic tart: try adding chopped fresh herbs, such as thyme, or, for meat-eaters, 115g/4oz/⅔ cup chopped smoked pancetta.

5 Preheat the oven to 190°C/375°F/Gas 5. Roll out the dough thinly and use to line a 23–25cm/9–10in loose-based flan tin (quiche pan). Line with baking parchment and baking beans, then bake blind for 10 minutes.

6 Remove the paper and baking beans and bake for 4–5 minutes more, until the pastry is lightly cooked to a pale brown colour (blond is quite a good description). Reduce the oven setting to 180°C/350°F/Gas 4.

7 Beat the egg, egg yolks and cream together. Season with salt, lots of black pepper and the grated nutmeg. Place half the onions in the pastry shell and add half the egg mixture. Add the remaining onions, then pour in as much of the remaining custard as you can.

8 Place on a baking sheet and bake on the middle shelf for 40–50 minutes, or until the custard is risen, browned and set in the centre. Serve warm rather than piping hot.

Energy 548Kcal/2271kJ; Protein 7.3g; Carbohydrate 35.4g, of which sugars 9.7g; Fat 42.9g, of which saturates 25.6g; Cholesterol 200mg; Calcium 115mg; Fibre 3g; Sodium 156mg.

SUMMER HERB RICOTTA FLAN

SIMPLE TO MAKE AND INFUSED WITH AROMATIC BASIL, CHIVES AND OREGANO, THIS DELICATE FLAN MAKES A DELIGHTFUL LUNCH DISH, ACCOMPANIED BY AN OLIVE AND GARLIC TAPENADE.

SERVES 4

INGREDIENTS
olive oil, for greasing and glazing
800g/1¾lb/3½ cups ricotta cheese
75g/3oz/1 cup finely grated
 Parmesan cheese
3 eggs, separated
60ml/4 tbsp torn fresh
 basil leaves
60ml/4 tbsp chopped fresh chives
45ml/3 tbsp fresh
 oregano leaves
2.5ml/½ tsp salt
ground black pepper
2.5ml/½ tsp paprika
fresh herb leaves, to garnish
For the tapenade
400g/14oz/3½ cups pitted black
 olives, rinsed and halved,
 reserving a few whole olives
 to garnish (optional)
5 garlic cloves, crushed
75ml/2½fl oz/⅓ cup olive oil

1 Preheat the oven to 180°C/350°F/ Gas 4. Lightly grease a 23cm/9in springform cake tin (pan) with olive oil. Mix together the ricotta, Parmesan and egg yolks in a food processor.

2 Add the herbs and the salt and pepper and blend until smooth.

3 Whisk the egg whites until they form soft peaks. Gently fold into the ricotta mixture, then spoon the mixture into the tin and smooth the top.

4 Bake for 1 hour 20 minutes, then remove from the oven and brush with olive oil, then sprinkle with paprika. Cool before removing from the tin.

5 Make the tapenade. Finely chop the olives and garlic in a food processor or blender. Gradually add the olive oil and blend to a coarse paste, then transfer to a serving bowl.

6 Garnish the flan with fresh herb leaves and serve with the tapenade.

RED ONION, THYME AND GOAT'S CHEESE PASTRIES

FRESH THYME ADDS A TASTY EDGE TO THE RED ONION IN THESE SCRUMPTIOUS PASTRIES. RING THE CHANGES BY SPREADING THE PASTRY BASE WITH PESTO OR TAPENADE BEFORE YOU ADD THE FILLING.

SERVES 4

INGREDIENTS
15ml/1 tbsp olive oil
450g/1lb red onions, sliced
30ml/2 tbsp fresh thyme
 or 10ml/2 tsp dried
15ml/1 tbsp balsamic vinegar
425g/15oz packet ready-rolled puff
 pastry, thawed if frozen
115g/4oz goat's cheese, cubed
1 egg, beaten
salt and ground
 black pepper
fresh oregano sprigs,
 to garnish
mixed green salad leaves,
 to serve

1 Heat the oil in a large, heavy frying pan, add the onions and fry over a gentle heat for 10 minutes, or until softened, stirring occasionally. Add the thyme, seasoning and vinegar, and cook for another 5 minutes. Remove the pan from the heat and leave to cool.

2 Preheat the oven to 220°C/425°F/ Gas 7. Unroll the puff pastry and, using a 15cm/6in plate as a guide, cut four rounds. Place the pastry rounds on a dampened baking sheet and, using the point of a knife, score a border, 2cm/¾in inside the edge of each round. (Do not cut through the pastry.)

3 Divide the onions among the pastry rounds and top with the goat's cheese. Brush the edge of each round with beaten egg.

4 Bake the pastries for 25–30 minutes, or until they are golden. Garnish with oregano sprigs before serving with mixed salad leaves.

Energy 730Kcal/3021kJ; Protein 32.7g; Carbohydrate 8.6g, of which sugars 6.7g; Fat 63g, of which saturates 26.7g; Cholesterol 245mg; Calcium 335mg; Fibre 4g; Sodium 2512mg.
Energy 595Kcal/2482kJ; Protein 15.4g; Carbohydrate 50.8g, of which sugars 8.1g; Fat 39.4g, of which saturates 5.9g; Cholesterol 74mg; Calcium 139mg; Fibre 1.6g; Sodium 543mg.

Pizzas and Breads

Let herbs bring diversity to your pizza and bread cooking. Add freshness to pizzas with a rocket or grilled fennel topping, or an exotic touch to breads with combinations of herbs, spices and vegetables. Mint, basil and coriander impart their unique taste, and olives and oregano give a full-bodied flavour to pizzas and savoury breads. This section contains recipes for every occasion, from quick supper dishes to dinner party accompaniments.

Above *Onion Rolls with Poppy Seeds*

Left *Bresaola and Rocket Pizza*

ROCKET AND TOMATO PIZZA

GARLIC AND BASIL FLAVOUR A TOMATO SAUCE THAT BLENDS BEAUTIFULLY WITH CREAMY MOZZARELLA.
ROCKET, WITH ITS PRONOUNCED FLAVOUR, ADDS THE FINAL TOUCH.

3 Cover the dough with the upturned bowl or a dish towel and leave to rest for about 5 minutes, then knead for a further 5 minutes, or until smooth and elastic. Place in a lightly oiled bowl and cover with clear film. Leave in a warm place for about 45 minutes, or until doubled in size.

4 Preheat the oven to 220°C/425°F/ Gas 7. To make the topping, heat the oil in a frying pan and fry the garlic for 1 minute. Add the canned tomatoes and sugar, and cook for 5–7 minutes, or until reduced and thickened. Stir in the basil and seasoning, then set aside.

SERVES 2

INGREDIENTS
    10ml/2 tsp olive oil, plus extra
       for drizzling and greasing
    1 garlic clove, crushed
    150g/5oz canned chopped tomatoes
    2.5ml/½ tsp sugar
    30ml/2 tbsp torn fresh basil leaves
    2 tomatoes, seeded and chopped
    150g/5oz mozzarella cheese, sliced
    20g/¾oz rocket (arugula) leaves
    coarse salt and ground black pepper
For the pizza base
    225g/8oz/2 cups strong white bread
       flour, sifted, plus extra for dusting
    5ml/1 tsp salt
    2.5ml/½ tsp easy-blend (rapid-rise)
       dried yeast
    15ml/1 tbsp olive oil, plus extra
       for greasing

1 To make the pizza base, place the flour, salt and easy-blend dried yeast in a large bowl. Make a well in the centre and add the oil and 150ml/¼ pint/⅔ cup warm water.

2 Mix with a round-bladed knife to form a soft dough. Turn out on to a lightly floured work surface and knead for 5 minutes.

5 Knead the risen dough lightly, then roll out to form a rough 30cm/12in round. Place on a lightly oiled baking sheet and push up the edges of the dough to form a shallow, even rim.

6 Spoon the tomato mixture over the pizza base, then top with the chopped fresh tomatoes, and the mozzarella. Season, then drizzle with olive oil. Bake in the top of the oven for 10–12 minutes, or until crisp and golden. Scatter with rocket and serve.

Energy 683Kcal/2874kJ; Protein 26.1g; Carbohydrate 92.3g, of which sugars 6.5g; Fat 25.8g, of which saturates 11.9g; Cholesterol 44mg; Calcium 494mg; Fibre 5.7g; Sodium 1312mg.

RICOTTA, OREGANO AND FONTINA PIZZA

PIZZA IS QUICK TO MAKE AND ALWAYS COMFORTING. THE EARTHY FLAVOUR OF THE MUSHROOMS IS DELICIOUS WHEN COMBINED WITH CHEESE AND OREGANO.

MAKES 4

INGREDIENTS
2.5ml/½ tsp active dried yeast
pinch of granulated sugar
450g/1lb/4 cups strong white
 bread flour
5ml/1 tsp salt
30ml/2 tbsp olive oil
For the tomato sauce
400g/14oz can chopped tomatoes
150ml/¼ pint/⅔ cup passata
1 large garlic clove, finely chopped
5ml/1 tsp dried oregano
1 bay leaf
10ml/2 tsp malt vinegar
salt and ground black pepper
For the topping
30ml/2 tbsp olive oil
1 garlic clove, finely chopped
350g/12oz/4 cups mixed mushrooms
 (chestnut, flat or button), sliced
30ml/2 tbsp chopped fresh oregano,
 plus whole leaves to garnish
250g/9oz/generous 1 cup
 ricotta cheese
225g/8oz Fontina cheese, sliced

1 Make the dough. Put 300ml/½ pint/ 1¼ cups warm water in a measuring jug. Add the yeast and the sugar and leave for 5–10 minutes until frothy. Sift the flour and salt into a large bowl and make a well in the centre. Gradually pour in the yeast mixture and the olive oil. Mix to make smooth dough.

2 Knead the dough on a lightly floured surface for about 10 minutes. Place in a floured bowl, cover and leave to rise in a warm place for 1½ hours.

3 Meanwhile, make the tomato sauce. Place all the ingredients in a pan, cover and bring to the boil. Lower the heat, remove the lid and simmer for 20 minutes, stirring occasionally, until reduced.

4 Make the topping. Heat the oil in a frying pan. Add the garlic and mushrooms, and season to taste. Cook, stirring, for 5 minutes or until the mushrooms are browned. Set aside.

5 Preheat the oven to 220°/425°F/ Gas 7. Brush four baking sheets with oil. Knead the dough for 2 minutes, then divide into four equal pieces. Roll out each piece to a 25cm/10in round and place on a baking sheet.

6 Spoon the tomato sauce over each and brush the edge with a little olive oil. Add the mushrooms, oregano and cheese. Bake for 15 minutes, then sprinkle the oregano leaves over.

Energy 821Kcal/3447kJ; Protein 33.9g; Carbohydrate 94g, of which sugars 8.1g; Fat 36.2g, of which saturates 16.6g; Cholesterol 66mg; Calcium 620mg; Fibre 5.8g; Sodium 1072mg.

BRESAOLA AND ROCKET PIZZA

HERE IS A QUICK AND TASTY PIZZA SPREAD WITH PESTO — A MIXTURE OF GROUND BASIL, PARSLEY AND PINE NUTS — AND TOPPED WITH GARLIC, TOMATOES, WILD MUSHROOMS AND BRESAOLA.

SERVES 4

INGREDIENTS
150g/5oz packet pizza
  base mix
120ml/4fl oz/½ cup
  lukewarm water
flour, for dusting
225g/8oz/3¼ cups mixed
  wild mushrooms
25g/1oz/2 tbsp butter
2 garlic cloves,
  coarsely chopped
60ml/4 tbsp pesto
8 slices bresaola
4 tomatoes, sliced
75g/3oz/scant ⅓ cup full-fat
  cream cheese
25g/1oz rocket (arugula)
salt and ground black pepper

1 Preheat the oven to 200°C/400°F/ Gas 6. Tip the packet of pizza base mix into a large mixing bowl and pour in enough of the lukewarm water to mix to a soft, not sticky, dough.

2 Turn out the dough on to a lightly floured surface and knead for about 5 minutes, or until smooth and elastic.

3 Divide the dough into two equal pieces, knead lightly to form two balls, then pat out the balls of dough into flat rounds.

COOK'S TIP
If you are in a hurry, you could buy two ready-made pizza bases instead of the pizza mix, add the topping and bake for 10 minutes.

4 Roll out each piece of the pizza dough on a lightly floured surface to a 23cm/9in round and then transfer to baking sheets.

5 Slice the wild mushrooms. Melt the butter in a frying pan, add the garlic and cook for 2 minutes.

6 Add the sliced mushrooms and cook them over a high heat for about 5 minutes, or until they have softened but are not overcooked.

7 Season to taste with salt and ground black pepper.

8 Spread pesto on the pizza bases, leaving a 2cm/¾in border around the edge of each one.

9 Arrange the bresaola and tomato slices around the rim, then spoon the garlic mushrooms into the centre.

10 Dot the cream cheese on top and then bake for 15–18 minutes.

11 Top each with a handful of the rocket leaves just before serving.

Energy 427Kcal/1781kJ; Protein 13.3g; Carbohydrate 32.7g, of which sugars 4g; Fat 27.9g, of which saturates 13g; Cholesterol 51mg; Calcium 244mg; Fibre 2.9g; Sodium 402mg.

HOT PEPPERONI <u>AND</u> OREGANO PIZZA

THERE IS NOTHING MORE MOUTHWATERING THAN A FRESHLY BAKED PIZZA, ESPECIALLY WHEN THE TOPPING INCLUDES TOMATOES, PEPPERONI, RED CHILLIES AND FRESH OREGANO.

SERVES 4

INGREDIENTS
225g/8oz/2 cups strong white
    bread flour
10ml/2 tsp easy-blend (rapid-rise)
    dried yeast
5ml/1 tsp granulated sugar
2.5ml/½ tsp salt
15ml/1 tbsp olive oil
175ml/6fl oz/¾ cup mixed lukewarm
    milk and water
400g/14oz can chopped tomatoes,
    strained
2 garlic cloves, crushed
5ml/1 tsp dried oregano
225g/8oz mozzarella cheese, grated
2 dried red chillies, crumbled
225g/8oz pepperoni, sliced
30ml/2 tbsp drained capers
fresh oregano, to garnish

1 Sift the flour into a bowl. Stir in the yeast, sugar and salt. Make a well in the centre. Stir the olive oil into the milk and water, then stir the liquid into the flour. Mix to a soft dough.

2 Knead the dough on a lightly floured surface for 10 minutes until it is smooth and elastic. Cover and leave in a warm place for about 30 minutes or until the dough has doubled in bulk.

3 Preheat the oven to 220°C/425°F/ Gas 7. Turn the dough out on to a lightly floured surface and knead lightly for 1 minute. Divide it in half and roll each piece out to a 25cm/10in circle. Place on lightly oiled pizza trays or baking sheets.

4 To make the topping, mix the tomatoes, garlic and oregano in a bowl. Spread half over each base, leaving a border around the edge.

5 Set half the mozzarella aside. Divide the rest between the pizzas.

6 Bake for 7–10 minutes until the dough rim on each pizza is pale golden.

7 Sprinkle the crumbled chillies over the pizzas, then arrange the pepperoni slices and capers on top. Sprinkle with the remaining mozzarella.

8 Return the pizzas to the oven and bake for 7–10 minutes more. Sprinkle over the oregano and serve immediately.

Energy 406Kcal/1700kJ; Protein 13.2g; Carbohydrate 43.8g, of which sugars 8.4g; Fat 21g, of which saturates 7.8g; Cholesterol 31mg; Calcium 232mg; Fibre 3.8g; Sodium 640mg

FRESH HERB PIZZA

WONDERFUL FRESH SUMMER HERBS COMBINE WITH CREAM AND GARLIC IN THIS HEAVENLY PIZZA.
SERVE WITH A CRISP GREEN SALAD WITH PLENTY OF DRESSING.

SERVES 2–3

INGREDIENTS

115g/4oz/4 cups mixed fresh herbs,
  such as parsley, basil and oregano
3 garlic cloves, crushed
120ml/4fl oz/½ cup double
  (heavy) cream
1 pizza base, 25–30cm/
  10–12in diameter
15ml/1 tbsp garlic oil
115g/4oz/1 cup grated
  Pecorino cheese
salt and ground
  black pepper

1 Preheat the oven to 220°C/425°F/
Gas 7.

2 Chop the herbs finely, in a food
processor if you have one. In a bowl
mix together the herbs, garlic, cream
and seasoning.

3 Brush the pizza base with the garlic
oil, then spread over the herb mixture.

4 Sprinkle over the Pecorino. Bake
the pizza in the preheated oven for
15–20 minutes, or until crisp and
golden and the topping is still moist.

5 Cut the pizza into thin wedges and
serve immediately.

Energy 247Kcal/1032kJ; Protein 8.8g; Carbohydrate 18.6g, of which sugars 1.6g; Fat 15.8g, of which saturates 8.2g; Cholesterol 35mg; Calcium 236mg; Fibre 1.4g; Sodium 250mg.

TOMATO, FENNEL AND PARSLEY PIZZA

THIS PIZZA RELIES ON THE WINNING COMBINATION OF TOMATOES, FENNEL AND PARSLEY. THE FENNEL ADDS BOTH A CRISP TEXTURE AND A DISTINCTIVE FLAVOUR.

SERVES 2–3

INGREDIENTS
    1 fennel bulb
    45ml/3 tbsp garlic oil
    1 pizza base, 25–30cm/
        10–12in diameter
    30ml/2 tbsp chopped fresh
        flat leaf parsley
    50g/2oz/½ cup grated
        mozzarella cheese
    50g/2oz/⅔ cup freshly grated
        Parmesan cheese
    salt and ground black pepper
For the tomato sauce
    15ml/1 tbsp olive oil
    1 onion, finely chopped
    1 garlic clove, crushed
    400g/14oz can
        chopped tomatoes
    15ml/1 tbsp tomato purée (paste)
    15ml/1 tbsp chopped fresh
        mixed herbs, such as parsley,
        thyme, basil and oregano
    pinch of sugar
    salt and ground black pepper

1 To make the tomato sauce, heat the oil in a pan and fry the onion and garlic until softened.

2 Add the tomatoes, tomato purée, herbs, sugar and seasoning. Simmer, stirring occasionally, until the tomatoes have reduced to a thick pulp.

3 Preheat the oven to 220°C/425°F/ Gas 7. Trim and quarter the fennel bulb lengthways. Remove the core and slice thinly.

4 Heat 30ml/2 tbsp of the oil in a frying pan and sauté the fennel for 4–5 minutes, or until just tender. Season.

5 Brush the pizza base with the remaining oil and spread over the tomato sauce. Spoon the fennel on top and sprinkle over the flat leaf parsley.

6 Mix together the mozzarella and Parmesan cheese in a bowl, then sprinkle the mixture evenly over the top of the pizza.

7 Bake the pizza in the preheated oven for 15–20 minutes, or until it is crisp and golden. Serve immediately.

Energy 487Kcal/2038kJ; Protein 17g; Carbohydrate 46.3g, of which sugars 9.6g; Fat 27.3g, of which saturates 7.9g; Cholesterol 26mg; Calcium 354mg; Fibre 5.2g; Sodium 463mg.

NEW POTATO, ROSEMARY AND GARLIC PIZZA

WAXY NEW POTATOES, SMOKED MOZZARELLA, ROSEMARY AND GARLIC MAKE THE FLAVOUR OF THIS PIZZA UNIQUE. FOR A DELICIOUS VARIATION, USE SAGE INSTEAD OF ROSEMARY.

SERVES 2–3

INGREDIENTS
   350g/12oz new potatoes
   45ml/3 tbsp olive oil
   2 garlic cloves, crushed
   1 pizza base, 25–30cm/
      10–12in diameter
   1 red onion, thinly sliced
   150g/5oz/1¼ cups grated smoked
      mozzarella cheese
   10ml/2 tsp chopped fresh rosemary
   salt and ground black pepper
   30ml/2 tbsp freshly grated Parmesan,
      to garnish

1 Preheat the oven to 220°C/425°F/ Gas 7. Scrape the potatoes and cook in boiling salted water for 5 minutes. Drain well. When cool, peel and slice thinly.

2 Heat 30ml/2 tbsp of the oil in a large frying pan. Add the sliced potatoes and garlic and fry for 5–8 minutes, or until the potatoes are tender.

3 Brush the pizza base with the remaining olive oil. Sprinkle over the onion, then arrange the fried potatoes on top.

4 Sprinkle the mozzarella and rosemary over the potatoe and onion.

5 Grind over plenty of black pepper and bake for 15–20 minutes, or until crisp and golden.

6 Remove from the oven and sprinkle over the Parmesan to serve.

Energy 532Kcal/2231kJ; Protein 18.7g; Carbohydrate 58.7g, of which sugars 4.8g; Fat 26.4g, of which saturates 9.6g; Cholesterol 34mg; Calcium 310mg; Fibre 2.8g; Sodium 447mg.

SAFFRON FOCACCIA WITH ROSEMARY TOPPING

A DAZZLING YELLOW BREAD WITH A DISTINCTIVE FLAVOUR, THIS SAFFRON FOCACCIA IS TOPPED WITH
GARLIC, ONION, ROSEMARY AND OLIVES. IT MAKES A TASTY SNACK OR ACCOMPANIMENT.

MAKES 1 LOAF

INGREDIENTS
pinch of saffron threads
150ml/¼ pint/⅔ cup boiling water
225g/8oz/2 cups plain (all-purpose)
flour, plus extra for dusting
2.5ml/½ tsp salt
5ml/1 tsp easy-blend
(rapid-rise) dried yeast
15ml/1 tbsp olive oil,
plus extra for greasing
For the topping
2 garlic cloves, sliced
1 red onion, cut into thin wedges
fresh rosemary sprigs
12 black olives, pitted and
coarsely chopped
15ml/1 tbsp olive oil

1 In a jug (pitcher), infuse (steep) the saffron in the boiling water. Set aside.

2 Place the flour, salt, yeast and oil in a food processor. Turn on, then gradually add the saffron liquid until the dough forms a ball. Alternatively, mix in a bowl.

3 Transfer to a lightly floured work surface and knead for 10–15 minutes, or until smooth and elastic.

4 Place in a bowl, cover and leave in a warm place for 30–40 minutes, or until the dough has doubled in bulk.

5 Lightly grease a baking sheet and set aside until required.

6 Knock back (punch down) the risen dough on a lightly floured surface.

7 Roll the dough out into an oval shape about 1cm/½in thick. Place on the prepared baking sheet and leave to rise in a warm place for 20–30 minutes.

8 Preheat the oven to 200°C/400°F/Gas 6. Use your fingers to press small indentations in the dough.

9 Cover the dough with the garlic, onion, rosemary and olives and brush lightly with the olive oil.

10 Bake the loaf in the oven for about 25 minutes, or until it sounds hollow when tapped underneath.

11 Transfer the bread to a wire rack and leave to cool. Serve the focaccia in slices or wedges.

Energy 1038Kcal/4377kJ; Protein 22.3g; Carbohydrate 179.6g, of which sugars 6.7g; Fat 30.5g, of which saturates 4.4g; Cholesterol 0mg; Calcium 361mg; Fibre 9.3g; Sodium 1134mg.

WARM HERBY BREAD

THIS MOUTHWATERING, ITALIAN-STYLE BREAD, FLAVOURED WITH BASIL, ROSEMARY, OLIVE OIL AND SUN-DRIED TOMATOES, IS ABSOLUTELY DELICIOUS SERVED WARM WITH SALADS AND SLICED MEATS.

MAKES 3 LOAVES

INGREDIENTS
- 20g/¾oz fresh yeast or
  15ml/1 tbsp dried yeast
- 5ml/1 tsp caster (superfine) sugar
- 900ml/1½ pints/3¾ cups warm water
- 1.3kg/3lb/12 cups strong white bread flour, plus extra for dusting
- 15ml/1 tbsp salt
- 75ml/5 tbsp mixed fresh chopped basil and rosemary leaves
- 50g/2oz/1 cup drained sun-dried tomatoes, roughly chopped
- 150ml/¼ pint/⅔ cup extra virgin olive oil, plus extra for greasing and brushing

To finish
- 15ml/1 tbsp rosemary leaves
- sea salt flakes

1 Cream the fresh yeast with the sugar, and gradually stir in 150ml/¼ pint/⅔ cup warm water. If you are using dried yeast, put the sugar into a small bowl, pour on the same amount of warm water, then sprinkle the yeast over the top.

2 Leave the mixture in a warm place for 10–15 minutes, or until it has reached a frothy consistency.

3 Put the flour, salt, chopped basil and rosemary leaves, and chopped sun-dried tomatoes into a large mixing bowl.

4 Add the oil together with the frothy yeast mixture, then gradually mix in the remaining warm water with a spoon.

5 As the mixture becomes stiffer, bring it together with your hands. Mix to a soft but not sticky dough, adding a little extra water if needed.

6 Turn the dough out on to a lightly floured surface and knead for 5 minutes until smooth and elastic.

7 Put back into the bowl, cover loosely with oiled clear film and then put in a warm place for 30–40 minutes, or until doubled in size.

8 Knead again until smooth and elastic, then cut into three pieces. Shape each into an oval loaf about 18cm/7in long, and arrange on oiled baking sheets. Slash the top of each loaf with a knife in a criss-cross pattern.

9 Loosely cover and leave in a warm place for 15–20 minutes, or until well risen. Preheat the oven to 220°C/425°F/Gas 7. Brush the loaves with a little olive oil and sprinkle with rosemary leaves and salt flakes. Cook for about 25 minutes, or until golden brown. The bases should sound hollow when they are tapped.

Energy 1789Kcal/7563kJ; Protein 41.5g; Carbohydrate 338.2g, of which sugars 7.9g; Fat 39.3g, of which saturates 5.7g; Cholesterol 0mg; Calcium 643mg; Fibre 14.6g; Sodium 1987mg.

ITALIAN FLAT BREAD WITH ROSEMARY

ROSEMARY LEAVES ADD THEIR UNMISTAKABLE FLAVOUR TO THE TUSCAN VERSION OF AN ITALIAN FLAT BREAD. IT CAN BE ROLLED TO VARYING THICKNESSES TO GIVE EITHER A CRISP OR SOFT FINISH.

MAKES 1 LARGE LOAF

INGREDIENTS
  60ml/4 tbsp extra virgin olive oil,
    plus extra for greasing
  350g/12oz/3 cups unbleached white
    bread flour, plus extra for dusting
  2.5ml/½ tsp salt
  15g/½oz fresh yeast
  200ml/7fl oz/scant 1 cup
    lukewarm water
For the topping
  30ml/2 tbsp extra virgin olive oil
  30ml/2 tbsp fresh rosemary leaves
  coarse salt, for sprinkling

1 Lightly oil a baking sheet. Sift the flour and salt into a bowl and make a well in the centre. Cream the yeast with half the water. Add to the well with the remaining water and oil and mix to a soft dough. Turn out on to a lightly floured surface and knead for 10 minutes, until smooth and elastic.

2 Place the dough in a lightly oiled bowl, cover with a layer of lightly oiled clear film and leave to rise in a warm place for about 1 hour, or until it has doubled in bulk.

3 Knock back (punch down) the dough, turn out on to a lightly floured surface and knead gently. Roll to a 30 × 20cm/ 12 × 8in rectangle and place on the prepared baking sheet. Brush with some of the olive oil for the topping and cover with lightly oiled clear film.

4 Leave the dough to rise once again in a warm place for about 20 minutes. Brush with the remaining olive oil, prick all over with a fork and sprinkle with fresh rosemary leaves and coarse salt. Leave to rise again in a warm place for a further 15 minutes.

5 Meanwhile, preheat the oven to 200°C/400°F/Gas 6. Bake the loaf for 30 minutes, or until light golden. Transfer to a wire rack to cool slightly. Serve while still warm.

Energy 1800Kcal/7571kJ; Protein 34.1g; Carbohydrate 273g, of which sugars 6.2g; Fat 71g, of which saturates 10.1g; Cholesterol 0mg; Calcium 570mg; Fibre 12.9g; Sodium 24mg.

RED ONION AND ROSEMARY FOCACCIA

THIS BREAD IS RICH IN OLIVE OIL AND IT HAS AN AROMATIC TOPPING OF RED ONION, FRESH ROSEMARY AND COARSE SALT.

2 Set the yeast aside in a warm, but not hot, place for 10 minutes, until it has turned frothy.

3 Add the yeast, the remaining water, 15ml/1 tbsp of the oil and the chopped rosemary to the flour.

4 Mix all the ingredients together to form a dough, then gather the dough into a ball and knead on a floured work surface for about 5 minutes, until smooth and elastic. You may need to add a little extra flour if the dough is very sticky.

5 Place the dough in a lightly oiled bowl and slip it into a polythene bag or cover with oiled clear film and leave to rise. The length of time you leave it for depends on the temperature: leave it all day in a cool place, overnight in the refrigerator, or for 1–2 hours in a warm, but not hot, place.

6 Lightly oil a baking sheet. Knead the dough to form a flat loaf that is about 30cm/12in round or square.

7 Place the dough on the prepared baking sheet, cover it with oiled clear fillm (plastic wrap) and leave it to rise again in a warm place for a further 40–60 minutes.

SERVES 4–5

INGREDIENTS
  450g/1lb/4 cups strong white bread
    flour, plus extra for dusting
  5ml/1 tsp salt
  7g/¼oz fresh yeast or generous 5ml/1
    tsp dried yeast
  2.5ml/½ tsp light muscovado
    (brown) sugar
  250ml/8fl oz/1 cup lukewarm water
  60ml/4 tbsp extra virgin olive oil,
    plus extra for greasing
  5ml/1 tsp very finely chopped fresh
    rosemary, plus 6–8 small sprigs
  1 red onion, thinly sliced
  coarse salt

1 Sift the flour and salt into a bowl. Set aside. Cream the fresh yeast with the sugar, and gradually stir in half the water. If using dried yeast, stir the sugar into the water and sprinkle the dried yeast over.

8 Preheat the oven to 220°C/425°F/ Gas 7. Toss the onion in 15ml/1 tbsp of the oil and sprinkle over the loaf with the rosemary sprigs and a sprinkling of coarse salt. Bake for 15–20 minutes until golden brown.

Energy 392Kcal/1657kJ; Protein 8.6g; Carbohydrate 71.4g, of which sugars 2.5g; Fat 10g, of which saturates 1.4g; Cholesterol 0mg; Calcium 129mg; Fibre 3g; Sodium 396mg.

CORIANDER AND CHEESE FLAT BREADS

THESE FLAT BREADS COMBINE THE SALTINESS OF HALLOUMI WITH THE VIBRANT DISTINCTIVE FLAVOUR OF CORIANDER, AND ARE BEST EATEN WITH A BOWL OF YOGURT DIP.

MAKES 10

INGREDIENTS
500g/1¼lb/4½ cups strong white
  bread flour
2 × 7g packets easy-blend
  (rapid-rise) dried yeast
5ml/1 tsp sugar
1 bunch fresh chives, chopped
60–90ml/4–6 tbsp chopped fresh
  coriander (cilantro)
45–75ml/3–5 tbsp dried
  onion flakes
200ml/7fl oz/scant 1 cup
  lukewarm water
60ml/4 tbsp natural
  (plain) yogurt
45ml/3 tbsp olive oil
250g/9oz halloumi cheese,
  finely diced

1 Mix the flour, yeast, sugar, chives, coriander and onion flakes in a bowl, mixer or food processor.

2 Add the water, yogurt and oil and mix together to form a dough.

3 Knead the dough for 5–10 minutes until it is smooth.

4 Lightly oil a large bowl and place the dough in it.

5 Cover with a clean dish towel and leave to rise in a warm place for about 1 hour, or until doubled in size.

VARIATION
For a less salty result, use finely diced Cheddar in place of the halloumi.

6 Turn the dough on to a lightly floured surface and punch down with your fists.

7 Knead in the cheese, then knead for a further 3–4 minutes.

8 Preheat the oven to 220°C/425°F/ Gas 7.

9 Divide the dough into 10 pieces and shape each into a flat round about 1cm/½in thick. Place on non-stick baking sheets and leave to rise for 10 minutes, or until doubled in size.

10 Bake for about 15 minutes until risen and golden brown. Eat immediately.

Energy 291Kcal/1222kJ; Protein 11.8g; Carbohydrate 39.4g, of which sugars 1.3g; Fat 10.2g, of which saturates 4.6g; Cholesterol 18mg; Calcium 290mg; Fibre 1.8g; Sodium 257mg.

SOUR RYE BREAD <u>WITH</u> CARAWAY SEEDS

AROMATIC CARAWAY SEEDS TOP THIS EAST EUROPEAN BREAD. IT USES A SOURDOUGH "STARTER", WHICH NEEDS TO BE MADE A DAY OR TWO IN ADVANCE.

MAKES 2 LOAVES

INGREDIENTS
  450g/1lb/4 cups rye flour
  450g/1lb/4 cups strong white bread
  flour, plus extra for dusting
  15ml/1 tbsp salt
  7g/¼oz sachet easy-blend
  (rapid-rise) dried yeast
  25g/1oz/2 tbsp butter, softened,
  plus extra for greasing
  600ml/1 pint/2½ cups warm water
  15ml/1 tbsp caraway seeds
For the sourdough starter
  60ml/4 tbsp rye flour
  45ml/3 tbsp warm milk

1 For the starter, mix the rye flour and milk in a bowl. Cover with clear film. Leave in a warm place for 1–2 days.

2 Sift together both types of flour and the salt into a large mixing bowl. Stir in the easy-blend dried yeast.

3 Make a well in the centre of the dry ingredients and add the butter, warm water and sourdough starter. Mix well with a wooden spoon until you have formed a soft dough.

4 Turn out the dough on to a lightly floured surface and knead for about 10 minutes, or until smooth and elastic. Put in a clean bowl, cover with greased clear film (plastic wrap) and leave to rise in a warm place for 1 hour, or until doubled in size.

5 Knead for 1 minute, then divide the dough in half. Shape each piece into a round 15cm/6in across.

6 Transfer to two greased baking sheets. Cover with greased clear film and leave to rise for 30 minutes.

7 Preheat the oven to 200°C/400°F/ Gas 6. Brush the loaves with water, then sprinkle with caraway seeds.

8 Bake for 35–40 minutes, or until the loaves are browned and sound hollow when tapped on the bottom. Cool on a wire rack.

COOK'S TIP
Sour rye bread keeps fresh for up to a week. This recipe can also be made without yeast, but the resulting bread will be much denser.

Energy 1725Kcal/7330kJ; Protein 42.9g; Carbohydrate 369.5g, of which sugars 4.5g; Fat 18.7g, of which saturates 8g; Cholesterol 28mg; Calcium 427mg; Fibre 36.8g; Sodium 3042mg.

WELSH CLAY-POT LOAVES WITH HERBS

THESE BREADS ARE FLAVOURED WITH CHIVES, PARSLEY, SAGE AND GARLIC, AND TOPPED WITH FENNEL SEEDS. YOU CAN USE ANY SELECTION OF YOUR FAVOURITE HERBS.

MAKES 2 LOAVES

INGREDIENTS
  50g/2oz/¼ cup butter, melted,
    plus extra for greasing
  115g/4oz/1 cup wholemeal
    (whole-wheat) bread flour
  350g/12oz/3 cups unbleached strong
    white bread flour, plus extra for dusting
  7.5ml/1½ tsp salt
  15g/½oz fresh yeast
  150ml/¼ pint/⅔ cup lukewarm milk
  120ml/4fl oz/½ cup lukewarm water
  15ml/1 tbsp chopped fresh chives
  15ml/1 tbsp chopped fresh parsley
  5ml/1 tsp chopped fresh sage
  1 garlic clove, crushed
  oil, for greasing
  beaten egg, for glazing
  fennel seeds, for sprinkling (optional)

1 Lightly grease two clean 14cm/5½in-diameter, 12cm/4½in-high clay flower pots. Sift the flours and salt together into a large bowl and make a well in the centre.

2 Blend the yeast with a little of the milk until smooth, then stir in the remaining milk. Pour the yeast liquid into the centre of the flour and sprinkle over a little of the flour from around the edge. Cover the bowl and leave in a warm place for 15 minutes.

3 Add the water, melted butter, herbs and garlic to the flour mixture and blend together to form a dough. Turn out on to a lightly floured surface and knead for about 10 minutes, or until the dough is smooth and elastic.

4 Place in a lightly oiled bowl, cover with lightly oiled clear film and leave to rise, in a warm place, for 1¼–1½ hours, or until doubled in bulk.

5 Turn the dough out on to a lightly floured surface and knock back (punch down). Divide in two. Shape and fit into the flower pots. It should about half fill the pots. Cover with oiled clear film and leave to rise for 30–45 minutes in a warm place, or until the dough is 2.5cm/1in from the top of the pots.

6 Meanwhile, preheat the oven to 200°C/400°F/Gas 6. Brush the tops with beaten egg and sprinkle with fennel seeds, if using. Bake for 35–40 minutes, or until golden. Turn out on to a wire rack to cool.

Energy 1003Kcal/4235kJ; Protein 27.1g; Carbohydrate 177g, of which sugars 8g; Fat 25.7g, of which saturates 14.4g; Cholesterol 58mg; Calcium 402mg; Fibre 11.6g; Sodium 198mg.

POPPY-SEEDED BLOOMER

THIS SATISFYING WHITE BREAD HAS A CRUNCHY, POPPY-SEED TOPPING. IT IS MADE BY A SLOWER RISING METHOD AND WITH LESS YEAST THAN USUAL. THIS PRODUCES A LONGER-KEEPING LOAF WITH A FULLER FLAVOUR. THE DOUGH TAKES ABOUT 8 HOURS TO RISE.

MAKES 1 LOAF

INGREDIENTS
  oil, for greasing
  675g/1½lb/6 cups unbleached
    strong white bread flour, plus
    extra for dusting
  10ml/2 tsp salt
  15g/½oz fresh yeast
  430ml/15fl oz/1⅞ cups water
For the topping
  2.5ml/½ tsp salt
  30ml/2 tbsp water
  poppy seeds,
    for sprinkling

1 Lightly grease a baking sheet. Sift the flour and salt together into a large bowl and make a well in the centre.

2 Mix the yeast and 150ml/¼ pint/ ⅔ cup of the water in a bowl. Mix in the remaining water and add to the centre of the flour.

3 Mix it in, gradually incorporating the surrounding flour, until the mixture forms a firm dough.

COOK'S TIPS
• The traditional cracked, crusty appearance of this loaf is difficult to achieve in a domestic oven. However, you can get a similar result by spraying the oven with water before baking.
• If the underneath of the loaf is not very crusty at the end of baking, turn the loaf over on the baking sheet, switch off the heat and leave in the oven for a further 5–10 minutes.

4 Turn out on to a lightly floured surface and knead for at least 10 minutes, or until smooth and elastic.

5 Place the dough in a lightly oiled bowl, cover with lightly oiled clear film (plastic wrap).

6 Leave to rise, at cool room temperature, about 15–18°C/60–65°F, for 5–6 hours, or until doubled in bulk.

7 Knock back (punch down) the dough, turn out on to a lightly floured surface and knead it thoroughly and quite hard for about 5 minutes.

8 Return the dough to the bowl, and re-cover. Leave it to rise, at cool room temperature, for a further 2 hours or slightly longer if you have time.

9 Knock back the dough again, turn it out and repeat the thorough kneading for about 5 minutes.

10 Leave to rest for 5 minutes, then roll out on a lightly floured surface into a rectangle 2.5cm/1in thick.

11 Roll the dough up from one long side and shape it into a square-ended thick baton shape, about 33 × 13cm/13 × 5in.

12 Place it seam-side up on a baking sheet, cover and leave to rest for 15 minutes. Turn over. Plump up by tucking the dough under the sides and ends. Using a sharp knife, cut six diagonal slashes on the top.

13 Leave to rest, covered, in a warm place, for 10 minutes. Meanwhile, preheat the oven to 230°C/450°F/Gas 8.

14 Mix the salt and water together and brush this glaze over the bread. Sprinkle with poppy seeds.

15 Bake the bread immediately for 20 minutes, then reduce the oven temperature to 200°C/400°F/Gas 6; bake for 25 minutes more, or until golden. Transfer to a wire rack to cool.

VARIATION
For a more rustic loaf, replace up to half the flour with wholemeal (whole-wheat) bread flour.

Energy 2302Kcal/9788kJ; Protein 63.5g; Carbohydrate 524.5g, of which sugars 10.1g; Fat 8.8g, of which saturates 1.4g; Cholesterol 0mg; Calcium 946mg; Fibre 20.9g; Sodium 3950mg.

OLIVE AND OREGANO BREAD

THIS TASTY ITALIAN BREAD IS HIGHLY FLAVOURED WITH OREGANO, PARSLEY AND OLIVES AND IS AN EXCELLENT ACCOMPANIMENT TO ALL SALADS. SERVE WARM FROM THE OVEN IN LARGE WEDGES, SPREAD WITH UNSALTED BUTTER TO ENJOY THE FLAVOURS AT THEIR BEST.

MAKES 1 LOAF

INGREDIENTS

7g/¼oz fresh yeast or
  5ml/1 tsp dried yeast
pinch of sugar
300ml/½ pint/1¼ cups
  warm water
15ml/1 tbsp olive oil, plus
  extra for greasing
1 onion, chopped
450g/1lb/4 cups strong
  white bread flour, plus
  extra for dusting
5ml/1 tsp salt
1.5ml/¼ tsp ground
  black pepper
50g/2oz/½ cup pitted
  black olives, roughly chopped
15ml/1 tbsp black
  olive paste
15ml/1 tbsp chopped
  fresh oregano
15ml/1 tbsp chopped
  fresh parsley

1 Cream the fresh yeast with the sugar, and then gradually stir in half the warm water. If you are using dried yeast, put half the warm water in a jug (pitcher) and then sprinkle the yeast on top.

2 Add the sugar, stir well and leave the mixture to stand in a warm place for 10 minutes, or until it is frothy.

VARIATION
For a change, you could subsitite an equal quantity of finely chopped fresh rosemary for the oregano.

3 Heat the oil in a frying pan and fry the onion until golden brown, stirring occasionally. Remove the pan from the heat and set aside.

4 Sift the flour into a mixing bowl with the salt and pepper. Make a well in the centre. Add the yeast mixture, onions (with the oil), olives, olive paste, oregano, parsley and remaining water.

5 Gradually incorporate the flour, and mix to a soft dough, adding a little extra water if necessary.

6 Turn the dough out on to a lightly floured surface and knead for 5 minutes, or until smooth and elastic.

7 Place in a mixing bowl, cover with a damp dish towel and leave to rise in a warm place for about 2 hours until the dough has doubled in bulk. Lightly grease a baking sheet and set aside.

8 Turn the dough out on to a lightly floured surface and knead again for a few minutes. Shape into a 20cm/8in flat round and place on the prepared baking sheet.

9 Using a sharp knife, make criss-cross cuts over the top of the dough. Cover and leave in a warm place for 30 minutes, or until well risen. Preheat the oven to 220°C/425°F/Gas 7.

10 Dust the loaf with a little flour. Bake for 10 minutes then lower the oven temperature to 200°C/400°F/Gas 6.

11 Bake for a further 20 minutes, or until the loaf sounds hollow when it is tapped underneath.

12 Transfer to a wire rack to cool. Serve the bread warm or cold in slices or wedges.

Energy 1718Kcal/7282kJ; Protein 43.7g; Carbohydrate 354.5g, of which sugars 10.2g; Fat 23.6g, of which saturates 3.5g; Cholesterol 0mg; Calcium 692mg; Fibre 16.8g; Sodium 1367mg.

ONION, THYME AND OLIVE BREAD

THIS BREAD IS DELICIOUSLY FLAVOURED WITH BLACK OLIVES, ONION AND THYME, AND IS GOOD FOR SANDWICHES OR CUT INTO THICK SLICES AND DIPPED IN OLIVE OIL. IT IS ALSO EXCELLENT TOASTED, MAKING A WONDERFUL BASE FOR BRUSCHETTA OR DELICIOUS CROÛTONS FOR TOSSING INTO SALAD.

**MAKES 1 LARGE OR
2 SMALL LOAVES**

INGREDIENTS
350g/12oz/3 cups unbleached
  strong white bread flour, plus
  extra for dusting
115g/4oz/1 cup cornmeal,
  plus a little extra
rounded 5ml/1 tsp salt
15g/½oz fresh yeast or
  10ml/2 tsp dried yeast
5ml/1 tsp muscovado
  (molasses) sugar
warm water
15ml/1 tbsp chopped fresh thyme
30ml/2 tbsp olive oil, plus extra
  for greasing
1 red onion, finely chopped
75g/3oz/1 cup freshly grated
  Parmesan cheese
90g/3½oz/scant 1 cup pitted
  black olives, halved

2 Make a well in the centre of the dry ingredients and pour in the yeast liquid and a further 150ml/¼ pint/⅔ cup of warm water.

3 Add the thyme and 15ml/1 tbsp of the olive oil and mix well with a wooden spoon, gradually drawing in the dry ingredients until fully incorporated.

4 Add a dash more warm water, if necessary, to make a soft, but not sticky, dough.

5 Knead the dough on a lightly floured work surface for 5 minutes, or until it is smooth and elastic.

6 Place in a clean, lightly oiled bowl and then place in a plastic bag or cover with oiled clear film (plastic wrap). Set aside to rise in a warm, but not hot, place for 1–2 hours, or until well risen.

8 Brush a baking sheet with olive oil. Turn out the risen dough on to a floured work surface. Gently knead in the cooked onions, followed by the freshly grated Parmesan cheese and, finally, the halved black olives.

9 Shape the dough into one or two oval loaves. Sprinkle the extra corn meal on to the work surface and roll the bread in it, then place the loaf or loaves on the prepared baking sheet.

1 Mix the flour, cornmeal and salt in a warmed bowl. If using fresh yeast, cream it with the sugar and gradually stir in 120ml/4fl oz/½ cup of the warm water. If using dried yeast, stir the sugar into the water and sprinkle the dried yeast over the surface. Leave the bowl in a warm place for 10 minutes, or until the yeast mixture is frothy.

COOK'S TIP
The best type of Parmesan is Parmigiano reggiano, which is made in the Reggio Emilia area of Italy. It will keep for several weeks in the refrigerator, wrapped in foil.

7 Meanwhile, heat the remaining olive oil in a large, heavy frying pan. Add the chopped onion and cook over a fairly gentle heat, stirring occasionally, for about 8 minutes, or until the onion has turned soft and golden, but is not at all browned. Set aside to cool.

VARIATION
If you prefer, shape the dough into a loaf, roll in cornmeal and place in a lightly oiled loaf tin (pan). Leave to rise, as in step 9, until risen well above the rim of the tin. Bake for 35–40 minutes, or until it sounds hollow when turned out and tapped on the base.

10 Make several criss-cross lines across the top of the loaf or loaves.

11 Slip the baking sheet into the plastic bag, or cover the dough with a layer of oiled clear film.

12 Leave the dough to rise once again in a warm place for about 1 hour, or until well risen. Preheat the oven to 200°C/400°F/Gas 6.

13 Bake the loaf or loaves for 30–35 minutes, or until the bread sounds hollow when tapped on the base. Leave to cool on a wire rack.

Energy 1142Kcal/4803kJ; Protein 37.4g; Carbohydrate 182.5g, of which sugars 6.4g; Fat 32.5g, of which saturates 10.4g; Cholesterol 38mg; Calcium 733mg; Fibre 8.4g; Sodium 1428mg.

ONION ROLLS WITH POPPY SEEDS

SERVE THESE SWEET-SMELLING, SEED-TOPPED ROLLS HOT, SPREAD WITH BUTTER, OR COLD, FILLED WITH SANDWICH INGREDIENTS, OR EAT WITH A BOWL OF WARMING SOUP FOR A SATISFYING LUNCH.

3 Lightly oil a bowl. Place the dough in it and turn to coat. Cover with a dishtowel. Leave to rise in a warm place for about 1½ hours, or until doubled in size.

4 Turn the dough on to a lightly floured surface, punch down with your fists, knead for 3–4 minutes, then knead half the onions into the dough.

5 Form the dough into egg-size balls, then press each ball into a round 1cm/½in thick. Place on a baking sheet.

6 Lightly beat the remaining egg with 30ml/2 tbsp water and a pinch of salt.

7 Press an indentation on top of each round of dough and brush with the egg mixture. Sprinkle the remaining onions and the poppy seeds on to the rolls.

8 Leave to rise in a warm place for 45 minutes, or until doubled in size.

9 Preheat the oven to 190°C/375°F/Gas 5. Bake the rolls for 20 minutes, or until pale golden brown. They are equally delicious served hot from the oven or when they are cool.

MAKES 12–14

INGREDIENTS
15ml/1 tbsp dried active yeast
15ml/1 tbsp sugar
250ml/8fl oz/1 cup
  lukewarm water
30ml/2 tbsp vegetable oil
2 eggs, lightly beaten
500g/1¼lb/4½ cups strong
  white bread flour
3–4 onions, very
  finely chopped
60ml/4 tbsp poppy seeds
salt

1 In a mixer fitted with a dough hook, a food processor fitted with a dough blade, or a large bowl, mix together the yeast, sugar and water. Sprinkle with a little flour, cover and leave for 10–12 minutes until bubbles appear on the surface.

2 Beat 5ml/1 tsp salt, the oil and one of the eggs into the mixture until well mixed, then gradually add the flour and knead for 5–10 minutes until the dough leaves the sides of the bowl. If the dough is still slightly sticky, add a little more flour.

Energy 161Kcal/681kJ; Protein 4.6g; Carbohydrate 31.1g, of which sugars 3.3g; Fat 2.9g, of which saturates 0.5g; Cholesterol 27mg; Calcium 62mg; Fibre 1.5g; Sodium 12mg.

Syrian Onion Bread <u>with</u> Mint

FRESH MINT CONTRASTS WITH GROUND CUMIN AND CORIANDER SEEDS AND ONION ON TOP OF THESE
SAVOURY BREADS FROM SYRIA. THEY MAKE AN EXCELLENT ACCOMPANIMENT TO SOUPS OR SALADS.

MAKES 8

INGREDIENTS
450g/1lb/4 cups unbleached strong
  white bread flour, plus extra
  for dusting
5ml/1 tsp salt
20g/¾oz fresh yeast
280ml/9fl oz/scant 1¼ cups
  lukewarm water
oil, for greasing
For the topping
60ml/4 tbsp finely chopped onion
5ml/1 tsp ground cumin
10ml/2 tsp ground coriander seeds
10ml/2 tsp chopped fresh mint
30ml/2 tbsp olive oil

1 Lightly flour two baking sheets. Sift the flour and salt together into a large bowl and make a well in the centre. Cream the yeast with a little of the water, then mix in the remainder.

2 Add the yeast mixture to the centre of the flour and mix to a firm dough. Turn out on to a lightly floured surface and knead for 8–10 minutes, or until smooth and elastic.

3 Place the dough in a lightly oiled bowl, cover with lightly oiled clear film (plastic wrap) and leave to rise, in a warm place, for about 1 hour, or until doubled in size.

COOK'S TIP
If you haven't any fresh mint to hand, then add 15ml/1 tbsp dried mint. Use the freeze-dried variety if you can as it has much more flavour.

4 Knock back (punch down) the dough and turn out on to a lightly floured surface. Divide into eight equal pieces and roll into 13–15cm/5–6in rounds. Make them slightly concave. Prick all over and space well apart on the baking sheets. Cover with lightly oiled clear film and leave to rise for 15–20 minutes.

5 Meanwhile, preheat the oven to 200°C/400°F/Gas 6. Mix the chopped onion, ground cumin, ground coriander and chopped mint in a bowl. Brush the breads with the olive oil for the topping, sprinkle evenly with the spicy onion mixture and bake for 15–20 minutes. Serve the onion breads warm.

Energy 220Kcal/932kJ; Protein 5.5g; Carbohydrate 44.4g, of which sugars 1.3g; Fat 3.5g, of which saturates 0.5g; Cholesterol 0mg; Calcium 85mg; Fibre 1.9g; Sodium 248mg.

GARLIC AND HERB BREAD

THIS IRRESISTIBLE GARLIC BREAD INCLUDES PLENTY OF FRESH MIXED HERBS. YOU CAN VARY THE OVERALL FLAVOUR ACCORDING TO THE COMBINATION OF HERBS YOU CHOOSE.

SERVES 3–4

INGREDIENTS
  1 baguette or bloomer loaf
For the garlic and herb butter
  115g/4oz/½ cup unsalted (sweet)
    butter, softened
  5–6 large garlic cloves, finely
    chopped or crushed
  30–45ml/2–3 tbsp chopped fresh
    herbs (such as parsley, chervil and
    a little tarragon)
  15ml/1 tbsp chopped fresh chives
  coarse salt and ground black pepper

1 Preheat the oven to 200°C/400°F/ Gas 6. Make the garlic and herb butter by beating the butter with the garlic, herbs, chives and seasoning.

VARIATIONS
• Use 105ml/7 tbsp extra virgin olive oil instead of the butter.
• Flavour the butter with garlic, a little chopped fresh chilli, grated lime rind and chopped fresh coriander (cilantro).
• Add chopped, pitted black olives or sun-dried tomatoes to the butter with a little grated lemon rind.

2 Cut the bread into 1cm/½in thick diagonal slices, but be sure to leave them attached at the base so that the loaf stays intact.

3 Spread the garlic and herb butter between the slices evenly, being careful not to detach them, and then spread any remaining butter over the top of the loaf.

4 Wrap the loaf in foil and bake in the preheated oven for 20–25 minutes, until the butter is melted and the crust is golden and crisp. Cut the loaf into slices to serve.

COOK'S TIP
This loaf makes an excellent addition to a barbecue. If space permits, place the foil-wrapped loaf on the top of the barbecue and cook for about the same length of time as for oven baking. Turn the foil parcel over several times to ensure it cooks evenly.

Energy 491Kcal/2057kJ; Protein 10.3g; Carbohydrate 58.4g, of which sugars 3.3g; Fat 25.7g, of which saturates 15.3g; Cholesterol 61mg; Calcium 136mg; Fibre 3.1g; Sodium 792mg.

SAFFRON AND BASIL BREADSTICKS

THESE TASTY BREADSTICKS HAVE THE DELICATE AROMA AND FLAVOUR OF SAFFRON, AS WELL AS ITS
RICH YELLOW COLOUR. THEY ARE IDEAL AS AN ACCOMPANIMENT TO SOUPS OR SALADS OR AS A SNACK.

MAKES 32

INGREDIENTS
   generous pinch of saffron strands
   30ml/2 tbsp hot water
   450g/1lb/4 cups strong white bread
     flour, plus extra for dusting
   5ml/1 tsp salt
   10ml/2 tsp easy-blend (rapid-rise)
     dried yeast
   300ml/½ pint/1¼ cups lukewarm water
   45ml/3 tbsp olive oil, plus extra
     for greasing
   45ml/3 tbsp chopped fresh basil

1 In a small bowl, infuse (steep) the saffron strands in the hot water for 10 minutes.

2 Sift the flour and salt into a large mixing bowl. Stir in the yeast, then make a well in the centre of the dry ingredients. Pour in the lukewarm water and the saffron liquid and start to mix together a little.

3 Add the oil and basil and continue to mix to form a soft dough, then transfer to a lightly floured surface and knead for about 10 minutes, or until the dough is smooth and elastic.

4 Place in a greased bowl, cover with clear film (plastic wrap) and leave to rise in a warm place for about 1 hour, or until the dough has doubled in bulk.

5 Knock back (punch down) the dough and transfer it to a lightly floured surface. Knead it for 2–3 minutes until the dough is smooth and elastic. Preheat the oven to 220°C/425°F/Gas 7.

6 Lightly grease two baking sheets and set them aside. Divide the dough into 32 even pieces and shape each into long, thin sticks. Place them well apart on the prepared baking sheets, then leave them for a further 15–20 minutes, or until they become puffy. Bake in the oven for about 15 minutes, or until crisp and golden. Transfer to a wire rack to cool. Serve warm or cold.

Energy 57Kcal/242kJ; Protein 1.3g; Carbohydrate 10.9g, of which sugars 0.2g; Fat 1.2g, of which saturates 0.2g; Cholesterol 0mg; Calcium 20mg; Fibre 0.4g; Sodium 62mg

Desserts and Cakes

Bring the delightful tastes of herbs to divine desserts and cakes. In this mouthwatering section, lemon grass is combined with fresh fruit and bay leaves to add a twist to a tropical dessert, and the delicate scent of rose petals transforms a simple apple dessert into a fragrant feast. Saffron subtly enhances the delicate flavour of pears, lavender flowers perfume cakes and cookies, and sunflower and poppy seeds add a tasty crunch to cakes and scones.

Above *Minted Pomegranate Yogurt with Grapefruit Salad*

Left *Lavender Cake*

LEMON GRASS SKEWERS WITH BAY LEAVES

LEMON GRASS SKEWERS GIVE THE FRUIT A SUBTLE LEMON TANG THAT IS COMPLEMENTED BY THE FLAVOUR OF THE BAY LEAVES IN THIS FRESH DESSERT. ALMOST ANY SOFT FRUITS CAN BE SUBSTITUTED.

SERVES 4

INGREDIENTS
    4 long fresh lemon grass stalks
    1 mango, peeled, stoned (pitted)
      and cut into chunks
    1 papaya, peeled, seeded and
      cut into chunks
    1 star fruit, cut into chunks
    8 fresh bay leaves
    oil, for greasing
    a little nutmeg
    60ml/4 tbsp maple syrup
    50g/2oz/¼ cup demerara
      (raw) sugar
For the lime cheese
    150g/5oz/⅔ cup curd (farmer's)
      cheese or low-fat soft cheese
    120ml/4fl oz/½ cup double
      (heavy) cream
    grated rind and juice of ½ lime
    30ml/2 tbsp icing
      (confectioners') sugar

1 Prepare the barbecue or preheat the grill (broiler). Cut the top of each lemon grass stalk into a point with a sharp knife.

2 Discard the outer leaves, then use the back of the knife to bruise the length of each stalk to release the oils.

3 Thread each lemon grass stalk, skewer-style, with a selection of the fruit pieces and two bay leaves.

4 Support a piece of foil on a baking sheet and roll up the edges to make a rim. Grease the foil, lay the kebabs on top and grate a little nutmeg over each.

5 Drizzle the maple syrup over each kebab and dust liberally with the demerara sugar. Grill (broil) or cook on a barbecue or 5 minutes, until the kebabs are lightly charred.

6 Meanwhile, make the lime cheese. Mix together the cheese, cream, grated lime rind and juice, and icing sugar in a bowl.

7 Serve at once with the lightly charred fruit kebabs.

COOK'S TIP
Only fresh lemon grass will work as skewers. It is now possible to buy lemon grass stalks in jars.

Energy 370Kcal/1551kJ; Protein 6.9g; Carbohydrate 46.5g, of which sugars 46.4g; Fat 19.3g, of which saturates 12g; Cholesterol 50mg; Calcium 93mg; Fibre 2.6g; Sodium 217mg.

BANANAS WITH LIME AND CARDAMOM SAUCE

AROMATIC CARDAMOM AND FRESH LIME GIVE AN EXOTIC HINT TO THE FLAKED ALMONDS IN THIS DELICIOUS SAUCE FOR POURING OVER BANANAS.

SERVES 4

INGREDIENTS

6 small bananas
50g/2oz/¼ cup butter
50g/2oz/½ cup flaked (sliced) almonds
seeds from 4 cardamom
　pods, crushed
thinly pared rind and juice
　of 2 limes
50g/2oz/¼ cup light muscovado
　(molasses) sugar
30ml/2 tbsp dark rum
vanilla ice cream, to serve

VARIATIONS

If you prefer not to use alcohol in your cooking, replace the rum with a fruit juice of your choice, such as orange or even pineapple juice. The sauce is equally good poured over folded crêpes.

1 Peel the bananas and cut them in half lengthways. Heat half the butter in a large frying pan. Add half the bananas, and cook until the undersides are golden. Turn carefully, using a fish slice or metal spatula. Cook until golden.

2 As they cook, transfer the bananas to a heatproof serving dish. Cook the remaining bananas in the same way.

3 Melt the remaining butter, then add the almonds and cardamom seeds. Cook, stirring until golden.

4 Stir in the lime rind and juice, then the sugar. Cook, stirring, until the mixture is smooth, bubbling and slightly reduced. Stir in the rum. Pour the sauce over the bananas and serve immediately, with vanilla ice cream.

Energy 388Kcal/1623kJ; Protein 4.7g; Carbohydrate 51.1g, of which sugars 47.1g; Fat 17.7g, of which saturates 7.2g; Cholesterol 27mg; Calcium 49mg; Fibre 2.7g; Sodium 80mg.

POACHED PEARS IN SAFFRON SCENTED HONEY SYRUP

FRUIT HAS BEEN POACHED IN HONEY SINCE ANCIENT TIMES. THE ROMANS DID IT, AS DID THE PERSIANS, ARABS, MOORS AND OTTOMANS. DELICATE AND PRETTY TO LOOK AT, THESE SAFFRON-SCENTED PEARS WOULD PROVIDE AN EXQUISITE FINISHING TOUCH TO ANY MEAL.

SERVES 4

INGREDIENTS
   45ml/3 tbsp clear honey
   juice of 1 lemon
   250ml/8fl oz/1 cup water
   pinch of saffron threads
   1 cinnamon stick
   2–3 dried lavender heads
   4 firm pears

1 Heat the honey and lemon juice in a heavy pan that will hold the pears snugly. Stir over a gentle heat until the honey has dissolved. Add the water, saffron threads, cinnamon stick and flowers from 1–2 lavender heads.

2 Bring the mixture to the boil, then reduce the heat and simmer the liquid for 5 minutes.

3 Peel the pears, leaving the stalks attached. Add the pears to the pan and simmer for 20 minutes, turning and basting at regular intervals, until they are tender.

4 Leave the pears to cool in the syrup and serve at room temperature, decorated with a few lavender flowers.

VARIATION
Use whole, peeled nectarines or peaches instead of pears.

Energy 66Kcal/278kJ; Protein 0.5g; Carbohydrate 16.5g, of which sugars 16.5g; Fat 0.2g, of which saturates 0g; Cholesterol 0mg; Calcium 17mg; Fibre 3.3g; Sodium 5mg.

MINTED POMEGRANATE YOGURT
WITH GRAPEFRUIT SALAD

THE JEWEL-LIKE SEEDS OF THE POMEGRANATE ARE STIRRED INTO YOGURT TO MAKE A DELICATE SAUCE FOR A FRESH-TASTING GRAPEFRUIT SALAD IN THIS DESSERT. THE FLECKS OF GREEN ARE FINELY CHOPPED FRESH MINT, WHICH COMPLEMENT THE CITRUS FLAVOURS PERFECTLY.

SERVES 3–4

INGREDIENTS
300ml/½ pint/1¼ cups Greek
(US strained plain) yogurt
2–3 ripe pomegranates
small bunch of fresh mint,
finely chopped
clear honey or caster (superfine)
sugar, to taste (optional)
For the grapefruit salad
2 red grapefruits
2 pink grapefruits
1 white grapefruit
15–30ml/1–2 tbsp orange
flower water
To decorate
handful of pomegranate seeds
fresh mint leaves

1 Put the yogurt in a bowl and beat well. Cut open the pomegranates and scoop out the seeds, removing and discarding all the bitter pith.

2 Fold the pomegranate seeds and chopped mint into the yogurt.

3 Sweeten with a little honey or sugar, if using, then chill until ready to serve.

4 Peel the red, pink and white grapefruits, cutting off and discarding all the pith. Cut between the membranes to remove the segments, holding the fruit over a bowl to catch the juices.

5 Discard the membranes and mix the fruit segments with the reserved juices. Sprinkle with the orange flower water and add a little honey or sugar, if using.

6 Stir gently then decorate with a few pomegranate seeds.

7 Decorate the chilled yogurt with a sprinkling of pomegranate seeds and mint leaves, and serve with the grapefruit salad.

VARIATION
Alternatively, you can use a mixture of oranges and blood oranges, interspersed with thin segments of lemon. Lime segments work well with the grapefruit and mandarins or tangerines could be used too. Juicy melons and kiwi fruit would also be ideal.

Energy 188Kcal/784kJ; Protein 8.8g; Carbohydrate 18g, of which sugars 18g; Fat 10.5g, of which saturates 5.2g; Cholesterol 0mg; Calcium 202mg; Fibre 3.6g; Sodium 82mg.

GOOSEBERRY AND ELDERFLOWER FOOL

ELDERFLOWERS AND GOOSEBERRIES ARE A MATCH MADE IN HEAVEN, EACH BRINGING OUT THE FLAVOUR OF THE OTHER. SERVE WITH AMARETTI OR OTHER DESSERT BISCUITS FOR DIPPING.

SERVES 6

INGREDIENTS
   450g/1lb/4 cups
      gooseberries, trimmed
   30ml/2 tbsp water
   50–75g/2–3oz/¼–⅓ cup caster
      (superfine) sugar
   30ml/2 tbsp elderflower cordial
   400g/14oz carton ready-made
      custard sauce
   300ml/½ pint/1¼ cups double
      (heavy) cream
   crushed amaretti, to decorate
   amaretti, to serve

1 Put the gooseberries and water in a pan. Cover and cook for 5–6 minutes.

2 Add the sugar and elderflower cordial to the gooseberries, then stir vigorously or mash until the fruit forms a pulp.

3 Remove the pan from the heat, spoon the gooseberry pulp into a bowl and set aside to cool.

4 Stir the custard into the fruit. Whip the cream to form soft peaks, then fold it into the mixture and chill.

5 Serve in dessert glasses, decorated with crushed amaretti, and accompanied by amaretti.

Energy 366Kcal/1521kJ; Protein 3.5g; Carbohydrate 24.2g, of which sugars 21.8g; Fat 28.4g, of which saturates 16.7g; Cholesterol 70mg; Calcium 111mg; Fibre 1.9g; Sodium 41mg.

APPLE AND ROSE-PETAL SNOW

THIS IS A LOVELY, LIGHT AND REFRESHING DESSERT. THE ROSE PETALS GIVE A DELICATE FRAGRANCE BUT OTHER EDIBLE PETALS SUCH AS HONEYSUCKLE, LAVENDER AND GERANIUM COULD ALSO BE USED.

SERVES 4

INGREDIENTS

2 large cooking apples
150ml/¼ pint/⅔ cup thick
   apple juice
30ml/2 tbsp rose water
2 egg whites
75g/3oz/6 tbsp caster (superfine) sugar
a few rose petals from an
   unsprayed rose
crystallized rose petals, to decorate
crisp biscuits (cookies) or brandy
   snaps, to serve

VARIATION

Make an Apple and Rose-petal Fool. Fold 150ml/¼ pint/⅔ cup each custard and whipped cream into the apple purée.

1 Peel and chop the apples and cook them with the apple juice until they are soft. Sieve, add the rose water and leave to cool.

2 Whisk the egg whites until they form stiff peaks, then gently whisk in the caster sugar.

3 Gently fold together the apple and rose water purée and the egg whites. Stir in most of the rose petals.

4 Spoon the snow into four glasses and chill. Decorate with the crystallized rose petals and serve with some crisp biscuits or brandy snaps.

Energy 113Kcal/483kJ; Protein 1.7g; Carbohydrate 28.1g, of which sugars 28.1g; Fat 0.1g, of which saturates 0g; Cholesterol 0mg; Calcium 16mg; Fibre 0.9g; Sodium 33mg.

LAVENDER AND PEACH PAVLOVA

PAVLOVA MUST BE ONE OF THE MOST LAVISH DESSERTS. HERE IT IS PERFUMED WITH LAVENDER SUGAR, FILLED WITH FRESH PEACHES AND CREAM, AND DECORATED WITH SUGARED FLOWERS.

SERVES 8

INGREDIENTS
  5 large egg whites
  250g/9oz/1¼ cups lavender sugar
  5ml/1 tsp cornflour (cornstarch)
  5ml/1 tsp white wine vinegar
  sugared flowers,
    to decorate
For the filling
  300ml/½ pint/1¼ cups double
    (heavy) cream
  2 ripe peaches

COOK'S TIP
To make lavender sugar, mix 15ml/1 tbsp dried culinary lavender with 1kg/2¼lb/ 5 cups caster (superfine) sugar. Store in an airtight container. Shake regularly.

1 Preheat the oven to 110°C/225°F/ Gas ¼. Line two baking sheets with baking parchment and draw a 23cm/9in circle on one and a 16cm/6¼in circle on the second.

2 Put the egg whites in a large bowl and whisk until they form stiff but moist-looking peaks. Gradually whisk in the sugar, a spoonful at a time, and continue whisking for 2 minutes until the meringue is thick and glossy.

3 Mix the cornflour and vinegar together and fold into the meringue mixture. Using two dessertspoons, drop spoonfuls of meringue over the smaller circle. Make the larger circle in the same way, and level the centre slightly.

4 Cook for 1¼ hours, or until pale golden. (Swap the positions of the baking sheets during cooking so that the layers cook to an even colour.) The meringues should come away from the paper easily; test by peeling away an edge of the paper but leave the meringues on the paper to cool.

5 To serve, remove the paper and put the larger meringue on a large, flat serving plate. Softly whip the cream, and spoon over the meringue. Halve, stone (pit) and slice the peaches and arrange on the cream. Place the second meringue on top of the peaches. Chill. When ready to serve, decorate with a selection of crystallized flowers and serve immediately.

Energy 325Kcal/1357kJ; Protein 2.8g; Carbohydrate 35.2g, of which sugars 35.2g; Fat 20.2g, of which saturates 12.5g; Cholesterol 51mg; Calcium 38mg; Fibre 0.4g; Sodium 48mg.

CURD TARTS WITH COINTREAU AND NUTMEG

LEMON EMPHASIZES THE ORANGE AND COINTREAU FILLING, AND A LITTLE NUTMEG ADDS A WARM AND SPICY TOUCH TO THESE TRADITIONAL ENGLISH TARTS. EXCELLENT SERVED WITH HOME-MADE CUSTARD.

SERVES 6

INGREDIENTS

175g/6oz/1½ cups plain (all-purpose) flour, plus extra for dusting
40g/1½oz/3 tbsp block margarine, diced
40g/1½oz/3 tbsp white vegetable fat (shortening), diced
30ml/2 tbsp caster (superfine) sugar
1 egg yolk
2.5ml/½ tsp ground nutmeg
orange segments and thinly pared orange rind, to decorate
For the filling
25g/1oz/2 tbsp butter, melted
50g/2oz/¼ cup caster (superfine) sugar
1 egg
175g/6oz/¾ cup curd (farmer's) cheese
30ml/2 tbsp double (heavy) cream
50g/2oz/¼ cup currants
15ml/1 tbsp grated lemon rind
15ml/1 tbsp grated orange rind
15ml/1 tbsp Cointreau

1 Start by making the pastry. Sift the flour into a large mixing bowl and rub in the margarine and vegetable fat until the mixture resembles fine breadcrumbs.

2 Stir in the sugar and egg yolk and then add enough cold water to make a firm dough.

3 Wrap the pastry in clear film and chill for 30 minutes. Preheat the oven to 190°C/375°F/Gas 5.

COOK'S TIPS

• Curd cheese is a soft, unripened cheese with a milky, tangy flavour. If it is not available, cottage cheese can be used instead, although it will not have the same tang. Process in a food processor or press through a sieve (strainer), then use as curd cheese.
• To make a large tart, use the pastry to line an 18cm/7in flan tin (quiche pan). Spoon in the filling and bake at the same temperature for 45–55 minutes.

4 Roll out the dough on a lightly floured surface and use it to line six 10cm/4in fluted flan tins (tart pans).

5 To make the filling, combine the melted butter, sugar, egg, curd cheese, cream, currants, grated lemon and orange rinds and Cointreau in a bowl. Mix well. Spoon the mixture into the pastry cases and smooth out, sprinkle over the nutmeg and bake for 30–35 minutes. Serve decorated with orange segments and the pared orange rind.

Energy 395Kcal/1654kJ; Protein 9g; Carbohydrate 43.5g, of which sugars 21.2g; Fat 21.6g, of which saturates 8.6g; Cholesterol 89mg; Calcium 102mg; Fibre 1.1g; Sodium 263mg.

DATE, FIG AND ORANGE PUDDING

THE FULL AND RICH FLAVOUR OF FIGS AND DATES IS HIGHLIGHTED BY ZESTY ORANGE IN THIS WARM AND COMFORTING PUDDING. IDEAL TO SERVE ON COLD, WINTRY DAYS.

3 Leave the fruit mixture to cool, then transfer to a food processor or blender and process until smooth. Press the mixture through a sieve (strainer) to remove the fig seeds, if you wish.

4 Cream the butter and sugar until pale and fluffy, then beat in the fig purée. Beat in the eggs, then fold in the flours and mix until combined.

SERVES 6

INGREDIENTS
   juice and grated rind of 2 oranges
   115g/4oz/⅔ cup pitted, chopped, ready-to-eat dried dates
   115g/4oz/⅔ cup chopped ready-to-eat dried figs
   30ml/2 tbsp orange liqueur (optional)
   175g/6oz/¾ cup unsalted (sweet) butter, plus extra for greasing
   175g/6oz/¾ cup soft light brown sugar
   3 eggs
   75g/3oz/⅔ cup self-raising (self-rising) wholemeal (whole-wheat) flour
   115g/4oz/1 cup unbleached self-raising (self-rising) flour
   30ml/2 tbsp golden (light corn) syrup (optional)

1 Reserve a few strips of orange rind for the decoration and put the rest in a pan with the orange juice.

2 Add the dates and figs, then pour in the orange liqueur, if using. Cook, covered, over a gentle heat for 8–10 minutes, or until soft.

5 Grease a 1.5 litre/2½ pint/6¼ cup pudding basin, and pour in the golden syrup, if using. Tilt the bowl to cover the inside with a layer of syrup. Spoon in the pudding mixture. Cover the top with greaseproof (waxed) paper, with a pleat down the centre, and then with pleated foil, and tie down with string.

6 Place the bowl in a large pan and pour in enough water to come halfway up the sides of the bowl. Cover with a tight-fitting lid and steam for 2 hours. Check the water occasionally and top up if necessary.

7 Turn the pudding out and decorate with the reserved orange rind. Serve piping hot.

Energy 583Kcal/2447kJ; Protein 7.7g; Carbohydrate 81.4g, of which sugars 57.6g; Fat 27.5g, of which saturates 16.1g; Cholesterol 157mg; Calcium 177mg; Fibre 3.1g; Sodium 312mg.

SOUFFLÉED RICE PUDDING WITH NUTMEG

VANILLA AND NUTMEG ADD THEIR DELICATE FLAVOURS TO THIS CREAMY SOUFFLÉED RICE PUDDING.
IT IS EQUALLY DELICIOUS SERVED COLD.

SERVES 4

INGREDIENTS
65g/2½oz/⅓ cup short grain
   pudding rice
45ml/3 tbsp clear honey
750ml/1¼ pints/3 cups milk
1 vanilla pod (bean) or
   2.5ml/½ tsp vanilla extract
butter, for greasing
2 egg whites
5ml/1 tsp freshly grated nutmeg
wafer biscuits (cookies),
   to serve (optional)

1 Place the rice, honey and milk in a heavy or non-stick pan, and bring the milk to just below boiling point, watching it closely to prevent it from boiling over. Add the vanilla pod, if using.

2 Reduce the heat to the lowest setting and cover the pan.

3 Leave to cook for 1–1¼ hours, stirring occasionally to prevent sticking, until most of the liquid has been absorbed.

4 Remove the vanilla pod or, if using vanilla essence, add this to the rice mixture now.

5 Preheat the oven to 220°C/425°F/ Gas 7. Grease a 1 litre/1¾ pint/4 cup baking dish with butter.

COOK'S TIP
This pudding is especially delicious topped with a stewed, dried-fruit salad, although a fresh summer-fruit compote would also work well.

6 Place the egg whites in a large grease-free bowl and whisk until they hold soft peaks. Using either a metal spoon, a fish slice or a metal spatula, fold the egg whites evenly into the rice and milk mixture. Tip into the baking dish.

7 Sprinkle with grated nutmeg and then bake in the oven for 15–20 minutes, or until the rice pudding has risen well and the surface is golden brown. Serve the rice pudding hot, with wafer biscuits, if you like.

Energy 183Kcal/773kJ; Protein 9.2g; Carbohydrate 29.6g, of which sugars 17.4g; Fat 3.5g, of which saturates 2g; Cholesterol 11mg; Calcium 229mg; Fibre 0g; Sodium 113mg.

SWEET COUSCOUS WITH ROSE-SCENTED FRUIT COMPOTE

THIS SWEET, NUTRITIOUS MIXTURE TASTES GREAT WITH A DRIED FRUIT COMPOTE. MAKE THE COMPOTE A FEW DAYS AHEAD, SO THAT THE FLAVOURS OF THE ROSE WATER, CINNAMON AND FRUIT CAN MINGLE, AND SERVE IT WARM, WITH THE FRESHLY COOKED SWEET COUSCOUS.

1 Prepare the fruit compote a couple of days in advance. Put the dried fruit and almonds in a bowl and pour in just enough water to cover.

2 Gently stir in the sugar and rose water, and add the cinnamon stick. Cover and leave the fruit and nuts to soak for 48 hours, during which time the water and sugar will form a lovely golden-coloured syrup.

3 To make the couscous, bring the water to the boil in a pan. Stir in the couscous and raisins, and cook gently for 1–2 minutes, until the water has been absorbed. Remove the pan from the heat, cover tightly and leave the couscous to steam for 10–15 minutes. Meanwhile, poach the compote over a gentle heat until warmed through.

4 Tip the couscous into a bowl and separate the grains with your fingertips.

5 Melt the butter and pour it over the couscous. Sprinkle the sugar over, then, using your fingertips, rub the butter and sugar into the couscous. Divide the mixture between six bowls.

6 Heat the milk and cream together in a small, heavy pan until they are just about to boil, then pour the mixture over the couscous. Serve immediately, with the dried fruit compote.

SERVES 6

INGREDIENTS
300ml/½ pint/1¼ cups water
225g/8oz/1⅓ cups couscous
50g/2oz/scant ⅓ cup raisins
50g/2oz/¼ cup butter
50g/2oz/¼ cup granulated sugar
120ml/4fl oz/½ cup milk
120ml/4fl oz/½ cup double
 (heavy) cream

For the fruit compote
225g/8oz/1 cup dried apricots
225g/8oz/1 cup stoned
 (pitted) prunes
115g/4oz/¾ cup sultanas
 (golden raisins)
115g/4oz/⅔ cup blanched almonds
175g/6oz/generous ¾ cup
 granulated sugar
30ml/2 tbsp rose water
1 cinnamon stick

Energy 661Kcal/2771kJ; Protein 9.4g; Carbohydrate 95.6g, of which sugars 75.9g; Fat 29.3g, of which saturates 12.1g; Cholesterol 46mg; Calcium 143mg; Fibre 4.8g; Sodium 82mg.

SAFFRON AND CARDAMOM CRÈME CARAMEL WITH BUTTER COOKIES

THE SUBTLE FLAVOURS AND AROMAS OF SAFFRON AND CARDAMOM ADD AN INDULGENT AND UNUSUAL TWIST TO THESE DELICIOUS, CREAMY, CHILLED DESSERTS. THE RICH, BUTTERY COOKIES ARE AN IRRESISTIBLE ACCOMPANIMENT AND ADD SOME WELCOME CRUNCH.

SERVES 4–6

INGREDIENTS
  600ml/1 pint/2½ cups milk
  115g/4oz/⅔ cup granulated sugar,
    plus 60ml/4 tbsp for caramel
  pinch of saffron threads
  2.5ml/½ tsp cardamom seeds
  15–30ml/1–2 tbsp rose water
  4 eggs, lightly beaten
  60ml/4 tbsp boiling water
For the cookies
  200g/7oz/scant 1 cup butter
  130g/4½oz/generous 1 cup icing
    (confectioners') sugar, sifted
  5–10ml/1–2 tsp orange
    flower water
  250g/9oz/2¼ cups plain
    (all-purpose) flour, sifted
  handful of whole
    blanched almonds

1 Preheat the oven to 180°C/350°F/ Gas 4. Heat the milk, sugar, saffron and cardamom in a pan until the milk is just about to boil. Remove the pan from the heat and set aside to cool. Add the rose water, then gradually pour the mixture on to the eggs in a bowl, beating all the time. Set aside.

2 To make the caramel, heat the 60ml/ 4 tbsp sugar in a small, heavy pan, until melted and dark brown. Stir in the water, holding the pan at arm's length as the caramel will spit. Let it bubble before tipping it into individual ovenproof dishes. Swirl the dishes to coat the base and sides evenly. Leave to cool.

3 Pour the custard into the dishes and then stand them in a roasting pan. Pour in enough cold water to come two-thirds of the way up the outsides of the dishes. Bake in the oven for about 1 hour, or until the custard has set. Cool, then chill in the refrigerator for several hours or overnight.

4 To make the cookies, melt the butter in a pan over a low heat and then leave to cool until lukewarm. Stir in the icing sugar and orange flower water, then gradually beat in the flour to form a smooth, stiff dough. Wrap in clear film (plastic wrap) and chill for 15 minutes.

5 Preheat the oven to 180°C/350°F/ Gas 4. Grease a baking sheet. Break off walnut-size pieces of dough and roll them into balls. Place on the baking sheet and flatten slightly. Press a whole blanched almond into the centre of each. Bake for 20 minutes, or until golden.

6 Allow to cool slightly on the baking sheet; when firm, transfer to a wire rack.

7 To serve, run a knife around the edges of the crème caramel dishes and invert on to plates. Serve immediately with the butter cookies.

Energy 969Kcal/4064kJ; Protein 17.8g; Carbohydrate 119.9g, of which sugars 72.3g; Fat 50g, of which saturates 29.3g; Cholesterol 306mg; Calcium 338mg; Fibre 2g; Sodium 443mg.

SWEET PEAR AND CARDAMOM SPONGE

SCENTED CARDAMOM SEEDS COMPLEMENT DESSERT PEARS IN THIS MOIST SPONGE. IT MAKES A
DELICIOUS DESSERT SERVED WITH A DOLLOP OF WHIPPED CREAM OR ICE CREAM.

SERVES 4

INGREDIENTS
   115g/4oz/½ cup butter, softened,
    plus extra for greasing
   115g/4oz/1 cup self-raising (self-
    rising) flour, plus extra for dusting
   5 pears
   10 green cardamom pods
   5ml/1 tsp baking powder
   115g/4oz/generous ½ cup caster
    (superfine) sugar
   3 egg yolks
   30–45ml/2–3 tbsp warm water

1 Preheat the oven to 190°C/375°F/Gas 5.
Line the base of a 20cm/8in-diameter
cake tin (pan) with baking parchment
and then butter and lightly flour
the sides.

2 Peel the pears, cut them in half and
remove the cores with a sharp knife.
Arrange the fruit cut-side up in a circle
in the bottom of the tin.

COOK'S TIP
Choose very sweet dessert pears, like
Comice or Williams. They need to be
completely ripe and very juicy.

3 Remove the cardamom seeds from
the pods and crush the seeds lightly
using a mortar and pestle.

4 Sift together the flour and baking
powder. Add the sugar, the crushed
cardamom seeds, butter, egg yolks and
30ml/2 tbsp of the water. Beat with an
electric or hand whisk until creamy. The
mixture should fall off a spoon; if it does
not, add a little more water.

5 Place the mixture on top of the pears
and level with a knife. Bake the cake
for 45–60 minutes, or until firm.

6 Turn the cake out on to a wire rack
and peel off the baking parchment. Cool
before serving.

Energy 530Kcal/2217kJ; Protein 5.6g; Carbohydrate 67g, of which sugars 45.6g; Fat 28.4g, of which saturates 16.3g; Cholesterol 218mg; Calcium 156mg; Fibre 4.2g; Sodium 291mg.

GREEK YOGURT AND FIG CAKE

BAKED FRESH FIGS, THICKLY SLICED, MAKE A DELECTABLE TOPPING FOR A FEATHERLIGHT SPONGE.
FIGS THAT ARE A BIT ON THE FIRM SIDE WORK BEST FOR THIS PARTICULAR RECIPE.

SERVES 6–8

INGREDIENTS
6 firm fresh figs, thickly sliced
45ml/3 tbsp clear honey, plus extra
 for glazing
200g/7oz/scant 1 cup butter,
 softened, plus extra for greasing
175g/6oz/scant 1 cup caster
 (superfine) sugar
grated rind of 1 lemon
grated rind of 1 orange
4 eggs, separated
225g/8oz/2 cups plain
 (all-purpose) flour
5ml/1 tsp baking powder
5ml/1 tsp bicarbonate of soda
 (baking soda)
250ml/8fl oz/1 cup Greek
 (US strained plain) yogurt

1 Preheat the oven to 180°C/350°F/
Gas 4. Grease a 23cm/9in cake tin
(pan) and line the base.

2 Arrange the figs over the base of the
tin and drizzle over the honey.

3 Cream the butter and caster sugar
with the lemon and orange rinds.

4 When the mixture is pale and fluffy,
gradually beat in the egg yolks.

5 Sift the dry ingredients together in
a separate bowl. Add a little to the
creamed mixture, beat well, then beat
in a spoonful of yogurt. Repeat until all
the dry ingredients and yogurt have been
incorporated into the creamed mixture.

6 Whisk the egg whites in a grease-free
bowl until they form stiff peaks.

7 Stir half the whites into the cake
mixture to slacken it slightly, then fold
in the rest.

8 Pour the mixture over the figs in the
base of the cake tin.

9 Bake in the preheated oven for
1¼ hours, or until golden and a skewer
inserted in the centre of the cake
comes out clean.

10 Turn the cake out on to a wire rack,
peel off the lining paper and cool.

11 Drizzle the figs with a little extra
honey before serving.

Energy 484Kcal/2027kJ; Protein 8.1g; Carbohydrate 58.7g, of which sugars 37.2g; Fat 25.8g, of which saturates 15.2g; Cholesterol 153mg; Calcium 154mg; Fibre 2g; Sodium 245mg.

LAVENDER CAKE

BAKE A SUMMER-SCENTED CAKE THAT IS REMINISCENT OF THOSE DISTANT ELIZABETHAN TIMES WHEN LAVENDER WAS AN EXTREMELY POPULAR CULINARY HERB.

SERVES 8

INGREDIENTS

175g/6oz/¾ cup unsalted (sweet) butter, plus extra for greasing
175g/6oz/scant 1 cup caster (superfine) sugar
3 eggs, lightly beaten
175g/6oz/1⅔ cups self-raising (self-rising) flour, sifted, plus extra
30ml/2 tbsp fresh lavender florets
2.5ml/½ tsp vanilla extract
30ml/2 tbsp milk
50g/2oz/½ cup icing (confectioners') sugar, sifted
2.5ml/½ tsp water
a few fresh lavender florets

1 Preheat the oven to 180°C/350°F/ Gas 4. Lightly grease and flour a ring tin (pan) or a deep 20cm/8in round, loose-based cake tin (pan).

2 Cream the butter and sugar together thoroughly until the mixture is light and fluffy.

3 Add the beaten egg gradually, beating thoroughly between each separate addition, until the mixture has become thick and glossy.

4 Gently fold in the flour, together with the lavender florets, vanilla essence and milk.

5 Spoon the mixture into the tin and bake for 1 hour.

6 Leave to stand for 5 minutes, then turn out on to a wire rack to cool.

7 Mix the icing sugar with the water until smooth.

8 Pour the icing over the cooled cake and decorate it with a few fresh lavender florets.

VARIATION
For a pretty colour contrast, add a little orange food colouring to the icing before pouring over the cake.

Energy 375Kcal/1572kJ; Protein 4.7g; Carbohydrate 46.2g, of which sugars 30g; Fat 20.4g, of which saturates 12.1g; Cholesterol 118mg; Calcium 111mg; Fibre 0.7g; Sodium 241mg.

DATE AND WALNUT SPICE CAKE

NUTMEG, MIXED SPICE AND WALNUTS FLAVOUR THIS SCRUMPTIOUS CAKE, AND DATES MAKE IT DELICIOUSLY MOIST. IT GOES VERY WELL WITH MORNING COFFEE.

SERVES 8

INGREDIENTS
- 115g/4oz/½ cup unsalted (sweet) butter, plus extra for greasing
- 175g/6oz/1½ cups unbleached self-raising (self-rising) flour, plus extra for dusting
- 175g/6oz/¾ cup soft dark brown sugar
- 2 eggs
- 5ml/1 tsp bicarbonate of soda (baking soda)
- 2.5ml/½ tsp freshly grated nutmeg
- 5ml/1 tsp mixed (apple pie) spice
- pinch of salt
- 175ml/6fl oz/¾ cup buttermilk
- 50g/2oz/⅓ cup ready-to-eat pitted dates, chopped
- 25g/1oz/¼ cup chopped walnuts

For the topping
- 60ml/4 tbsp clear honey
- 45ml/3 tbsp fresh orange juice
- 15ml/1 tbsp coarsely grated orange rind, plus extra to decorate

1 Grease and lightly flour a 23cm/9in springform cake tin (pan). Preheat the oven to 180°C/350°F/Gas 4.

2 Cream together the butter and sugar until the mixture is fluffy and creamy. Add the eggs, one at a time, and then beat well to combine.

3 Sift together the flour, bicarbonate of soda, nutmeg, mixed spice and salt. Gradually add this to the creamed mixture, alternating with the buttermilk. Add the chopped dates and walnuts, and stir well.

4 Spoon the mixture into the prepared cake tin and level the top. Bake for 50 minutes, or until a skewer inserted into the centre comes out clean. Leave to cool for 5 minutes, then turn out on to a wire rack to cool completely.

5 To make the topping, heat the clear honey, orange juice and rind in a small, heavy pan. Bring to the boil and boil rapidly for 3 minutes, without stirring, until syrupy.

6 Make small holes all over the top of the warm cake using the skewer, and then pour over the hot syrup. Decorate with the orange rind. Serve immediately in generous slices.

COOK'S TIP
To make a quite acceptable buttermilk substitute, simply mix 15ml/1 tbsp lemon juice with 250ml/8fl oz/1 cup semi-skimmed (low-fat) milk.

Energy 350Kcal/1472kJ; Protein 5.1g; Carbohydrate 50.3g, of which sugars 34.1g; Fat 15.7g, of which saturates 8.1g; Cholesterol 79mg; Calcium 131mg; Fibre 1g; Sodium 196mg.

LEMON AND WALNUT CAKE

DON'T STINT ON THE LEMON RIND — IT GIVES THIS CAKE A WONDERFUL ZESTY TANG THAT BLENDS PERFECTLY WITH THE WARM FLAVOUR OF THE WALNUTS.

SERVES 8–10

INGREDIENTS
1 large banana, about 150g/5oz
225g/8oz/1 cup butter, plus extra
for greasing
150g/5oz/1 cup dried, pitted
dates, chopped
5 small (US medium) eggs
300g/11oz/scant 3 cups wholemeal
(whole-wheat) flour, or half
wholemeal and half plain (all-
purpose) white flour
75g/3oz/¾ cup walnut pieces
4 large lemons

1 Preheat the oven to 180°C/350°F/
Gas 4. Grease a deep 20cm/8in springform cake tin (pan). Line the base of
the tin with baking parchment.

2 Peel and chop the banana. Process
with the butter and dates in a food
processor or blender.

3 Add one egg and 15ml/1 tbsp of the
flour to the creamed mixture. Process
briefly to mix, then add the remaining
eggs one at a time, each with a further
15ml/1 tbsp flour.

4 Scrape the mixture into a bowl and
fold in the remaining flour, with the
walnut pieces.

5 Grate the rind from three lemons
and thinly pare the rind from the fourth
(reserve for the decoration). Squeeze
the juice from two lemons, then stir the
grated lemon rind and juice into the
cake mixture.

6 Spoon the mixture into the prepared
tin. Bake for 50–60 minutes, or until a
fine skewer inserted in the centre of the
cake comes out clean.

7 Cool on a wire rack. Decorate the
cake with the pared lemon rind.

COOK'S TIPS
• If the dried dates are very hard, soften
them in boiling water for 10 minutes
before draining and using.
• Make sure that you buy plain dried
dates and not the kind that are chopped
and coated with sugar.
• Look out for packets of walnut pieces
in supermarkets, as they are usually
much less expensive than either shelled
walnuts or walnut halves.

Energy 404Kcal/1683kJ; Protein 8.9g; Carbohydrate 33.2g, of which sugars 14.3g; Fat 27.1g, of which saturates 13g; Cholesterol 143mg; Calcium 44mg; Fibre 3.7g; Sodium 174mg.

RICH LEMON POPPY-SEED CAKE

THE CLASSIC COMBINATION OF POPPY SEEDS AND LEMON IS USED FOR THIS LIGHT CAKE, WHICH HAS A DELICIOUS LEMON CURD AND FROMAGE FRAIS FILLING.

SERVES 8

INGREDIENTS
  350g/12oz/1½ cups unsalted
    (sweet) butter, plus extra
    for greasing
  350g/12oz/1¾ cups golden
    caster (superfine) sugar
  45ml/3 tbsp poppy seeds
  20ml/4 tsp finely grated lemon rind
  70ml/4½ tbsp luxury lemon curd
  6 eggs, separated
  120ml/4fl oz/½ cup semi-skimmed
    (low-fat) milk
  350g/12oz/3 cups unbleached
    self-raising (self-rising) flour,
    plus extra for dusting
  icing (confectioners') sugar,
    to decorate
For the filling
  150g/5oz/½ cup luxury lemon curd
  150ml/¼ pint/⅔ cup fromage frais
    or natural (plain) yogurt

1 Butter and lightly flour two 23cm/9in springform cake tins (pans). Preheat the oven to 180°C/350°F/Gas 4.

2 Cream the butter and sugar until light and fluffy. Add the poppy seeds, lemon rind, lemon curd and egg yolks and beat well, then add the milk and mix well. Fold in the flour until combined.

3 Whisk the egg whites using a hand-held electric mixer or whisk until they form soft peaks.

4 Carefully fold the egg whites into the cake mixture until just combined. Divide between the prepared tins.

5 Bake for 40–45 minutes, or until a skewer inserted into the centre of the cakes comes out clean and the tops are golden.

6 Leave the cakes to cool in the tins for 5 minutes, then remove from the tins and leave to cool on wire racks.

VARIATION
Replace the lemon curd and fromage frais filling with a lemon syrup. Boil 45ml/3 tbsp lemon juice, 15ml/1 tbsp lemon rind and 30ml/2 tbsp caster sugar for 3 minutes until syrupy and glossy. Make a single cake using half the ingredients. Pour the syrup over the warm cake and leave to cool.

7 To finish, spread one cake with the lemon curd and spoon the fromage frais or yogurt evenly over the lemon curd.

8 Put the second cake on top, press down gently, then dust the top with icing sugar before serving.

Energy 805Kcal/3374kJ; Protein 10.7g; Carbohydrate 99.6g, of which sugars 60.9g; Fat 43.3g, of which saturates 25.3g; Cholesterol 246mg; Calcium 242mg; Fibre 1.4g; Sodium 509mg.

RASPBERRY AND ROSE-PETAL SHORTCAKES

ROSE-WATER-SCENTED CREAM AND FRESH RASPBERRIES FORM THE FILLING FOR THIS DELECTABLE AND LUXURIOUS DESSERT. ALTHOUGH THEY LOOK IMPRESSIVE, THESE SHORTCAKES ARE EASY TO MAKE AND WOULD BE AN EXCELLENT CHOICE FOR A DINNER PARTY.

MAKES 6

INGREDIENTS
    115g/4oz/½ cup unsalted (sweet)
    butter, softened
    50g/2oz/¼ cup caster
    (superfine) sugar
    ½ vanilla pod (bean), split and
    seeds reserved
    115g/4oz/1 cup plain (all-purpose)
    flour, plus extra for dusting
    50g/2oz/⅓ cup semolina
For the filling
    300ml/½ pint/1¼ cups double
    (heavy) cream
    15ml/1 tbsp icing (confectioners')
    sugar, plus extra for dusting
    2.5ml/½ tsp rose water
    450g/1lb/2⅔ cups raspberries
For the decoration
    12 miniature roses, unsprayed
    6 mint sprigs
    1 egg white, beaten
    caster (superfine) sugar, for dusting

1 Cream the butter, sugar and vanilla seeds together in a bowl until the mixture is pale and fluffy. Sift the flour and semolina together, then gradually work the dry ingredients into the creamed mixture to make a biscuit (cookie) dough.

VARIATIONS
Other soft, red summer berries, such as mulberries, loganberries and tayberries, would be equally good in this dessert. You might also like to use different shapes of cutter for the shortcakes, such as flowers and hearts.

2 Gently knead the dough on a lightly floured surface until smooth. Roll out quite thinly and prick all over with a fork. Using a 7.5cm/3in fluted cutter, cut out 12 rounds. Place these on a baking sheet and then chill in the refrigerator for 30 minutes.

3 Meanwhile, make the filling. Whisk the double cream with the icing sugar until soft peaks form. Gently fold the rose water into the mixture and then chill until required.

4 Preheat the oven to 180°C/350°F/ Gas 4. Paint the roses and mint sprigs with the beaten egg white. Dust with sugar; place on a wire rack to dry.

5 Bake the shortcakes in the preheated oven for 15 minutes, or until they are lightly golden. Remove them from the oven, then lift them off the baking sheet with a metal fish slice or metal spatula and transfer to a wire rack to cool.

6 To assemble the shortcakes, spoon the rose-water cream on to half the cooled shortcakes.

7 Arrange a layer of raspberries on top of the cream, then top with a second shortcake.

8 Dust the filled shortcakes with icing sugar. Decorate with the frosted roses and mint sprigs.

COOK'S TIPS
• For best results, serve the shortcakes as soon as possible after assembling them. Otherwise, they are likely to turn soggy from the raspberries' liquid.
• If necessary, ground rice can be substituted for the semolina used for making the shortcakes.
• For the best-flavoured shortcakes, always use butter and not margarine.

Energy 537Kcal/2231kJ; Protein 4.7g; Carbohydrate 34.5g, of which sugars 13.4g; Fat 43.2g, of which saturates 26.8g; Cholesterol 109mg; Calcium 80mg; Fibre 2.7g; Sodium 132mg.

LAVENDER HEART COOKIES

IN FOLKLORE, LAVENDER HAS ALWAYS BEEN LINKED WITH LOVE, AS HAS FOOD. SO MAKE SOME OF THESE DELICIOUS HEART-SHAPED COOKIES AND SERVE THEM TO YOUR LOVED ONE ON VALENTINE'S DAY, OR ON ANY OTHER ROMANTIC ANNIVERSARY.

1 Cream the butter and sugar together until light and fluffy. Mix together the flour and lavender, and add to the creamed mixture.

2 Bring the mixture together in a soft ball. Cover with clear film (plastic wrap) and chill for 15 minutes. Meanwhile, preheat the oven to 200°C/400°F/Gas 6.

3 Roll out the mixture on a lightly floured surface and stamp out about 18 biscuits (cookies), using a 5cm/2in heart-shaped cutter.

4 Place the biscuits on a heavy baking sheet and bake them in the preheated oven for about 10 minutes, or until they are golden brown.

5 Leave the biscuits to stand for about 5 minutes to firm up.

6 Using a metal spatula, transfer them carefully from the baking sheet on to a wire rack to cool.

7 Sprinkle with icing sugar. You can store the biscuits in an airtight container for up to 1 week.

COOK'S TIPS
• Metal cutters make cutting easier, but remember to ensure that they are completely dry before putting them away, or they will turn rusty.
• Biscuits such as these can be made in advance and frozen very successfully, if you like, as long as they are well wrapped in foil.

MAKES 16–18

INGREDIENTS
 115g/4oz/½ cup unsalted (sweet) butter, softened
 50g/2oz/¼ cup caster (superfine) sugar
 175g/6oz/1½ cups plain (all-purpose) flour, plus extra for dusting
 30ml/2 tbsp fresh lavender florets or 15ml/1 tbsp dried culinary lavender, roughly chopped
 25g/1oz/¼ cup icing (confectioners') sugar, for sprinkling

Energy 97Kcal/406kJ; Protein 1g; Carbohydrate 11.9g, of which sugars 4.5g; Fat 5.4g, of which saturates 3.4g; Cholesterol 14mg; Calcium 17mg; Fibre 0.3g; Sodium 39mg.

LAVENDER SCONES

THE FRAGRANCE OF LAVENDER MARRIES WELL WITH THE SWEETNESS OF SUMMER SOFT FRUIT, AND MAKES FOR AN ELEGANT TEA-TIME TREAT. THE LAVENDER'S SCENTED QUALITY GIVES THE WELL-KNOWN TEA SCONE A FLAVOUR, WHICH NOWADAYS CAN SEEM PLEASANTLY UNUSUAL AND SURPRISING.

MAKES 12

INGREDIENTS
225g/8oz/2 cups plain (all-purpose) flour, plus extra for dusting
15ml/1 tbsp baking powder
50g/2oz/¼ cup butter
50g/2oz/¼ cup sugar
10ml/2 tsp fresh lavender florets or 5ml/1 tsp dried culinary lavender, roughly chopped
about 150ml/¼ pint/⅔ cup milk
plum jam and clotted cream, to serve

1 Preheat the oven to 220°C/425°F/ Gas 7. Sift the flour and baking powder together. Rub the butter into the flour mixture until it resembles fine breadcrumbs.

2 Stir in the sugar and chopped lavender, reserving a pinch to sprinkle on the top of the scones before baking them. Add enough milk so that the mixture forms a soft, sticky dough. Bind the dough together and then turn it out on to a floured surface.

3 Shape the dough into a round, gently patting down the top to give a 2.5cm/ 1in depth. Using a floured cutter, stamp out 12 scones.

4 Place the scones on a baking sheet. Brush the tops of each scone with a little milk and sprinkle over the reserved lavender.

5 Bake the scones for 10–12 minutes, or until golden. Serve warm with plum jam and clotted cream.

Energy 117Kcal/494kJ; Protein 2.2g; Carbohydrate 19.5g, of which sugars 5.3g; Fat 3.9g, of which saturates 2.3g; Cholesterol 10mg; Calcium 44mg; Fibre 0.6g; Sodium 31mg.

SUNFLOWER SULTANA SCONES

THESE FRUITY SCONES HAVE A CRUNCHY AND TASTY SUNFLOWER-SEED TOPPING. THEY MAKE A TEMPTING TEA-TIME TREAT SPREAD WITH BUTTER AND JAM.

MAKES 10–12

INGREDIENTS
    oil, for greasing
    225g/8oz/2 cups self-raising (self-
        rising) flour, plus extra for dusting
    5ml/1 tsp baking powder
    25g/1oz/2 tbsp butter
    30ml/2 tbsp golden caster (superfine)
        sugar
    50g/2oz/⅓ cup sultanas (golden raisins)
    30ml/2 tbsp sunflower seeds
    150g/5oz/⅔ cup natural (plain) yogurt
    about 30–45ml/2–3 tbsp skimmed
        (low-fat) milk
    butter and jam, to serve (optional)

1 Preheat the oven to 230°C/450°F/ Gas 8. Lightly oil a baking sheet. Sift the flour and baking powder into a bowl and rub in the butter.

2 Stir in the sugar, sultanas and half the sunflower seeds, then mix in the yogurt, with just enough milk to make a fairly soft, but not sticky dough.

3 Roll out the dough on a lightly floured surface to a thickness of about 2cm/¾in. Cut into 6cm/2½in rounds with a biscuit (cookie) cutter and lift on to the baking sheet.

4 Brush the scones with milk and then sprinkle them with the reserved sunflower seeds.

5 Bake 10–12 minutes, or until they are well risen and golden brown.

6 Cool the scones on a wire rack. Serve them split and spread with butter and jam, if you like.

Energy 114Kcal/481kJ; Protein 2.8g; Carbohydrate 21g, of which sugars 6.8g; Fat 2.7g, of which saturates 1.2g; Cholesterol 5mg; Calcium 98mg; Fibre 0.7g; Sodium 93mg.

POPPY-SEED ROLL

THIS SWEET YEAST BAKE WITH ITS SPIRAL FILLING OF DRIED FRUITS, POPPY SEEDS AND LEMON IS A WONDERFUL EXAMPLE OF TRADITIONAL POLISH COOKING.

SERVES 12

INGREDIENTS
 450g/1lb/4 cups plain (all-purpose)
  flour, plus extra for dusting
 pinch of salt
 30ml/2 tbsp caster (superfine) sugar
 10ml/2 tsp easy-blend
  (rapid-rise) dried yeast
 175ml/6fl oz/¾ cup milk
 finely grated rind of 1 lemon
 50g/2oz/¼ cup butter
For the filling and glaze
 50g/2oz/¼ cup butter
 115g/4oz/⅔ cup poppy seeds
 50ml/2fl oz/¼ cup set
  (crystallized) honey
 65g/2½oz/½ cup raisins
 65g/2½oz/scant ½ cup finely
  chopped candied orange peel
 50g/2oz/½ cup ground almonds
 1 egg yolk
 50g/2oz/¼ cup caster
  (superfine) sugar
 oil, for greasing
 15ml/1 tbsp milk
 60ml/4 tbsp apricot jam
 15ml/1 tbsp lemon juice
 15ml/1 tbsp rum or brandy
 25g/1oz/¼ cup toasted flaked
  (sliced) almonds

1 Sift the flour, salt and sugar into a bowl. Stir in the easy-blend dried yeast. Make a well in the centre.

2 Heat the milk and lemon rind in a pan with the butter, until melted. Cool a little, then add to the dry ingredients and mix to a dough.

3 Knead the dough on a lightly floured surface for 10 minutes, until smooth and elastic. Put the dough in a clean bowl, cover and leave in a warm place to rise for 45–50 minutes, or until doubled in size.

4 For the filling, melt the butter in a pan. Reserve 15ml/1 tbsp of the poppy seeds, then process the rest in a food processor.

5 Add the processed poppy seeds to the pan with the honey, raisins and candied orange peel. Cook gently for 5 minutes. Stir in the ground almonds, then leave to cool.

6 Whisk the egg yolk and sugar together in a bowl until pale, then fold into the poppy seed mixture. Roll out the dough on a lightly floured surface to form a rectangle that measures 30 × 35cm/ 12 × 14in. Spread the filling to within 2.5cm/1in of the edges.

7 Roll both ends towards the centre. Place on a baking sheet, cover with oiled clear film and leave to rise for 30 minutes. Preheat the oven to 190°C/375°F/Gas 5.

8 Brush with the milk, then sprinkle with the reserved poppy seeds. Bake for 30 minutes, until golden brown.

9 Heat the jam and lemon juice gently until bubbling. Strain, then stir in the rum or brandy. Brush over the roll while still warm and scatter with almonds.

Energy 351Kcal/1475kJ; Protein 7.7g; Carbohydrate 45.8g, of which sugars 15.4g; Fat 16.2g, of which saturates 5.4g; Cholesterol 36mg; Calcium 112mg; Fibre 2.6g; Sodium 80mg.

Ices and Sorbets

From everyday favourites, such as vanilla or chocolate double mint ice creams to Turkish Delight Sorbet or Bay and Ratafia Slice, this section is sure to have some new and exciting ideas for you to enjoy. Summer flowers – rose geranium, elderflowers and lavender – bring their subtle flavours to ices and sorbets. Or, discover the unusual tastes that bay and rosemary bring to sweet iced desserts. Add an exotic touch with lemon grass or cardamoms.

Above *Strawberry and Lavender Sorbet*

Left *Lemon and Cardamom Ice Cream*

CINNAMON AND COFFEE PARFAIT

THIS FRENCH-STYLE ICE CREAM IS FLECKED WITH CINNAMON AND MIXED WITH JUST A HINT OF COFFEE. AS IT IS MADE WITH A BOILING SUGAR SYRUP IT DOESN'T REQUIRE BEATING DURING FREEZING, SO CAN BE POURED STRAIGHT INTO FREEZERPROOF SERVING DISHES.

SERVES 6

INGREDIENTS
    15ml/1 tbsp instant
      coffee granules
    30ml/2 tbsp boiling water
    7.5ml/1½ tsp ground cinnamon
    4 egg yolks
    115g/4oz/generous ½ cup
      granulated sugar
    120ml/4fl oz/½ cup cold water
    300ml/½ pint/1¼ cups
      double (heavy) cream,
      lightly whipped
    200g/7oz/scant 1 cup crème fraîche
    extra ground cinnamon,
      to decorate

1 Spoon the coffee into a heatproof bowl, stir in the boiling water until dissolved, then stir in the cinnamon.

2 Put the egg yolks in a large, heatproof bowl and whisk them lightly until frothy.

3 Bring a medium pan of water to the boil and lower the heat so that it simmers gently. Put the sugar in a small pan, add the cold water and heat gently, stirring occasionally, until the sugar has completely dissolved.

4 Increase the heat and boil the sugar syrup for 4–5 minutes, without stirring, until the syrup registers 115°C/239°F on a sugar thermometer. Alternatively, test whether or not it is ready by dropping a little of the syrup into a cup of cold water. Pour the water away. If the syrup can be moulded in to a soft ball, it is ready to be used.

5 Put the bowl of egg yolks over the pan of simmering water and whisk in the sugar syrup. Whisk until the mixture is very thick and then remove from the heat. Continue whisking until it is cool.

6 Whisk the coffee and cinnamon into the yolk mixture, then fold in the cream and crème fraîche. Pour into a tub or individual freezerproof glass dishes. Freeze for 4 hours, or until firm.

7 If frozen in a tub, scoop into bowls and decorate with cinnamon.

COOK'S TIP
Test the syrup regularly. When it is nearly ready the syrup will fall slowly from the spoon. If the syrup fails to form a ball when tested in cold water, boil it for a few minutes more; if the syrup forms strands that snap it is overdone and you must start again.

Energy 490Kcal/2030kJ; Protein 3.6g; Carbohydrate 21.7g, of which sugars 21.6g; Fat 43.9g, of which saturates 26.8g; Cholesterol 241mg; Calcium 70mg; Fibre 0g; Sodium 26mg.

GINGERED SEMI-FREDDO

THIS ICE CREAM IS LUXURIOUSLY CREAMY AND GENEROUSLY SPECKLED WITH SMALL CHUNKS OF CHOPPED STEM GINGER. SEMI-FREDDO IS AN ITALIAN SEMI-FROZEN ICE CREAM THAT IS NEVER BEATEN DURING FREEZING. IT WILL STAY SOFT WHEN FROZEN.

SERVES 6

INGREDIENTS
  4 egg yolks
  115g/4oz/generous ½ cup caster
    (superfine) sugar
  120ml/4fl oz/½ cup cold water
  300ml/½ pint/1¼ cups double
    (heavy) cream
  115g/4oz/⅔ cup drained preserved
    stem ginger, finely chopped, plus
    extra slices, to decorate
  45ml/3 tbsp whisky (optional)

1 Put the egg yolks in a large, heatproof bowl and whisk until frothy. Bring a pan of water to the boil and simmer gently.

2 Mix the sugar and measured cold water in a pan and heat gently, stirring occasionally, until the sugar has completely dissolved.

3 Increase the heat and boil for 4–5 minutes without stirring until the syrup registers 115°C/239°F on a sugar thermometer. Alternatively, test by dropping a little of the syrup into a cup of cold water. Pour the water away. You should be able to mould the syrup into a ball.

4 Put the bowl of egg yolks over the pan of simmering water and whisk in the sugar syrup.

5 Continue whisking until the mixture is very thick. Remove from the heat and whisk until cool.

6 Whip the cream and lightly fold it into the yolk mixture, with the chopped ginger and whisky, if using. Pour into a plastic tub or similar freezerproof container and freeze for 1 hour.

7 Stir the semi-freddo to bring any ginger that has sunk to the bottom of the tub to the top, then return to the freezer for 5–6 hours, or until firm. Scoop into dishes or chocolate cases (see Cook's Tip). Decorate with slices of ginger.

COOK'S TIP
Semi-freddo looks wonderful in chocolate cases, made by spreading melted chocolate over squares of non-stick baking paper and then draping them over upturned tumblers. Peel the paper off when the chocolate has set and turn the cases the right way up before filling.

Energy 371Kcal/1539kJ; Protein 3g; Carbohydrate 22.4g, of which sugars 22.3g; Fat 30.6g, of which saturates 17.8g; Cholesterol 203mg; Calcium 55mg; Fibre 0.5g; Sodium 23mg.

CLASSIC VANILLA ICE CREAM

NOTHING BEATS THE CREAMY SIMPLICITY OF TRUE VANILLA ICE CREAM. VANILLA PODS ARE EXPENSIVE, BUT WELL WORTH BUYING FOR THE SUPERB FLAVOUR THEY IMPART.

2 Lift the vanilla pod up. Holding it over the pan, scrape the black seeds out of the pod with a small knife so that they fall back into the milk. Set the vanilla pod aside and bring the milk back to the boil.

3 Whisk the egg yolks, sugar and cornflour in a bowl until the mixture is thick and foamy. Gradually pour on the hot milk, whisking constantly. Return the mixture to the pan and cook over a gentle heat, stirring all the time.

4 When the custard thickens and is smooth, pour it back into the bowl. Cool it, then chill.

SERVES 4

INGREDIENTS
1 vanilla pod (bean)
300ml/½ pint/1¼ cups semi-skimmed (low-fat) milk
4 egg yolks
75g/3oz/6 tbsp caster (superfine) sugar
5ml/1 tsp cornflour (cornstarch)
300ml/½ pint/1¼ cups double (heavy) cream

COOK'S TIP
Don't discard the vanilla pod after use. Instead make vanilla sugar by rinsing it, drying it and putting it in the sugar jar.

1 Using a small knife, slit the vanilla pod lengthways. Pour the milk into a heavy pan, add the vanilla pod and bring to the boil. Remove from the heat and leave for 15 minutes to allow the flavours to infuse (steep).

5 By hand: Whip the cream until it has thickened. Fold it into the custard, and pour into a plastic tub or freezerproof container. Freeze for 6 hours, or until firm enough to scoop, beating twice with a fork, or in a food processor.
Using an ice cream maker: Stir the cream into the custard and churn the mixture until thick.

6 Scoop the ice cream into dishes, bowls or bought cones.

Energy 545Kcal/2260kJ; Protein 6.8g; Carbohydrate 25.3g, of which sugars 24.4g; Fat 47.1g, of which saturates 27.4g; Cholesterol 309mg; Calcium 160mg; Fibre 0g; Sodium 60mg.

ROSEMARY ICE CREAM

FRESH ROSEMARY HAS A LOVELY FRAGRANCE THAT WORKS AS WELL IN SWEET DISHES AS IT DOES IN SAVOURY. SERVE THIS ICE CREAM AS AN ACCOMPANIMENT TO SOFT FRUIT OR PLUM COMPOTE.

SERVES 6

INGREDIENTS

300ml/½ pint/1¼ cups milk
4 large fresh rosemary sprigs
3 egg yolks
75g/3oz/6 tbsp caster (superfine)
  sugar
10ml/2 tsp cornflour (cornstarch)
400ml/14fl oz/1⅔ cups crème fraîche
about 15ml/1 tbsp demerara (raw)
  sugar
fresh rosemary sprigs and herb
  flowers, to decorate
amaretti or ratafia biscuits (almond
  macaroons), to serve (optional)

6 Strain the custard through a sieve (strainer) into a bowl. Cover the surface closely with baking parchment and leave to cool. Chill until very cold, then stir in the crème fraîche.

7 By hand: Pour the mixture into a freezerproof container. Freeze for about 6 hours, beating twice using a fork, a whisk or a food processor to break up the ice crystals. Freeze until firm.
Using an ice cream maker: Churn the mixture in an ice cream maker until it is thick, then scrape it into a tub or similar freezerproof container. Freeze until ready to serve.

8 Scoop the ice cream into dessert dishes, sprinkle lightly with demerara sugar and decorate with rosemary sprigs and herb flowers. Offer amaretti or ratafia biscuits, if you like.

1 Put the milk and rosemary sprigs in a heavy pan. Bring almost to the boil, then remove from the heat and leave to infuse (steep) for 20 minutes.

2 Whisk the egg yolks in a bowl with the sugar and cornflour.

3 Remove the rosemary sprigs from the milk, then return the pan to the heat and bring the milk almost to the boil.

4 Pour it over the egg yolk mixture in the bowl, stirring well.

5 Return the mixture to the pan and cook it over a very gentle heat, stirring constantly until the custard thickens. Do not let it boil or the mixture may curdle.

COOK'S TIP
A mixture of rosemary, lavender and chive flowers would look very attractive for the decoration.

Energy 371Kcal/1538kJ; Protein 4.7g; Carbohydrate 21.2g, of which sugars 19.4g; Fat 30.3g, of which saturates 19.4g; Cholesterol 179mg; Calcium 119mg; Fibre 0g; Sodium 43mg.

MINT ICE CREAM

THIS REFRESHING AND INVIGORATING FRESH MINT ICE CREAM WILL BE DELICIOUSLY COOLING ON A HOT SUMMER'S DAY AND MAKES AN UNUSUAL DESSERT.

2 In a separate pan, bring the cream to the boil with the vanilla pod.

3 Remove the vanilla pod and pour on to the egg mixture, whisking briskly.

4 Continue whisking to ensure the eggs are mixed into the cream.

5 Gently heat the mixture until the custard thickens enough to coat the back of a wooden spoon. Remove from the heat and leave to cool.

6 By hand: Stir in the mint, then transfer to a freezerproof container. Freeze until the mixture is mushy then beat using a fork, a whisk or a food processor to break up the ice crystals. Freeze for another 3 hours, or until it is softly frozen, then whisk again. Finally, freeze until the ice cream is firm (this will take at least 6 hours).
Using an ice cream maker: Stir in the mint and churn in an ice cream maker until firm.

7 Transfer to the refrigerator for 20 minutes before serving, so that it will soften a little. Decorate with mint sprigs.

SERVES 8

INGREDIENTS
    8 egg yolks
    75g/3oz/6 tbsp caster
      (superfine) sugar
    600ml/1 pint/2½ cups
      single (light) cream
    1 vanilla pod (bean)
    60ml/4 tbsp chopped
      fresh mint
    mint sprigs,
      to decorate

1 Beat the egg yolks and sugar until pale and light. Transfer to a small pan.

Energy 212Kcal/879kJ; Protein 5.8g; Carbohydrate 2.1g, of which sugars 1.7g; Fat 20.2g, of which saturates 10.8g; Cholesterol 254mg; Calcium 107mg; Fibre 0g; Sodium 32mg.

CHOCOLATE DOUBLE MINT ICE CREAM

FULL OF BODY AND FLAVOUR, THIS CREAMY ICE CREAM COMBINES THE SOPHISTICATION OF DARK CHOCOLATE WITH THE COOLNESS OF FRESH CHOPPED MINT. CRUSHED PEPPERMINTS PROVIDE CRUNCH.

SERVES 4

INGREDIENTS
4 egg yolks
75g/3oz/6 tbsp caster
  (superfine) sugar
5ml/1 tsp cornflour (cornstarch)
300ml/½ pint/1¼ cups semi-skimmed
  (low-fat) milk
200g/7oz dark (bittersweet)
  chocolate, broken into squares
40g/1½oz/¼ cup peppermints
60ml/4 tbsp chopped
  fresh mint
300ml/½ pint/1¼ cups
  whipping cream
sprigs of fresh mint dusted
  with icing (confectioners') sugar,
  to decorate

1 Put the egg yolks, sugar and cornflour in a bowl and whisk until thick and foamy. Pour the milk into a heavy pan, bring to the boil, then gradually whisk into the yolk mixture.

2 Scrape the mixture back into the pan and cook over a gentle heat, stirring constantly until the custard thickens and is smooth.

3 Scrape it back into the bowl, add the chocolate, a little at a time, and stir until melted. Cool, then chill.

COOK'S TIP
If you freeze the ice cream in a tub, don't beat it in a food processor when breaking up the ice crystals or the crunchy texture of the crushed peppermints will be lost.

4 Put the peppermints in a strong plastic bag and crush them with a rolling pin. Stir them into the custard with the chopped mint.

5 By hand: Whip the cream until it has thickened, but is still soft enough to fall from a spoon. Fold it into the custard, scrape the mixture into a plastic tub or similar freezerproof container and freeze for 6–7 hours, beating once or twice with a fork or electric whisk to break up the ice crystals.
Using an ice cream maker: Mix the custard and cream together and churn the mixture until firm enough to scoop.

6 Serve the ice cream in scoops and then decorate with mint sprigs dusted with sifted icing sugar.

Energy 757Kcal/3159kJ; Protein 9.8g; Carbohydrate 68.3g, of which sugars 66.7g; Fat 51.4g, of which saturates 29.8g; Cholesterol 299mg; Calcium 186mg; Fibre 1.3g; Sodium 66mg.

LEMON AND CARDAMOM ICE CREAM

THE CLASSIC PARTNERSHIP OF LEMON AND CARDAMOM GIVES THIS RICH ICE CREAM A LOVELY TANG.
IT IS PERFECT AFTER A SPICY MAIN COURSE.

SERVES 6

INGREDIENTS

15ml/1 tbsp cardamom pods
4 egg yolks
115g/4oz/generous ½ cup caster
   (superfine) sugar
10ml/2 tsp cornflour (cornstarch)
finely grated rind and juice of
   3 lemons
300ml/½ pint/1¼ cups milk
300ml/½ pint/1¼ cups
   whipping cream
fresh lemon balm sprigs and
   icing (confectioners') sugar,
   to decorate (optional)

1 Put the cardamom pods in a mortar and crush them with a pestle to release the seeds. Pick out and discard the shells, then grind the seeds to break them up slightly.

2 Put the yolks, sugar, cornflour, lemon rind and juice in a bowl. Add the cardamom seeds and whisk.

3 Bring the milk to the boil in a heavy pan, then pour it over the egg yolk and cardamom mixture in the bowl, stirring.

4 Return the mixture to the pan and cook over a very gentle heat, stirring constantly with a wooden spoon until the custard thickens. Do not allow it to boil or it may start to curdle.

5 Pour the custard into a bowl, cover the surface with greaseproof (waxed) paper and leave to cool. Chill in the refrigerator until it is very cold.

6 By hand: Whip the cream until it has thickened but still falls from the whisk, and then stir into the custard. Transfer to a freezerproof container. Freeze for about 6 hours, beating twice, either using a fork or whisk or in a food processor, to break up the ice crystals. Freeze until firm.
Using an ice cream maker: Whisk the cream lightly into the chilled custard, then churn the mixture in an ice cream maker until it holds its shape. Transfer to a plastic tub or similar freezerproof container and freeze the ice cream until needed.

7 Transfer the ice cream to the refrigerator 30 minutes before serving.

8 Scoop into glasses. Decorate with the sprigs of lemon balm, dusted with icing sugar, if you like.

Energy 338Kcal/1406kJ; Protein 4.9g; Carbohydrate 25.3g, of which sugars 23.7g; Fat 24.9g, of which saturates 14.3g; Cholesterol 197mg; Calcium 116mg; Fibre 0g; Sodium 42mg.

KULFI <u>WITH</u> CARDAMOM

THIS INDIAN ICE CREAM IS TRADITIONALLY MADE BY REDUCING MLLK. CARDAMOMS ARE SIMMERED WITH THE MILK SO THAT IT IS INFUSED WITH THEIR DELICATE, SPICY FLAVOUR.

SERVES 4

INGREDIENTS
1.5 litres/2½ pints/6¼ cups full-fat
(whole) milk
3 cardamom pods
25g/1oz/2 tbsp caster
(superfine) sugar
50g/2oz/⅓ cup pistachio
nuts, skinned
a few pink rose petals from an
unsprayed rose, to decorate

1 Pour the milk into a large pan. Bring to the boil, lower the heat and simmer gently for 1 hour, stirring occasionally.

2 Put the cardamom pods in a mortar and crush them with a pestle.

3 Add the pods and the seeds to the hot milk in the pan and continue to simmer the milk for 1–1½ hours, or until the volume of milk has reduced to about 475ml/16fl oz/2 cups.

4 Strain the flavoured milk into a jug (pitcher) or bowl, stir in the caster sugar and then leave to cool.

5 Grind half the skinned pistachio nuts to a smooth powder in a blender, nut grinder or cleaned coffee grinder. Cut the remaining nuts into thin slivers and set them aside for the decoration. Stir the ground pistachio nuts into the milk mixture.

6 Pour the milk mixture into four kulfi moulds. Freeze overnight until the kulfi is firm.

7 To unmould the kulfi, half-fill a plastic container or bowl with very hot water, stand the moulds in the water and count to ten. Immediately lift out the moulds and invert them on a baking sheet.

8 Transfer the ice creams to a platter or individual plates, cut a cross in the top of each and strew the sliced pistachios and rose petals around. Serve at once.

COOK'S TIPS
• Stay in the kitchen while the milk is simmering, so that you can control the heat to keep the milk gently bubbling without boiling over.
• If you don't have any kulfi moulds, use lolly (popsicle) moulds without the tops or even disposable plastic cups. If the ices won't turn out, dip a cloth in very hot water, wring it out and place it on the tops of the moulds, or plunge the moulds back into hot water for a few seconds.

Energy 272Kcal/1147kJ; Protein 15g; Carbohydrate 25.2g, of which sugars 24.9g; Fat 13.3g, of which saturates 5g; Cholesterol 22mg; Calcium 467mg; Fibre 0.8g; Sodium 228mg.

COCONUT AND LEMON GRASS ICE CREAM

LEMON GRASS, A VERSATILE FLAVOURING WHICH IS WIDELY USED IN ASIAN COOKING, MELDS WITH LIME TO ADD AN EXOTIC FRAGRANCE TO ICE CREAM. IF YOU CANNOT GET FRESH LEMON GRASS STALKS, USE THE DRIED STALKS THAT COME IN JARS.

2 Whisk the egg yolks in a bowl with the sugar and cornflour until smooth.

3 Gradually pour the coconut and lemon grass milk over the mixture, whisking well.

4 Return the mixture to the pan and heat gently, stirring until the custard starts to thicken. Do not let it boil.

5 Remove the custard from the heat and strain it into a clean bowl. Cover with a circle of dampened greaseproof (waxed) paper to prevent a skin forming. Leave to cool.

6 By hand: Whip the cream until it has thickened but still falls from the whisk, and stir into the custard with the lime rind. Transfer the mixture to a freezerproof container and freeze for 2 hours. Remove from the freezer and beat using a fork, a whisk or a food processor to break up the ice crystals. Freeze for another 2 hours then beat the mixture again.
Using an ice cream maker: Stir the cream and lime rind into the cooled custard. Churn.

7 Spoon the mixture into five or six dariole moulds. Freeze for at least 3 hours.

8 Meanwhile, make the lime syrup. Heat the sugar and water in a small, heavy pan until the sugar dissolves. Bring to the boil and allow to boil for 5 minutes without stirring. Reduce the heat, add the thinly sliced lime and the lime juice and simmer the syrup gently for 5 minutes more. Leave to cool.

9 To serve, loosen the edges of the dariole moulds with a knife. Dip them in very hot water for 2 seconds then turn out the ice creams on to dessert plates.

10 Serve with the lime syrup and the lime slices spooned around.

SERVES 5–6

INGREDIENTS
    4 lemon grass stalks
    400ml/14fl oz/1⅔ cups coconut milk
    3 egg yolks
    90g/3½oz/½ cup caster
      (superfine) sugar
    10ml/2 tsp cornflour (cornstarch)
    150ml/¼ pint/⅔ cup whipping cream
    finely grated (shredded)
      rind of 1 lime
    lime slices, to decorate
For the lime syrup
    75g/3oz/6 tbsp caster
      (superfine) sugar
    75ml/5 tbsp water
    1 lime, very thinly sliced, plus
      30ml/2 tbsp lime juice

1 Cut the lemon grass stalks in half lengthways and bruise the stalks by tapping them with a rolling pin. Put them in a heavy pan, add the coconut milk and bring to just below boiling point. Remove from the heat and leave to infuse (steep) for 30 minutes, then remove the lemon grass.

CASHEW AND ORANGE FLOWER ICE CREAM

A CASHEW-NUT CREAM FORMS THE BASIS OF THIS DELICIOUS ICE CREAM, WHICH IS DELICATELY PERFUMED WITH ORANGE FLOWER WATER AND GRATED ORANGE RIND. IT EVOKES IMAGES OF ALL KINDS OF DESSERTS THAT ARE POPULAR IN THE MIDDLE EAST.

SERVES 4–6

INGREDIENTS

4 egg yolks
75g/3oz/6 tbsp caster
  (superfine) sugar
5ml/1 tsp cornflour (cornstarch)
300ml/½ pint/1¼ cups
  semi-skimmed (low-fat) milk
150g/5oz/scant 1 cup
  cashew nuts
300ml/½ pint/1¼ cups
  whipping cream
15ml/1 tbsp orange flower water
grated rind of ½ orange, plus curls
  of thinly pared orange rind,
  to decorate

4 Very finely chop the cashew nuts. Heat the cream in a small pan. When it boils, stir in the nuts. Leave to cool.

5 Stir the orange flower water and grated orange rind into the chilled custard. Process the nut cream in a food processor or blender until it forms a fine paste, then stir it into the orange custard mixture.

6 By hand: Pour the mixture into a freezerproof container and freeze for 6 hours, beating twice with a fork, a whisk or an electric mixer to break up the ice crystals.
Using an ice cream maker: Churn the mixture until it is firm enough to scoop.

7 Scoop the ice cream into dishes and decorate with orange rind curls.

1 Whisk the egg yolks, sugar and cornflour in a bowl until the mixture is thick and foamy.

2 Pour the milk into a heavy pan, bring it to the boil, then gradually whisk it into the yolk mixture.

3 Return the mixture to the pan and cook it over a gentle heat, stirring constantly until the custard thickens and is smooth. Do not let it boil or it may curdle. Pour it back into the bowl. Leave to cool, then chill.

COOK'S TIPS
• For a more intense flavour, roast the cashew nuts under the grill (broiler) or dry-fry before chopping them.
• To curl the pared orange rind, wrap each strip in turn around a cocktail stick (toothpick) and leave it for a minute.

Energy 464Kcal/1928kJ; Protein 9.9g; Carbohydrate 23g, of which sugars 18.2g; Fat 37.6g, of which saturates 16.8g; Cholesterol 197mg; Calcium 121mg; Fibre 0.8g; Sodium 115mg.

LAVENDER AND HONEY ICE CREAM

HONEY AND LAVENDER MAKE A MEMORABLE PARTNERSHIP IN THIS OLD-FASHIONED ICE CREAM. SERVE SCOOPED INTO GLASSES OR SET IN LITTLE MOULDS AND TOP WITH LIGHTLY WHIPPED CREAM.

SERVES 6–8

INGREDIENTS
90ml/6 tbsp clear honey
4 egg yolks
10ml/2 tsp cornflour (cornstarch)
8 lavender spikes, plus extra,
  to decorate
450ml/¾ pint/scant 2 cups milk
450ml/¾ pint/scant 2 cups
  whipping cream
dessert biscuits (cookies), to serve

1 Put the honey in a bowl together with the egg yolks and cornflour.

2 Pull the lavender flowers from the spikes and add them to the mixture in the bowl with a little of the milk. Whisk lightly to combine the ingredients.

3 Pour the remaining milk into a heavy pan and bring it to the boil.

4 Pour it over the egg yolk mixture in the bowl, stirring well with a wooden spoon as you pour.

5 Return the custard mixture to the pan and cook it very gently over a low heat, stirring constantly with the wooden spoon until the mixture thickens. Do not let the mixture boil or it may curdle.

6 Pour the custard into a large bowl and cover the surface closely with baking parchment. Leave to cool, then chill.

7 By hand: Whip the cream until it is thickened but still falls from the whisk, and stir into the custard. Transfer the mixture to a freezerproof container. Freeze for about 6 hours, beating twice using a fork, a whisk or a food processor to break up the ice crystals. Freeze until firm.
Using an ice cream maker: Stir the cream into the custard, then churn the mixture in an ice cream maker until it holds its shape. Transfer to a tub or similar freezerproof container and freeze until ready to serve.

8 Transfer the ice cream to the refrigerator 30 minutes before serving, so that it softens slightly.

9 Scoop the ice cream into small dishes, decorate with lavender flowers and serve with dessert biscuits.

Energy 309Kcal/1282kJ; Protein 4.6g; Carbohydrate 13.9g, of which sugars 12.8g; Fat 26.5g, of which saturates 15.6g; Cholesterol 169mg; Calcium 113mg; Fibre 0g; Sodium 45mg.

STRAWBERRY AND LAVENDER SORBET

DELICATELY PERFUMED WITH JUST A HINT OF LAVENDER, THIS DELIGHTFUL, PASTEL PINK SORBET IS PERFECT FOR A SPECIAL-OCCASION DINNER.

SERVES 6

INGREDIENTS
 150g/5oz/¾ cup caster
  (superfine) sugar
 300ml/½ pint/1¼ cups water
 6 fresh lavender flowers
 500g/1¼lb/5 cups strawberries,
  washed and hulled
 1 egg white
 lavender flowers, to decorate

1 Put the sugar and water into a pan and bring to the boil, stirring constantly until the sugar has dissolved.

2 Take the pan off the heat, add the lavender flowers and leave to infuse (steep) for 1 hour. If time permits, chill the syrup before using.

3 Purée the strawberries in a food processor or in batches in a blender, then press the purée (paste) through a large sieve (strainer) into a bowl.

4 By hand: Spoon into a plastic tub or similar freezerproof container, strain in the lavender syrup and freeze for 4 hours, or until the mixture is mushy.

Using an ice cream maker: Pour the strawberry purée into the bowl of an ice cream maker and strain in the lavender syrup. Churn for 20 minutes, or until the mixture is thick.

5 Whisk the egg white until it has just turned frothy.

6 By hand: Scoop the sorbet from the plastic tub into a food processor, process it until smooth, then add the whisked egg white. Mix well to combine, then spoon the sorbet back into the tub and freeze for a further 4 hours, or until it is firm.

Using an ice cream maker: Add the egg white to the ice cream maker and continue to churn until the sorbet is firm enough to scoop.

7 Serve the sorbet in scoops, decorated with lavender flowers.

COOK'S TIP
The size of the lavender flowers may vary; if they are very small you may need to use eight instead of six. To double check, taste a little of the cooled lavender syrup. If you think the flavour is a little mild, add 2–3 more flowers, reheat and cool again before using.

Energy 123Kcal/523kJ; Protein 1.3g; Carbohydrate 31.1g, of which sugars 31.1g; Fat 0.1g, of which saturates 0g; Cholesterol 0mg; Calcium 27mg; Fibre 0.9g; Sodium 17mg.

LYCHEE <u>AND</u> ELDERFLOWER SORBET

THE MUSCAT FLAVOUR OF ELDERFLOWERS IS WONDERFUL WITH SCENTED LYCHEES. SERVE THIS SOPHISTICATED SORBET AFTER A RICH MAIN COURSE.

SERVES 4

INGREDIENTS
175g/6oz/scant 1 cup caster
  (superfine) sugar
400ml/14fl oz/1⅔ cups water
500g/1¼lb fresh lychees, peeled
  and pitted
15ml/1 tbsp elderflower cordial
dessert biscuits (cookies), to serve

COOK'S TIPS
• Switch the freezer to the coldest setting before making the sorbet – the faster the mixture freezes, the smaller the ice crystals and the better the texture.
• Use a metal freezerproof container for best results.

1 Place the sugar and water in a pan and heat gently until the sugar has dissolved. Increase the heat and boil for 5 minutes, then add the lychees. Reduce the heat and simmer the mixture for 7 minutes. Remove from the heat and allow to cool completely.

2 Purée in a food processor or blender, then press as much as you can through a sieve (strainer) into a bowl.

3 By hand: Stir the elderflower cordial into the purée (paste), pour into a freezerproof container. Freeze for 2 hours, or until crystals form around the edge. Process briefly in a food processor or blender to break up the crystals. Repeat twice, then freeze until firm.
Using an ice cream maker: Pour the elderflower cordial and the purée into an ice cream maker. Churn until the sorbet is firm enough to scoop.

4 Transfer to the refrigerator for 10 minutes to soften. Serve with biscuits.

Energy 249Kcal/1064kJ; Protein 1.4g; Carbohydrate 64.7g, of which sugars 64.7g; Fat 0.1g, of which saturates 0g; Cholesterol 0mg; Calcium 31mg; Fibre 0.9g; Sodium 4mg.

GOOSEBERRY AND ELDERFLOWER SORBET

A CLASSIC COMBINATION THAT MAKES A REALLY REFRESHING SORBET. MAKE IT IN SUMMER, AS A STUNNING FINALE TO AN AL FRESCO MEAL, OR SAVE IT FOR SERVING AFTER A HEARTY WINTER STEW.

SERVES 6

INGREDIENTS
150g/5oz/¾ cup caster
    (superfine) sugar
175ml/6fl oz/¾ cup water
10 elderflower heads
500g/1¼lb/5 cups gooseberries
200ml/7fl oz/scant 1 cup apple juice
dash of green food colouring (optional)
a little beaten egg white and caster
    (superfine) sugar, to decorate
    the glasses
elderflowers, to decorate

1 Put 30ml/2 tbsp of the sugar in a pan with 30ml/2 tbsp of the water. Set aside. Mix the remaining sugar and water in a separate, heavy pan. Heat them gently, stirring occasionally, until dissolved. Bring to the boil and boil for 1 minute, without stirring, to make a syrup.

2 Remove from the heat and add the elderflower heads, pressing them into the syrup with a wooden spoon. Leave to infuse (steep) for about 1 hour.

3 Strain the elderflower syrup through a sieve (strainer) placed over a bowl. Set the syrup aside. Add the gooseberries to the pan containing the reserved sugar and water. Cover and cook very gently for about 5 minutes until the gooseberries have softened and the juices have started to run.

COOK'S TIP
Elderflowers can only be picked for a very short time. At other times, use 90ml/6 tbsp elderflower cordial.

4 Tip the mixture into a food processor and add the apple juice. Process until smooth, then press the purée (paste) through a sieve into a bowl. Leave to cool. Stir in the elderflower syrup, with a dash of green food colouring, if you like. Chill until very cold.

5 By hand: Pour into a freezerproof container. Freeze for 2 hours, or until crystals start to form around the edges. Process briefly in a food processor or blender to break up the crystals. Repeat twice more, then freeze until firm.
Using an ice cream maker: Churn the mixture until it holds its shape. Scrape it into a freezer container and freeze for several hours or overnight, until firm.

6 To decorate the glasses, put a little egg white in a bowl. Spread out the caster sugar on a plate. Dip the rim of each glass in the egg white, then into the sugar. Allow to dry for a few minutes. Soften the sorbet in the refrigerator and serve, decorated with elderflowers.

Energy 127Kcal/543kJ; Protein 1.1g; Carbohydrate 31.9g, of which sugars 31.9g; Fat 0.4g, of which saturates 0g; Cholesterol 0mg; Calcium 39mg; Fibre 2g; Sodium 4mg.

BASIL AND ORANGE SORBET

BASIL HAS A SWEET, AROMATIC FLAVOUR THAT GOES VERY WELL WITH CITRUS FRUITS. THIS DELICIOUS SORBET IS REFRESHING AND NOT TOO CLOYING – PERFECT AFTER A RICH MAIN COURSE.

3 Put half the orange juice in a food processor or blender with the basil leaves and process the mixture in short bursts until the basil has been chopped into small pieces.

4 Using an ice cream maker: Pour the syrup, basil-specked orange juice and remaining orange juice into the ice cream maker and churn until the mixture is thick.
By hand: Pour the mixture into a freezerproof container and mix well. Freeze for 2 hours, or until crystals start to form around the edges. Process briefly in a food processor or blender to break up the crystals. Repeat twice more, then freeze until firm.

5 Scoop into bowls and decorate with basil leaves or turn into a freezer container and freeze until it is required.

COOK'S TIPS
• If you prefer a sweeter sorbet, substitute extra orange juice for the lemon and lime juice.
• You can use good quality freshly squeezed orange juice as an alternative to squeezing your own, if you prefer.

SERVES 6

INGREDIENTS
175g/6oz/scant 1 cup caster (superfine) sugar
105ml/7 tbsp water
30ml/2 tbsp lemon or lime juice
10–12 small oranges
15g/½oz fresh basil leaves
tiny basil leaves, to decorate

1 Put the sugar and water in a pan and bring slowly to the boil, stirring until all of the sugar has dissolved.

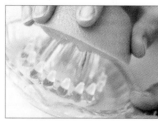

2 Leave the liquid to cool and then stir in the lemon or lime juice. Squeeze the oranges until you have 500ml/17fl oz/ generous 2 cups orange juice.

Energy 189Kcal/806kJ; Protein 2.4g; Carbohydrate 47.5g, of which sugars 47.5g; Fat 0.2g, of which saturates 0g; Cholesterol 0mg; Calcium 110mg; Fibre 3.4g; Sodium 12mg.

LEMON SORBET

THIS IS PROBABLY THE MOST CLASSIC SORBET OF ALL. MADE WITH FRESH, JUICY LEMONS, IT IS
REFRESHINGLY TANGY AND YET DELICIOUSLY SMOOTH. IT QUITE LITERALLY MELTS IN THE MOUTH.

SERVES 6

INGREDIENTS

200g/7oz/1 cup caster
(superfine) sugar
300ml/½ pint/1¼ cups water
4 lemons, well scrubbed
1 egg white
sugared lemon rind,
to decorate

1 Put the sugar and water into a pan
and bring to the boil, stirring
occasionally until the sugar dissolves.

2 Pare the rind thinly from two lemons
so that it falls straight into the pan.
Simmer for 2 minutes without stirring,
then take the pan off the heat. Leave
to cool, then chill.

3 Squeeze the juice from all the lemons
and add it to the syrup.
By hand: Strain the syrup into a shallow
freezerproof container, reserving the
rind. Freeze the mixture for 4 hours
until it is mushy.
Using an ice cream maker: Strain the
syrup and lemon juice, and churn
the mixture until thick.

4 By hand: Scoop the sorbet into a food
processor and beat it until smooth.
Lightly whisk the egg white with a fork
until it is just frothy. Spoon the sorbet
back into the tub, beat in the egg white
and return the mixture to the freezer for
4 hours.
Using an ice cream maker: Add the egg
white to the mixture and continue to
churn for 10–15 minutes, or until firm
enough to scoop.

5 Scoop into bowls or glasses and
decorate with sugared lemon rind.

COOK'S TIP
Cut the top off a lemon and retain as a
lid. Squeeze the juice out of the larger
portion. Remove any membrane and use
the shell as a container. Scoop sorbet
into the shell, top with the lid and add
lemon leaves or small bay leaves. Allow
one lemon for each person.

VARIATION
Sorbet can be made from any citrus fruit.
As a guide you will need 300ml/½ pint/
1¼ cups fresh fruit juice and the pared
rind of half the squeezed fruit. Use 4
oranges or 2 oranges and 2 lemons, or,
for a grapefruit sorbet, use the rind of
1 ruby grapefruit and the juice of 2. For
lime sorbet, combine the rind of 3 limes
with the juice of 6.

Energy 135Kcal/574kJ; Protein 0.7g; Carbohydrate 35.1g, of which sugars 35.1g; Fat 0g, of which saturates 0g; Cholesterol 0mg; Calcium 19mg; Fibre 0g; Sodium 12mg.

ROSE-PETAL SORBET

THIS SORBET MAKES A WONDERFUL END TO A SUMMER MEAL WITH ITS FABULOUS FLAVOUR OF ROSES.
REMEMBER TO USE THE MOST SCENTED VARIETY YOU CAN FIND IN THE GARDEN. PICK FRESH BLOOMS
WHICH ARE NEWLY OPENED, IDEALLY IN THE LATE MORNING.

SERVES 4–6

INGREDIENTS
    115g/4oz/generous ½ cup caster
      (superfine) sugar
    300ml/½ pint/1¼ cups boiling water
    petals of 3 large, scented red or
      deep-pink roses from an unsprayed
      rose, white ends of petals removed
    juice of 2 lemons
    300ml/½ pint/1¼ cups rosé wine
    whole crystallized roses or rose
      petals, to decorate

1 Place the sugar in a large heatproof
bowl and pour over the boiling water.

2 Stir the mixture until the sugar has
completely dissolved.

3 Add the rose petals and leave the
liquid to cool completely.

4 Pour the mixture in to a food
processor, process until smooth, then
strain through a sieve (strainer). Add
the lemon juice and wine.

5 By hand: Pour into a freezerproof
container. Freeze for several hours, or
until ice crystals form around the edges.
Whisk or use a food processor to break
up the crystals. Re-freeze until frozen
around the edges. Repeat the whisking
and freezing process once or twice
more, until the sorbet is pale and
smooth. Freeze until firm.
Using an ice cream maker: Churn until
firm with a good texture.

6 Serve in scoops, decorated with
crystallized roses or rose petals.

COOK'S TIPS
• If the sorbet is too hard to scoop,
transfer it to the refrigerator and leave
it for about 30 minutes before you are
ready to serve.
• For a stunning presentation idea, scoop
the sorbet into a rose ice bowl. The bowl
and sorbet can be left in the freezer until
they are needed.

VARIATION
If you prefer, a yellow version of this dish
can be made using yellow rose petals
and white wine instead of rosé.

Energy 111Kcal/469kJ; Protein 0.2g; Carbohydrate 21.3g, of which sugars 21.3g; Fat 0g, of which saturates 0g; Cholesterol 0mg; Calcium 16mg; Fibre 0g; Sodium 3mg.

TURKISH DELIGHT SORBET

LOVE TURKISH DELIGHT, BUT DON'T WANT STICKY FINGERS? SERVE THIS SUPERB SORBET INSTEAD. IT HAS ALL THE FLAVOUR AND AROMA OF THE SWEETMEAT FROM WHICH IT IS MADE, BUT IS EASIER TO EAT. SERVE IT IN SMALL PORTIONS WITH A POT OF STRONG COFFEE.

SERVES 4

INGREDIENTS
    250g/9oz rose water-flavoured
    Turkish delight
    30ml/2 tbsp granulated (white) sugar
    750ml/1¼ pints/3 cups water
    30ml/2 tbsp lemon juice
    50g/2oz white chocolate, broken
    into squares
    roughly chopped almonds,
    to decorate

1 Cut the Turkish delight into small pieces with a pair of scissors.

2 Put half the pieces of Turkish delight in a heavy pan with the sugar.

3 Pour in half the water. Heat gently over a low heat until the Turkish delight has dissolved, stirring.

4 Remove from the heat. Cool, then stir in the lemon juice with the remaining water and Turkish delight. Chill in the refrigerator for several hours.

5 By hand: Pour the mixture into a shallow freezerproof container and freeze for 3–4 hours, beating twice as it thickens. Return to the freezer until ready to serve.
Using an ice cream maker: Churn the mixture until it holds its shape.

6 While the sorbet is freezing, dampen eight very small plastic cups or glasses, then line them with clear film (plastic wrap).

7 Spoon the sorbet into the cups and tap them lightly on the surface to compact the mixture. Cover with the overlapping clear film and freeze for at least 3 hours or overnight.

8 Make a paper piping bag. Put the chocolate in a heatproof bowl and melt it over a pan of gently simmering water. Remove the sorbets from the freezer, let them stand for 5 minutes, then pull them out of the cups.

9 Transfer to serving plates and peel off the clear film. Spoon the melted chocolate into the piping bag, snip off the tip and scribble a design on the sorbet and the plate. Sprinkle the almonds over the top and serve.

Energy 280Kcal/1188kJ; Protein 1.4g; Carbohydrate 63.8g, of which sugars 58g; Fat 3.9g, of which saturates 2.3g; Cholesterol 0mg; Calcium 44mg; Fibre 0g; Sodium 34mg.

ROSE GERANIUM MARQUISE

THIS DESSERT MAKES A GOOD CHOICE FOR A DINNER PARTY AS IT CAN BE MADE IN ADVANCE. ROSE GERANIUM LEAVES GIVE THE ICE CREAM A DELICATE, SCENTED FLAVOUR IN THIS ELEGANT DESSERT.

SERVES 8

INGREDIENTS
  225g/8oz/generous 1 cup caster
    (superfine) sugar
  400ml/14fl oz/1⅔ cups water
  24 fresh rose geranium leaves
  45ml/3 tbsp lemon juice
  250g/9oz/generous 1 cup
    mascarpone cheese
  300ml/½ pint/1¼ cups double
    (heavy) or whipping cream
  200g/7oz savoiardi or sponge
    finger biscuits (cookies)
  90g/3½oz/generous ½ cup almonds,
    finely chopped and toasted
  geranium flowers and icing
    (confectioners') sugar,
    to decorate

1 Put the sugar and water in a heavy pan and heat gently, stirring occasionally, until the sugar has dissolved completely.

2 Add the rose geranium leaves to the pan and cook gently for 2 minutes. Leave to cool.

VARIATION
If you prefer, use other kinds of nuts instead of the almonds used here. Macadamia nuts and walnuts would both work well.

COOK'S TIP
If you cannot get savoiardi biscuits, use ordinary sponge finger biscuits instead. These tend to be smaller, though, so you will need to adjust the size of the rectangle accordingly.

3 Strain the cooled geranium syrup into a measuring jug (pitcher) and then stir in the lemon juice.

4 Put the mascarpone in a bowl and beat it until it has softened. Gradually beat in 150ml/¼ pint/⅔ cup of the syrup mixture.

5 Whip the cream until it forms peaks, then fold it into the mascarpone and syrup mixture. At this stage the mixture should hold its shape. If necessary, whip the mixture a little more.

6 Spoon a little of the mixture on to a flat, freezerproof serving plate and spread it out with a palette knife (metal spatula) to a 21 × 12cm/8½ × 4½in rectangle.

7 Pour the remaining geranium syrup into a shallow bowl. Dip a savoiardi or sponge finger biscuit into the syrup and moisten it until it is moist but not disintegrating.

8 Place the biscuit on to the rectangle. Repeat with a third of the biscuits to cover the rectangle completely.

9 Spread another even, thin layer of the cream mixture over the biscuits.

10 Set aside 15ml/1 tbsp of the nuts for the topping. Sprinkle half the remainder over the cream.

11 Make another two layers of the syrup-steeped biscuits, sandwiching them with more of the cream mixture and the remaining nuts, but leaving enough cream mixture to coat the dessert completely.

12 Spread the remaining cream mixture over the top and sides of the cake until it is evenly coated all over.

13 Sprinkle the reserved nuts over the top of the marquise. Freeze the cake for at least 5 hours, or overnight if you have time.

14 Transfer the marquise to the refrigerator and leave it for around 30 minutes before serving, so that it softens slightly.

15 Sprinkle with geranium flowers, dust with icing sugar, and serve in slices.

Energy 454Kcal/1896kJ; Protein 8.6g; Carbohydrate 45.4g, of which sugars 39.6g; Fat 27.7g, of which saturates 13.3g; Cholesterol 109mg; Calcium 83mg; Fibre 1.1g; Sodium 34mg.

MAPLE AND WALNUT MERINGUE GATEAU

RICH WALNUTS AND SWEET MAPLE SYRUP ARE GREAT PARTNERS AND GO PARTICULARLY WELL WITH PALE-GOLDEN MERINGUE. THIS ICED DESSERT IS A FEAST FOR ALL MERINGUE LOVERS AND MAKES A STUNNING CONCLUSION TO A DINNER PARTY.

SERVES 10–12

INGREDIENTS
  4 egg whites
  200g/7oz/scant 1 cup light
    muscovado (brown) sugar
  150g/5oz/1¼ cups walnut pieces
  600ml/1 pint/2½ cups double
    (heavy) cream
  150ml/¼ pint/⅔ cup maple syrup,
    plus extra, to serve

1 Preheat the oven to 140°C/275°F/ Gas 1.

2 Draw three 23cm/9in circles on separate sheets of baking parchment.

3 Invert the baking parchment circles on three baking sheets.

4 Whisk the egg whites in a grease-free bowl until stiff.

5 Whisk in the sugar, about 15ml/1 tbsp at a time, whisking well after each addition until the meringue is stiff and glossy.

6 Spread the meringue to within 1cm/½in of the edge of each baking parchment circle.

7 Bake the meringue for about 1 hour or until crisp, swapping the baking sheets around halfway through cooking. Leave to cool.

8 Set aside 45ml/3 tbsp of the walnuts. Finely chop the remainder.

9 Whip the cream with the maple syrup until it forms soft peaks. Fold in the chopped walnuts.

10 Use about a third of the mixture to sandwich the meringues together on a flat, freezerproof serving plate.

11 Using a palette knife (metal spatula), spread the remaining cream mixture in an even layer over the top and sides of the gateau.

12 Sprinkle with the reserved walnuts and freeze overnight.

13 Transfer to the refrigerator about 1 hour before serving so that the cream filling softens slightly.

14 Drizzle a little of the extra maple syrup over the top of the gateau, just before serving. Serve in slices.

Energy 441Kcal/1831kJ; Protein 3.7g; Carbohydrate 28.6g, of which sugars 28.5g; Fat 35.4g, of which saturates 17.4g; Cholesterol 69mg; Calcium 48mg; Fibre 0.4g; Sodium 67mg.

BAY ᴬᴺᴰ RATAFIA SLICE

THE WARM BUT DELICATE FLAVOUR OF BAY LEAVES COMBINES PARTICULARLY WELL WITH ALMOND
FLAVOURS. SERVE THIS SUMPTUOUS SLICE WITH FRESH APRICOTS, PLUMS, PEACHES OR SOFT FRUITS.
AN EXCELLENT DINNER-PARTY DESSERT THAT CAN BE MADE IN ADVANCE.

SERVES 6

INGREDIENTS
   300ml/½ pint/1¼ cups milk
   4 fresh bay leaves
   4 egg yolks
   75g/3oz/6 tbsp caster
    (superfine) sugar
   10ml/2 tsp cornflour (cornstarch)
   150g/5oz ratafia (almond macaroons)
    or macaroon biscuits (cookies)
   300ml/½ pint/1¼ cups
    whipping cream

1 Put the milk in a pan, add the bay leaves and bring slowly to the boil. Remove from the heat and infuse (steep) for 30 minutes. Meanwhile, whisk the egg yolks in a bowl with the sugar and cornflour.

2 Strain the milk over the egg yolk mixture and stir well.

3 Return to the pan and cook over a gentle heat, stirring constantly until the custard thickens. Do not let it boil or it may curdle.

4 Transfer the custard to a bowl, cover closely with baking parchment and leave to cool completely. Chill until very cold.

5 Crush the biscuits in a strong plastic bag, using a rolling pin.

COOK'S TIP
If the ice cream is not firm enough to roll, freeze for a couple of hours more.

6 By hand: Whip the cream until it has thickened but still falls from the whisk, and stir into the custard. Transfer to a freezerproof container. Freeze for about 4 hours, beating twice using a fork, a hand whisk or a food processor to break up the ice crystals. Stir in 50g/2oz of the crushed biscuits and freeze for a further 2 hours.
Using an ice cream maker: Add the cream to the custard and churn until it is very thick. Scrape it into a bowl and add 50g/2oz of the crushed biscuits. Return to the ice cream maker and churn for 2 minutes more.

7 Working quickly, spoon the ice cream on to a sheet of baking parchment, packing it into a log shape, about 5cm/2in thick and 25cm/10in long. Bring the baking parchment up around the ice cream to pack it together tightly.

8 Support on a baking sheet and freeze for at least 3 hours or overnight.

9 Spread the remaining crushed biscuits in a layer on a sheet of baking parchment. Unwrap the ice cream log and roll it quickly in the crumbs until it is completely coated. Return to the freezer until needed. Serve in slices.

Energy 451Kcal/1881kJ; Protein 7.7g; Carbohydrate 38.1g, of which sugars 25.7g; Fat 30.9g, of which saturates 16.5g; Cholesterol 298mg; Calcium 157mg; Fibre 0.4g; Sodium 129mg.

GLOSSARY

Above Salvia officinalis *'Icterina'*

ALKALOID – a nitrogen-based compound contained in a plant, usually capable of having a powerful effect on bodily systems, such as painkilling or poisoning.

ALLERGEN – a substance which causes an allergic reaction.

ALTERNATE – refers to leaves arranged successively on either side of a stem.

ANALGESIC – pain relieving.

ANTISCORBUTIC – counteracts scurvy, a disease caused by Vitamin C deficiency.

ARIL – seed-covering, often fleshy and brightly coloured, of certain plants, such as Taxus baccata (common yew).

ASTRINGENT – has a binding, contracting effect on bodily tissue and stops bleeding.

AXIL – the upper angle between a leaf or bract and the stem on which it grows.

AXILLARY – growing in the axil.

BASAL (of leaves) – growing or forming at the base of the stem.

BOLT – to run to seed prematurely.

BRACT – a small, modified leaf.

BULBIL – a small, bulb-like structure growing in a leaf axil or flower cluster.

CALCAREOUS – containing lime; chalky.

CALYX (pl. CALYCES) – the outer circle of sepals, joined or divided, which surround a flower head or bud.

CORYMB – a flat-topped or convex flower cluster having flower stalks arising from different points on the stem.

CULTIVAR – a plant produced or selected from a natural species, its distinctive characteristics maintained by cultivation.

DECIDUOUS – describes a tree or shrub that loses its leaves annually, regrowing them the following season.

DECOCTION – an extraction of the water-soluble constituents of a medicinal plant, made by boiling it in water.

DECUMBENT – growing along the ground, with a tendency to turn upwards at the tips.

DIOECIOUS – produces male and female flowers on different plants.

DISC-FLORET – small, often tubular floret, which, along with many, forms the centre of a compound flower head, such as a daisy.

DIURETIC – promotes the flow of urine.

DROPSY – (oedema) a disease that is characterized by excessive build-up of fluid in bodily tissues.

DRUPE – fleshy fruit with one or more seeds enclosed in a stony casing.

ELLIPTIC – oval-shaped, tapering to a point at each end.

EMETIC – causes vomiting.

EMOLLIENT – softens and smoothes the skin.

ENTIRE – refers to smooth, untoothed leaf margins.

EXPECTORANT – encourages the ejection of phlegm from the respiratory tract.

GLOBOSE – spherical.

Below *A colourful border display.*

Below *An espaliered fruit tree.*

Below Calendula officinalis

Above *A border of purple and green sage.*

Above *A bed of mixed thymes.*

HYBRID – a plant produced by cross-fertilization between two species.

INFUSION – an extraction of water-soluble constituents of a medicinal plant, made by steeping it in water that has been brought to boiling point.

LANCEOLATE – (of leaves) narrow and tapering to a point at the tip.

MONOECIOUS – bears separate male and female flowers on the same plant.

MUCILAGE – a glutinous substance contained in a plant.

OBOVATE – an inverted egg-shape, which is narrow at the base and broader at the top.

OPPOSITE – (of leaves) growing in pairs at the same level, on opposite sides of the stem.

OVATE – egg-shaped, with the broader part at the base, narrow at the top.

OVOID – a solid egg-shape with the broader end at the base, usually applied to fruit.

PALMATE – describes a compound leaf with several leaflets arising from a common point.

PANICLE – branched, compound flower cluster.

PERFOLIATE – describes a stalkless leaf, or leaves, which encircle and enclose the stem.

PINNATE – describes a compound leaf, made up of two rows of leaflets on either side of the central stem.

PROPHYLACTIC – protects from disease.

PURGATIVE – strongly laxative.

RACEME – an unbranched, often conical-shaped, flower cluster.

RAY-FLORET – the usually strap-shaped outer petal (floret) of a compound flower head such as a daisy.

RHIZOME – an underground, often ground-level, branched, swollen root-like stem, that usually grows horizontally and bears leafy shoots.

SPADIX – a flower spike with a thick, fleshy stem, which is usually encased in a spathe.

SPATHE – a leaf or bract wrapped round a central spike of flowers.

Below *Catmint and a yellow climbing rose.*

TAPROOT – the main, downward-growing root of a plant, which is often cylindrical or a cone shape.

TINCTURE – a solution, usually in alcohol, of the active constituents of a medicinal plant.

TRIFOLIATE – describes leaves with three lobes or leaflets.

UMBEL – an umbrella-shaped flower cluster.

VERMIFUGE – expels or destroys intestinal worms.

VULNERARY – promotes the healing of wounds.

WHORL – leaves or flowers arising from the same point and encircling the stem.

USEFUL SOURCES <u>AND</u> SUPPLIERS

Above *Feverfew*

UNITED KINGDOM

SUPPLIERS OF ESSENTIAL OILS

The Fragrant Earth Co. Ltd
Beckery Road
Glastonbury BA6 9NX
Tel 01458 831216
www.fragrantearth.com

Napiers the Herbalists
31 Townsend Street
Glasgow G4 0LF
Tel 0131 263 1860
napiers.net

Neal's Yard Remedies
Peacemarsh, Gillingham
Dorset SP8 4EU
Tel 01747 834 600
www.nealsyardremedies.com

Norfolk Herbs
Blackberry Farm
Dillington, Dereham
Norfolk NR19 2QD
Tel 01362 860812
www.norfolkherbs.co.uk

The Organic Herb Trading Company
Milverton
Somerset TA4 1ND
Tel 01823 401205
www.organicherbtrading.com

Right *A deeply coloured knot garden.*

Shirley Price Aromatherapy Limited,
8 Hawley Road, Hinckley
Leicestershire LE10 0PR
Tel 01455 615466
www.shirleyprice.co.uk

MEDICINAL AND CULINARY HERBS

G. Baldwin & Co.
171–173 Walworth Road
London SE17 1RW
Tel 020 7703 5550
www.baldwins.co.uk

Potters Herbal Supplies
Potters Division
Vifor Pharma UK Ltd,
1 Botanic Court
Wigan WN5 0JZ
Tel 01202 449752
www.pottersherbals.co.uk

Poyntzfield Herb Nursery
By Dingwall Ross & Cromarty
Dingwall
Ross-Shire IV7 8LX
Tel 01381 610352
www.poyntzfieldherbs.co.uk

Iden Croft Herbs
Frittenden Road
Kent TN12 0DH
Tel 01580 891432
www.uk-herbs.com

NORTH AMERICA

SUPPLIERS OF ESSENTIAL OILS

The Body Shop
1811 24000th Road
Parsons, Kansas 67357
Tel (620) 421-1919
www.thebodyshop-usa.com

Lorann Oils
4518 Aurelius Road
Lansing, Michigan 48910
Tel (517) 882-0215
www.lorannoils.com

MEDICINAL AND CULINARY HERBS

Caprilands Herb Farm
P.O. Box 190, Coventry
Connecticut 06238
Tel 1-800-568-7132
www.caprilands.com

Above Helianthus annuus

Horizon Herbs, LLC
PO Box 69
Williams
Oregon 97544
Tel (541) 846-6704
www.horizonherbs.com

Richter's Herbs
357 Durham Regional Hwy 47
Goodwood
Ontario L0C 1A0
Tel 1-800-668-4372
www.richters.com

MEDICINAL AND CULINARY HERBS

Bundanoon Village Nursery
29 Railway Avenue
Bundanoon
NSW 2578
Tel (02) 4883-7859
www.bundanoonbloomery.com.au

Darling Mills Farm
15-17 McCallums Avenue
Berrilee
NSW 2159
Tel (02) 9655 1339
www.darlingmillsfarm.com.au

Above Monarda didyma *'Cambridge Scarlet'*

Happy Herb Company
PO Box 3157
Uki
NSW 2484
Tel (02) 6679 4103
happyherbcompany.com

Herbie's Spices
745 Darling Street
Rozelle 2039
NSW
Tel (02) 9555-6035
www.herbies.com.au
All culinary herbs and spices in one place.
Huge range. Mail order for dried herbs
nationally and throughout the Pacific.

Mudbrick Cottage Herb Farm
491 Gold Coast Springbrook Road
Mudgeeraba Gold Coast
Queensland 4213
Tel 07 55 303 253
www.herbcottage.com.au

Pindari Herb Farm
200 Norwich Drive
Longford
Tasmania 7301
Tel (03) 6391 1799
www.pindariherbfarm.com

Above *Wild strawberry and marjoram pot.*

Pleasance Herbs
11935 Summerland Way
NSW 2470
Tel 0438 373 681
www.pleasanceherbs.com.au

Renaissance Herbs
www.renaissanceherbs.com.au
Largest range – supplies to nurseries
nationally through franchised growers
throughout Australia and New Zealand.

Below Melilot

Index

Above *Frittata with Tomatoes and Thyme*

Below *Garlic and Herb Bread*

Above *Cornflower*

Below *Linguine with Rocket*

ACKNOWLEDGEMENTS

JESSICA HOUDRET'S ACKNOWLEDGEMENTS

My thanks to the following people for specialist information: Alan Gear of the Henry Doubleday Research Association, on the use of comfrey in the garden; Dr. Stanley Deans on thyme oil; Duncan Ross of Poyntzfield Herb Nursery on ginseng; Dr. Rosita Arvigo and the Traditional Healers Foundation of Belize, on plants of Central America; and also to Dr. Katya Svoboda of the Scottish Agricultural College, Dr. Rosemary Cole of the National Herb Centre and Dr. Charles Hill.

THE PUBLISHER WOULD LIKE TO THANK THE FOLLOWING PEOPLE FOR THEIR HELP WITH THE GARDENING SECTION OF THIS BOOK:

Roger and Linda Bastin; Christine and Peter Bench; Mrs Chris and Mandie Dennis; Adam Gordon; Henry Doubleday Research Association; Simon and Judith Hopkinson (and Anne); Victoria Ker; Anne Marie Powell; Letta Proper Pranger; Sally Reed; Duncan and Susan Ross; The Royal Botanic Gardens; Lord Salisbury/ Michael Pickard (Curator); Richard Scott; The Shakespeare Birthplace Trust; The Shrewsbury Quest; Roger Souvereyns; Phillip C Stallard; Peter Turner; Stijn Vanormelingen; Susie & Kevin White.

Below *Soothing bath oil*

THE PUBLISHER WOULD LIKE TO THANK THE FOLLOWING PEOPLE FOR THEIR HELP WITH THE RECIPE SECTION OF THIS BOOK:

PHOTOGRAPHERS: Karl Adamson, Edward Allwright, Steve Baxter, Nicki Dowey, James Duncan, Gus Filgate, John Freeman, Ian Garlick, Michelle Garrett, Peter Henley, John Heseltine, Amanda Heywood, Janine Hosegood, Andrea Jones, Dave Jordan, Dave King, Don Last, William Lingwood, Patrick McLeavey, Michael Michaels, Steve Moss, Thomas Odulate, Debbie Patterson, Craig Robertson, Sam Stowell, Polly Wreford.

RECIPES: Catherine Atkinson, Alex Barker, Angela Boggiano, Ruby Le Bois, Carla Capalbo, Lesley Chamberlain, Kit Chan, Jacqueline Clarke, Maxine Clark Cleary, Frances Cleary, Carole Clements, Andi Clevely, Trish Davies, Roz Denny, Patrizia Diemling, Stephanie Donaldson, Matthew Drennan, Joanna Farrow, Rafi Fernandez, Christine France, Silvano Franco, Sarah Gates, Shirley Gill, Brian Glover, Nicola Graimes, Rosamund Grant, Juliet Harbutt, Jessica Houdret, Deh-Ta Hsiung, Shehzad Hussain, Christine Ingram, Judy Jackson, Peter Jordan, Manisha Kanini, Soheila Kimberley, Lucy Knox, Masaki Ko, Sara Lewis, Patricia Lousada, Gilly Love, Norma MacMillan, Sue Maggs, Sally Mansfield, Maggie Mayhew, Norma Miller, Sallie Morris, Janice Murfitt, Annie Nichols, Elizabeth Lambert Oritz, Katherine Richmond, Anne Sheasby, Jenni Shapter, Liz Trigg, Hilaire Walden, Laura Washburn, Stuart Walton, Steven Wheeler, Kate Whiteman, Elizabeth Wolf-Cohen, Jenni Wright.

STYLISTS: Alison Austin, Shannon Beare, Madeleine Brehaut, Frances Cleary, Tessa Evelegh, Marilyn Forbes, Annabel Ford, Nicola Fowler, Michelle Garrett, Carole Handslip, Cara Hobday, Kate Jay, Maria Kelly, Lucy McKelvie, Marion McLornan, Marion Price,

Above *Garden pinks*

Jane Stevenson, Helen Trent, Sophie Wheeler, Judy Williams, Elizabeth Wolf-Cohen.

HOME ECONOMISTS: Eliza Baird, Alex Barker, Julie Beresford, Sascha Brodie, Stephanie England, Annabel Ford, Christine France, Carole Handslip, Kate Jay, Jill Jones, Clare Lewis, Sara Lewis, Bridget Sargeson, Joy Skipper, Jenni Shapter, Carole Tennant.

PICTURE CREDITS FOR THE GARDENING SECTION OF THIS BOOK
key t = top, b = bottom, c = centre, l = left, r = right
Page 191 tl Alamy. Pages 12 bl, 16 bl, 19 tl ET Archive; pages 16 tr, 17 bl Edimedia; pages 17 tr, 18 bl, 19br, 22 bl The Bridgeman Art Library; pages 13 tr & 113 Vaughn Fleming, 22 tr Clay Perry, 28 rc David Askham, 45 br Steven Wooster, 90 tl, 124 tr, 135 tr John Glover, 113 bc, 118 tr Brigitte Thomas, 125 tr Sunniva Harte, 126 tr Clive Boursnell, 134 tl Lamontagne, 134/5 tc Christopher Gallagher, 139 tr Ron Evans, 203 b Clive Nichols – The Garden Picture Library; pages 23t, 43 br, 55 cl, 80 tr & cr, 81, 87 bc, 88 tl, 90 br, 96 tl, 97 tl, 98 tc, 103 bl, 108 tl, 109 tl, 111 tr, 112 tl, 115 tl, 119 tl, 122 tl, 133 tc, 137 bl, tr, 135 tc, 136, 137 tl, 139 bc, 154 tl,

Above *Flax*

155 tl, 161 bc, 171 tr, 187 tr, 194 tr, 198 tr, 199 tl, tr, 203 t, 204 br, 205 tr, 206 b, 208 tl, 212 tl Jessica Houdret; pages 23 bl, 42 bl, 43 bl, 92 tr Lucy Mason; pages 23 tr, 26 tr, 38 bl, 50 tr, 53 br, 61 tr Jacqui Hurst; pages 34 br, 216 tr Adrian Thomas, 46 bl Neil Joy, 59 Michael Jones, 62 tr Geoffrey S. Chapman, 114 tc K. Jayara, 117 bl Malcolm Richards, 128 tr Michael R. Chandler, 222 tl Anthony Cooper, 223 tr E. Mole, 225 tl Bjorn Svensson 225 tr – A–Z Botanical Collection Ltd; pages 36 bl, 43 tr & tl, 69, 70, 71 tl, tc, tr, 75 tr & bl, 112 cr, br, 139 br, 143 br, 151 bl, 159 br, 161c, 208 tl, 234/5, 236 br, 239 tr, 240 tr Michelle Garrett; pages 236 bl, 237 br, 239 br & bl, 241 cr Polly Wreford; pages 85 tr, 116 tl, 124 tc, 126 tl, 141 tr, 184 tl, 187 bl, 215 tl Harry Smith Collection; page 88 tr Brenda Szabo – Kirstenbosch Botanic Garden, South Africa; pages 89 tl, 194 tl Dr. Eckart Pott, 103 br Bob & Clara Calhoun, 175 tc, tr, 181 tl Staffen Widstrand, 181 cl N. Schwihtz, 196 tl Harald Lange, 196 cr Hans Reinhard – Bruce Coleman Ltd.; pages 106 tl, 175 tl, 182 tr Deni Bown; pages 130 tl, 132 tl, 146 br, 148 tl Dr. John Feltwell, Garden & Wildlife Matters; page 184 br Duncan Ross, Poyntzfield Nursery.